Beginning Visual Basic .NET Databases

Denise Gosnell
Matthew Reynolds
Bill Forgey

Wrox Press Ltd. ®

Beginning Visual Basic .NET Databases

Published by Wrox Press Ltd,
Arden House, 1102 Warwick Road, Acocks Green,
Birmingham, B27 6BH, UK
Printed in the United States
ISBN 1861005555

Trademark Acknowledgements

Credits

Authors
Denise Gosnell
Matthew Reynolds
Bill Forgey

Technical Reviewers
Beth Breidenbach
PJ Burke
Mike Clark
Simon Delamare
Damien Foggon
Zach Greenvoss
Mark Horner
Wendy Lanning
Carl Mayes
Dale Onyon
Sumit Pal
Rachelle Reese
Sean M Schade
David Schultz
Brian Sherwin
Phillip Sidari
Konstantinos Vlassis
David Williams
Thearon Willis

Technical Architect
Paul Jeffcoat

Technical Editors
Victoria Blackburn
Richard Deeson

Author Agent
Laura Jones

Project Administrator
Rob Hesketh

Category Manager
Sarah Drew

Production Manager
Liz Toy

Production Coordinator
Pip Wonson

Production Assistant
Matt Clark

Index
Michael Brinkman

Proof Reader
Agnes Wiggers

Cover
Dawn Chellingworth

About the Authors

Denise Gosnell

Denise Gosnell is a consultant in the Microsoft Consulting Services Public Sector Practice at Microsoft (dgosnell@microsoft.com). Denise has a unique background in both law and technology and uses her background to help federal, state, and local governments implement hi-tech solutions.

She received a bachelor's degree in Computer Science – Business (summa cum laude) from Anderson University and a Doctor of Jurisprudence from Indiana University School of Law in Indianapolis. Denise is an attorney licensed to practice law in Indiana and is an active member of the Indiana and Indianapolis Bar Associations. Her legal areas of expertise are intellectual property law and real estate law. Denise is also a Microsoft Certified Solution Developer.

Denise has worked in the computer industry since 1994 in a variety of roles ranging from Systems Engineer, Programmer, IS Manager, and Senior Consultant. Denise is also an avid writer, and has co-authored the following books: *MSDE Bible* (IDG Books), *Professional SQL Server 2000 XML* (Wrox Press), and *Professional .NET Framework* (Wrox Press).

When Denise isn't working, writing, or studying, she and her husband Jake enjoy traveling around the globe to interesting places such as Russia, China, and Poland.

To my husband Jake for his patience and understanding this year while I was simultaneously working on three books with Wrox on most evenings and weekends. To the fine folks at Wrox Press for making this book a reality.

Matthew Reynolds

After working with Wrox Press on a number of projects since 1999, Matthew is now an in-house author for Wrox Press writing about and working with virtually all aspects of Microsoft .NET. He's also a regular contributor to Wrox's *ASPToday* and C# *Today*, and *Web Services Architect.* He lives and works in North London and can be reached on matthewr@wrox.com.

For Fanjeev Sarin.

Thanks very much to the following in their support and assistance in writing this book: Len, Edward, Darren, Alex, Jo, Tim, Clare, Martin, Niahm, Tom, Ollie, Amir, Gretchen, Ben, Brandon, Denise, Rob, Waggy, Mark, Elaine, James, Zoe, Faye and Sarah. And, also thanks to my new friends at Wrox, which include Charlotte, Laura, Karli, Dom S, Dom L, Ian, Kate, Joy, Pete, Helen, Vickie, John, Dave, Adam, Craig, Jake, Julian, Rob and Paul.

Bill Forgey

Bill writes: "I began my career in the early 1990's, originally an Electronic Engineering major and, soon after, the US Navy. I soon found myself in a shutdown engineering firm and was too stubborn to take anything less. My shipmate introduced me to VB 3.0 and Access 2.0 and, for the next few months, I found myself learning everything I could about VB. I began developing a phonebook program using VB and MS Access. I would program 12 to 14 hours a day, including all nighters or until my hands got numb. I read every book I could on VB, many of which were references and how to's. Everything I wanted to do in VB I was able to, thanks to the language. After four months of steady learning, I landed a contract position writing VB software to control data acquisition modules – luckily the majority of the work was with VB and Access. I thought I knew everything after that. I earned a grand a week and soon forgot about school. For my first three years I worked very hard and put in lots of hours, and I bought and read even more books. Books like Dan Appleman's *Programmer's API*, which I didn't understand for over a year after I bought it. As soon as Wrox books came out I was hooked. My first book was the *Revolutionary Guide to Visual C++*. I liked the style as well as the straightforward information not found anywhere else. As the years have passed, I have found learning new and other types of technology much easier. I found it just takes time, dedication, and some common sense to succeed in this business.

I am the Technical Lead in my current position, introducing project methodology, new technologies, standards, and training to development teams. I have spent some time consulting and have been exposed to technologies such as ASP, Delphi, Pascal, COM, C/C++, SQL, Java, ADO, Visual Basic, and now .NET. I currently live in Sacramento, California, and can be contacted via e-mail at bforgey@vbcentral.net."

Thanks goes out to Wrox Press, Paul, Richard, Rob, Laura, these are wonderful people to work with. Also thanks to the team of technical reviewers.

I'd also like to thank Desiree for being so forgiving for all those late nights and lost moments. I could never write the words to express my feelings about you.

Table of Contents

Introduction

All software is based on the principle of manipulating data. Whether it's the code that runs inside your VCR to start recording at a specific time, or air traffic control software, code is always working with data in one form or another.

Today, we find that sophisticated applications store their data in a "database", a central repository of data overseen by a Database Management System, or DBMS. A DBMS does two things. Firstly, it handles the storage of the data. Secondly, it provides mechanisms for retrieving data as well as adding, removing, and changing data. A DBMS endeavors to do this in the most efficient way possible.

Over the years, the DBMS market has grown into a mature sophisticated industry in its own right, offering products designed for use in large enterprise environments like Oracle 9i or Microsoft SQL Server 2000, down to products designed for use on the desktop like Microsoft Access. In some cases, you even find that software packages include their own DBMS software for managing their own proprietary databases.

You'll find in your work as a programmer that applications often require access to data managed by a DBMS. In fact, you'll most likely find that using a DBMS is *the* easiest way to store and manipulate your application's data. However, with a wide variety of vendors to choose from, how can we write application code that can work with any database our customer cares to choose?

The trick here is to build your application to work with a "data access layer" of some kind. Rather than writing code that specifically requires a specific DBMS, you write code that talks to the layer. It's then the layer's responsibility to switch to the "native" calls that the DBMS itself uses. Microsoft calls this vision "Universal Data Access", or UDA. Microsoft's latest tool for UDA is ADO.NET, a comprehensive set of objects that work together to make up a data access layer.

This book is all about building Visual Basic .NET applications that harness the power of ADO.NET. We will show how to use this technology in a variety of different ways: with desktop applications using Windows Forms; with web applications using ASP.NET; and with Web Services.

Who Is This Book for?

This book is for programmers with some basic experience of Visual Basic .NET, who want to begin programming database applications.

It might be useful if you have some limited experience of Access, although this is not strictly necessary.

Note that this book is *not* an introduction to Visual Basic .NET. If you are completely new to Visual Basic .NET, you will probably find *Beginning Visual Basic .NET* (Wrox Press, ISBN 1861004966) a better choice to get you off the ground.

Likewise, this book is *not* aimed at getting experienced VB6 developers up to speed with the changes between VB6 and Visual Basic .NET. If you fall into this category, try *Professional VB.NET* (Wrox Press, ISBN 1861004974) instead.

What Does This Book Cover?

Visual Basic .NET is tightly coupled to very comprehensive and flexible data access technologies, so the potential range of things that might fall under the title of this book is huge. Rather than trying to cover too much, we have concentrated on providing a detailed introduction to the following strands:

- Basic database design principles.
- The SQL Server Desktop Engine.
- Querying the database using T-SQL.
- Using Visual Studio .NET's Server Explorer to run queries, views, stored procedures, etc.
- ADO.NET and the `DataSet` object.
- Reading data into the `DataSet`, binding it to a control on the user interface, changing data in the `DataSet`, and saving those changes back in the underlying database.
- XML's role in ADO.NET.
- Internet database applications using Web Forms and Web Services.

What Do I Need To Use this Book?

All you'll need is a PC running:

- Windows 2000, XP, or NT4 Server.
- IIS 5, which comes with Windows 2000 and Windows XP.
- Internet Explorer.
- Access XP (or 2000).

- Visual Studio .NET Professional edition. (Higher versions of Visual Studio, for example,. the Enterprise editions, should work fine too. However, at the time of writing, they were unavailable and so this book was written using the Professional edition.)
- SQL Server 2000 Desktop Engine. This comes with Visual Studio .NET.

> **This book was written before the final release of Visual Studio .NET. If there are any substantial changes between the instructions given in this book and those required to work with the final release of Visual Studio .NET, we will provide free updates on the Wrox online errata service.**

Conventions

We've used a number of different styles of text and layout in this book to help differentiate between the different kinds of information. Here are examples of the styles we used and an explanation of what they mean.

Try It Outs – How Do They Work?

1. Each step has a number.
2. Follow the steps through.
3. Then read the *How It Works* section to find out what's going on.

> **These boxes hold important, not-to-be forgotten, mission-critical details that are directly relevant to the surrounding text.**

Background information, asides, and references appear in text like this.

Bullets appear indented, with each new bullet marked as follows:

- **Important words** are in a bold type font
- Words that appear on the screen, or in menus like the File or Window, are in a similar font to the one you would see on a Windows desktop
- Keys that you press on the keyboard, like *Ctrl* and *Enter*, are in italics

Code has several fonts. If it's a word that we're talking about in the text, for example, when discussing a `For ... Next` loop, it's in this font. If it's a block of code that can be typed as a program and run, then it's also in a gray box:

```
Private Sub btnAdd_Click(ByVal sender As System.Object, _
          ByVal e As System.EventArgs) Handles btnAdd.Click

   Dim n As Integer
   n = 27

   MessageBox.Show(n)

End Sub
```

Sometimes we'll see code in a mixture of styles, like this:

```
Private Sub btnAdd_Click(ByVal sender As System.Object, _
          ByVal e As System.EventArgs) Handles btnAdd.Click

   Dim n As Integer
   n = 27

   n = n + 2

   MessageBox.Show(n)

End Sub
```

In cases like this, the code with a white background is code that we are already familiar with; the line highlighted in gray is a new addition to the code since we last looked at it.

Customer Support

We always value hearing from our readers, and we want to know what you think about this book: what you liked, what you didn't like, and what you think we can do better next time. You can send us your comments, either by returning the reply card in the back of the book, or by e-mail to feedback@wrox.com. Please be sure to mention the book title in your message.

How To Download the Sample Code for the Book

When you visit the Wrox site, http://www.wrox.com/, simply locate the title through our Search facility or by using one of the title lists. Click on Download in the Code column, or on Download Code on the book's detail page.

The files that are available for download from our site have been archived using WinZip. When you have saved the attachments to a folder on your hard drive, you need to extract the files using a decompression program such as WinZip or PKUnzip. When you extract the files, the code is usually extracted into chapter folders. When you start the extraction process, ensure your software (WinZip, PKUnzip, etc.) is set to use folder names.

Errata

We've made every effort to make sure that there are no errors in the text or in the code. However, no one is perfect and mistakes do occur. If you find an error in one of our books, like a spelling mistake or a faulty piece of code, we would be very grateful for feedback. By sending in errata, you may save another reader hours of frustration and, of course, you will be helping us provide even higher quality information. Simply e-mail the information to support@wrox.com. Your information will be checked and, if correct, posted to the errata page for that title, or used in subsequent editions of the book.

To find errata on the web site, go to http://www.wrox.com/ and simply locate the title through our Advanced Search or title list. Click on the Book Errata link, which is below the cover graphic on the book's detail page.

E-mail Support

If you wish to directly query a problem in the book with an expert who knows the book in detail then e-mail support@wrox.com, with the title of the book and the last four numbers of the ISBN in the subject field of the e-mail. A typical e-mail should include the following things:

- The **title of the book**, **last four digits of the ISBN**, and **page number** of the problem in the Subject field
- Your **name**, **contact information**, and the **problem** in the body of the message

We *won't* send you junk mail. We need the details to save your time and ours. When you send an e-mail message, it will go through the following chain of support:

- Customer Support – Your message is delivered to our customer support staff, who are the first people to read it. They have files on most frequently asked questions and will answer anything general about the book or the web site immediately.
- Editorial – Deeper queries are forwarded to the technical editor responsible for that book. They have experience with the programming language or particular product, and are able to answer detailed technical questions on the subject.
- The Authors – Finally, in the unlikely event that the editor cannot answer your problem, he or she will forward the request to the author. We do try to protect the author from any distractions to their writing; however, we are quite happy to forward specific requests to them. All Wrox authors help with the support on their books. They will e-mail the customer and the editor with their response, and again all readers should benefit.

The Wrox Support process can only offer support to issues that are directly pertinent to the content of our published title. Support for questions that fall outside the scope of normal book support, is provided via the community lists of our http://p2p.wrox.com/ forum.

p2p.wrox.com

For author and peer discussion, join the P2P mailing lists. Our unique system provides **programmer to programmer™** contact on mailing lists, forums, and newsgroups, all in addition to our one-to-one e-mail support system. If you post a query to P2P, you can be confident that it is being examined by the many Wrox authors and other industry experts who are present on our mailing lists. At p2p.wrox.com you will find a number of different lists that will help you, not only while you read this book, but also as you develop your own applications. Particularly appropriate to this book are the beginning_vb, vbbegin_databases, and vb_dotnet lists.

To subscribe to a mailing list just follow these steps:

1. Go to http://p2p.wrox.com/.
2. Choose the appropriate category from the left menu bar.
3. Click on the mailing list you wish to join.
4. Follow the instructions to subscribe and fill in your e-mail address and password.
5. Reply to the confirmation e-mail you receive.
6. Use the subscription manager to join more lists and set your e-mail preferences.

Why This System Offers the Best Support

You can choose to join the mailing lists or you can receive them as a weekly digest. If you don't have the time, or facility, to receive the mailing list, then you can search our online archives. Junk and spam mails are deleted, and your own e-mail address is protected by the unique Lyris system. Queries about joining or leaving lists, and any other general queries about lists, should be sent to listsupport@p2p.wrox.com.

Relational Database Design

In this chapter, we'll cover some of the background details for the design and implementation of a database. The great majority of applications, whether developed with Visual Basic .NET or some other programming language, involve a database in some capacity, so it is crucial to have a firm understanding of the principles of good database design. After a brief introduction to databases in general, the chapter narrows its focus to designing and implementing one specific type of database – the relational database. Don't worry if you don't understand all the database terms at the moment as, by the end of the chapter, you will have a good understanding of:

- What a database is
- How relational databases compare to flat file databases
- The advantages of relational databases
- How to analyze business needs to identify what information a database should contain
- How to identify suitable elements that a database will need to include based on the requirements of a particular business
- How to define keys and relationships
- The objectives of data normalization and the advantages it can bring
- How to define indexes
- Putting it all together to create the physical database

Finally, we review the key points to remember when designing relational databases.

What Is a Database?

A **database** is essentially an electronic means of storing **data** in an **organized** manner. Data can be anything that a business or individual needs to keep track of and that, prior to computers, could have only been tracked on one or more paper documents. Once stored, data in the database can be retrieved, processed, and displayed by programs as **information** to the reader. The actual structure that a database uses to store data can take one of many different forms, each of which offers certain advantages when that information is to be retrieved or updated. In the next section, we will look at how storing the database in a flat file structure differs from a relational database structure, and the advantages and disadvantages that each of those presents.

Flat File Versus Relational Databases

Flat files are the most basic form of a database – all of the information is stored in a single file. A flat file includes a field for every item of information that you need to store. While they are easy to create and can be useful in certain situations, flat files are not very efficient. They can be quite wasteful of storage space, containing a lot of duplicated information, especially in a complex system where multiple files hold connected information. This can make information harder to maintain and retrieve. If you have worked with **spreadsheets** before, then you have already worked with one of the most common examples of a flat file database. To further demonstrate how the data in flat files is organized and why this can be problematic, let's walk through a hypothetical example.

Suppose you use the spreadsheet shown in the table below to track orders placed by your customers:

Order #	Order Date	Item Description	Quantity	Quantity Per Unit	Price	Customer Name	Customer Address
1000	**1-Aug-01**	**Tofu**	1	**40 - 100 g pkgs**	**23.25**	**Jane Doe**	**123 Somewhere St., Anytown, IN 46060 USA**
1000	**1-Aug-01**	**Jack's New England Clam Chowder**	1	**12 - 12 oz cans**	**9.65**	**Jane Doe**	**123 Somewhere St., Anytown, IN 46060 USA**
1000	**1-Aug-01**	**Grandma's Boysenberry Spread**	3	**12 - 8 oz jars**	**25**	**Jane Doe**	**123 Somewhere St., Anytown, IN 46060 USA**
1001	2-Aug-01	Uncle Bob's Organic Dried Pears	1	12 - 1 lb pkgs	30	John Smith	345 Anywhere St., Somewhere, IN 46001 USA
1001	2-Aug-01	Tofu	1	40 - 100 g pkgs	23.25	John Smith	345 Anywhere St., Somewhere, IN 46001 USA

Notice how this spreadsheet contains order information as well as customer information. Jane Doe, for example, placed order #1000 for Tofu, Jack's New England Clam Chowder, and Grandma's Boysenberry Spread. Each of those items is listed on a separate row in the spreadsheet. Further notice how the Order #, Order Date, as well as Jane Doe's name and address, are listed multiple times for each item in the order, as indicated by the gray entries above.

We say that the Order #, Order Date, Customer Name, and Customer Address fields contain **redundant** information – that is, the same information duplicated in several places. Redundant information causes a database to be larger than it really needs to be because it contains multiple entries with the same information. It also causes extra work when recording information about the order in the spreadsheet, due to the fact that the same information must be typed repeatedly. Unfortunately, typing the information multiple times greatly increases the likelihood that a mistake will be made – such as the misspelling of a name or address in one of the order items.

Another problem with flat files is **maintenance**. What happens, for example, when Jane Doe moves and you need to update her address in your spreadsheet? Well, in this flat file format, you will have to update her address multiple times – once for each item she has ever ordered. If she is a really good customer, that could mean hundreds of changes. If her address were stored in one place only, then that would be the only place you would have to update it. But that certainly isn't the case in our example. In this simple example, you have witnessed firsthand some of the most common problems of flat file databases: data redundancy and excessive maintenance requirements.

Now that we understand what a flat file database is, and are aware of areas where the format can be problematic, we are ready to look at a database type that addresses these shortcomings: the **relational database**. In its simplest terms, a relational database can be thought of as a collection of informational items broken down into different groups interrelated to each other in one or more ways. In database terms, these groups are often called **tables**. This concept may sound complicated, but it isn't really that bad. Let's modify our previous example to demonstrate what it would look like in a relational format – and then you can see for yourself that the big-picture concept isn't too complicated to understand.

Recall that our flat file spreadsheet contained information about Orders and Customers. Each order consisted of multiple order items and each order was placed by a single customer. A relational database storing this information might be split into three separate tables: `Customers`, `Orders`, and `OrderItems`, depicted in the diagram below:

Customers	**Orders**	**OrderItems**
Customer_Id	Order_Id	Item_Id
Customer_First_Name	Customer_Id	Order_Id
Customer_Last_Name	Order_Date	Item_Description
Customer_Address1		Quantity_Ordered
Customer_City		Item_Price
Customer_State		Quantity_Per_Unit
Customer_Zip		
Customer_Country		

The `Customers` table above contains a single entry for each customer. The `Orders` table contains a single entry for each order. And, finally, the `OrderItems` table contains a single entry for each item in the order, meaning there can be one or more items per order. Thus, customer information is stored separately from each order and each item of an order is stored separately from the orders themselves. Notice that the `Orders` table contains a `Customer_Id` that relates to the `Customer_Id` field in the `Customers` table. Further notice that the `OrderItems` table contains an `Order_Id` that relates to the `Order_Id` field in the `Orders` table. We will look at this concept of how tables relate together in the *Defining Relationships* section of this chapter. For now, just know that this is the mechanism that eliminates data redundancy, a problem we saw in the flat file format that duplicated customer names and addresses and so on. There is no such duplication in this relational database. If we want to update Jane Doe's address, for example, we merely have to update the single entry she has in the `Customers` table. Better yet, when Jane Doe places her order, we do not have to type in her address multiple times. If she has already ordered from us before, her details will already be held by an entry in the `Customers` table, and we simply have to use the `Customer_Id` from that existing entry. If she is a new customer on the other hand, all we need do is add her details once to the `Customers` table, where it will remain, ready to be reused should she reorder further items from us.

You may be wondering at this point how we came up with all these items for the above tables, or what exactly they mean. Don't worry too much about such details, the main thing is that, at this point, you at least have a grasp of the high-level concepts behind the relational database format: that it stores data in logical interrelated groups and that it eliminates redundant data. As long as this makes sense, we can move on to the details of how to determine database requirements and how we can then create a relational database from such requirements.

Determining Database Requirements

Before we jump in and start designing a database, we first need to undertake a variety of investigation and analysis processes to determine the information that needs to be captured. This section explores the steps that you should take to facilitate this process.

Analyzing Our Business Needs

The first step in determining the requirements for a database is a thorough analysis of the needs of the business or individual for whom the database is intended. Your objective at this stage is to invest the time to learn the customer's business and fully understand what they wish to accomplish. It can be tempting to skip this step and jump straight to creating the physical structure of the database. Of course, we are too wise to succumb to such a poor design strategy. In order to construct a database that truly meets the needs of the customer, it is critical to have a complete understanding of their objectives beforehand. The physical structure we then decide on will be heavily influenced by the particular objectives of their business.

Here are some guidelines to follow when completing an analysis:

- Analyze any current electronic databases that are to be replaced by the new system. Find out what works well with the present system and what areas need improvement. Ask questions to determine key fields (`order_date`, `item_description`, etc.) for the database: which ones are most often used, are any not really used at all, and whether there are any missing. You may find that certain information isn't actually used and can be omitted from the new database, or that there is critical information missing that needs to be added.

- Interview one-on-one and in groups to discuss the current procedures with people at every level of the business that will interact with the database or use the reports that it generates. Devise questions to find the objectives that they would like to accomplish, the information that they need to track, any frustrations of the present system, and details of how they presently work with the database.
- Get copies of existing forms and reports – whether paper or electronic – that are used in the data handling process. After obtaining these paper and electronic copies, make sure that they are populated with sample data so you can further clarify the type of information that they represent. From this information, and from talking with the employees, you are ready to start drafting a high-level "wish list" of the information that needs to be dealt with. This wish list will later be used to help determine the fields and tables in the database that need to be created.
- Carefully analyze existing reports and create drafts on paper of reports that you think will be needed, based on your fact-finding. Once you have some ideas on paper of the reports that will be needed, you will start to get an idea of the fields that will be required by the database. You can't generate a report from data that doesn't exist in the database, right?
- Make sure that you do a good job of documenting your analysis, what you learned, from whom, why it is important, and any other details that you feel may be relevant.

Once you have conducted the interviews, hosted group meetings, and have analyzed the current process and systems, you should compile a summary of what overall objectives are to be accomplished. As an example, this summary could look like the following for a typical hypothetical business:

- The overall objective of the database is to store information about products on offer, the company's inventory, outstanding and completed sales, and customers.
- They have several products available for order.
- Customers can place orders for one or more products at a time. Typically, an order is for one to three products, but no order is for more than four products.
- Each order will belong to just one customer, although it may include multiple products.
- They want to be able to take customer orders over the phone and enter them into the database application directly. In order to do this, they need accessible product information – such as quantity in stock and price – to allow product availability to be confirmed at the time that the order is placed.
- They need to be able to generate various reports from the data to show sales totals, orders awaiting fulfillment, out-of-stock products, and grand-total orders for each customer.
- They need a way to target customers for special promotions, either by phone or e-mail.

The summary should be a concise high-level recap of what you need to accomplish. It is essential that you share your findings with the company that you're doing the analysis for, so they can give feedback on whether you understand their needs correctly. You should also be able to hand the summary to a total stranger and they should be able to understand the purpose of the database at an abstract level. This summary and the detailed data that you compile and refine will then be used to further design the database.

Determining the Information To Be Tracked

Now that you have interviewed as many people as possible, studied the current process, and compiled all your findings, you can review your conclusions so far to determine individual data elements that need to be tracked. For example, read through your notes and, any time that you see something that you know will have to be tracked in the database, write it somewhere separately with all the other items that are likely to be required as a field. Continue this process until you have listed all of the pieces of information that need to be tracked.

When writing down this information, don't worry about any particular order or grouping of the items. At this stage, simply list anything that you feel is data that should be tracked. Also, list an example beside each element to show typical values that it might contain. This will come in handy later when you have to determine the appropriate data type that a particular field will allow. We are still early in the process and it is important to try to get a solid overall feel for the database's contents – there's no need to worry about being exact at this point.

From the requirements gathered in previous stages, our list of fields might look something like this:

Product Identifier (e.g. 12345)	Product Description (e.g. Tofu)	Product Unit Price (e.g. $23.25)
Product Quantity on Hand (e.g. 50)	Product Unit of Measure (e.g. 40 – 100 g pkgs)	Customer Name (e.g. Jane A. Doe)
Customer Number (e.g. 123456)	Customer Address (e.g. 123 Somewhere St., Anytown, IN 46060 USA)	Customer Email (e.g. jdoe@yahoo.com)
Customer Telephone (e.g. 317-111-2222)	Product Identifier for Items Ordered (e.g. 12345 for Tofu)	Quantity Ordered (e.g. 3)
Ordered by Customer Number (e.g. 123456)	Order Ship Date (e.g. Aug. 3, 2001)	Order Number (e.g. 1000)
Order Date (e.g. Aug. 1, 2001)	Unit Price as Ordered (e.g. $23.25)	

Notice how the fields are listed in no particular order and that they each contain typical examples in parentheses. The table includes fields that will allow us to connect information about customers, products, and sales orders.

In the next section, we look at how to use this sort of list to determine the structure for our database.

Determining the Logical Database Design

After you have determined high-level requirements and objectives for the database, you can begin to implement the relational database design on paper – a phase commonly termed **logical database design**. You need to have a sketch drafted out – a roadmap – detailing how your database is to look before you actually begin the task of creating it electronically.

Defining Tables (Entities) and Fields (Attributes)

The first step in creating the logical database design is to define your tables and fields. **Tables**, also called **entities**, are logical groupings of related information. Recall that, when we converted our flat file spreadsheet into tables at the beginning of the chapter, we ended up with the following `Customers`, `Orders`, and `OrderItems` tables:

Customers	Orders	OrderItems
`Customer_Id`	`Order_Id`	`Item_Id`
`Customer_First_Name`	`Customer_Id`	`Order_Id`
`Customer_Last_Name`	`Order_Date`	`Item_Description`
`Customer_Address1`		`Quantity_Ordered`
`Customer_City`		`Item_Price`
`Customer_State`		`Quantity_Per_Unit`
`Customer_Zip`		
`Customer_Country`		

Fields, also called **attributes,** are the individual data elements within the table – or you could say the attributes that together describe the entity. You see above that the `Customers` table contains several individual bits of information for any customer: `Customer_Id`, `Customer_First_Name`, `Customer_Last_Name`, and so on. We refer to these as the fields of the `Customers` table, or equivalently as the attributes that describe the `Customers` entity. Either terminology is acceptable, but the terms tables and fields tend to be the terms most commonly used so we shall use them throughout the remainder of the chapter.

Identifying Tables and Fields

Now that we understand the definition of tables and fields, let's step back and actually walk through the steps of how you get here – that is, how to identify tables and fields from the information gathered in the initial analysis phases.

Looking at the business requirements, we previously determined that the following fields need to be tracked, shown below in no particular order:

Product Identifier (e.g. 12345)	Product Description (e.g. Tofu)	Product Unit Price (e.g. $23.25)
Product Quantity on Hand (e.g. 50)	Product Unit of Measure (e.g. 40 – 100 g pkgs)	Customer Name (e.g. Jane A. Doe)
Customer Number (e.g. 123456)	Customer Address (e.g. 123 Somewhere St., Anytown, IN 46060 USA)	Customer Email (e.g. jdoe@yahoo.com)
Customer Telephone (e.g. 317-111-2222)	Product Identifier for Items Ordered (e.g. 12345 for Tofu)	Quantity Ordered (e.g. 3)
Ordered by Customer Number (e.g. 123456)	Order Ship Date (e.g. Aug. 3, 2001)	Order Number (e.g. 1000)
Order Date (e.g. Aug. 1, 2001)	Unit Price as Ordered (e.g. $23.25)	

What we can do now is take a detailed look at all elements to be covered by the system, and try to break them down into tables and fields. To do this, take a look over the list and see what could be readily grouped together into a table – as we now know, a table is a logical grouping of related data. This step is not an exact science. We can do our best to group the data into suitable tables but, depending on how many fields you have altogether and how complicated the requirements are, it will almost always take multiple attempts to get right – at this point in the process, you aren't even expected or likely to get the tables and fields exactly right. The later steps that we will look at, help us to decide on the modifications we should make to ensure that our database meets the requirements of good design.

So, let's see if we can turn our above example into a set of tables. Scan through all the elements in the list and see what type of information they each relate to. For example, in scanning the list above, each element either describes one of: the product, the customer, or the order. In database terms, this step is called defining the **entities**. An entity is used to describe a group of related information. After identifying the entities themselves, you can then create an **entity relationship diagram (ERD),** which shows the information describing each entity and the relationship each entity has to the other.

To create an ERD, you simply list each entity name in a separate box, and then list each piece of information underneath the entity that it corresponds to. You then make comments and draw arrows describing how each entity relates to each other, such as describing the fact that an order can contain one or more products. Here is an example of what the ERD looks like from applying these steps to our example:

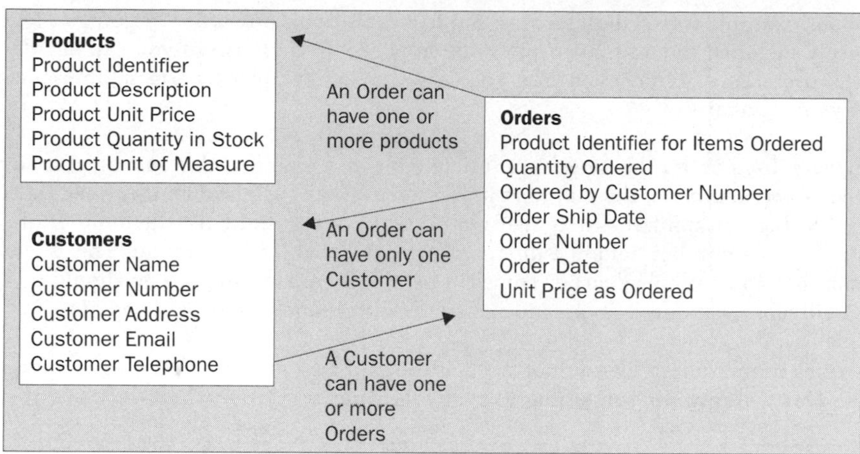

From the ERD, you can then begin to easily formulate ideas on what tables it looks like the database will need to contain. Upon analyzing the ERD above, for example, it looks like we will at least need the following tables:

- `Products` – to store information about all the products that our company offers for sale
- `Customers` – to store information for each customer
- `Orders` – to store information about each order

Now that we have some potential tables identified, let's assign fields for each of these tables. What this really means is that you will translate the pieces of information in the ERD that describe each entity into a name that will be meaningful in the database.

There are a couple of guidelines that we need to be aware of before we start this process. First, use a new sheet of paper (or file if you prefer to write on screen) for each potential table, and put each field as you consider it onto the sheet for the table that it seems to relate to the most. Always try to give fields meaningful names that concisely describe the kind of information they contain, thus facilitating the task of retrieving information in your applications later. Say, for example, that you called the customer number field something arbitrary like `field1`, and the customer name `field2`. When you come to retrieve the customer name in your applications later, you're in danger of having to open database fields at random to try to locate the one containing the customer name, unless you happen to remember which is which. Even if you do know that `field2` is the customer name, your code will be littered with confusing and unhelpful names, making it much harder to understand. In many cases, third-party developers will use your database in their applications, making the situation a potential nightmare. Choosing appropriate and descriptive field names is an aspect of good database design that is all too often neglected, and yet it is something that should never be underestimated.

Here is another essential tip when naming fields: use case appropriately to make the name easier on the eye. For example, instead of naming a field `customername` in all lower case, use the alternative form `CustomerName`. This mix of upper and lower case is sometimes referred to as "camel case", and it can make identifiers much easier to read than if just a single case is employed. Spaces are usually not allowed in field names but underscores can be used to designate spaces. You could use an underscore to separate `CustomerName`, making `Customer_Name`. This standard for separating words in identifiers is followed across multiple database languages, and either designation (`CustomerName` or `Customer_Name`) is equally acceptable.

In the previous example I used underscores. But from this point onward, I'm going to leave them out. I have purposely included them so far to show you how each style looks so you can decide which is your own personal preference. Whichever form you chose, try to be consistent, using the same standard throughout your database.

After listing each field under the most appropriate table and giving each a meaningful name, next to every field give an example of the data that it will contain, the type of data it is (text, date, number, and so on), and how big you think the field needs to be. If it is a text field, list the number of characters it must handle. If it is a number field, list the range of values that it may contain. This is where the example data that you compiled earlier comes in handy. By examining it, you should be able to make some educated guesses about the type and size of the information fields will contain.

With these rules in mind, let's list each of the fields identified so far under the most appropriate of the three tables. This will result in something like the following:

PRODUCTS TABLE

Field	**Example**	**Type of Data**	**Estimated Size of Data**
`ProductIdentifier`	12345	Numeric	Positive number with no decimals
`ProductDescription`	Tofu	Text	25 characters
`ProductUnitPrice`	$23.25	Currency	$00.00 to $10,000.00
`ProductQuantityOnHand`	50	Numeric	0 to 9,999
`ProductUnitOfMeasure`	40 – 100 g pkgs	Text	25 characters

CUSTOMERS TABLE

Field	**Example**	**Type of Data**	**Estimated Size of Data**
`CustomerNumber`	123456	Numeric	Positive number with no decimals
`CustomerName`	Jane A. Doe	Text	45 characters
`CustomerAddress`	123 Somewhere St., Anytown, IN 46060 USA	Text	65 characters
`Customer Telephone`	317-111-2222	Text	12 characters
`CustomerEmail`	jdoe@yahoo.com	Text	50 characters

ORDERS TABLE			
Field	**Example**	**Type of Data**	**Estimated Size of Data**
`OrderNumber`	1000	Numeric	Positive number with no decimals
`OrderDate`	Aug. 1, 2001	Date	Valid date
`ProductIdentifier1`	12345	Numeric	Positive number with no decimals
`PriceItem1`	$19.00	Currency	$00.00 to $10,000.00
`QuantityItem1`	2	Numeric	0 to 9,999
`ProductIdentifier2`	2345	Numeric	Positive number with no decimals
`PriceItem2`	$8.50	Currency	$00.00 to $10,000.00
`QuantityItem2`	3	Numeric	0 to 9,999
`ProductIdentifier3`	3456	Numeric	Positive number with no decimals
`PriceItem3`	$13.00	Currency	$00.00 to $10,000.00
`QuantityItem3`	4	Numeric	0 to 9,999
`ProductIdentifier4`	4567	Numeric	Positive number with no decimals
`PriceItem4`	$15.00	Currency	$00.00 to $10,000.00
`QuantityItem4`	5	Numeric	0 to 9,999
`CustomerNumber`	123456	Numeric	Positive number with no decimals
`OrderShipDate`	Aug. 3, 2001	Date	Valid date

Notice how we have listed our fields in the three tables called `Products`, `Customers`, and `Orders`. The `Products` table comprises fields that describe the products for sale and include product description, price, and so on. In the `Customers` table, we list fields pertinent to individual customers and include the customer name, address, and so on. Lastly, we have listed details pertaining to individual orders in the `Orders` table, including the order number, products ordered, customer number, and order ship date. We allow up to four products to be ordered and have corresponding fields for the price and quantity of each.

It is important to bear in mind that the structure outlined at this point is not yet in the final format, and you should be aware that we will be modifying it further to conform with the rules of good database design. For now, the objective is to just make an initial attempt at identifying the tables and fields that we might need. This gives us a starting point from which we can now move on to apply some database design rules that further refine what we have at the moment. So, without any further ado, let's identify the key fields for each of our tables, and see why this is important.

Identifying Keys

Once we have drawn up the above lists of possible tables and fields, the next step in the logical database design is to identify the primary and foreign keys for each table.

Primary Keys

A **primary key (PK)** consists of a field or a set of fields that uniquely identify each record in that table. The primary key is defined by the "primary" field. For example, in the `Customers` table, the `CustomerNumber` is the primary key. The customer number must be unique for every customer, and an attempt to add a new customer record with an existing number will fail. `ProductIdentifier` in the `Products` table is another example of a primary key, as is the `OrderNumber` in the `Orders` table. Each product in the `Products` table is uniquely defined by the `ProductIdentifier`, and every order must be allocated a unique value to use for the `OrderNumber` field. Because primary keys must be unique, they must contain a value (that is, they cannot be empty).

When deciding which field or fields to use as the primary key, try to pick numeric values whenever possible. This is because the primary key constitutes the main method of access to a record in the table and, as a rule, numeric keys generally out-perform non-numeric keys. However, text-based keys do work and may be used when a suitable numeric key isn't available. Text fields can pose problems of uniqueness, such that the customer name would not make a suitable primary key because many people share the same name. In such cases, you could make a **composite key** with a key based on the combination of multiple fields, such as the `Name` and `Address` fields. These two fields, when combined, would then constitute the primary key to uniquely identify any customer. Such a text-based key would work but is less suitable than a key based on a unique customer number, because it is possible that two people with the same name could share the same address.

In some cases, you may want to create a primary key that is system generated. A **system-generated key** is a key that the database assigns automatically when the record is inserted. You may already be familiar with what is called an AutoNumber in Access, which is one example of a system-generated key. Continuing with our example, suppose that you created a system-generated key for the `ProductIdentifier` field. Then, when a new product record is added to the database, the `ProductIdentifier` field gets filled in by the database automatically. You do not have to write any code in your programs to assign or insert the value in such a case. With non system-generated keys, on the other hand, you must assign and specifically insert a value into that key field when inserting a record into that table. When you design the keys for a table in the physical database, you must specify that a key field is to be system generated or, by default, it will not be.

The most important aspect of assigning keys is to make absolutely sure that the field or fields you pick for the key will always be unique. This means that you should not choose a field as the key that can possibly be duplicated in the same table for multiple records. As an example, you would not want to make the `OrderDate` the primary key in the `Orders` table because there could be more than one order for a given date in the table. If you did have the `OrderDate` as the primary key, when the second record with that same date is inserted, a key violation will occur because the new record has an identifier that has already been used. In such a case, the attempt to add the new record will fail.

Foreign Keys

A **foreign key (FK)** is a key comprised of a field or multiple fields that link to the primary key of another table. A good example of a foreign key is the `CustomerNumber` in the `Orders` table. The `CustomerNumber` is the primary key in the `Customers` table but, in the `Orders` table, it is a foreign key. Each `Order` contains a unique `OrderNumber` as the primary key, but it also contains a `CustomerNumber` foreign key to let us reference the details of the customer who placed the order, as contained in the `Customers` table. Of course, the `CustomerNumber` in the `Orders` table doesn't uniquely identify the order (the `OrderNumber` does) – it is just another piece of information about the order that happens to be the primary key of another table. The `ProductIdentifier` fields in the `Orders` table are also foreign keys, as they refer to the `ProductIdentifier` primary key of the `Products` table.

Shown below are our tables as before, but with the primary and foreign keys highlighted. Note that, for clarification, we've added PK for primary key and FK for foreign key for each field name cell as appropriate, but these designations won't actually be part of the field name in our database:

PRODUCTS TABLE			
Field	**Example**	**Type of Data**	**Estimated Size of Data**
`ProductIdentifier (PK)`	12345	Numeric	Positive number with no decimals
`ProductDescription`	Tofu	Text	25 characters
`ProductUnitPrice`	$23.25	Currency	$00.00 to $10,000.00
`ProductQuantityOnHand`	50	Numeric	0 to 9,999
`ProductUnitOfMeasure`	40 – 100 g pkgs	Text	25 characters

CUSTOMERS TABLE			
Field	**Example**	**Type of Data**	**Estimated Size of Data**
`CustomerNumber (PK)`	123456	Numeric	Positive number with no decimals
`CustomerName`	Jane A. Doe	Text	45 characters
`CustomerAddress`	123 Somewhere St., Anytown, IN 46060 USA	Text	65 characters
`CustomerTelephone`	317-111-2222	Text	12 characters
`CustomerEmail`	jdoe@yahoo.com	Text	50 characters

ORDERS TABLE			
Field	**Example**	**Type of Data**	**Estimated Size of Data**
OrderNumber (PK)	1000	Numeric	Positive number with no decimals
OrderDate	Aug. 1, 2001	Date	Valid date
ProductIdentifier1 (FK)	12345	Numeric	Positive number with no decimals
PriceItem1	$19.00	Currency	$00.00 to $10,000.00
QuantityItem1	2	Numeric	0 to 9,999
ProductIdentifier2 (FK)	2345	Numeric	Positive number with no decimals
PriceItem2	$8.50	Currency	$00.00 to $10,000.00
QuantityItem2	3	Numeric	0 to 9,999
ProductIdentifier3 (FK)	3456	Numeric	Positive number with no decimals
PriceItem3	$13.00	Currency	$00.00 to $10,000.00
QuantityItem3	4	Numeric	0 to 9,999
ProductIdentifier4 (FK)	4567	Numeric	Positive number with no decimals
PriceItem4	$15.00	Currency	$00.00 to $10,000.00
QuantityItem4	5	Numeric	0 to 9,999
CustomerNumber (FK)	123456	Numeric	Positive number with no decimals
OrderShipDate	Aug. 3, 2001	Date	Valid date

Now that we have identified the primary and foreign keys for the currently envisaged structure, we can move on to examine the relationships between each table.

Defining Relationships

The next step in our logical database design is to define the relationships between the tables. A **relationship** is the term used to describe a connection between related tables. Stated another way, it means having shared fields in different tables that allow records to reference records in other tables. For example, suppose we want to find the description of a product that a customer ordered. The `Orders` table doesn't need the full product description, but simply the `ProductIdentifier` for each product ordered. We can use these fields (`ProductIdentifier1` is the first product code, `ProductIdentifier2` the second, and so on) to pull out the corresponding product record from the `Products` table – the entry in that table with the same `ProductIdentifier` entry – and so we can retrieve the `ProductDescription` for any ordered item. In Chapter 3, we will cover how to use Structured Query Language (SQL) for this very purpose.

Now that we have an understanding of what we mean by the term relationship in this context, we're ready to look at the three possible types of relationships: One-To-One, One-To-Many, and Many-To-Many.

One-To-One Relationships

A **one-to-one relationship** indicates that each record in a table may relate to only one record in another table. For example, suppose that we have three hundred fields for each customer. Further, suppose that our database doesn't support records with this many fields. One solution would be to break the customers table into two separate tables, such as `Customers` and `CustomersDetail`. Tables with one-to-one relationships have the same primary key, which serves to link two related records – this field is sometimes referred to as the **join column**. In our hypothetical scenario, the tables would link to each other by both using the unique `CustomerNumber` field as their primary key. Tables that have such a one-to-one relationship can be viewed as simply extensions of each other. In practice, true one-to-one relationships do not actually occur very often. Often, when they are found in a database system, they are there to get around some limitation of the database such as the one we've just described.

An example of our hypothetical one-to-one relationship is shown here:

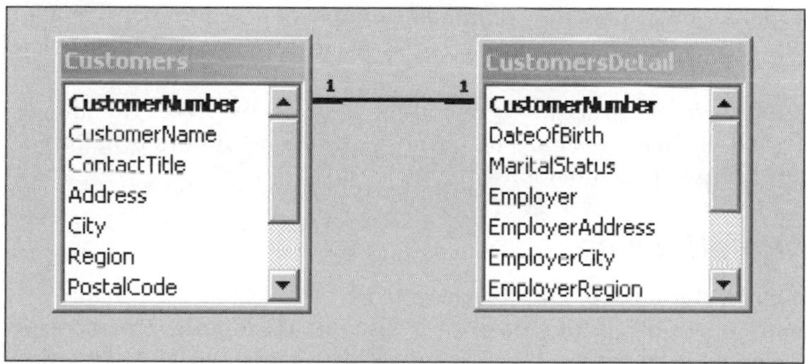

Notice how the hypothetical `Customers` table above joins to the hypothetical `CustomersDetail` table by the common `CustomerNumber` field. This field is the primary key for both tables and the information contained in each table is, in effect, just an extension of the other.

> **It is important to note that `CustomerNumber` is in bold in the tables above as it is the primary key. Bolding of entries always designates them as the primary key.**

One-To-Many Relationships

In a **one-to-many relationship**, any record in a table can relate to multiple records in a second table. This is the type of relationship that will exist between the `Customers` and `Orders` tables of our example database setup. A single customer can place many orders, but each order may have only one customer – we say that the `Customers` table has a one-to-many relationship with the `Orders` table (one customer to many orders). Note that this means that any record in the first table (`Customers`) can have zero or one corresponding records in the second table (`Orders`), though not necessarily more than one. Looked at from another angle, each customer in the `Customers` table can place zero, one, or many orders.

An example of this one-to-many relationship from our work-in-progress database structure is shown below:

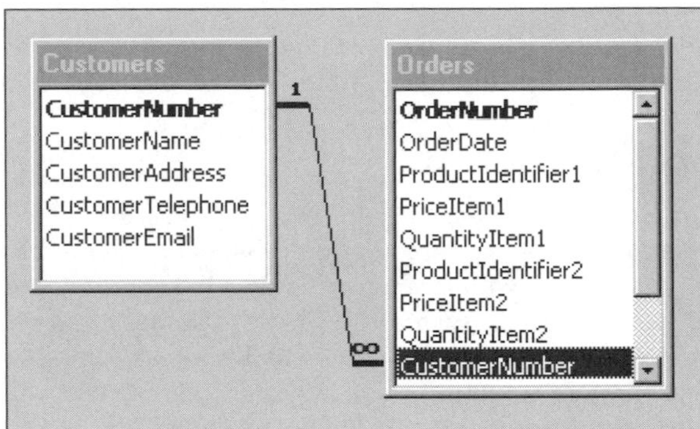

Notice how the `CustomerNumber` entry in the `Customers` table relates directly to multiple `CustomerNumber` entries in the `Orders` table, and that a customer may not have any outstanding orders in the `Orders` table, even though they have a record in the `Customers` table. The symbols above are the standard typically employed for designating relationships – with the one symbol ("`1`") next to the `CustomerNumber` in the `Customers` table and the many symbol ("∞") next to the `CustomerNumber` in the `Orders` table. This scenario is a very common example of a one-to-many relationship: we have a primary key for one table relating to another table where that same key is the foreign key.

Don't get too used to the table structure shown in the figure above. We will change it shortly to better meet the rules of good database design. The purpose of showing it here is merely as an example of a one-to-many relationship between database tables.

Many-To-Many Relationships

With a **many-to-many relationship**, many records in one table can link to many records in the second table. Many-to-many relationships are resolved by use of a third table, created especially to store the relationships between records in the other two tables. This table breaks the relationship down into multiple one-to-many relationships. Without this third table, many-to-many relationships would be impossible to implement due to restrictions of database systems.

Suppose that you have many users of a system and each user can be assigned to multiple roles. In such a case, you could say that one user could have many roles and that one role could have many users. How could you actually accomplish this? It is not possible to just create a users table and a roles table and then link them together. What you can do, on the other hand, is create a third (intermediate) table to store the relationships between users and roles. An example of how this can be accomplished is opposite:

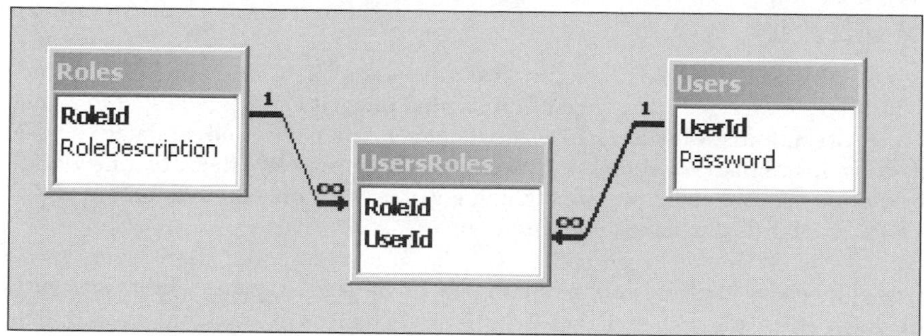

Notice how there is a one-to-many relationship between the `Roles` and `UserRoles` tables, as designated by the one and many symbols. This means that for each role, there can be many users. Further notice how there is a one-to-many relationship between the `Users` and `UsersRoles` tables. This means that each user can have many roles. You can see how the intermediate table, `UserRoles`, brings these two tables together. A good way of thinking of it is that the `UsersRoles` is a bride table which brings the `Roles` and `Users` tables together. The diagram below shows some sample data to further illustrate this concept:

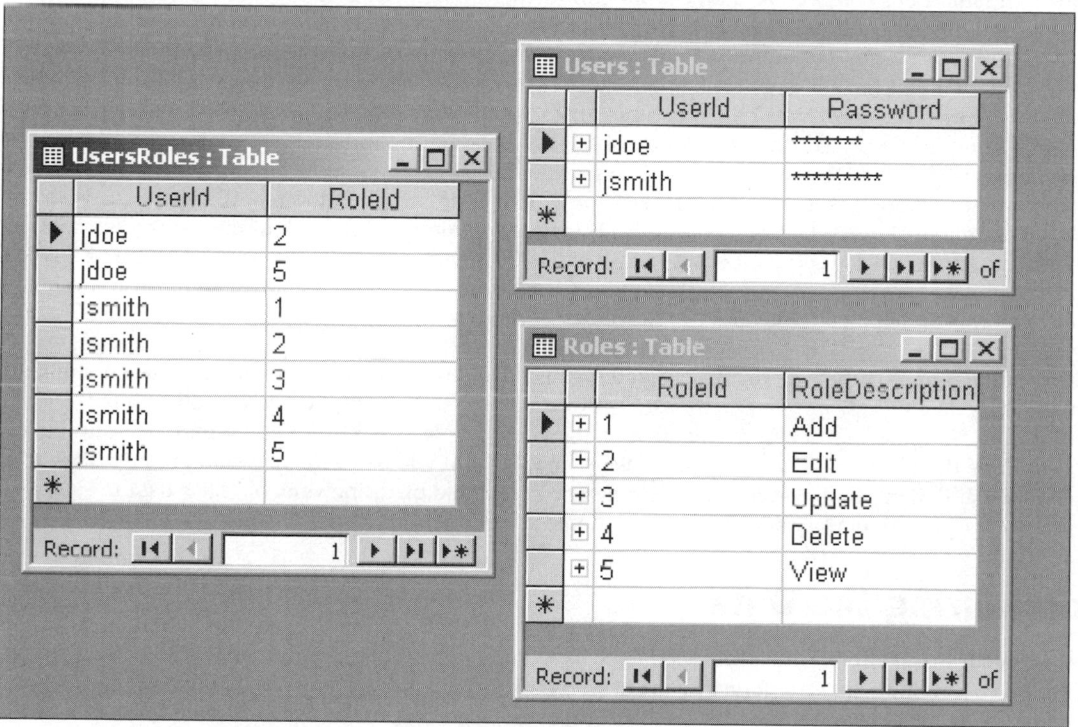

Notice that in the UsersRoles table, the user jdoe is assigned the RoleIds of 2 and 5. By looking at the RoleId in the Roles table, you will see that this means he has been assigned to the Edit and View roles. You will also notice that the same role is contained multiple times in the UsersRoles table: both jdoe and jsmith have RoleIds of 2 and 5. Thus, by using this intermediate UsersRoles table, we are able to overcome the limitations of most database platforms and accomplish the same end result as a many-to-many relationship.

Referential Integrity

By defining our table relationships in the physical database (which we discuss later in the chapter), we are setting ourselves up to take advantage of **referential integrity**. When enabled for a database, referential integrity automatically ensures that, whenever data is inserted, updated, or deleted, these defined relationships remain consistent. For example, the foreign key fields of a new or altered record can be checked to ensure that there is a matching entry in the table where that field is the primary key, thus avoid adding records that have invalid references.

With referential integrity in place, you may also take advantage of features known as **cascade update** and **cascade delete**. Cascade update means that, if a key changes in any table, the value in all tables where that key is present will be updated to reflect the new value. Similarly, with the cascade delete option enabled, if a record is deleted, all related records in the database will be deleted. By enforcing referential integrity, you can save yourself a lot of extra coding effort to modify multiple tables any time that a key value changes or records are deleted that would impact multiple tables.

We have already mentioned that referential integrity is a very important consideration. It is important to note that there are times, however, when referential integrity and cascading updates or deletes are problematic. Let's take a look at an example to further illustrate this concept of referential integrity, as well as to describe the problems that can occur when you do or don't take advantage of it.

Suppose that you have a database containing the table structure that we have designed so far in this chapter. Further, suppose that the database tables do not have referential integrity enabled. If you change the `ProductIdentifier` value of a given product in the `Products` table, you then would have to write code to manually change every occurrence of that same `ProductIdentifier` in every single place where it is used in the `Orders` table. If you do not, then the records in the `Orders` table will become **orphaned.** Orphaned records no longer contain the link back to the parent key that they were based on. To state it another way – the value for `ProductIdentifier` in the `Orders` table no longer exists in the `Products` table, so the `Order` record has become an orphan and cannot be joined back to the `Products` table because the values no longer match.

Also, depending on the way that your database has been designed, there are situations when enabling cascading deletes may not be exactly what you want. For example, suppose you need to remove a customer from the `Customers` table (maybe they haven't placed an order in the past year and you want to archive them). If you have cascading deletes enabled and you delete the customer record, then all of the orders that that customer placed are also deleted. You would be losing valuable sales data in such a case. Whenever you enable cascade deletes, you should make doubly sure that it will have the effect you desire.

Normalizing the Data

Once your initial efforts have established likely keys and relationships for your tables, the next step in the logical database design is to normalize the data. **Normalization** is the process of simplifying the database design to achieve the optimum structure. The steps in this process are known as **normal forms**. These normal forms are a sequence of rules that are applied to progressively simplify a database design. The higher the normal form of a database, the more efficient its underlying design is. This is because, for a database to be simplified into third normal form, it must first meet the criteria of the first and second normal forms.

In the real world, a database is generally said to be of good design if it meets the third normal form. In fact, there are normal forms beyond the third but, since such forms have little practical use in most real world situations, we only need concern ourselves with the first three. So, let's jump right in and take a look at the first three normal forms and start to apply their rules to our work-in-progress example.

First Normal Form

To achieve First Normal Form, we must eliminate any repeating groups.

In **First Normal Form**, we simplify our database structure to eliminate any repeating groups. In other words, First Normal Form includes the concept that fields must be "atomic" or a field represents one type of value for all records. Examples of these repeating groups can be:

- A list of multiple values in the same field. An example would be a field containing the single string "5 – Tofu, 4 – Jack's New England Clam Chowder". The problem here is that it is inefficient to retrieve individual items from such fields, as the contents have to be laboriously read and split up (parsed). It wouldn't be easy to examine the different products ordered by a customer. It would be an even more difficult task to examine products according to the quantities ordered.
- Repeated fields – that is, multiple occurrences of very similar fields to hold similar data (`Product1`, `Price1`, `Quantity1`, `Product2`, `Price2`, `Quantity2`, for example). Such fields are problematic for a couple of reasons. Firstly, they could impose a limit on how many products a customer might order at one time. You would have to modify the database structure to add additional columns if you wish to change this maximum later. Secondly, you waste space every time a customer places an order for less than the number of columns you have allocated. In other words, if you have fields to hold up to five products, and the customer only orders one product, then space in the database is taken up unnecessarily for the other four empty product fields. The third problem with repeating fields is that data analysis is much more complicated. For example, the analysis of sales data would be an awkward task if you had to join to each of the repeating fields to find the total of what was sold to each customer.

So, now that we know what we're looking for, let's look at our in-progress table structure to see where it violates first normal form, and make any necessary changes for compliance. The following figures recap the current table structure:

PRODUCTS TABLE

Field	**Example**	**Type of Data**	**Estimated Size of Data**
`ProductIdentifier (PK)`	12345	Numeric	Positive number with no decimals
`ProductDescription`	Tofu	Text	25 characters
`ProductUnitPrice`	$23.25	Currency	$00.00 to $10,000.00
`ProductQuantityOnHand`	50	Numeric	0 to 9,999
`ProductUnitOfMeasure`	40 – 100 g pkgs	Text	25 characters

CUSTOMERS TABLE			
Field	**Example**	**Type of Data**	**Estimated Size of Data**
`CustomerNumber (PK)`	123456	Numeric	Positive number with no decimals
`CustomerName`	Jane A. Doe	Text	45 characters
`CustomerAddress`	123 Somewhere St., Anytown, IN 46060 USA	Text	65 characters
`CustomerTelephone`	317-111-2222	Text	12 characters
`CustomerEmail`	jdoe@yahoo.com	Text	50 characters

ORDERS TABLE			
Field	**Example**	**Type of Data**	**Estimated Size of Data**
`OrderNumber (PK)`	1000	Numeric	Positive number with no decimals
`OrderDate`	Aug. 1, 2001	Date	Valid date
`ProductIdentifier1 (FK)`	12345	Numeric	Positive number with no decimals
`PriceItem1`	$19.00	Currency	$00.00 to $10,000.00
`QuantityItem1`	2	Numeric	0 to 9,999
`ProductIdentifier2 (FK)`	2345	Numeric	Positive number with no decimals
`PriceItem2`	$8.50	Currency	$00.00 to $10,000.00
`QuantityItem2`	3	Numeric	0 to 9,999
`ProductIdentifier3 (FK)`	3456	Numeric	Positive number with no decimals
`PriceItem3`	$13.00	Currency	$00.00 to $10,000.00
`QuantityItem3`	4	Numeric	0 to 9,999
`ProductIdentifier4 (FK)`	4567	Numeric	Positive number with no decimals
`PriceItem4`	$15.00	Currency	$00.00 to $10,000.00
`QuantityItem4`	5	Numeric	0 to 9,999
`CustomerNumber (FK)`	123456	Numeric	Positive number with no decimals
`OrderShipDate`	Aug. 3, 2001	Date	Valid date

Look at the tables and fields above – can you spot any multiple values listed together in a single field? The `Products` table doesn't include any – all of its fields contain just a single, discreet data item. Is the same true for the `Customer` table though? Well, not really. Notice how one field holds the complete customer name, including the first name, middle initial, and last name:

CustomerName	**Jane A. Doe**	Text	45 characters

If we wanted to analyze the data by last name, for example, such a structure would require us to devise an algorithm that would reliably split up the string held in this field. This is prone to error and would certainly have a negative impact on our database performance. It makes sense for us to separate the `CustomerName` field out into three separate fields; say `CustomerFirstName`, `CustomerLastName`, and `CustomerMiddleName`. The same holds true for the `CustomerAddress` field as well, where we have the entire customer address in just one field:

CustomerAddress	**123 Somewhere St., Anytown, IN 46060 USA**	Text	65 characters

Once again, to achieve a first normal form, we need to break the street address, city, state, zip, and country values into separate fields as well. After our modifications to the `Customers` table to eliminate such multiple data items in a single field, the new structure looks something like this:

CUSTOMERS TABLE			
Field	**Example**	**Type of Data**	**Estimated Size of Data**
CustomerNumber (PK)	123456	Numeric	Positive number with no decimals
CustomerFirstName	Jane	Text	15 characters
CustomerMiddleName	A.	Text	15 characters
CustomerLastName	Doe	Text	25 characters
CustomerAddress	123 Somewhere St.	Text	30 characters
CustomerCity	Anytown	Text	20 characters
CustomerState	IN	Text	2 characters
CustomerZip	46060	Text	9 characters
CustomerCountry	USA	Text	20 characters
CustomerTelephone	317-111-2222	Text	12 characters
CustomerEmail	jdoe@yahoo.com	Text	50 characters

Now that we have separated the `Name` and `Address` fields so that each data item has its own field, data will be much easier to retrieve using this revised format. It greatly facilitates such things as retrieving information about all customers in the state of Indiana for example. Before, you would have been required to parse the entire address field to search for the state part of the field, and there'd be no guarantee that that information had even been included for every customer.

The `Customers` table is, in fact, the only table with fields containing multiple values in the same field. Now let's look to see whether we have any tables that actually have fields that repeat themselves. We don't have to look very hard to see that our `Orders` table has several repeating fields for each product ordered, namely `ProductIdentifier`, `PriceItem`, and `QuantityItem`, as listed below:

ProductIdentifier1 (FK)	12345	Numeric	Positive number with no decimals
PriceItem1	$19.00	Currency	$00.00 to $10,000.00
QuantityItem1	2	Numeric	0 to 9,999
ProductIdentifier2 (FK)	2345	Numeric	Positive number with no decimals
PriceItem2	$8.50	Currency	$00.00 to $10,000.00
QuantityItem2	3	Numeric	0 to 9,999
ProductIdentifier3 (FK)	3456	Numeric	Positive number with no decimals
PriceItem3	$13.00	Currency	$00.00 to $10,000.00
QuantityItem3	4	Numeric	0 to 9,999
ProductIdentifier4 (FK)	4567	Numeric	Positive number with no decimals
PriceItem4	$15.00	Currency	$00.00 to $10,000.00
QuantityItem4	5	Numeric	0 to 9,999

We will run into problems when a customer wants to order more than four products, or when we analyze sales because we would have to search all four fields to calculate what was ordered. One way that we can modify our `Orders` table to comply with First Normal Form is to break up an order into a separate record for each item of the order, as shown opposite:

ORDERS TABLE			
Field	**Example**	**Type of Data**	**Estimated Size of Data**
`OrderNumber (PK)`	1000	Numeric	Positive number with no decimals
`ProductIdentifier (PK)`	12345	Numeric	Positive number with no decimals
`OrderDate`	Aug. 1, 2001	Date	Valid date
`CustomerNumber (FK)`	123456	Numeric	Positive number with no decimals
`Price`	$ 15.00	Currency	$00.00 to $10,000.00
`Quantity`	5	Numeric	0 to 9,999
`OrderShipDate`	Aug. 3, 2001	Date	Valid date

Below is a screenshot showing how our database might look after this modification:

Orders : Table

OrderNumber	ProductIdentifier	OrderDate	CustomerNumber	Price	Quantity	OrderShipDate
1000	14	5/27/2001	12345	$ 15.00	5	5/28/2001
1000	23	5/27/2001	12345	$ 13.25	1	5/28/2001
1000	25	5/27/2001	12345	$ 9.99	2	5/28/2001
1001	7	5/27/2001	23456	$ 17.32	1	5/28/2001
1001	10	5/27/2001	23456	$ 25.00	2	5/28/2001

Notice that now there are multiple records for each product in a given order. You might think this to be an inefficient duplication of data – you'd be right, but don't worry because we will address this when we refine the design to Second Normal Form in a minute. The important thing is that we are no longer limited to how many products can be included in a given order and, in addition, we could now easily retrieve the totals for each product ordered. With this format, if an order consists of just one product, then only one record needs to be created in the `Orders` table. On the other hand, if the order consisted of five separate products, then five records would be created in the `Orders` table. To allow this and yet ensure that each record in the `Orders` table still has a unique primary key, the primary key has to be changed to a combination of the `OrderNumber` and `ProductIdentifier` fields.

With respect to the `Products` table, we do not need to make any modifications to make it comply with First Normal Form. None of the fields in the `Products` table violate the two rules described above. In other words, none of the fields in the `Products` table contain multiple values in the same field, nor do they contain any repeated fields.

At this point, all of our tables comply with First Normal Form – we have eliminated inefficient repeating groups from the structure, achieving a better design that will make our lives much easier later. So let's move on to Second Normal Form and see what further changes, if any, we need to make our database structure comply.

Second Normal Form

To achieve Second Normal Form, we make sure that non-key fields depend on all of the fields in the primary key.

In **Second Normal Form**, we aim to streamline our design to ensure that every field that is not itself a key is specific to the entire primary key. Every field in the table should be dependent upon the entire primary key so that, when new records are added, the same values will not be repeated from record to record unnecessarily. Let's look at our sample database design to illustrate this issue.

In the First Normal Form step, we modified the `Orders` table to allow multiple records for every product ordered (as opposed to having a fixed set of fields for up to four products). To allow this, the `OrderNumber` and `ProductIdentifier` fields became the primary key for the `Orders` table. While that satisfied the rule for first normal form, it violates Second Normal Form because the `OrderDate`, `CustomerNumber`, and `OrderShipDate` fields are not dependent solely on the entire primary key – that is, the combination of `OrderNumber` and `ProductIdentifier`. These fields depend only on the `OrderNumber` and are irrespective of the `ProductIdentifier` field. It should be possible to find values for the `OrderDate`, `CustomerNumber`, and `OrderShipDate` fields without needing to know the value of `ProductIdentifier` of any products that were ordered. The effect of this is that the current design repeats information (`CustomerNumber` and `OrderShipDate`) in multiple records of the `Orders` table when, ideally, we should only provide this information once. By duplicating the `CustomerNumber` and `OrderShipDate` multiple times for each item in the order, you open yourself up to the same maintenance nightmare associated with spreadsheets, as discussed earlier in this chapter. If either of those fields ever needs to be updated, you would have multiple places to update the information.

So how do we solve this problem and make the database comply with the Second Normal Form? The answer is that we must create a new table (`OrdersProducts`) to store multiple products for each order. Fields specific to the order in general can remain in the `Orders` table, but the details for each product of an individual order will be moved into the new `OrdersProducts` table. Here is how the modified `Orders` table and the new `OrdersProducts` table might look:

ORDERS TABLE			
Field	**Example**	**Type of Data**	**Estimated Size of Data**
OrderNumber (PK)	1000	Numeric	Positive number with no decimals
OrderDate	Aug. 1, 2001	Date	Valid date
CustomerNumber (FK)	123456	Numeric	Positive number with no decimals
OrderShipDate	Aug. 3, 2001	Date	Valid date

ORDERSPRODUCTS TABLE			
Field	**Example**	**Type of Data**	**Estimated Size of Data**
OrderNumber (PK)	1000	Numeric	Positive number with no decimals
ProductIdentifier (PK)	12345	Numeric	Positive number with no decimals
Price	$23.25	Currency	
Quantity	2	Numeric	

Now, all non-primary key fields in the `Orders` table (`OrderDate`, `CustomerNumber`, and `OrderShipDate`) depend on the whole key – the `OrderNumber` – and are not unnecessarily repeated. In addition, all non-key fields in the `OrderProducts` table depend on that table's complete primary key, composed of the `OrderNumber` and `ProductIdentifier`. This means that `Price` and `Quantity` are information that describes the situation represented by the whole key – that is, each product of any given order.

Now that all of our tables comply with Second Normal Form, we're ready to learn about the next stage up: Third Normal Form.

Third Normal Form

To achieve Third Normal Form, we make sure that no fields depend on other non-key fields.

In **Third Normal Form**, we make sure that no fields depend on other non-key fields. A common example of this would be a calculated field derived from other fields in the table (such as a `TaxPrice` field made from adjusting the `Price` field). In such a case, if the fields that the calculated field is dependant upon change, the calculated field would have to be updated too. Updating fields to reflect changes to fields that they are based on can represent a management nightmare.

Now, our example doesn't in fact contain any fields dependent on other non-key fields. So – just to illustrate – let's consider a slightly different `Orders` table that includes a `CustomerLastName` field to illustrate a violation of the Third Normal Form:

ORDERS TABLE			
Field	**Example**	**Type of Data**	**Estimated Size of Data**
`OrderNumber (PK)`	1000	Numeric	
`OrderDate`	Aug. 1, 2001	Date	
`CustomerNumber (FK)`	123456	Numeric	Positive numbers with no decimals
`CustomerLastName`	Doe	Text	25 characters
`OrderShipDate`	Aug. 3, 2001	Date	

The new CustomerLastName field depends on the CustomerNumber field, which is not the primary key. As with the calculated field example, this dependency creates a problem because, any time that the CustomerLastName changes in the Customers table, this field in the Orders table must also be updated. Not only is there a dependency problem but there is a redundancy problem too, because you are duplicating information unnecessarily. To solve these kinds of problems, we need to remove such fields and add them to the appropriate table if it is not already present there. Of course, in this example, CustomerLastName already exists as a field in the Customers table, so, to comply with Third Normal Form, all we would need to do is remove the CustomerLastName field from the Orders table.

When To Denormalize

There are times when business objectives (such as database performance) greatly outweigh the benefits to a database from obeying Third Normal Form. In such cases, it is acceptable to break one or more of the rules of normalization, thus **denormalizing** the data. Here are a couple of situations when you might denormalize your data:

- When you can significantly cut down the number of tables that you need to search against to retrieve needed information, by adding an additional field to a given table.
- When a calculated field in a table will allow you to run queries and/or reports much faster and that particular field is very commonly used.

The most important consideration when deciding whether to denormalize is to analyze risk versus benefit. For example, if the speed improvement is significant, you may decide that the cost of dealing with maintaining consistency is worth paying in such a case. However, when in doubt, you should err on the side of normalization. These normalization rules were designed to help you create good robust database structures and they should be followed unless you are confident that the benefits far outweigh the risks.

It is important to note that there is no bell that rings to tell you that you have violated one of the rules of normalization. This means that you have to be careful when designing your databases because the quality of your data will be affected by the design considerations you make. It is also good to keep in mind that, when you get some strange results with your data, you should look into whether the normalization (or lack thereof) is causing the unexpected results. Lastly, don't get frustrated when trying to master the techniques of normalization versus denormalization. It will take time to learn and you will make some mistakes in the process, as we all have.

Defining Indexes

The final step in the logical design of our database is to define indexes. **Indexes** in a database are similar to indexes in a book – they allow rapid location of required information. Indexes are important to good database design, because all of the data in the world wouldn't be much good without a means to quickly retrieve it. The database engine uses indexes to rapidly locate one particular piece of information, but the database engine doesn't contain indexes unless you explicitly set them up. So, what are the types of indexes available to us, and when should each be used?

Indexes should be created for fields that are frequently used to retrieve information. Most databases allow you to define an index that is either unique or non-unique, and clustered or non-clustered. We'll take a look at what each of these means in more detail.

Unique indexes are indexes that do not allow duplicate records. Unique indexes are typically used for the primary keys of a table.

Conversely, **non-unique indexes** are indexes on fields that do allow duplicate values (typically fields that need to be indexed for speed, such as foreign keys, but are not the primary key).

With **clustered indexes**, the data is physically stored in the table in the same order as the clustered index. This saves the database engine having to look up a location and then access that location in a second step to retrieve the information, as you would have to do with an index in a book, for example. There can only be one clustered index per table and it will commonly be defined on the primary key.

There are certain situations where a clustered index will actually perform slowly – for example, when you make a lot of data inserts. Remember that, with a clustered index, the table records are physically stored mirroring the order of the index, much like the table of contents at the beginning of a book. Any time you insert a new record, all of the records after the one being inserted are typically rewritten to a different physical section of the database file and your clustered index file would require a correspondingly disruptive change. Continuing with the table of contents of a book example, if you insert several new sections in different parts throughout the book, you would also have to change the listing at the front of the book to mirror the new order. This shifting around of chunks of information can adversely impact speed in some cases. However, it is relatively rare to have a high enough volume of inserts taking place all of the time to seriously impact in this way and, in general, the clustered index is a fantastic choice for data-retrieval speed. You should define a clustered index on the field that is most frequently used to retrieve the data in a given table, such as the primary key.

With **non-clustered indexes**, on the other hand, the database engine will find the location in the index and then move to that location in the table to retrieve the information. Stated another way, the pages in the index are just pointers to the pages in the database that contain the database records, just as an index in a book points to the pages in the book where the topic can be found. You can have more than one non-clustered index per table. Thus, you most commonly see non-clustered indexes defined for fields in a table that are frequently used to retrieve data, but which are not that table's primary key.

For example, in our `Orders` table, we might define a clustered index on the `OrderNumber` field and a non-clustered index on the `CustomerNumber` field. The `OrderNumber` field is the primary key of the `Orders` table and is the likely candidate to be used most frequently to look up order information – so the fastest possible approach for retrieving an order is to define the `OrderNumber` as a clustered index. With the `OrderNumber`, we will have a list of all of the `Orders` in numeric order so, if we know the number that we are looking for, it will speed up the process. The `CustomerNumber` field is also a field likely to be searched frequently, but not quite as frequently as the `OrderNumber`. Since there can only be one clustered index per table (in this case, on the `OrderNumber`), but we still need fast retrieval of `CustomerNumbers`, a non-clustered index is a good choice for this field. To properly define the other indexes, you will need to take into account the information that will be retrieved and which fields will be used most frequently to retrieve that information.

Once the indexes for your tables have been identified, we have finally completed the last step in the database design process.

Testing the Logical Database Design

At the end of the logical database design process, we now have a "roadmap" on paper of what our database looks like, and we can test the design to make sure it works. You are probably thinking, "How can I test a logical database design that exists only on paper?" It's not difficult really – we simply walk through some examples on paper simulating how they would be handled when our database is live. Try adding a hypothetical customer to the table on paper and see how it looks. Then, have that customer place an order and write down what that record would look like. Very often, just by walking through a design on paper in this way, we can discover some essential field that we've overlooked, or some other requirement that has not been addressed as yet.

Implementing the Physical Database Design

A **physical database** can now be created electronically to the exact specifications determined by the completed logical design. By physical database, I refer to the files and their structure as created by the database software we are using – according to the details we give it and as established during the design process. In the next chapter, we will be creating a database with Microsoft SQL Server 2000 Desktop Engine.

Create, Test, and Refine

The first step in implementing the physical database is to create it using appropriate software. As we have followed all of the previous steps and obtained a good design, this step should be pretty straightforward. You should be able to simply read the requirements outlined on paper by your database design and create an electronic version that corresponds directly.

Once you have set up all of the required tables, fields, keys, and indexes, you are ready to test your database with sample data. You can just open each table directly and input data by hand into each field. It is not necessary to have the user interface for your application up and running before you test the database design. In fact, it is a good idea to have your database sound before you even begin designing the user interface. This can help you quickly determine if you have any fields that are too small, or if any are missing, and such like.

Testing will highlight any refinements necessary, such as increasing field sizes or adding an overlooked field. This process of create, test, and refine should be repeated on the physical database structure until you are satisfied that it will meet the business objectives you wish to accomplish. Often, this refinement process will continue as your user interface is developed. It is often only when creating the user interface that you realize you are missing some fields or that some field sizes are too small. Additionally, database indexes are often refined after reports or queries are tested later in the process. Hopefully, as long as you've followed the steps discussed in this chapter, such changes later in the development cycle will be minimal.

Now that you have learned the basics of building databases on paper, you should consider spending some time experimenting with normalization and indexes. This will not only give you a feel for observing and testing the concepts mentioned, but it will also help prepare you for the next chapter where you will be physically creating the database.

Summary

Naturally, becoming a master of database design will take some practice. However, we have covered a lot of concepts in this chapter that should give you quite a head start in becoming an expert. In this chapter, you have learned about the following concepts:

- What a database is and how relational databases compare to flat file databases.
- Analyzing business needs to determine the information that a database should contain and using your analysis to create the initial tables and fields.
- Defining keys and relationships for the logical database structure.
- Progressively modifying the logical database design to comply with first, second, and third normal forms.
- Determining what indexes are most appropriate for the logical database.
- Creating the physical database from the logical design.

Now that you have a good handle on the steps involved in creating databases on paper, we'll move on to the next chapter where we learn the details about working with SQL Server Desktop Engine to physically create the database.

Exercises

1. What is the difference between a flat file database and a relational database?
2. What advantages does a relational database offer over a flat file arrangement?
3. List the steps you would take to determine the database requirements of a customer.
4. What is a primary key? What is a foreign key? What do we mean by relationships?
5. Briefly describe the first three Normal Forms.
6. What are indexes, and what advantages can they bring?
7. What is the difference between the logical and physical database?

Answers are available at http://p2p.wrox.com/exercises/.

Microsoft SQL Server 2000 Desktop Engine

This chapter delves into the details of the Microsoft SQL Server 2000 Desktop Engine. After setting the stage by comparing the Desktop Engine with other editions of SQL Server, we then explore the Desktop Engine in great detail. We look at why the Desktop Engine is preferable for storing database information to Microsoft Access, and we run through all the steps necessary for getting it up and running. Specifically, this chapter covers:

- The various editions of Microsoft SQL Server 2000 available
- How the SQL Server Desktop Engine compares with the other varieties
- Why the Desktop Engine is a better choice than Access
- How the Desktop Engine bridges the gap between Access and SQL Server
- Where to obtain a copy of the Desktop Engine and how to install it
- What services are installed along with it
- What an Access project file is
- How to create a new SQL Server Desktop Engine database from scratch using Access
- How to use the Upsizing Wizard to convert an existing Access database to a Desktop Engine database format

Finally, we summarize what we have learned and leave you with some additional questions to test your understanding of the Desktop Engine.

The Microsoft SQL Server 2000 Desktop Engine

We use the Microsoft SQL Server Desktop Engine for database development throughout this book. Before wading too far into this topic, it is worthwhile to first understand what Microsoft SQL Server 2000 is, what different editions of it are available, and how the Desktop Engine we will be using in this book compares with other editions of SQL Server 2000.

Microsoft SQL Server 2000 Defined

Microsoft SQL Server 2000 is a relational database management system that can be used by individuals or businesses for storing and managing data. It also offers powerful functionality for data analysis and reporting. There are actually seven versions of Microsoft SQL Server 2000 to choose from. Two of these, the Enterprise and Standard Editions, are for deployment on servers in production environments. The other five versions each have a special purpose and are not licensed for deployment on production servers. Each of the seven versions of SQL Server are briefly described below:

For more information on SQL Server, please see Beginning SQL Server 2000 Programming by Wrox Press (ISBN 1861005237).

- **SQL Server 2000 Enterprise Edition** – This is the most comprehensive version of SQL Server 2000 and supports the full set of SQL Server 2000 features. This version is most appropriate for large organizations that need to manage immense amounts of data quickly and efficiently.

- **SQL Server 2000 Standard Edition** – This version of SQL Server 2000 supports many of the available features, with the notable exception of those that enable the quick and efficient management of large amounts of data. Hence, this version is primarily aimed at small to medium sized organizations that do not have the complex database requirements of larger firms. SQL Server 2000 Standard Edition is nonetheless an extremely powerful version of SQL Server and supports Analysis Services (with a few exceptions), Replication, Full-Text Search, Data Transformation Services, English Query, and other advanced SQL Server features.

- **SQL Server 2000 Personal Edition** – This version of SQL Server 2000 supports basically the same features as the Standard Edition, with the exception of transactional replication. Additionally, Analysis Services and Full-Text Search are only available on certain operating systems with this edition. This version is most appropriate for users who spend some time disconnected from the network but access SQL Server data on their local machine while disconnected. A common example would be mobile users – say, a company's sales force who require access to data while out in the field. This version limits the number of concurrent database activities that can be running at any one time. This simply means that it isn't designed to handle a great many users or database activities.

- **SQL Server 2000 Windows CE Edition** – This version of SQL Server 2000 runs on mobile devices that run under Windows CE. It is a compact edition of SQL Server 2000 and allows relational databases to be stored and managed on a Windows CE device for later synchronization with the main database. It also allows users to manage a SQL Server database remotely over the Internet from their CE device.

- **SQL Server 2000 Developer Edition** – This version of SQL Server 2000 supports all available features just like the Enterprise Edition, with the proviso that it not be deployed on a production server. As the name indicates, this version is designed for developers, consultants, and solution providers while developing and testing SQL applications.

- **SQL Server 2000 Evaluation Edition** – This version is a fully functional version of SQL Server 2000 Enterprise Edition that stops working after 120 days. It allows organizations to evaluate the full product without charge.

- **SQL Server 2000 Desktop Engine** – This is a redistributable version of the SQL Server database engine. This means that you can include it in your setup programs for applications that use SQL Server to store data. The Desktop Engine doesn't include any of the SQL Server 2000 graphical user interface tools, such as SQL Server Enterprise Manager, so other products (such as Visual Studio .NET Server Explorer, Access, or SQL Server 2000 APIs) must be used to create and manage databases stored in this version of SQL Server. (Note: This is not the same version as the SQL Server 7 Desktop Edition. The SQL Server 7 Desktop Edition became the Personal Edition in SQL Server 2000. The SQL Server 2000 Desktop Engine was called the **Microsoft Data Engine**, or **MSDE**, in SQL Server 7).

Now that we understand a little bit about each version of SQL Server 2000, let's narrow our focus to the Microsoft SQL Server 2000 Desktop Engine, as used in the remainder of this book. As mentioned in the feature list above, the SQL Server 2000 Desktop Engine that came with SQL Server 7 was called the Microsoft Data Engine, or MSDE. Even though the MSDE abbreviation is in fact derived from this older name, Microsoft Data Engine, it is still widely used today to refer to the latest SQL Server 2000 Desktop Engine version. Thus, you should be aware that both Desktop Engine and MSDE are acceptable names for referring to the SQL Server 2000 Desktop Engine. In fact, without knowing the history, you would probably just conclude that MSDE is the abbreviation for Microsoft SQL Server Desktop Engine anyway. This seemingly appropriate abbreviation is probably the reason why the term is still accepted despite the product renaming that occurred in SQL Server 2000.

Why Use Desktop Engine Instead of Access?

Now that we've sorted out the origin of the MSDE acronym, let's begin to look at the features that Desktop Engine offers in a little more detail. MSDE was introduced by Microsoft to bridge the gap between two of its other database products, namely Access and SQL Server. A large number of applications were built using Microsoft Access as the database engine, often with a front end created using Access tools. As such applications increase in popularity, and the number of simultaneous users and/or data volumes hit certain thresholds, they start outgrowing the capabilities of Access. At that point, many developers find themselves having to modify code to port the applications to a SQL Server database. This can be a monumental task in many cases and may require a complete re-write of data access code. The underlying Jet database engine used by Access is very different from the underlying SQL Server engine. This means that several data types are inconsistent and have to be modified, certain Jet statements have to be entirely rewritten for SQL, and so on.

So how does Desktop Engine help you overcome this divide between Access and SQL Server to make the transition easier than before? One big advantage is that Desktop Engine is actually a real version of SQL Server 2000. It includes the same relational database engine and replication features as the Personal Edition, except for the full-text search feature, and the graphical database administration tools. Bear in mind, though, that database sizes in Desktop Engine may not exceed 2 Gigabytes, and database usage is limited to five concurrent batches, which means that no more than five database tasks can be processed at a given time. For example, five concurrent batches could occur if five different users are logged in or if an application with a single open connection processes five tasks concurrently. Thus, Desktop Engine, by design, isn't capable of handling a large number of users or very extensive databases. Furthermore, Desktop Engine is limited in that it doesn't support Analysis Services. What this really boils down to is the fact that Desktop Engine is a small-scale version of SQL Server, one that cannot exceed the 2 GB limitation and that cannot have more than five concurrent users or transactions hitting the database at once.

Another key benefit of Desktop Engine is its **freely distributable** format. There is no requirement to pay a license fee to use Desktop Engine in a standalone environment, and you are free to distribute it with standalone applications. A free version of SQL Server is not a thing to be laughed at. Desktop Engine can be packaged with your application's setup program and installed with it on third party computers. There are some exceptions to this free license, as detailed in the licensing agreement that accompanies the package. One example is using Desktop Engine as the client to connect to another SQL Server database; in that scenario it requires a client access license for communicating with the other SQL Server database under the terms of that agreement.

An additional advantage that Desktop Engine offers many companies is that it can simplify the process of creating demo CDs of their products. Suppose that you have an enterprise-wide SQL Server-based application that you want to give to a prospective client on a demo CD. In the past, many companies had to write an Access version of their application solely to avoid violating the SQL Server licensing agreement for purposes of the demo CD. In such cases, the data was stored in an Access file that could be freely distributed with a runtime version of Access. The alternative of including links to trial versions of SQL Server that can be downloaded is not much better. As a free distribution version of SQL Server, Desktop Engine solves this, allowing demo CDs to be easily created without having to rewrite any code to that end.

You can see why Desktop Engine offers a very serious alternative when you are considering Access for smaller database requirements. In addition to being a true version of SQL Server (facilitating upgrade to a production SQL variant later), it has the advantage of being client-server based rather than file-based like Access. You may already be aware that Access stores all its data in a single file (the `.mdb` file). Desktop Engine, on the other hand, is a true client-server application where it is installed on a machine that acts as the server. This does not mean that Desktop Engine has to be installed on a separate machine, and it is perfectly happy running on the same machine as the client. What this really means is that, with client-server based databases, the process on the server looks for the data for you. With Access, on the other hand, all of the processing for data takes place on the client and can consume valuable client resources.

As a proper version of SQL Server, you don't have to make *any* modifications to your code (SQL statements, table structures, etc.) should you later decide to upsize to a full version of SQL Server to support a larger database size or more concurrent users. All you would have to do is purchase the higher version of SQL Server and simply import the existing database into the new installation without modification. Thus, when your application becomes extremely popular and justifies the power of one of the premium versions of SQL Server, you are all set. This is an incredible advantage. The gap has finally been closed between Access and SQL Server, thanks to Desktop Engine.

Obtaining and Installing Desktop Engine

In this section, we will look at where you can obtain a copy of Desktop Engine and will then walk through the steps of installing it.

Please note that, if you are already running another version of SQL Server 2000, you can use that version instead of Desktop Engine. The code in this book will work on any version of SQL Server 2000, but we will focus on Desktop Engine as it is the only version of SQL Server that is completely free.

Where To Get a Copy of Desktop Engine

Desktop Engine is available from many sources, including Visual Studio .NET and SQL Server 2000. In this section, we look at how to install Desktop Engine from the Visual Studio .NET CDs. Check the installation requirements for Desktop Engine described below to make sure your system can support it.

Installation Requirements

Desktop Engine can be installed on a machine running Microsoft Windows 98, Windows NT 4.0, Windows ME, or Windows 2000. It is also likely to be supported by Windows XP when released. 64 MB of RAM is the minimum to run Desktop Engine on Windows 2000, but the other operating systems listed can get away with just 32 MB. Desktop Engine requires 44 MB of disk space for the database engine software itself.

How To Install Desktop Engine

In this section, I shall lead you through the steps required to install Desktop Engine on your machine.

Step 1 – Insert the Visual Studio .NET Setup CD

Insert the second Visual Studio .NET setup CD. Open Windows Explorer and navigate to the `D:\Program Files\Microsoft.Net\FrameworkSDK\Samples\Setup` directory (where `D:` is the letter corresponding to your CD drive). Note that you are looking for the `InstMSDE.exe` file; the precise location of this file may change to a different CD or directory by the time of final release of Visual Studio .NET.

> *On some versions of Visual Studio .NET, you may need to use the `SQL2000.exe` file, rather than `InstMSDE.exe`.*

Step 2 – Launch the Desktop Engine Setup Program

Next, double-click on the `InstMSDE.exe` program to launch the setup program. You may be prompted to update some files on your system before setup can continue. If so, then follow the prompts on the screen to update your system with the necessary files. This may require that you reboot your machine and restart the setup program again.

After launching setup, the Windows Installer Program will flash for a few seconds as it initiates the setup procedure. It will then begin copying files to your system without requiring any further interaction from the user.

Desktop Engine will be installed with the default configuration settings for SQL Server, as specified by the `setup.ini` file in the Setup directory. The SQL Server instance that gets installed will be called MyComputer\NetSDK, where MyComputer is the name of your machine. If you want to modify these default installation settings (and/or specify additional installation settings), you will need to copy all the install files to a directory on your hard drive or network so you can modify the `setup.ini` file in that directory. When you run the install program from that directory, it will then use whatever configuration information you specified in the new `setup.ini` file.

Step 3 - Confirm That the Installation Was Successful

The Desktop Engine install process should add a new icon to the Windows Startup menu. To verify that Desktop Engine installed correctly, go to Start | Programs | Startup and check that the program called Service Manager now resides there. Placing this program in the Startup menu ensures that, each time you start your computer, it will run automatically.

Rather than restarting your computer to execute it, click on the Service Manager icon shown in the Startup menu to run it manually. When you do this, you will notice that a new icon depicting a server appears in the taskbar System Tray – the set of miniature icons that usually appears next to the clock. We will examine the workings of Service Manager in more detail later on in the chapter.

Understanding What was Installed

Now that the installation is complete, let's look at what exactly has been installed. Altogether, three services get installed with Desktop Engine: SQL Server, SQL Server Agent, and Distributed Transaction Coordinator. SQL Server Service Manager, which we just started manually, is a utility that allows you to manage each of these services. We will now look at each of the services and the Service Manager utility in more detail.

SQL Server Service

The **SQL Server** service is the core of Desktop Engine. In fact, it is the core engine used by all other versions of SQL Server. It consists of the SQL Server storage engine and the query processor. The storage engine is responsible for reading and writing all data to and from the database. The query processor is responsible for receiving and executing SQL statements. There are also a few other components in addition to the storage engine and query processor, but they are not needed for our purposes so we will not be discussing them.

The SQL Server service must be running for any data to be retrieved, inserted, updated, or deleted from Desktop Engine. The default installation sets this service to automatically run on the startup of the computer. When we look at the SQL Server Service Manager in a moment, we will find out how to manage the SQL Server service.

SQL Server Agent

A second service that gets installed is the **SQL Server Agent**. This service can schedule jobs and alerts for your database. If, for instance, you wish to back up your database each night, the SQL Server Agent lets you schedule a job to automatically perform this task, and reports any problems encountered. While this service is not always required, in many cases SQL Server Agent can be a very useful tool.

Distributed Transaction Coordinator

The third service installed is the **Distributed Transaction Coordinator** (**DTC** or sometimes **MSDTC**). The DTC service allows transactions to span more than one computer across a network. We won't be using the DTC in this book, but will look at transactions in Chapter 10.

Managing the Services with SQL Server Service Manager

As we've already mentioned, the **SQL Server Service Manager** utility allows you to manage the three previous services. When it has been initiated, either automatically on startup or manually after installation, an icon is displayed in the system tray area typically located in the lower right of the screen, as shown here:

In this screenshot, the SQL Server Service Manager Utility icon appears immediately to the left of the clock, and depicts a server with an inset green arrow, resembling the play symbol of a VCR. Sometimes, the icon shows a red square, like a stop symbol, denoting the suspension of one of the three services as described later in this section. If you double-click this icon, the SQL Server Service Manager screen shown next will appear:

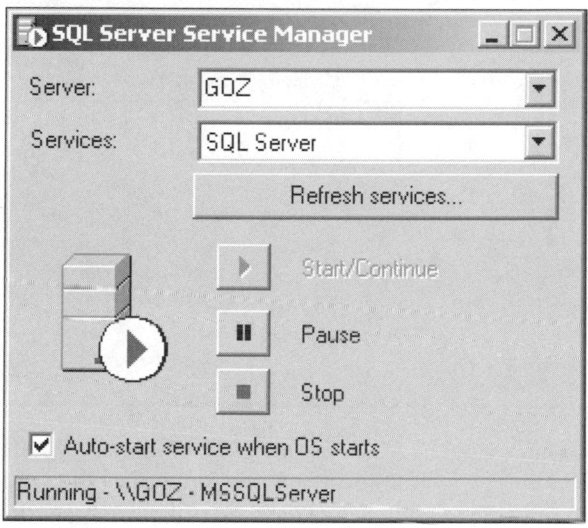

This window displays the settings for the selected Server and Services, along with the status of the selected service. The Server and Services boxes have drop-down lists that allow you to choose from those available. The Server drop-down, for example, contains all the SQL Server instances that this particular computer is aware of. The Services drop-down contains choices for selecting one of the three services we've already learned about: SQL Server Service, SQL Server Agent, and Distributed Transaction Coordinator.

There are also buttons for Start/Continue, Pause, and Stop, which are available or grayed out according to the current status. In the case depicted above, the Pause and Stop buttons are enabled. If we wanted to temporarily suspend all database activities, we would simply click the Pause button on this screen. If we wanted to turn off database activities entirely, we would click the Stop button. To re-start the service later, we would click the Start/Continue button.

The SQL Server Service shown in the above screen is running on a server called GOZ (yours will be running on a server with a different name). Note the status bar at the bottom that shows the message Running - \\GOZ - MSSQLServer, and the green arrow appearing in the circle on the picture of the server. This green arrow would be replaced by a red square if this service were suspended, and the red square would also be displayed on the small icon in the system tray.

Further, notice how the indicator to Auto-start service when OS starts is checked, which means that SQL Server will start whenever the operating system boots up. It is a good idea to have this setting turned on for the SQL Server Service so that database inserts, updates, deletes, reads, etc. will be allowed without having to manually start the service every time. Check this value to enable auto-start if it isn't already set.

Now let's take a look at how we can manage the SQL Server Agent using the SQL Server Service Manager Utility. In the next screenshot, the SQL Server Agent service has been chosen in the Services drop-down, and the current inactive status of SQL Server Agent is indicated by the red square:

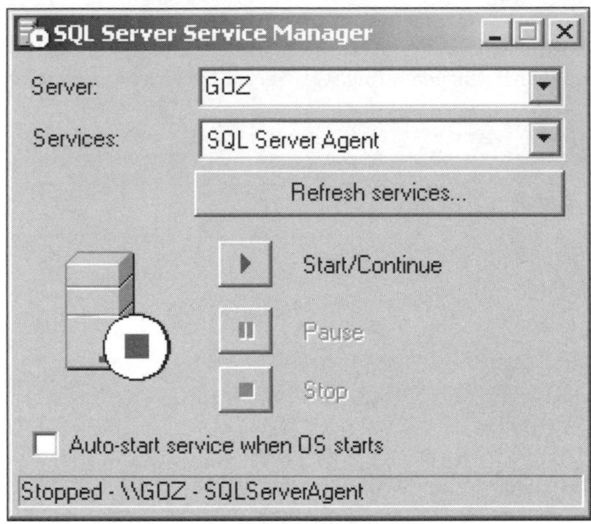

Notice above that we are managing the SQL Server Agent on the server called GOZ, and that the service is stopped. We could click the Start/Continue button to start the service. Also, notice that the Auto-start service when OS starts option is *not* enabled. This is because we don't wish to take advantage of the scheduled jobs feature at the moment, and thus don't want the service to start up whenever we switch on our machine. There is no reason to have a service running, and consuming valuable system resources, if you are not taking advantage of it.

As you can see from these examples, it's a pretty straightforward job to manage the three services that come with Desktop Engine using the SQL Server Service Manager Utility. Now that we have covered the basics of setting up Desktop Engine and we are able to start and stop database services, we can move on to the fun part of working with Desktop Engine databases in Access.

Using Access to Work with Desktop Engine / SQL Server

Since the Desktop Engine version of SQL Server doesn't come with any user interface tools for managing databases (such as the SQL Server Enterprise Manager that comes with other versions of SQL Server), you will have to use Microsoft Access, the Visual Studio .NET Server Explorer, or some other external means for managing SQL Server databases. The good news is that Microsoft Access 2000, Microsoft Access XP (2002), and the Visual Studio .NET Server Explorer all provide tight integration with SQL Server databases. These tools allow you to create and manage new SQL Server databases. They also allow you to view database views (a type of query) and other database objects associated with a database. In the rest of this chapter, we will be using Access XP to manage SQL Server databases. Later in the book, we look at how to use the Visual Studio .NET Server Explorer to perform SQL management.

Access provides upsizing wizards that can convert existing Access databases to any version of SQL Server. Prior versions of Access did not allow you to manage the table structure, create new databases, or manage other objects like views. All they allowed you to do was link to existing SQL Server tables to view, create, delete, or update the data they contained. The new close integration with SQL Server that Access 2000 and Access XP offer is a huge improvement over these past situations.

Microsoft Access 2000 first introduced the concept of the **Microsoft Access project**. A Microsoft Access project is a file that connects to a SQL Server database and can be used to create client-server applications. The project file (with a `.adp` extension) does not contain any data, tables, or other such information. It simply stores details about the SQL Server database that enable Access to retrieve any required information on demand.

Creating a New Desktop Engine / SQL Server Database from Microsoft Access

In this section, we will use Access XP (2002) to create a new database with the `Products`, `Customers`, `Orders`, and `OrdersProducts` tables that we devised in Chapter 1. To create a new SQL Server database from Access, we first need to create an empty Access project. We will then create each table in design view and then open them to add some sample data. Please note that the steps for Access 2000 are a bit different, as will be indicated briefly in the background text.

Try It Out – Creating a New SQL Server Database from Microsoft Access

1. Open Microsoft Access.

2. Select File | New and the task pane will appear in the right-hand of the screen. Choose Project (New Data) and click the OK button.

   For Access 2000, select File | New and choose Project (New Database) in the dialog box that appears and click OK. Then work through the steps below. Note that some of the steps will be slightly different than those described.

   Please note that if you are using Access 2000, see Microsoft Knowledge Base Article q269824 for a potential problem that could generate a database error on this step. A service pack is available to fix this problem. You can read this article at the following URL:
   http://support.microsoft.com/support/kb/articles/Q269/8/24.ASP.

3. Name the project `SampleDatabase` in the File New Database dialog box, and browse to the location where you want to save the new project. Click the Create button to create the new project file in the specified location of your hard drive or network.

4. Once the new `SampleDatabase` project has been created, the Microsoft SQL Server Database Wizard dialog box will appear, as shown overleaf:

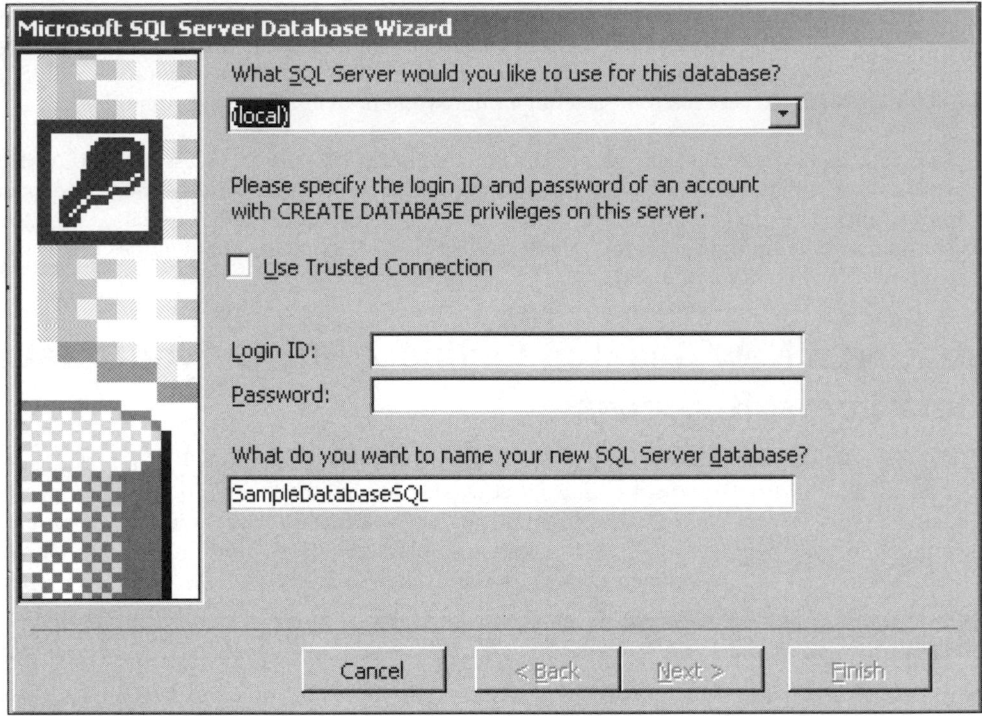

5. The Wizard starts by prompting you for the SQL Server database that will be used, and the Login ID and Password to use for it. At the bottom, it asks us to specify the name we want to use for our database in SQL Server. Fill in the information giving the proper SQL Server for the database. Fill in the Login ID and Password (which will be "sa" and blank, respectively, unless you changed them earlier). Lastly, enter SampleDatabaseSQL in the database name box at the bottom. This can be different to the name we previously gave our Access project file in Step 3 above, as this will be the name of the database itself in SQL Server. After you have filled in all these fields, click the Next button.

6. The next screen will indicate that the wizard has all of the information it needs in order to create your database. On that screen, click the Finish button.

7. For a brief moment, we see a progress bar on screen as it creates the new database for us. Once it completes, the Wizard is finished, leaving us with the empty database, as shown here:

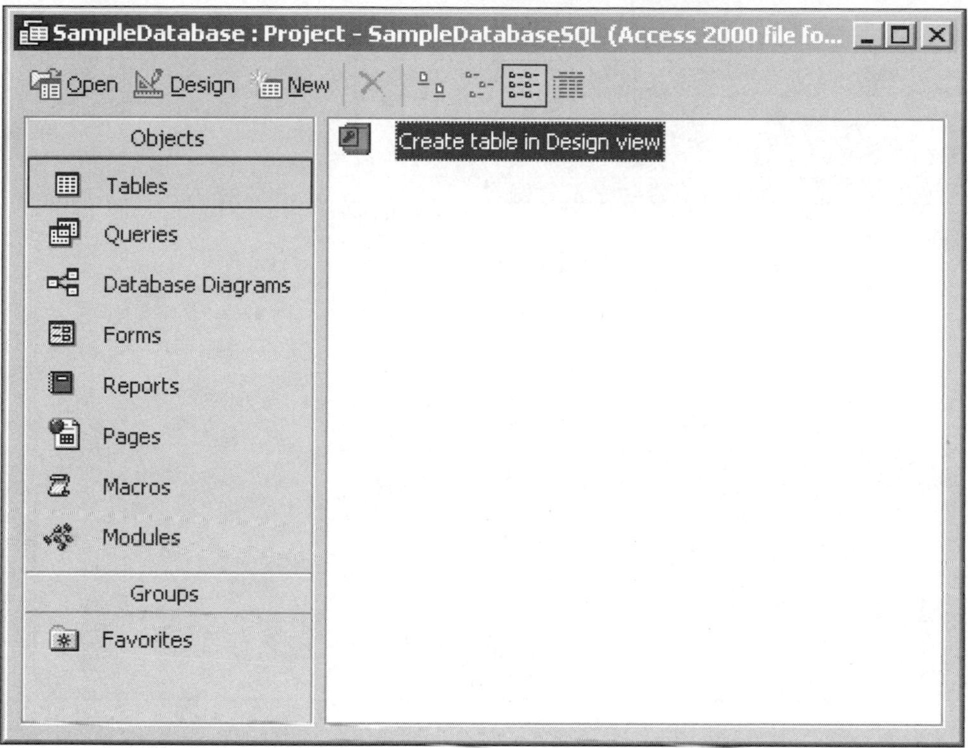

8. Our next step is to create a new table, and we do this by double-clicking the line that says Create table in Design view.

9. An empty table design will appear on the screen. First, we shall create the `Products` table. Recall from Chapter 1 that the `Products` table has the following structure:

PRODUCTS TABLE			
Field	**Example**	**Type of Data**	**Estimated Size of Data**
`ProductIdentifier (PK)`	12345	Numeric	Positive number with no decimals
`ProductDescription`	Tofu	Text	25 characters
`ProductUnitPrice`	$23.25	Currency	$00.00 to $10,000.00
`ProductQuantityOnHand`	50	Numeric	0 to 9,999
`ProductUnitOfMeasure`	40 – 100 g pkgs	Text	25 characters

Fill in the fields just as in the screenshot below, making sure not to overlook the Allow Nulls column:

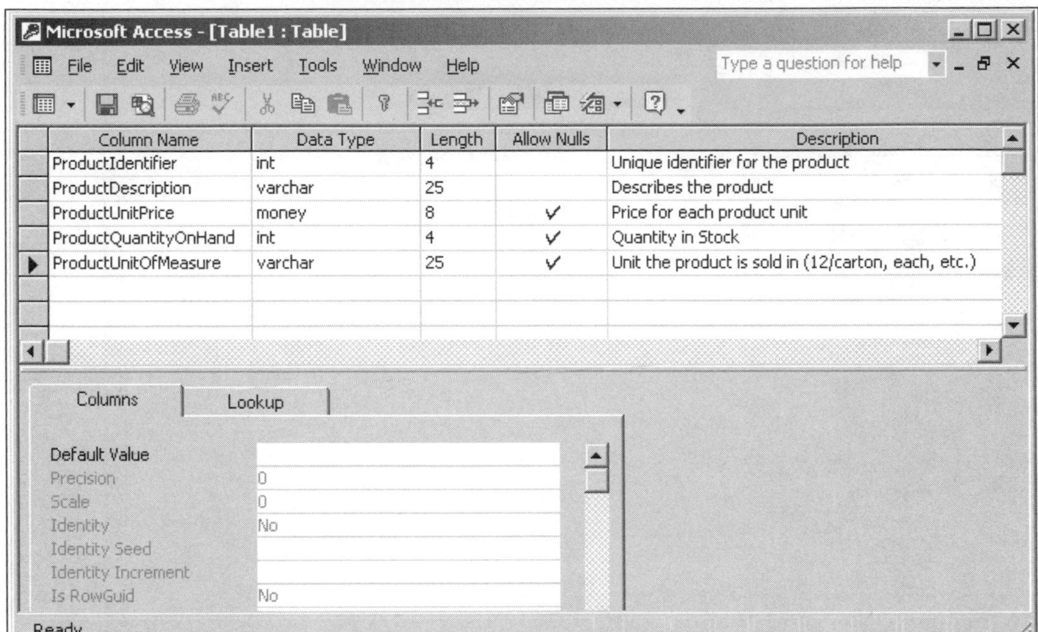

After you have filled in the fields as specified above, take a closer look at the field names, data types, and sizes that you have just assigned for each. Notice that we have specified the `ProductIdentifier` field as an integer. We will be using the `ProductIdentifier` as the unique value that identifies each product, which we will assign momentarily. Also notice that we specified the `ProductDescription` and `ProductUnitOfMeasure` as `VarChar`, because they are text based fields of variable length up to the maximum specified, depending on the data that they will hold. The `ProductUnitPrice` is given as the `Money` data type, which is how SQL Server represents currency. The field named `ProductQuantityOnHand` is an `Int`, which will hold any integer value. Also notice that the `ProductIdentifier` and `ProductDescription` fields cannot be `Null`, as indicated by the absence of a tick in the Allow Nulls column. The effect of this is to make that field required, so that if a new product record is added without values given for the `ProductIdentifier` and `ProductDescription` fields, the record will not be added and an error will occur.

10. Not only do we want the `ProductIdentifier` to be our primary key, but we also want it to be automatically generated by SQL Server, starting with a value of one and incremented by one with each new product. So before we set `ProductIdentifier` as the primary key, we need to specify that it is an **Identity Column**, starting with the value one (the **Identity Seed**) and is to be incremented by one (the **Identity Increment**). Select the `ProductIdentifier` field and modify the Identity, Identify Seed, and Identity Increment (default values of 1) attributes that appear in the box underneath the table, as this screenshot shows:

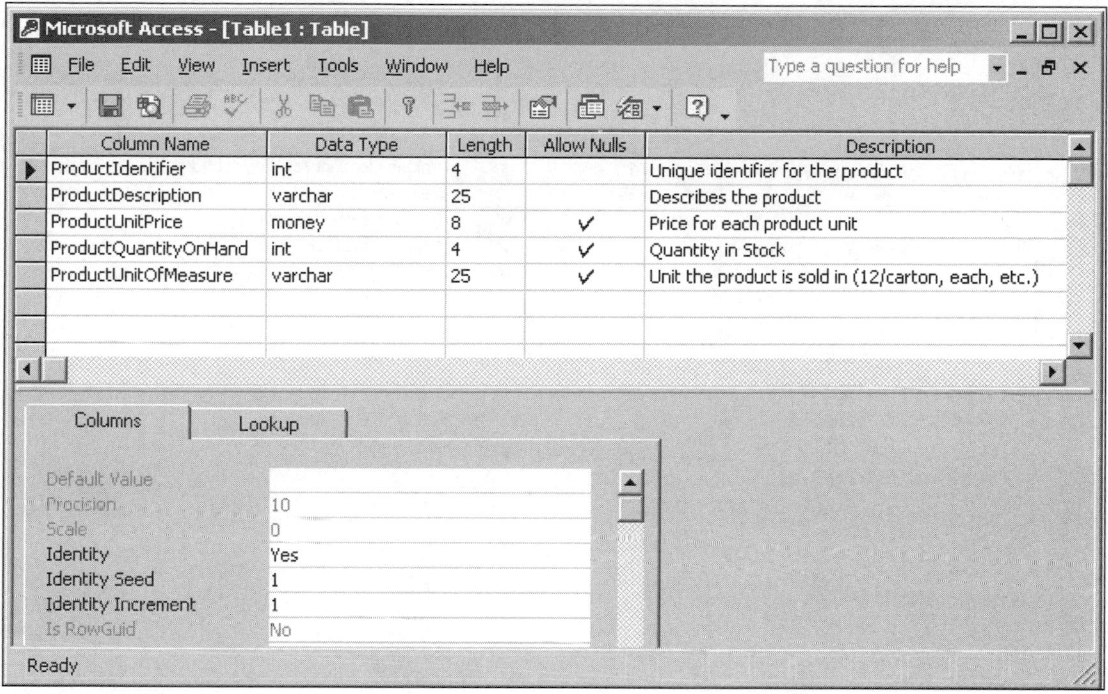

11. Now that we have specified that the `ProductIdentifier` field is an `Identity` column to be automatically generated by SQL Server, we are ready to select it as the Primary Key for our table. Highlight the row where it says `ProductIdentifier`, and then select **Edit | Primary Key**, as shown overleaf:

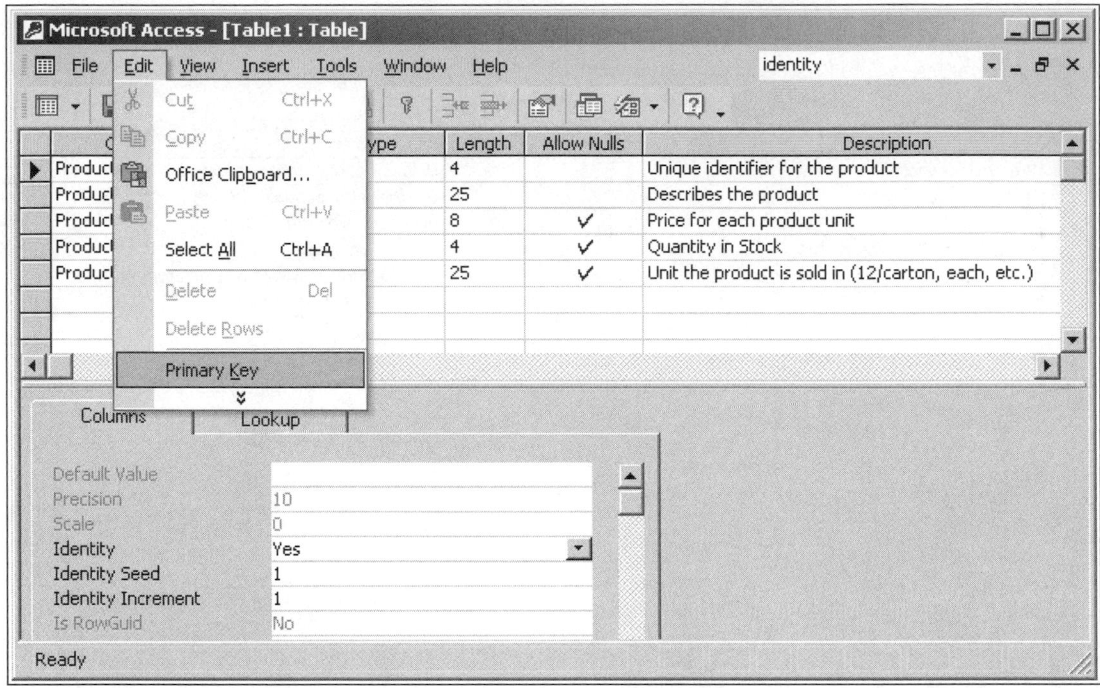

Notice how an image of a key appears in the left most column of the `ProductIdentifier` field. This is a visual indicator to tell us that the `ProductIdentifier` field is now the primary key for the table.

12. We are ready to save the table to the database. To do so, select File | Save. You will be prompted to specify a name for the table so enter the name Products, and click on OK.

13. After saving your table, close the design view by clicking the cross in the upper right hand corner of the `Products` table window. You should now be returned to the database explorer where the new `Products` table should appear as the only table currently in the database:

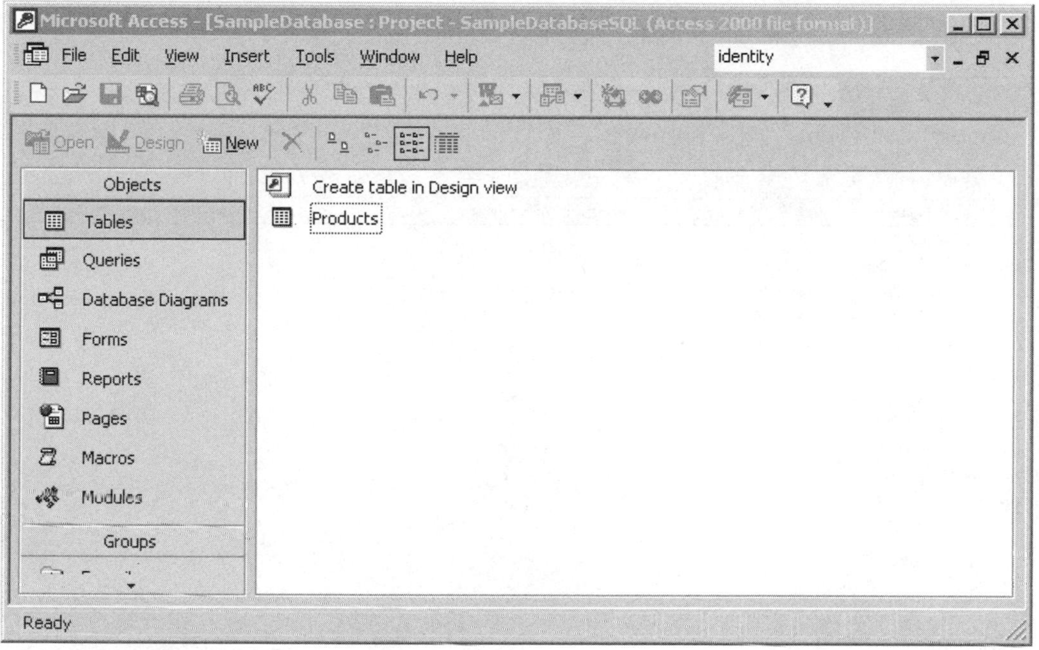

14. We can now repeat this process to create the `Customers` table. Double-click where it says Create table in Design view.

15. The logical design for the `Customers` table that we devised in Chapter 1 is repeated here:

CUSTOMERS TABLE			
Field	**Example**	**Type of Data**	**Estimated Size of Data**
`CustomerNumber (PK)`	123456	Numeric	Positive number with no decimals
`CustomerFirstName`	Jane	Text	15 characters
`CustomerMiddleName`	A.	Text	15 characters
`CustomerLastName`	Doe	Text	25 characters
`CustomerAddress`	123 Somewhere St.	Text	30 characters
`CustomerCity`	Anytown	Text	20 characters
`CustomerState`	IN	Text	2 characters
`CustomerZip`	46060	Text	9 characters
`CustomerCountry`	USA	Text	20 characters
`CustomerTelephone`	317-111-2222	Text	12 characters
`CustomerEmail`	jdoe@yahoo.com	Text	50 characters

Create the `Customers` table with the settings shown below:

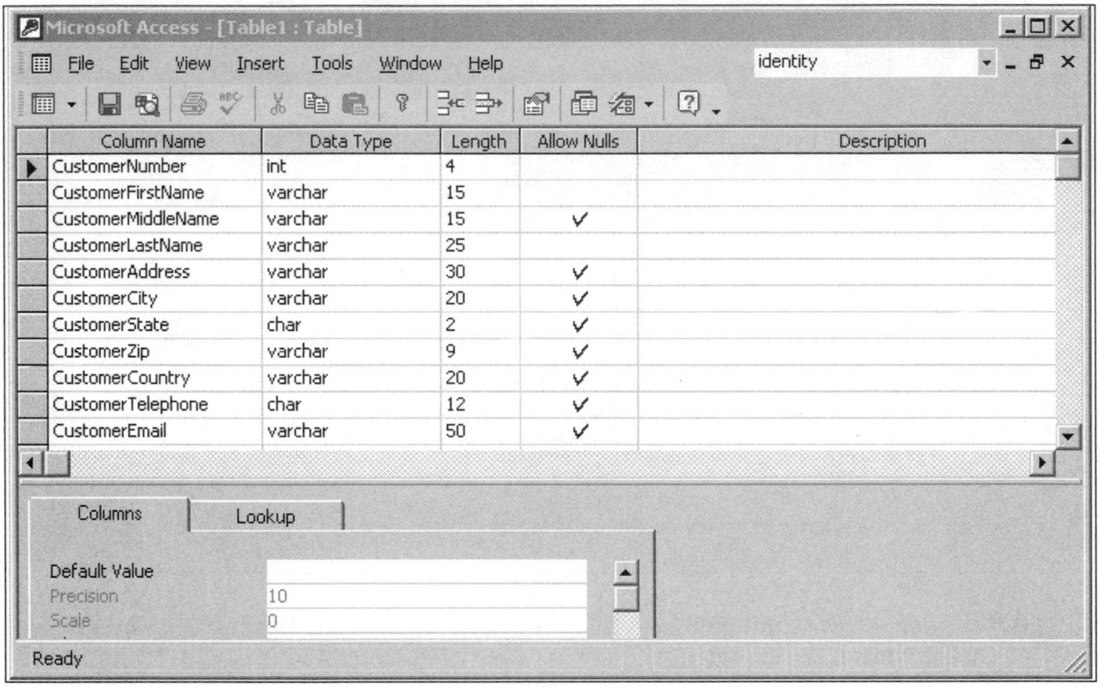

Microsoft Access - [Table1 : Table]

Column Name	Data Type	Length	Allow Nulls	Description
CustomerNumber	int	4		
CustomerFirstName	varchar	15		
CustomerMiddleName	varchar	15	✓	
CustomerLastName	varchar	25		
CustomerAddress	varchar	30	✓	
CustomerCity	varchar	20	✓	
CustomerState	char	2	✓	
CustomerZip	varchar	9	✓	
CustomerCountry	varchar	20	✓	
CustomerTelephone	char	12	✓	
CustomerEmail	varchar	50	✓	

Columns | Lookup

Default Value:
Precision: 10
Scale: 0

Ready

Notice how the majority of the fields are declared as the `varchar` data type. That is because this is the best type to use for variable length text values. However, the `CustomerState` and `CustomerTelephone` fields are the `Char` type, because they will always contain a fixed number of characters and in such cases `Char` is the better option. For example, the `CustomerState` field will always contain the two letter state abbreviation for US customers. Further notice that the `CustomerNumber`, `CustomerFirstName`, and `CustomerLastName` fields may not be `Null`, so that when a new customer record is added, the `CustomerNumber`, `CustomerFirstName`, and `CustomerLastName` fields will have to be specified at least.

16. Repeat the process described in Steps 10 and 11 to set the `CustomerNumber` as an Identity field, with the same default values for the Identity Seed and the Identity Increment, and also then set it as the Primary Key.

17. Select File | Save and save the table with the name `Customers` before closing it and returning to the view showing all the tables created so far.

18. Now, repeat the process to create the `Orders` table. Again, start by double-clicking on Create table in Design view.

19. Recall from Chapter 1 that the logical design of the `Orders` table is as follows:

ORDERS TABLE			
Field	**Example**	**Type of Data**	**Estimated Size of Data**
OrderNumber (PK)	1000	Numeric	Positive number with no decimals
OrderDate	Aug. 1, 2001	Date	Valid date
CustomerNumber (FK)	123456	Numeric	Positive number with no decimals
OrderShipDate	Aug. 3, 2001	Date	Valid date

Create the `Orders` table with the settings shown below:

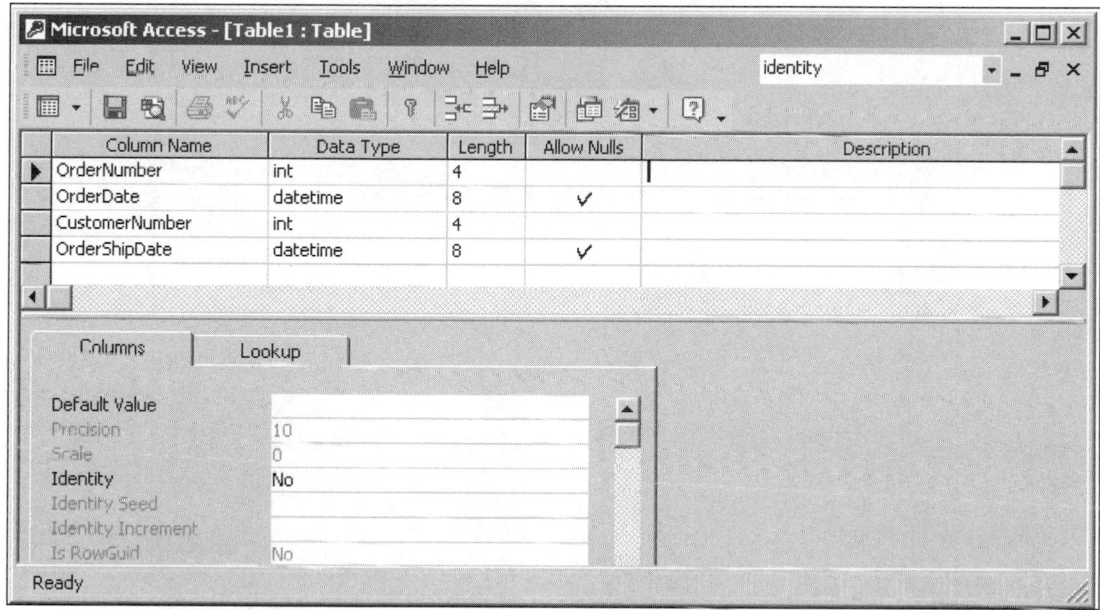

Notice that the `OrderDate` and `OrderShipDate` fields are of `DateTime` type, the SQL Server type for specifying date values. The `OrderNumber` and `CustomerNumber` fields are both `int` data types and may not be `Null`. Thus, when a new record is added, `OrderNumber` and `CustomerNumber` must be provided as a minimum.

20. Again, repeat the process described in Steps 10 and 11 to set the `OrderNumber` as an Identity field and also as the Primary Key.

21. Select File | Save and save the `Orders` table, but don't close the window this time, as we wish to remain in the design view.

22. Recall from the logical design that the `CustomerNumber` of the `Orders` table is a Foreign Key linked to the `CustomerNumber` Primary Key of the `Customers` table. We're now going to set up the `CustomerNumber` field as such a Foreign Key. Select View | Relationships from the drop-down menu, and the following screen should appear:

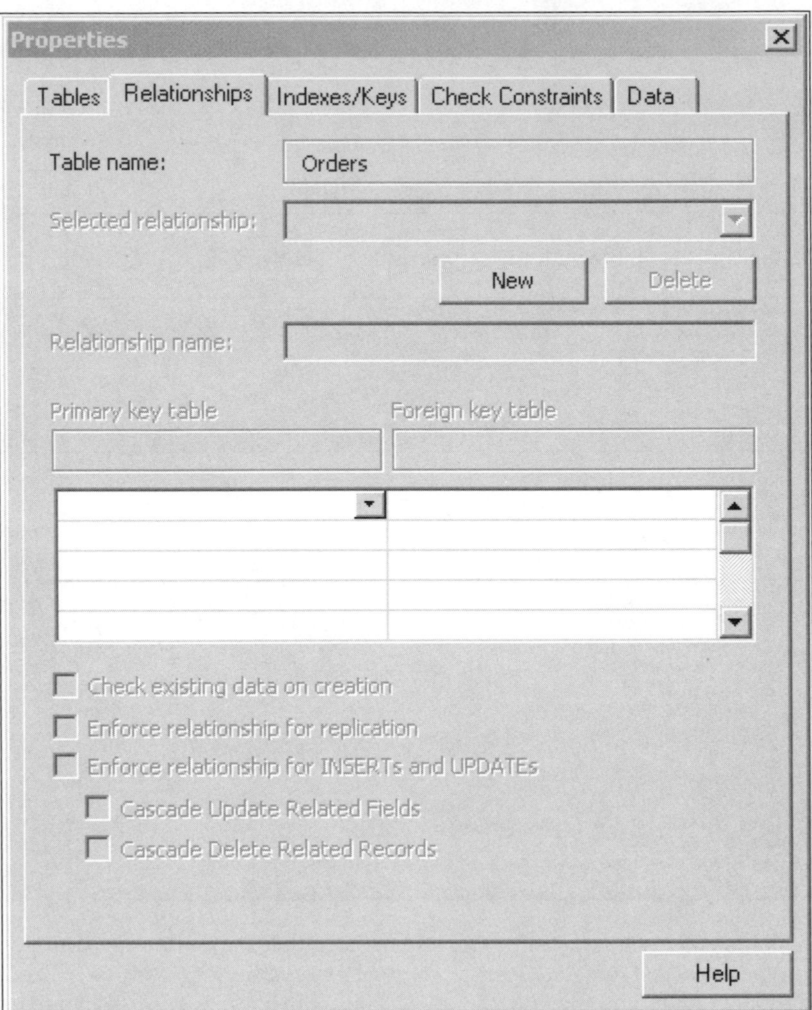

23. Click the New button and you will notice that it will automatically assume you want to create a relationship with the `Customers` table, as shown opposite:

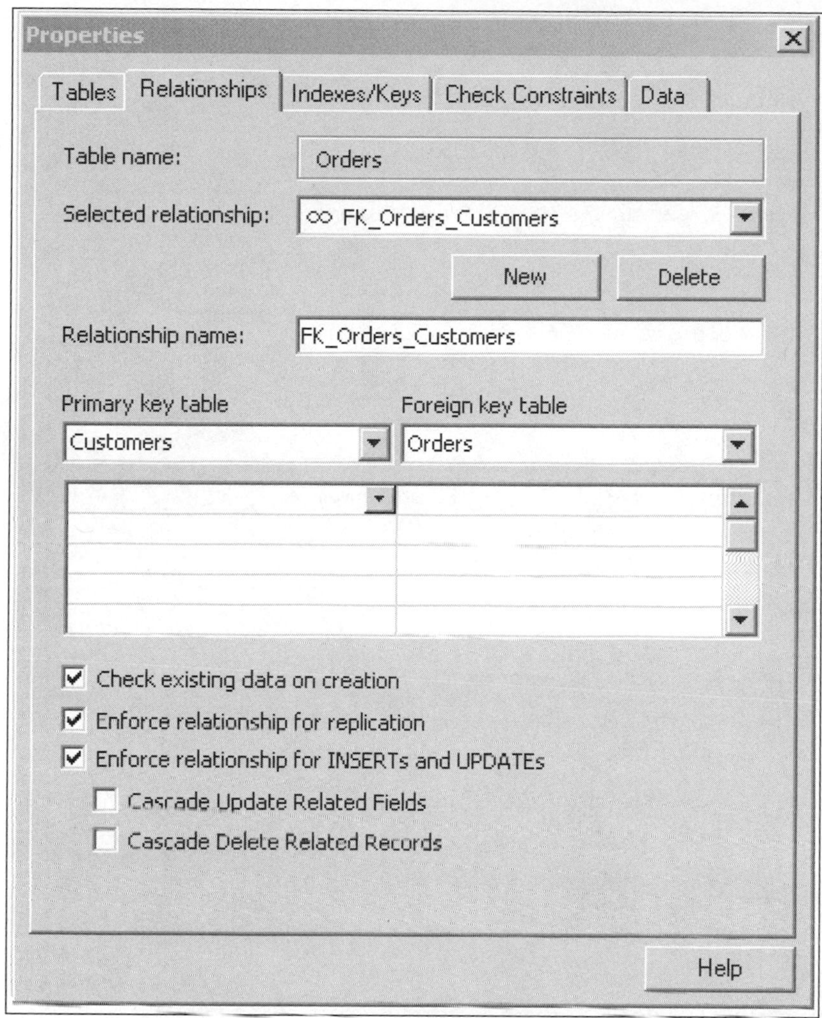

The option to Check existing data on creation means that the relationship will be verified upon creation and, if any records do not have proper relationships, an error will be raised. By enforcing the relationship for replication, the relationship will be maintained if the data is replicated on another server. If the relationship is enforced for `INSERT`s and `UPDATE`s, then any attempt to insert or update a record that doesn't meet the relationship will cause the insert or update to fail.

24. It has automatically filled in Customers as the Primary key table and Orders as the Foreign key table, which is just what we want it to do. It isn't being as clever as you might think though, as basically it just defaults to the first table alphabetically, which will not always be the one you actually want to use. In such cases, you can specify the appropriate Primary and Foreign Key tables using drop-down lists. In our case, we're lucky, and all we need to do now is specify which fields within each table are related to each other, namely the `CustomerNumber` in the `Customers` table to the `CustomerNumber` in the `Orders` table, as shown here:

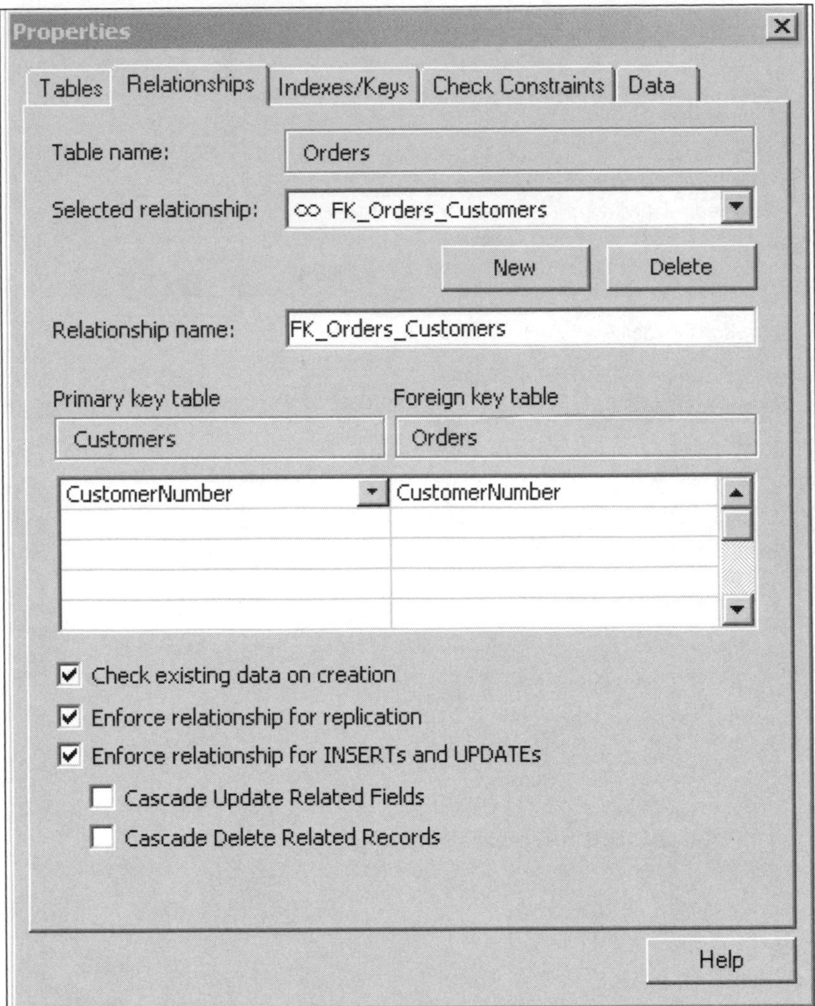

This creates the desired relationship between the two tables that we want. That's all you have to do in order to create a Foreign Key relationship!

25. While this screen is still open, let's take a quick look at the Indexes/Keys tab to see how it automatically creates a Clustered Index when you specify a Primary Key for a table. Clustered Indexes were explained in Chapter 1.

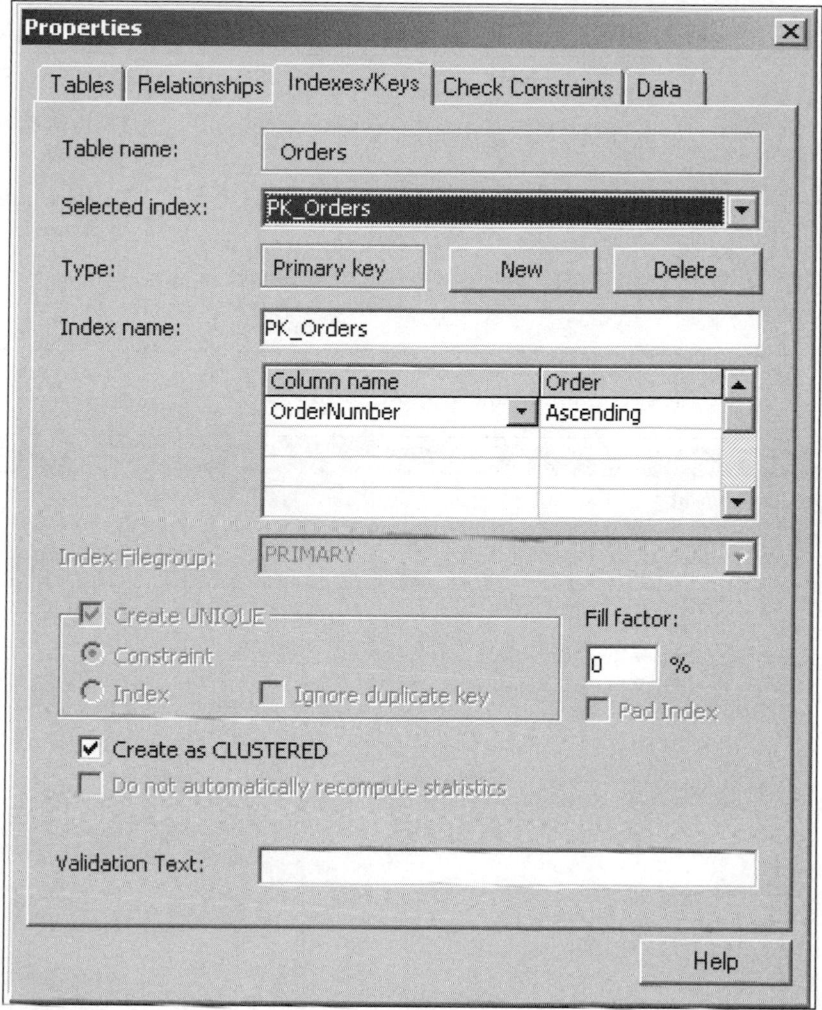

26. Now close the Properties dialog and then the `Orders` table so that you are returned to the view of all defined tables. You may be prompted to save your changes to the table, in which case click Yes.

27. Now, repeat the process one last time to create the `OrdersProducts` table. As before, double-click Create table in Design view to begin.

28. Recall from Chapter 1 that the `OrdersProducts` table is to have the following structure:

ORDERSPRODUCTS TABLE			
Field	**Example**	**Type of Data**	**Estimated Size of Data**
OrderNumber (PK)	1000	Numeric	Positive number with no decimals
ProductIdentifier (PK)	12345	Numeric	Positive number with no decimals
Price	$23.25	Currency	
Quantity	2	Numeric	

Create the `OrdersProducts` table as shown below:

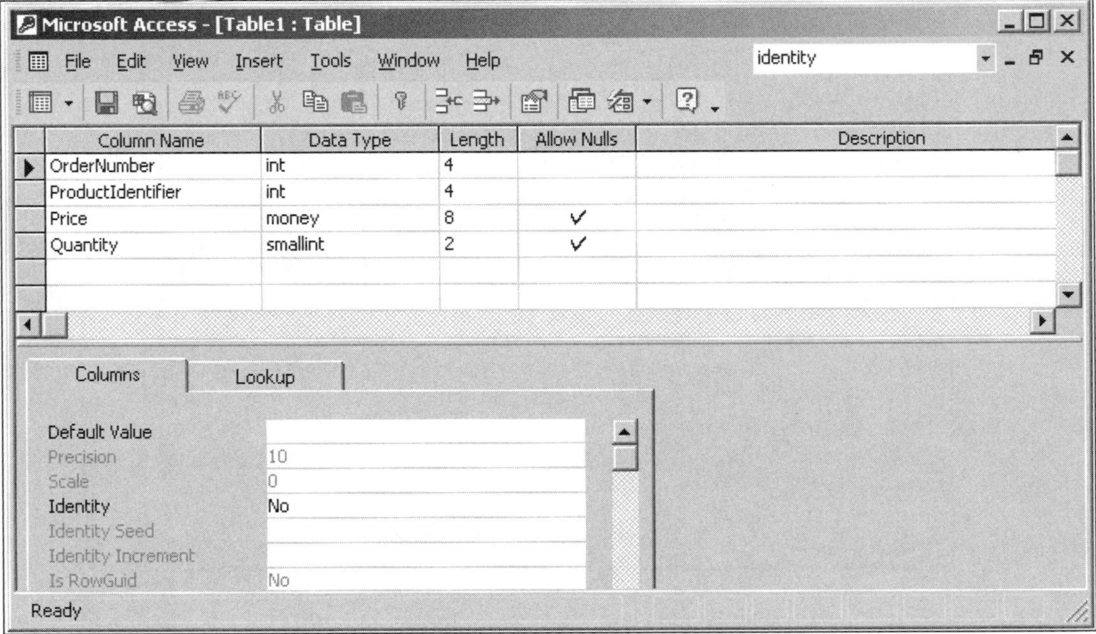

Notice that the `OrderNumber` and `ProductIdentifier` both have the `int` data type and that the `Quantity` field is `smallint`. The `smallint` data type in SQL Server can hold whole number values in the range -32,768 to 32,767 and should be used when a given integer field will not need to exceed that range. Thus, as even the most dedicated customer is highly unlikely to ever want to order more than 32,767 items of any particular product, `smallint` is appropriate for the `Quantity` field. Also notice that the `OrderNumber` and `ProductIdentifier` fields cannot be `Null` and therefore must be specified when creating a new record in this table.

29. In this case, we are going to specify that the combination of the `OrderNumber` and `ProductIdentifier` fields make up the Primary Key. It is the combination of both of these that makes a Unique Record Identifier, thus allowing multiple products for any one order. Note however that we are NOT going to set them up as identity columns because they are not initially created by this table, but by the tables that they refer to. The `OrderNumber` is generated in the `Orders` table, while the `ProductIdentifier` is generated in the `Products` table. So all we need to do this time to make the Primary Key for the table is to select both `OrderNumber` and `ProductIdentifier` fields and then choose the Edit | Primary Key option.

30. After doing so, the graphic of the key should appear next to both the `OrderNumber` and `ProductIdentifier` fields.

31. Now select File | Save to save the `OrdersProducts` table but, again, don't close it straight away.

32. `OrderNumber` and `ProductIdentifier` are Primary Keys in this table, but they are Foreign Keys in the `Orders` and `Products` tables. Thus, we need to create Foreign Key relationships with these tables like we did between the `Orders` table and the `Customers` table. To do so, select View | Relationships and click the New button.

33. Again, it defaults to a relationship with the `Customers` table, which this time is *not* what we want. So, in the Primary key table drop down, select Orders so we can first create our Foreign Key relationship to the `OrderNumber` field of the `Orders` table.

34. Notice how, when you change the Primary Key table to the `Orders` table and then move to a different field, the Selected relationship and the Relationship name are automatically updated, as shown overleaf:

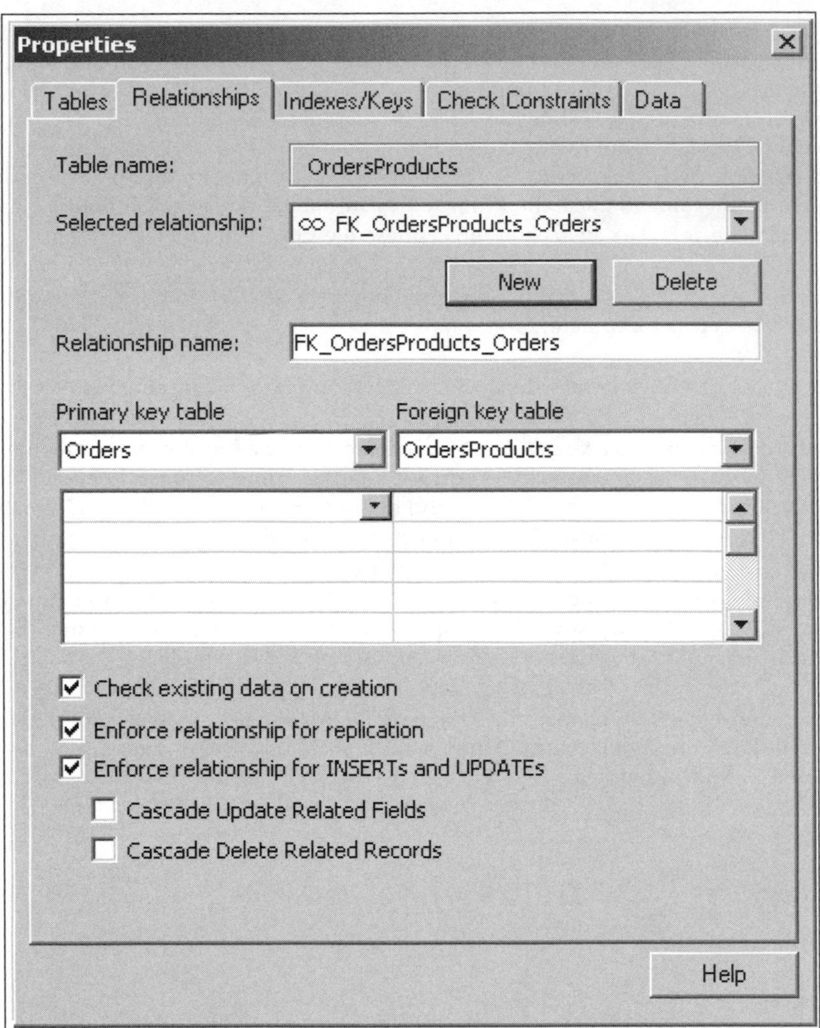

35. Now select OrderNumber for the Primary Key value from the `Orders` table and OrderNumber for the Foreign Key value from the `OrdersProducts` table, as shown opposite:

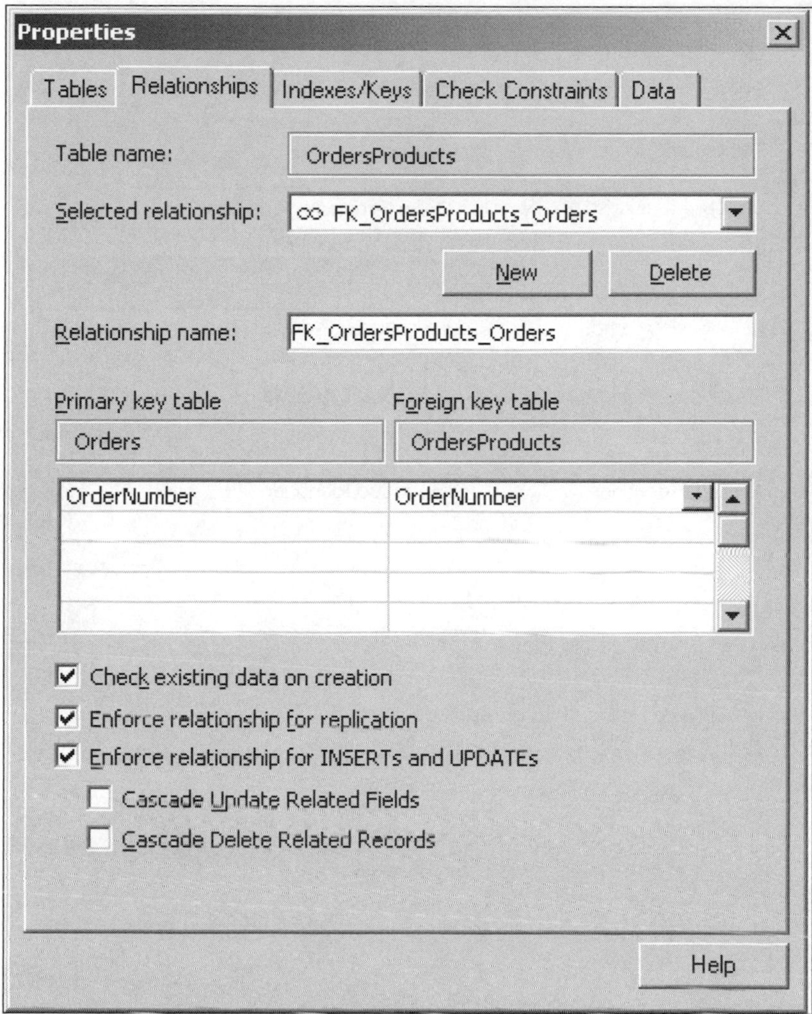

36. This creates the relationship with the `Orders` table, so now we're ready to create the relationship with the `Products` table. To do so, click the New button.

37. Now change the Primary key table to show the Products table. Again, when you leave the field, the Selected relationship and Relationship name are automatically updated. The OrdersProducts table should still be showing as the Foreign Key table. Now select the ProductIdentifier in both the Primary Key and Foreign Key drop-down lists. At this point, you have created the relationship with the Products table too.

38. To see a list of existing relationships on the OrdersProducts table, select the Selected relationship drop-down at the top of the Relationships dialog to see all those currently defined:

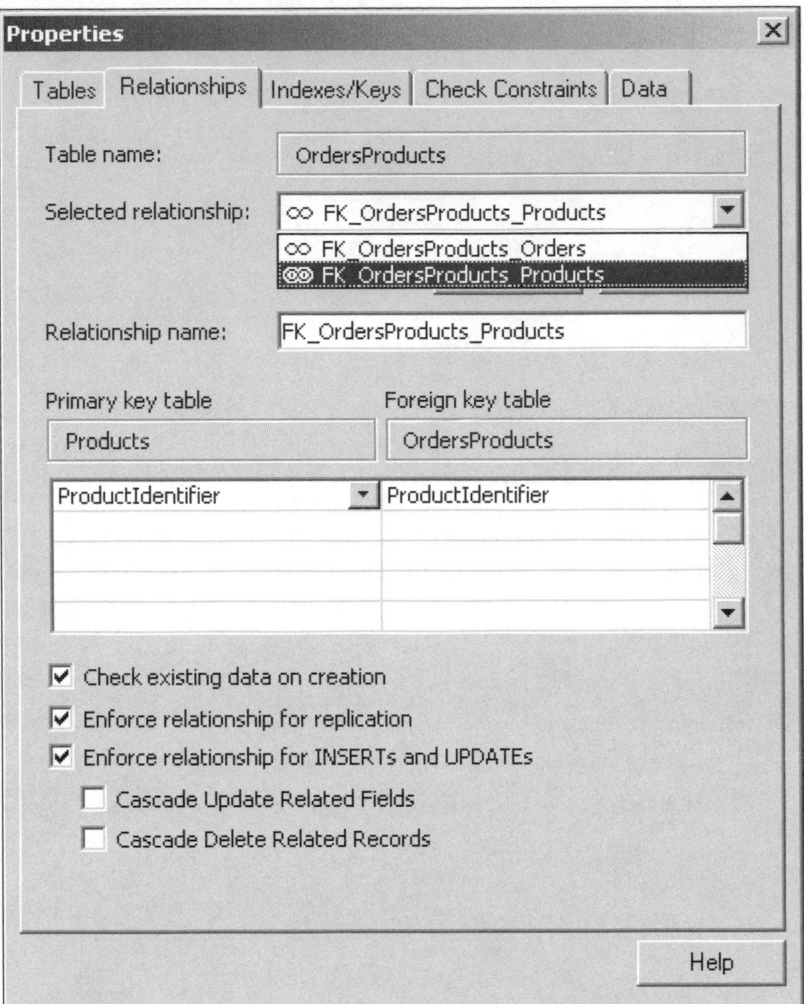

39. Notice that both the relationships we have just created appear in the drop-down list. Close this window and the `OrdersProducts` table by clicking on the cross in the top right corner of each so that you return to the tables view. If you are prompted to save table changes, click Yes.

40. Double-click on the `Products` table and add some sample data. Remember that the `ProductIdentifier` field is generated by SQL Server, so you do not have to fill in this field yourself. Try adding the record without entering values for the required fields, just to see what happens. Then add a few valid records and close the datasheet view.

41. Then, open the `Customers` table and add some new customers. Again, recall that you do not need to specify the `CustomerNumber`, as it is automatically generated by SQL Server. Try adding a record without specifying one of the required fields to see what happens. Then, add a couple of customers to the table and then close the datasheet view.

42. Open the `Orders` record and fill in some information there too. See what happens when you try to specify a `CustomerNumber` that doesn't exist in the `Customers` table (the Foreign Key relationship we defined requires this value to exist in the `Customers` table before it may be added to the `Orders` table). Then, add a valid order that links to a `CustomerNumber` that does exist in the `Customers` table.

43. Last of all, open the `OrdersProducts` table and fill in some sample data. See what happens when you type in an `OrderNumber` or `ProductIdentifier` that do not already exist in their respective main tables. Recall that we previously defined a Foreign Key relationship which requires that these values exist in their main tables (Orders and Products) before they may be used in the `OrdersProducts` table. Fill in some valid values designating existing `OrderNumbers` and `ProductIdentifiers` from their respective tables. Add the same `OrderNumber` multiple times with different `ProductIdentifiers` (more than one product per order) to verify that this is allowed.

Congratulations! You have now successfully created a new database with four tables in your Desktop Engine / SQL Server database by using a Microsoft Access project.

Now that we have learned the basics of database design and implemented our basic physical Desktop Engine database, we can begin working with a more complicated database that will be used for the majority of this book. We will use the Northwind sample database that comes with Access for this purpose. It is similar in many ways to the database we've just created, and has similar `Products`, `Customers`, `Orders`, and `OrdersProducts` tables. However, the Northwind database is more complex, contains additional tables, and is designed around the needs of a fictitious retailer called Northwind.

In this next section, we look at how to use the Upsizing Wizard to convert the existing Northwind Access database into a SQL Server database. During this process, the wizard will automatically create a new Access project for us to link to the database. Once the Northwind database is converted to SQL Server, we will then be able to use it for the examples in the rest of this book.

Upsizing an Existing Access Database To SQL Server 2000 Desktop Engine

The Upsizing Wizard of Access 2000 and Access XP allows you to open an existing Access database and convert it to the equivalent SQL Server database. In this section, we are going to convert the sample Northwind database from Access to SQL Server. Once the conversion is complete, we will analyze the report produced to ensure that no errors occurred. We will then take a look at the resulting project file that allows us to view and manage the newly created SQL Server database.

Note that Access 2000's Upsizing Wizard works differently to the Upsizing Wizard in Access XP and, if you use the 2000 Wizard, you may end up with slight differences in the resulting upsized database (such as different views, stored procedures, or functions).

Try It Out – Upsizing the Northwind Database from Access to SQL Server

1. Open Microsoft Access XP.

2. Select File | Open and browse to find the Northwind sample database (`northwind.mdb`) supplied with Access and click the Open button to open it up. A common location for this database file is `C:\Program Files\Microsoft Office\Samples`. This may not necessarily be its location on your machine if you installed the sample databases somewhere else. You can search for the file using the Start | Search menu option. If you still cannot find the Northwind database on your hard drive, then you can rerun Microsoft Access setup and install the sample databases.

3. Close the Main Switchboard of the Northwind application so that you are left with the database design view.

4. From the Tools menu, select Database Utilities | Upsizing Wizard, as shown below:

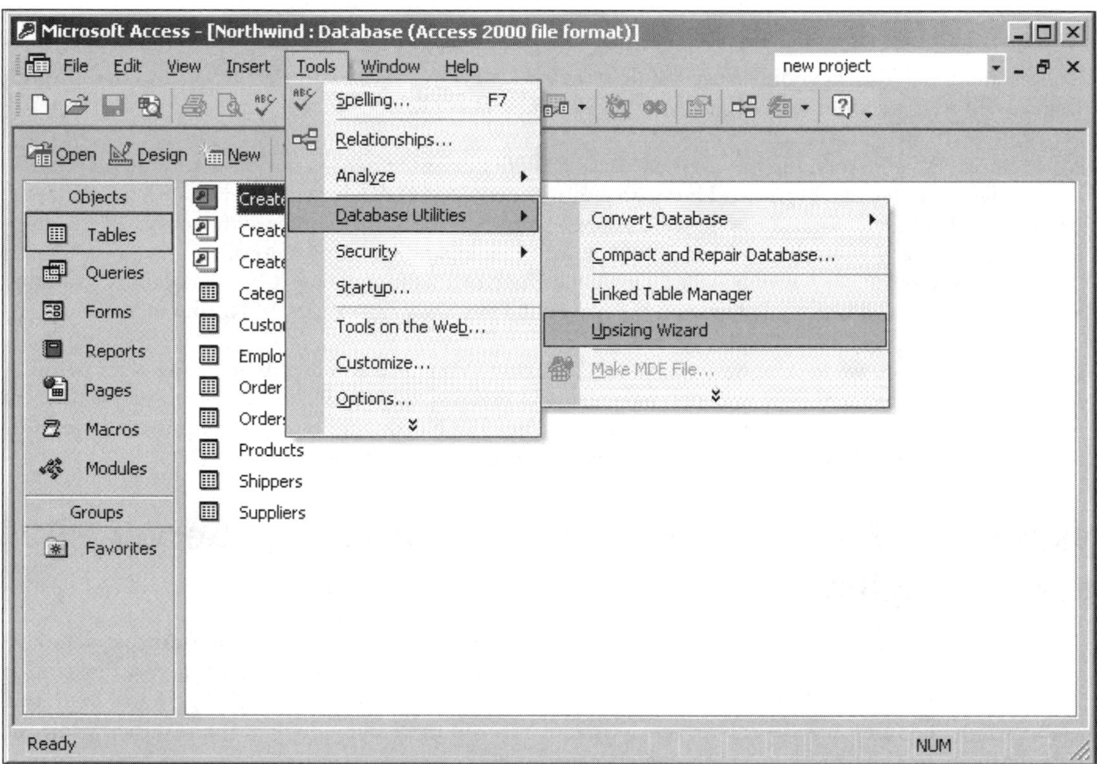

5. The Upsizing Wizard will begin, and the following screen will appear:

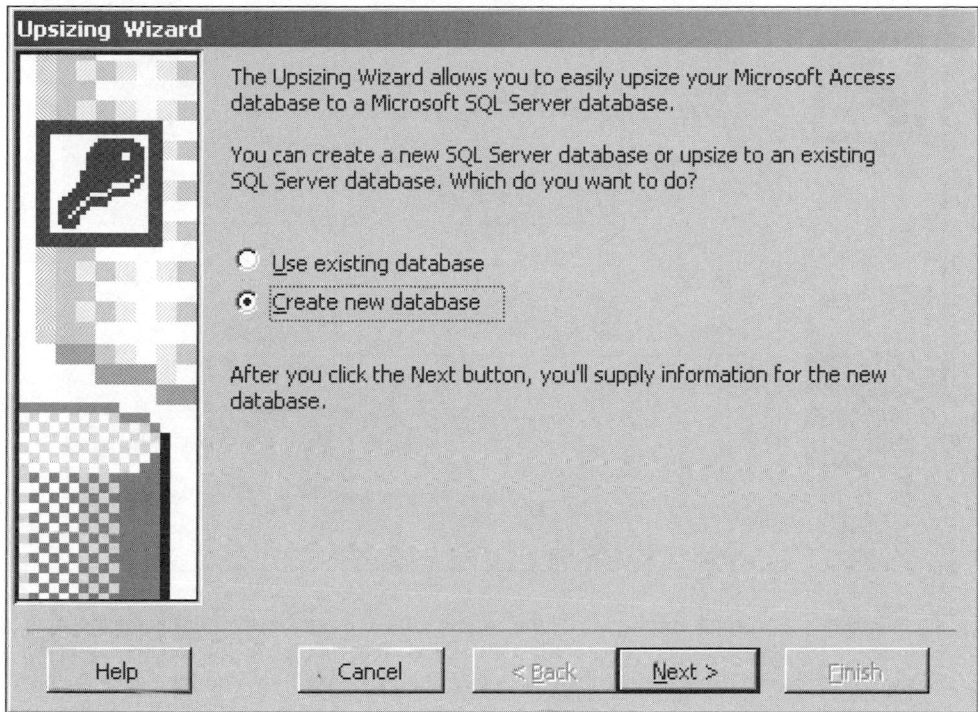

6. Select the **Create new database** option if it isn't already selected and click the **Next** button so we can create a brand new SQL Server database from the existing Northwind Access database.

7. Fill in information about the SQL Server (which in our case will be the name of our Desktop Engine installation) that you want to create the new database on, as shown in the example overleaf. A list of available servers should be in the drop-down list. In some cases, (local) will be the correct one if you are creating the database on a version of Desktop Engine on the current computer. For the User Id and Password, fill in information for a valid SQL Server user with create database permissions. By default, you can use "sa" (system administrator) with a blank password. Of course, when you have a database containing sensitive information, you really need to change these user details to something less obvious.

   Below the UserId and Password boxes, specify the name you want to use when referring to the new Northwind database from Desktop Engine. I'm going to call mine NorthwindSQL and, to keep things simple, it's a good idea if you do the same. Once all necessary information is filled in, click the Next button.

   Please note that, with Access 2000, you may receive an "Overflow" dialog box at this step. The solution is to apply a patch that can be downloaded from the Microsoft Web Site. There is a knowledge base article that discusses this issue. You can read this article at the following URL: http://support.microsoft.com/support/kb/ articles/Q272/3/84.ASP.

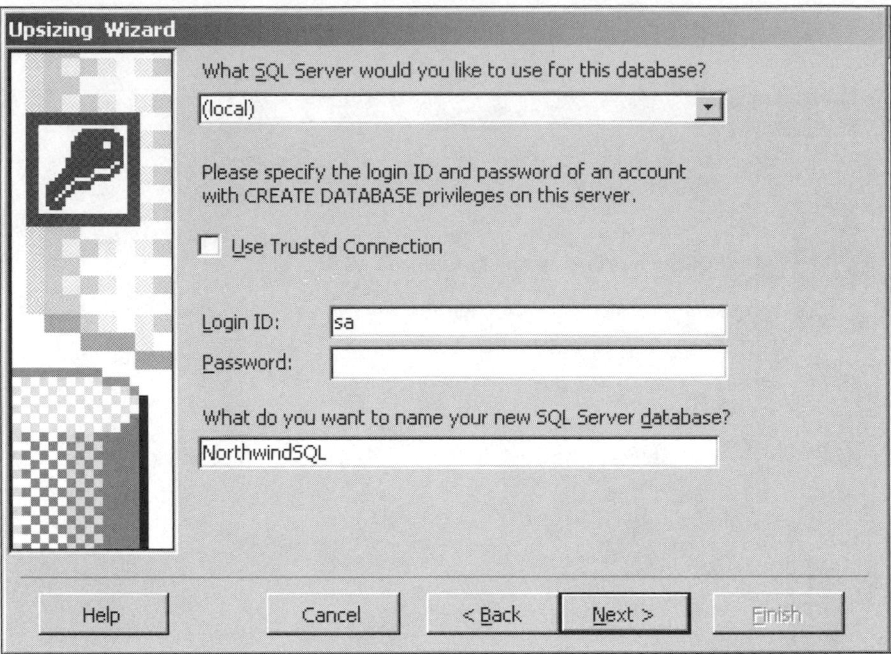

8. The next screen prompts you to specify the tables in the existing Northwind database that are to be included in the new SQL Server database. Click the double right arrow button on the screen so that all the tables are moved to the list of tables to export, as shown below, and then click the Next button.

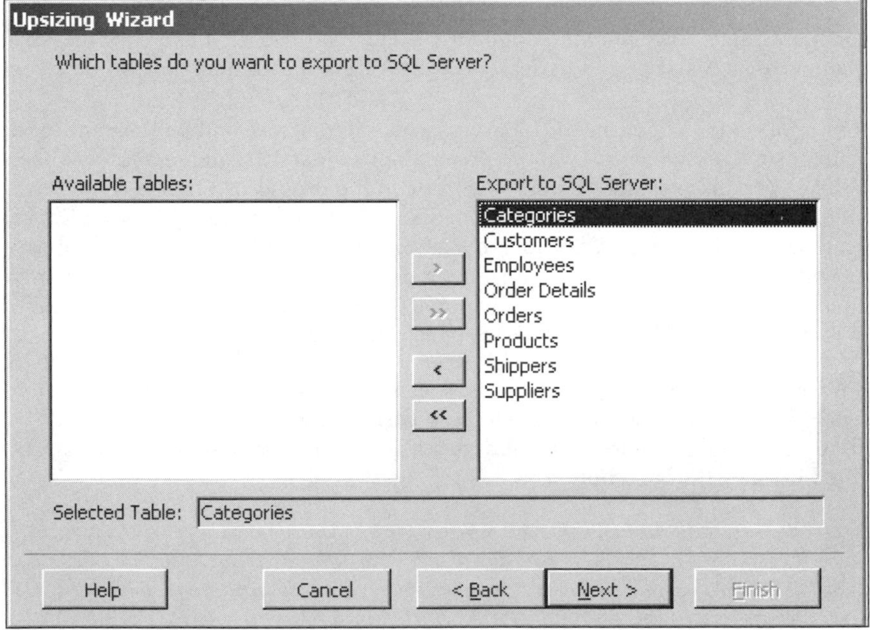

9. The next screen allows us to specify which database attributes (that is, fields) we wish to carry over to the upsized version. In this case, we want to upsize the table structure as well as the data, and thus should make sure that the following options are checked before clicking **Next**:

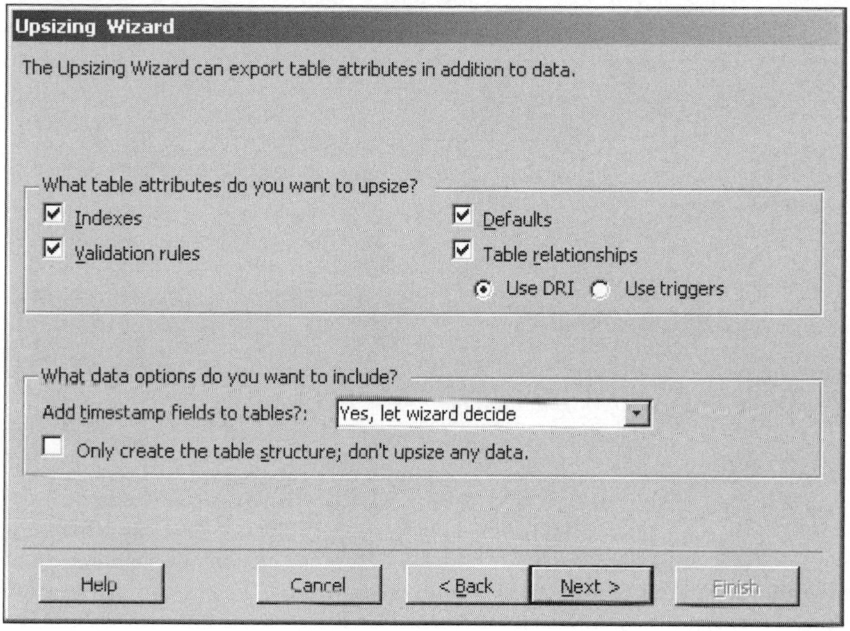

Note that for the table relationships, you have the option to **Use DRI** or **Use triggers**. DRI creates relationships between the tables during the creation of the table. Triggers, on the other hand, should be selected when you need to support cascading updates and deletes.

For the timestamp option, generally, you should allow the wizard to determine whether a timestamp should be used. Using a timestamp column in a table makes sure that its timestamp column is updated with a value that reflects that last time it was updated.

10. The next screen allows us to specify where we want to create the Access project file and what we want it to be called. This screen gives us the option to link to an existing application or create a new client-server Access application. We are going to do the latter, which will convert all the database details from the Access database to the SQL Server version, while leaving the user interface components in Access. This allows us to create a client-server application with Access as the front-end and SQL Server as the back-end. You can change the file location to whatever destination on your computer you wish to place the Access project file, but save it with the name `NorthwindSQL.adp`.

We could also specify to save the password and user ID so that the user ID and password you use for connecting will be stored in a connection string that the project uses.

Once this is done, the **Finish** button becomes enabled, as you can see overleaf. However, we aren't going to click **Finish** just yet; instead we're going to click the **Next** button to see what other choices are available.

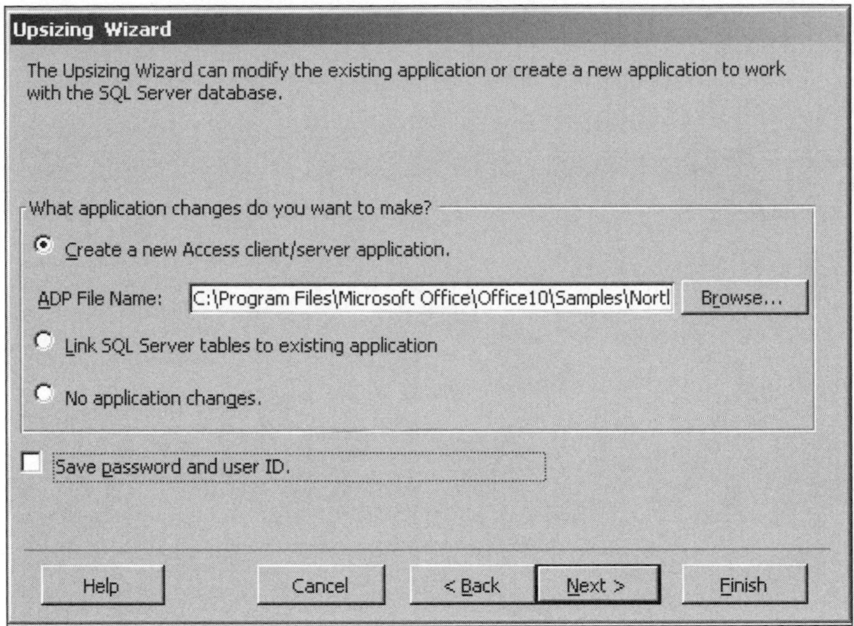

11. The screen shown below is the final one of the wizard. Notice how the Next button is no longer enabled while the Finish button still is. Here we can decide whether we want to Open the new ADP file (our new client-server project) once the wizard completes, or whether we wish to remain in the original Access Northwind file.

We are going to select the option to Open the new ADP file, as we are eager to see what it looks like.

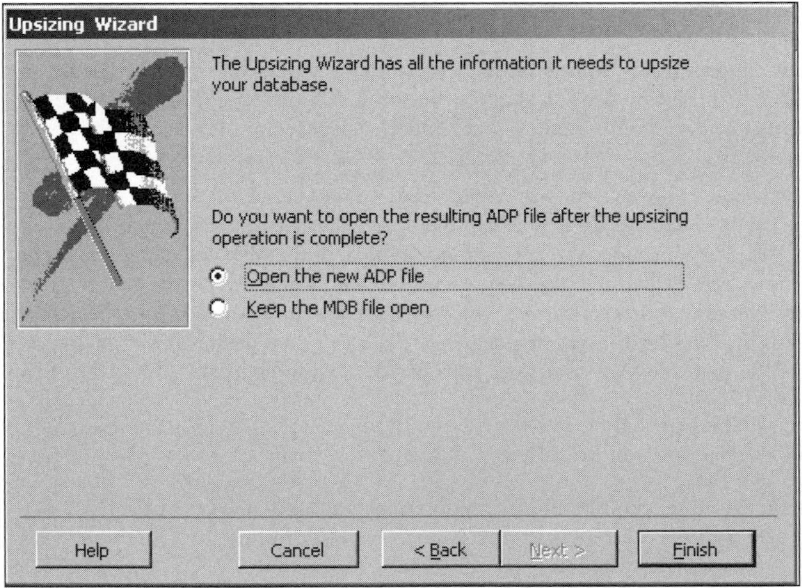

12. After clicking the Finish button, Microsoft Access works its magic and converts our Access Northwind database to a SQL Server database with a client-server Access front-end. You will see a progress bar as shown below detailing each step as it is taken, and the overall progress of the upsizing process:

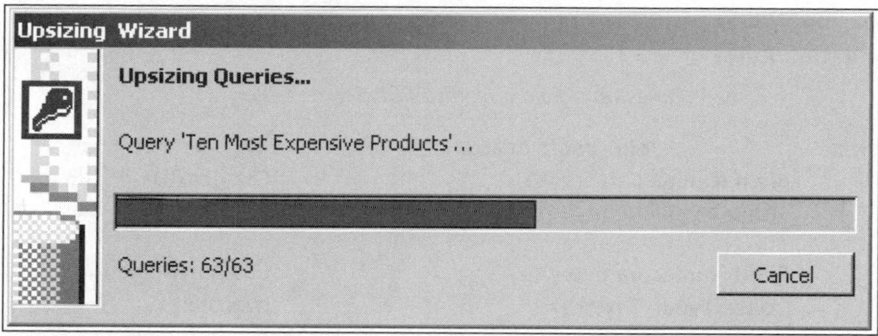

13. Any errors with the upsizing attempt will be displayed in dialog boxes. For example, in this instance, a syntax error was encountered while copying a particular record into the newly created tables. This error was caused by attempting to place the text value `Qtr` into an integer field. The wizard notifies you of any such error, and continues with the upsizing process once you have clicked OK.

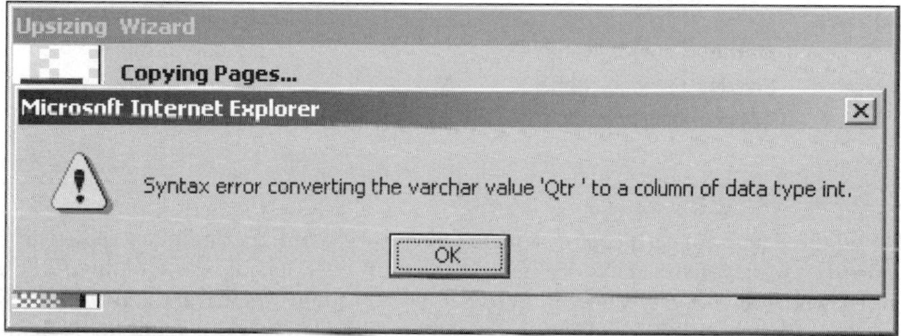

14. Once the upsizing is complete, a summary report will be displayed on the screen. The summary report gives you a record of the work you did and helps you determine why database objects failed to update. The first piece of important information in this report is the detailed listing of each table that was converted, what data type it was converted to, which indexes were converted, etc. An example of the sort of information described for each table is shown overleaf. Notice how the original Access values are shown on the left and the SQL Server values they were translated to appear on the right. The `CategoryID`, for example, was a `Number (Long)` in Access but, in SQL Server, it was converted to the `int` data type. At the bottom we see that the original `CategoryName` index was successfully converted to a `CategoryName` index in SQL Server. This tells us that the index was and is a Unique Index on the `CategoryName` field, which, you may recall from Chapter 1, means that the index is based on a field that may contain unique values only.

Table: Categories

	Microsoft Access	SQL Server
Table Name:	Categories	Categories
Attached Table Name:		
Aliasing Query:		
Validation Rule:		

Timestamp field added to SQL Server table.

Fields

	Microsoft Access	SQL Server
Field Name:	CategoryID	CategoryID
Data Type:	Number (Long)	int
Field Name:	CategoryName	CategoryName
Data Type:	Text(15)	nvarchar(15)
Field Name:	Description	Description
Data Type:	Memo	text
Field Name:	Picture	Picture
Data Type:	OLE Object	image

Indexes

	Microsoft Access	SQL Server
Name:	CategoryName	CategoryName
Fields:	CategoryName	CategoryName
Type:	Unique	Unique

15. After all the details for each converted table have been listed, the summary report describes the queries that were converted. Notice how, in the example opposite, some of the stored Access Queries were converted to Views in SQL Server, and some others were converted to Stored Procedures. Views and Stored Procedures will be explained in more detail in the next two chapters but, for now, it is enough to know that Views and Stored Procedures in SQL Server are similar in concept to the Stored Query in Access, and that the report shows the results of the conversion.

Queries

Query Alphabetical List of Products

Upsized using SQL:

```
CREATE VIEW "Alphabetical List of Products"
AS
SELECT Products.*, Categories.CategoryName AS Expr1001
FROM Categories INNER JOIN Products ON (Categories.CategoryID=Products.CategoryID)
WHERE (((Products.Discontinued)=0))
```

Query Product Sales for 1997

Upsized using SQL:

```
CREATE VIEW "Product Sales for 1997"
AS
SELECT Categories.CategoryName, Products.ProductName, sum(convert(money,"Order
Details".UnitPrice*Quantity*(1-Discount)/100)*100) AS ProductSales, 'Qtr ' +
datepart(q,ShippedDate) AS ShippedQuarter
FROM (Categories INNER JOIN Products ON (Categories.CategoryID=Products.CategoryID))


INNER JOIN (Orders INNER JOIN "Order Details" ON (Orders.OrderID="Order Details".OrderID))
ON (Products.ProductID="Order Details".ProductID)
WHERE (((Orders.ShippedDate) Between '1/1/1997' And '12/31/1997'))
GROUP BY Categories.CategoryName, Products.ProductName, 'Qtr ' + datepart(q,ShippedDate)
```

16. You can print the log file or use the report that is created and saved automatically for you.

Congratulations again! You have now successfully upsized the Northwind database to create a client-server project, including the table structure of your SQL Server database and an Access project file containing the user interface elements (forms, and so on) that links the tables to the SQL Server database.

We should have the new Access project open (`NorthwindSQL.adp`) since, above, we chose the option to open it after the wizard completed. Take a moment to look around the project and get a feel for the new structure. You will see that it doesn't look very different to the standalone Access Northwind database prior to the upsizing process. The biggest difference takes place behind the scenes. The tables are displayed just like before but now the data in the tables and the tables themselves are physically located in a Desktop Engine database as opposed to an Access file.

Other Ways of Creating and Managing Desktop Engine Databases

Since the Desktop Engine edition of SQL Server does not include any SQL Server graphical user interface management tools (Enterprise Manager, Query Analyzer), you have to use other means to create and manage SQL Server databases. The exception to this, of course, is if you installed Desktop Engine from the SQL Server 2000 installation CDs – in which case, you can install SQL Server's graphical user interface tools like Enterprise Manager.

In this chapter, we have studied one way of creating and managing SQL Server databases, through Access projects. Another way to create and manage SQL Server databases is using the Server Explorer that comes with Visual Studio .NET, and we will look at this in more detail in the next chapter. There are also APIs available that allow you to create and manage SQL Server databases programmatically through Visual Basic and other such languages. However, we will not be covering the programmatic creation and management of Desktop Engine databases in this book, as it is a complex and advanced task suited to experienced database programmers. However, creating database applications using Visual Basic .NET that read, update, insert, and delete data in SQL Server databases that have already been set up is well within the scope of this book and will be covered extensively. For the creation and management of databases, Access or the Visual Studio .NET Server Explorer are adequate for our purposes, leaving us to concentrate fully on our first forays into the world of database programming.

Summary

In this chapter, we have learned a lot about Microsoft SQL Server 2000 Desktop Engine and how it can help us overcome the gap between Access databases and their SQL Server equivalents. To begin with, we examined differences between the Desktop Engine and other editions of Microsoft SQL Server 2000, before narrowing our focus to explore the Desktop Engine in greater depth. We learned:

- That Desktop Engine is a freely distributable version of Microsoft SQL Server 2000.
- That Desktop Engine solves the problems previously posed when having to migrate from Access to SQL Server, since no changes to the database are necessary when you need to upgrade to a more powerful version of SQL Server.
- Where to find a copy of the setup program and how to install it onto your computer.
- How to create a new Desktop Engine/SQL Server database from scratch using Microsoft Access.
- How to upsize an existing Microsoft Access database to a Desktop Engine database. In the process, we found out what an Access project file is and how it can create client-server applications. The project file doesn't store any data or data structures, but contains only links to the SQL Server database and user interface elements (forms, etc.) for the database.

In Chapter 1, we learned some of the theory behind the design of a database. In this chapter, we have seen how to put our design into practice by creating a new SQL Server database using Access. In the next chapter, we will find out how to pass information into and out of SQL Server databases using the Visual Studio .NET Server Explorer. We will, among other things, explore the SQL language and learn how to run queries and create Views.

Exercises

1. What is Desktop Engine? How does it compare to other versions of Microsoft SQL Server 2000?
2. Why should you use it instead of Access? What problems does it solve?
3. Why is Access a great companion to Desktop Engine/SQL Server?
4. Describe what an Access Project File is and how to go about creating one.

Answers are available at http://p2p.wrox.com/exercises/.

Querying the Database

In this chapter, we will take a look at how to retrieve information from SQL Server Desktop Engine databases. We will also learn how to add, update, and delete data that is in the database. In this process, we will specifically cover the following topics:

- How Transact SQL (T-SQL) differs from Microsoft Access Jet in its syntax.
- How to retrieve information from Desktop Engine databases using T-SQL.
- Creating a View in Server Explorer to run SQL statements.
- Selecting and filtering information in the database.
- Inserting, updating, and deleting information in the database.
- Sorting the data results in a specific order.
- Retrieving database information from multiple tables.
- How to summarize information in the database meaningfully.
- Some complex ways to retrieve the information you need.

After covering these areas, we will summarize what we learned and present you with some questions to ensure you have fully grasped these concepts.

Querying SQL Server Desktop Engine Databases

Having data stored in a database does not provide much value unless you have an easy way to retrieve the information when you need it. We query a database to process data to create information that is meaningful to the user. In this chapter, we will look at how to use the Server Explorer and the Transact SQL language to manage information in SQL Server Desktop Engine databases.

Transact SQL (T-SQL) versus Jet SQL

You have most likely already heard the term Structured Query Language, most commonly known as SQL (pronounced "sequel"). You also probably already know that you can use SQL statements to retrieve data from databases. There are different dialects of SQL in use depending on the database platform.

For example, all versions of Microsoft SQL Server, including the SQL Server Desktop Engine, utilize the Transact SQL (T-SQL) language for retrieving and modifying information in the database. Microsoft Access, on the other hand, employs the language called Jet SQL. Although T-SQL and Jet SQL are alike in many ways, they are also very different. The need to change from one SQL syntax to another constitutes one of the primary problem areas that people migrating applications from Access to SQL Server must overcome.

In order to make the transition from one database platform to another as smooth as possible, the American National Standards Institute (ANSI) has created standards for SQL that aim to ensure that SQL statements written for one database will run against other databases also following that standard, even if running on a different platform. There are two different versions of the ANSI Standard: ANSI 89 and ANSI 92. The ANSI 89 standard was adopted in 1989, and this was consolidated and much improved into a new standard adopted in 1992, named, perhaps unimaginatively, the ANSI 92 standard. Both of these standards offer multiple levels of adherence that databases can conform to. Most database vendors that provide some degree of compliance with the ANSI 92 standards have aimed at Level 1, the lowest compliance level.

Jet SQL, the Access version of SQL, adheres to most of the Level 1 requirements for ANSI 89, but does not meet the ANSI 92 standard. T-SQL, the SQL Server version of SQL, on the other hand, is fully compliant with the ANSI 92 Level 1 standard, making SQL Server Desktop Engine a much better choice than Jet for many professional applications. In addition to supporting the features required by the ANSI 92 standard, SQL Server also supports many additional features not defined by that standard. This is both a good thing and a bad thing. Clearly, such features provide enhanced functionality, but in order to run on other database platforms, those statements will have to be modified. Statements that use syntax that does conform to ANSI 92, on the other hand, will not need modification to run on other ANSI 92 compliant databases.

With this history as the backdrop, let's delve into the details of how to use the T-SQL language to retrieve and modify information in Desktop Engine databases.

The Basics of T-SQL

The T-SQL language allows you to retrieve, modify, update, and delete data in SQL Server (and therefore Desktop Engine) databases. It also allows you to sort, filter, summarize, and group information in many meaningful ways. This section will demonstrate each of these features in more detail. After learning the T-SQL syntax itself, we will see how to run statements against our upsized NorthwindSQL database.

Selecting Data from the Database

You are probably already aware of the most basic type of SQL statement: the `SELECT` statement. Use the `SELECT` statement to retrieve records from a database. For example, if we want to see all information in the `Products` table, we would run the following SQL statement:

```
SELECT * FROM Products
```

The asterisk (`*`) above designates that we want to see *all* fields in the `Products` table. If, instead, we only wanted to find the name of the product, the price, and units that are in stock, the SQL statement below would accomplish this:

```
SELECT ProductName, UnitPrice, UnitsInStock FROM Products
```

In this example, the specific fields we want to see are listed, followed by the `FROM` clause that indicates which table to retrieve the information from. The `SELECT` and `FROM` keywords are capitalized to make the statement more readable, but it is not a requirement and does not affect the meaning of the code. You should always consider capitalizing SQL keywords for this reason.

So how do we run this SQL statement and see the results? SQL Server Desktop Engine doesn't have a user interface, so we have to make use of the graphical interface in Access XP or Visual Studio .NET to run queries. We will run the queries in Visual Studio .NET, since it is convenient and takes advantage of the single environment that we'll be using throughout the rest of this book. Visual Studio .NET uses the Server Explorer tool to let us run SQL statements. Note that Server Explorer can do a lot more than just running T-SQL queries. We will look at these other options later, but for now we are only concerned with running SQL queries.

Try It Out – Running a Query in Server Explorer

1. Start up Visual Studio .NET.

2. Locate the Server Explorer window. If it is already open, it will be tucked away in the left-hand corner of the screen near the Toolbox. If not, you may have to open it using View | Server Explorer (or pressing *Ctrl-Alt-S*). It should appear similar to the following screenshot, except of course that the listings under Data Connections and Servers will reflect those set up on your particular system:

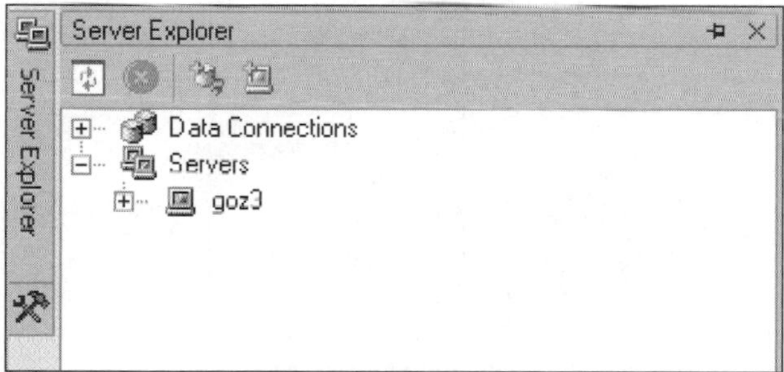

3. Now we want to show the NorthwindSQL database node. It will be found in the tree located underneath the Servers node, so expand the node labeled with the name of your particular server (where above there is goz3). This will bring up several new nodes – we're after our SQL Server, so expand the node labeled SQL Servers. Next, expand the node corresponding to the name of your Desktop Engine server (GOZ3 in the following screenshot). This brings up the names of all the SQL databases installed on your machine, as shown opposite (you may well have different databases in your tree):

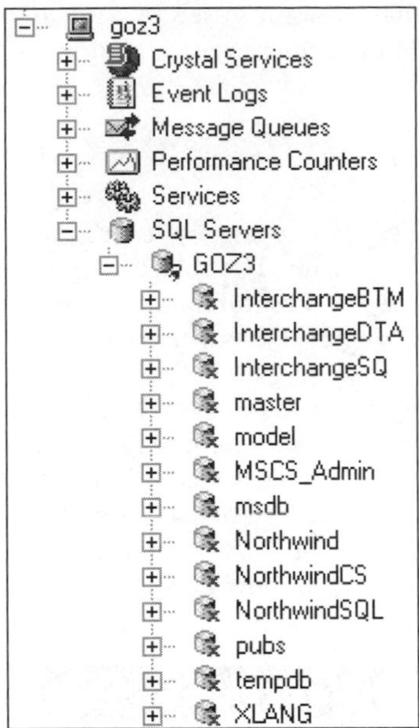

4. We're only interested in the NorthwindSQL database, so expand that node, and then expand the Tables node that now appears underneath NorthwindSQL, and you should be able to recognize the database we upsized:

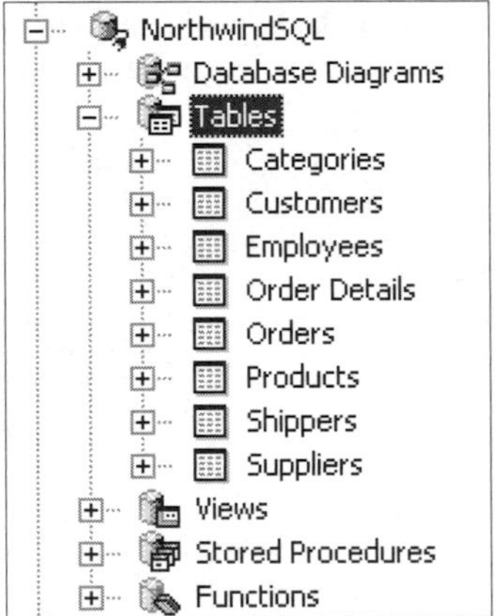

5. We will use the Server Explorer's ability to create views to run our SQL queries. This will be explained in more detail shortly. For now, right-click on the Views node in Server Explorer for the NorthwindSQL database. Some options should pop up as shown below:

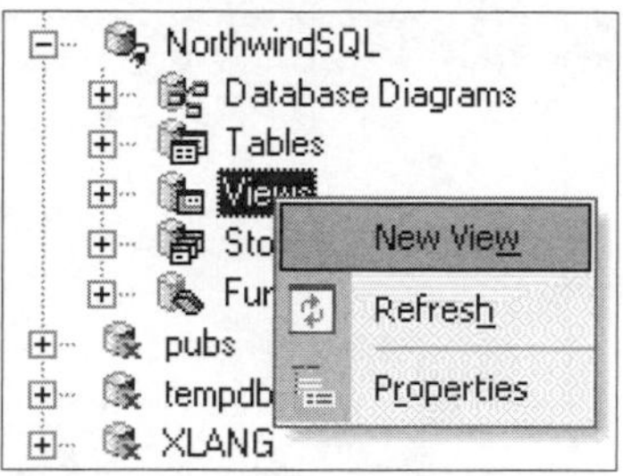

6. Select the New View option from this menu to create a new view. An Add Table window will appear prompting you to choose which tables to include in the view. Click the Close button to ignore this for now, as we shall add the tables that we need manually. We now have the View designer open, as shown below:

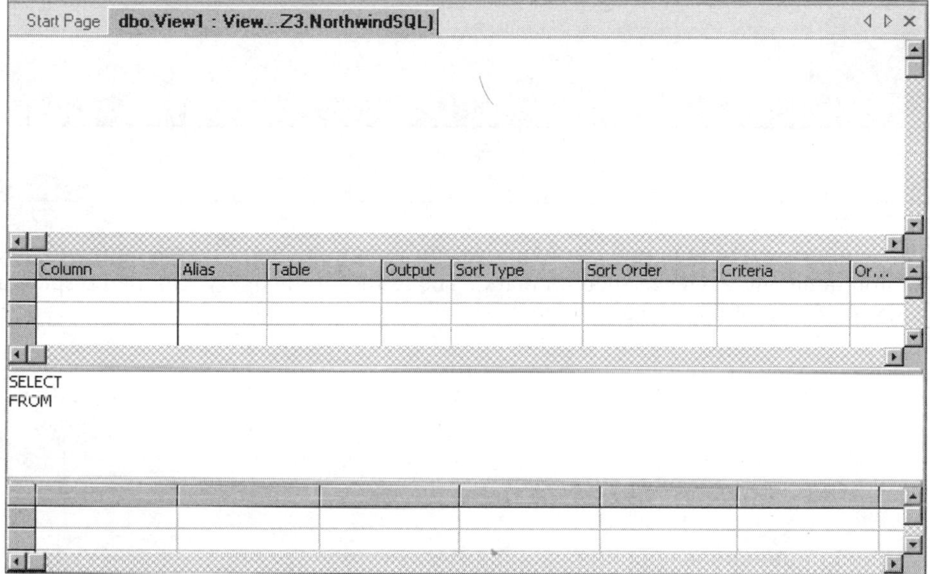

7. Use the SELECT FROM area of the designer to create the SQL statement you wish to run. An example is shown overleaf:

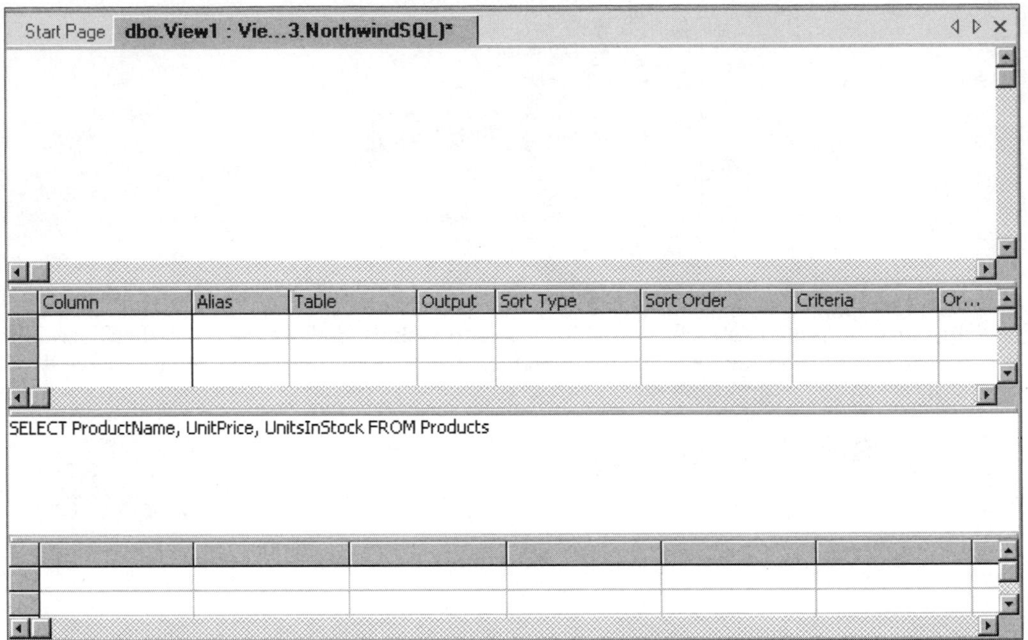

8. To actually run the SQL statement entered, click the Run Query button on the toolbar (the button depicting a red exclamation mark). The results of the query will then display in the Output section of the screen:

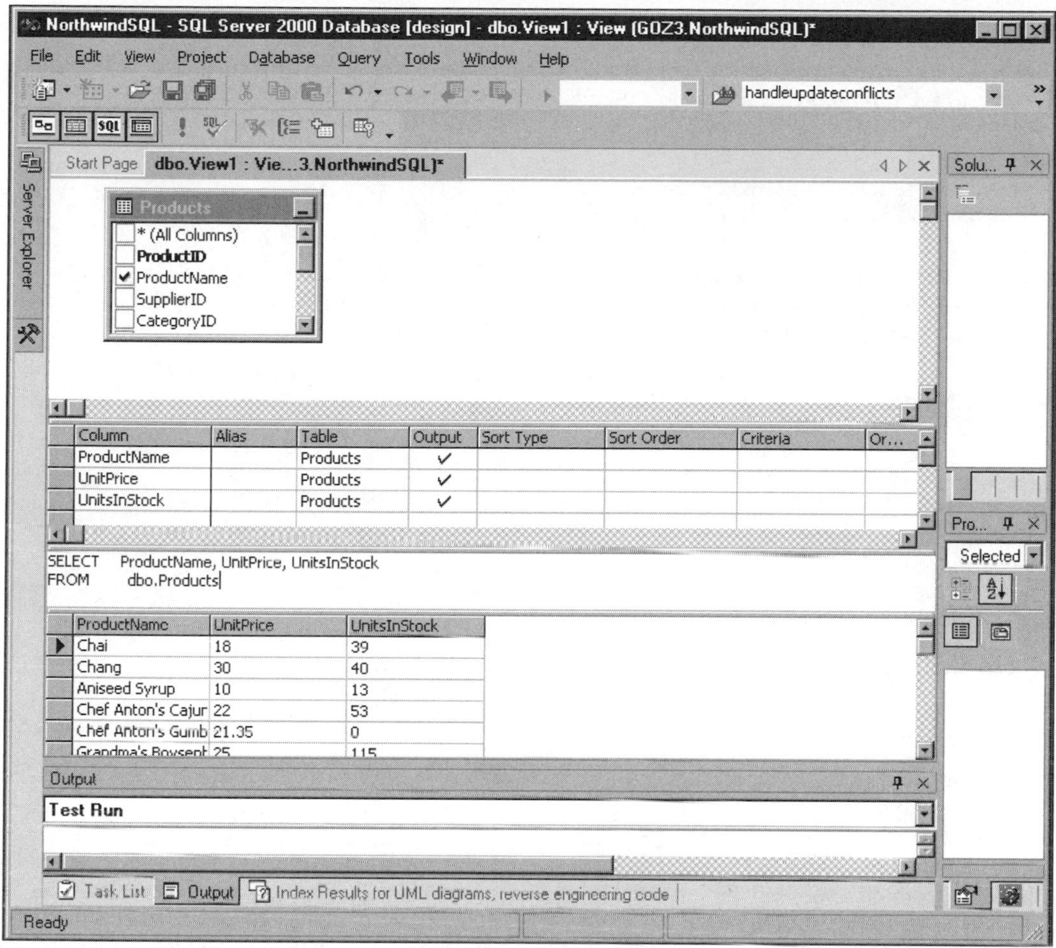

How It Works

Server Explorer lets us run SQL statements and display the results by creating a new view. Views are a new concept that will be explained in greater detail in Chapter 4. For now, we just need to know that a View is a SQL statement that can be saved to a database and treated as a "virtual table". Here we used the View designer to create and run SQL statements.

After we navigated to the NorthwindSQL node in the Server Explorer, we expanded the nodes to show the tables that the database contained. After confirming that this was indeed the database that we upsized, we created an empty View and ran a sample SQL statement. This SQL statement selected the `ProductName`, `UnitPrice`, and `UnitsInStock` columns from the database, and displayed its results in the Output section of the screen.

Use the View designer to run the SQL Statements given throughout this chapter to see them in action. Let's now look at some more examples of SQL statements that access the database.

Filtering Data with WHERE

In the previous example, we selected all records from certain columns in the `Products` table. What if we only want to see products that sell for less than $25? When we want to filter data so that only records meeting certain criteria are retrieved, we can use a `WHERE` clause in our SQL statement, as shown below:

```
SELECT ProductName, UnitPrice, UnitsInStock FROM Products
WHERE UnitPrice < 25
```

The `WHERE` clause specifies that the `UnitPrice` should be less than 25, so that the above SQL statement will return the specified three columns for all products less than $25. Run this SQL statement in Server Explorer in the View designer, and you should get results similar to these:

ProductName	UnitPrice	UnitsInStock
Chai	18	39
Aniseed Syrup	10	13
Chef Anton's Cajun Seasoning	22	53
Chef Anton's Gumbo Mix	21.35	0
Queso Cabrales	21	22
Konbu	6	24

This is a very simple example of a `WHERE` clause, so let's now look at some of the more complicated ways to filter data.

The table below shows some examples of the most commonly used Comparison Operators in `WHERE` clauses. In our previous examples, we used the 'less than' (<) operator to return only the products that cost less than $25. We could just as easily have substituted one of the other comparison operators in its stead. Have a look through the table now, paying particular attention to the last four entries, and we will then look at them in more detail.

Comparison Operator	Description
>	Greater than.
<	Less than.
=	Equals.
>=	Greater than or equal to.
<=	Less than or equal to.
<>	Not equal to.
`BETWEEN x AND y`	Matches values that fall between `x` and `y` inclusive – that is, both `x` and `y` satisfy the condition.

Comparison Operator	Description
`LIKE`	Returns fields that start with, end with, or contain this particular value. `NOT LIKE` is also valid, matching anything that does not correspond to the given pattern.
`IN`	Matches values given in the subsequent parentheses. `NOT IN` is also valid and finds a match on anything but the particular values specified.
`IS NULL`	Column contains a `Null` value.

You should already understand how to use the greater-than and less-than operators from the previous example. The other standard comparison operators act as we would expect them to. So, to return all products that cost $25 exactly, we can replace the less-than sign with the equal sign:

```
SELECT ProductName, UnitPrice, UnitsInStock FROM Products
WHERE UnitPrice = 25
```

Now, the statement returns only the records in the `Products` table that have a price of exactly $25. Run this in the View designer if you wish to check how it works.

You could replace the other comparison operators in a similar manner to achieve different filtering effects, such as to show all products that cost $25 and higher (>=), those that cost $25 and lower (<=), and those that do not cost $25 (<>). Play around with these in the query window to see the impact of each variation. Now let's take a look at a few of the other filters which are not so obvious.

BETWEEN

The `BETWEEN` operator allows you to return all records in the specified range. For example, if you want to see all products with prices in the range $25-$35, you could use the following SQL statement:

```
SELECT ProductName, UnitPrice, UnitsInStock FROM Products
WHERE (UnitPrice BETWEEN 25 AND 35)
```

Don't forget that this is an inclusive range, so items priced at exactly $25 and $35 will be returned. Here, we want to find records based on a numeric range – price – but the `BETWEEN` operator works fine with alphabetical ranges as well. For example, suppose you want to see all products with names that appear alphabetically between A and C, inclusive. This can be accomplished with the following statement:

```
SELECT ProductName, UnitPrice, UnitsInStock FROM Products
WHERE (ProductName BETWEEN 'A' AND 'C')
```

Executing this statement will return results containing any product name starting with A and B. But why have no product names starting with C been returned? This is because of how SQL treats alphabetical groupings, such that anything that starts with C but is not the letter C itself would be classed as falling *after* C. For example, "Camembert Pierrot" would be considered as coming after the letter C alphabetically, and thus would not be returned by the above SQL statement. If you wanted to specify a `BETWEEN` range that *would* return those product names starting with C, you could use something like the following:

```
SELECT ProductName, UnitPrice, UnitsInStock FROM Products
WHERE (ProductName BETWEEN 'A' AND 'D' AND <> 'D')
```

The above statement should yield results like this:

ProductName	UnitPrice	UnitsInStock
Alice Mutton	39	0
Aniseed Syrup	10	13
Boston Crab Meat	18.4	123
Camembert Pierrot	34	19
Carnarvon Tigers	62.5	42
Chai	18	39
Chang	30	40
Chartreuse verte	18	69
Chef Anton's Cajun Seasoning	22	53
Chef Anton's Gumbo Mix	21.35	0
Chocolade	12.75	15
Côte de Blaye	263.5	17

LIKE

The `LIKE` operator allows you to perform partial string matching to filter records where a particular field starts with, ends with, or contains a certain set of characters. For example, if you wanted to see all product names that start with 'G', you could use the following statement:

```
SELECT ProductName, UnitPrice, UnitsInStock FROM Products
WHERE ProductName LIKE 'G%'
```

Notice the percent sign (`%`) following the G. If you're used to Access queries, you might expect this to be a `*` sign – this is just one of those differences that we touched upon earlier. The percent sign's purpose is to denote any sequence of characters, so that the database knows to search for all records that have a product name beginning with G, as shown below:

ProductName	UnitPrice	UnitsInStock
Geitost	2.5	112
Genen Shouyu	15.5	39
Gnocchi di nonna Alice	38	21
Gorgonzola Telino	12.5	0

ProductName	UnitPrice	UnitsInStock
Grandma's Boysenberry Spread	25	115
Gravad lax	26	11
Guaraná Fantástica	4.5	20
Gudbrandsdalsost	36	26
Gula Malacca	19.45	27
Gumbär Gummibärchen	31.23	15
Gustaf's Knäckebröd	21	104

To see a list of all products *ending* with G, you would put the percent sign *before* the G, like this:

```
SELECT ProductName, UnitPrice, UnitsInStock FROM Products
WHERE ProductName LIKE '%G'
```

This statement returns results something like this:

ProductName	UnitPrice	UnitsInStock
Chang	30	40
Chef Anton's Cajun Seasoning	22	53
Nord-Ost Matjeshering	25.89	10

Notice how only those products that end in the letter G are returned. You could specify more than one letter if you wanted to. For example, you could have just as easily asked to see all of the products that begin with 'GO', or all the products that end with 'GO'.

The third way of using the `LIKE` operator returns any records that contain a certain character or sequence of characters. For example, suppose you want to see all products that have the word `BERRY` somewhere in the product name – you could use a SQL statement like this:

```
SELECT ProductName, UnitPrice, UnitsInStock FROM Products
WHERE ProductName LIKE '%BERRY%'
```

Notice how in this instance, the percent signs come before *and* after the letters you want to filter. This lets the database know that you want to return records that contain the letters `berry` at any point in the product name field. As SQL is not case sensitive, `BERRY` is treated identically to `berry`, and so the statement will match 'Berry', 'Grandma's Boisenberry Spread', 'Northwoods Cranberry Sauce', and so on:

ProductName	UnitPrice	UnitsInStock
Grandma's Boysenberry Spread	25	115
Northwoods Cranberry Sauce	40	6

Serving a similar purpose to the percent sign in LIKE clauses is the underscore character that indicates a *single* occurrence of any character. Also, we can indicate one of a set of characters, rather than just any character, by listing the allowed characters within square brackets:

```
SELECT ProductName, UnitPrice, UnitsInStock FROM Products
WHERE ProductName LIKE [cs]ha_
```

This SQL statement will return products with a name of Chai, Shaz, and so on, but not Chang, because the underscore will match one and only one character. If the above WHERE clause had the percent sign in place of the underscore, then Chang would be returned, as well as Chai and Shaz.

IN

You can use the IN comparison operator to provide a specific set of values. For example, if you want to see all products where the price is exactly $5, $10, or $20, you could use the following:

```
SELECT ProductName, UnitPrice, UnitsInStock FROM Products
WHERE UnitPrice IN (5, 10, 20)
```

Notice how the IN clause is followed by parentheses, and the values you want to retrieve are separated by commas. In this instance, the filter applies to a numeric value (UnitPrice), so we do not need to use single quotes. Any products with unit prices matching any of those three values is returned:

ProductName	UnitPrice	UnitsInStock
Aniseed Syrup	10	13
Sir Rodney's Scones	10	3
Maxilaku	20	10
Longlife Tofu	10	4

Note that you could accomplish the same result with the following SQL statement:

```
SELECT ProductName, UnitPrice, UnitsInStock FROM Products
WHERE UnitPrice = 5 OR UnitPrice = 10 OR UnitPrice = 20
```

We can filter text fields of a record using the IN clause, although we must remember to use single quotes around each text value for ProductName. For example, suppose we want to return any records where the product name is either 'Alice Mutton' or 'Aniseed Syrup', we could use the IN operator like this:

```
SELECT ProductName, UnitPrice, UnitsInStock FROM Products
WHERE ProductName IN ('Alice Mutton', 'Aniseed Syrup')
```

In this instance, the values are surrounded by the single quotes since they correspond to a text field in the database. This statement will return both the Alice Mutton and Aniseed Syrup product records, as long as they exist in the database of course. An alternative notation for this statement's WHERE clause would be: WHERE ProductName='Alice Mutton' OR ProductName= 'Aniseed Syrup'.

IS NULL

There will be times when you specifically want to see when certain fields are explicitly `Null`. Be aware that `Null` is quite different from zero, or an empty string. It is a special value that any type of column may have, and indicates that no data is stored in that column. If you wanted to see all of the products where the `Price` field is `Null`, you could use a SQL statement containing the `IS NULL` keyword like this:

```
SELECT ProductName, UnitPrice, UnitsInStock FROM Products
WHERE UnitPrice IS NULL
```

Specifying Multiple Filters with AND/OR

We have seen a couple of examples that specify multiple filters in the `WHERE` clause to limit the records retrieved using the `AND` and `OR` keywords. For example, suppose that you want to see all products where the price is less than $25 and the `UnitsInStock` is greater than 10. Such a statement looks like this:

```
SELECT ProductName, UnitPrice, UnitsInStock FROM Products
WHERE (UnitPrice < 25) AND (UnitsInStock > 10)
```

Notice how the `AND` keyword is used between the two sets of criteria and how each separate condition is contained within parentheses. Running this SQL statement should return results similar to these:

ProductName	UnitPrice	UnitsInStock
Chai	18	39
Aniseed Syrup	10	13
Chef Anton's Cajun Seasoning	22	53
Queso Cabrales	21	22
Konbu	6	24
Tofu	23.25	35

If instead you wanted to see all products that are less than $25 *or* have more than 10 in stock, you would use this statement:

```
SELECT ProductName, UnitPrice, UnitsInStock FROM Products
WHERE (UnitPrice < 25) OR (UnitsInStock > 10)
```

Notice that records are returned if either criterion is met:

ProductName	UnitPrice	UnitsInStock
Chai	18	39
Chang	30	40
Aniseed Syrup	10	13
Chef Anton's Cajun Seasoning	22	53

You can specify many criteria to restrict the returned results to exactly what you need. Suppose you only want to see products priced between $25 and $50, with a `ProductName` that starts with C, and that have over 10 units in stock. No problem. You can do that with the following SQL statement:

```
SELECT ProductName, UnitPrice, UnitsInStock FROM Products
WHERE (UnitPrice BETWEEN 25 AND 50)
AND (ProductName LIKE 'C%')
AND (UnitsInStock > 10)
```

This returns the following records:

ProductName	UnitPrice	UnitsInStock
Camembert Pierrot	34	19
Chang	30	40

You can see how easy it is to specify multiple filters to achieve the exact results you need for a given scenario. Now that we've learnt the T-SQL syntax for retrieving data from a database, let's take a look at how to change distinct records.

Modifying Data with INSERT, UPDATE, and DELETE

T-SQL provides you with the means to insert data into a database, update existing records with new values, or delete existing records. Let's look at each of these in more detail.

INSERT

The `INSERT` statement can be used to add new records to a database. Suppose you want to add details of a new product line to the `Products` table. The product is called Belgian Waffles, has a price of $5, and is provided by the Supplier with an ID of 3. Suppose that you do not know the Category ID and other information yet (and that our database allows `Null` values for `CategoryId` and certain other columns that we don't specify). To add this partial information, you can use the following T-SQL statement:

```
INSERT INTO Products (ProductName, UnitPrice, SupplierId) VALUES ('Belgian
Waffles', 5, 3)
```

Let's look at this syntax in more detail. First, there is the `INSERT INTO` statement followed by the name of the table to insert the record into. The following parentheses contain the name of the fields that we have the data for. Next, after the `VALUES` keyword, are parentheses containing the values for the field names previously listed, and in the same order. It is critical that the order of the values match with the order of the field names, otherwise data will be inserted into the wrong fields. Last of all, notice how the Belgian Waffles value is surrounded by single quotes but the `UnitPrice` and `SupplierId` values are not. This is because the `ProductName` field is textual and the `UnitPrice` and `SupplierId` fields are numerical. You will need to know the data types of the fields you are inserting data into in order to know whether quotes are required or not. When inserting a record, be sure to provide values for all columns unless you know that a column has a default value or that it allows `nulls`.

Go ahead and run the SQL statement above in the View designer. Note that you will first receive a dialog box such as the following:

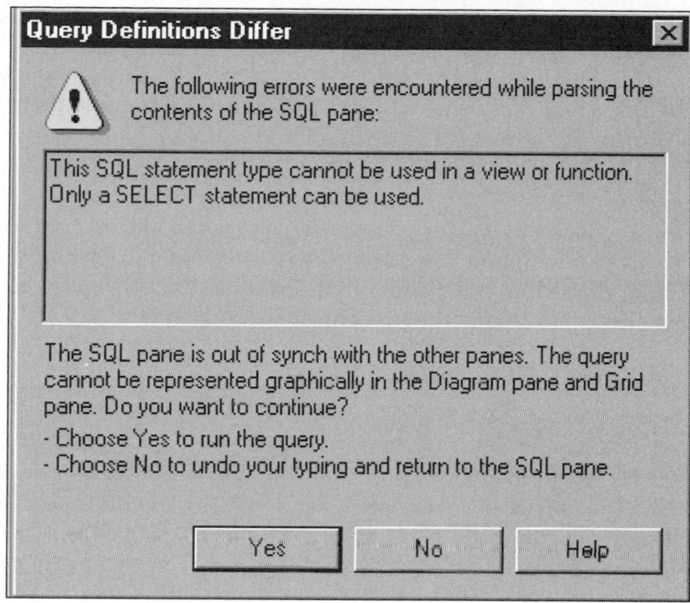

This message box is essentially just a warning that you will not be able save the View if it contains an `INSERT` statement. We are not planning on saving this SQL statement anyway, and are simply using the View designer window to run it, so we can ignore this message. Click the Yes button to continue. A message box will then appear indicating how many rows the `INSERT` statement affected (that is, how many rows were added).

This example inserts a new record into the `Products` table using information specified in the SQL statement itself. You might find it useful here to think of the SQL `SELECT` statement that would retrieve this new record from the database to verify that it was indeed added.

There is also another way to insert values: by inserting the results of a `SELECT` statement. This means that you can use a `SELECT` statement to retrieve records from one table and insert them into another table. Let's walk through a quick example. Suppose you have a `TempProducts` table that gets populated temporarily with any new `Products` that your company is going to start carrying. You could use the following to select all the records it contains, and insert them in the same step into the `Products` table:

```
INSERT INTO Products
(SELECT * FROM TempProducts)
```

Note that the fields do not have to be named identically, they just have to appear in the same order and be of the same data type. Furthermore, the `Products` table must already exist for this to work. If you only wanted to insert certain fields instead of all of them, you could specify those fields individually, like this:

```
INSERT INTO Products (ProductName, UnitPrice, SupplierId)
(SELECT ProductName, UnitPrice, SupplierId FROM TempProducts)
```

There is also a way to insert the results of a SELECT into a totally new table altogether. Suppose that for some reason you wanted to create a temporary copy of the Products table that you could manipulate without harming the live Products table. The SELECT INTO statement will allow you to create a brand new table from the results of a select statement. Here's an example that creates a TempProducts table from all the current records in the Products table:

```
SELECT * INTO TempProducts FROM Products
```

Notice that, in this instance, we're using the SELECT INTO statement instead of the INSERT INTO statement. SELECT INTO is used when you want to create a new table from the returned results, while INSERT INTO is used when you are inserting records into an existing table.

Now let's move on to see how to update existing records.

UPDATE

The UPDATE statement allows you to update existing records in the database. For example, when we first added the Belgian Waffles record, we only knew the ProductName, UnitPrice, and SupplierId. Suppose that we now know the CategoryId, QuantityPerUnit, and UnitsInStock values and want to update that record in the database. The following statement shows how we might do this:

```
UPDATE Products
SET CategoryId = 3, QuantityPerUnit = '12 per box', UnitsInStock = 50
WHERE ProductName = 'Belgian Waffles'
```

The UPDATE key word is followed by the name of the table to update, and the SET statement is followed by the individual fields to be updated, along with their corresponding values – with each field separated by commas. Last of all, the WHERE clause specifies which records to update. Don't forget the WHERE clause when appropriate to limit the records which are to be updated. If the WHERE clause is not supplied, then all records in the table will be updated with these new values. Of course, there are certain situations where this is really what you want – such as for a mass update where you need to update the fields of all records. In general though, the WHERE clause is an essential part of UPDATE statements, as it is here.

It is also possible to use an UPDATE statement to update records in one table based on information taken from another table. You can do this using an UPDATE FROM clause, as shown below:

```
UPDATE Products
SET CategoryId = 3, QuantityPerUnit = '12 per box', UnitsInStock = 50
FROM Products, Categories
WHERE Products.CategoryId = Categories.CategoryId AND
      Products.ProductName = 'Belgian Waffles'
```

OK, this may not be the best example, but it shows how you can update one table based on certain criteria for joining multiple tables.

DELETE

In addition to updating data in databases, you can also easily delete data. The DELETE statement allows you to remove records that you no longer want. For example, suppose that all of the products in the TempProducts table have been successfully added to the main Products table. At this point, you are ready to delete all the records from the TempProducts table. The following SQL statement will accomplish this:

```
DELETE FROM TempProducts
```

This will delete **all** records in the TempProducts table because there is no WHERE clause to limit affected records. Use caution when running a DELETE statement without a qualifying WHERE clause. It is a common mistake to forget to include one when you really want to delete a single or few records, with potentially disastrous results. For example, to delete just the Belgian Waffles record from the TempProducts table, the SQL statement would be:

```
DELETE FROM TempProducts WHERE ProductName = 'Belgian Waffles'
```

Note that when deleting records from a database, it is always best to use the primary key whenever possible, such as the ProductId or SupplierId fields in this case. You can then be sure that you will only delete the record you intended, because other fields do not provide a guarantee of uniqueness (for instance, in the above statement, there could be more than one record with a ProductName field of 'Belgian Waffles').

Beyond the Basics

T-SQL offers a rich set of features for data manipulation and analysis. You have seen several of these features throughout this chapter already. In this section, we will look at examples of more complicated ways to retrieve data. T-SQL supports many advanced features beyond those given, but I hope that this section gives a flavor of what can be accomplished.

Sorting Data with ORDER BY and GROUP BY

If you don't specify a particular order for returned results, they will simply be returned in the order they appear in the tables. This will quite likely not be the most meaningful order for your purposes. Fortunately, you can specify how the returned information should be ordered or grouped so that it is suitable for what you plan to do with it.

ORDER BY

The ORDER BY clause allows you to specify in which order you want results returned. Recall this example from earlier in the chapter:

```
SELECT ProductName, UnitPrice, UnitsInStock FROM Products
```

You might want to sort these results by ProductName to produce an alphabetical listing of Products. The statement above will return them in no particular order, which isn't great, unless of course our database is sorted alphabetically on this field. As this is not the case, we have to specify that the results are to be returned in alphabetical order by ProductName, using the following ORDER BY clause:

```
SELECT ProductName, UnitPrice, UnitsInStock FROM Products
ORDER BY ProductName
```

The above statement returns the data as shown below:

ProductName	UnitPrice	UnitsInStock
Alice Mutton	39	0
Aniseed Syrup	10	13
Belgian Waffles	5	0
Boston Crab Meat	18.4	123
Camembert Pierrot	34	19

This uses the default order of ascending, and the statement could have equally been written as:

```
SELECT ProductName, UnitPrice, UnitsInStock FROM Products
ORDER BY ProductName ASC
```

Here, the `ASC` keyword (for ascending) is explicitly specified. You can also return the records in reverse alphabetical order, that is, descending order. Use the `DESC` keyword as shown:

```
SELECT ProductName, UnitPrice, UnitsInStock FROM Products
ORDER BY ProductName DESC
```

This will return a list of all the products in reverse alphabetical order:

ProductName	UnitPrice	UnitsInStock
Zaanse koeken	9.5	36
Wimmers gute Semmelknödel	33.25	22
Vegie-spread	43.9	24
Valkoinen suklaa	16.25	65
Uncle Bob's Organic Dried Pears	30	15
Tunnbröd	9	61

Note that the order is based on the data type, which will not necessarily be alphanumeric.

You can also specify multiple fields to sort by. For example, suppose you want to sort descending by price (to see the most expensive first), but that you want to further sort on `ProductName` alphabetically so that products with the same price will be listed in alphabetical order. The SQL statement shown below would achieve this:

```
SELECT ProductName, UnitPrice, UnitsInStock FROM Products
ORDER BY UnitPrice DESC,
ProductName ASC
```

Notice how the multiple sort fields are separated by commas and each specifies the type of sort to use, either ascending or descending. The ordering priority follows the order that they appear in the ORDER BY clause. This statement will return results similar to those shown below:

ProductName	UnitPrice	UnitsInStock
Côte de Blaye	263.5000	17
Thüringer Rostbratwurst	123.7900	0
Mishi Kobe Niku	97.0000	29
Sir Rodney's Marmalade	81.0000	40
Carnarvon Tigers	62.5000	42
Raclette Courdavault	55.0000	79
Manjimup Dried Apples	53.0000	20
Tarte au sucre	49.3000	17
Ipoh Coffee	46.0000	17
Rössle Sauerkraut	45.6000	26
Schoggi Schokolade	43.9000	49
Vegie-spread	43.9000	24

Notice how the most expensive products are listed first. Take special notice of the last two lines: the Schoggi Schokolade and Vegie-spread products. They are both the same price: 43.9000, and are thus then sorted alphabetically so that the Schoggi Schokolade comes first.

GROUP BY

There will be times when you want to summarize information in the database rather than retrieving individual records. For example, you might want to find the total number of products that you have available, the total sales on a given day, and so on. You can accomplish this in T-SQL using an appropriate **aggregate function** combined with a GROUP BY clause. The table below lists some of the most common aggregate functions:

Aggregate Function	Description
AVG	Returns the average
COUNT	Returns the total occurrences
MAX	Returns the highest value
MIN	Returns the lowest value
SUM	Returns the mathematical sum

The following statement uses the AVG function to produce the average price of all products in the Products table:

```
SELECT AVG(UnitPrice)
FROM Products
```

Running the above SQL statement in the View designer returns something like 26.5895.

Aggregate functions used as in the example shown above return a single record as the resultset. Thus, when you want to summarize data in groups, you must use the GROUP BY clause in conjunction with the aggregate functions. Let's look at an example to make this clearer. If you want to see the average price by Supplier, you would use the following SQL statement:

```
SELECT AVG(UnitPrice) AS 'Average Price', SupplierId
FROM Products
GROUP BY SupplierId
```

The SQL statement above yields results similar to the following:

Average Price	SupplierID
10.2842	1
16.4857	2
20	3
46	4
29.5	5
14.9166	6

Notice how the average function (AVG) is given the UnitPrice field and a more meaningful name, a column **alias**, of Average Price. You can use column aliases to give any column you wish a more meaningful name. The second and final item in the SELECT list is the SupplierId, which is also specified in the GROUP BY clause. Whenever you use an aggregate function in a SQL statement, any item in the SELECT list that isn't part of the aggregate must be included in the GROUP BY clause. The effect of running the above statement is that multiple rows will be returned: one record for each supplier that will contain their average product price.

You can add the equivalent of a WHERE clause to a GROUP BY with the HAVING keyword. Hence, we could modify the above statement to return only details for suppliers whose average price is greater or equal to $20 as shown:

```
SELECT AVG(UnitPrice) AS 'Average Price', SupplierId
FROM Products
GROUP BY SupplierId
HAVING AVG(UnitPrice) >= 20
```

Let's look at some of the other aggregate functions, starting with the COUNT function, which returns the number of items matching the condition specified, as in this example that returns the number of products in the Products table:

```
SELECT COUNT(ProductId)
FROM Products
```

Running the above SQL statement in our View designer returns a single number indicating how many relevant records there are.

Let's now see how MIN, MAX, and SUM work. The SQL statement below will return the least price of all products offered, the greatest price, and the total of all prices:

```
SELECT MIN(UnitPrice), MAX(UnitPrice), SUM(UnitPrice)
FROM Products
```

In the View designer, this statement will show three numbers in the Output window representing the requested information.

Retrieving Data from Multiple Tables Using JOINS

Up to this point, all of our T-SQL examples have only retrieved information in a single table at a time. T-SQL is able to select or update information in multiple tables together using table **joins**. Joins allow us to set up the table relationships that we discussed in Chapter 1. However, the join operation in SQL is a very powerful and versatile technique that is hard to do justice in the limited space available in this chapter. If you require more detailed information than I can provide here, Chapter 8 of *Beginning SQL Programming*, also from Wrox Press, covers the issue in more depth.

With an **inner join**, the records in one table that have a matching record in the other table will be returned. With an **outer join**, on the other hand, all of the records from one table are returned even if they don't have a match with the other table. Let's look at an example of each of these.

Suppose that you want to see a list of all products with the corresponding CompanyName field from the Suppliers table. The Products table contains the SupplierId, but to get the CompanyName of the supplier, we need to join to the Suppliers table. We want to use an inner join to make sure that only records with a match in both tables are returned:

```
SELECT Products.ProductName, Suppliers.CompanyName FROM Products JOIN Suppliers ON
Products.SupplierId = Suppliers.SupplierId
```

Notice how the JOIN takes place in the FROM clause. The first table is listed immediately after the FROM clause and then the table to be joined to is listed after the JOIN clause. Following the table names comes the ON clause describing how the two tables relate together.

It is worth mentioning that the above syntax uses the ANSI 92 standard. The older syntax, ANSI 89 mentioned earlier, may still be encountered in some systems' existing code. These statements still run on SQL Server 2000, but Microsoft has plans to stop supporting this outdated syntax in the future. Thus, it is highly recommended that you only use the ANSI 92 standard as shown above.

Just for your own understanding, however, an example of this older syntax is shown overleaf:

```
SELECT Products.ProductName, Suppliers.CompanyName
FROM Products, Suppliers
WHERE Products.SupplierId = Suppliers.SupplierId
```

Notice that the distinction lies in where the joins take place. In the older syntax, the table names are both listed in the `FROM` clause but the join itself is in the `WHERE` clause.

Now for outer joins. There are actually three types of outer join: `LEFT OUTER JOIN`, `RIGHT OUTER JOIN`, and `FULL OUTER JOIN`. Left and right outer joins return all rows from the table on the left or on the right of the `OUTER JOIN` phrase, respectively, even if that table doesn't have a match with the other table. Here's an example:

```
SELECT LastName, FirstName, OrderId FROM Employees LEFT OUTER JOIN Orders ON
Employees.EmployeeId = Orders.EmployeeId
```

The effect of this statement is that all records from the `Employees` table are listed even if they never had a sale. Under the older syntax, the above example would look like this:

```
SELECT LastName, FirstName, OrderId FROM Employees, Orders WHERE
Employees.EmployeeId *= Orders.EmployeeId
```

A full outer join, in contrast to left and right outer joins, will return all rows from both tables even if there aren't matches. It has the same syntax as the other joins, except that you specify `FULL OUTER JOIN` as part of the statement.

T-SQL can also join a table to itself: the **self join**. To conduct a self join, you simply list the same table multiple times but with a different alias using the `AS` keyword. You can then treat them as though they were independent and separate tables. The most commonly used example to demonstrate this concept is a personnel table that contains each `EmployeeId` with a separate field containing the ID of that employee's supervisor. Each supervisor is also an employee in the table, so the `SupervisorId` field links back to the `EmployeeId` field. Selecting information from the table with a self join might look something like this:

```
SELECT Emp1.LastName AS Employee, Emp2.LastName AS Supervisor FROM Employees Emp1
JOIN Employees Emp2 ON Emp1.ManagerId = Emp2.EmployeeId
```

Notice how the same table, `Employees`, is listed twice but with the aliases `Emp1` and `Emp2`. The rest of the SQL statement treats the one table as though they are two separate tables. This statement will return details for all employees along with the name of their supervisor.

Retrieving Distinct Data

In some cases the data returned will contain duplicate values. Note, please don't confuse this with duplicate records – we should have none of those if we followed the good design rules discussed earlier in this book. You can use the `DISTINCT` keyword to ensure that only unique records are returned.

Let's look at an example where we want to list all the different prices that our products presently have, without regard to what products they go with. The statement below would return such a list:

```
SELECT UnitPrice FROM Products ORDER BY UnitPrice
```

The above statement will produce results similar to the following:

```
0
0
0
0
0
2.5
4
4
4.5
5
6
```

You can see the problem with this statement as it stands. Since some products have the same price, such prices are listed more than once in the results. To return a unique list of possible prices, we just need to add the `DISTINCT` keyword like so:

```
SELECT DISTINCT UnitPrice
FROM Products ORDER BY UnitPrice
```

After making this change, each price will only appear once in the results list:

```
0
2.5
4
4.5
5
6
```

This makes the results much easier to view, since duplicate values are eliminated.

Note that `Null` fields are not included in any result set produced when the `DISTINCT` operator is used in conjunction with an aggregate function.

Using Subqueries

T-SQL allows you to have a query nested within a query: also called a **subquery**. For example, suppose that you want to return a list of all `ProductNames` and the `CompanyName` for the supplier with the ID of 3. In the `Products` table, you have the `SupplierId`, but not their name. You would traditionally just join to the `Suppliers` table in order to get their name, like below:

```
SELECT ProductName, CompanyName FROM Products JOIN Suppliers ON
Products.SupplierId = Suppliers.SupplierId WHERE Products.SupplierId = 3
```

The exact same result can be accomplished by using a subquery instead of the `JOIN` clause:

```
SELECT ProductName, (Select CompanyName FROM Suppliers WHERE SupplierId = 3) as
CompanyName FROM Products WHERE SupplierId = 3
```

Notice the subquery that replaces the CompanyName field in the original statement, avoiding the need to join to the Suppliers table in the FROM clause of the statement. There are times when the joins get so complicated that a subquery can be used to help accomplish the same result more effectively.

Unions

Another advanced T-SQL feature is the UNION keyword that allows you to combine the results of multiple SELECT statements into a single result set. The type of fields being selected must correspond across each SELECT statement, but the field names themselves do not have to be the same.

Let's look at a simple example to show you how this works. Suppose that you have a table called ProductsArchived as well as the Products table that we've already been using, and that the ProductsArchived table contains products that are no longer dealt with. The following SQL statement would bring up any product you are currently offering or have ever offered by using the UNION operator to combine the results from two separate SELECT statements:

```
SELECT ProductName FROM ProductsArchived
UNION
SELECT ProductName FROM Products
```

The UNION operator can only be used when the data types of all fields correspond to each other. In our example above, the ProductName field in the ProductsArchived table corresponds to the ProductName in the Products table. Here they are also named the same, but that is not a requirement, and the example would work if the name in the ProductsArchived table were OldName for instance.

Summary

In this chapter, we learnt a lot about T-SQL and how we can use it to manipulate data in SQL Server Desktop Engine databases. We learnt the syntax of T-SQL, and how to view the results of SQL statements by creating a new view in Server Explorer. The following topics were covered in this chapter:

- What T-SQL is and how it compares to Access Jet
- What ANSI 92 is and the fact that T-SQL is Level 1 compliant
- How to retrieve data using SELECT statements
- Using Views in Server Explorer to run SQL statements
- How to filter results by specifying WHERE criteria
- How to add, update, and delete records in the database
- Joining multiple tables together using inner and outer joins
- A quick look at subqueries and unions

I hope you have gained a good understanding of how to modify and retrieve data in SQL Server Desktop Engine databases from this chapter. In the next, we will explore the Server Explorer in greater detail.

Exercises

1. How does T-SQL compare and contrast with Access Jet?

2. Describe the purpose of the `WHERE` clause in a SQL statement.

3. What is the difference between an inner join and an outer join?

4. Describe how to run a SQL Statement from the Visual Studio .NET environment.

5. Suggest a suitable SQL statement for obtaining a list of all products in the Northwind catalog that are out of stock?

Answers are available at http://p2p.wrox.com/exercises/

Exploring the Server Explorer

In Chapter 3, we learned how to use Server Explorer to run SQL statements against the database. In this chapter, we will build upon these concepts and delve into the details of the Visual Studio .NET Server Explorer. This chapter will specifically cover:

- What Visual Studio .NET Server Explorer is and what it allows you to manage
- How to view existing SQL Server databases using Server Explorer
- How to manage and modify existing SQL Server databases using Server Explorer
- How to create new SQL Server database objects (tables, views, and stored procedures) with Server Explorer
- How to create database diagrams with Server Explorer
- Brief explanations of Data Connections and all Server nodes listed in Server Explorer
- How to create new SQL Server databases with Server Explorer

Managing SQL Server Databases Using Server Explorer

In this section, we will delve into the details of using Server Explorer to work with SQL Server databases. We will explore the NorthwindSQL database that we created in previous chapters and will also create a new database. After this whirlwind tour, you should start to become familiar with how to create and manage SQL Server databases using Server Explorer.

The Views Node

Views are virtual tables that allow you to view information in a different way than in the underlying tables. They are technically just queries that have been saved to the SQL Server Desktop Engine database and can be accessed with the view name in the same places you would use a table name.

When we upsized the Northwind database to SQL Server Desktop Engine (NorthwindSQL) in Chapter 2, the Access queries were converted to Views and Stored Procedures on the SQL Server Desktop Engine database, depending on the purpose they served. Let's look at some examples of what was converted to a View.

Navigate to the NorthwindSQL database in Server Explorer. You should be familiar with this from Chapter 3. Expand the **Views** node under **NorthwindSQL**, as shown below:

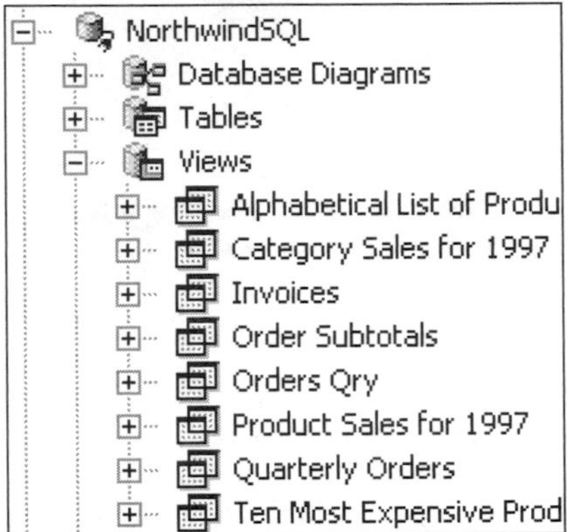

Right-click on **Ten Most Expensive Products** and select **Design View** from the pop-up menu. The following view will appear where the `ProductNames` of the `TOP 10` most expensive products that are in the `Products` table are selected. The `ProductNames` will be listed in descending (most expensive to least) order according to their `UnitPrice`.

```
SELECT TOP 10 ProductName AS TenMostExpensiveProducts, UnitPrice
FROM dbo.Products
ORDER BY UnitPrice DESC
```

By having this SQL statement stored in a View, you don't have to keep typing it each time you want to run it. After it is saved in a View, you can treat it as though it is a table and can issue a `SELECT` statement like this against it:

```
SELECT * FROM [Ten Most Expensive Products]
```

Notice how the View name `[Ten Most Expensive Products]` is specified in the `FROM` clause in the place where you would normally have a table name. You can put a View name anywhere that you could also put a table name, since a View is actually a virtual table.

Take a minute to look at some of the other Views in the NorthwindSQL project before continuing on.

The ability to create a virtual table out of your most commonly used SQL statements for easier retrieval later is a big advantage to using Views. Another advantage is they are an easy way to implement row and column level security. Row level security means restricting the values that a particular user can see down to the record level. Column level security means restricting which fields they can see.

A common example of a View being used for row level security is the case of an employee being allowed to see his/her own personal information but not anyone else's:

```
SELECT * FROM Employees WHERE EmployeeId = 15
```

After creating a View like the one above, you would then give Employee 15 permission to run that View instead of giving him/her permission to access the whole `Employees` table. In this sense, you are restricting the employee to only being able to see his/her own information but not the information of others. As a practical matter, you would not want to do this for all employees in a large company, as it could become very unmanageable to maintain Views for every employee. This is just meant to show you a simple example of row level security.

A common example of column level security is not allowing anyone outside the Human Resources department to see confidential information, such as salary information. Suppose that the `Employees` table contains the `salary` of each employee along with their name, address, and job title. In this case, you would want people outside Human Resources to have access to the name and title of each employee only. Thus, you might create a View with the following SQL Statement:

```
SELECT LastName, FirstName, Title FROM Employees
```

If you save this in a View called `EmployeeList`, you can then give all employees access to this View instead of to the table containing confidential salary and other such information. You should see very quickly why Views are useful in saving you efforts from retyping commonly executed queries and from helping you with row and column level security.

Let's walk through the process of creating a new View from scratch. We are going to create the View just described above: `EmployeeList`.

Try It Out – Create a New View

1. Navigate to the Views node in the NorthwindSQL database and right-click on Views. Select the New View option in the pop-up list as shown below:

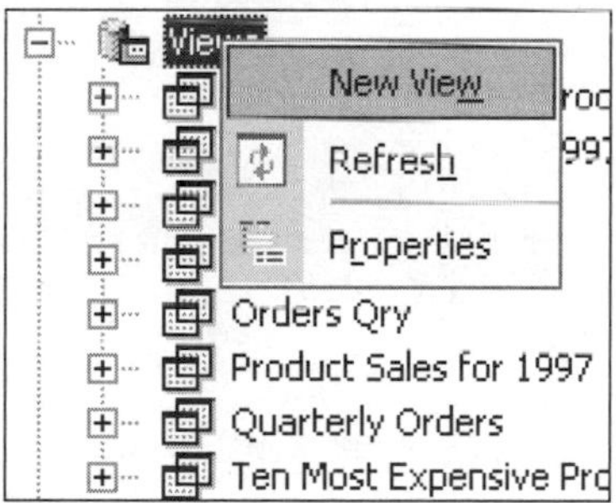

2. Close the Add Tables dialog box that appears so that we can add the SQL statement manually. Create the View with the SQL statement as follows:

```
SELECT LastName, FirstName, Title FROM Employees
```

3. Save and close the View and name it `EmployeeList` when prompted.

4. Now that the View has been created, browse in Server Explorer to see the current list of Views for the database. Notice how the View you just created (`EmployeeList`) appears in the list along with the other Views that already existed previously.

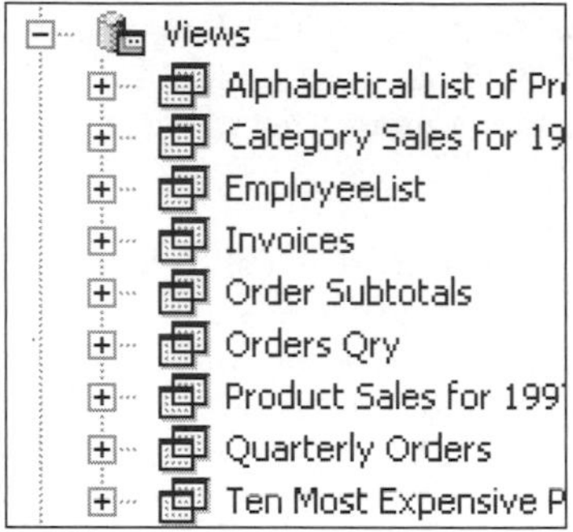

5. Right-click the EmployeeList View and select Retrieve Data from View. Results similar to the following will appear:

Start Page | dbo.EmployeeLis...Z3.NorthwindSQL)

LastName	FirstName	Title
Davolio	Nancy	Sales Representative
Fuller	Andrew	Vice President, Sales
Leverling	Janet	Sales Representative
Peacock	Margaret	Sales Representative
Buchanan	Steven	Sales Manager
Suyama	Michael	Sales Representative
King	Robert	Sales Representative
Callahan	Laura	Inside Sales Coordinator
Dodsworth	Anne	Sales Representative

How It Works

First, we created a new View using Server Explorer and named it `EmployeeList`. The View implements column level security and selects only the `LastName`, `FirstName`, and `Title` columns from the `Employees` table in the database.

```
SELECT LastName, FirstName, Title FROM Employees
```

When we retrieved the data using this View, the `EmployeeList` with LastName, FirstName, and Title was returned and displayed in the grid. This View works exactly as we designed it. Close the results window and return to Server Explorer so we can take a look at the Stored Procedures node next.

The Stored Procedures Node

Stored Procedures are procedures that are stored in the SQL Server Desktop Engine database. They allow you to take frequently used T-SQL statements and save them into a procedure for easy reuse. You can then execute the stored procedure any time you need it. In many ways, a stored procedure is similar in concept to a Visual Basic procedure. The biggest difference is that stored procedures are stored in the SQL Server database itself. Stored procedures are also more efficient than passing SQL statements to the database on the fly, since stored procedures are precompiled and thus execute faster.

You are probably wondering how Stored Procedures differ from Views. Views are best for retrieving data: they are virtual tables that can help make some common retrieval efforts easier or more secure. Stored Procedures, on the other hand, can be used more like what we think of as procedures: with parameters being passed in and database actions being taken as a result (inserts, updates, deletes, or selects). Stored procedures can also include flow-of-control statements, such as `IF` statements, variable declarations, etc.

A Stored Procedure Example

The NorthwindSQL database contains a stored procedure which was a query in the Access database prior to the upsizing. Navigate to the Stored Procedures node of the database.

Right-click on the Stored Procedure named "Customers and Suppliers by City" and then select Edit Stored Procedure to open it in Design Mode. Let's take a look at this in more detail to better understand it.

```
ALTER PROCEDURE [Customers and Suppliers by City]
AS
SELECT City, CompanyName, ContactName, 'Customers' AS Relationship
FROM Customers UNION SELECT City, CompanyName, ContactName, 'Suppliers'
AS _Suppliers_
FROM Suppliers
ORDER BY City, CompanyName
```

First you see the `ALTER PROCEDURE` statement, which is just the T-SQL syntax for creating a new stored procedure if it doesn't already exist or altering the existing one if it does exist. You will also sometimes see `CREATE PROCEDURE`, which simply creates the procedure if a stored procedure with the specified name does not already exist.

After the `ALTER PROCEDURE` designation, the `SELECT` statements retrieve the information from the various tables, in this case the `Customers` table and the `Suppliers` table. The `ORDER BY` clause gives the fields to use in sorting the data that is retrieved.

Later, if you want to run this Stored Procedure, you could use a T-SQL statement similar to the following:

```
EXEC [Customers and Suppliers by City]
```

The `Exec` statement is followed by the Stored Procedure name that you want to run. After the stored procedure name come the parameters that the procedure expects, if there are any. You don't necessarily have to specify the parameter names if you're passing in the parameters in the correct order. However, it is always a good idea to be explicit to be on the safe side. In a moment we will run this stored procedure using the Server Explorer graphical tool.

Try It Out – Create a New Stored Procedure

1. Navigate to the Stored Procedures node in the NorthwindSQL database and right-click on Stored Procedures.

2. Select the New Stored Procedure option in the pop-up list. Create a stored procedure with the T-SQL statements as follows:

```
CREATE PROCEDURE dbo.SupplierList
    (
        @SupplierId int
    )

AS
    SELECT * FROM Suppliers WHERE SupplierId = @SupplierId
    RETURN
```

3. Save and close the Stored Procedure.

4. From Server Explorer, browse to the Stored Procedures node in the NorthwindSQL database. Expand the tree so you can see the list of Stored Procedures, as shown below. Notice that the SupplierList stored procedure we just created is listed along with the other Stored Procedures:

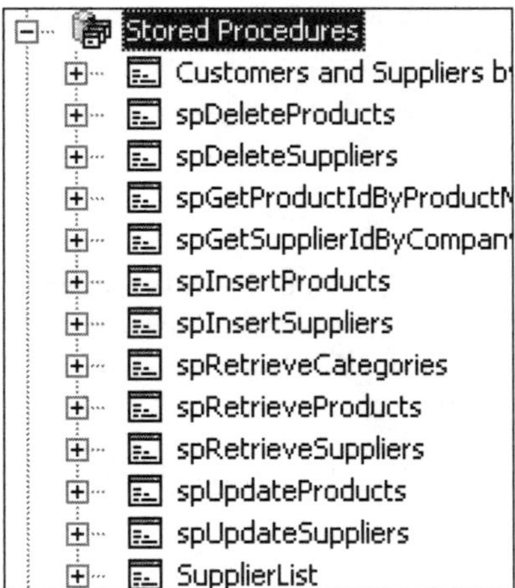

5. Right-click on the SupplierList Stored Procedure and a pop-up menu will appear:

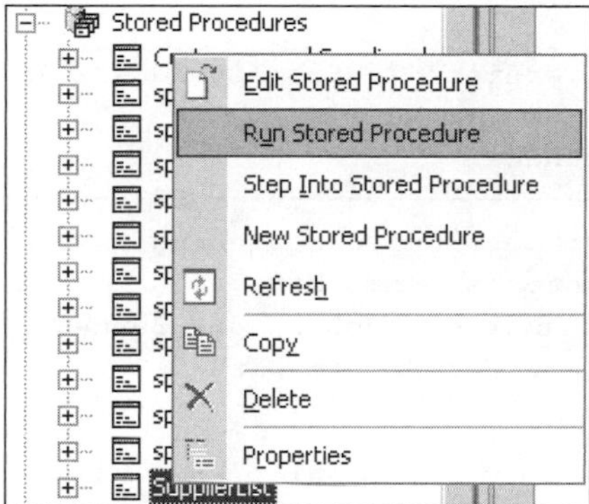

6. Select Run Stored Procedure from the list and then you will be prompted to specify the `@SupplierId` parameter:

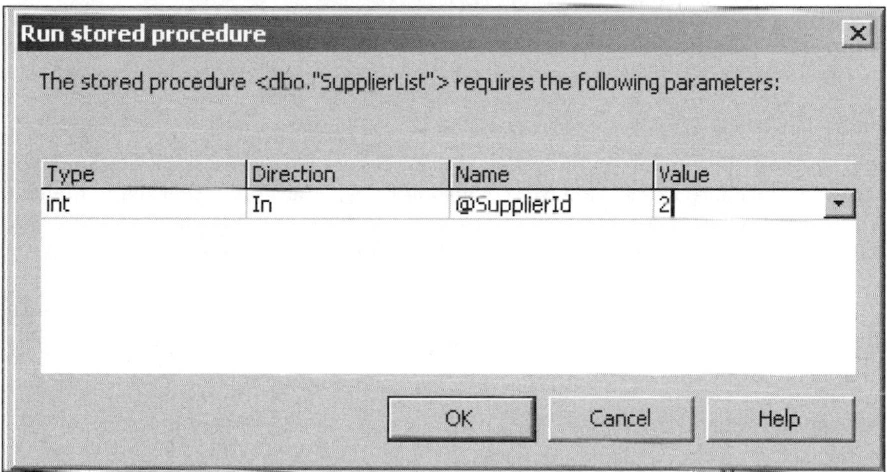

7. Specify a value of 2 for `@SupplierId`. After clicking OK, the results are displayed in the `Output` window. You may need to resize it in order to see all of the results, as shown overleaf:

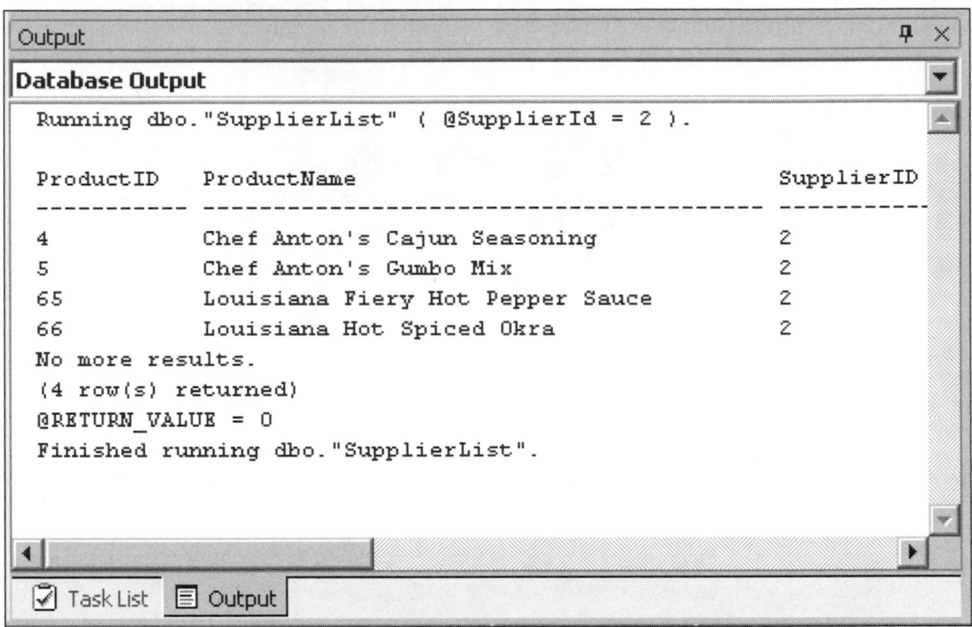
Output

Database Output

```
Running dbo."SupplierList" ( @SupplierId = 2 ).

ProductID   ProductName                                    SupplierID
----------- ---------------------------------------------- ----------
4           Chef Anton's Cajun Seasoning                   2
5           Chef Anton's Gumbo Mix                         2
65          Louisiana Fiery Hot Pepper Sauce               2
66          Louisiana Hot Spiced Okra                      2
No more results.
(4 row(s) returned)
@RETURN_VALUE = 0
Finished running dbo."SupplierList".
```


How It Works

We created a new stored procedure in the database using Server Explorer. Visual Studio .NET automatically created the stored procedure for us when we specified to create a new one. After filling in the details of the stored procedure and saving it, the procedure was created with the name specified in the `CREATE PROCEDURE` statement, `SupplierList`. The stored procedure receives a `SupplierId` as a parameter:

```
(
    @SupplierId int
)
```

and then selects the `Supplier` record based on the `SupplierId` passed in:

```
SELECT * FROM Suppliers WHERE SupplierId = @SupplierId
```

Now, let's have a look at how that stored procedure works in action. We ran the stored procedure and specified a value of 2 for the `SupplierId` parameter. This returned the details about Supplier 2 into the `Output` window when the stored procedure was run.

Now that we are familiar with the Stored Procedures node in Server Explorer, let's move on to learning about the Tables node.

The Tables Node

Next, expand the Tables node to see a list of all the tables in the database. Click on Products and expand it as well and you will notice that it lists all of the fields in that table, as shown opposite:

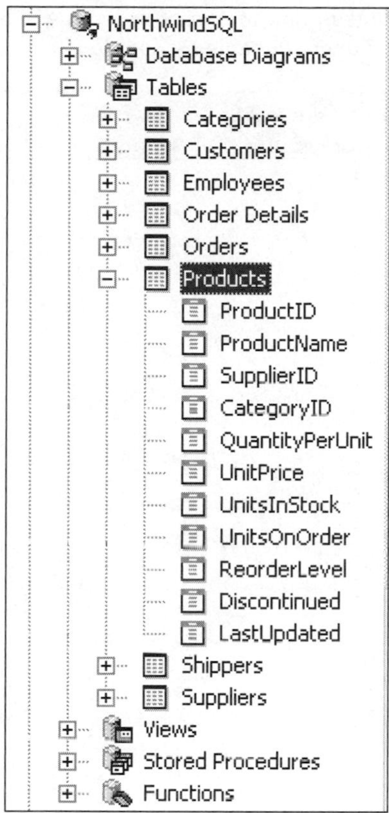

Next, let's retrieve some data from the Products table. To do so, right-click the Products table in the list. A pop-up menu will appear like below:

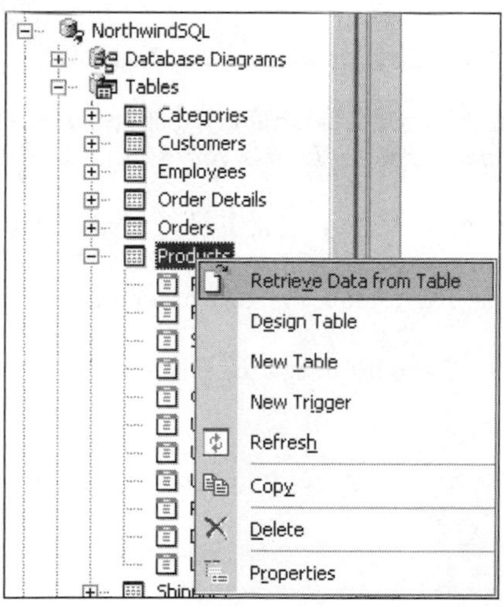

Select the Retrieve Data from Table option in the list and you will be able to see the following results. You can also retrieve the data and open the table by double-clicking on Products.

Start Page | dbo.Products : T...Z3.NorthwindSQL)

ProductID	ProductName	SupplierID	CategoryID	QuantityPerUnit	UnitPrice
1	Chai	1	1	10 boxes x 20 bag:	18
2	Chang	2	2	5 per box	30
3	Aniseed Syrup	1	2	12 - 550 ml bottles	10
4	Chef Anton's Cajur	2	2	48 - 6 oz jars	22
5	Chef Anton's Gumb	2	2	36 boxes	21.35
6	Grandma's Boysenk	3	2	12 - 8 oz jars	25
7	Uncle Bob's Organi	3	7	12 - 1 lb pkgs.	30
8	Northwoods Cranb	3	2	12 - 12 oz jars	40
9	Mishi Kobe Niku	4	6	18 - 500 g pkgs.	97
10	Ikura	4	8	12 - 200 ml jars	31
11	Queso Cabrales	5	4	1 kg pkg.	21
12	Queso Manchego L	5	4	10 - 500 g pkgs.	38
13	Konbu	6	8	2 kg box	6
14	Tofu	6	7	40 - 100 g pkgs.	23.25
15	Genen Shouyu	6	2	24 - 250 ml bottles	15.5
16	Pavlova	7	3	32 - 500 g boxes	17.45
17	Alice Mutton	7	6	20 - 1 kg tins	39
18	Carnarvon Tigers	7	8	16 kg pkg.	62.5
19	Teatime Chocolate	8	3	10 boxes x 12 piec	9.2
20	Sir Rodney's Marm	8	3	30 gift boxes	81
21	Sir Rodney's Scone	8	3	24 pkgs. x 4 pieces	10
22	Gustaf's Knäckebrö	9	5	24 - 500 g pkgs.	21
23	Tunnbröd	9	5	12 - 250 g pkgs.	9
24	Guaraná Fantástic	10	1	12 - 355 ml cans	4.5
25	NuNuCa Nuß-Noug	11	3	20 - 450 g glasses	14
26	Gumbär Gummibärc	11	3	100 - 250 g bags	31.23
27	Schoggi Schokolad	11	3	100 - 100 g pieces	43.9
28	Rössle Sauerkraut	12	7	25 - 825 g cans	45.6
29	Thüringer Rostbrat	12	6	50 bags x 30 sausc	123.79

Notice how all of the records in the Products table are displayed in a grid on the screen. From this view, you can edit data and add new data as well. This is very similar to the Access datasheet view.

Now that we have looked at how easy it is to view data in a table, let's look at a table in design mode. Close this data display window and return to Server Explorer. Navigate to the NorthwindSQL database again and locate the Tables node. Right-click the Customers table.

Click on the Design Table option in the list to see the Customers table in Design View, as shown opposite:

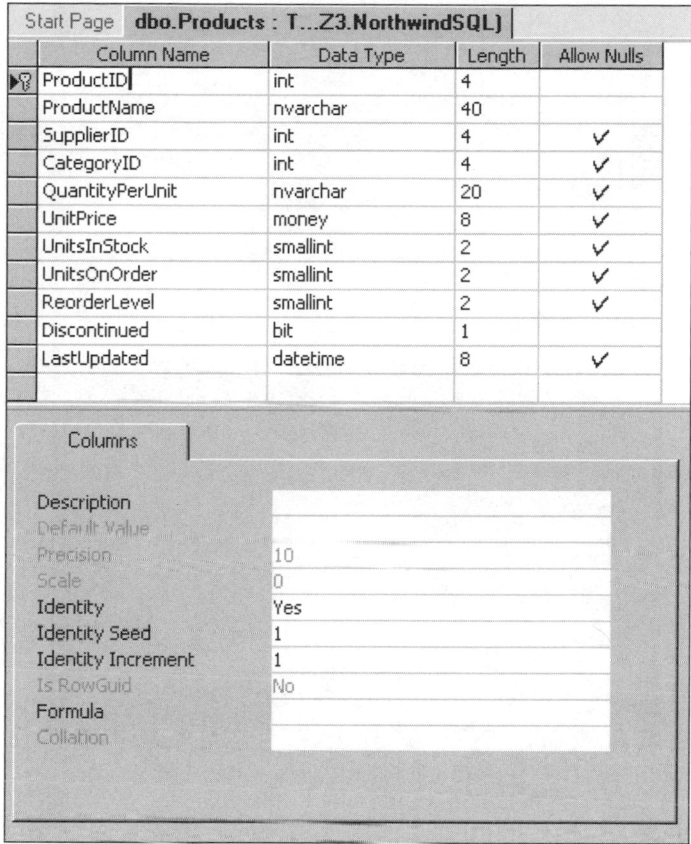

In this screen, you can modify the table to rename columns, add new columns, etc. Click the X in the upper right-hand corner of the design window to close it and return to the Server Explorer.

Try It Out – Create a New Table

1. Navigate to the Tables node in the NorthwindSQL database and right-click on Tables.

2. Select the New Table option in the pop-up list.

3. Create a new table with the fields shown overleaf. Note that this is just for demonstration purposes; it doesn't make a lot of sense to have this as an additional table.

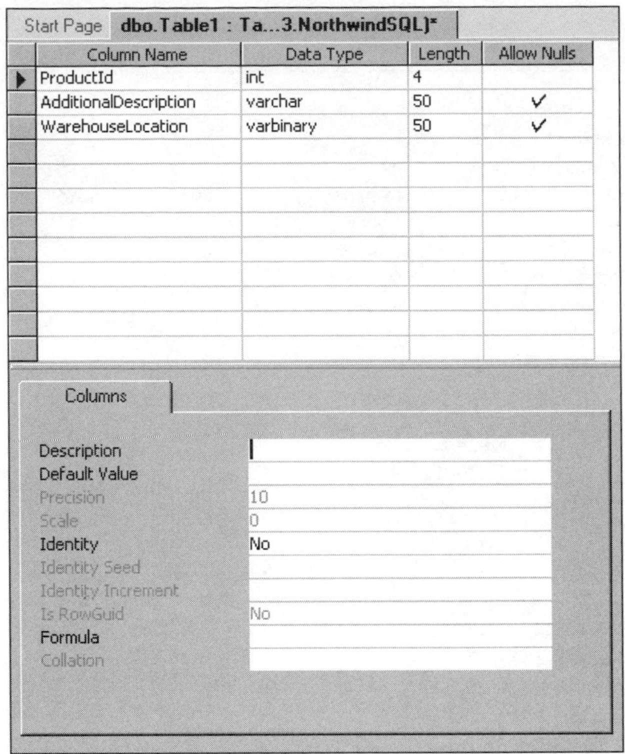

4. Select the `ProductId` field and set it as the Primary Key by clicking the Primary Key button on the toolbar.

5. Next to the Set Primary Key icon are icons for Relationships, Manage Indexes and Keys, and Manage Check Constraints. Clicking any of them brings up the Property Pages window with multiple tabs:

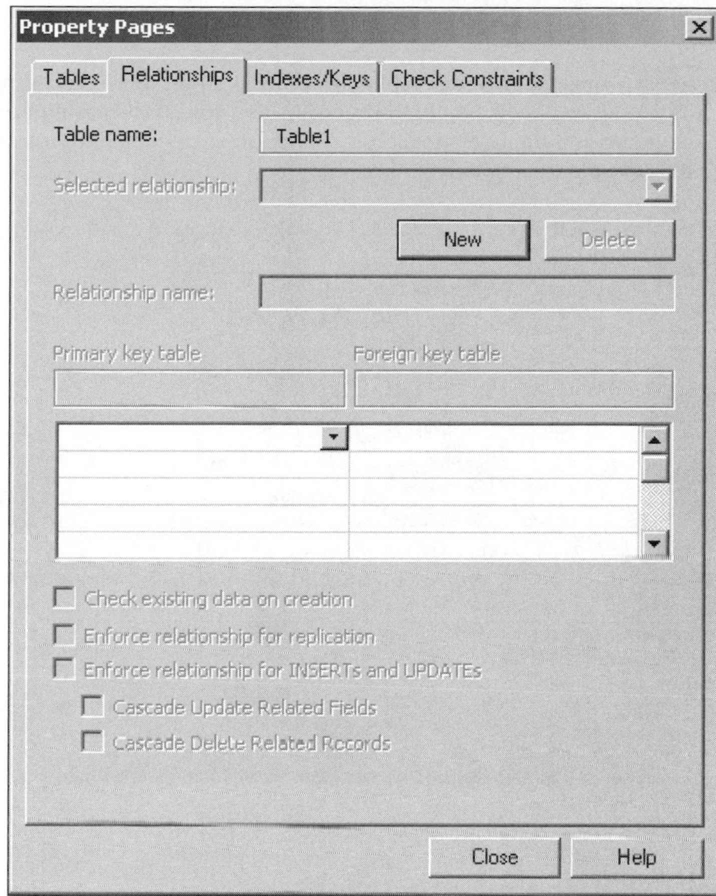

6. Close the table and specify the name ProductsExtended when prompted.

How It Works

Using the Tables node in Server Explorer, we are able to add new tables and modify existing tables. In this instance, we created a new table called `ProductsExtended` that contains a few fields for demonstration purposes only. The graphical table designer allows you to add new fields, specify primary keys, set table relationships, etc. Upon closing the table, you will be prompted to give the table a name if it has never been saved before.

Go back to Server Explorer and navigate to this newly created ProductsExtended table in the database. Right-click on the ProductsExtended table and select Retrieve Data from Table. Fill in a few records for test data.

The Database Diagrams Node

Now that we know how to view and manage tables, views, and stored procedures in Server Explorer, let's look at a new topic that we haven't covered so far in this book. **Database diagrams** are visual representations of the tables and their relationships to each other. Server Explorer allows you to view existing database diagrams and to create new ones.

Navigate in Server Explorer to the NorthwindSQL Database Diagrams node and right-click on it:

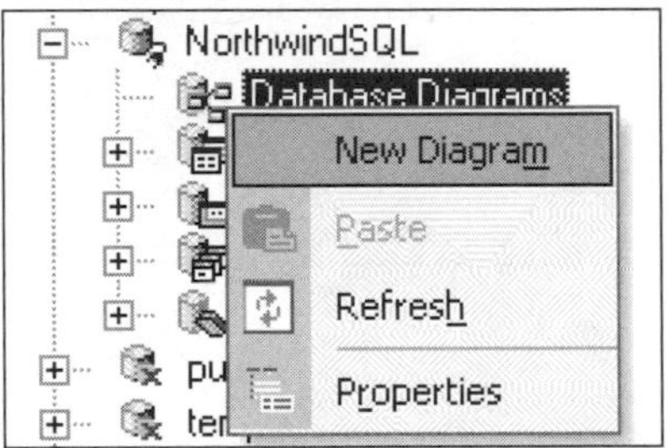

Click the New Diagram option on the pop-up menu, and the Add Table dialog box will appear:

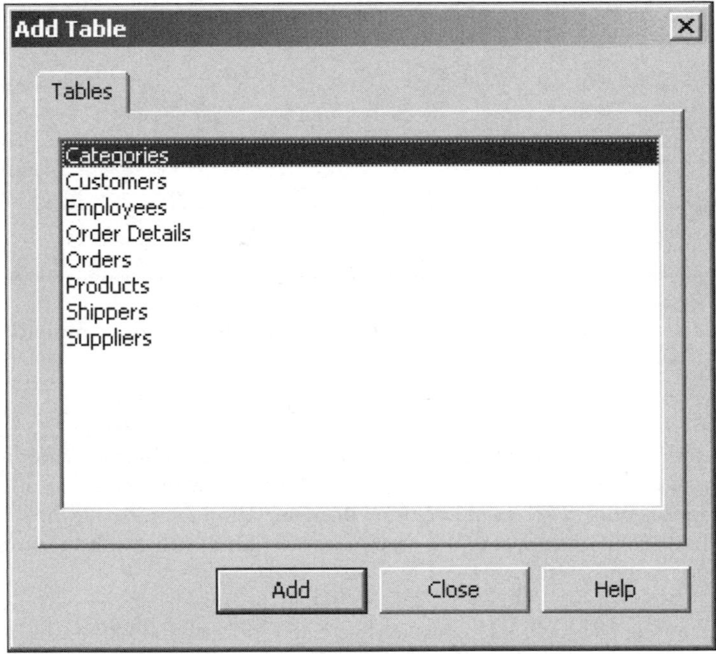

Select all tables in the list and click the Add button. After all tables have been added (are no longer in the list), click the Close button. The following screen will appear:

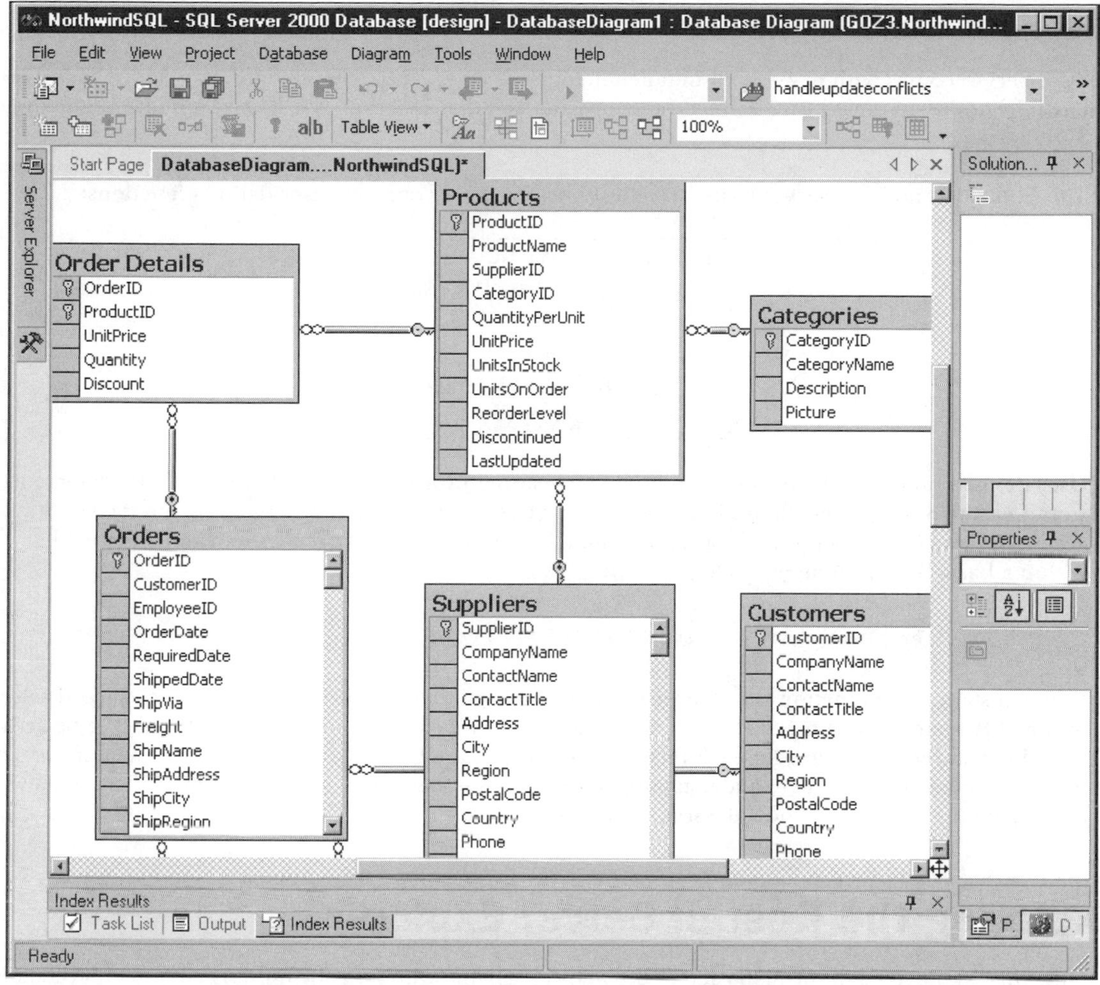

Notice how it automatically displays the table relationships based on the Primary and Foreign Keys. We did not have to do anything beyond this in order to make the table relationships automatically appear in the diagram. The Primary Keys are indicated with the picture of a key. The Foreign Key relationships are represented by the lines to different tables with the Primary Key in the relationship highlighted with a key on the end of its line.

Database diagrams are very valuable to keep handy throughout your application development process. They serve as a quick visual indicator of your table structure and field names. The ability to customize and create database diagrams containing only the tables you want on a given diagram is extremely useful, especially in scenarios where you have hundreds of tables in a database and want to create a special view of certain ones.

Next, close the database diagram. You will be prompted to save it. Give it any name you desire, such as DatabaseDiagram. Note that although we did not look at database diagrams in the chapters dealing with Access Projects, they can also be created in Access Projects as well.

The Functions Node

SQL Server comes with many built-in functions such as `GetDate`, `RTrim`, and many more. You also have the ability to create user-defined functions and call that function as if it were a built-in function of SQL Server.

The **Functions** node in Server Explorer allows you to create your own user-defined functions:

User defined functions have a lot in common with stored procedures as both are just SQL statements stored on the SQL Server. Both the `CREATE function` and the `CREATE procedure` declarations accept parameters. However, a user-defined function, unlike a stored procedure, can be embedded within a basic SQL statement, such as below:

```
SELECT FormatDescription(ProductName) FROM Products
```

In this instance, the function is called `FormatDescription` and will be called for each record selected in the SQL statement. If this code were within a stored procedure, then a loop would have to be created to call the stored procedure for each record. These topics are beyond the scope of this chapter, but at least take away the high-level understanding of what a function is and know that you can create new ones using the Functions Node of Server Explorer.

Exploring the Rest of Server Explorer

Now that we have been through each of the nodes available with NorthwindSQL, or any other database for that matter, we can now move on to look at the other parts of the Server Explorer. In the following sections, we will work our way back up through the Server Explorer tree, starting with the SQL Server Databases node and finishing with Data Connections.

SQL Server Databases Node

Collapse the NorthwindSQL database we've been working with and navigate up one level on the node list. You will notice that the SQL Servers node in the Server Explorer lists all of the SQL Server databases on that particular server selected and allows you to view and manage them. Recall in Chapter 2 how we used an Access Project to manage our Desktop Engine databases. The SQL Servers node offers the same functionality as Access Projects plus some additional features. The main advantage to using Server Explorer instead of Access is that you are in the same integrated development environment and do not have to open up a separate program (for example Access).

The example below shows the SQL Server databases available on a server called Goz3:

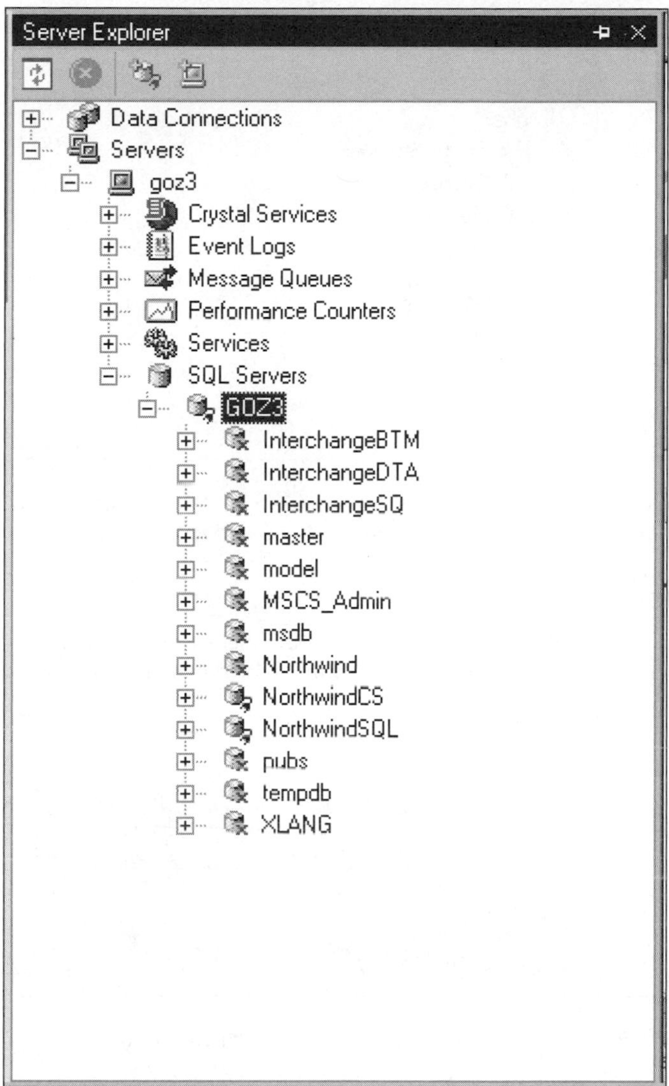

SQL Server Instances Node

Next, collapse the databases listed under the server you were just looking at and notice that this level lists all of the SQL Servers available to you from the Visual Studio .NET environment:

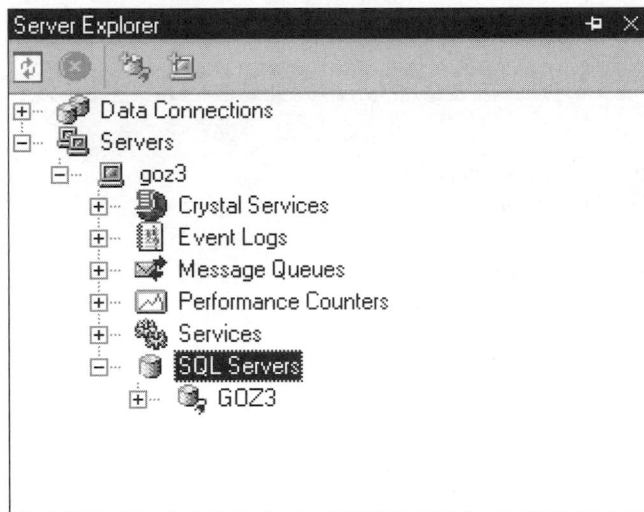

From this level, you can navigate to any of the available SQL Server instances or you can create a new database. Let's take quick look at how you can create a new database from here.

Creating Databases

To create a new SQL Server database in Server Explorer, select the name of the SQL Server instance where you want to create the database. Right-click on the server name, as shown below:

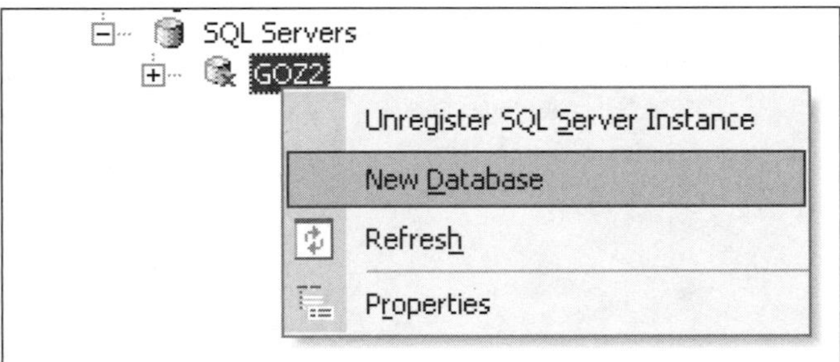

Select New Database from the pop-up menu and the Create Database screen will appear:

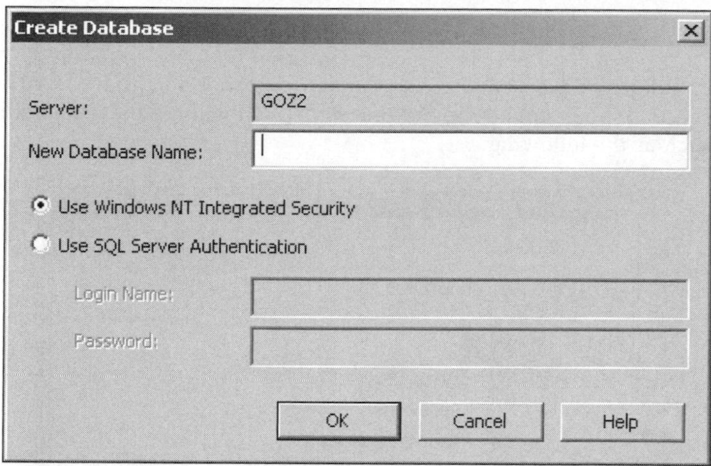

Next, type "Test" for the New Database Name field. You have the option to specify Windows NT Integrated Security or SQL Server Authentication. Select the SQL Server Authentication option and then specify the Login Name of sa and leave the password blank (unless you changed the default password after installation, as you should have).

Upon clicking the OK button, Visual Studio .NET creates the SQL Server database for you and it will appear in the Server Explorer list as one of the SQL Server databases on our local server. Navigate to the newly created Test database, as shown below:

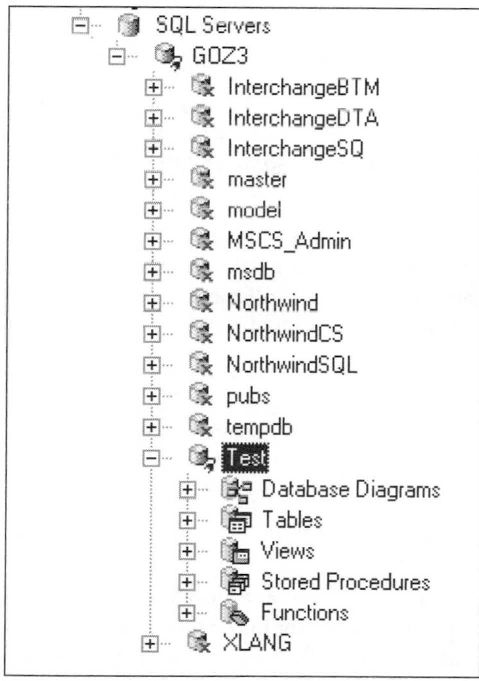

Notice how the new Test database did indeed appear in the list of databases for that SQL Server instance.

Servers Node

Collapse the nodes you just expanded to create the new database and go to the level where you see a list of all of the Servers. If you expand the Servers node, you will see that it contains multiple servers/services, such as the following:

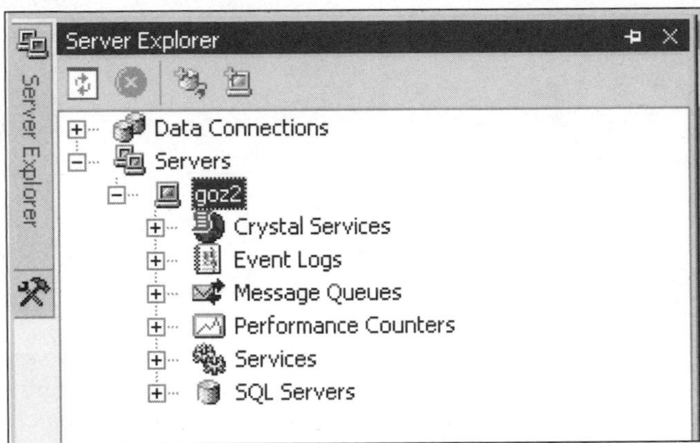

Displayed under the server name are the SQL Servers and other resources that are available on that server for use. Most of these are beyond the scope of the book so we will only give a brief definition of what they do. After that, we will look at Services in a bit more detail.

- **Crystal Services** – allows you to view the Crystal Reports options available for your application. Examples of what you might use the Crystal Services node in Server Explorer for include viewing the Crystal Reports available on the server and looking up their location and filename.
- **Event Logs** – allows you to view the Application, Security, and System event logs for the selected server. There is a lot of valuable information in the event logs. In your applications, for example, you might want to write some events to log when the application starts and completes for each user.
- **Message Queues** – allows the Administrator of the local machine to view all messages in the Public, Private, and System queue categories as well as create new Public and Private queue categories. Additionally, you can view all message entries. A normal user, however, cannot access message queues on the server at all.
- **Performance Counters** – allows Administrators of the local machine to view all performance counters and create new categories and counters. Normal users, however, can only explore the performance counters (as long as they were not created by the Administrator) but cannot create any new ones. Performance counters can be used to keep track of how certain features and tasks are performing and this node allows you to view those that are available or are actually being used.

Services

The Services node in Server Explorer allows you to manage the services available on that particular server. By **service**, we are referring to a program with no user interface that runs in the background performing a particular function. Generally, a service starts automatically when the machine is booted up and runs while the computer is on. If you are interested in what services are currently running on your computer, go to Start | Settings | Control Panel | Administrative Tools | Services and you should see something similar to the following:

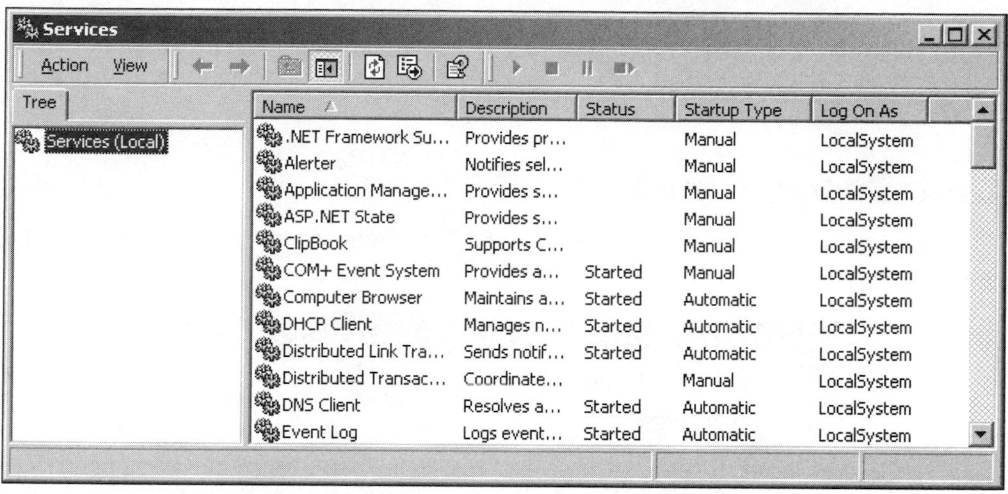

Now, let's look at an example. Recall that in Chapter 2 we learned how to use SQL Server Service Manager in the taskbar to start and stop the SQL Server, SQL Server Agent, and Distributed Transaction Coordinator services of SQL Server. The Services node in Server Explorer allows you to do the same thing: manage those services and many others as well.

Expand the Services node and browse until you see **MSSQLSERVER**, the name of SQL Server Service, in the list. Right-click **MSSQLSERVER** on the list and a similar screen to below will appear:

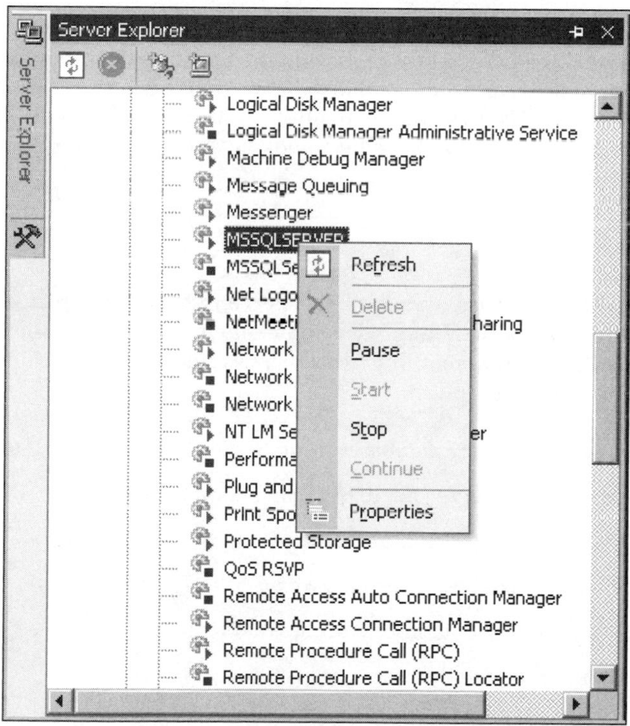

Notice that there are options for **Refresh**, **Pause**, **Stop**, and **Properties**. By selecting **Pause**, the SQL Server database service will be paused and by selecting **Stop**, all database activities will be stopped. The SQL Server Agent and Distributed Transaction Coordinator services also appear alphabetically in the list and can be managed in a similar way.

The Data Connections Node

The last node in the Server Explorer to mention is the **Data Connections** node. Collapse all of the nodes in the list until you see just the highest level, like below:

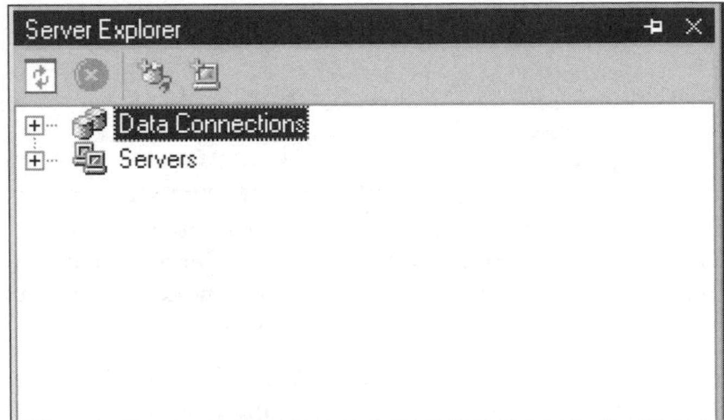

You can add a data connection to any database that you can connect to. Once a data connection has been added for a particular database, you can expand the data connection node and view and manage the database. Data connections can be created for Oracle, SQL Server, and other such types of databases. However, it is important to note that SQL Server databases can also be managed in Server Explorer under the Servers node, as we have been looking at earlier in this chapter.

Summary

In this chapter, we explored the Visual Studio .NET Server Explorer in great detail. The Server Explorer is integrated into the Visual Studio development environment to allow for management of servers without leaving the environment. It greatly increases developer productivity for this reason. We specifically covered the following topics:

- Viewing existing SQL Server databases using Server Explorer
- Modifying existing SQL Server databases using Server Explorer
- Creating tables, views, and stored procedures with Server Explorer
- Viewing and creating database diagrams with Server Explorer
- Creating new SQL Server databases with Server Explorer
- A quick look at the nodes within the Servers node
- The Data Connections node

In this chapter we gained a detailed understanding of how to use Server Explorer to create and manage databases and their objects (tables, stored procedures, views, etc.). In the next chapter, we will learn how Visual Basic .NET ties in with database programming.

Exercises

1. Name at least three features that Server Explorer allows you to view and/or manage for a given server.

2. Describe some of the tasks that you can perform on a SQL Server database using Server Explorer.

3. Create a stored procedure that accepts a customer Last Name as a parameter and returns a list of all matching records with that last name.

Answers are available at http://p2p.wrox.com/exercises/.

The User Interface for the Database

Up to now, we've looked at ways of designing a database and querying the information within it using various SQL statements and stored procedures. In this chapter, we will now put some of that knowledge to use.

Capable database application designers and builders are invariably considered a great asset to a company or business, and rightly so. Such people are able to solve a number of problems in situations where users need to interact with data, be it accessed over a LAN, WAN, or the Internet. Once you have acquired the knowledge to build database systems, there really only remains the know-how to build an interface that allows users to talk to these systems. There are other aspects of development you need to be aware of, for instance designing a system geared towards a three-tier architecture, and these will be discussed later. Banks, stores, and most businesses today all depend on some type of database system for their day-to-day operations and, without it, they would no longer be able to run efficiently. This is where you as the developer have a crucial role to play. To be able to tie a user interface, and other related business components if desired, to a data source is a valuable asset. Think of the last application you used around your office, perhaps an employee phonebook, customer database, inventory program, or finance program, and how they all gathered data and presented it to you in a friendly manner. Being able to build these types of application that have the potential to make dealing with information so much easier, can bring great benefits throughout a company, and so it is that such programmers become highly valued assets.

Many companies nowadays employ a person or group solely for the management of existing databases – the database administrators (DBAs) – and have a separate team of developers whose job it is to build the applications themselves. Often, however, you as the database developer will be playing both roles, and so you will need a basic understanding of both tasks. The DBA's responsibilities include:

- Knowledge of the structure of the database and how to use and store information in an efficient manner
- The ability to normalize a database, as talked about in the Chapter 1
- Insight into the changing demands of the company as it grows and expands – will the database in its present form be able to handle ten or even a hundred times the amount of information and remain efficient?

- A logical methodology when it comes to the user interface design, so screens are organized in a way that makes sense to the user – for instance grouping related controls together, such as customer and address fields
- The ability to work closely with the user to design these systems

This will all help when it comes to developing client-server applications. When we develop databases we need to consider such things as efficiency, flexibility, handling multiple users, data locking, data growth, integrity, and performance. The person developing the client-side of the application needs to worry about how the user interface will look as well as the performance and efficiency of the application. Having a clear idea of how users will interact with your database system will help in determining how it should be built. Users will often perform certain procedures in a certain order when undertaking tasks, and some tasks will be much more common than others. For instance, if you are designing a stock inventory application, you might want your system to start up with the screen that allows users to make changes to the inventory, rather than, say, the screen for adding new product lines.

In this chapter, we look at the fundamentals of building a basic user interface to a SQL data source. We'll also look at some good practices that you should apply when building more sophisticated database applications. Here are the topics we will cover to this end:

- A simple user interface for accessing a database
- How to populate a DataGrid
- Using Wizards
- The code generated behind the scenes
- Good practices for general user interface design

The User Interface

So you've learned how to design a database and how to update information in it using suitable SQL statements. We can't expect our users to open up an administrative database tool and manipulate the data directly like this, so our next step is to create some way for users to access information. This is the role of the **user interface** – to provide a means of communication between the user and the database.

Through the user interface, users may interact with data and manipulate it in order to accomplish certain tasks such as to view, add, update, or delete details. The user interface and database go hand in hand, and with the right combination, users are able to handle massive amounts of information without any particular technical knowledge.

Some type of thought process or methodology is required to come up with a good design for the interface: we want to create a consistent and appropriate look so that the interface is readily accessible to those who are to use it. We should be aware of existing business logic when allowing the user to do things like add or delete information to ensure it's done correctly and to prevent users from inadvertently manipulating data in a way that could potentially result in irrecoverable losses to the business. Security and data integrity are important, for they provide the mechanisms to ensure users are not able to adjust their own bank balances, modify prices themselves, or view or even change other people's information. We need a way to hide the checks and balances behind the scenes. Most of this can be accomplished through good design of forms, to build in the capability to call upon, validate, and protect this information: either through the code behind the forms or by having the forms call another object. There is also the possibility that a malicious user could bypass these forms entirely, and attempt to directly access the database, so watertight security is vital. To achieve this, our forms can be made to access the database with a secret user ID and password, and we can hide our checks and balances through stored procedures – that is, procedures stored on the database server. These stored procedures can perform some validation based on what parameters are passed, and only return information when correct security information has been passed. All this is accomplished through business rules, which dictate how data will be maintained in the particular scenarios relevant to our business.

Now that we know a little about the issues involved with the user interface, we can move on to look at how we can build an interface in Visual Basic .NET. The fundamental component of this type of application is the Windows Form, which can be viewed as an empty canvas waiting to be painted on. We can place controls on such a form to create a logical look and feel for our interface, and provide a natural and intuitive way for the user to communicate with our database.

Creating a Simple Database Application

So now we can start the task of creating a very simple database application with a basic Windows Form user interface. The application will connect to the `Customers` table in the NorthwindSQL database using your SQL Server Desktop Engine. (As you may remember, we upsized the sample `Northwind.mdb` file from Access to SQL Server 2000 Desktop Engine and named the database `NorthwindSQL`.) We will refer to this database throughout this chapter as simply the Northwind database. Our application will retrieve and display a list of customers in a `DataGrid` control on a Windows Form. Once we've finished, you should be able to build similar applications based on different databases using the techniques I shall introduce. I recommend that you experiment with other tables of the Northwind database until you feel comfortable with these techniques.

Our finished application will consist of a form that simply displays all information in the `Customers` table when the user clicks a button, as in the screenshot here:

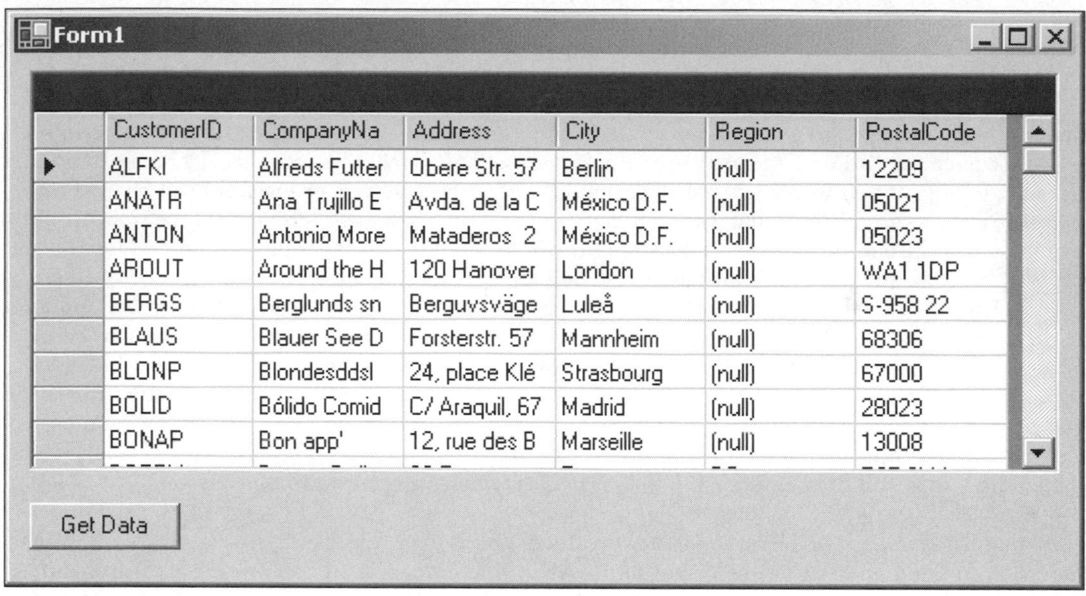

	CustomerID	CompanyNa	Address	City	Region	PostalCode
▶	ALFKI	Alfreds Futter	Obere Str. 57	Berlin	(null)	12209
	ANATR	Ana Trujillo E	Avda. de la C	México D.F.	(null)	05021
	ANTON	Antonio More	Mataderos 2	México D.F.	(null)	05023
	AROUT	Around the H	120 Hanover	London	(null)	WA1 1DP
	BERGS	Berglunds sn	Berguvsväge	Luleå	(null)	S-958 22
	BLAUS	Blauer See D	Forsterstr. 57	Mannheim	(null)	68306
	BLONP	Blondesddsl	24, place Klé	Strasbourg	(null)	67000
	BOLID	Bólido Comid	C/ Araquil, 67	Madrid	(null)	28023
	BONAP	Bon app'	12, rue des B	Marseille	(null)	13008

A Brief Introduction to ADO.NET

Before we can begin creating our application we need to learn about some basic components of ADO.NET and wizards that our application is to use. We will go into greater detail on ADO.NET in the next chapter so, for now, we'll learn just enough to get us through this simple database project.

ADO.NET provides us with a way of gathering data and information and presenting it through a user interface. By using some components, we're able to connect to various data sources and can then build a user interface that accesses a database.

We need four pieces to build our ADO.NET project:

1. A **data source** – where the actual data is stored, our database.
2. A **`Connection` object** – for connecting us to our database.
3. A **`DataAdapter` object** – to provide a mechanism for reading and writing data to the database.
4. A **`DataSet` object** – this will contain the table(s) that we will use.

The following figure shows how all these pieces tie together. Firstly, we need a connection to the data source, provided by a `Connection` object. The `Connection` object requires certain information for it to connect to the data source. The `Connection` object is called by the `DataAdapter` object, which handles commands to select, update, insert, and delete data in the data source. Finally we have a `DataSet` that contains our tables and which uses the `DataAdapter` to populate itself and to update information in the data source.

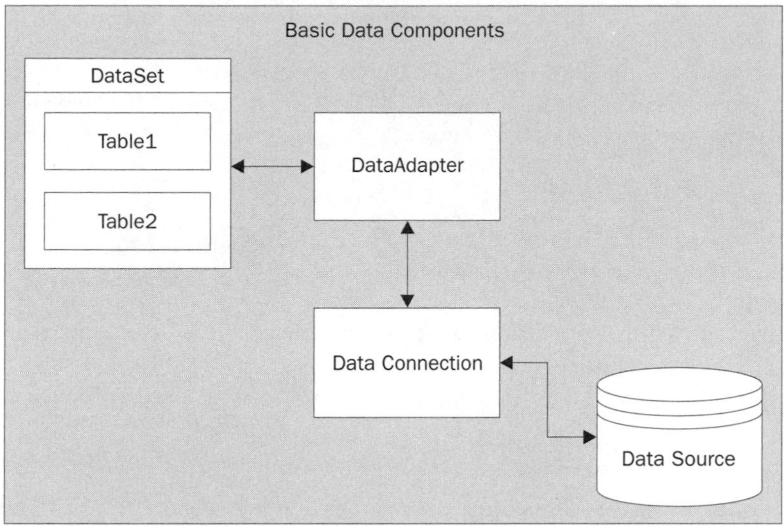

We will now cover these components in a bit more detail, taking each of the data source, `Connection`, `DataAdapter`, and `DataSet` in turn.

The Data Source

A data source is the term used to describe any collection of information that can provide data to us. It can take the form of a database, an XML document, a Microsoft Excel spreadsheet, or even a flat text or binary file. It only takes one or two lines of code for us to change the kind of data source that we connect to. The Windows environment provides us with a shared set of classes for use in our programs to communicate with these different sources using similar code.

The Data Connection

The first thing we need to connect to a database is the data `Connection` object. This comes in two versions – either a `SqlConnection` or `OleDbConnection` object. As we are working with the SQL Server Desktop Engine, we will use the **`SqlConnection`** object.

When we create a connection using a `SqlConnection` object, we need to feed it the following connection parameters:

- `Data Source` – the name of the server where your data source is located. The data source can be anywhere, be it on your network or somewhere over the Internet. Usually, you will be working on your local network and so you need to specify the name of the computer that holds the data source here. Alternatively, we can give the name `localhost` or `(local)` to signify that we want to use the computer that is actually running the application. This terminology is used by many Windows applications when it is necessary to identify the current, local computer.
- `User ID` and `Password` – the authentication details required to communicate with the data source. The ID and password is set up by the database administrator and helps prevent people from viewing or modifying the database without permission.

- Initial Catalog – this is the name of the database we want to work with – in this case, NorthwindSQL.

To create a new connection, we declare a new SqlConnection and set the ConnectionString property using these parameters as shown here:

```
Dim myConnection As New SqlClient.SqlConnection()
myConnection.ConnectionString = "Data Source=localhost;" & _
                                "Initial Catalog=NorthwindSQL;User
                      Id=sa;Password=sa;"
```

Alternatively, we can pass the connection string as a parameter to the SqlConnection as follows:

```
Dim myConnection As New SqlClient.SqlConnection("Data Source=localhost;" & _
                                     "Initial Catalog=NorthwindSQL;User
                    Id=sa;Password=sa;"")
```

Creating a new OleDbConnection object is similar, except that we also need a Provider parameter to describe the type of data source that we are connecting to. So why don't we need that parameter with the SqlConnection object? You've got it – because the provider type will always be SQL and, in fact, if you do try to set the Provider parameter for an SqlConnection object, you will get an error.

Now we can look at the component that requires a data Connection object to be set up in order to function, namely the DataAdapter.

The DataAdapters

The DataAdapter is the mechanism that sits between the data source and the DataSet. We have two types of DataAdapters, the SqlDataAdapter, which is used exclusively for SQL Server databases, and the OleDbDataAdapter, which is used for all other data sources and goes through another layer called OLE DB. Consequently, by avoiding the need for this extra layer, the SqlDataAdapter provides much faster access to data. The OleDbDataAdapter can be used to access SQL Server but, as it then goes through the OLE DB layer, you are well advised to stick with the SqlDataAdapter for optimum performance if you don't anticipate using anything other than SQL Server. This applies to our simple database application in this chapter, and so we work strictly with SqlDataAdapter.

The DataAdapter allows selecting, updating, deleting, or inserting data in the data source. These methods are accomplished through the use of the SelectCommand, UpdateCommand, InsertCommand, and DeleteCommand properties to set the database command string required for that particular operation. Each of these properties is an instance of a Command object, whose job it is to execute a SQL statement or stored procedure and return a result set. For a SQL database, the Command object will hold the actual SELECT, UPDATE, INSERT, and DELETE statement required for a given operation, such as "SELECT * FROM Products" or "DELETE FROM Orders WHERE CustomerID='ABC'". The Command object also stores connection information so it may connect to the database to execute the SQL statement that it contains. Note that, in our simplified case, we will only be working with a SelectCommand as we only need to select information from our database for viewing.

As we are dealing with a SQL database, we will be working with the SqlCommand object (as opposed to the OleDBCommand object). When we use the DataAdapter Wizards, for each table you work with you will have a corresponding DataAdapter. When we use the Wizards, the DataAdapters are configured specifically for the chosen table such that all of the methods for updating and retrieving information point to that specific table. To reuse the adapter for another table, we have to essentially rebuild the objects that make up the DataAdapter, which means all of the Command objects. The simpler solution is to assign one DataAdapter per table, and this helps keep your code nice and clean and easy to maintain. When you build a DataAdapter, you can specify more than one table if needed. For example, we could create a DataAdapter that links the Customers table and the Orders table – to enable us to view information from both tables using a single DataAdapter, without needing any code to link them. This method of linking multiple tables into a single view doesn't work really well when it comes to updating information, however, as the DataAdapter Wizard isn't able to properly link tables together to cascade updates or deletes, reinforcing the case for using one DataAdapter per table.

This diagram shows the basic structure of a DataAdapter:

The DataSet

Finally, a DataSet is a container or collection of tables; it can contain one or more tables and is maintained in memory. Relationships between tables are also stored here. The tables it holds contain information such as customer details or product information in the form of records, or **rows**. A table may consist of thousands of such rows.

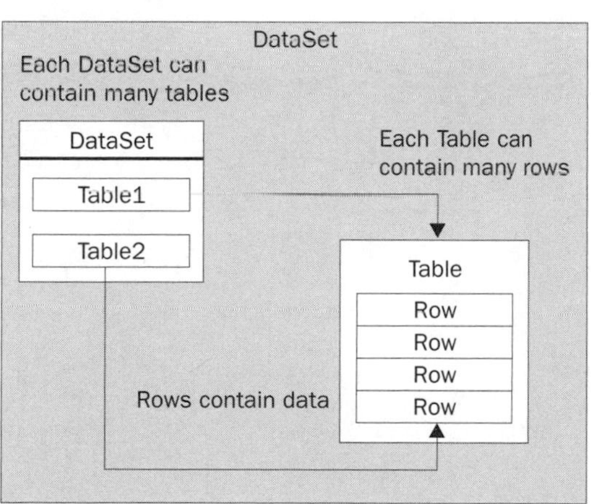

One useful illustration is to think of a DataSet as holding details of a book publisher. A technical publisher might publish books in several categories such as .NET, Java, ASP, and C++. Within each category are individual books – so that a .NET category could have books such as Professional VB.NET, Beginning VB.NET, Professional C#, and Introducing .NET. A table could represent each of these categories, and each book in a category would be represented by a row in the appropriate table. Each row holds details for each book – for example, title, price, ISBN number, publishing date, and the number of pages.

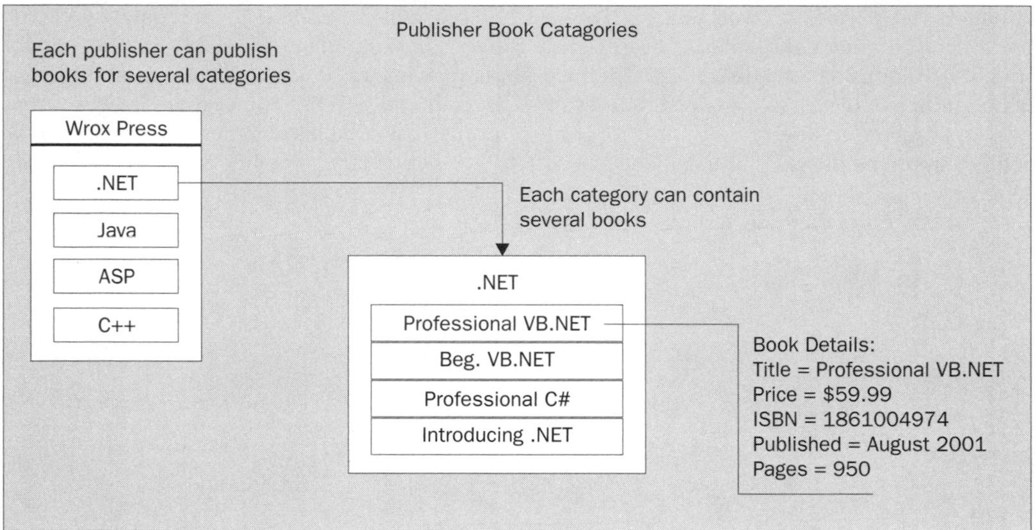

There is no limit to the type of information you can store in a DataSet. Now that we have looked at the internals of a DataSet, let's take a look at how we can put one to use in an application. The components shown in the figure below will be demonstrated in our application:

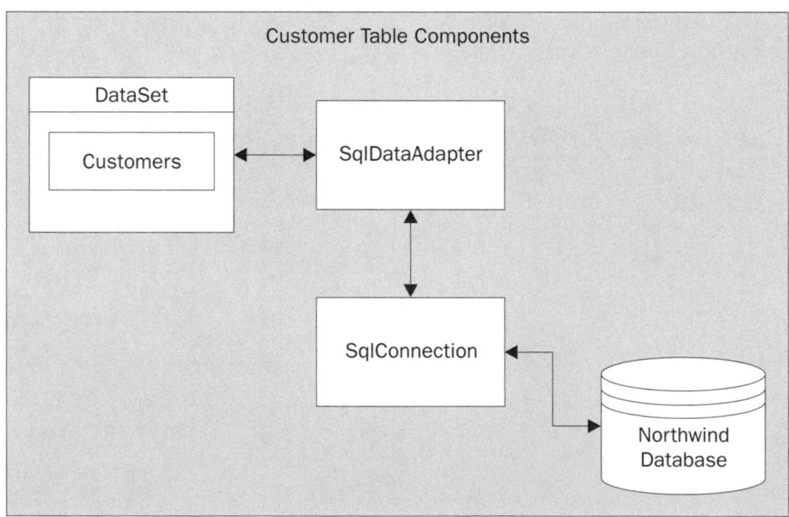

For our program, we will need to create a `SqlDataAdapter` object to select customer records from the Northwind database via a `SqlConnection` object. This connection will be opened only long enough to complete the SQL `SELECT` operation. Our `DataSet` will be populated with data from our customer table using the `SqlDataAdapter` object. Linking, or **data binding**, to a visual component such as the `DataGrid` control will then display the `DataSet`'s contents on a Windows Form.

Now we can begin implementing these components in our simple database application. Here's an overview of the tasks ahead:

- Creating a Windows Application
- Connecting to a data source
- Adding a `DataAdapter` to our form
- Generating a `DataSet` from the `DataAdapter`
- Adding a `DataGrid` control to our form
- Displaying the contents of a customer table in our `DataGrid`

We start by creating a new Visual Studio .NET application and then adding a `SqlDataAdapter` to the project. We'll also have to create a connection to the NorthwindSQL database for the `DataAdapter`. From the `SqlDataAdapter` we'll create a new `DataSet`. Once we have a `DataSet`, we will add a `DataGrid` to our form and bind the `DataSet` to it. Lastly, we'll add a button that fills the `DataSet` with customer records and displays it in the `DataGrid`.

Visual Studio .NET's configuration wizards provide us with an easy way of doing all this. We're just a point and click away from creating our database application!

Try It Out – Creating a DataAdapter

1. Create a new Visual Basic .NET Windows Application. You can create this project in any directory. Name the project CustomerApp and click OK.

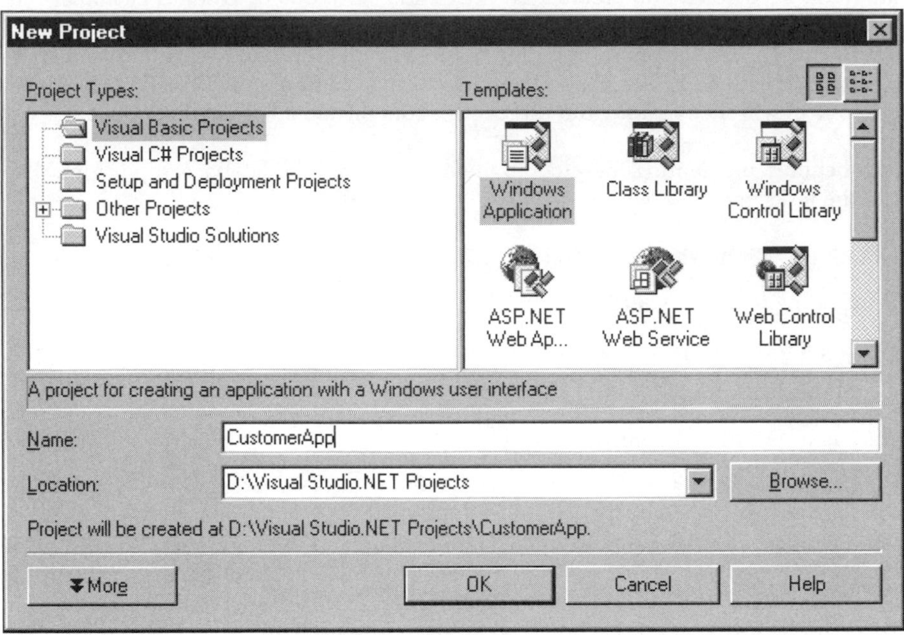

2. A new form will automatically be generated called Form1. Add a `SqlDataAdapter` to the form by double-clicking the SqlDataAdapter component from the Data tab of the Toolbox, usually found to the left of the Visual Studio screen.

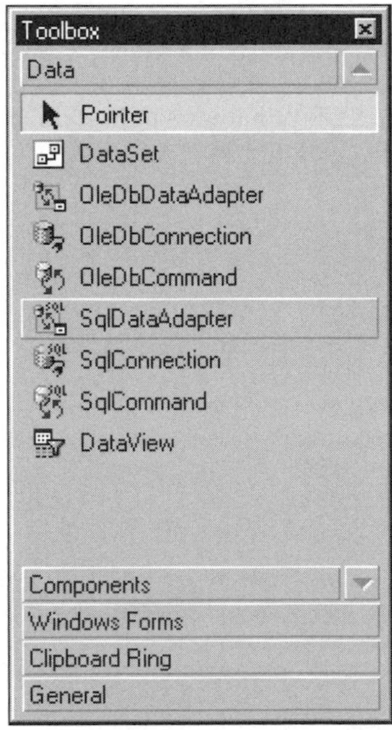

3. Click Next when the welcome page of the DataAdapter Configuration Wizard appears to bring up the window shown in the following screenshot, prompting for a connection to a database. If we had created other data connections already, they would be shown in the drop-down list. Since this is our first time connecting, however, it will be empty and we must create a new connection by clicking the New Connection... button.

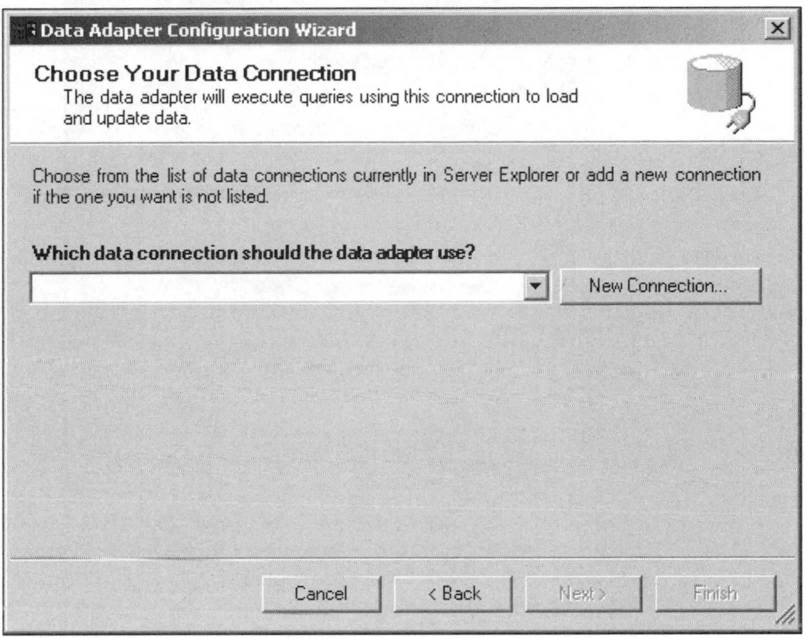

4. Now we are presented with the Data Link Properties window. In the top drop-down list for selecting the server name, if you can find your computer's name there, then choose it – otherwise type in localhost or whatever is the server name where the SQL Server containing the NorthwindSQL database resides. In item two, you choose to either use your current Windows logon details to authenticate or to enter a different user name and password as used by SQL Server. You should try selecting the Windows NT Integrated security first as this often works; if it doesn't, then try a specific username and password as set by the database administrator. In this case we use a SQL Server ID of sa (for system administrator) with no password. In general, of course, you would not use a blank password because of security concerns. Item three requires you to choose an existing database on the server, so type in NorthwindSQL here. Click the Test Connection button to test your connection if you wish, although you can be fairly sure that the connection is valid if the correct list of databases appears in item three's drop-down.

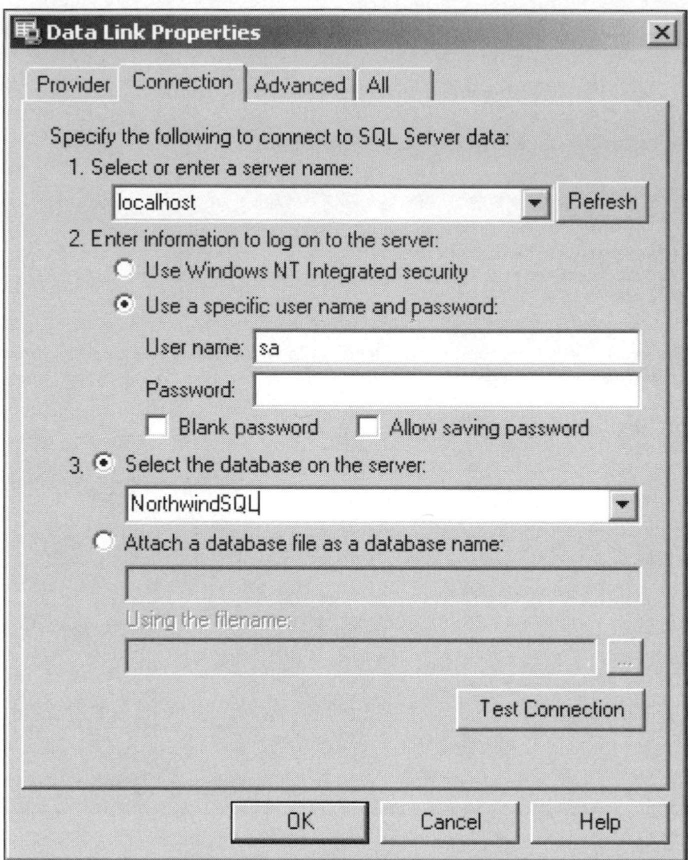

5. Click OK to proceed, and then Next to get to the Choose a Query Type window for determining the access method for the data in the Northwind database. You can use a SQL statement, or new or existing stored procedures. For the first option you must specify the SQL statement to use. The second option also asks you to specify a SQL statement but, this time, the wizard will create corresponding stored procedures rather than plain SQL statements. We will use the first option and specify a SQL statement to select our records. Click on Use SQL statements, and then click Next.

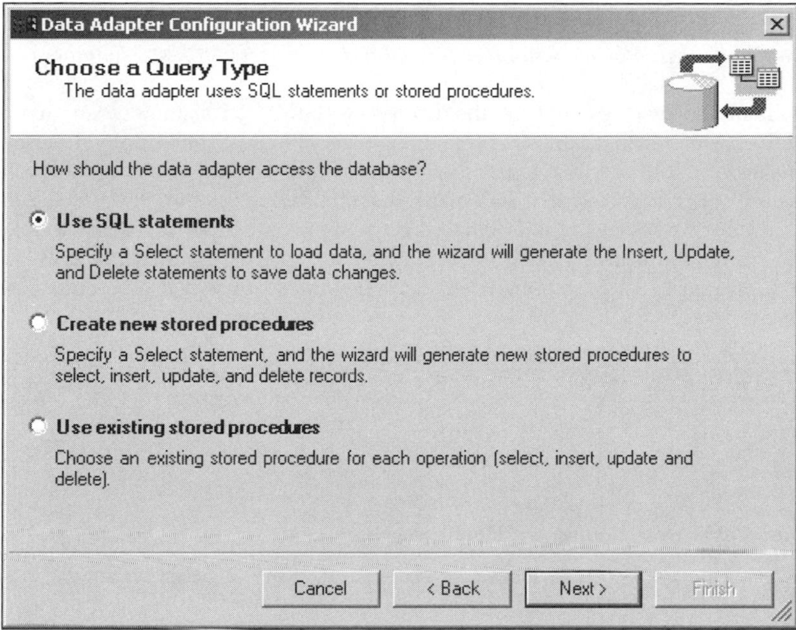

6. Now we need to enter the `SELECT` statement for selecting our customer records. Turn back to Chapter 3 to refresh your memory of SQL commands if you wish. We will be using the Query Builder to help us build a SQL statement rather than typing in a SQL statement directly. The builder is similar to the one provided with Microsoft Access and SQL Server. First, we need to change some options so click the Advanced Options button.

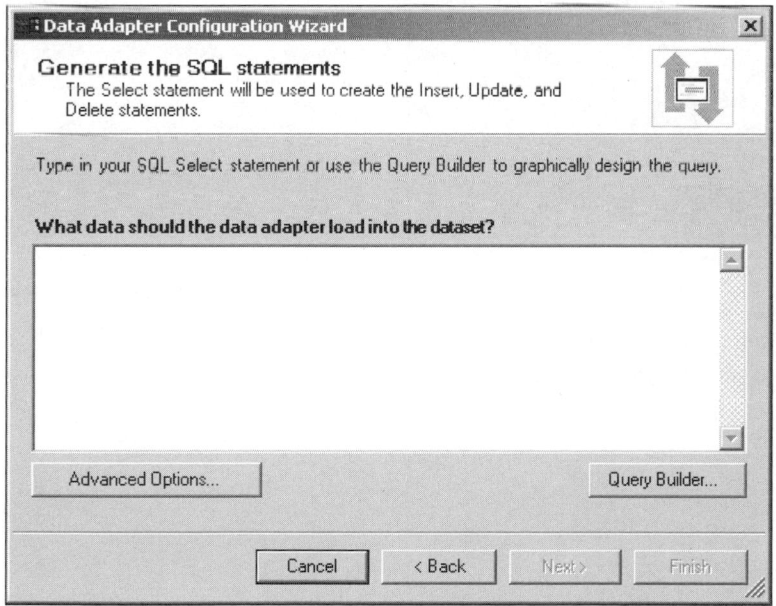

7. This advanced dialog gives us three options. The first option tells us that all of the SQL commands to insert, update, and delete will be generated based on your `SELECT` statement.

We will only be viewing data from the database with `SELECT` statements so unselect the first CheckBox, which then disables the remaining CheckBoxes. I shall briefly describe the other options now, should you wish to use them in later applications. Use optimistic concurrency generates `UPDATE` and `DELETE` statements that check to make sure that none of the columns have changed since we retrieved the original records, to prevent data from being changed by more than one user at the same time. The Refresh the Dataset option generates a `SELECT` statement after each `UPDATE` or `DELETE` statement, so that the updated row will also be updated in your `DataSet`.

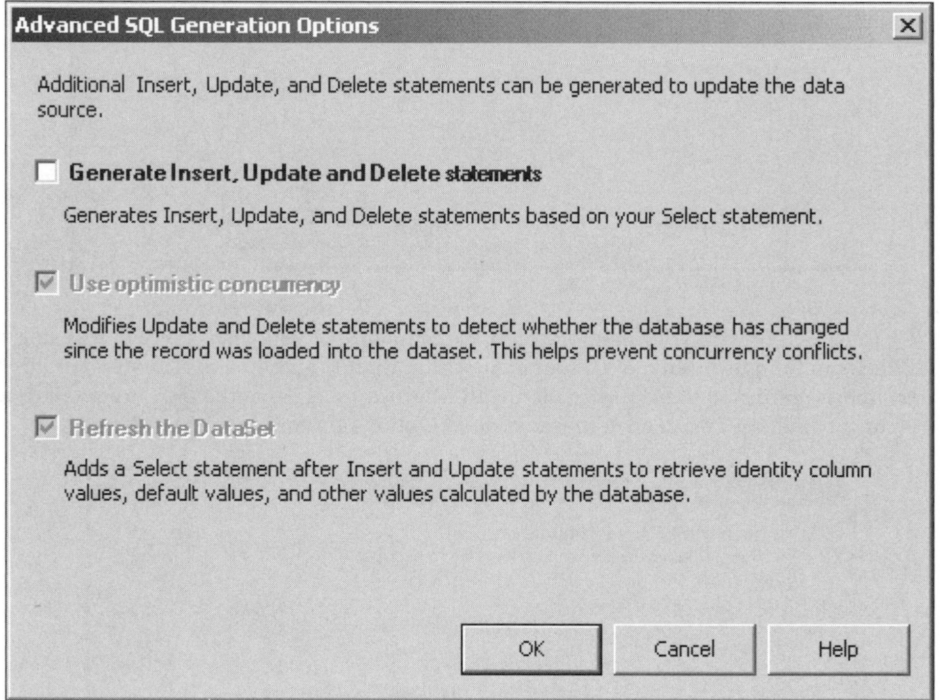

8. Click OK when you're finished to return to the previous screen. Now, click the Query Builder button.

You can add as many tables to your query as you want, but we just need the `Customers` table so double-click its name; the table should then appear in the window in the background. Now click the Close button.

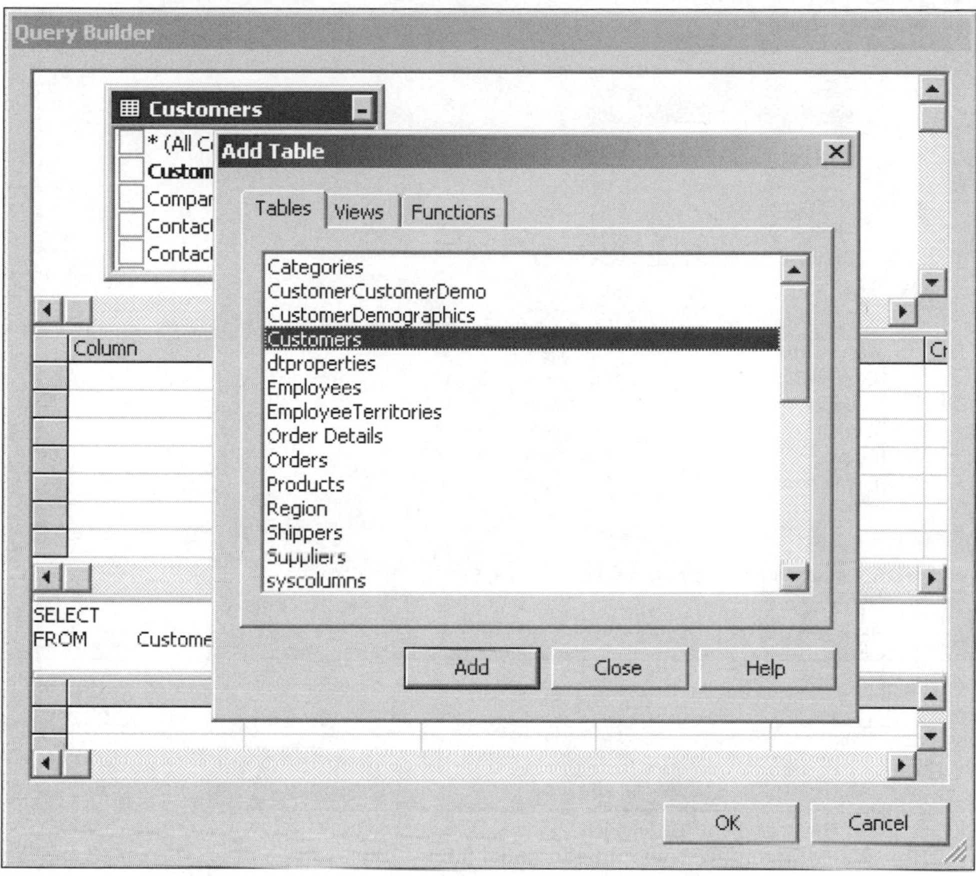

9. Next, select the columns to display: CustomerID, CompanyName, Address, City, Region, and PostalCode. As you select columns, the `SELECT` statement will change accordingly. Once you have selected all of the columns, right-click anywhere in the Query Builder area to bring up the context menu, and select Run to show the query results in the area below.

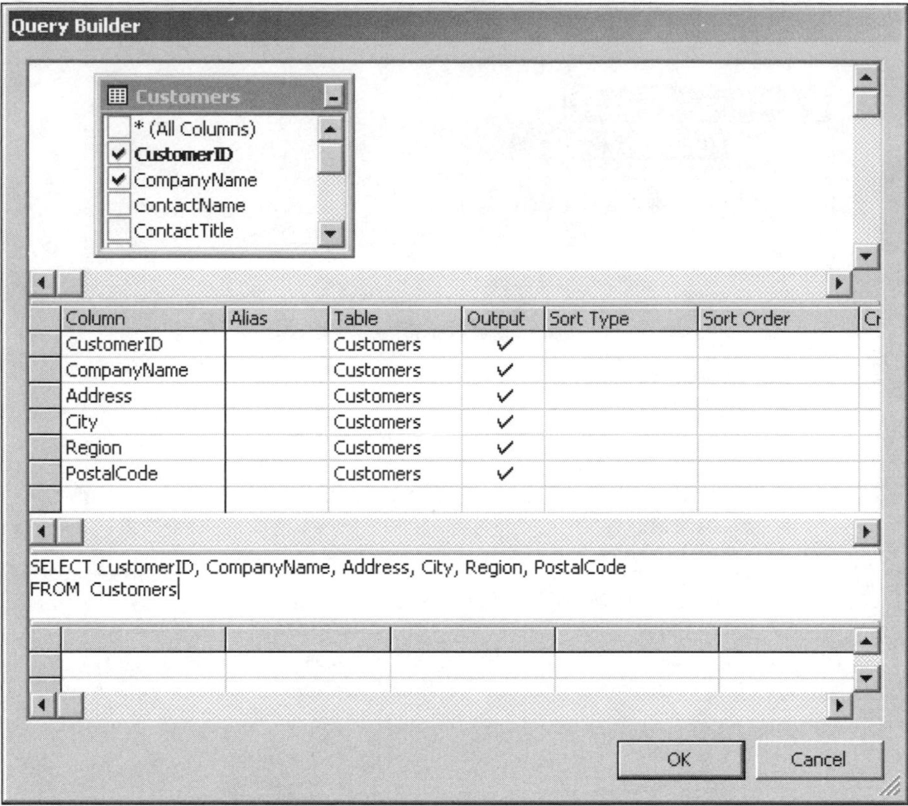

This context menu lets you add additional tables if you want but, for now, we will leave it as is. You can also specify an alias for each column, which can be useful if the names in the database don't match your conventions or are not obvious.

As an example, set the Alias of CompanyName to Company and PostalCode to Zip. Notice how the SQL statement changes from "`SELECT CustomerID, CompanyName, Address, City, Region, PostalCode`" to "`SELECT CustomerID, CompanyName AS Company, Address, City, Region, PostalCode AS Zip`".

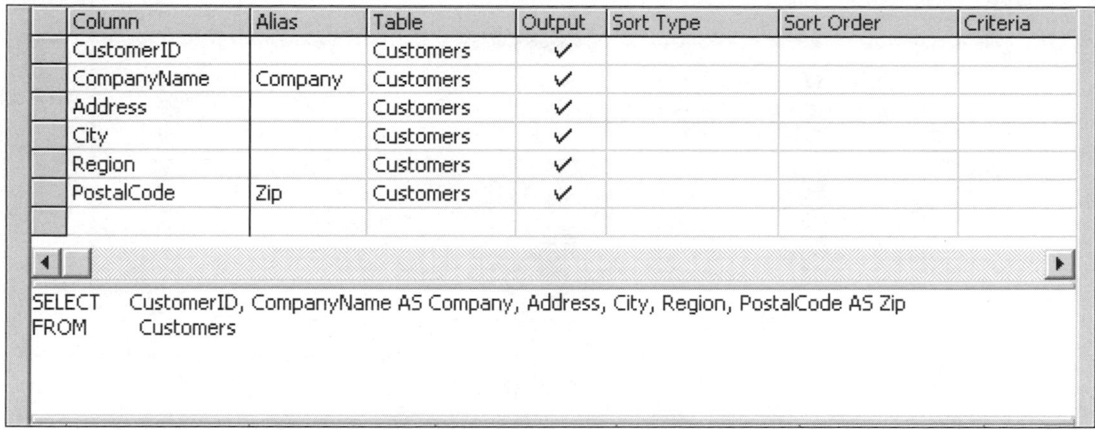

We won't be using the Alias feature so remove any you may have set before continuing. When finished, click OK.

10. Our new `SELECT` statement should now appear in the dialog. Check that it is correct and click Next.

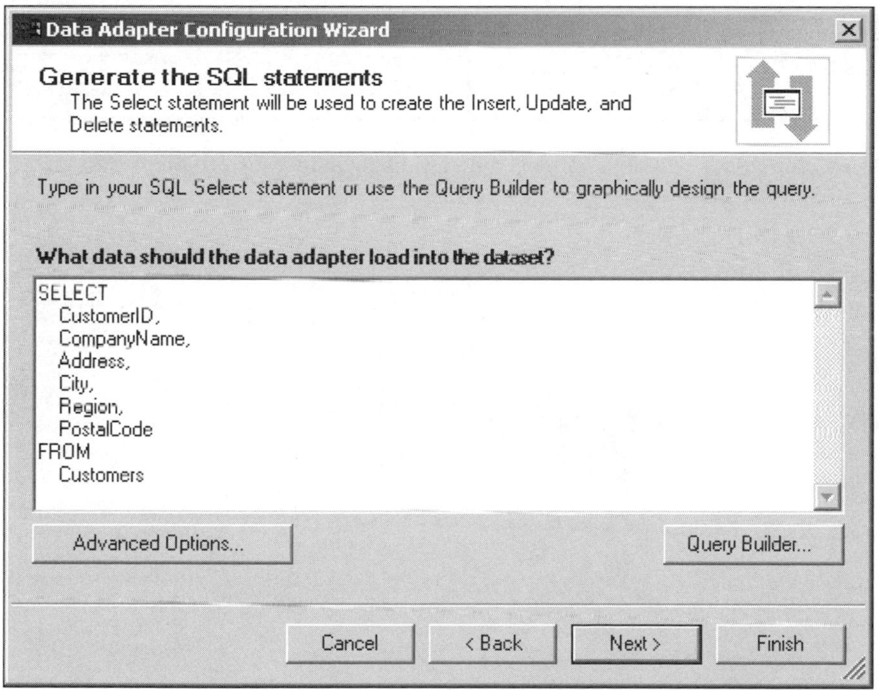

The last screen provides us with a summary of the wizard's actions. Click the Finish button.

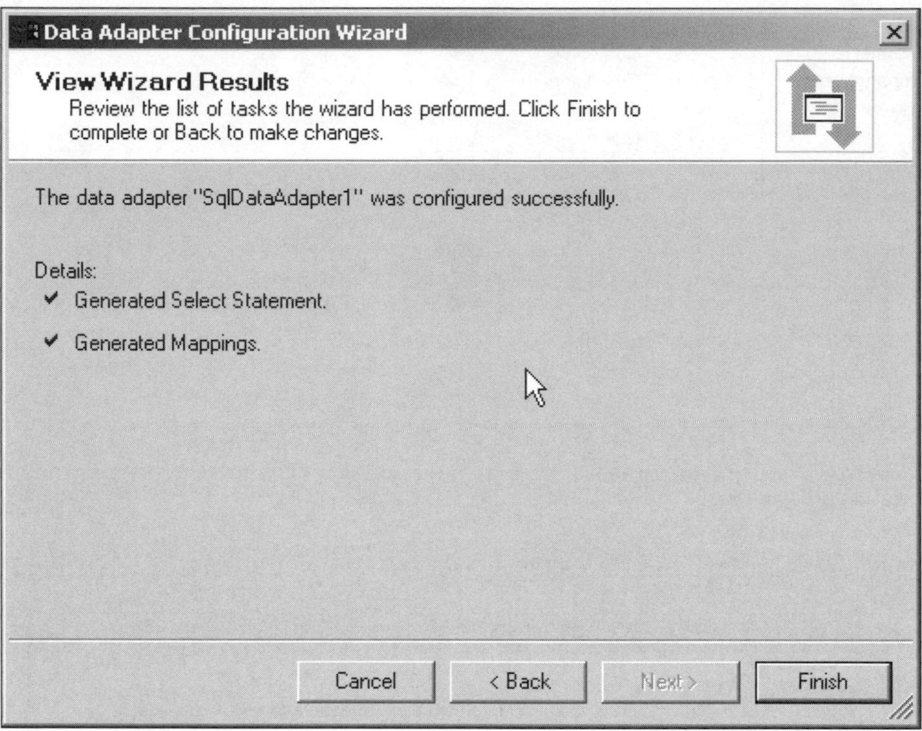

Two components will now be placed under the form in your project: `SqlDataAdapter1` and `SqlConnection1`.

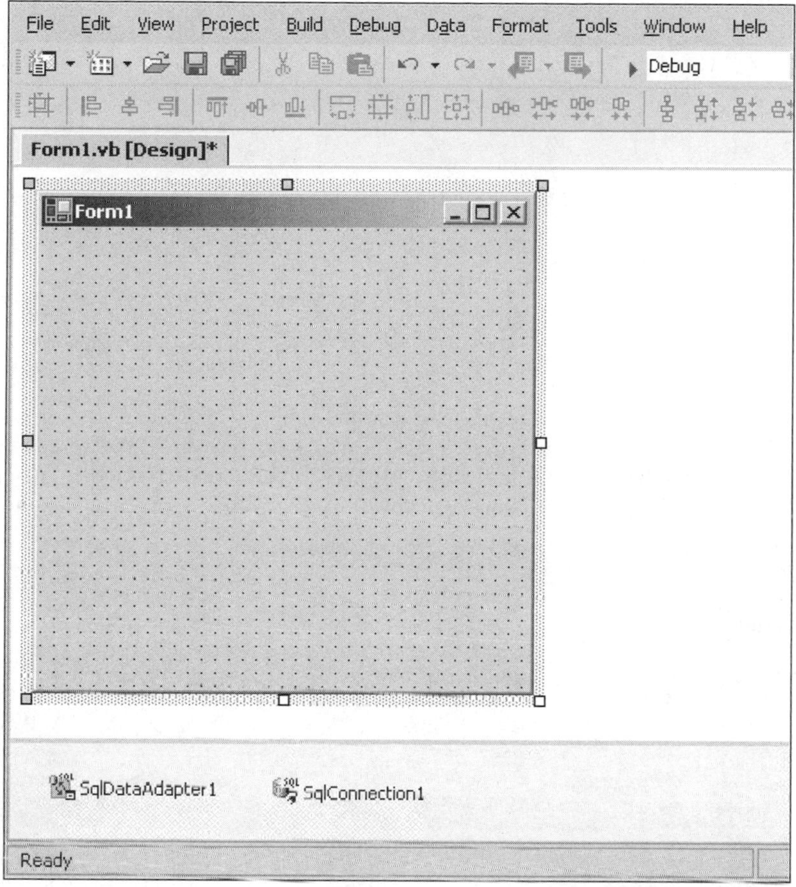

Building the Data Container

We need to build a data container to hold our results. The data container we shall use will be a `DataSet`.

Try It Out – Generating a DataSet

1. Generate a `DataSet` by right-clicking on the `SqlDataAdapter1` control and selecting Generate Dataset.

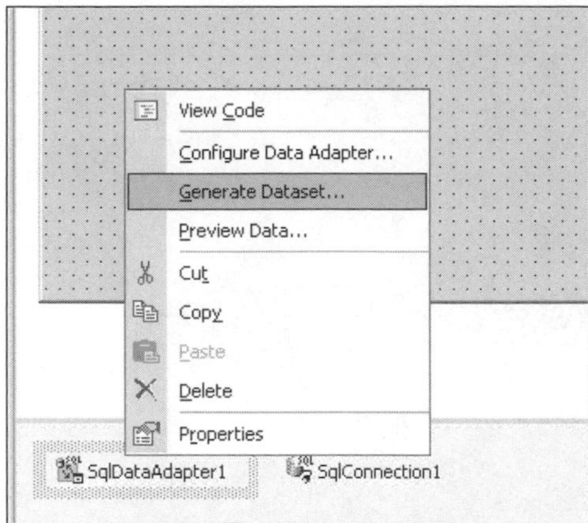

This context menu provides some other options that you may find useful at some point. Configure DataAdapter lets you reconfigure the `DataSet`, taking you through a similar sequence of steps as we just followed when building our `DataAdapter`. We can also preview the data in our `DataAdapter` with the Preview Data option. If you select this item you will see a screen as shown:

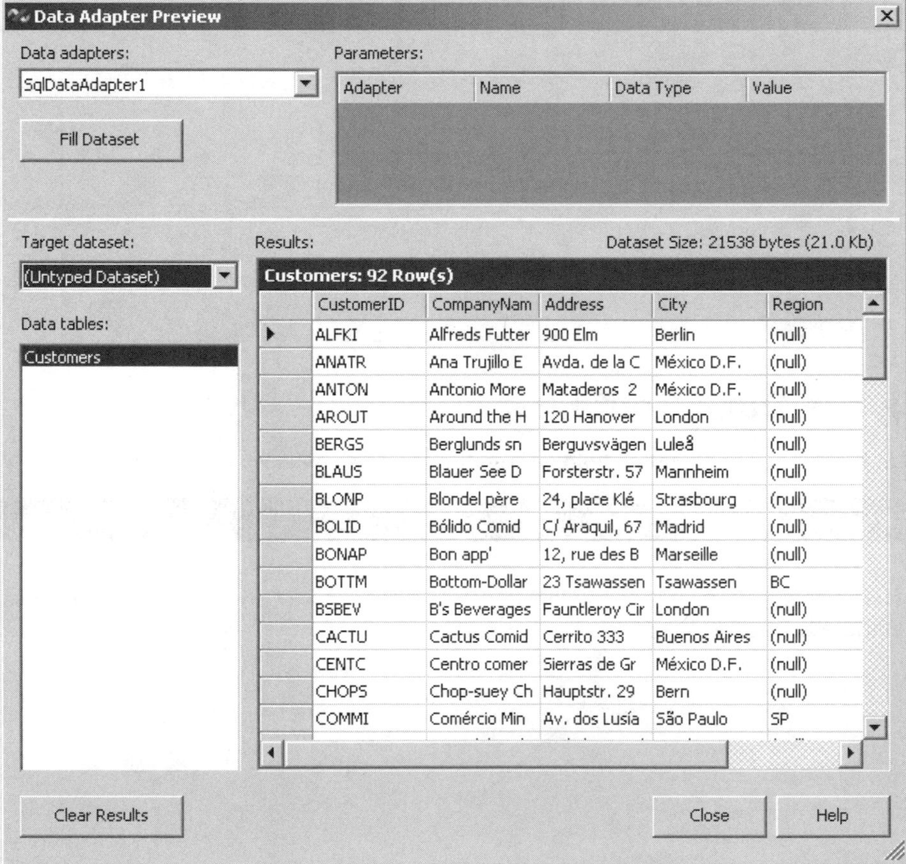

The **Data adapters** drop-down box shows a list of all `DataAdapters` in your project. Select the `DataAdapter` you want to view the data of, in this case `SqlDataAdapter1`, and then click the **Fill Dataset** button. This will call the `Fill` method of the `DataAdapter` and will show you the results obtained. The **Target dataset** drop-down lists all `DataSets` in your project. If, as in our case, there are none yet, it will show **Untyped Dataset** as the default `DataSet`. This is a sort of temporary `DataSet` for displaying the results. The **Parameters** area shows any parameters required to run the SQL `SELECT` statement or stored procedure associated with the selected `DataAdapter`. **Clear Results** will clear the results shown if you wish to regenerate the results or choose another `DataAdapter`.

2. Going back to the context menu, at the **Generate Dataset** dialog, select the option to create a new `DataSet` and enter the name **CustomerDataSet**. Check the **Add this dataset to the designer** box to indicate that we want the new `DataSet` object added to the initialization section of our form, and for it to be instantiated. Whether or not this box is checked, an XML schema file is generated that defines the structure of the tables within our `DataSet`. We will look at XML and its role in ADO.NET in Chapter 12. Click **OK** when finished:

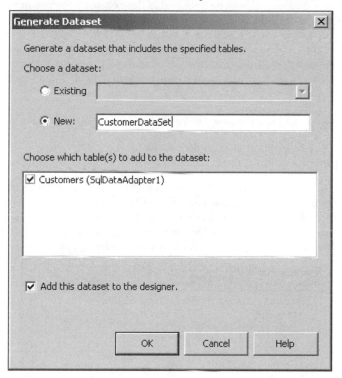

We should now have a `DataSet` control on our form called **CustomerDataSet1**, as well as an associated XML schema file called `CustomerDataSet.xsd`. Our form should now contain the three components shown below:

How It Works

The purpose of these steps was to create a new DataSet object called CustomerDataSet1. Whenever we reference the DataSet, we will use the name CustomerDataSet1. This is not to be confused with the actual DataSet name of CustomerDataSet. Also, note that the DataSet is empty until we populate it through the DataAdapter in code. The wizard generates code to link the DataSet to the XML schema file, CustomerDataSet.xsd. This XML schema describes the layout of the DataSet, based on the columns that we selected in the Query Builder. We won't be using the XML features of the DataSet here, so we don't need to concern ourselves with it yet (Chapter 12 looks at XML in detail). SqlDataAdapter1 contains our SELECT statement to retrieve data from the Customers table, and it connects to the database using SqlConnection1 – remember that we need both a DataAdapter and Connection object to get data from a database.

Binding Data to Controls

Most of the controls in the Toolbox are bindable, which means that we can assign a column, or sometimes a group of columns, from a database table to be displayed as their contents. As you move through the rows of a table, the contents of the chosen column or columns will appear in the control. Other bindable controls include TextBoxes, Labels, CheckBoxes, ComboBoxes and ListBoxes. Most of these controls work by setting their DataBindings.Text property to the name of the table column that you want to bind to. According to the property you're dealing with, you would check the DataBinding properties for a corresponding property to set – with experience you will learn which controls support which data binding properties. Other controls like the DataGrid use the DataSource and DataMember properties for binding. DataGrids are capable of showing the data in all columns of a table, rather than just one. Combo and ListBoxes use a DataSource and DisplayMember property and work similarly to TextBoxes in that they only show single columns of data.

To populate a ListBox or ComboBox with data taken from a given column, set their DataSource and DisplayMember properties appropriately. There are two methods for displaying data:

- As a **bound list** – this will display a list of items in the control and will be in synch with any navigation control on the form. The control can also act as a navigation control so that, when you select a different record to display, all other bound controls change in synch to display the relevant data of the new record. This is done by setting the DataSource property to a DataSet object and the DisplayMember property to the column name of the table, as shown here:

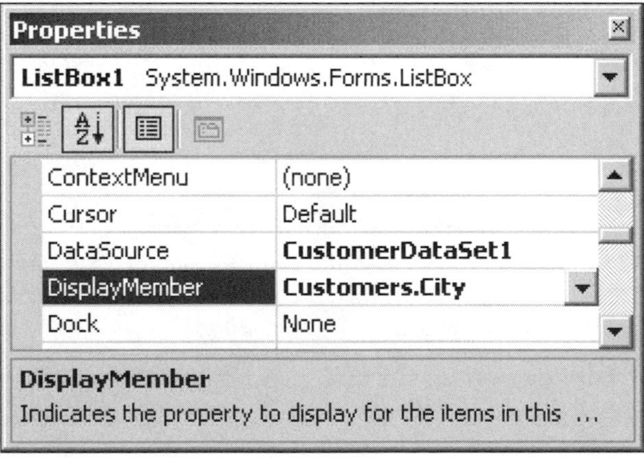

- As a **general list** – this will display a list of items in the control and will not change to match any navigation controls. This is achieved by setting DataSource to a `DataSet.Table` object and DisplayMember to a column:

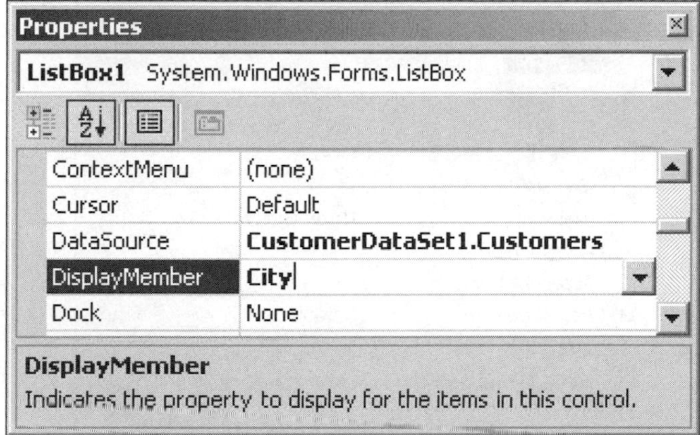

You can apply these same methods and properties when using a `ComboBox`.

To populate the `Checked` property of a `CheckBox`, set the `DataBindings.Checked` property to a `Boolean` (`True` or `False`) column of the database:

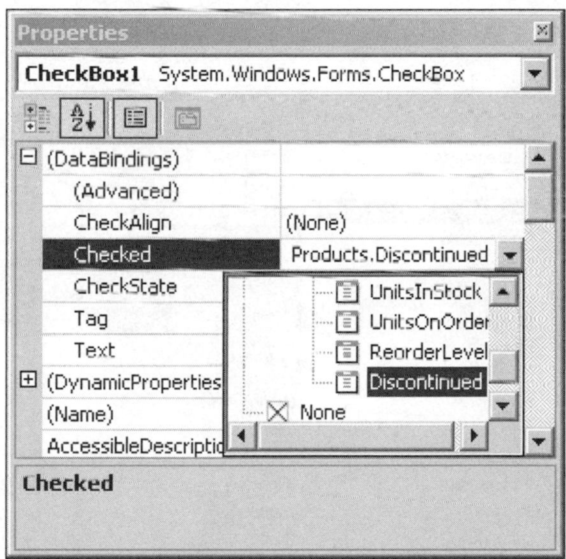

The `RadioButton` control is a little different to the `CheckBox`. We really only have one useable `DataBindings` property: the `Text` property. There is also a `Checked` property, but it's hidden under the `Advanced` property. Click on the Advanced property's ellipsis button (...) to bring up the Advanced Data Binding dialog:

Under the Advanced Data Binding dialog we can set the Checked property. As a matter of fact, we can set any property in this dialog to a column in a database, as long as that column is of the correct type or format for that property:

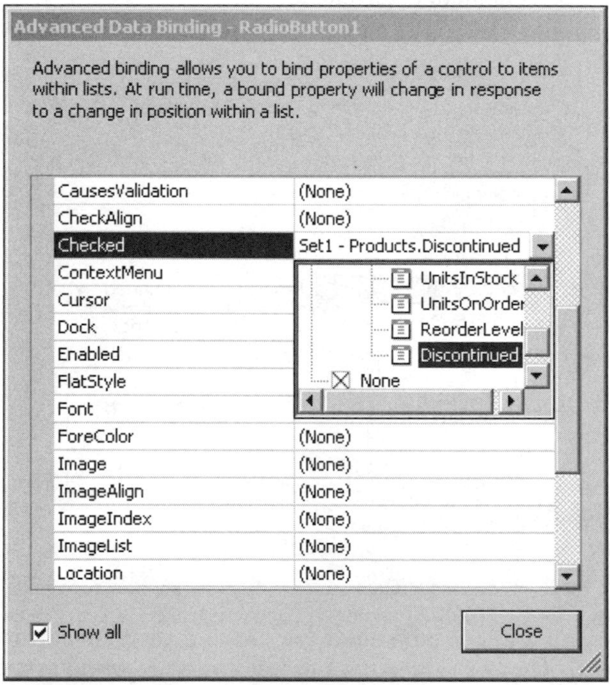

Besides setting these controls by pointing and clicking, we can also bind these controls at runtime, which would allow us to display different tables or columns in our controls, based on a user's request. In this way, we can use just one control to display a variety of information, instead of limiting each control to displaying a single set of data. The following code shows how to bind to a control manually:

```
TextBox1.DataBindings.Add("Text", CustomerDataSet1, "Customers.Address")
```

The arguments of the `DataBindings.Add` method are the `DataBinding` property of the control we wish to set (`Text` in this case). For every property of a control that you want to set, you should check for a matching `DataBinding` property. The remaining two parameters are the `DataSet` (`CustomerDataSet1`) and the table name plus column name, separated by a period (`Customers.Address`).

An alternative way to call the `DataBindings.Add` method is to pass in a `Binding` object:

```
Dim myBinding As New Binding("Text", CustomerDataSet1, "Customers.Address")
TextBox1.DataBindings.Add(myBinding)
```

Let's take a look at some other common controls and their data-binding properties for the display of data:

Control	Property	Example
TextBox	Text	TextBox1.DataBindings.Add("Text", myDataSet, "Customers.Address")
Label	Text	Label1.DataBindings.Add("Text", myDataSet, "Customers.Address")
Check Box	Text	CheckBox1.DataBindings.Add("Text", myDataSet, "Products.ProductName")
	Checked	CheckBox1.DataBindings.Add("Checked", myDataSet, _ "Products.Discontinued")
Radio Button	Text	RadioButton1.DataBindings.Add("CheckState", myDataSet, _ "Products.ProductName")
	Checked	RadioButton1.DataBindings.Add("CheckState", myDataSet, _ "Products.Discontinued")
ListBox		DataSource = myDataSet DisplayMember = myTable.myColumnName
Combo Box		Same as ListBox
Data Grid	Results	DataSource = myDataSet DataMember = myTable

Binding is a great way to display information in controls without having to write any code to do so. As you navigate through your records, all bound controls are automatically updated. In addition, as you change the row shown in one control, other bound controls stay in synch.

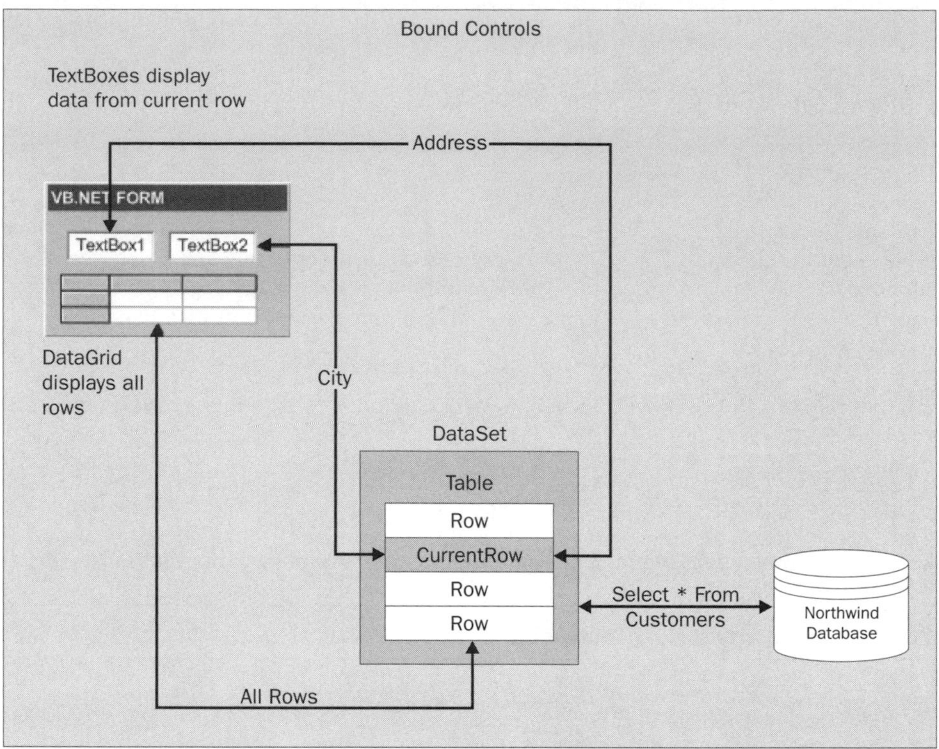

Try It Out – Adding a Data Bound DataGrid

In this section, I'll take you through the process of adding a bound control to our project.

1. Add a `DataGrid` from the Windows Forms tab in the Toolbox to Form1 of the `CustomerApp` project.

2. Add a `Button` to the form and change its Name in the Properties window to btnGetData, and the Text property to Get Data.

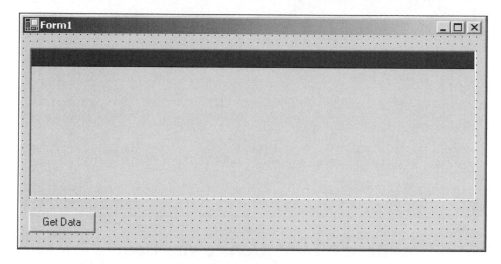

3. Set `DataGrid1`'s DataSource property to CustomerDataSet1 and set the DataMember property to Customers.

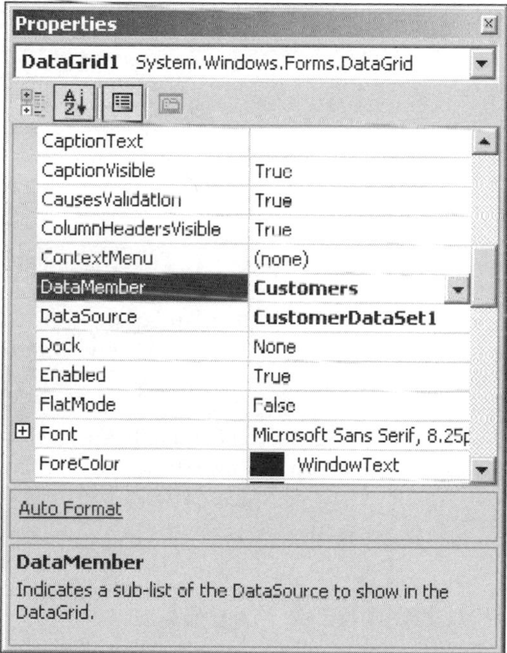

How It Works

We added a `DataGrid` and button to the form. By setting the DataSource and DataMember properties, we tell the `DataGrid` to bind to our `DataSet` and that we want to show the Customers table. Once we set these properties, the grid will automatically be bound to the table specified and the columns formatted with the columns from our SQL `SELECT` statement, as shown overleaf:

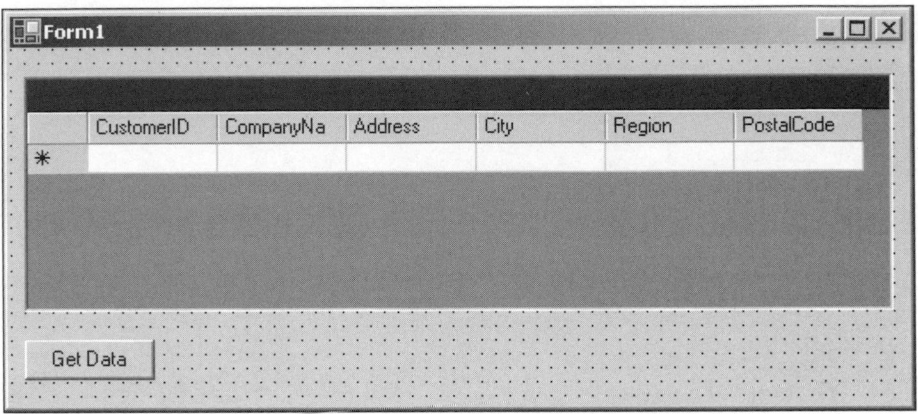

Displaying Database Information to the User

One thing our wizards didn't do is add code to actually fill the `DataSet` with the desired information from the database. We have to call the `Fill` method of the `DataAdapter` to accomplish this. Double-click on the Get Data button in Visual Studio, and add the following for the click event:

```
Private Sub btnGetData_Click(ByVal sender As System.Object, _
                             ByVal e As System.EventArgs) _
                             Handles btnGetData.Click

       SqlDataAdapter1.Fill(CustomerDataSet1)

End Sub
```

When we call the `Fill` method of `SqlDataAdapter1`, we retrieve data from the data source using a SQL `SELECT` statement. The `Fill` method then populates the `DataSet` passed as its parameter. As the `DataGrid` binds to the `DataSet`, when the `DataSet` updates, the `DataGrid` will also change – it is in synch. The data connection will open using our `Connection` object to retrieve the customer listing, and close once the operation is complete.

The `Fill` method returns an integer value that tells you the number of records that were added to the `DataSet`, as long as your SQL statement is set up to return rows, that is. This can be useful for error checking.

```
Dim RecordsAdded As Integer = SqlDataAdapter1.Fill(CustomerDataSet1)
```

Compiling and Running the Project

We've added all the components to our application, so build and run the project. You will notice there is no data displayed. Click the Get Data button to fill the `DataGrid` with a list of customers. Here is what our finished product should look like:

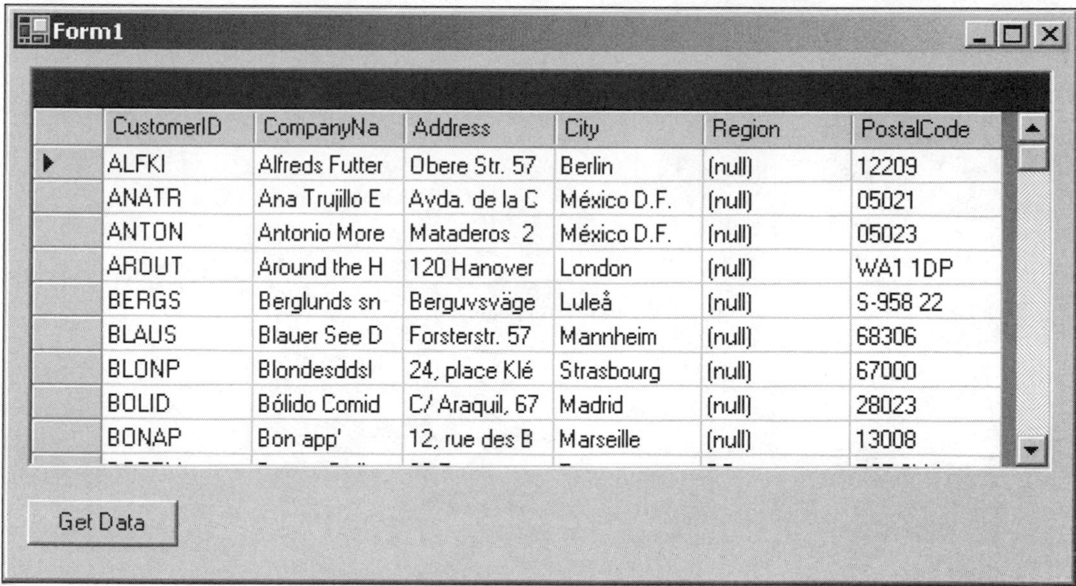

It's that easy!

So what's going on to make this work?

1. From the user interface – our Windows Form – we click the **Get Data** button, which calls the `Fill` method of the `SqlDataAdapter` to tell the database that we want some records.

2. Next, the `SqlDataAdapter` requests a connection to be opened through the `SqlConnection` object.

3. The `SqlConnection` object uses the logon information we provided to open a connection to the database. Once the connection is opened, a `SelectCommand` is issued to actually retrieve the records. As you may remember, this command is created from a `SqlCommand` object.

4. Once the connection is open and we issue a `SELECT` command, the results are sent through the connection.

5. The results are then passed through the `SqlDataAdapter`.

6. Finally, the `SqlDataAdapter` populates the `DataSet`.

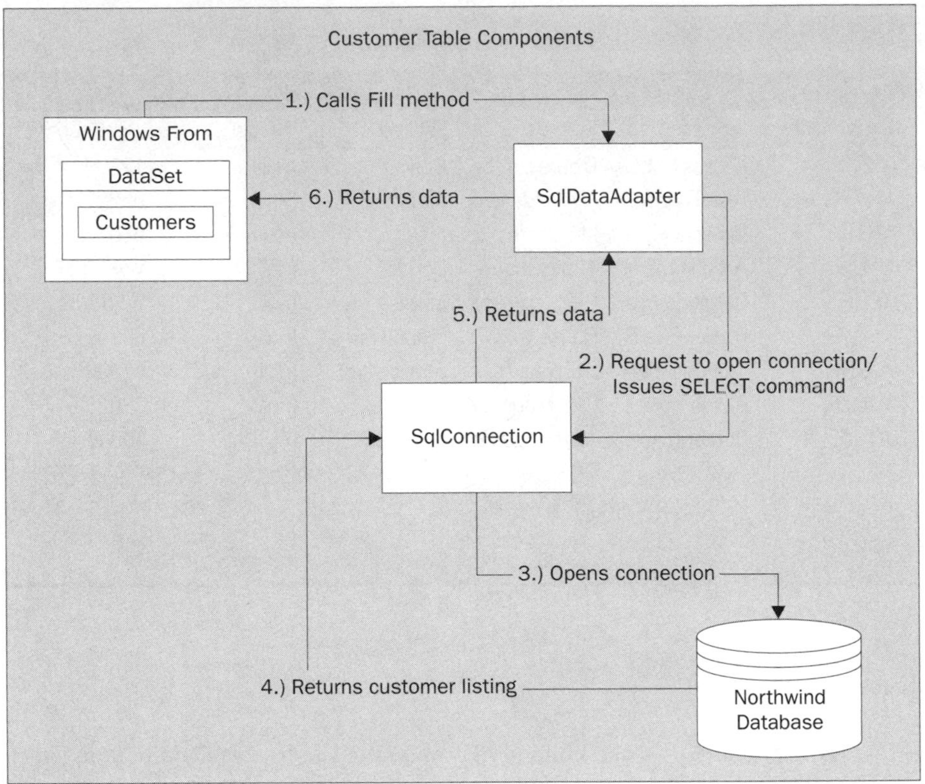

Once we have filled our `DataSet`, the connection is closed and we are free to use the `DataSet` however we wish. In the last example, we displayed the data on the user interface by binding the `DataSet` to a `DataGrid` control on our Windows Form.

What's Behind the Curtain?

So what exactly was the code that those wizards created for us? You're probably thinking how neat they are to create this code but, if something breaks, would we be able to fix it? To solve any such problems, we need to know how the program works and what is happening behind the scenes.

Let's begin by looking at the code that was generated by the Windows Form Designer – right-click on Form1 and select View Source.

```
#Region " Windows Form Designer generated code "

    Public Sub New()
        MyBase.New()

        'This call is required by the Windows Form Designer.
        InitializeComponent()

        'Add any initialization after the InitializeComponent() call
```

```
        End Sub

        'Form overrides dispose to clean up the component list.
        Protected Overloads Overrides Sub Dispose(ByVal disposing As Boolean)
            If disposing Then
                If Not (components Is Nothing) Then
                    components.Dispose()
                End If
            End If
            MyBase.Dispose(disposing)
        End Sub
        Friend WithEvents SqlDataAdapter1 As System.Data.SqlClient.SqlDataAdapter
        Friend WithEvents SqlConnection1 As System.Data.SqlClient.SqlConnection
        Friend WithEvents DataGrid1 As System.Windows.Forms.DataGrid
        Friend WithEvents btnGetData As System.Windows.Forms.Button
        Friend WithEvents CustomerDataSet1 As CustomerApp.CustomerDataSet
        Friend WithEvents SqlSelectCommand1 As System.Data.SqlClient.SqlCommand

        'Required by the Windows Form Designer
        Private components As System.ComponentModel.Container
```

We can see the standard constructor and destructor code here, and then we have declarations for our `DataAdapter`, `SQLConnection`, `DataGrid`, `Button`, `DataSet`, and `SqlCommand`. These are just declarations and do not create actual instances just yet. You can trap events created by these objects if needed, since they are declared with the `WithEvents` keyword. The `Friend` keyword signifies that the declaration is valid anywhere within the same assembly or program, so we can reference these objects anywhere in our program.

Let's look at the `InitializeComponent` procedure. Instances of our `DataAdapter`, `SqlConnection`, `DataGrid`, `Button`, `DataSet`, and `SqlCommand` objects are set up here:

```
        'NOTE: The following procedure is required by the Windows Form Designer
        'It can be modified using the Windows Form Designer.
        'Do not modify it using the code editor.
        <System.Diagnostics.DebuggerStepThrough()> Private Sub InitializeComponent()
            Me.SqlDataAdapter1 = New System.Data.SqlClient.SqlDataAdapter()
            Me.SqlConnection1 = New System.Data.SqlClient.SqlConnection()
            Me.DataGrid1 = New System.Windows.Forms.DataGrid()
            Me.btnGetData = New System.Windows.Forms.Button()
            Me.CustomerDataSet1 = New CustomerApp.CustomerDataSet()
            Me.SqlSelectCommand1 = New System.Data.SqlClient.SqlCommand()
```

To prevent other objects from accessing our controls, we call the `BeginInit` method on our `DataGrid` and `DataSet` objects:

```
            CType(Me.DataGrid1, System.ComponentModel.ISupportInitialize).BeginInit()
            CType(Me.CustomerDataSet1,
    System.ComponentModel.ISupportInitialize).BeginInit()
            Me.SuspendLayout()
```

These are called to avoid any access to these components before initialization. Certain controls require that some properties be initialized before others in order to work properly. By using `BeginInit`, we temporarily place our control in a frozen state, preventing any events or validation from occurring. Not all controls have this requirement so, if you come across a control that doesn't support this method, you can safely assume that it doesn't need initializing in a particular order like those here do.

In this next block of code, we assign our SELECT statement reference:

```
'
'SqlDataAdapter1
'
Me.SqlDataAdapter1.SelectCommand = Me.SqlSelectCommand1
```

We set the SelectCommand property to our SELECT statement so that, when we later call the DataAdapter's Fill method, this statement will get executed. In the code below, we assign the table mappings, table name, and column names:

```
Me.SqlDataAdapter1.TableMappings.AddRange( _
     New System.Data.Common.DataTableMapping()
    {New System.Data.Common.DataTableMapping("Table", "Customers",
     New System.Data.Common.DataColumnMapping()
    {New System.Data.Common.DataColumnMapping("CustomerID", "CustomerID"),
     New System.Data.Common.DataColumnMapping("CompanyName",
     "CompanyName"),
     New System.Data.Common.DataColumnMapping("Address", "Address"),
     New System.Data.Common.DataColumnMapping("City", "City"),
     New System.Data.Common.DataColumnMapping("Region", "Region"),
     New System.Data.Common.DataColumnMapping("PostalCode",
     "PostalCode")})})
```

By default, when you create a new table, it is simply called Table but, since we're using the Customers table, it is renamed. We also have our column mappings. We didn't change any of the column names in the Query Builder so all of the names will be left with their original names. If we had used an alias when building our SQL statement and used Company for CompanyName, for example, it would be mapped with the new name provided as the second parameter. This section of code builds the DataSet's structure in memory. We use the DataAdapter to fill this in-memory object with data.

Next, the connection string is made up from the parameters for connecting to the database. These same properties were set in the Data Link Properties dialog earlier and, consequently, your connection string may vary slightly from this one:

```
'
'SqlConnection1
'
Me.SqlConnection1.ConnectionString = _
    "data source=localhost;initial catalog=NorthwindSQL;persist security
    " & _
    "info=False;user id=sa;workstation id=MyWorkstation;packet size=4096"
```

The data source value specifies the computer where the data is located, the initial catalog value represents the database we want to communicate with, persist security info states whether or not sensitive security information should be returned in the connection string, user id and password give the user account to connect to the database, and, finally, packet size sets the size of the data blocks for transmissions to and from the database server. This size depends on your network and the default is 4096 bytes.

The behavior of the DataGrid gets configured next:

```
            '
            'DataGrid1
            '
            Me.DataGrid1.DataMember = "Customers"
            Me.DataGrid1.DataSource = Me.CustomerDataSet1
            Me.DataGrid1.Location = New System.Drawing.Point(8, 16)
            Me.DataGrid1.Name = "DataGrid1"
            Me.DataGrid1.Size = New System.Drawing.Size(504, 168)
            Me.DataGrid1.TabIndex = 0
```

Properties of the DataGrid are set to reference the DataSet and the Customers table to show the results of our query. The Location, Name, Size, and TabIndex properties are assigned at this point too. Our code now places the button and sets its characteristics:

```
            '
            'btnGetData
            '
            Me.btnGetData.Location = New System.Drawing.Point(8, 200)
            Me.btnGetData.Name = "btnGetData"
            Me.btnGetData.TabIndex = 1
            Me.btnGetData.Text = "Get Data"
```

The TabIndex is set to one, indicating that it will be the second tab item. The button Text property sets the label to show on the button, which is "Get Data" in this case. Properties of our DataSet are then set:

```
            '
            'CustomerDataSet1
            '
            Me.CustomerDataSet1.DataSetName = "CustomerDataSet"
            Me.CustomerDataSet1.Locale = New System.Globalization.CultureInfo("")
```

Our DataSet object, which is called CustomerDataSet1, uses the DataSet name of CustomerDataSet.

The Locale property is set to a CultureInfo object. This class holds culture-specific information, such as language, sublanguage, country/region, and cultural conventions. This class also provides the information to perform certain tasks, such as formatting dates and numbers, sorting and comparing strings, and determining character type information. The culture information is based on which country you are in. For example, you might specify "en-AU" which is English – Australia, "en-GB" which indicates English – United Kingdom, and "en-US" which is English – United States. There are many other specifiers available for you to use. If you don't specify a type, then the culture information specific to your computer will be used.

The Namespace property is used when reading and writing an XML document into the DataSet using the ReadXml, WriteXml, ReadXmlSchema, or WriteXmlSchema methods:

```
            Me.CustomerDataSet1.Namespace =
    "http://www.tempuri.org/CustomerDataSet.xsd"
```

By default, this points to www.tempuri.org. You can point this to your web site or directory to read the schema. You can also leave this as is and it will work without any problems. Again, we will get onto XML and its role in ADO.NET in Chapter 12.

The records from the database become available for retrieval when a connection is opened and a SQL statement is executed, as shown here:

```
        '
        'SqlSelectCommand1
        '
        Me.SqlSelectCommand1.CommandText = _
             "SELECT CustomerID, CompanyName, Address, City, Region, PostalCode
             FROM Customers"
        Me.SqlSelectCommand1.Connection = Me.SqlConnection1
```

To begin with, a `SELECT` statement is assigned to the `CommandText` property and is executed when the connection opens. The columns shown are the same as the ones that we selected in the Query Builder earlier. This property can be a SQL statement or the name of a stored procedure. Once we set our `SELECT` statement, we assign a connection so that, when the command is executed, it opens the connection specified.

The code for the other controls on the form (the `Button` and `DataGrid`) is added to the `Controls.AddRange` method. This is used by the Windows Form to track all of the controls that are on the form. It also exposes the ability for the developer to iterate through the controls collection on a form. We then call the `EndInit` methods of the `DataGrid` and `DataSet` to let the system know that we can now access the components.

```
        '
        'Form1
        '
        Me.AutoScaleBaseSize = New System.Drawing.Size(5, 13)
        Me.ClientSize = New System.Drawing.Size(520, 237)
        Me.Controls.AddRange(New System.Windows.Forms.Control() {Me.btnGetData,
        Me.DataGrid1})
        Me.Name = "Form1"
        Me.Text = "Form1"
        CType(Me.DataGrid1, System.ComponentModel.ISupportInitialize).EndInit()
        CType(Me.CustomerDataSet1,
        System.ComponentModel.ISupportInitialize).EndInit()
        Me.ResumeLayout(False)

    End Sub

#End Region
```

Finally, let's consolidate the essential pieces of our code to see what we've really done:

```
Dim CustomerDataSet1 As DataSet

Dim SqlConnection1 As New System.Data.SqlClient.SqlConnection()
SqlConnection1.ConnectionString = "data source=localhost;initial
catalog=NorthwindSQL; " & _
        "persist security info=False;user id=sa;workstation id=
MyWorkstation;packet size=4096"

Dim SqlSelectCommand1 As New System.Data.SqlClient.SqlCommand()
SqlSelectCommand1.CommandText = "SELECT CustomerID, CompanyName, Address," & _
                                "City, Region, PostalCode FROM Customers"
```

```
SqlSelectCommand1.Connection = SqlConnection1

Dim SqlDataAdapter1 As New System.Data.SqlClient.SqlDataAdapter()
SqlDataAdapter1.SelectCommand = SqlSelectCommand1

CustomerDataSet1 = New DataSet("CustomerDataSet")


DataGrid1.DataMember = "Customers"
DataGrid1.DataSource = CustomerDataSet1

SqlDataAdapter1.Fill(CustomerDataSet1)
```

To recap:

- We created a new connection to the database using a `SqlConnection` object and by setting the connection string
- We created a SQL `SELECT` statement to retrieve customer information
- We created a `SqlCommand` object to call our SQL `SELECT` statement
- The command was configured so that, any time that we select records, a connection is opened by assigning the `Connection` object to the `SqlCommand` object
- We configured a `DataAdapter`, `SqlDataAdapter1`, to return the appropriate records any time that we call the `Fill` method
- We created a new `DataSet` to hold our tables
- We configured our `DataGrid` so that it displays the `Customers` table using the `DataSet`
- We called the `Fill` method, which filled our table up with customer records and displayed it in the `DataGrid`

Adding Additional Tables

We have seen how to display a single table to the user. What if we wanted to display multiple tables? We can add more tables to view in our `DataGrid` by adding another `SqlDataAdapter`. For example, if we want to view suppliers in our `DataGrid`, we can add another `DataAdapter` and use the *same* connection to display this information.

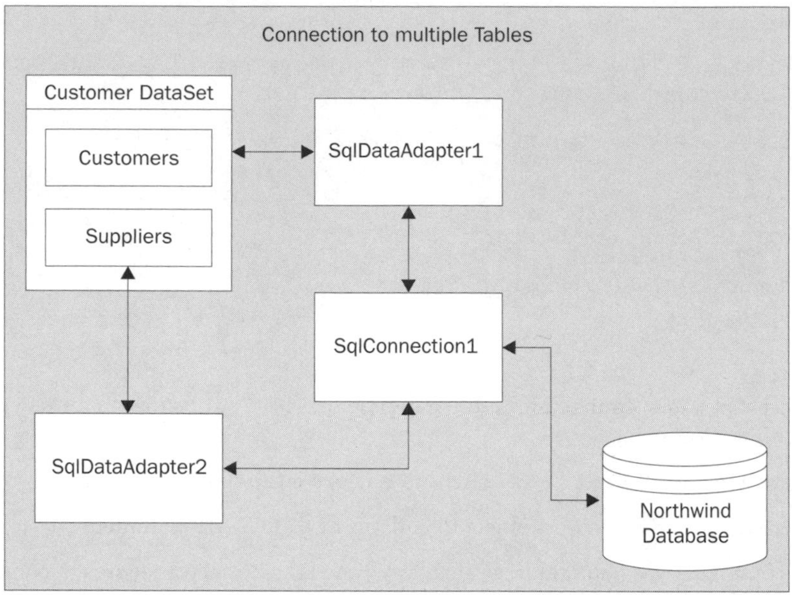

Try It Out – Adding a Second DataAdapter

In this section, I will take you through the steps for adding an additional `DataAdapter`.

1. In the form design view, add another `SqlDataAdapter` control to your form from the Data tab of the Toolbox. You will be guided through the same steps that we followed earlier.

   As you will notice, this time an existing data connection is listed from the connection we created earlier. This will show up as Computername.NorthwindSQL.dbo, where Computername is the name of the computer that you're connected to. Click the Next button.

2. The Query Type window will be shown next. Choose Use SQL statement, as we did before and click Next.

3. Now you will be prompted for the SQL statement used to select information from the Suppliers table. Once again, since we are only going to view records, we will turn off the option to have the wizard automatically generate insert, update, and delete commands. Click the Advanced Options button. Uncheck the first checkbox. Click OK when you're done.

4. You should be back at the Generate the SQL Statements screen. Click on the Query Builder button. Add the Suppliers table and select the following columns: SupplierID, CompanyName, Address, City, Region, and PostalCode. Click the OK button when completed.

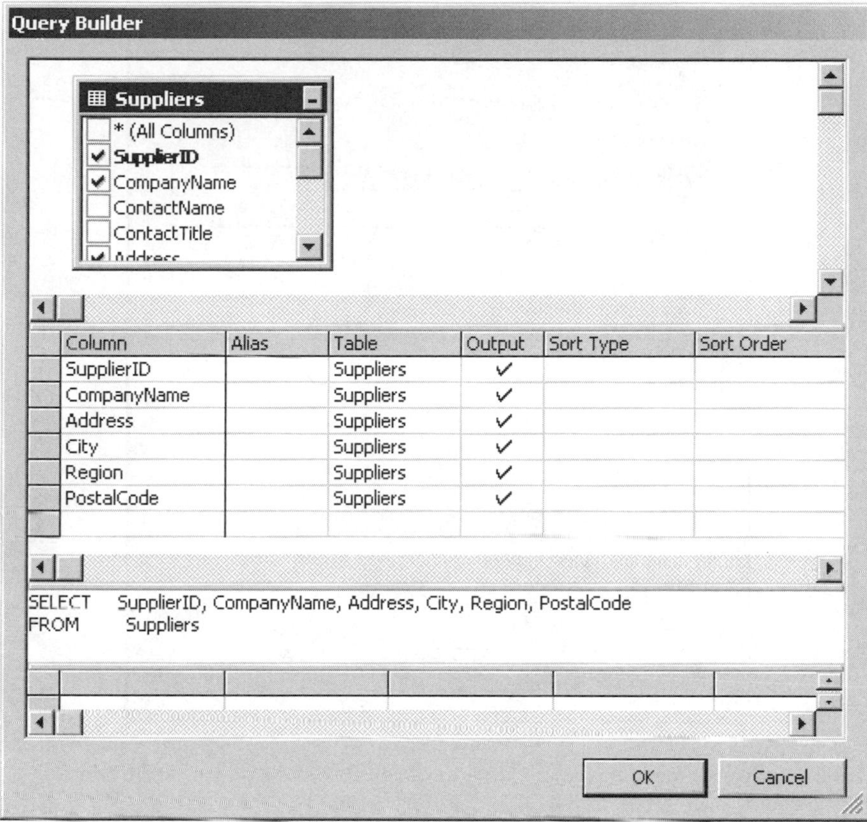

5. Again, we'll be back at the previous window. Review the SQL statement and click **Next**.

The final dialog will appear. Click **Finish**. This will add a new `DataAdapter` called **SqlDataAdapter2** below your form.

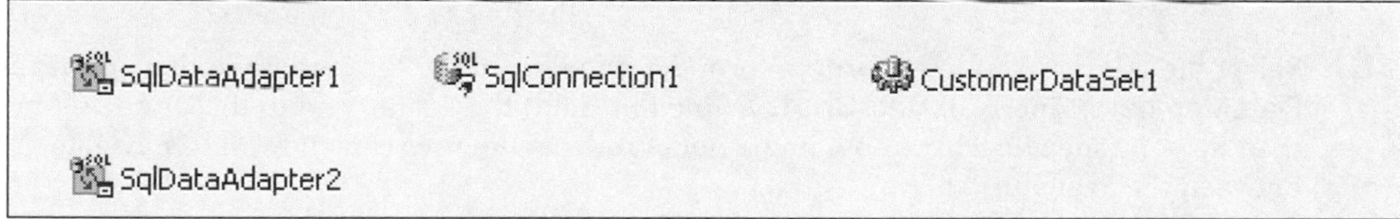

6. Next we need to update our existing `DataSet` to hold this second table. Right-click on `SqlDataAdapter2` and select **Generate Dataset**. The **Generate Dataset** window will appear and we can choose to use the existing `DataSet` or create a new one. We will use the existing one. Also, there will be a list that shows two tables: the **Customer** table (our original one) and now the **Suppliers** table. The **Suppliers** table will already be selected so just click **OK**. This will add the table to the existing `DataSet`.

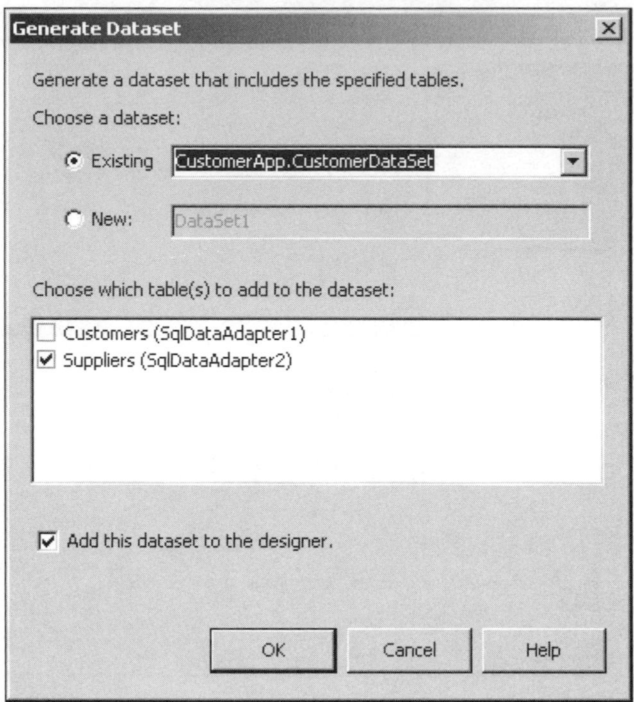

7. Add the following code in the click event of the **Get Data** button to fill the `Supplier` table:

```
Private Sub btnGetData_Click(ByVal sender As System.Object, _
                             ByVal e As System.EventArgs) _
                             Handles btnGetData.Click

        SqlDataAdapter1.Fill(CustomerDataSet1)
        SqlDataAdapter2.Fill(CustomerDataSet1)
End Sub
```

8. Select the `DataGrid` on the form in form design view. In the Properties window, clear the **DataMember** property of **DataGrid1**. Doing this binds the `DataGrid` to the `DataSet` rather than just one specific table, providing a node tree that the user can click on to navigate between the available tables.

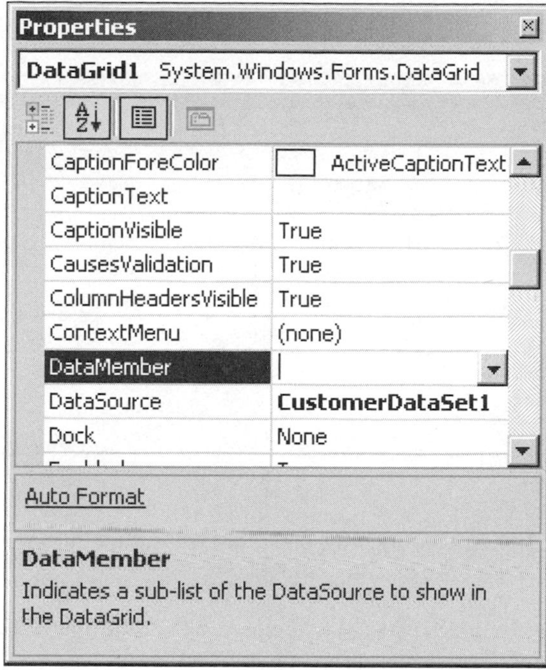

9. Compile and run the project. Click the Get Data button. Then click the plus symbol to expand the nodes in the node tree. We should see a Customer and Suppliers link.

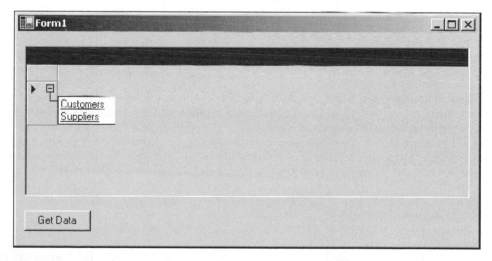

If we click on either of the links, we should see the data for each table. To get back to the parent, click the left arrow in the upper right corner of the grid.

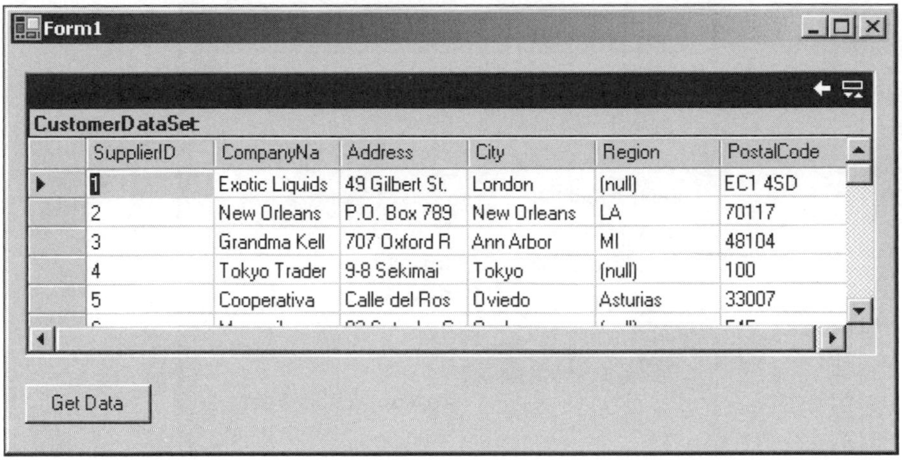

Form1

CustomerDataSet

SupplierID	CompanyNa	Address	City	Region	PostalCode
1	Exotic Liquids	49 Gilbert St.	London	(null)	EC1 4SD
2	New Orleans	P.O. Box 789	New Orleans	LA	70117
3	Grandma Kell	707 Oxford R	Ann Arbor	MI	48104
4	Tokyo Trader	9-8 Sekimai	Tokyo	(null)	100
5	Cooperativa	Calle del Ros	Oviedo	Asturias	33007

Get Data

How It Works

We added a new `DataAdapter` to work with the additional table, but we tied the new table to the existing `DataSet`. We also used the existing connection.

In the code above, the connection is opened and closed twice, automatically. It would be more efficient to open and close our connections once, with code like this:

```
Private Sub btnGetData_Click(ByVal sender As System.Object, _
                             ByVal e As System.EventArgs) _
                             Handles btnGetData.Click

        SqlConnection1.Open()
        SqlDataAdapter1.Fill(CustomerDataSet1)
        SqlDataAdapter2.Fill(CustomerDataSet1)
        SqlConnection1.Close()
End Sub
```

In this block of code, a connection is opened explicitly by calling the `SqlConnection Open` method, which leaves our connection open. The `Fill` method is called and the connection is closed by a call to the `Close` method. Normally, we would want the `Fill` method to leave the connection in the state that it found it. In other words, if the connection to the data source is already open, it should leave it open; if the connection is closed, then it will close it when it is done. We can use the `State` property to determine whether our connection is open or closed, as the code below demonstrates:

```
If SqlConnection1.State <> ConnectionState.Open Then SqlConnection1.Open()
' Make database calls.
If SqlConnection1.State <> ConnectionState.Closed Then SqlConnection1.Close()
```

We need to check the state before opening or closing the connection because, if we try to call the `Open` method on an open connection, we will receive an error stating that the connection is already open. The same goes for the `Close` method. You should always close your connections when you're done with them to free up any resources that they might be taking up. Be aware though that opening and closing connections slows an application, and performance can be improved by keeping a connection open for database calls that occur in close proximity within your program.

Good Form Design

In the above sections, we developed a functional but trivial user interface for a database. Creating production standard database applications is a much more complex process, however, and requires a clear and effective design to be properly thought out in order for the finished product to be effective and to satisfy the end users. In the remainder of this chapter, we examine the aspects of design that you must consider if you wish to create professional, well-designed forms. These aspects include:

- Usability – a consistent and logical flow of controls and menus throughout the program, along with interactive help if practical and relevant, will make the user interface intuitive and simple to use. Try to provide plenty of functionality that allows the user to manipulate information quickly. Make the interface consistent with other frequently-used software interfaces, if possible.
- Presentation – aim for an attractive, friendly feel.
- Validation – alert the user to any mistakes that they may make by checking data against certain criteria.
- Ability to expand – keep this in mind so that future enhancements will not have to radically change the look and feel of the user interface.

Usability

Taking these in order, we'll first look at usability. One way to think of a form is as an ATM machine. The ATM machine is a user interface that allows us to interact with our bank. The ATM is simple, friendly, and easy to use – with only a very basic understanding, anyone can use it. The same goes for forms; we should aim to design them so that users can quickly learn how to use them, and quickly perform common actions. We must make our users feel comfortable with the interface, otherwise they won't use it at all and our efforts will have been wasted. For business applications, we need to make our customers as happy as possible if we want to keep their attention and retain their business.

If you have captured all of the functionality needed by the user and have made it readily accessible, you are most of the way there. You need to consult your users to find out which functions they need the most, and to determine which are "must have" features and which are merely "nice to have". You will find that users always want the icing on the cake and, if you're not careful, you can get sidetracked by attempting to provide too many additional features, possibly making the coding of the core functionality harder. There's an old programmers' principle known as the 80:20 rule, which states that 80% of a problem will be solved by 20% of the final code, and the remaining 80% of your code addresses only the other 20% of the problem. You especially want to avoid coding awkward functionality if just one or two users will use it; instead you should concentrate on things that most, if not all, potential users will use.

Microsoft publishes some design standards for interfaces at http://www.microsoft.com/winlogo/default.asp. You must adhere to these standards if you wish to be able to use the Windows Logo on your software. The standards encompass such things as particular ways of placing buttons, the standard Windows format for menus, and the nature of the Help program that your application must incorporate. This keeps your applications consistent with one another or with other programs adhering to the Microsoft design standards, and helps users to find their way around any application and make the most of it. Most, but not all, developers try to follow the Microsoft Windows standard. Users certainly appreciate being able to go from one application to the next, irrespective of vendor, knowing that certain features will be in the same place, and it lets your customers quickly get up to speed with new applications.

Useful books for designing Windows user interfaces include "About Face: The Essentials of User Interface Design" by Alan Cooper, "Developing User Interfaces for Microsoft Windows" by Everett McKay, or "Microsoft Windows User Experience".

Who Dreams of Forms?

A key principle for user interface development is that, ultimately, the application's users should dictate how the user interface looks.

In most large companies, software development generally follows this scenario. A development team is formed, consisting of a project manager and developers, and a representative of the client company. The team's job is to define, analyze, and document functional specifications for the application. These specifications will define each business rule – each and every function that the application should perform when it is finished. The users of the finished application will be asked to describe the functionality that would most benefit them, in light of the tasks that they currently perform every day. Prototypes will be built to test the technology being used and, at this point, the design of the user interface can be started. At regular intervals, the developers and project manager will sit with a number of end users to discuss the look and feel of the interface. Although the client's representative has final authority on what functionality should be included, it is the users who will actually use the application eventually – matching the application against their needs will produce a tool that is successful.

Presentation

The next quality to look at is the actual presentation of the form. If you've ever had to work with programs that had purple backgrounds, yellow buttons, and green text, then you'll know the value of an attractive user interface. If you're a commercial developer then presentation is all – its style reflects not only on you as the developer, but the brand of your whole company.

Validation

Another very useful capability of form controls is their provision of validation mechanisms that are transparent to the user. Controls can check input against certain criteria and alert the user if any discrepancy is found. A common use for this type of control is the case where certain fields on a form are required, such as the customer name and phone number. We can add some validation behind the form to check that these fields are not left blank, and display a pertinent message to the user if they are. Validation like this can be invaluable to users new to a system, helping them through a potentially frustrating process. Validation is covered in Chapter 8.

Ability to Expand

Last of all, there's the issue of making a program easy to expand. To properly understand this concern, I would like to introduce a couple of design models that you will encounter when building applications. The application developed in the first part of this chapter used a model where all of the processing takes place on the user's machine. Consequently, should we enhance or upgrade the application later – perhaps to view a different table in the database, for instance – then we would have to redistribute the updated software to each of our users. If we wanted to change the type of data source that we communicate with – for example, to an Oracle database instead of a SQL Server database – we couldn't do it easily either. To avoid this difficulty, it is sensible to split the processing up into multiple **tiers**. There is a detailed discussion of the issue of application architecture in the next chapter, so I will provide just a brief overview here.

The standard **client/server** or two-tier model consists of:

- A client application that sits on each workstation and contains **business logic**. Business logic or rules define the processes that are involved in the particular task that is being performed.
- A server component that is used to communicate to the data source.

The standard **three-tier** model consists of:

- A client application that sits on each workstation. Also known as the **client** tier.
- A server component that is used to communicate to the data source. Also known as a **data** tier.
- A **middle** tier containing components that contain the business logic. These components could sit on the client or data tiers instead, but it can be beneficial to centralize business logic processing in the middle tier so that services are not duplicated on each user's machine.

So, for the three-tier model, we split our processing up into smaller components than for the client/server model. There are also n-tier models where you break your services into even smaller components, but I shall leave talking about these until the next chapter.

Encapsulating code like this into relatively independent blocks reduces the amount of code that would have to be updated if part of our application is changed. As our systems grow larger, we may want to expand or modify some of the business logic of our application. Imagine that we have some validation code *on the client* that checks that the user inputs a minimum of eight characters for a password field. If we want to change this business logic so that only six characters are required, we would have to redistribute the updated client software to every client machine. If, however, this validation business logic is kept in a server-side component, we can just update that one piece of code on the server without affecting all of the clients. However, we would, of course, have to design our application beforehand to have this architecture from the start. Additionally, when changing business logic in objects, we need to be careful that we do not change the objects' interfaces. It helps to think long-term to avoid maintenance and expansion headaches later on. Strictly speaking, these issues are application design considerations, but they should be considered when designing the user interface as both go hand in hand.

Summary

So what have we learned in this chapter? We've seen that, by using the wizards in Visual Studio .NET, we can easily build our user interface and connect it to a data source to display information. We covered:

- The `DataSet` – how this object can hold tables of information, and how to fill it with data.
- The `DataAdapter` – how it provides us with methods for retrieving data through the use of `Command` objects, and methods to populate the tables of a `DataSet` through its `Fill` method.
- The `Connection` object – how a `SqlConnection` object linked us to our Northwind database. We also looked at the parameters required for such a connection: `Data Source`, `Initial Catalog`, `User ID`, and `Password`.
- Bindable controls – we learned how to place a `DataGrid` and other controls onto a form, and use them to display information from a database by binding a `DataSet` to them.

- How to display a second table in the DataGrid, using one DataSet and one Connection object – we learned that it's better to open our connection once, do all the work we need, and then close our connection.

You should now be comfortable with these fundamentals of data access in Visual Basic .NET. We will apply and expand these techniques in the rest of the book. In the next chapter, we look in detail at ADO.NET.

Questions

1. List the key principles to bear in mind when producing a well-designed form.
2. What are the core objects that we need to build an ADO.NET project?
3. What is a DataSet?
4. What is the relationship between a DataAdapter and Connection object?
5. What does it mean to say a control is "bindable"?
6. What is a significant benefit of separating the business rules from the client and data tiers?

Answers are available at http://p2p.wrox.com/exercises/.

Data Access with ADO.NET

In the last chapter we built a simple database application using some of the more basic ADO.NET components. This chapter aims to look in greater detail at each of the major components of ADO.NET and how they work together. We start with a brief look at the history of data access and the evolution of technology over the years, focusing on the strengths and weaknesses of ADO in its current state. We will build an ADO.NET application to familiarize you with the concepts discussed. When we're finished, you should be comfortable enough with ADO.NET to build basic database applications by yourself.

Data access has played a very crucial role in application development through the years, and it can be helpful to understand a little of its background, such as how and why it evolved. There have been many promising technologies available over the years and, as developers, we experimented with them all in the hope that they would neatly address all our business needs for gathering information and managing data, without which we wouldn't be able to accomplish many common business goals.

Many developers seek a more uniform and robust engine to communicate with their data sources. Many third-party vendors strive to find an engine that will permit them to communicate with multiple data sources without the need for separate code: the alternative, of maintaining different sets of code for every data source, can easily become a programmer's worst nightmare.

There are many different technologies available that store and retrieve data, indicated by the huge range of acronyms in the data access field, such as DAO, RDO, ODBC, OLE DB, and ADO. It can be hard to choose between the different technologies to determine the best tools for a particular job. Factors to consider include reliability, overall quality, robustness, how frequently the product is updated to fix problems and improve performance, and so on. Longevity is an issue when deciding on such products, because you want to use a solution from a company that is going to be around long enough to provide the support that your application may require. ADO.NET can make such decisions much easier, as we shall see in this chapter.

Data can come from a variety of sources, including comma separated value (CSV) files, XML, e-mail, spreadsheets, or one of a range of other text or binary formats. In general, however, you will more commonly be taking information from a database such as Microsoft Access, SQL Server, Visual Fox Pro, Oracle, DB2, Sybase, or Informix. At the moment, there is much demand for communication with data sources across platforms, such as accessing data on a mainframe running under Unix from a workstation running Windows. A great deal of data is being migrated to newer generation servers that are more robust and cost effective, so this trend is likely to continue, and there are a lot of companies that want to upgrade because their existing systems can no longer support the volume of data they now require. Now, of course, everyone is talking about Internet services and retrieving data through that means – the ultimate distributed model. How can we do this in a way that avoids having to rewrite our code or buy a new product whenever our systems get larger? ADO.NET is one product that can help in our quest.

Microsoft has come up with many different technologies through the years to try to tackle some of the hurdles facing developers concerned with data access. Developers need applications that can share data between end-points, receive orders for products online, retrieve marketing reports, provide e-mail alerts, customer listings, and stock reports, and more. These are just some of the problems that a sound data access system like the new ADO.NET must address.

In this chapter, we will cover the ADO.NET infrastructure in detail to give you a better understanding of its architecture and components. Specifically, the topics include:

- The history of data access
- The evolution of ADO.NET
- An analysis of the differences between ADO and ADO.NET
- The different components that make up the `DataSet`
- How to update the `DataSet`
- ADO.NET namespaces
- Data flow in ADO.NET
- The .NET data providers
- The `DataReader` class

A Short History of Data Access

Data access methods have been around since Microsoft Access 1.0 and Visual Basic 3.0. Access databases were made to work very well with Visual Basic, as they still do for simple desktop applications.

The first data model in Visual Basic was called Data Access Objects (DAO), introduced in Visual Basic 3.0. It could interact with Microsoft Access and other types of databases, although it was optimized for databases located on your desktop computer. It was easy to work with because it provided simple data access methods and tools from within the Visual Basic IDE environment, such as the data binding controls. These tools and the abundance of resources such as books and technical articles meant that you were able to get a database application up and running in next to no time. The Visual Basic environment came with a data manager that allowed the creation and management of Access databases and, when you distributed your apps, the setup utilities allowed for easy selection of any required data access libraries. It also allowed you to write code to access different data sources using one set of code, as the only thing to change was the type of data source you wanted to connect to. These data sources were mainly non-relational databases.

Non-relational databases are typically flat-files stored as a sequential binary stream. ISAM (Indexed Sequential Access Method) databases fall into this category and provide a way of managing how a computer accesses records and files stored on hard disk. The data is stored sequentially and direct access to a specific record requires use of an index. The structure of these files is pretty complex. Most engines that read this kind of data are very quick and efficient at accessing records because there are no extra layers to go through, and they can directly access the data. This has the unfortunate implication that they lack any security mechanism to protect the data, and anyone can go in and view or edit the information in the database, and no transaction history is kept of who, what, or when items are changed. Such systems are not designed for multi-server configurations, where processing can be split up to make the client computer do much of the data processing work. They are poorly suited to multi-user environments, and don't provide an intrinsic mechanism for preventing users from stepping on each other's toes by making concurrent alterations.

Data Access Technologies

Briefly, the evolution of modern data access technologies can be summarized as below. Each new development resolved certain issues with its predecessors, and generally enhanced the tools available to database developers:

- **ODBC**, Open Database Connectivity, has been the most successful data provider to date. It is supported by more development languages than any other data access technology. The SQL Access Group (SAG) was set up in 1989 to define and promote standards to allow developers to switch data systems, either local or remote, without rewriting their code, and to enable companies to centralize their databases instead of requiring separate copies to be installed on each client computer. The group included a number of software and hardware vendors, chiefly Hewlett-Packard, Digital, Sun, Informix, IBM, Oracle, and Microsoft. In 1990, the group combined the required features into an Application Programming Interface (API) that would allow client-server applications to access a variety of different databases, although it wasn't until 1992 that a standard suitable for commercial software products was published.

  Microsoft was the first to commercialize this specification with ODBC 1.0 in the same year. Many other database vendors have since added Microsoft ODBC support to their products and, today, there are over 170 different types of ODBC drivers available. Microsoft supplies its ODBC Software Development Kit (SDK), incorporating a number of tools to aid in the development of drivers that will fit into Microsoft's ODBC structure. The SDK is also available for non-Windows environments such as UNIX, OS/2, and Macintosh, although vendors can write their own API that conforms to SAG standards rather than use Microsoft's SDK. For further information on the internals of ODBC, read *Inside ODBC* by Kyle Geiger, published in 1995 by Microsoft Press.

  ODBC provides a standard set of API functions that you can use to access a wide range of data sources. Through the use of a driver manager, it translates the statement requested to the native syntax, and returns the results to your application. This mechanism provides the developer with a single set of statements for a range of systems, independent of platform, vendor, database, and language. However, the ODBC API was complex and unintuitive to work, and there were inconsistencies in some of the drivers that required custom code be written to cater for those drivers.

  In the Windows environment, an ODBC control panel is available to manage ODBC connections. You can create a connection by giving it a name, and use this name to reference that connection in your Visual Basic applications or web pages.

- **DAO**, Data Access Objects, introduced in Access 1.0 back in 1992, is a technology built around the JET engine capable of accessing Microsoft Access databases, external ISAM databases including Btrieve, dBase, Paradox, FoxPro, and ODBC data sources. Visual Basic 3.0 provided support for DAO and the Microsoft JET database engine and, for a while, it was the most popular method of communicating with Access and ISAM data sources.

  Everything has to go through the JET engine, even when accessing other data sources through the ODBC API. It supports 16-bit operations, making it the primary choice of the time for Windows 3.x's 16-bit environment. DAO provided the capability to access JET and ODBC sources with a common set of code. However, the syntax wasn't as simple as it could have been, and it was slow and resource-hungry. In addition, it was designed for desktop applications where the database and application were both on one machine. JET was optimized for Microsoft Access databases; any other sources suffered in performance because commands were required to be translated before being sent to the database server. However, it was widely available and, because it was supplied with Microsoft Office products, any user with Office could use the technology.

- **RDO**, Remote Data Objects, was introduced with the 32-bit version of VB4 in 1995 specifically to access remote ODBC data sources, such as Microsoft SQL Server and Oracle, but without the complex syntax of the ODBC API. RDO's object model was based on DAO, and it included some of the best features of DAO's interface and core functionality, without the requirement to use the JET Engine. This led to improved performance over DAO for non-Access databases. RDO had an intelligent cursor, making for faster data processing. Compared to DAO, it had better handling for queries and result sets, was faster, and required less overhead. Much of this performance advantage derives from the fact that RDO communicates directly with the ODBC API without going through any other layers. It didn't stay around long however due to the arrival of yet better technologies.

- **ODBCDirect** was introduced with Visual Basic 5.0 in 1997 as an alternative form of DAO that switches between the JET Engine and RDO. It provided access to the ODBC data sources directly, bypassing the Microsoft JET Engine. Internally, it uses the RDO engine and, in fact, it's very much the same as RDO but with DAO object names. Compared to DAO, ODBCDirect has better performance, better resources, better access to server-side functionality, and better update and query methods. The downside was that it couldn't access non-ODBC sources.

- **OLE DB**, Object Linking and Embedding for Databases, Microsoft's API for universal data access, allows communication to relational and non-relational data sources including legacy and mainframe data using a Component Object Model (COM). It was introduced in 1996, and provides all the capabilities of ODBC but is divided into two components: consumers and providers. The consumer components use the data, while providers talk to the data and expose an interface to the consumers. It can handle different types of non-relational data sources such as e-mail, file systems, graphics, and many other custom data sources. It's the core of Microsoft's database technology today. Only C++ applications originally had direct access to OLE DB and the code required to use it can quickly become very convoluted.

- **ADO**, ActiveX Data Objects, is a wrapper around OLE DB that was first released in 1996 to hide the complicated syntax of OLE DB. It has similar features to DAO and RDO and, although it is designed for minimal network traffic, it has good performance and is easy to learn. ADO provides all the capabilities of OLE DB, which means we can access data stores from various different vendors. This model was designed towards a tightly-coupled connected architecture, while still allowing for a disconnected setup. Disconnected means data is kept in memory without any active connection to the database, to allow work to be done on the data without having to rely on a network that might be slow or not be available all the time. It also allows greater scalability in that server resources are freed up, hence allowing more connections. Tightly coupled means that the components or objects of a system must be connected to each other, as opposed to loosely coupled where the components can work independently of each other and only communicate when needed.

- **RDS**, Remote Data Service, is similar to ADO but was designed to provide OLE DB technology for web-based applications. It allows data to be manipulated on the web client without making additional calls – or round trips – to the server, thus freeing up resources from the server. It is designed more for disconnected data sources than ADO.

- **ADO.NET**, introduced in 2000, is the latest Microsoft ADO and RDS technology. As it is built in XML, the industry standard which hopes to reshape the way we deal with data, it can be managed by any application that can read this standard regardless of the platform concerned – be it Windows, Linux, or Unix – or the language – be it C++, VB, Delphi, or whatever.

The following table provides a recap of each technology's pros and cons:

Technology	Pros	Cons
ODBC	Allows connection to multiple data sources.	Initially was hard to work with the ODBC API.
DAO	Optimized for Microsoft Access databases. Readily accessible with Office products, great for desktop applications. A reliable and proven technology.	Performance wasn't as great with non-Microsoft Access databases. Syntax can get overly complex at times.
RDO	Can access remote data sources such as SQL Server and Oracle. Using core functionality of DAO, but quicker and has less overhead than DAO.	Superseded by ADO.
ODBCDirect	An alternative mode to DAO to bypass the JET engine and communicate directly with ODBC.	No access to non-ODBC data sources.
OLE DB	Allows communication with both relational and non-relational data using COM. Has all the capabilities of ODBC.	Coding with it is very hard. Initially only available to C++ developers.
ADO	Provides a wrapper around OLE DB. High performance and easy to use.	Initially designed for a connected architecture.

Table continued on following page

Technology	Pros	Cons
RDS	Allows web applications to get to a data source through OLE DB technology. Similar to ADO. Designed primarily for a disconnected architecture.	Only available for web applications.
ADO.NET	Designed similarly to ADO and RDS. Built-in XML support. Simplifies communication between different environments and languages.	None yet.

ODBC, OLE DB, ADO, and RDS were later brought together in a single package known as the Microsoft Data Access Components (MDAC) – see http://www.microsoft.com/data/.

Application Architectures

Changes in the architectures underlying applications drove the development of these different data access technologies. There are three typical application architectures in use today:

- Client-Server (2-tier)
- 3-Tier
- n-Tier

Client-Server

Client-server architecture consists of one or more client applications communicating with another application or service known as the server. The client and the server can reside on the same computer, or on separate computers. In the early days of the client-server model, each database application (or client) would access information from a copy of the database on the same computer, as shown in the figure below. With hundreds or even thousands of clients, this quickly becomes a big headache to maintain, because any time data is changed on one computer, other computers won't know about it as each client's database is not in sync. This model required changes to be collated at some suitable time, often at the end of the business day, and the updated database would then have to be redistributed to each client machine. There's no easy way to track or follow up on a customer's activity for the current day, or generate up-to-the-minute reports from one central system. Reasons such as these underlined the need for a system based on a central database.

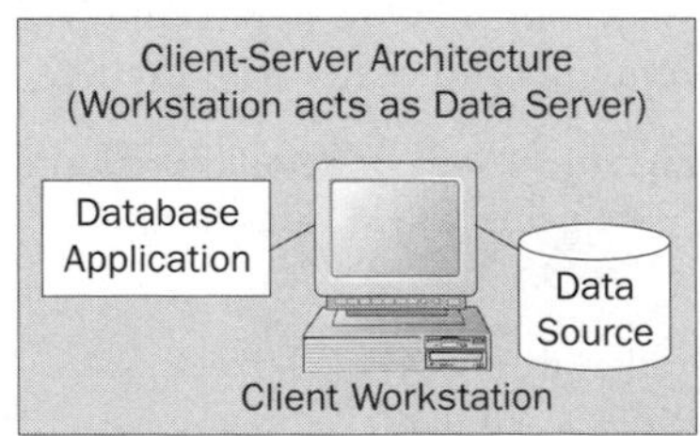

This state of affairs improved considerably when data was moved onto its own computer – either a dedicated server or just one particular client workstation – so that multiple clients could access the same data source simultaneously. This introduced the issue of concurrent updates, where there is a risk of conflict if two users attempt to update the same record at once. **Locking** is one solution that arose in response – if one person is editing a record, that record is locked so that other users cannot update the same information until the first has finished. It is still possible to read this data; it just can't be modified. Despite this, separating and centralizing the data from the client applications was a major step forward. In the early systems, most of the code to access the data still resided on the client's computer. Also, the data server was often just a file server with no engine to process commands from clients, meaning that all the actual work had to be done client-side. This was especially true for non-relational databases.

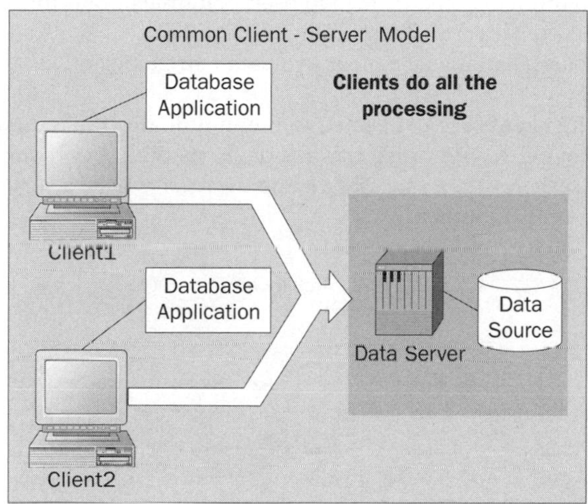

The diagram above shows how multiple clients access one data server, reading and updating one database simultaneously. Not all applications will need a centralized database however, and you will have to make that decision according to the particular application you're developing. If only one or two clients will use an application, and there is unlikely to be a future requirement to add more users, then a single computer client-server application may be the simpler and most efficient choice. Many software vendors use this type of architecture because it's quick and easy to build and maintain databases for such applications as a contact manager that holds addresses and phone numbers, or an inventory application for a small store. Many of these smaller applications will use a package such as Microsoft Access because applications can be designed and built at much lower cost than the same application using Microsoft SQL Server or Oracle. Smaller database systems usually require less security and are simpler to maintain. Should data become corrupt, you can very easily restore it because backing up data is just as straightforward. Of course, such applications do not offer the security required for a publicly distributed database, nor can they match the performance of the top engines. Which is right for you will only become clear once you have weighed up all the pros and cons.

3-Tier

3-Tier architecture arrived as a consequence of improvements in technology, resulting in more powerful equipment and operating systems. In a 3-tier system you can move most of the processing off the client's computer onto dedicated servers. 3-Tier architecture comprises services that reside between the client and server (on the **middle-tier**). The middle-tier must be independent of the client and server in order to be considered a true 3-tier model, although it may reside on the same machine as the server, as in many systems. Ideally, all business requirements, such as data validation and methods for retrieving data, are moved to the middle-tier. As much processing as possible is removed from the client machine. Although there is a small performance penalty involved with this architecture – because we can now no longer directly access our data source but must instead go through a middle man to process transactions – this architecture enabled servers such as Microsoft SQL Server, Microsoft Transaction Server (MTS), COM+, and web servers to all run databases, process transactions, and manage memory much more efficiently than ever before.

In the next illustration, the clients are connected to the middle tier that contains our business logic for data retrieval. This middle tier would preferably reside on its own server such as an MTS Server, a COM+ server, or a web server. On the far right is the data-tier where a server manages the database with an application such as SQL Server.

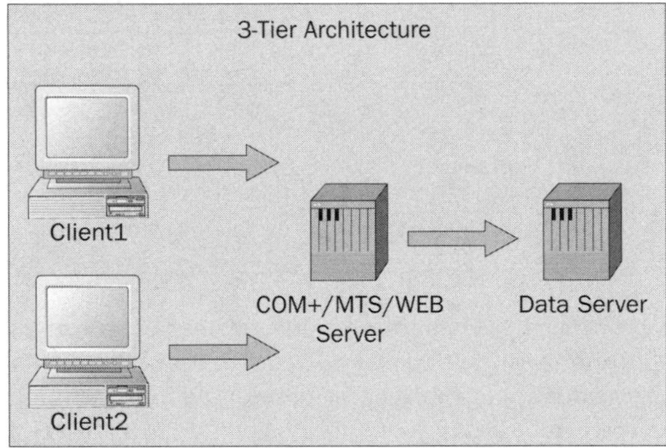

To sum up, a 3-tier application is divided into three parts, or tiers, namely the client tier, the middle tier, and the data tier. The client tier consists of a user interface, such as a Windows Form containing menus and controls. This tier will communicate with the middle tier to retrieve data or perform some action.

The middle tier, sometimes called the **business tier**, houses the business logic code to carry out the actual work required by the clients in the form of classes such as `Customer`, `Orders`, or `Products`. Our client Windows Form, for example, could have a button that shows a message box with a customer's last name taken from the customer table of the NorthwindSQL database. The business component would contain code to validate data coming in to or out of our database. The code behind the button on the Windows Form would simply call the relevant business component in the middle tier, and show the result that it returns. Placing code in this tier takes it off the client, greatly assisting maintainability. In many cases, we can change our business rules whenever we want without affecting the client in any way.

The final tier, the **data tier**, is where our data server, such as Microsoft SQL Server, resides.

n-Tier

As we move into the new century, more and more Internet applications are upon us. There is an increased need for systems based on the disconnected model where we connect to our data source, download the data to the client, and then close the connection. We maintain a cached set of records locally for manipulating data that must then be uploaded to the server if changes are made. Not only does this mean that our client has to spend less time waiting on a potentially slow network or Internet connection, but also that our server has to maintain less connections, so requiring less resources, and thus is able to support more connections (that is, users).

When we talk about n-tier applications, we mean there could be any number ("n") of tiers. For an application to fall into an n-tier model, it needs to have one or more business logic components and one or more business data access components. The business data access components house definitions of specific tables or fields, methods for extracting information required by a particular application and the like. The data access component in the case of an n-tiered application is fairly generic and contains methods and properties designed to work with any application and database.

n-Tier architectures encourage highly distributed systems where we break our services up making them more scalable and maintainable. This also allows for better disconnected databases. However, as we break up our services, they tend to become more specialized and geared more towards a particular task. As a result, we cannot move them around tiers as easily. For example, we might have a data access class that works with just Oracle, or components that just work in MTS or COM+ environments. Such objects would be suitable for one task and one task only.

Most companies have moved to a distributed system where products and services are no longer held on just one server. In the diagram below, clients running some type of database application, such as a stock inventory or a phonebook program, communicate directly with the web server containing the business logic such as data validation. The web server in turn talks to an MTS or COM+ server where the business data components reside to manage database transactions. There is a separate database server that performs the actual database accesses required. These systems can readily communicate with clients across a WAN or Internet.

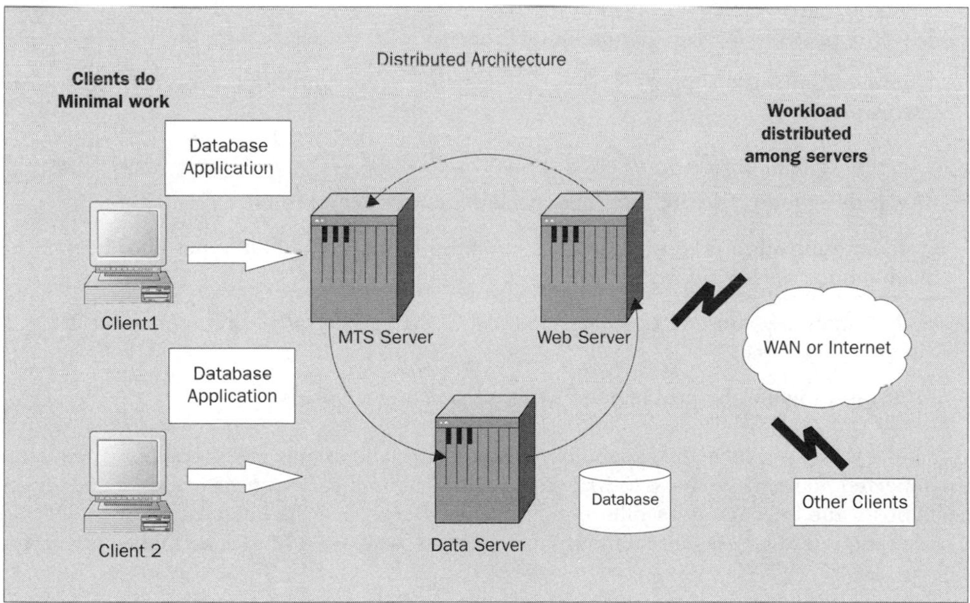

Current State of ADO

ActiveX Data Objects (ADO), the child of DAO and RDO, has been the most efficient data access model up to now, and is supported by a wide range of development languages. Many objects were streamlined or dropped to make a more lightweight model capable of rapid data access in a variety of architectures, from single to n-tier. It achieves this by being a wrapper for underlying OLE DB calls.

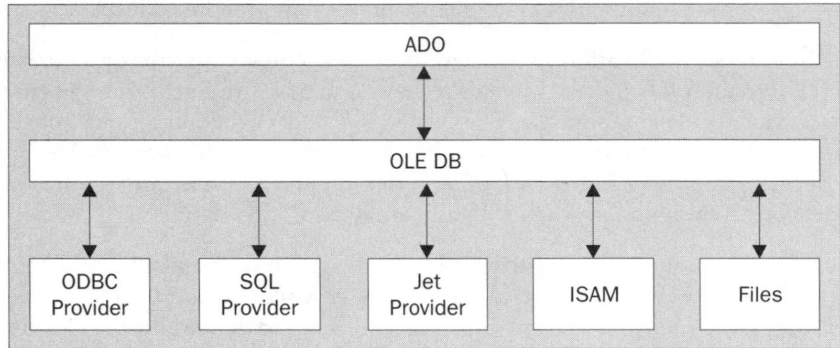

ADO's Strengths and Weaknesses

ADO has stabilized to the point where it is very reliable and supported worldwide. You can easily apply the model to Windows and web applications. As it is supported by all Microsoft products, including Office, anyone with such a product on their system can run ADO applications. It can also be used for displaying or managing data in web pages.

The following list provides a summary of ADO's main weaknesses:

- It's only possible to manage one table or one set of records at a time
- There's no intrinsic support for XML, invaluable when communicating between various environments
- We can't easily create relationships between tables on the fly
- It was designed primarily with a connected architecture in mind
- As communication is based on COM, you are limited to the data types COM supports; a problem for non-Windows platforms
- ADO data types must be translated to their COM counterparts, taking up valuable system time and resources
- COM is known to be problematic when penetrating firewalls

Unfortunately, we do not have the capability of accessing relational, non-relational, or other data sources in a disconnected manner. We have to write many different applications for each level of data access, whether it be for the Internet or for different data stores. Because of the different versions of libraries and sets of code required to access these different technologies, we have a hard time managing our code.

This has led to the situation often referred to as "DLL hell", where applications have to package multiple library components since one won't provide all the required functionality. Versioning problems are rife in this scenario, because applications that support ADO require that the correct runtime libraries are located on the client's computer. Microsoft, being Microsoft, continually updates its libraries with bug fixes and enhancements and, if one application is only compatible with an older version, or a new library is shipped with some other software, problems are going to occur unless that application is rewritten for the new DLL. From the developer's standpoint, several versions have to be maintained and compiled using different methods just to maintain applications.

Ideally, we need to have all these features in one package that encapsulates key ADO and RDS functionality and preferably throws in XML support for communication with diverse platforms, including legacy systems. We also need support for more flexible data types over the Web.

ADO.NET

ADO.NET provides database connectivity between relational and non-relational systems through a common set of components.

It also enables truly disconnected data access. Client-server applications have traditionally had to maintain an open connection to the database while running, or provide their own method of caching data locally, which is impractical for a number of reasons:

- Open database connections take up valuable system resources. In most cases, databases can maintain only a given number of concurrent connections, and the overhead of a large number of connections detracts from overall application performance. In some cases, however, a constant connection may be required, and it may not be desirable or practical to close a connection.
- Applications that require an open database connection are extremely difficult to scale up, so that an application that performs acceptably with 100 users may well not do so with 1000.
- A model based on connected data can make it difficult and impractical to exchange data across application and organizational boundaries. If two components need to share the same data, both have to be connected to the same data source, or a reliable way of passing data back and forth between components must be implemented.

Because of these reasons, ADO.NET was built for a disconnected architecture. Data is read into a component (an object to be precise) called a `DataSet`, which acts as a temporary scratch-pad for data. The `DataSet` holds data even when the connection to the data store is broken and is good for as long as it is in scope. Data in the disconnected `DataSet` can be manipulated by an application before reconnecting to the data store to update it with any changes. Changes are made in an **optimistic approach**. When connection is re-established for an update, original versions of data used to populate the `DataSet` are compared to the data currently held by the server. If someone else has altered the same information in the meantime, an error is generated and the operation rejected.

The ADO.NET `DataSet` uses XML to transfer data. XML is a language that marks up data with customizable tags in a standard manner that allows independent organizations and applications to readily understand each other's data. Standards for XML have been developed by the World Wide Web Consortium (W3C), an independent body established to develop standardized communications protocols. Rather than having XML support as an add-on, as in old-style ADO, XML is built in to the `DataSet`. For more information on ADO.NET and XML, see Chapter 12.

ADO.NET's model bears, not surprisingly, many similarities to that of ADO, so developers conversant with ADO do not face an insurmountable learning curve before getting up to speed with the new syntax.

ADO still exists in the new environment; backwards compatibility is provided by another layer so that developers can slowly convert their existing applications. The optimum approach is to continue to maintain old applications using vanilla ADO, while using ADO.NET for any new applications.

Comparisons to ADO

Apart from its disconnected nature, the other key advantages of ADO.NET over ADO are:

- Whereas ADO.NET uses `DataSets` to hold data, ADO uses the `RecordSet` object. An ADO `RecordSet` represents a single table so, even if you join multiple tables, its view will be of a single table – it is not possible to work with multiple tables at once. The ADO.NET `DataSet`, on the other hand, contains a collection of tables and the relationships between them, so is able to handle a much more complex data structure.
- The ADO.NET `DataSet` provides both a table-based relational view and an XML-based hierarchical view, and either can be used interchangeably. See Chapter 12 for more on this.
- The ADO `RecordSet` stores data in binary format, which can be a problem because firewalls tend to block binary data transfers. XML is a text-based data format, so ADO.NET can transfer data more easily and reliably through firewalls.
- XML also permits an unlimited variety of data types, and incorporates ways to validate that the correct data types are used. Because ADO uses COM as a transportation mechanism, performance can be hindered by translation to and from the limited COM data types.
- With ADO, there was always the problem of having the correct version of MDAC to access your data, but ADO.NET supports side-by-side versions of ADO.NET without having to worry about versioning issues.

ADO.NET Architecture

The main components of ADO.NET are the **.NET Data Providers** and the `DataSet` object. By separating the components that manage the data (Data Providers) from the components that store the data (`DataSets`), we allow for a loosely-coupled flexible system. These components are able to work quite independently from each other. The `DataSet` is able to use the services of the Data Providers to retrieve information. The providers make connections just long enough to retrieve data for the `DataSet`, and then close them.

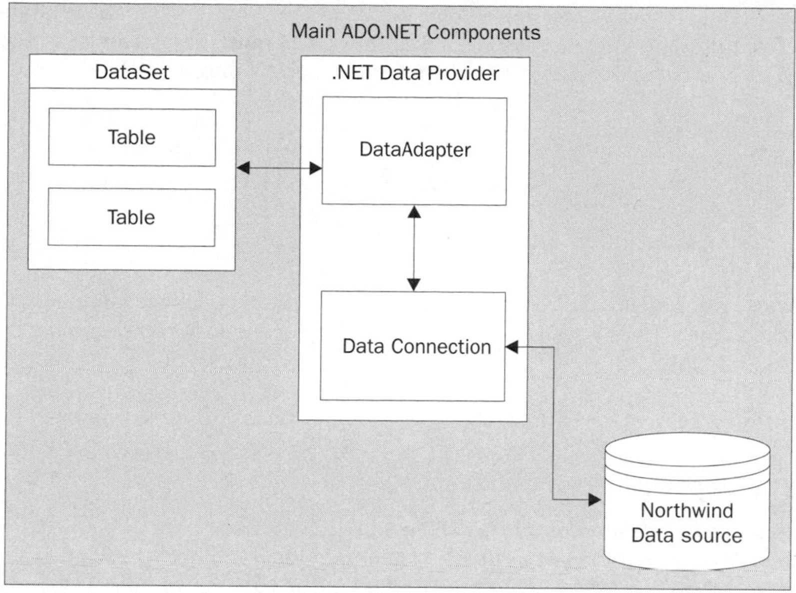

As you can see above, we have our `DataSet`, which is made up of tables. There is also the .NET Data Provider which connects to the database and executes our commands.

The DataSet Object

As mentioned earlier, the `DataSet` is an in-memory representation of data entirely independent of the original data source. It is a disconnected data object, so that once it's filled with data, it will work independently of any other objects and needs no connection to the data source.

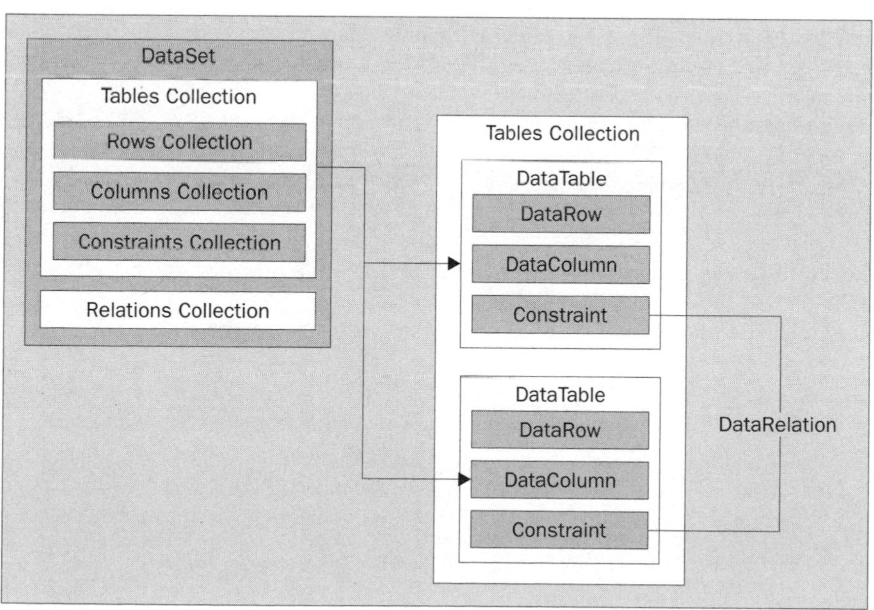

The methods and objects that we use are similar to that of the relational database model. The DataSet is made up of five different types of object: **Tables**, **Rows**, **Columns**, **Constraints**, and **Relations collections**, just as in a database. A DataSet can contain zero or more tables.

Let's look at how to create a new DataSet:

```
Dim myDataSet As DataSet = New DataSet()
' or
Dim myDataSet As DataSet = New DataSet("MyCustomerDataSet")
```

We can create a new instance of a DataSet just by calling the New keyword on our DataSet object. You can pass the name of the DataSet as a parameter if you want. If you don't, the default name of NewDataSet will be used.

DataSets are "filing cabinets" of information that you can access anytime you need to.

The DataTable Object

A DataSet contains a collection of tables as a DataTableCollection. The DataSet stores a reference to this object in its Tables property. Each individual memory-resident table is referred to as a DataTable, and there could be zero or more tables in the collection. DataTables contain rows of data, and each row is made up of columns.

You can create a new DataTable object as follows:

```
Dim myCustomerTable As DataTable = New DataTable()

' or by specifying the name for the DataTable
Dim myCustomerTable As DataTable = New DataTable("CustomersTable")
```

The first line creates a new table without any table name parameter, so that the table name will remain blank. The second line creates a new table but specifies a new table name of CustomersTable.

You can add a new table to a DataSet by the Add method of the DataSet's Tables property:

```
Dim myDataSet As DataSet = New DataSet("MyDataSet")
Dim myCustomerTable As DataTable = myDataSet.Tables.Add("CustomersTable")
```

This code will add a new table called CustomersTable to the new DataSet MyDataSet.

You can add an existing table to a DataSet by passing in a DataTable object:

```
' Create a new DataSet called MyDataSet.
Dim myDataSet As DataSet = New DataSet("MyDataSet")

' Create a new table called MyDataTable.
Dim myDataTable As DataSet = New DataTable("CustomersTable")

' Add the existing table to the DataSet.
Dim myCustomerTable As DataTable = myDataSet.Tables.Add(myDataTable)
```

If you don't specify a table name when adding a new table to a `DataSet`, the default name of `TableN` will be assigned, where `N` starts at one and is incremented by one with each use, producing names such as `Table1`, `Table2`, or `Table8`. It is a good habit to always name your tables yourself, and to choose more descriptive names than `Table1`, `Table2`, and so on. If you try to add a table with the same name as a table already contained by the `DataSet`, an exception is generated.

To reference a particular table by name in the `DataSet`:

```
Dim myCustomerTable As DataTable = myDataSet.Tables("CustomersTable")
```

Note that ADO.NET is case-sensitive, so you can define two tables with the same name but different casing if you want. On the other hand, if each table in the `DataSet` has a unique name, then table references become case-insensitive so you can reference the table using any case you want.

You can reference a particular table by its index in the `DataSet`:

```
Dim myCustomerTable As DataTable = myDataSet.Tables(0)
```

With tables in a `DataSet` the index reference always starts at zero, so this code references the first table. The first table you add to a `DataSet` will be index 0, the second table you add will be index 1, and so on. You may find it better to reference these tables by index rather than their names to help maintainability. Should you change your table names, any developer who reads the code later will not be confused by a table referred to as `Customers` instead of `CustomerBilling` for example. It may be better to leave comments within the code that give the table names used. At the same time, using indexes can make your code that much less readable. If you decide on the table names yourself, be sure to use some sort of standard that will withstand the test of time and avoid confusion in the future. It all depends on how well the code is maintained and kept up to date, and on any standards used within your company. You should also apply these concepts to `DataSets` as well.

To remove a table from a `DataSet`:

```
myDataSet.Tables.Remove("CustomersTable")
' or

Dim myCustomerTable as DataTable = myDataSet.Tables("CustomersTable")
     myDataSet.Tables.Remove(myCustomerTable)
```

This removes the table named `CustomersTable`. We can also remove the table by passing in a `DataTable` object. The `DataSet.Table` property holds a reference to the `DataTableCollection` object as mentioned earlier that lists all contained tables. We can maintain this collection by calling the methods of the object, such as `Add` and `Remove`. These are the only two methods for removing a table from a `DataSet` – you cannot remove it by index.

The DataColumn Object

Before you can add any rows to a table you must define its schema. This is typically created when you create a new `DataSet` by right-clicking on the `DataAdapter` control. The schema defines the structure of the table and, when first created, a table doesn't have any schema associated with it until you add columns to the table. A column is represented by a `DataColumn` object.

You can also call other methods to assign a schema to the table such as the `ReadXmlSchema` or `ReadXml` methods of the `DataAdapter`.

The `DataColumn` is the key to creating a schema of a `DataTable`; by adding columns to a `DataColumn` collection we build a schema. Within our table we have a collection of columns called `DataColumnCollection`. Each collection item will refer to each column name in our table. We can access these column names by referring to the `Columns` property of the `DataTable`.

To view the entire column names in the `DataColumnCollection`, iterate through the collection as you would any other collection:

```
Dim myDataColumn As DataColumn
For Each myDataColumn in myCustomerTable.Columns
    Console.WriteLine(myDataColumn.ColumnName)
Next
```

If we have a table with the column names Address, City, State, and Zip, we would have a corresponding `DataColumnCollection` of these names. We reference these column names by referencing the collection, as we would any other collection object.

To reference a column by name, use the `DataTable`'s `Columns` property specifying the column name:

```
Dim myColumn As DataColumn
myColumn = myCustomerTable.Columns("Address")
```

We can also reference the column by index:

```
Dim myColumn As DataColumn
myColumn = myCustomerTable.Columns(0)
```

This is a zero-based index again. In general, you will find that most indexes are zero-based because that is closer to the internal mechanisms used to access such data types.

To add a new column to a table, use the `Add` method of the table's `Columns` property:

```
Dim myDataSet As DataSet = New DataSet()

' Add one new table...
myDataSet.Tables.Add("CustomersTable")

' Reference the new table...
Dim myCustomerTable as DataTable = myDataSet.Tables("CustomersTable")

' Add an address column to the new table.
myCustomerTable.Columns.Add("Address", Type.GetType("System.String"))
```

You must specify a column name and the type as parameters for the `Add` method. This type can be any .NET Framework type since we are not tied to any one type of data source. In this case, we create a column called `Address` and specify a data type of `String`.

Just like the table object, if you don't specify a column name when adding a new column to a table, the default name of `ColumnN` will be assigned, where `N` is incremented by one to give default names starting with `Column1`.

Primary Keys

Most tables have some type of unique column or combination of columns identifying each row of data, which is called the primary key. This primary key can be used to quickly and easily identify which row of data you want to work with. All database engines are optimized to locate a record quickest when the primary key is given. Primary keys, as unique values for a record, also help enforce data integrity.

You can add a primary key by setting the `AllowDBNull` property of the `DataColumn` to `False` and the `Unique` property to `True`:

```
Dim myColumn As DataColumn = myCustomerTable.Columns.Add("Address",
Type.GetType("System.String"))
myColumn.AllowDBNull = False
myColumn.Unique = True
```

Or you can specify the `PrimaryKey` property of the table object, which accepts an array of one or more `DataColumn` objects.

```
Dim myColumn(1) As DataColumn
myColumn(0) = myCustomerTable.Columns("CustomerID")
myCustomerTable.PrimaryKey = myColumn
```

In the code above, we declare an array with a size of one and use the `ColumnID` column as an identifier. Again, the first array item is referenced by an index of `0` since arrays are zero-based.

If you have a composite key made from multiple fields, you can specify a combination of column names to use for the primary key in the array passed to the `PrimaryKey` property:

```
Dim myColumn(2) As DataColumn
myColumn(0) = myCustomerTable.Columns("CustomerID")
myColumn(1) = myCustomerTable.Columns("PostalCode")
myCustomerTable.PrimaryKey = myColumn
```

We declare an array with a size representing the total number of columns we need to use for our key – in this case two. We then assign each array item with the relevant columns of our table, `CustomerID` and `PostalCode`, both of which are required to make the unique primary key for this hypothetical table.

The DataRow Object

The `DataRow` and `DataColumn` objects make up the `DataTable`. Using these objects' properties and methods, you can view, update, insert, and delete information from the tables. The `DataRow` represents the actual data in the table and is contained within a `DataRowCollection` collection object. Like the `DataColumnCollection`, we can access multiple items within the collection using standard collection methods.

Rows are represented by a collection within the table called `Rows`, so if we wanted to access the first row of data in a table we could do so as shown below, using a zero-based index:

```
myCustomerTable.Rows(0)
```

To view all the items in the DataRow collection, iterate through the collection as follows:

```
CONST ADDRESS_COLUMN As Integer = 2
Dim myDataRow As DataRow
For Each myDataRow in myCustomerTable.Rows
Console.WriteLine(myDataRow(ADDRESS_COLUMN).ToString())
    Console.WriteLine(myDataRow("Address").ToString())' Alternative method
Next
```

This will display the contents of the third column index in the table using the constant ADDRESS_COLUMN. This is another zero-based collection so the first row is zero, the second row one, and so on. We must use a number that represents the index of the column value we are trying to access, or we can use the column name or a column object.

Next we will talk about how to update the rows in our tables. It's important to be aware that, since we are disconnected from the database, changes will not be reflected on the server until we apply them on the database server using the DataAdapter as described later.

To add a new row to a table, use the NewRow method which creates a new empty DataRow object with the same schema as the table. Bear in mind that this new row is not associated with the table at all at this point, it just has the same characteristics. Once you have created a new DataRow object, you can assign the field values, and add the new object to your table using the Add method of the table's Rows property, passing in the DataRow object as the parameter.

```
' Create a new row.
Dim myRow As DataRow
myRow = myCustomerTable.NewRow()

' Set the field values.
myRow("Address") = "100 Elm Street"
myRow("City") = "Sacramento"
myRow("PostalCode") = "95825"

' Add the new row to the collection.
myCustomerTable.Rows.Add(myRow)
```

Every DataRow has a RowState property indicating the state of that row. State is examined in more detail in the next section. We can check the state of a row before performing any operations on it to ensure that it meets any conditions we may have. This line will output the current state of the first row in our table:

```
Console.WriteLine("My Row State is " &
myCustomerTable.Rows(0).RowState.ToString())
```

To access an individual column, use the Item property of the DataRow. We can use an index value, column name, or column object to access the column as shown:

```
Dim myRowNumber As Integer = 0
Dim myColumnNumber As Integer = 2

myCustomerTable.Rows(myRowNumber).Item(myColumnNumber)
' or...
```

```
myCustomerTable.Rows(myRowNumber).Item("Address")
' or...
Dim AddressColumn As DataColumn
AddressColumn =
myCustomerTable.Columns("Address")myCustomerTable.Rows(myRowNumber).Item(AddressCo
lumn)
```

We can also access the column by using the column name as a parameter of the `DataRow` we are looking at. This is the preferred method of referencing a row:

```
Dim myRow as DataRow = myCustomerTable.Rows(0)
MessageBox.Show(myRow("Address"))
```

Here we are looking at the first row in the table, `Rows(0)`, and assigning it to a `DataRow` object. Once we have the `DataRow`, we can display the contents of the required column by passing in its name, which here is `"Address"`.

Row States

Row states have an important role to play in determining which rows are to be updated. A row can have various states. Typically, when you modify a record, the corresponding row is flagged as modified, allowing you to review changes before actually committing them by calling the table's `AcceptChanges` method. This method is available for `DataSet`, `DataTable`, and `DataRow` objects and simply places each altered object's `RowState` back to the normal unedited value. This will commit all the changes you have made since the last `AcceptChanges` method was called for the table you're working with. We can also call this method on an individual row as well as an entire table or `DataSet`.

Here is a list of the `RowState` values available:

`RowState` Value	Description
`Unchanged`	Indicates that the row has not changed since `AcceptChanges` was last called.
`Added`	A new row has been added and `AcceptChanges` has not yet been called.
`Modified`	The row has been changed and `AcceptChanges` has not yet been called.
`Deleted`	The row has been deleted and `AcceptChanges` has not yet been called.

Once a row is `Added` or `Modified` and `AcceptChanges` is called, the `RowState` property is returned to the `Unchanged` state. If a row is marked `Deleted` then those rows will be deleted when the table's `AcceptChanges` method is called.

In the next diagram, when the user modifies the `Address` column in the `DataTable` called `myTable`, the `RowState` changes from `UnChanged` to `Modified`. The user can continue to modify other columns and rows and, as they do, the corresponding `RowState` will change to reflect the action performed on each row. In Step 3), they click the **Save** button and thus call the `AcceptChanges` method of our `DataTable`. The `RowState` value of every row in the table is then checked to see if it is anything other than `UnChanged`. When a `Modified` or `Added` row is discovered, the `RowState` is simply set back to `UnChanged`. If a `Deleted` row is found, then it will delete the row (but only locally in the `DataSet`) and change `RowState` back to `UnChanged`. Note that we are still not connected to any outside data source, such as SQL Server, and all work here is performed in the client application.

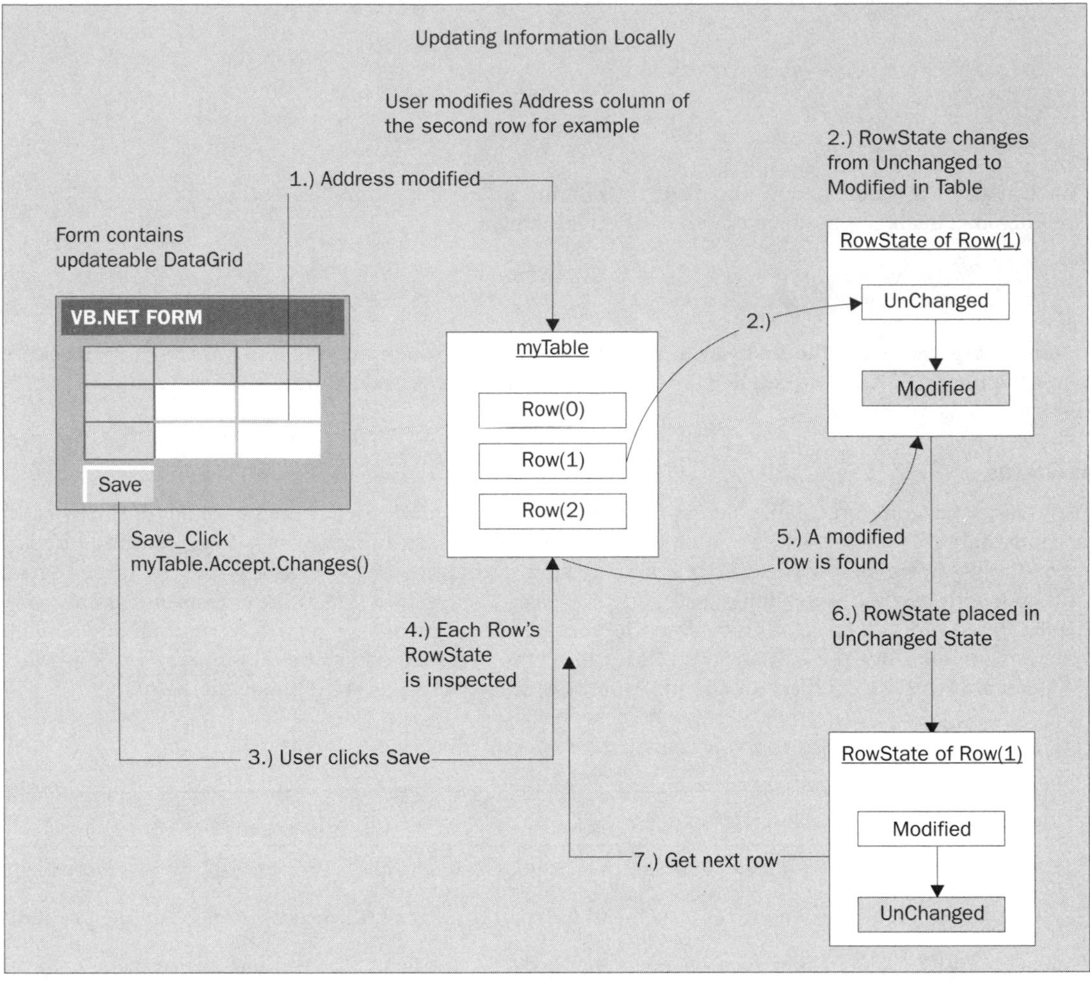

If we need to modify an existing row, access the row and column and assign the new value:

```
Dim myRow As DataRow = myCustomerTable.Rows(0)
myRow("Address") = "200 Elm Street"
myCustomerTable.AcceptChanges()
```

In this example, we access the first row of data (row 0) and update the `Address` field with new details. Once this new value is assigned, the `RowState` changes to `Modified`. Calling the `AcceptChanges` method reverts the `RowState` property to a value of `Unchanged`.

> **Please note that these methods only update the local `DataSet` tables and are *not* reflected on the database server. You must explicitly post your changes to the server using the Data Adapter.**

Updating many rows at a time can hinder performance since it causes events to fire at each step. You can temporarily suspend these events by using the `BeginEdit` method while you make any necessary changes and ensure all appropriate or missing data is provided. This also disables any constraints, which we talk about later, that may be set for the table. When you're finished with your modifications, you must call the `EndEdit` method, or the `CancelEdit` method to undo changes and place the row back in its normal state. Internally, `AcceptChanges` calls the `EndEdit` method itself. By committing updates all at once at the end, you inhibit any validation checks until all your operations are complete.

Here is an example of using `BeginEdit` and `EndEdit`:

```
' Get the first row.
Dim myFirstRow as DataRow = myCustomerTable.Rows(0)

' Edit the first row.
myFirstRow.BeginEdit()
myFirstRow("PostalCode") = "90210"
myFirstRow.EndEdit()
```

In this example, we call `BeginEdit` to suspend the state of the row while we assign a new value to the `PostalCode` column. Even though we have modified the column, its `RowState` remains `UnChanged` because of the `BeginEdit` call. It's not until we then call `EndEdit` that the `RowState` for this row is changed to `Modified`. Of course, even then, until we call `AcceptChanges` on the `DataSet`, or a particular table or row, none of these changes will be committed. The `AcceptChanges` call restores the `RowState` property to `UnChanged`.

Alternatively, you can omit the explicit `EndEdit` call, and just call `AcceptChanges` on the `DataSet`, table, or row, which implicitly calls `EndEdit` on all rows that were placed in edit mode with `BeginEdit`:

```
' Get the first row.
Dim myFirstRow as DataRow = myCustomerTable.Rows(0)
' Get the second row.
Dim mySecondRow as DataRow = myCustomerTable.Rows(1)

' Edit the first row.
myFirstRow.BeginEdit()
myFirstRow("PostalCode") = "90210"

' Edit the second row.
mySecondRow.BeginEdit()
mySecondRow("PostalCode") = "90210"

' Save changes for each row modified.
myFirstRow.AcceptChanges()
mySecondRow.AcceptChanges()

' Or

' Save all changes in the table.
myCustomerTable.AcceptChanges()

' Or

' Save changes in all the DataSet.
myDataSet.AcceptChanges()
```

We can also call CancelEdit on a row to take it out of the BeginEdit state. In the previous example, if we call myFirstRow.CancelUpdate or mySecondRow.CancelUpdate before the AcceptChanges call, then those rows will not be updated. You must call CancelEdit before any call to EndEdit.

While the DataRow is in this BeginEdit state, all new changes to a row are stored separately to the original values in what are known as the **proposed version** and the **original version**, respectively. When you call EndEdit, the original values in the database are replaced by the values in the proposed version. The values contained by these versions can be accessed by passing DataRowVersion.Original or DataRowVersion.Proposed as parameters to the Item property of the DataRow. This is handy when you want to validate new information provided by the user before saving in the database.

```
Dim myFirstRow As DataRow = myCustomerTable.Rows(0)

' Edit the PostalCode of the first row.
myFirstRow.BeginEdit
myFirstRow("PostalCode") = "90210"
```

```
' Get the first row.
Dim myRow as DataRow = myCustomerTable.Rows(0)
' Review original and proposed values of the first row.
If myRow.HasVersion(DataRowVersion.Proposed) = True Then
    Console.WriteLine(myRow("PostalCode", DataRowVersion.Original))
    Console.WriteLine(myRow("PostalCode", DataRowVersion.Proposed))
End If

' Save all changes, returns RowState back to normal.
myCustomerTable.AcceptChanges()
```

If you don't call AcceptChanges or EndEdit, RowState will remain as Modified.

To delete a row in a table, call the Delete method of the DataRowCollection. This will mark the row for deletion, and is the primary method for deleting rows:

```
Dim myRow As DataRow = myCustomerTable.Rows(0)
myRow.Delete()

myCustomerTable.AcceptChanges()
```

This deletes the first row in the table. Once you call Delete, the DataRow's RowState is changed to Deleted, and you must call the table's AcceptChanges method to actually delete the row and move up all other rows to fill in the vacated space.

You can call the RejectChanges method of the DataRow to restore a row that has been marked as Deleted. Like AcceptChanges, this method is also supported by entire DataSets and DataTables.

```
Dim myRow As DataRow = myCustomerTable.Rows(0)
myRow.Delete()
myRow.RejectChanges()
```

In this code snippet, we take a row from our table (the first row) and assign it to a DataRow object called myRow. We then call the Delete method of the collection, marking the row for deletion. We can now use the table's RejectChanges method should we decide not to delete the specified row, assuming that you haven't already called the AcceptChanges method.

The Remove method on the other hand removes a row from a table as if it never existed, and takes a DataRow object as the single argument. Unlike the Delete method, which marks the row for deletion, Remove actually deletes the row from the DataRowCollection but doesn't affect the database. There is no need to call AcceptChanges with this method since removal of the record is immediate, and once you remove a row in this way, the only way to get it back is to refresh the DataSet using the Fill method (RejectChanges won't work).

```
Dim myRow As DataRow = myCustomerTable.Rows(2)
myCustomerTable.Rows.Remove(myRow)
```

In this case, the third row in the table was removed (don't forget that zero-based index!).

The diagram below shows what our table looks like internally. We have rows on the left and a column along the top for each field name in the table, here Customer, Address, Region, and PostalCode. Each row contains the data pertaining to a particular record; the first row has Bill, 100 Elm Street, Los Angeles, and 90210:

DataTable				
	Column(0)	Column(1)	Column(2)	Column(3)
	Customer	Address	Region	PostalCode
Row(0)	Bill	100 Elm Street	Los Angeles	90210
Row(1)	Paul	1215 Jackson Rd	Phoenix	85523
Row(2)	Kate	998 Boardwalk	Redwood City	96125
Row(3)	Rob	223 Rocky Rd	Colorado	95516
Row(4)	Laura	4120 Williby	Lake Placid	85678

Now is a good time to quickly recap some of the methods we have discussed:

Method Name	Description
AcceptChanges	Removes any rows where the RowState is marked as Deleted. Sets any rows where RowState is Modified or Added to UnChanged. Also calls EndEdit on any rows that may have been edited with BeginEdit but had no explicit EndEdit. Applies to DataSet, DataTable, and DataRow objects.
RejectChanges	This method calls CancelEdit. Any row that has a RowState of Modified or Deleted will be changed to UnChanged. If a row has a RowState of Added then the row will be removed. Can be called after EndEdit method but before any AcceptChanges method is called. Applies to DataSet, DataTable, and DataRow objects.
Delete	Marks a row for deletion by setting RowState to Deleted. Rows are deleted when AcceptChanges is next called. Call RejectChanges to return the RowState to UnChanged. Applies to DataRow objects.

Table continued on following page

Method Name	Description
Remove	Removes a row from the DataRowCollection. You cannot retrieve the row without repopulating your table. Doesn't commit changes to the database during an Update call.
BeginEdit	Places a DataRow in edit mode. Suspends any event triggering until EndEdit is called. Applies only to DataRow objects.
EndEdit	Ends the suspended edit mode for a row and resumes event triggering.
CancelEdit	Takes a row out of edit mode. Can only be called if EndEdit hasn't yet been called.

The DataRelation Object

You can relate one column to another column in a separate table through what's known as a DataRelation. All relations within a DataSet are kept in a DataRelationCollection, which maintains all child and parent relations.

If we had two tables, a customer table and an order table, and both contain a CustomerID column, we could relate the two to show the customer's orders along with their other details. The Customer table would be the parent and the Orders table would be the child. If you cast your mind back to Chapter 1 where normalization was discussed, this arrangement allows several orders per customer, but any order is uniquely linked to just one particular customer.

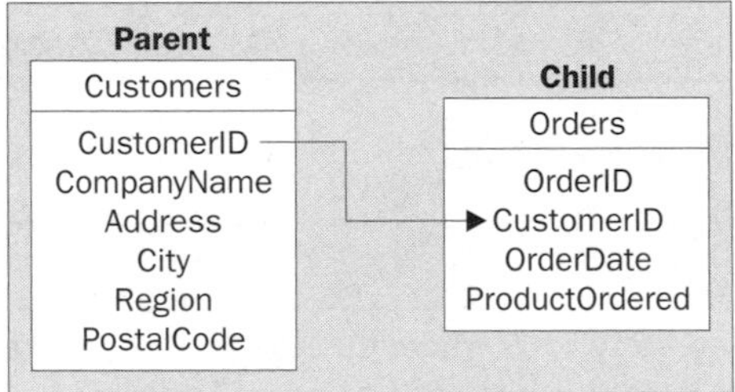

Relationships may only be created between matching columns in the parent and child tables, so the column in each table must contain identical data types – if the parent column is an integer, then the child column must also be an integer.

Below, we reference two columns: the first column is the CustomerID field in the Customers table; the second is also called CustomerID but this is in the Orders table. We assign these to a DataColumn object since that is what a DataRelation object needs to create a relation. The field names don't have to be the same, just as long as the data types are the same type. Next we create a DataRelation object passing in the parent and child DataColumn object as properties. We give the DataRelation the name CustomerOrders, and we finally call Add to add the relationship to the relationship collection of the DataSet.

```
Dim parentColumn As DataColumn
Dim childColumn As DataColumn
```

```
' Get DataColumn objects.
parentColumn = myDataSet.Tables("Customers").Columns("CustomerID")
childColumn = myDataSet.Tables("Orders").Columns("CustomerID")

' Create DataRelation.
Dim relCustomerOrders As DataRelation
relCustomerOrders = New DataRelation("CustomersOrders", parentColumn, childColumn)

' Add the relation to the DataSet.
myDataSet.Relations.Add(relCustomerOrders)
```

Now when we display a particular customer, let's say a customer with a `CustomerID` of `1001`, all records from the `Orders` table with a `CustomerID` of `1001` will show as well. We have essentially linked the two tables together.

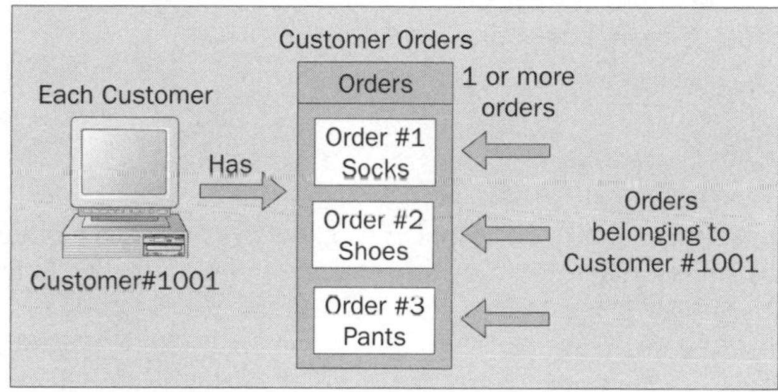

We can add as many relationships as we want to the `DataSet`, as they are kept in a collection which has no size limit.

The Constraints Object

Constraints help to enforce data integrity and specify what action to take when records are updated or deleted. A table has what's called a `ConstraintCollection` that can hold two types of constraints, `UniqueConstraints` and `ForeignKeyConstraints`. A customer table usually has a value – the primary key – uniquely identifying each customer. To ensure this stays unique you assign the field a `UniqueConstraint` ensuring that any value given for the column is unique. If you try to assign a non-unique value, an exception will be thrown. You can turn these constraints on or off by changing the `EnforceConstraints` property to `True` or `False` respectively. Most constraints are set on the server by the DBA, and are often in stored procedures.

You can cascade changes down to the child from the parent by adding different constraints to the `ConstraintsCollection` such as a `ForeignKeyConstraint`. `ForeignKeyConstraints` control what action is taken when a column item is updated or deleted in the parent table, so when a parent row is deleted for example, you may choose to also delete the child row, or to set the child column value to `Null` or some default value, or to generate an exception, depending on your business requirements.

Here is an example of setting up a `ForeignKeyConstraint`:

```
Dim myFkey As ForeignKeyConstraint

Dim parentColumn As DataColumn
Dim childColumn As DataColumn

' Set parent and child column variables.
parentColumn = myDataSet.Tables("Customers").Columns("CustomerID")
childColumn = myDataSet.Tables("Orders").Columns("CustomerID")

' Create a new foreign constraint.
myFkey = New ForeignKeyConstraint("CustomerFKConstraint", parentColumn,
childColumn)

' Set Null values when a value is deleted.
myFkey.DeleteRule = Rule.Cascade
myFkey.UpdateRule = Rule.Cascade
myFkey.AcceptRejectRule = AcceptRejectRule.Cascade

' Add the constraint, and set EnforceConstraints to true.
myDataSet.Tables("Customers").Constraints.Add(myFkey)
myDataSet.EnforceConstraints = True
```

To start with, we declare a `ForeignKeyConstraint` called `myFKey`, and a parent and child `DataColumn` object. These `DataColumns` point to the `CustomerID` column in each table, in this case `Customer` and `Suppliers`. We then instantiate a new `ForeignKeyConstraint` by passing in a constraint name, and the parent and child columns. We set up the `DeleteRule` that specifies how to handle the child table when a parent row is deleted. Here, we are using `Rule.Cascade`, the default rule, which means delete all related rows. We also set the `UpdateRule` to specify what is to happen in the case of an update to the parent row. Again, we use `Rule.Cascade` so that any child rows are updated to match.

Here are the rules available for the `DeleteRule` and `UpdateRule` properties of a `ForeignKeyConstraint`:

Rule	Description
`Cascade` (Default)	Deletes or updates all child rows that contain the parent column value
`SetDefault`	All child rows that contain the parent column value are set to the default row value
`SetNull`	All child rows that contain the parent column value are set to `Null`
`None`	No action is taken with the child rows

The `AcceptRejectRule` is invoked any time the `AcceptChanges` or `RejectChanges` method of a `DataSet`, `DataTable`, or `DataRow` is called. There are only two rules for this property, `Rule.Cascade` or `Rule.None`, and the default is `Rule.None`. Once we set these properties in the preceding code sample, we add the constraint to the `ConstraintCollection` of our `DataSet`. Finally, we set the `EnforceConstraints` property to `True` to enable the constraints.

We can also add a `UniqueConstraint` to the `ConstraintCollection` to ensure that the primary key of a column is unique. This is a very similar process to setting the primary key shown earlier.

```
' Declare a ConstraintCollection.
Dim myCKey As ConstraintCollection

Dim myColumn As DataColumn

' Get the column we want to place a unique constraint on.
myColumn = myDataSet.Tables("Customers").Columns("CustomerID")

' Add the constraint to the constraint collection.
myCKey.Add("MyConstraint", myColumn, True)

' Add the constraint collection to the table's constraint collection.
myDataSet.Tables("Customers").Constraints.Add(mCKey)
```

This code starts with declarations for a `ConstraintCollection` and a `DataColumn` object to hold the column we want to set the constraint for (in this case the `CustomerID` column). We use the `Add` method of the `ConstraintCollection`, passing in the name of a constraint, the `DataColumn` object, and a Boolean parameter indicating if this is a primary key. We then call the `Add` method of the `Tables.Constraints` property and pass in the `ConstraintCollection` object.

There are many objects that work together to make up the `DataSet` object. They all work hand in hand to build the tables' schema as well as manage the data.

Next we will see how to save changes that are made to a `DataSet` on the server.

Updating the Database

Once changes are made to a `DataSet` how do we update those changes back to the database? Earlier we showed how calling the `AcceptChanges` method updates only local records and not the database proper. These methods we use next assume you haven't called `AcceptChanges` on any of your modified records before you post changes to the server. We have a couple of methods for updating our database. To update a `DataSet` call the `Update` method of the `DataAdapter`. This can take a `DataSet`, `DataTables`, or an array of `DataRow` objects, and examines the `RowState` property to determine which rows have changed. Then `Insert`, `Update`, or `Delete` is executed depending on the state of the changed row.

When you call a `DataAdapter`'s `Update` method, you update your changes on the server. As you can see from the illustration overleaf, we follow a similar process as with the `AcceptChanges` method:

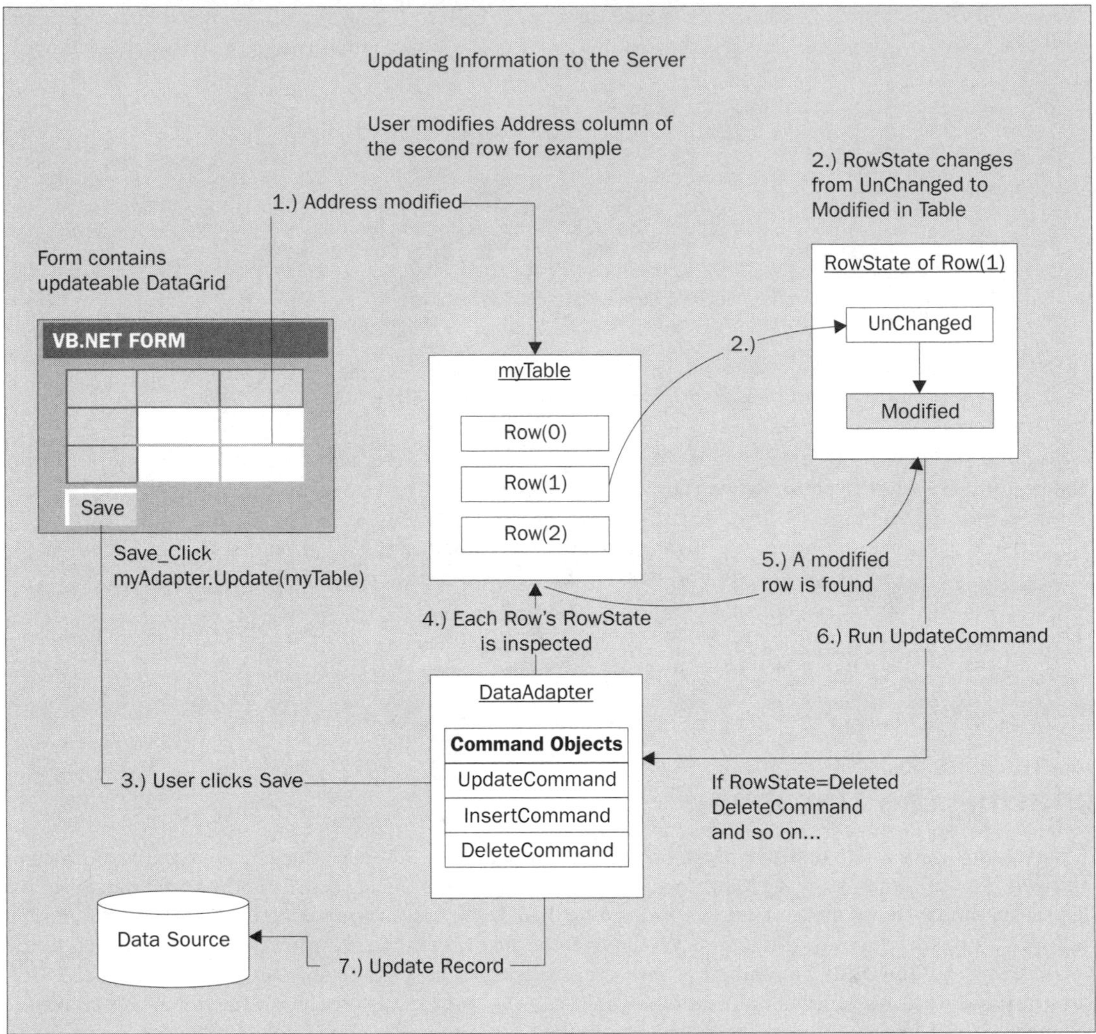

In the above diagram, when the user modifies the `Address` column in the `DataTable` called `myTable`, the `RowState` changes from `UnChanged` to `Modified`. The user can keep modifying other columns and other rows and, as they do, the `RowState` will change depending on what they did to the row. When they click on the Save button, which contains a `DataAdapter` called `myAdapter`, the `Update` method of the `DataAdapter` is called and the `DataTables` object, `myTable`, is passed as a parameter. The `DataAdapter` inspects all the rows of that table to see if any `RowState` values are anything other than `UnChanged`. When the `DataAdapter` discovers, in this case, a `Modified` row, the `UpdateCommand` is performed with the values of the modified row. The data source gets updated and the next row in the table is inspected until all the rows have been evaluated. Also note that, as an action is performed on a row, the `RowState` is changed back to `UnChanged`. If the `DataAdapter` discovers an `Added` or `Deleted` `RowState`, then it will run the corresponding `InsertCommand` or `DeleteCommand` object.

We can control which updates are completed first if we need to. By default, the `DataAdapter` will update each row depending on its order, one row could be deleted and the row after it added. We can use the `GetChanges` method of a `DataSet` or `DataTable` to control which updates we want to occur first. `GetChanges` returns a `DataSet` containing changes that match the `RowState` parameter you specify, thus allowing us to retrieve only records marked as modified, deleted, or inserted, as the code below shows:

```
Dim myDataSetChanges As New DataSet()

' Gets all changes.
myDataSetChanges = myCustomerDataSet.GetChanges()

' Get records that have been modified only.
myDataSetChanges = myCustomerDataSet.GetChanges(DataRowState.Modified)

' Get records that have been deleted only.
myDataSetChanges = myCustomerDataSet.GetChanges(DataRowState.Deleted)

' Get records that have been added only.
myDataSetChanges = myCustomerDataSet.GetChanges(DataRowState.Inserted)

' Update changes back to actual database.
myDataAdapter.Update(myDataSetChanges)
```

Once we have a `DataSet` with only records that have changed, we call the `DataAdapter`'s `Update` method passing in this `DataSet` as shown above.

This allows you to perform updates where you have **referential integrity**. Let's say you have a Customer table and an Address table and the Address table contains the primary key of the customer. You would want to delete the addresses before the customer otherwise you could experience an error. If we were to delete the customer first, we would have a record that points to another record that doesn't exist. This would leave "orphaned" records in the database that referential integrity prohibits.

A related method is the `Merge` method, which merges one `DataSet` into another keeping all the original `DataSet`'s row state information:

```
' Create a new dataset with only the modified records.
Dim myDataSetChanges As New DataSet()
myDataSetChanges = myCustomerDataSet.GetChanges(DataRowState.Modified)

' Merge the changes back into our local dataset.
myNewDataSet.Merge(myDataSet)

' Commit the changes.
myNewDataSet.AcceptChanges()
```

When we call the `Merge` method passing in `myDataSet`, any records in the `DataSet` are added to `myNewDataSet` that now has the records that were in `myDataSet` along with the row state information of each record. This is useful when we get data from an outside source or a source not part of our system that we want to merge into our current set of data. Once we call the `AcceptChanges` method of `myNewDataSet`, we no longer have a modified `RowState` and we lose any changes we may have had.

As a final note, you must ensure you have updated your changes back to the database by calling the `Update` method of your `DataAdapter`, otherwise the changes will be lost. This must be done before the `AcceptChanges` method is called since `AcceptChanges` clears any and all row states. The `Update` needs the row state information to determine which records need updating.

DataSet Sample

Next, we will expand the customer application created in the last chapter to add the capability to insert, update, and delete data. As it currently stands, our application provides a read-only view of the database. This is only a quick sample: we will develop a more complex application in later chapters.

Here is what our final result will look like:

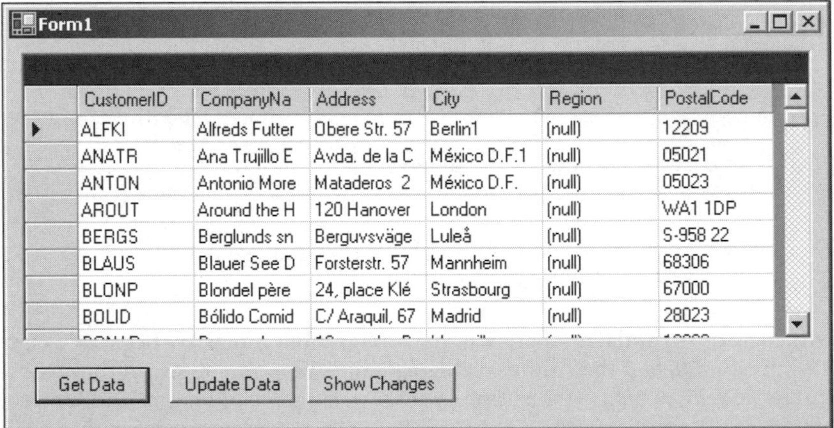

Try It Out – Reconfiguring the DataAdapters

1. Open the project from the previous chapter called **CustomerApp**.

We need to reconfigure the data adapter for our customer table so we can perform `Insert`, `Update`, and `Delete` commands on the table. Right-click on `SqlDataAdpter1` and select Configure Data Adapter.

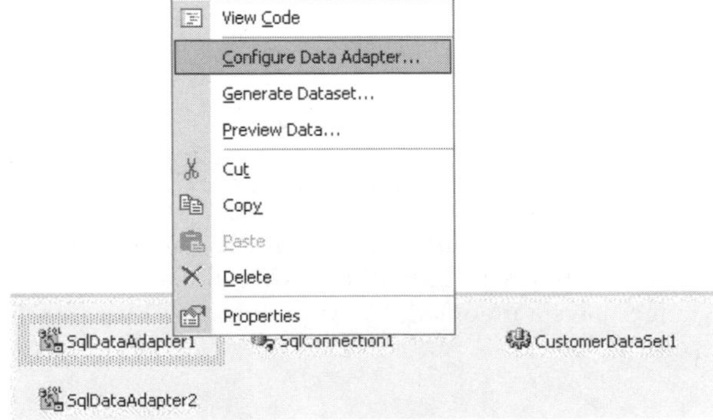

2. The Data Adapter Configuration Wizard dialog will appear prompting for a connection to a database. The name of our previous connection should appear which will be listed as Servername.Northwind SQL.dbo where Servername is the name of your particular computer. If the connection doesn't appear, create a new connection by clicking on the New Connection button.

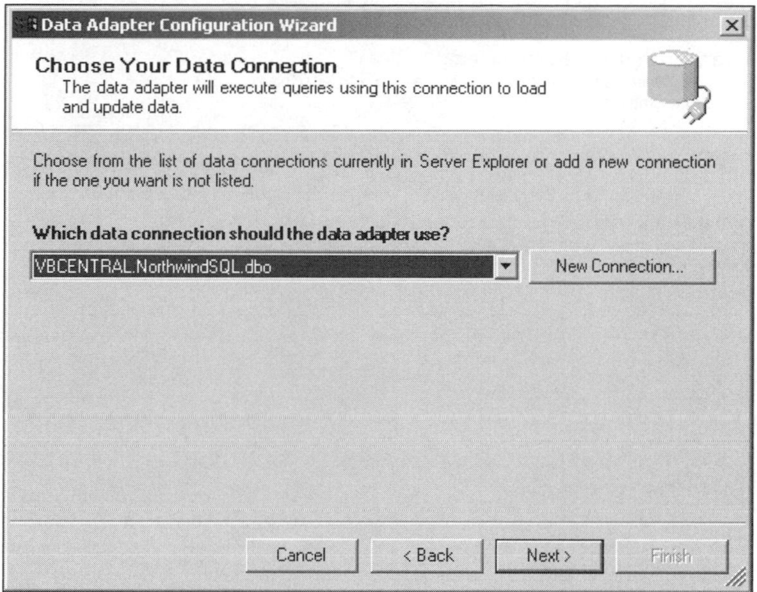

Click Next when you're finished.

3. The Use SQL statements option should already be selected. Ensure that it is and click Next:

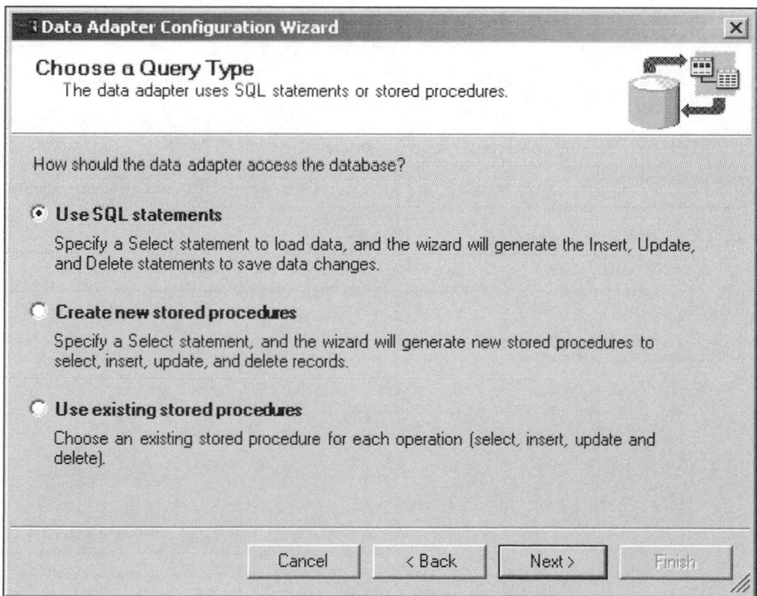

4. The existing SQL SELECT statement should appear on the next pop-up window. As we are now going to insert, update, and delete records, we want to enable the wizard's automatic generation of INSERT, UPDATE, and DELETE commands. Click the Advanced Options button:

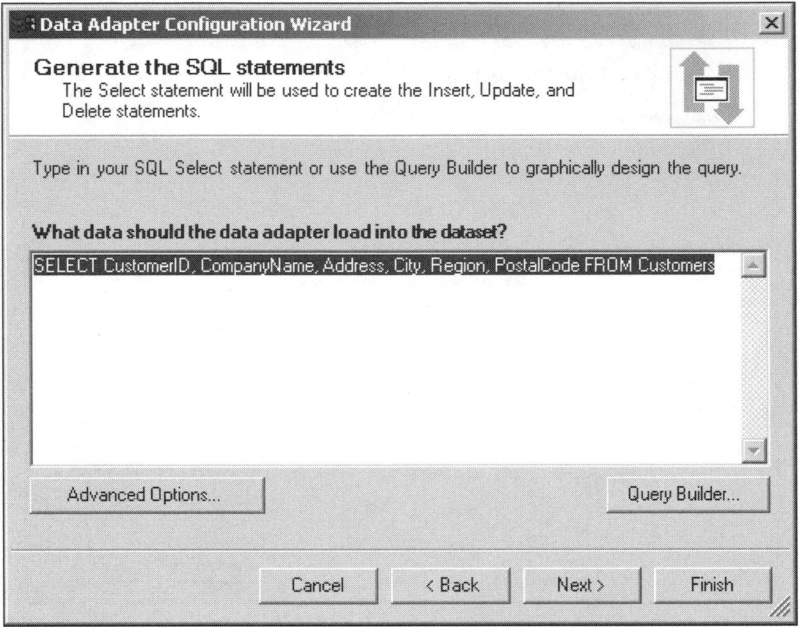

5. The advanced dialog gives us three options. Select the first checkbox, which will enable the rest of the checkboxes. We want all of the options selected. Click OK when you're finished:

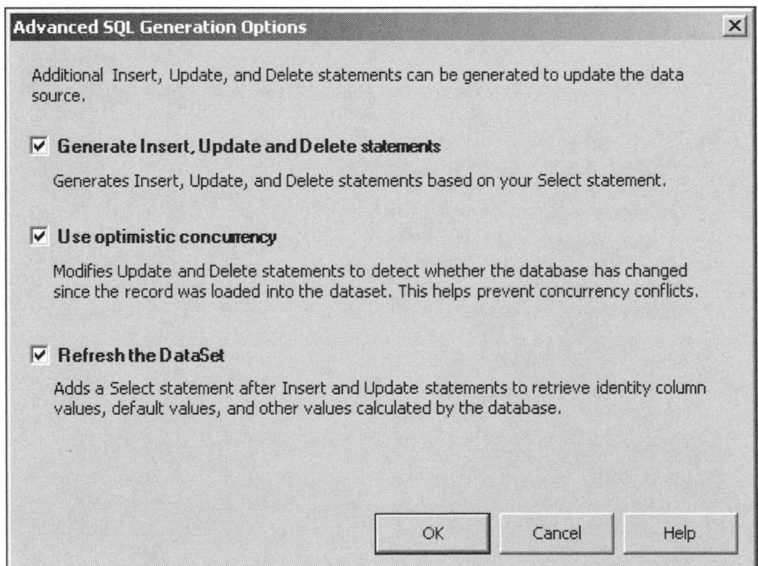

Review the SELECT statement on the next screen and click Next.

6. The last screen to be shown is a review of what will be built, and it should indicate that we are going to generate INSERT, UPDATE, and DELETE statements. Click the Finish button:

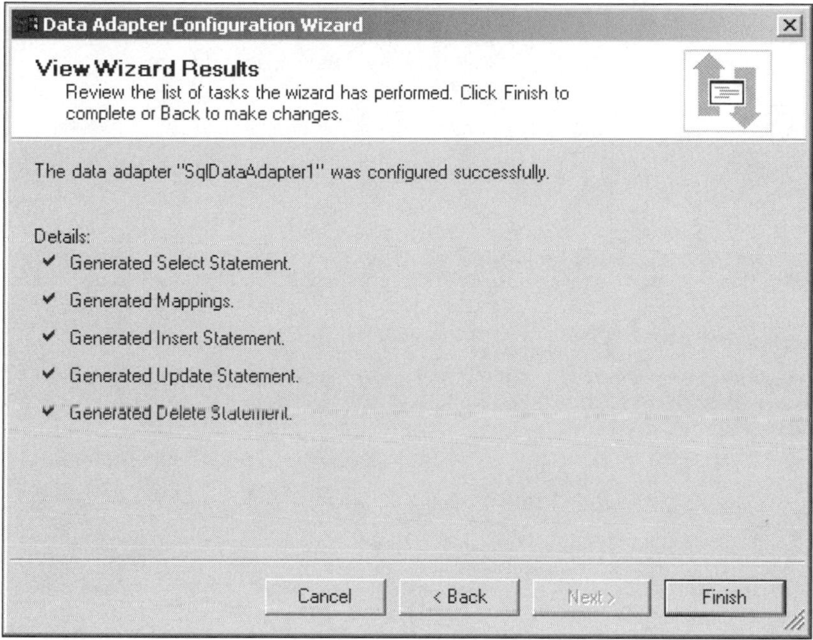

7. Repeat the above steps for the second data adapter, SqlDataAdapter2, so that we will be able to make changes to the Suppliers table.

Try It Out – Update

1. Add a new button to the form and call it btnUpdateData. Set the Text property to Update. Add one more button to the form and call it btnShowChanges. Set its Text property to Show Changes.

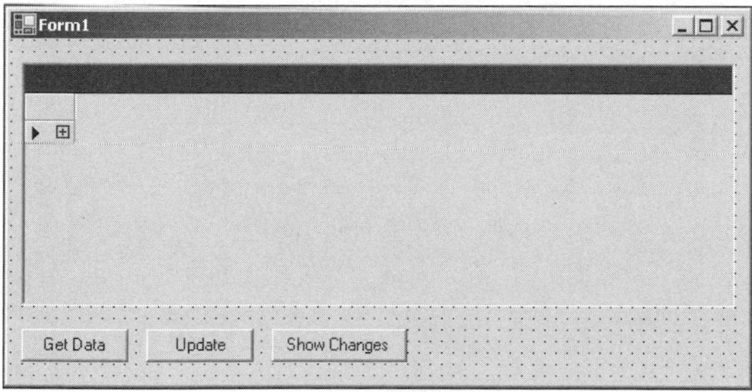

2. The Update button we added will be used to update any changes we have made to the records in our `DataGrid`. The Show Changes button will show us any changes we have made to the data.

   Add some code to the click event of the Update button by double-clicking on the button:

```
Private Sub btnUpdateData_Click(ByVal sender As System.Object, _
                                ByVal e As System.EventArgs) _
                                Handles btnUpdateData.Click

        Dim RecordsUpdated As Integer

        If CustomerDataSet1.HasChanges Then

            ' Update any customer table changes.
            RecordsUpdated = SqlDataAdapter1.Update(CustomerDataSet1)
            MessageBox.Show(RecordsUpdated.ToString & " customer record(s)
updated.")

            ' Update any supplier table changes.
            RecordsUpdated = SqlDataAdapter2.Update(CustomerDataSet1)
            MessageBox.Show(RecordsUpdated.ToString & " supplier record(s)
updated.")

            ' Refresh the grid.
            btnGetData_Click(sender, e)
        Else
            MessageBox.Show("There are no changed records to update.")
        End If
End Sub
```

3. Add some code to the click event of the Show Changes button by double-clicking on the button.

```
Private Sub btnShowChanges_Click(ByVal sender As System.Object, _
                                 ByVal e As System.EventArgs) _
                                 Handles btnShowChanges.Click

        ' Make sure we have changes to show.
        If CustomerDataSet1.HasChanges = False Then
            MessageBox.Show("There are no changed records to show.")
            Exit Sub
        End If

        ' Create a dataset with all changes.
        Dim myDataSet As New DataSet()
        myDataSet = CustomerDataSet1.GetChanges()

        ' Make sure we have no errors.
        If myDataSet.HasErrors = 0 Then

                ' Show only the changed records.
                DataGrid1.DataSource = Nothing
                DataGrid1.DataSource = myDataSet
        End If

End Sub
```

4. Add some code to rebind the `DataSource` to our original `DataSet` and to expand the rows:

```
Private Sub btnGetData_Click(ByVal sender As System.Object, _
                             ByVal e As System.EventArgs) _
                             Handles btnGetData.Click

        ' If connection isn't open then open it.
        If SqlConnection1.State <> ConnectionState.Open Then SqlConnection1.Open()

        ' Fill our customer table.
        SqlDataAdapter1.Fill(CustomerDataSet1)
        ' Fill our suppliers table.
        SqlDataAdapter2.Fill(CustomerDataSet1)

        ' If connection isn't closed then close it.
        If SqlConnection1.State <> ConnectionState.Closed Then
           SqlConnection1.Close()
        End If

        ' Rebind data source in case it's not bound to original dataset.
        DataGrid1.DataSource = Nothing
        DataGrid1.DataSource = CustomerDataSet1

        ' Expand all the child rows.
        DataGrid1.Expand(-1)

End Sub
```

How It Works

First let's look at the code we added under the **Update** button. We start by checking to see if the `CustomerDataSet1` `DataSet` has any changes in any of the tables that it contains and, if there are any changes, we update the database server by calling the `Update` method of both `DataAdapters`. If there are no changes, then these methods won't be called.

```
        If CustomerDataSet1.HasChanges Then

            ' Update any customer table changes.
            RecordsUpdated = SqlDataAdapter1.Update(CustomerDataSet1)
```

We show the number of records updated by passing back the result from the `Update` method.

```
            MessageBox.Show(RecordsUpdated.ToString & " customer record(s)
updated.")
```

The same goes for the supplier table; we call the `Update` method of `SqlDataAdapter2` and display the number of records as well.

```
            ' Update any supplier table changes.
            RecordsUpdated = SqlDataAdapter2.Update(CustomerDataSet1)
            MessageBox.Show(RecordsUpdated.ToString & " supplier record(s)
updated.")
```

Once we update any changes, we refresh the DataGrid by calling the **Get Data** button's click method:

```
' Refresh the grid.
btnGetData_Click(sender, e)
```

Now let's see the code behind the **Show Changes** button in the btnShowChanges_click event that shows only changed records:

```
' Make sure we have changes to show.
If CustomerDataSet1.HasChanges = False Then
    MessageBox.Show("There are no changed records to show.")
    Exit Sub
End If

' Create a dataset with all changes.
Dim myDataSet As New DataSet()
myDataSet = CustomerDataSet1.GetChanges()

' Make sure we have no errors.
If myDataSet.HasErrors = 0 Then

    ' Show only the changed records.
    DataGrid1.DataSource = Nothing
    DataGrid1.DataSource = myDataSet

End If
```

First we check to see if there are any changes in our DataSet, CustomerDataSet1, and display a message box to the user indicating that no changes have been made if that is the case. When we show our changed records in the DataGrid, we are binding it to a DataSet that contains just the changed records. We do this by calling the GetChanges method of our customer DataSet. This method returns a new DataSet with only changed records; we then verify that it doesn't contain any errors by checking the HasErrors property. The HasErrors property can be used for DataRow, DataTable, and DataSet objects, so you are not limited to just checking errors for whole DataSets. As long as there are no errors, we display the contents of the changed DataSet, myDataSet, in the DataGrid. We then call the Expand method of DataGrid1 to display any child rows. Once you view the changed records, you can click the **Update** button to save the changes to the database. If you don't click the **Update** button but instead click the **Get Data** button, the DataGrid is refreshed with a new DataSet and, as a result, any changes that you may have made will be lost.

Lastly, we added code in the **Get Data** button. To view our original DataSet we have to re-assign the original DataSet, CustomerDataSet1, back to the DataGrid. We first set the DataSource to Nothing to clear any existing DataSource.

```
' Rebind data source in case it's not bound to original dataset
DataGrid1.DataSource = Nothing
DataGrid1.DataSource = CustomerDataSet1
```

We then call the DataGrid's Expand method, using a value of -1 to expand all the child rows. We can also expand an individual row by passing in a number representing that row.

```
' Expand all the child rows.
DataGrid1.Expand(-1)
```

Now that we have added code to actually update our DataGrid information, let's go ahead and try it out.

Try It Out – Updating DataGrid Information

1. Compile and run the application using the *F5* key.

2. Click the Get Data button.

3. Expand the node if not already expanded so that the Customer and Supplier links show.

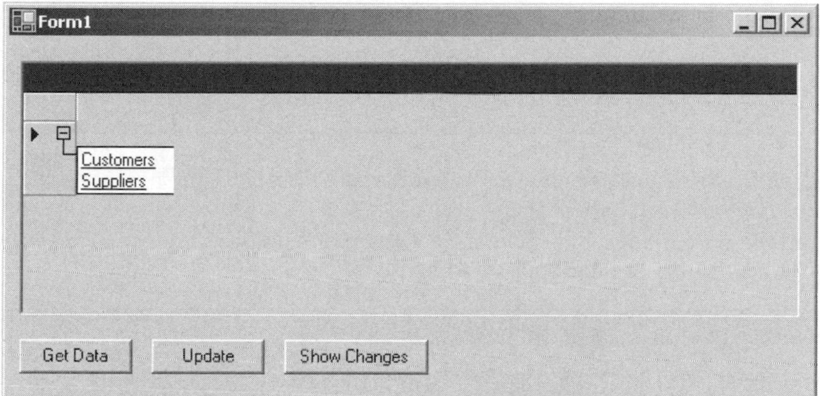

4. Select the Customers link and modify the second PostalCode record from 05021 to 05023.

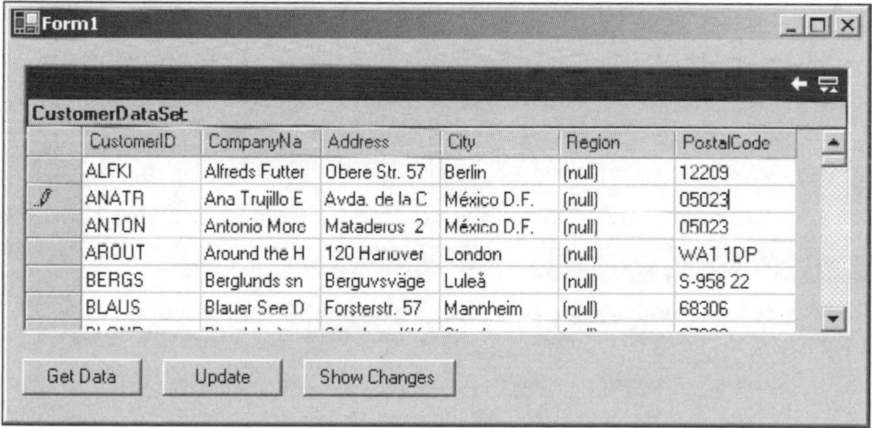

5. Click the navigate back button at the top right of the grid to navigate back to the parent. Click the Suppliers table and modify the first address record from 49 Gilbert Street to 100 Elm Street.

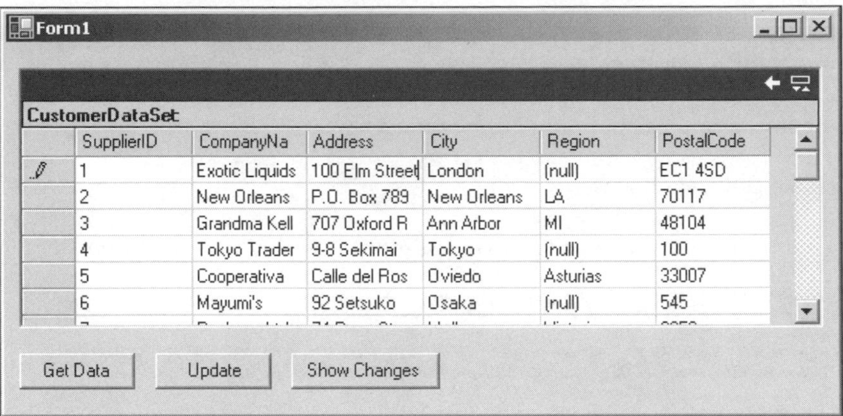

6. Click the Show Changes button. This will bring you back to the parent node.

7. Expand the parent node and click on the Customers link to show the changes made in the table. Do the same for the Suppliers link also.

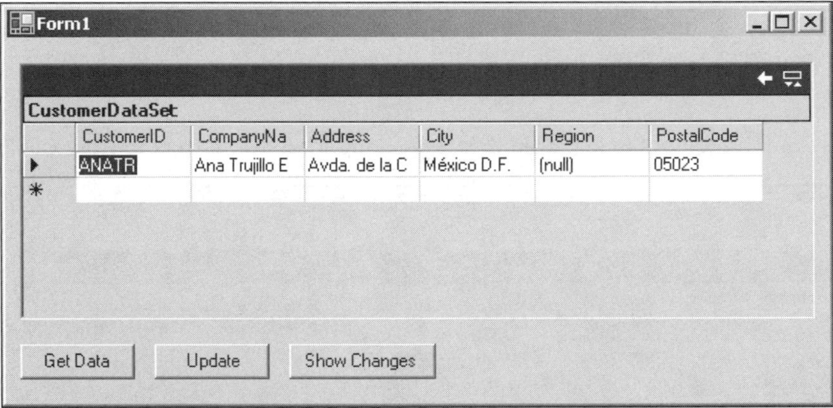

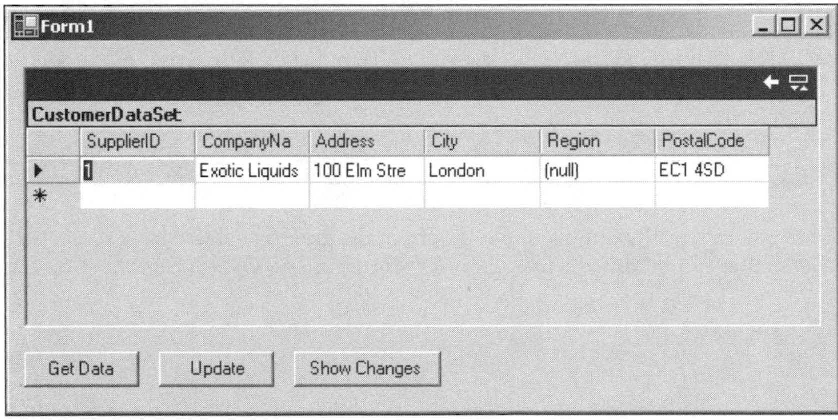

8. Once you're finished reviewing the changes, click the Update button. You will get messages indicating how many records were updated in each table. In this case there was one in each.

How It Works

We clicked the Get Data button to fill our `DataSet`, `CustomerDataSet1`, with our table information. This opens the database connection, retrieves the data, then closes the connection. Once our `DataSet` is filled, we are disconnected from the data source.

We then modified a customer record and a supplier record and clicked the Show Changes button to view all changes for each table. When we clicked the Update button, the `Update` method was called for the entire `DataSet`. The `Update` method examines the `RowState` property of the data tables to determine which records were modified. According to the value of `RowState`, the `DataAdapter` calls an `INSERT`, `UPDATE`, or `DELETE` statement to perform the required action.

The `GetChanges` method determines all the changes made, which were just the two, and which we can then store in a local `DataSet` that we bind to the `DataGrid` to view the changes. By selecting each link, Customers or Suppliers, we were able to view the changes in the corresponding table.

As you can see, we can update our records with very little code.

ADO.NET Namespaces

In this next section, we will look at the different namespaces that make up ADO.NET and how they are used.

Namespaces help identify a class or hierarchy. The namespace uses the assembly name as part of its naming convention. It's a way of referencing many assembly files together by tying the assemblies together.

Any time you create a new project, `System.Data` and `System.XML` are automatically referenced by the project, automatically giving you access to their underlying classes.

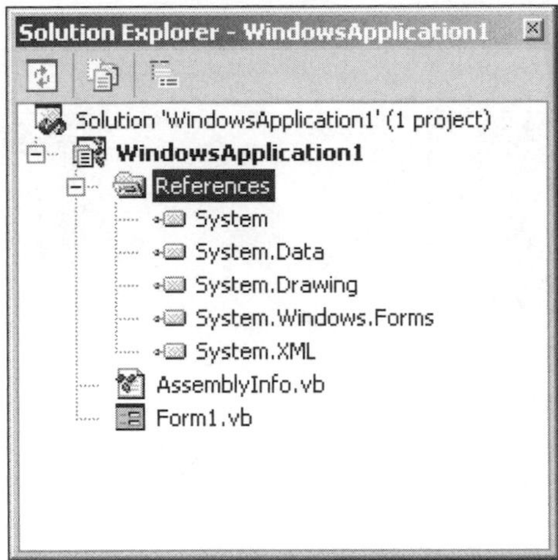

If we examine the properties of the `System.Data` reference, we can see the assembly's name, description, location, and version information:

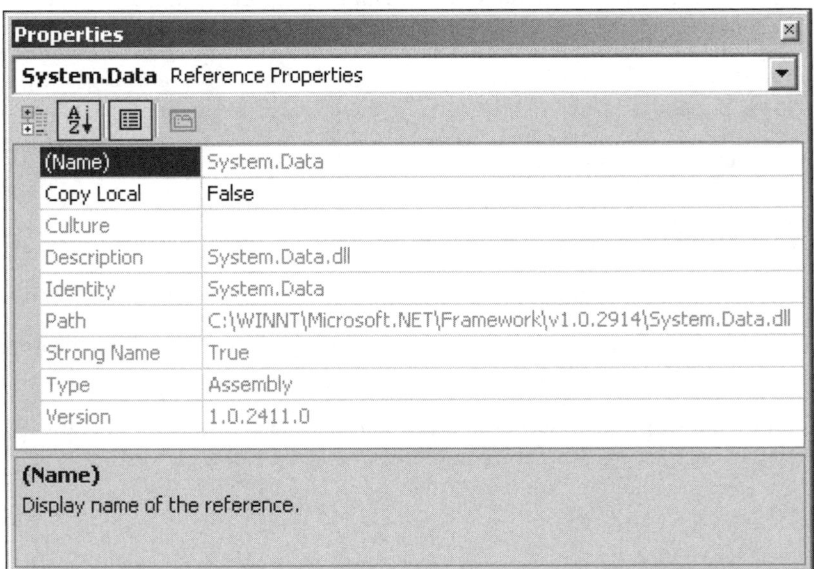

Let's take a look at the five commonly used ADO.NET namespaces:

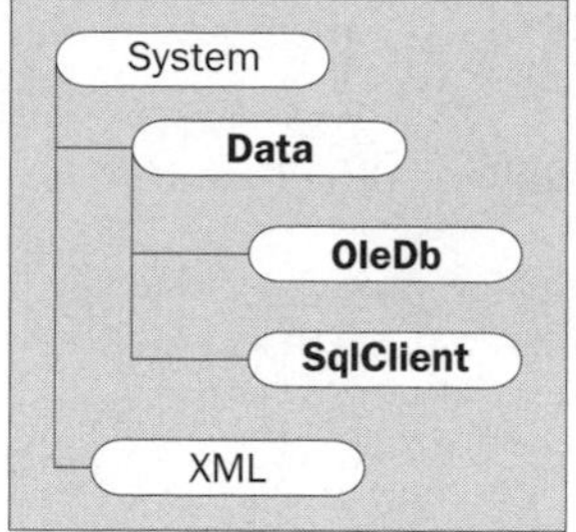

- `System` – the core namespace that contains the fundamental classes and base classes that define commonly-used value and reference data types, events and event handlers, interfaces, attributes, and processing exceptions.
- `System.Data` – this consists of classes that make up the ADO.NET architecture. Contains components to help manage data efficiently along with tools to view and update data.
- `System.Data.OleDb` – consists of classes to allow you to connect to OLE DB providers, execute commands, and view results.
- `System.Data.SqlClient` – contains classes to be used with a SQL data provider and is optimized to access SQL Server 7.0 or greater. The SQL Server version of the `System.Data.OleDb` namespace.
- `System.XML` – provides classes to support XML-based operations. The `DataSet` uses this for reading and writing XML data including schema files.

The System.Data Namespace

Underneath the `System.Data` namespace are five classes that support data management:

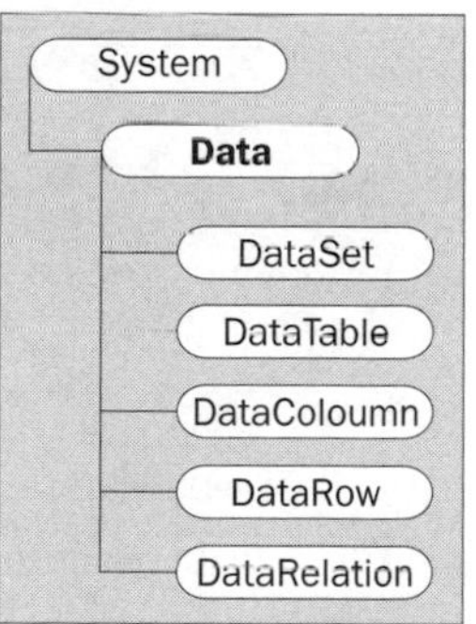

The `System.Data` namespace essentially provides all the tools required for management of our data: table creation, relation management, data management, and schema information.

When we need to declare a class within the namespace, we simply use the `New` keyword to create a new instance of the object:

```
Dim myDataSet As New DataSet()
Dim myTable As New DataTable()
Dim myColumn As New DataColumn()
Dim myRow As DataRow
```

We can also declare them with their fully qualified names:

```
Dim myDataSet As New System.Data.DataSet()
Dim myTable As New System.Data.DataTable()
Dim myColumn As New System.Data.DataColumn()
Dim myRow As System.Data.DataSet
```

We can set up an alias – an alternative way of referring to an object – for a namespace. This is a handy way to set up shorthand identifiers for some of the longer names. In a new Windows project, we would use an `Import` statement for the `System.Data` at the top of the module in order to set up the alias `MyADO` as shown:

```
Imports MyADO = System.Data
Public Class Form1
    Inherits System.Windows.Forms.Form

Windows Form Designer generated code

    Private Sub Form1_Load(ByVal sender As System.Object, _
                       ByVal e As System.EventArgs) Handles MyBase.Load

        Dim myDataSet As New MyADO.DataSet()
        Dim myTable As New MyADO.DataTable()
        Dim myColumn As New MyADO.DataColumn()
        Dim myRow As MyADO.DataRow

    End Sub
End Class
```

The System.Data.OleDb and System.Data.SqlClient Namespaces

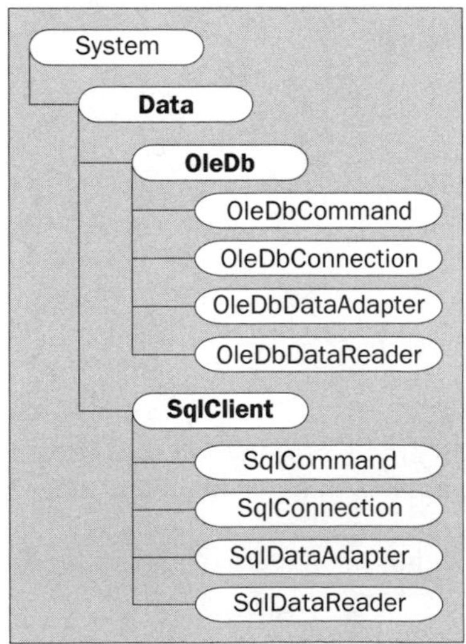

Chapter 5 introduced us to the `Command`, `Connection`, and `DataAdapter` classes, and we will look at these in more detail shortly. We will also take a look at the `DataReader` class. Note that there are OLE DB and SQL versions of each class. Since we are using the SQL Server Desktop Engine in this book, we can use the `SqlClient` namespace instead of `OleDb` since it is much quicker and cuts out much of the overhead of the OLE DB layer.

The System.Xml Namespace

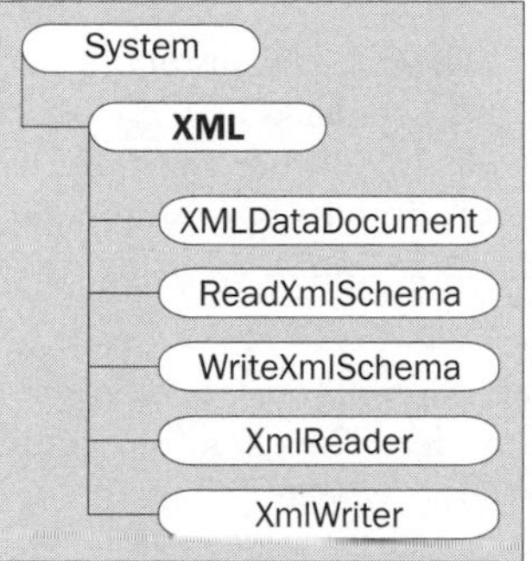

Since ADO.NET has built-in XML support, the `System.XML` namespace is an important namespace to become familiar with. Amongst other things, this namespace helps to define our table schemas, which – as you may remember – specify the structure of our tables. There is no need to worry about this namespace right now; this diagram has been included for completeness here. In Chapter 12, we look at ADO.NET and XML in further detail, and the classes listed above will be used throughout the final chapters of this book.

Dataflow in ADO.NET

Now that we have discussed the components of ADO.NET, let's see how they complement each other and how they would flow in a real-world application.

The data tier contains the data source, to which the managed provider must connect to retrieve information and fill our tables with information as requested by the client. The following figure summarizes the basic components of ADO.NET:

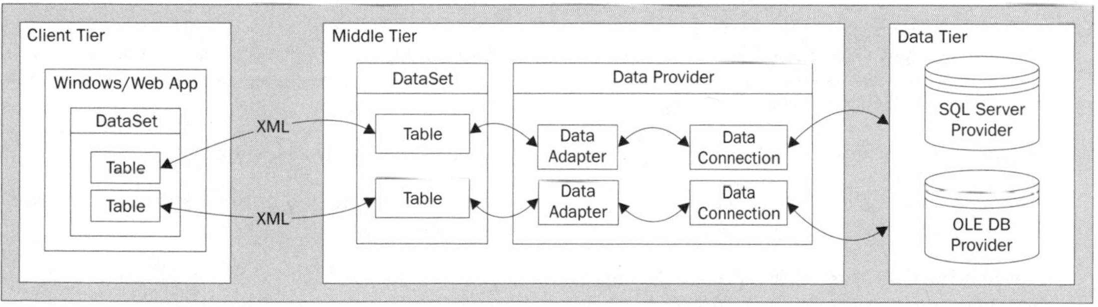

This diagram shows how ADO.NET is designed to work with a 3-tier or n-tier architecture. In our client tier, we use a `DataSet` that is entirely separate and independent from the middle tier. The client tier `DataSet` is a mirror image of the `DataSet` contained within the middle tier, and they communicate with each other through XML. The middle tier `DataSet` communicates with the Data Providers to select, add, update, or delete information. The Data Providers establish a connection to the data tier whenever information needs to be managed. Each tier can work quite independently of all others.

- The **data tier** is where the data store is located, as a SQL Server or an OLE DB data provider.
- Next, we have the **middle tier**, where the brains of the system are – the business logic. In this tier resides our `DataSet`, which gets populated by the Data Providers selecting records as appropriate. The Data Providers located in the middle tier constitute a business data tier component because they contain business logic that defines how we communicate with the database, and which is specific to this solution. The `System.Data` assembly is used to retrieve the data directly from the database.
- Lastly we have the **client tier**, where the users interface with our system; this is sometimes referred to as the **presentation tier**. The client tier could comprise a Windows or web application that interacts with the system.

.NET Data Providers

The .NET Data Providers consist of a number of classes used to connect to a data source, execute commands, and return records. They form the data tier. The .NET Data Providers are sometimes called Managed Providers.

There are two types of .NET Data Providers:

- The **OLE DB Data Provider** – to access any OLE DB provider including ODBC drivers for Oracle, Microsoft Access, Excel, FoxPro, Paradox, dBase, and any other native ODBC or OLE DB driver. It uses the `System.Data.OleDb` namespace.
- The **SQL Server Data Provider**– specific to SQL Server 7.0 and greater. It is faster than the OLE DB provider because it doesn't have to go through the OLE DB layer – it communicates directly with SQL Server. It uses the `System.Data.SqlClient` namespace.

Your application's performance and functional requirements will determine the best provider for your purposes. The chart below sums up when to choose one over the other:

Use the OLE DB Data Provider when:	**Use the SQL Server Data Provider when:**
Using Microsoft SQL Server 6.5 or earlier	Using SQL Server 7.0 or greater
You need to use Oracle	Using the Microsoft Data Engine
You need to use Microsoft Access	You require the best performance possible and are only using SQL Server
You need support for OLE DB Provider (use the SQL Data Provider instead of OLE DB Provider for SQL Server)	There is no future need for other database types besides Microsoft SQL Server (SQL Server 7.0 and above)
You need support for any native ODBC drivers	

To use the OLE DB data provider in your project, you must include the `OleDb` namespace in your code modules:

```
Imports System.Data.OleDb
```

To use the SQL Server data provider in your project, you include the `SqlClient` namespace in your code modules:

```
Imports System.Data.SqlClient
```

Within each managed provider are four components: the `Connection`, `DataAdapter`, `Command`, and `DataReader` objects.

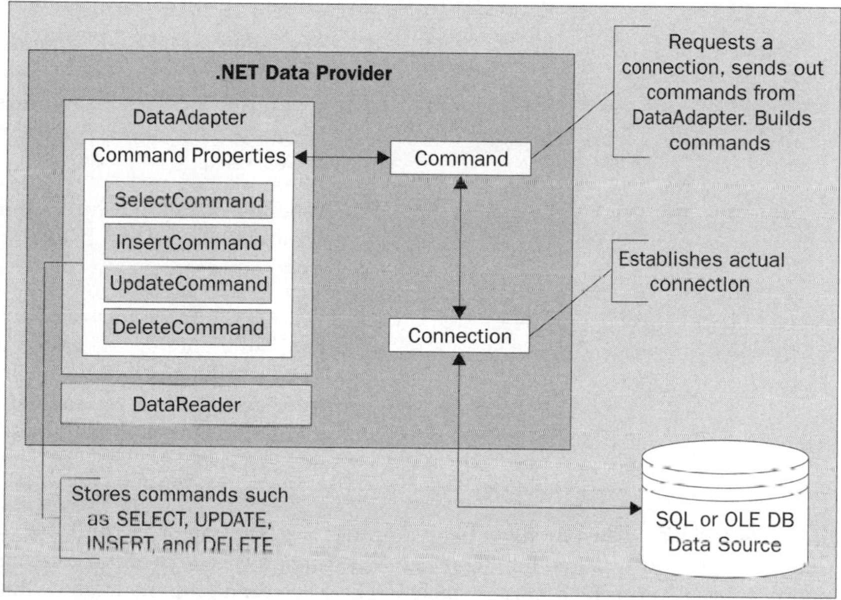

If you're using the SQL Server Data Provider, you use the `SQLDataAdapter`, `SqlCommand`, `SQLDataReader`, and `SqlConnection` form of these objects. For OLE DB Data providers, use the `OleDbDataAdapter`, `OleDbCommand`, `OleDbDataReader`, and `OleDbConnection` objects.

Now, let's next look at each of these objects individually.

The Connection Object

This opens a connection to the data source. You can use either the `OleDbConnection` or the `SqlConnection` object. For the OLE DB provider, you use a `Provider`, `Data Source`, `User ID`, and `Password` in the connection string. For the SQL provider, you need the same arguments as for the OLE DB provider, but omit the `Provider` type (which is always `SQLOLEDB`). If the connection string for a SQL provider does specify a `Provider` parameter, an exception is generated.

The connection string has several commonly used properties:

Property	Default Value	Description
`Provider`	*(Required)*	Used with OLE DB provider only. Specifies the provider to use.
`Data Source` or `Server`	*(Required)*	The name of the server to connect to, for example: localhost, MYSERVER.
`Initial Catalog` or `Database`	*(Required)*	The database to connect to, for example: `Northwind`, `Pubs`.
`User ID`	*(Required if set)*	The login account username.
`Password` or `PWD`	*(Required if set)*	The password for server logon.
`Connect Timeout` or `Connection Timeout`	`15`	The length of time (in seconds) to wait for a connection to the server before generating an error. Make sure this is adequate when using particularly slow networks.
`Persist Security Info`	`False`	Whether or not to return security-sensitive information back as part of the connection string.
`Integrated Security` or `Trusted_Connection`	`False`	Whether to use a secure connection or not. Either `True`, `False`, or `sspi` (same as `True`). Security Service Provider Interface (SSPI) is a means of secure authentication when communicating to a data source.

The connection must be closed when modifying the `ConnectionString` property. When you set the property, the connection string is parsed for errors and an exception is generated if it contains incorrect syntax or property values. A semicolon must be included between each property to allow the parser to distinguish between them. You can use single quotes or none around a value to set. Any value left blank will be ignored. Lastly, for `true` or `false` values, you can use '`yes`' and '`no`' as well as '`True`' and '`False`'.

The minimum arguments to connect to a data source are `Provider` (in the case of an OLE DB provider), `Data Source`, and `Initial Catalog`. If a username and password is set on the database, then you will also need those two pieces of information. Now let's take a look at some sample connection strings.

This one connects to a Microsoft Access database:

```
"Provider=Microsoft.Jet.OLEDB.4.0;Data Source=C:\Samples\Northwind.mdb;User
ID=;Password=;"
```

This one connects to an Oracle database:

```
"Provider=MSDAORA;Data Source=MyOracleDB;User ID=myID;Password=myPWD;"
```

The next one connects an `OleDbConnection` object to a SQL Server database. Wherever possible, use the SQL Data Provider if you know you are using a SQL database which doesn't require the `Provider` parameter, although you will come across applications that select a data provider at runtime.

```
"Provider=SQLOLEDB;Data Source=localhost;Initial Catalog=Pubs;Password=;User ID=;"
```

You can set the time before a connection fails to open by modifying your connection string to include a timeout value:

```
Dim myConnString As String = "Data Source=localhost;" & _
                             "Initial Catalog=NorthwindSQL;User ID=sa;" & _
                             "Connect Timeout=30;"
```

The `ConnectionTimeout` property of the `Connection` object is used to read the timeout value. This property is read-only and has a default of `15` seconds:

```
Timeout = myConnection.ConnectionTimeout
```

Connection Pooling

Connection pooling is enabled by default, and can provide improved performance of your applications and servers. When you create a new connection, a pool is created based on the connection string. The next time you create a connection, if the connection string hasn't changed then the same pool will be used. If the connection string has changed in any way, then a new pool will be required.

Consider a short example. The following code creates a new connection pool:

```
' Connection creates a new pool.
myConnString = "Data Source=localhost;Initial Catalog=NorthwindSQL;User Id=sa;"
myConnection = New SqlConnection(myConnString)
myConnection.Open()
```

If we then create another connection with the exact same connection string, it will simply be added to our first pool, thus avoiding the overhead imposed when a connection is set up:

```
' Connection added to existing pool.
myConnString2 = "Data Source=localhost;Initial Catalog=NorthwindSQL;User Id=sa;"
myConnection2 = New SqlConnection(myConnString2)
myConnection2.Open()
```

Now let's say we create another connection, but this time we have an `Initial Catalog` argument of `Pubs` instead of `NorthwindSQL`. This will cause a new pool to be created:

```
' Connection added to a new pool.
myConnString3 = "Data Source=localhost;Initial Catalog=Pubs;User Id=sa;"
myConnection3 = New SqlConnection(myConnString2)
myConnection3.Open()
```

The DataAdapter Object

The DataAdapter is the physical means of communication between the data source and the DataSet, and is either a SqlDataAdapter or an OleDbDataAdapter. If the application wants to retrieve or update records, it uses properties of the DataAdapter that reference Command objects that contain SELECT, INSERT, UPDATE, and DELETE commands. It is these referenced Command objects that communicate directly with the data source to manipulate data according to the user's request.

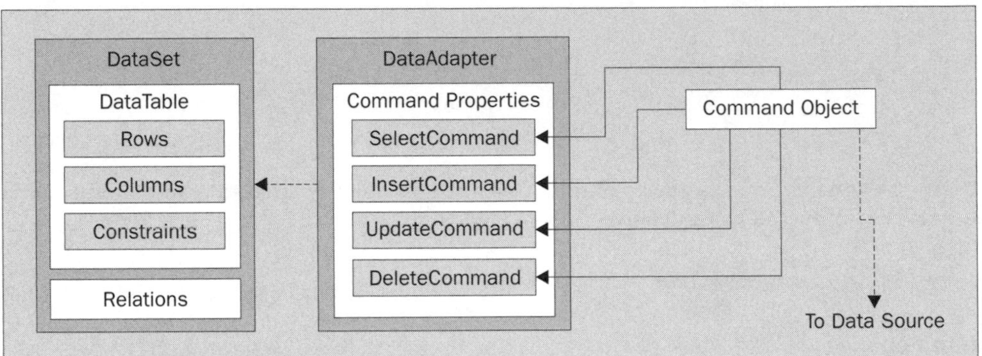

The most useful methods of the DataAdapter are the Fill and Update methods. The Fill method populates a DataSet or table with the specified information. To fill a DataSet, use the Fill method of a DataAdapter as in the following lines:

```
Dim myDataSet As New DataSet()
myAdapter.Fill(myDataSet)
```

We can also use the DataAdapter's Fill method with a DataTable:

```
Dim myCustomerTable As New DataTable()
myAdapter.Fill(myCustomerTable)
```

The Update method, as you may have guessed, serves to update records. Edit any rows in your DataSet, and call the Update method to persist those changes in the data source:

```
myAdapter.Update(myDataSet)
```

Use this method in the following fashion when dealing with a DataTable object:

```
myAdapter.Update(myTable)
```

Command Object

The Command object is used to set up SELECT, INSERT, UPDATE, and DELETE commands or stored procedures for a DataAdapter object. There are two types, OleDbCommand and SqlCommand, and four subtypes: SelectCommand, InsertCommand, UpdateCommand, and DeleteCommand.

This object is used to send commands to a database by way of a connection object.

```
Dim myConnection As New SqlConnection(myConnString)
Dim myAdapter As New SqlDataAdapter()

Dim mySelectQuery As String = "SELECT Address, City, PostalCode FROM Customers"
myAdapter.SelectCommand = New SqlCommand(mySelectQuery, myConnection)
```

This sets the `SelectCommand` property of the adapter to a new `SqlCommand` object, based on the `SELECT` query assembled in `mySelectQuery`, and using the connection called `myConnection`.

Setting up an `InsertCommand` is similar: create a new `SqlCommand` object with the required `INSERT` statement and connection object as parameters, and assign it to the `InsertCommand` property of a `DataAdapter`:

```
Dim myInsertQuery As String = "INSERT INTO Customers(Address, City, PostalCode) "
& _
                              "VALUES (@Address, @City, @PostalCode)"
myAdapter.InsertCommand = New SqlCommand(myInsertQuery, myConnection)
```

Assigning other commands follows the same pattern. For an `UPDATE` query, use code like this:

```
Dim myUpdateQuery As String = "UPDATE Customers SET Address='200 ABC Street', "  &
_
                              "City='Beverly Hills' WHERE CustomerID='DUMON'"
myAdapter.UpdateCommand = New SqlCommand(myUpdateQuery, myConnection)
```

Likewise, for a `DELETE` query, create a new `SqlCommand` object and assign it to the `DeleteCommand` property of a `DataAdapter`:

```
Dim myDeleteQuery As String = "DELETE FROM Customers WHERE CustomerID='DUMON'"
myAdapter.DeleteCommand = New SqlCommand(myDeleteQuery, myConnection)
```

If you create your `Command` objects manually instead of using the data wizards, the `SqlCommandBuilder` class provides an easy way to generate the SQL `INSERT`, `UPDATE`, and `DELETE` commands that the data wizards automatically produce. This class generates SQL statements to `INSERT`, `UPDATE`, and `DELETE` single tables based on the `SELECT` statement provided. Be aware though that, with this approach, you won't have as much control as if you were to create such commands yourself and the performance isn't the best it could be, because the class must query the database schema for information such as table column names, size, type, and key information. The generated statements provide for optimistic concurrency (see Chapter 10) and for refreshing the `DataSet`, as provided by the Data Adapter Wizard. This can be really useful if our application allows the users to design their own `SELECT` statements, because it gives us the ability to change any related `INSERT`, `UPDATE`, and `DELETE` commands programmatically. You can only use single tables with your `DataAdapters` so, if you're linked to multiple tables, you will get an exception.

Using the `SqlCommandBuilder` is quite straightforward: just declare a new object and pass in a `DataAdapter`:

```
Dim myBuilder As New SqlCommandBuilder(myAdapter)

' Show the INSERT statement that was generated.
MessageBox.Show(myBuilder.GetInsertCommand.CommandText)
```

After the above code, you will be able to execute the Update method of your DataAdapter to run the appropriate INSERT, UPDATE, and DELETE commands as required. These commands are built on the fly when the Update method is called, so you won't be able to see any of the Command object properties by inspecting your DataAdapter's contents. To retrieve the commands that will be used during an update, use the GetInsertCommand, GetUpdateCommand, and GetDeleteCommand properties of the SqlCommandBuilder object.

We're not limited to just SQL statements when we create our Command object, as we can also call stored procedures:

```
Dim mySelectCommand As SqlCommand
mySelectCommand = New SqlCommand("DeleteCustomer", myConnection)

mySelectCommand.CommandType = CommandType.StoredProcedure

Dim myParm As SqlParameter
myParm = mySelectCommand.Parameters.Add("@CustID", SqlDbType.NVarChar, 10)
myParm.Value = "DUMON"

myConnection.Open()

Dim RecordsAffected As Integer = mySelectCommand.ExecuteNoQuery()
myConnection.Close()
```

We create a new Command object and pass in the name of our stored procedure, which is DeleteCustomer. Within the DeleteCustomer stored procedure, there would be a SQL statement as shown below. We have to specify the type of command we want to execute, namely a stored procedure, using the CommandType.StoredProcedure property value. We then create a new SqlParameter to contain our parameter name, type, size, and value. We must then open our connection and execute the stored procedure using the ExecuteNoQuery method of the Command object. ExecuteNoQuery executes the SQL statement or procedure associated with the Command object and returns the number of records affected by the operation. When finished, we close the connection.

```
CREATE PROCEDURE dbo.DeleteCustomer
(
      @ReturnValue INT = Null OUTPUT,
      @CustID INT
)
AS
      DELETE FROM Customers WHERE CustomerID = @CustID
      SELECT @ReturnValue = @@ROWCOUNT
```

The DataReader Object

If you don't need to manipulate or modify records, you can greatly increase performance by using a DataReader. This is a forward only reader that can only read, not write, data. You're working directly with a data stream and not in-memory objects as with the DataSet. If you just want a quick display of your data then the DataReader is the object to use. Since we don't have all the bells and whistles of the DataSet that allow it to manipulate records, go backwards, and jump to specific records, we cut out all the associated overhead, resulting in much improved performance. Internally, the DataAdapter itself uses a DataReader to populate a DataSet and, as you may expect, there are two types of data reader: the OleDbDataReader and the SqlDataReader. Unfortunately the DataReader can't bind to a DataGrid like the DataSet can, so you must manually display any information read from a DataReader.

To populate a DataReader, you follow all the same steps of populating a DataSet as far as setting up your Command objects and connections. Since we don't have the capability to UPDATE, DELETE, or INSERT data with a DataReader, we don't need a DataAdapter.

To initialize a DataReader object, call the ExecuteReader method of the Command class:

```
Dim myReader As SqlClient.SqlDataReader = mySelectCommand.ExecuteReader()
```

The following constructs a DataReader object. The type of reader you create, whether SQL or OLE DB, will depend on the Command and Connection object you are using:

```
Dim myConnection As New SqlClient.SqlConnection()
myConnection.ConnectionString = "Data Source=localhost;" & _
                                "Initial Catalog=NorthwindSQL;User Id=sa;"

Dim mySelectQuery As String = "SELECT Address, City FROM Customers"
Dim mySelectCommand As New SqlClient.SqlCommand(mySelectQuery, myConnection)
myConnection.Open()

Dim myReader As SqlDataReader
myReader = mySelectCommand.ExecuteReader()
```

Use the Item property to get a value for a particular field. Pass the name of the field you want to retrieve or the index value representing the ordinal position of that field:

```
Console.WriteLine(myReader.Item("Address"))
```

To read records, use the Read method of the DataReader to load the next row into the Reader object. Read returns True as long as there are more records to read. Since a DataReader is a forward only reader, there are no methods to move backwards through the result set. Initially, the reader is located just prior to the first record, so you must call Read *before* you may access any records:

```
While myReader.Read()
        Console.WriteLine(myReader.Item("Address"))
End While
```

You can also call the methods GetString, GetInt16, GetDouble, or GetDateTime according to the specific type of the column in question. We can call GetName to get the name of the field, and GetType to determine the type of the field. These methods all take a zero-based index as the single argument so, to access the first field in your result set, you would use index 0. In this example, we retrieve the first column value, which is taken to be of type String:

```
CONST CUSTOMERID_COLUMN As Integer = 0

While myReader.Read()
        Console.WriteLine(myReader.GetString(CONST CUSTOMERID_COLUMN))
End While
```

If you try to display a record that is Null you will get an exception. This isn't difficult to avoid, as in the next code extract which uses the IsDBNull property to check whether a field is Null. This property takes a zero-based index representing the ordinal position of the field you want to check.

```
CONST ADDRESS_COLUMN As Integer = 1

' Always call Read before accessing data.
While myReader.Read()
    If myReader.IsDBNull(ADDRESS_COLUMN) = False Then ' make sure City field is
not Null
        Console.WriteLine(myReader.Item("Address") & ", " & myReader.Item("City"))
    End If
End While
```

Now let's see how to create a `DataReader` using the OLE DB data provider:

```
' Specify a SELECT statement.
Dim mySelectQuery As String = "SELECT Address, City FROM Customers"
' Create a new connection object.
Dim myConnection As New OleDbConnection(myConnString)
' Create a new command object.
Dim myCommand As New OleDbCommand(mySelectQuery, myConnection)
' Open the connection.
myConnection.Open()

' Call ExecuteReader which returns a DataReader object.
Dim myReader As OleDbDataReader
myReader = myCommand.ExecuteReader()

' Always call Read before accessing data.
While myReader.Read()
    Console.WriteLine(myReader.GetString(1) & ", " & myReader.GetString(2))
End While

' Always call Close when done reading.
myReader.Close()

' Close the connection when done with it.
myConnection.Close()
```

To create a `DataReader` for the SQL Server data provider, you would only need to change a few declarations:

```
Dim mySelectQuery As String = "SELECT Address, City FROM Customers"

' Create a new connection object.
Dim myConnection As New SqlConnection(myConnString)

' Create a new command object.
Dim myCommand As New SqlCommand(mySelectQuery, myConnection)

' Open the connection.
myConnection.Open()

' Call ExecuteReader which returns a DataReader object.
Dim myReader As SqlDataReader
myReader = myCommand.ExecuteReader()

' Always call Read before accessing data.
While myReader.Read()
```

```
        Console.WriteLine((myReader.GetString(1) & ", " & myReader.GetString(2))
    End While

    ' Always call Close when done reading.
    myReader.Close()

    ' Close the connection when done with it.
    myConnection.Close()
```

The Common Model

The common model uses the same set of code for both the OLE DB provider and the SQL Server provider. Just by changing the initial declarations, we can switch between the two different data providers while keeping most of the remaining code intact.

Here is how we may use the OLE DB data provider:

```
Dim myDataSet As DataSet

Dim myConnection1 As New OleDb.OleDbConnection()
myConnection1.ConnectionString = "Provider=SQLOLEDB;Data Source=localhost;" & _
                                 "Initial Catalog=NorthwindSQL;User Id=sa;"

Dim mySelectCommand1 As New OleDb.OleDbCommand()
mySelectCommand1.CommandText = "SELECT Address, City, Region, PostalCode FROM
Customers"

mySelectCommand1.Connection = myConnection1

Dim myDataAdapter1 As New OleDb.OleDbDataAdapter()
myDataAdapter1.SelectCommand = mySelectCommand1

myDataSet = New DataSet("MyNewDataSet")

myDataAdapter1.Fill(myDataSet)
```

If we then decide to use the SQL data provider, we only need to change our declarations and connection string. Everything else, including our method calls, stays the same.

```
Dim myDataSet As DataSet

Dim myConnection1 As New SqlClient.SqlConnection()
myConnection1.ConnectionString = "Data Source=localhost;" & _
                                 "Initial Catalog=NorthwindSQL;User Id=sa;"

Dim mySelectCommand1 As New SqlClient.SqlCommand()
mySelectCommand1.CommandText = "SELECT Address, City, Region, PostalCode FROM
Customers"

mySelectCommand1.Connection = myConnection1

Dim myDataAdapter1 As New SqlClient.SqlDataAdapter()
myDataAdapter1.SelectCommand = mySelectCommand1

myDataSet = New DataSet("MyNewDataSet")

myDataAdapter1.Fill(myDataSet)
```

ADO.NET's syntax lends itself to easily and painlessly switching our data sources. If our code uses only a SQL Data Provider, and we wish to add support for other OLE DB providers, the code rewriting required would be similarly minimal.

We could create a function to determine whether we should use a SQL Data Provider or an OLE DB Data Provider by checking the connection string to see if it contains the word "Provider", as shown below:

```
Public Function GetDataSet(ByVal myConnection as String) As DataSet

    ' Convert myConnection to upper case and look for the word PROVIDER.
    Dim UseOleDbProvider As Boolean

    If myConnection.ToUpper.IndexOf("PROVIDER") <> -1 Then UseOleDbProvider = True

    If UseOleDbProvider = False Then ' The word Provider was not found in the
string.
      ' Get DataSet from SqlDataAdapter.
    Else ' The word Provider was found in the string, so use an OLE DB Provider.
      ' Get DataSet from OleDbDataAdapter.
    End If

End Function
```

Here, we have a Boolean variable, `UseOleDbProvider`, that, if set to `True`, indicates that we should use an `OleDbDataAdapter`; otherwise, we should use a `SqlDataAdapter`. The `IndexOf` method searches the connection string for the substring `"PROVIDER"`, returning the starting position of where the text was found, or `-1` if it is not found. If it returns something other than `-1`, then we know the connection string contains a `Provider` argument, and is hence suitable for an `OleDbDataAdapter`. We can then use `UseOleDbProvider` to programmatically choose between the SQL Data Provider and the OLE DB Data Provider.

When there is a `Provider` argument, we can further check whether we can use the SQL Data Provider anyway if the OLE DB Provider is `SQLOLEDB`, as in the highlighted code below:

```
Public Function GetDataSet(ByVal myConnection as String) As DataSet

    ' Convert myConnection to uppercase and look for the word PROVIDER.
    Dim UseOleDbProvider As Boolean

    If myConnection.ToUpper.IndexOf("PROVIDER") <> -1 Then UseOleDbProvider = True

    ' Check to see if we can still use the SQL Data Adapter even though
    ' an OLE DB Provider was chosen.
    If UseOleDbProvider = True Then ' We are using an OLE DB Provider.
        If myConnection.ToUpper.IndexOf("SQLOLEDB") <> -1 Then UseOleDbProvider =
False
    End If

    If UseOleDbProvider = False Then ' The word Provider was not found in the
string.
      ' Get DataSet from SqlDataAdapter.
    Else ' The word Provider was found in the string so we are using an OLE DB
provider.
      ' Get DataSet from OleDbDataAdapter.
    End If

End Function
```

These are just a couple of ways that you can use the common model to your advantage.

DataReader Sample Project

We are going to create an application to monitor the level of product supplies in stock for the fictional Northwind company, and display an alert if the quantity of items in stock falls to or below a given reorder level. This can be set up with a timer to monitor daily, hourly, or even every minute.

In our application, we're going to open the NorthwindSQL database and read a list of products and display a warning for any products where the quantity in stock falls below a certain level, after checking to make sure there are none already on order. We shall display product records in a `ListView` control. The `ListView` control is commonly used for displaying information, and produces output similar to that produced by Windows Explorer when it shows you the files in a directory, along with the details of each file. It is suitable for our purposes, unlike the `DataGrid`, because the latter does not support the use of a `DataReader`.

Try It Out – Building our DataReader

1. Create a new Visual Basic Windows Application using the built-in template and name it ProductSupplyMonitor:

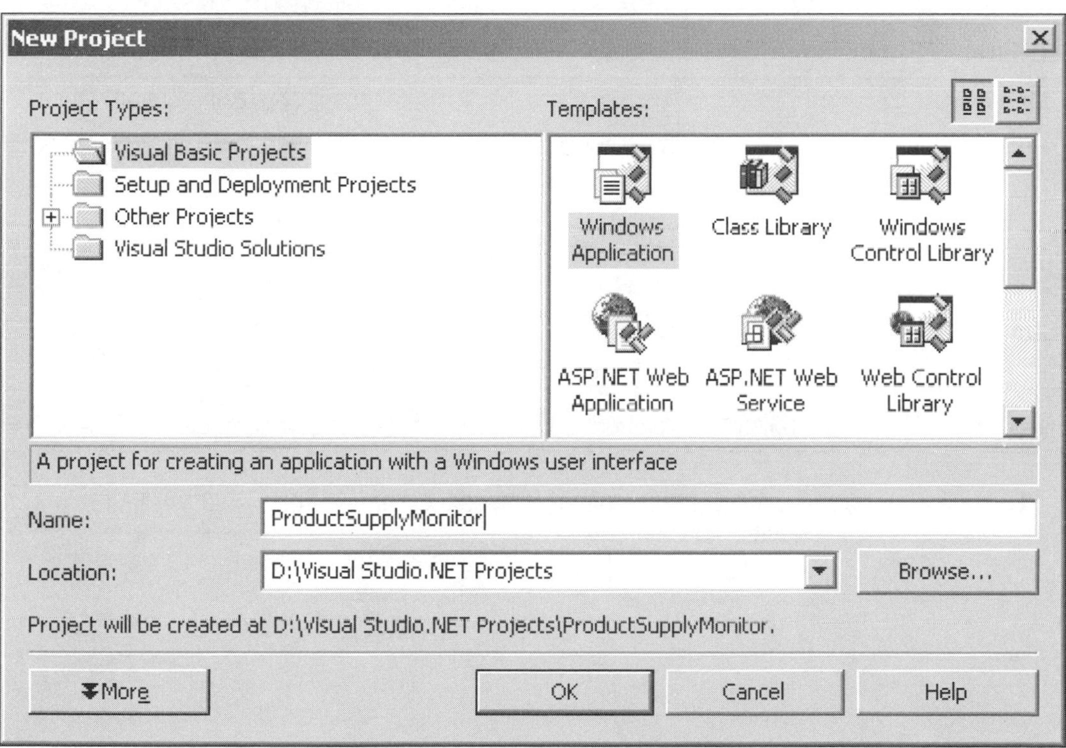

2. Find the ListView control in the Toolbox and place one on Form1, along with a Button as shown:

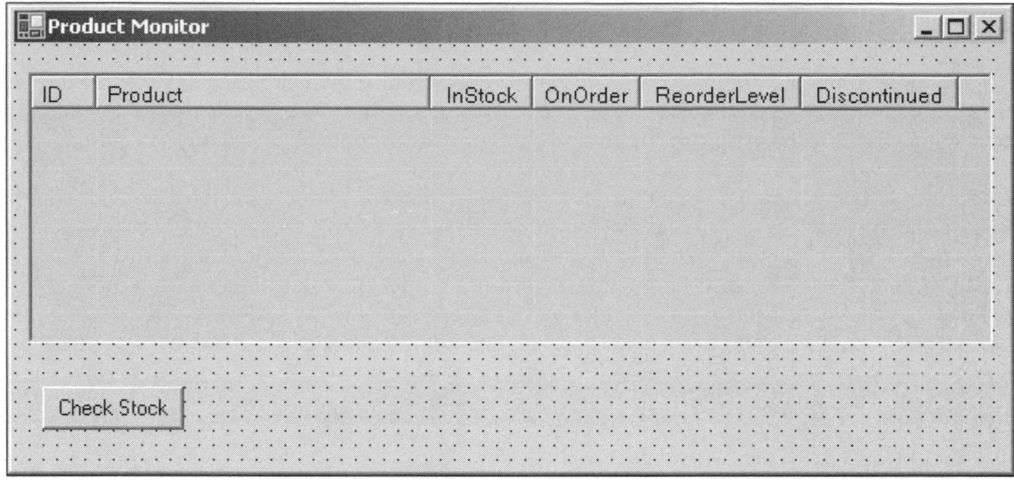

3. Set the following properties for the ListView and Button controls:

Control	Property	Value
ListView1	Anchor	Top, Bottom, Left, Right
	BackColor	255,192,128
	GridLines	True
	Font	Microsoft Sans Serif, 9pt
	View	Details
Button1	Name	btnCheckStock
	Text	Check Stock
	Anchor	Bottom, Left

4. In the Properties window for ListView1, select the Columns property ellipsis button to bring up the ColumnHeader Collection Editor.

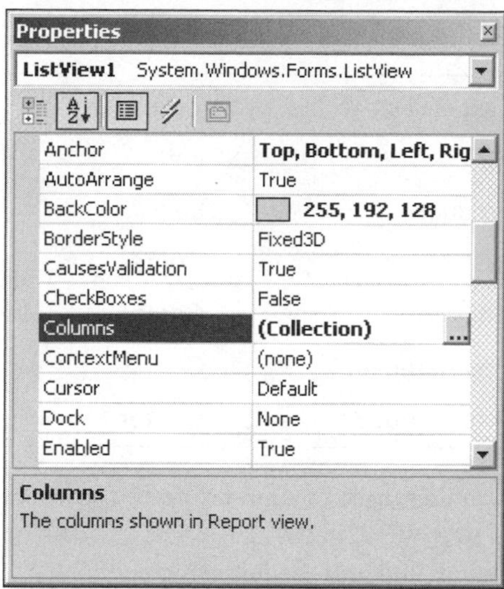

5. Click on the Add button five times to add five columns to the ListView. We're going to add columns for ID, Product, InStock, OnOrder, ReorderLevel, and Discontinued.

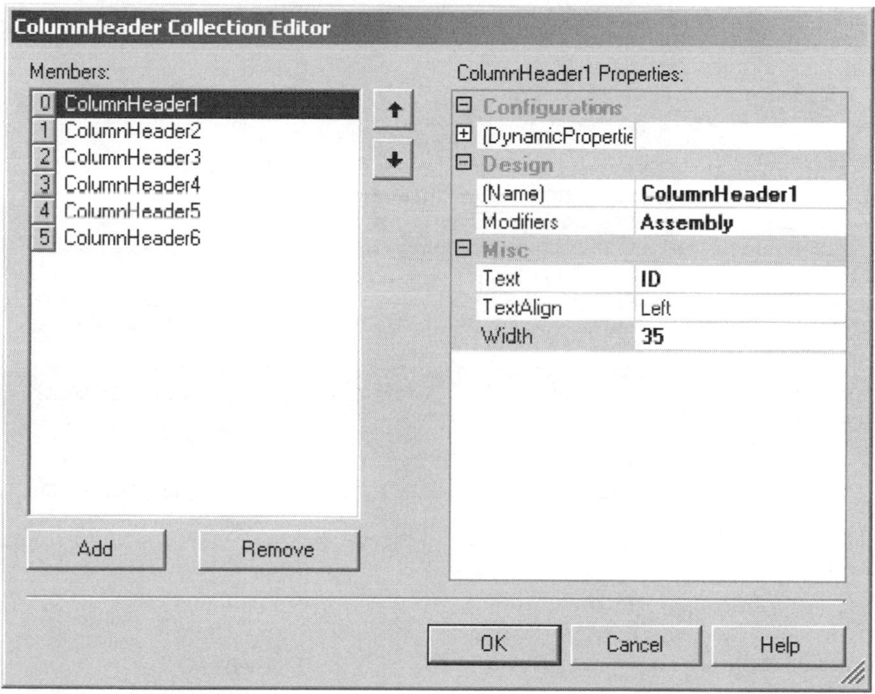

6. Set the `ColumnHeader` properties for all five as shown:

Member	Text	TextAlign	Width
ColumnHeader1	ID	Left	35
ColumnHeader2	Product	Left	185
ColumnHeader3	InStock	Center	60
ColumnHeader4	OnOrder	Center	60
ColumnHeader5	ReorderLevel	Center	90
ColumnHeader6	Discontinued	Center	90

When you're finished setting these column properties, click OK.

7. Double-click on the button and add the following code:

```
Private Sub btnCheckStock_Click(ByVal sender As System.Object, _
                                ByVal e As System.EventArgs) Handles
btnCheckStock.Click
```

```
        ' Track what row we're adding to the ListView.
        Dim currentRow As Integer

        ' Define the column indexes.
        Const PRODUCTID_COLUMN As Integer = 0
        Const PRODUCTNAME_COLUMN As Integer = 1
        Const UNITS_INSTOCK_COLUMN As Integer = 2
        Const UNITS_ONORDER_COLUMN As Integer = 3
        Const REORDERLEVEL_COLUMN As Integer = 4
        Const DISCONTINUED_COLUMN As Integer = 5

        ' Create a new connection object.
        Dim myConnection As New SqlClient.SqlConnection()
        ' Define the connection string.
        myConnection.ConnectionString = "Data Source=localhost;" & _
                                        "Initial Catalog=NorthwindSQL;User
Id=sa;Password=;"

        ' Define the SQL statement.
        Dim mySQLString As String = "SELECT ProductID, ProductName, UnitsInStock,
" & _
                                    "UnitsOnOrder, ReorderLevel, Discontinued FROM
Products"

        ' Create a new command object.
        Dim mySelectCommand1 As New SqlClient.SqlCommand(mySQLString,
myConnection)
        ' Open the connection.
        mySelectCommand1.Connection.Open()
        ' Assign the product listing to a DataReader.
```

```
        Dim myReader As SqlClient.SqlDataReader = mySelectCommand1.ExecuteReader()

        ' Clear out existing items in ListView.
        ListView1.Items.Clear()

        ' Read all the rows of data.
        While myReader.Read() = True
            Try
                ' Add items to ListView.
                ListView1.Items.Add(myReader.Item("ProductID"))

ListView1.Items.Item(currentRow).SubItems.Add(myReader.Item("ProductName"))

ListView1.Items.Item(currentRow).SubItems.Add(myReader.Item("UnitsInStock"))

ListView1.Items.Item(currentRow).SubItems.Add(myReader.Item("UnitsOnOrder"))

ListView1.Items.Item(currentRow).SubItems.Add(myReader.Item("ReorderLevel"))

ListView1.Items.Item(currentRow).SubItems.Add(myReader.Item("Discontinued"))

                ' If items in stock is less than reorder level and...
                ' If there are no units on order and...
                ' The item hasn't been discontinued then... Flag It!
                If myReader.GetInt16(UNITS_INSTOCK_COLUMN) <= _
                     myReader.GetInt16(REORDERLEVEL_COLUMN) And _
                       myReader.GetInt16(UNITS_ONORDER_COLUMN) = 0 And _
                         myReader.GetBoolean(DISCONTINUED_COLUMN) = False Then

                    ' Change In Stock Qty to RED.
                    ListView1.Items.Item(currentRow).SubItems.Item( _
                                    UNITS_INSTOCK_COLUMN).ForeColor =
Drawing.Color.White
                    ListView1.Items.Item(currentRow).SubItems.Item( _
                                    UNITS_INSTOCK_COLUMN).BackColor =
Drawing.Color.DarkRed

                End If
                ' Increment current row counter.
                currentRow = currentRow + 1
            Catch
                ' Handle Nulls.
            End Try
        End While
End Sub
```

8. Compile and run the project, and click the CheckStock button to bring up a display like that shown overleaf. You may need to make some adjustments to the InStock field of your database to ensure some items require reordering.

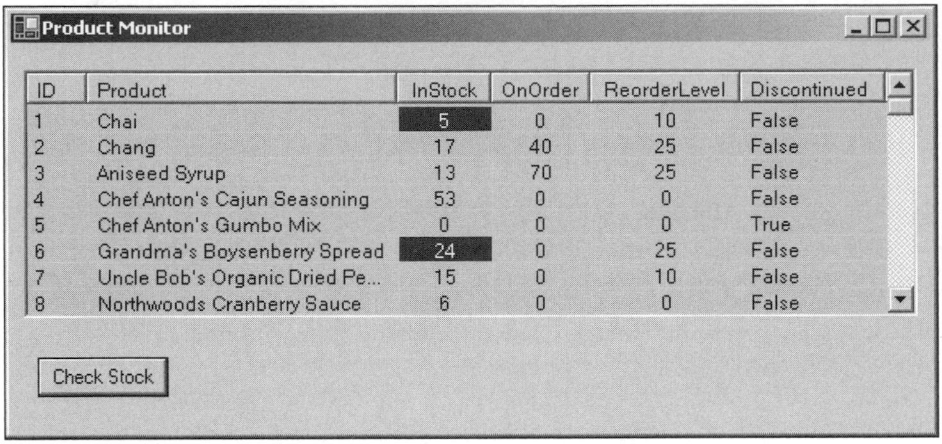

Product Monitor

ID	Product	InStock	OnOrder	ReorderLevel	Discontinued
1	Chai	5	0	10	False
2	Chang	17	40	25	False
3	Aniseed Syrup	13	70	25	False
4	Chef Anton's Cajun Seasoning	53	0	0	False
5	Chef Anton's Gumbo Mix	0	0	0	True
6	Grandma's Boysenberry Spread	24	0	25	False
7	Uncle Bob's Organic Dried Pe...	15	0	10	False
8	Northwoods Cranberry Sauce	6	0	0	False

Check Stock

Above is the final result of our project. We can see that the first item, with ID 1, only has five items in stock, below the reorder level of 10, that there aren't any on order, and that the item hasn't been discontinued. Consequently, this item is flagged up for reorder. If we look at the second row, we see that, although we are below our reorder level, there are some already on order, so this item doesn't need to be flagged, nor is the product with ID 5, because that is discontinued. Item number 6 is also flagged because it is below the reorder level.

The reorder levels are a field in the database like any other, so your interface application would allow users to adjust this value as appropriate, just as any other column. The stock check program could be configured to e-mail someone when stock drops below certain thresholds. You can learn about e-mailing, services and other advanced features in Wrox Press's *Professional Visual Basic .NET*.

How It Works

First, we declared a counter called `currentRow` to keep track of which row we're currently adding to the `ListView`. As each row is added, we increment this counter by one. Notice how we have defined all the column indexes as constants so we can easily reference them when retrieving column values. For the purposes of this example, these constants have been placed inside our local procedure, but we would often have them elsewhere in a module or class that would readily allow us to include them in any other routine as required. The constants denote the ordinal positions of each column, in sync with the `SELECT` statement that we will be using:

```
Private Sub btnCheckStock_Click(ByVal sender As System.Object, _
                                ByVal e As System.EventArgs) Handles
btnCheckStock.Click

        ' Track what row we're adding to ListView.
        Dim currentRow As Integer

        ' Define the column indexes from the SELECT statement.
        Const PRODUCTID_COLUMN As Integer = 0
        Const PRODUCTNAME_COLUMN As Integer = 1
        Const UNITS_INSTOCK_COLUMN As Integer = 2
        Const UNITS_ONORDER_COLUMN As Integer = 3
        Const REORDERLEVEL_COLUMN As Integer = 4
        Const DISCONTINUED_COLUMN As Integer = 5
```

Next, we created a new `SqlConnection` object and assigned a connection string to the `ConnectionString` property. This includes the name of the server we are connecting to (here we use `localhost`, but this may vary depending on where your SQL Server is situated), the name of the database we want to connect to (the `NorthwindSQL` database), and the user ID and password that our SQL Server requires.

```
        Dim myConnection As New SqlClient.SqlConnection()
        myConnection.ConnectionString = "Data Source=localhost;" & _
                                        "Initial Catalog=NorthwindSQL;User
Id=sa;Password=;"
```

Then we built a `SELECT` command by creating a new `SqlCommand` object and passing in the `SELECT` statement to be used, along with the `Connection` object. Notice our column constant values are defined from 0 through 5, representing each column's position in the `SELECT` statement. When our records are returned, we will have a total of six columns.

Next we open the connection using the `Open` method. If any information in the connection string is incorrect, an exception will occur.

```
        Dim mySQLString As String = "SELECT ProductID, ProductName, UnitsInStock,
" & _
                                    "UnitsOnOrder, ReorderLevel, Discontinued FROM
Products"

        Dim mySelectCommand1 As New SqlClient.SqlCommand(mySQLString,
myConnection)

        mySelectCommand1.Connection.Open()
```

To populate the `DataReader`, we call the `ExecuteReader` method of the `Command` object:

```
        Dim myReader As SqlClient.SqlDataReader = mySelectCommand1.ExecuteReader()
```

Since we will be repopulating the `ListView` every time we need to check the stock levels, we need to make sure we clear it first with the `Items Clear` method, otherwise rows will just get stacked on top of rows.

```
        ' Clear out existing items in ListView.
        ListView1.Items.Clear()
```

Now we can read each record by calling the `Read` method of our `DataReader`. Remember that this method returns `True` as long as there are records left to read. To access each field or column, use the `DataReader`'s `Item` property, passing in the name of the column to display. The records will be displayed on the `ListView` one row at a time. The first item is added to the `ListView` by calling the `Items.Add` method to add it to the first column. Any column on the same row after that must be added by calling the `SubItems.Add` method of the `Item` object for the current row, adding the column as a 'sub-item'.

```
        ' Read all the rows of data.
        While myReader.Read() = True
            Try
                ' Add items to ListView.
                ListView1.Items.Add(myReader.Item("ProductID"))
```

```
ListView1.Items.Item(currentRow).SubItems.Add(myReader.Item("ProductName"))

ListView1.Items.Item(currentRow).SubItems.Add(myReader.Item("UnitsInStock"))

ListView1.Items.Item(currentRow).SubItems.Add(myReader.Item("UnitsOnOrder"))

ListView1.Items.Item(currentRow).SubItems.Add(myReader.Item("ReorderLevel"))

ListView1.Items.Item(currentRow).SubItems.Add(myReader.Item("Discontinued"))
```

If any field is `Null`, an exception is produced, so we place these statements within a `Try...Catch` block to resume at the next record and ignore any `Null` values. In general, though, it is preferable to handle `Nulls` using the `IsDbNull` method of the `DataRow` object.

Once we have added all the column data for the current row, we check to see if the quantity in stock is less than or equal to the value of the reorder level column. If it is, we then check to see if there are any more on order or if the item has been discontinued. If neither of those are the case, then we mark the `InStock` column in red so it stands out and warns the user that this particular item is low on stock.

```
                ' If items in stock is less than reorder level and...
                ' If there are no units on order and...
                ' The item hasn't been discontinued then... Flag It!
                If myReader.GetInt16(UNITS_INSTOCK_COLUMN) <= _
                     myReader.GetInt16(REORDERLEVEL_COLUMN) And _
                       myReader.GetInt16(UNITS_ONORDER_COLUMN) = 0 And _
                         myReader.GetBoolean(DISCONTINUED_COLUMN) = False Then

                    ' Change In Stock Qty to RED.
                    ListView1.Items.Item(currentRow).SubItems.Item( _
                                    UNITS_INSTOCK_COLUMN).ForeColor =
Drawing.Color.White
                    ListView1.Items.Item(currentRow).SubItems.Item( _
                                    UNITS_INSTOCK_COLUMN).BackColor =
Drawing.Color.DarkRed

                End If
```

Finally, we increment our current row counter and restart our `While` loop.

```
                ' Increment current row counter.
                currentRow = currentRow + 1
            Catch
                ' Handle Nulls.
            End Try
        End While
End Sub
```

Summary

So what have we learned in this chapter? We've had a little look at the history and evolution of data access that has led to today's ADO.NET. We compared it with the previous incarnation of ADO, and learned that ADO.NET is designed with disconnected data access strongly in mind, and we saw how the disconnected model readily lends itself to working with the Internet. ADO.NET's key feature to enable this is that the `DataSet` is a disconnected object held completely in memory. We also looked at ADO.NET namespaces and the different components that make up the `DataSet`, before examining data flow, and building a simple application based on the `DataReader` object. I hope that you are now pretty comfortable with ADO.NET, and have a solid foundation on which to grow your understanding of this important and very useful technology. In the next chapters, we will dissect the `DataSet` further, and work through the process for updating data in a data store step by step.

Questions

1. What is a `DataSet`?
2. What are the two .NET Data Providers (sometimes called Managed Providers)?
3. What are the four components of the .NET Data Providers?
4. What method do you use to fill a `DataSet`?
5. What is a `DataReader` and why would we use it?
6. Can you update records with a `DataReader`?
7. What are the different namespaces used with ADO.NET?
8. What is the means used by ADO.NET to send a `SELECT` command to the database?
9. What method do you use to retrieve the changes you have made to a `DataSet` or table?

Answers are available at http://p2p.wrox.com/exercises/.

Reading Data into the DataSet

Over the course of the next four chapters, we shall build a Product Management System for the NorthwindSQL database. The Product Management System is based on what a real-world company might expect from a database application. In this chapter, we start off by implementing one of the user interfaces, before moving on to cover how a `DataSet` can be populated according to the requirements entered via the user interface. Specifically, we shall:

- Introduce the Product Management System
- Introduce the four Product Management System chapters and the steps we will undertake in each
- Build the Search Screens to allow searching for products and suppliers
- Populate the `DataSet` programmatically instead of with a wizard
- Using stored procedures, fill a `DataSet` with complete tables from the database and then create relationships between the tables
- Write the business logic to dynamically build a SQL statement to fulfill the user's criteria given on the Search Screen
- Fill a `DataSet` with the results of the SQL query
- Verify in the Output window that the data in the `DataSet` correctly reflects the user criteria entered on the Search Screen

At the end of this chapter, we recap what we've learned and, to ensure you have a good grasp on these concepts, present a short quiz before moving on to part two in Chapter 8.

The Product Management System Overview

In this chapter, we commence our Product Management System – a typical example of the sort of application you may be asked to write in your professional career – and we continue its development in Chapters 8 through 10. After reading this book and completing the exercises at the end of each chapter, you should have sufficient knowledge to build such applications unassisted. As your career develops, you will undoubtedly refine the procedures suggested here, but this sample project will give you a firm foundation to begin building database applications with Visual Basic .NET.

The Product Management System is based on the NorthwindSQL database used throughout this book. The basic purpose of the system is to provide a means for Northwind employees to manage the products they sell. This management includes adding details of new products, updating existing product information, adding new product suppliers, or updating existing supplier information. The Product Management System will consist of the following three key screens:

- Product Search Screen. Allows for ad-hoc searching of product information. The user can specify particular criteria to search on. Multiple criteria can be specified, and all matching records are then displayed in a grid. The user will be able to double-click on a particular record in the results pane to open the record in View/Edit mode on a separate screen. An example of the Products Search Screen is shown below with some search results in the grid:

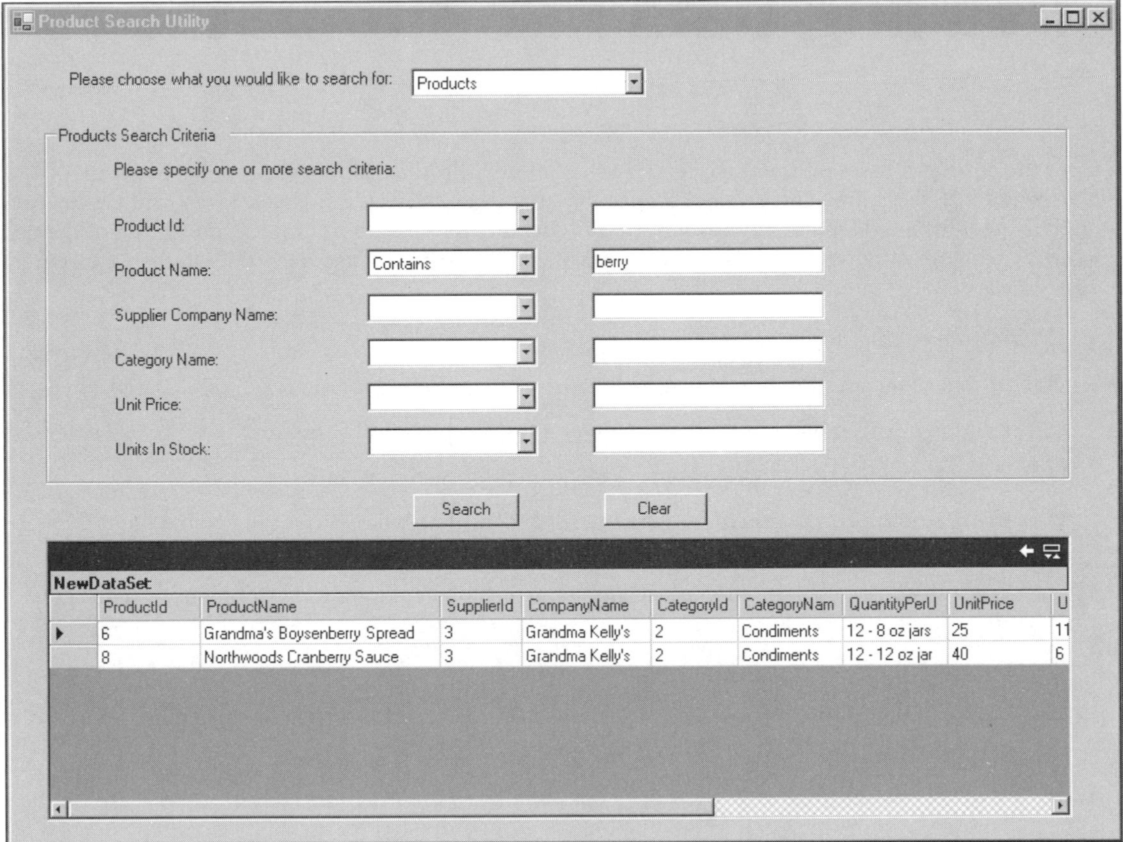

- Supplier Search Screen. Allows for ad-hoc searching of supplier information. It functions in the same manner as the Products Search Screen described above. The user can switch from the Products Search Screen to the Suppliers Search Screen by specifying the search method option on the form. An example of the Suppliers Search Screen is shown opposite:

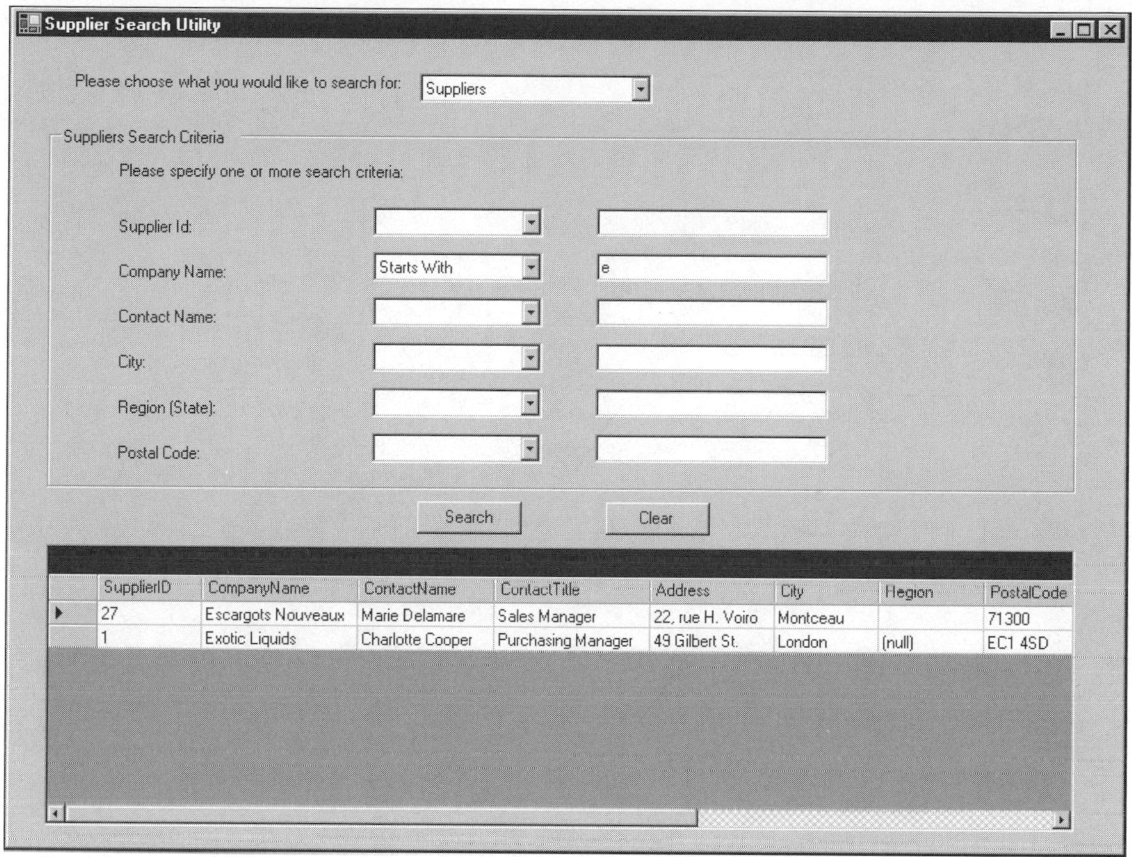

- Add/View/Edit Products Screen. When a Product record in the grid of results returned by the Products Search Screen is double-clicked, this screen will appear. It shows details of the given product record and allows the user to modify existing values. There will be a button on this form to allow for new products to be added. An example of this screen is shown overleaf:

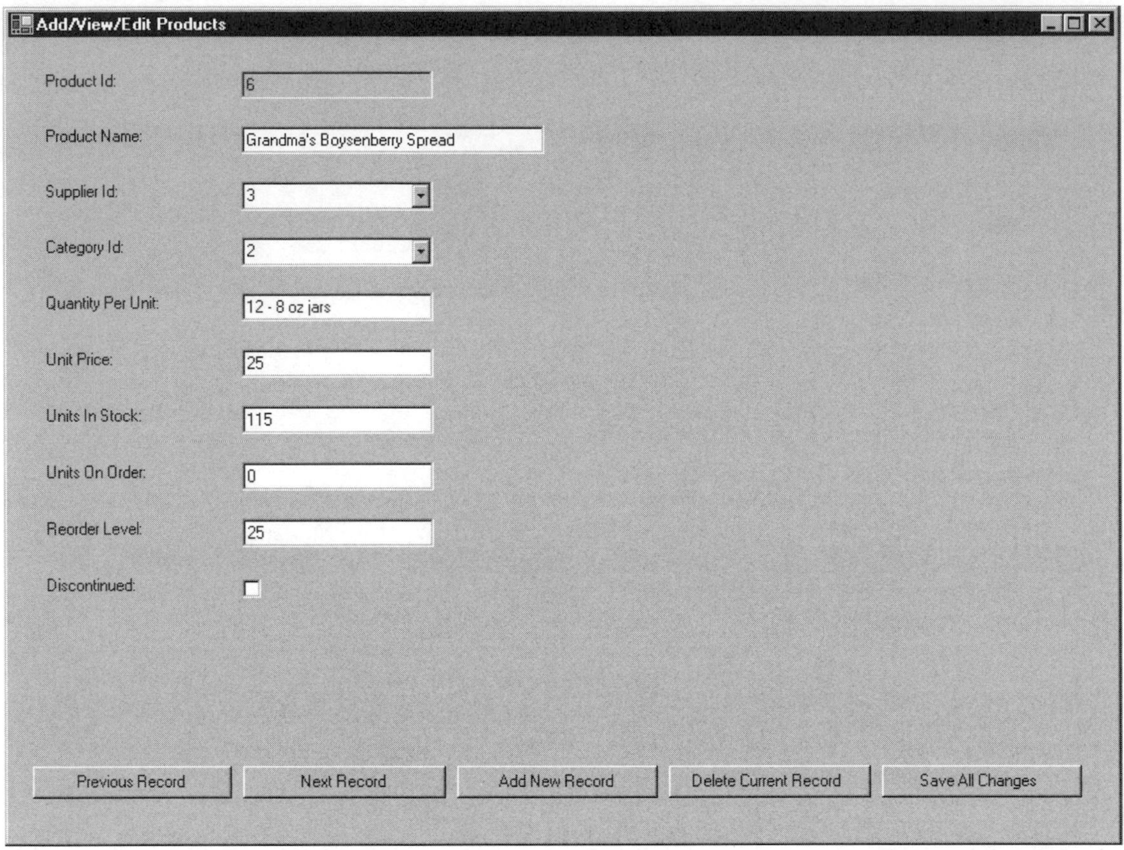

- Add/View/Edit Suppliers Screen: When a Supplier record in the grid on the Suppliers Search Screen is double-clicked, this screen will appear. It functions in the same manner as the Products Screen described above. An example of this screen is shown opposite:

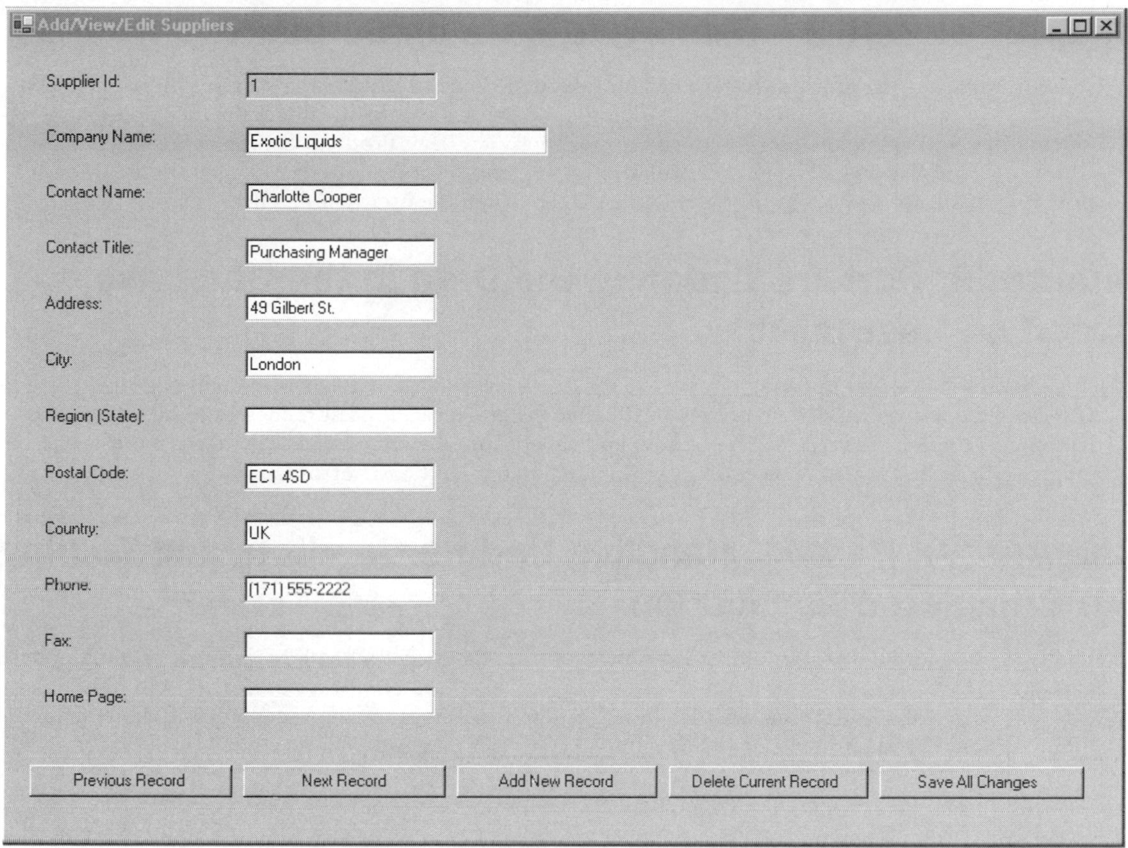

You should now have some idea what we intend to achieve, so let's look at a breakdown of the steps we will take to build it.

Chapter 7: Part 1 – Retrieving Data from the Database

Later in this chapter, we will build the Search Screen user interface to allow the user to specify criteria for searching for products or suppliers. We will build two `DataSets`: one to hold complete tables that will later be used as code tables and the other to hold the results of the user's search. A significant portion of this chapter will consist of building the user interface for the Search Screen and coding the SQL statement that reflects the user's input. Most importantly, however, we will see the `DataSet`, described in detail in Chapter 6, put to good use.

At the end of this chapter, we will have implemented code that builds a SQL statement according to the requirements provided by the user, retrieves matching records into a `DataGrid`, and outputs the results to the Output window (so we can verify that it worked properly). In the next chapter, we write the code to display the contents of the `DataGrid` on the Search Screen.

Chapter 8: Part 2 – Displaying Data on Screen

Chapter 8 picks up from where we left off to provide the code to display the search results on screen for the user. We will cover various methods of binding to `DataSets` that facilitate the display of information, and create the user interface for the Add/View/Edit Products Screen and the Add/View/Edit Suppliers Screen. We will also implement the code to open either of these screens to show full details for records in the `DataGrid` display when the user double-clicks them.

Chapter 9: Part 3 – Updating the Data in the Database Based on User Input

This chapter focuses on updating data in the database according to any changes made on the Add/Edit/View screens. We cover how to get changes in a local `DataSet` back into the underlying database. Stored procedures will be created and called from the code to actually make the database updates. We will also add some coding for input validation and basic error handling.

Chapter 10: Part 4 – Handling Update Conflicts and Touring the Completed Application

Finally, we explore how to handle concurrency conflicts that occur when a record that is being updated is modified by some other user in the interim. We look at a variety of ways of dealing with this situation. Most excitingly of all, we recap what we have accomplished over the four chapters and demonstrate our fully functional Product Management System.

Without further ado, let's get stuck into the details of part one. We should first work through all the steps involved in building the Search Screens that the user uses to specify what information we need to pull out into the `DataSet`.

Creating the User Interface for the Search Screens

Before we delve into creating the user interface for the search screens, it is important to give you some background on a critical topic – inheritance – that plays a key role in what we will be doing shortly. **Inheritance** is a powerful new feature of Visual Basic .NET that provides numerous advantages. Inheritance allows you to base a new class on an existing class and then make whatever necessary changes or additions you need in order to customize it. The biggest advantage to using inheritance is that you can reuse code that you've already written instead of repeating the code for slightly different variations of the same thing.

The **base class** is what we call the original class. The **subclass** (also called **child class**) is the class that inherits all of the functionality from the base class. Virtually any class we create can act as a base class from which other classes can be derived. By adding a single line of code to a class module, you can inherit all of the functionality from some other class. Here is an example:

```
Public Class clsCustomer
    Inherits clsPerson
```

In the code example above, the `clsCustomer` class inherits all functionality from `clsPerson`, plus then allows you to add new functionality to expand upon the person class. People sometimes refer to inheritance as **subclassing**, although inheritance is typically the more preferred term.

Visual inheritance is a type of inheritance that allows you to inherit both the user interface and other code aspects from a class. When a class module has user interface elements (such as if it is a form), then, when you add the `Inherits` statement as shown above, you inherit the user interface aspects as well. For example, visual inheritance allows you to define certain user interface elements once and then use them multiple times across projects. A good example might be to create a form that contains the menus, logo, size, etc. in the standard manner that your organization wants for each application. Instead of re-creating these preferences for each form you build, you can simply build these preferences once in a base form and then inherit from that form in all other forms that you add to your projects.

In our Product Management System, we are going to use visual inheritance to create a base search form that contains the functionality that both the products and suppliers search forms have in common. Then, to each subclass (the product search form and supplier search form), we will add the functionality that makes that particular form unique. The advantage that this provides us with is code reuse. Both forms have about 75% of the same code in common, and then about 25% that makes them unique. By putting the 75% they have in common in the base class and then inheriting from that base class, we save a large amount of duplication. Now that you understand the high level concept of inheritance, let's jump right into creating the base search form and see this in action.

Creating the Base Search Form Project

In the Product Management System we are building, we can build the base search form based on functionality common to all searches. We then inherit from the base search form and make the specific changes that make the products or suppliers search forms unique. In this section, we will create the base search form. Then, in the next section, we will create separate products and suppliers search forms that inherit the generic functionality from the base search form.

Try It Out – Creating the Base Search Form

1. Select File | New | Project, and select Visual Basic Projects and then Windows Application. Browse to the directory where you want to place the new project, such as a directory called ProdMgmtSystem. Name the project BaseForms and click OK.

2. In the Solution Explorer, select Form1.vb, right-click, and choose Rename. Change the filename of the form from Form1.vb to BaseSearchForm.vb.

3. Change the project type to Class Library so other forms can inherit from this form. Right-click on the BaseForms project name in Solution Explorer and select Properties. Change the Output Type from Windows Application to Class Library and click OK.

4. Double-click on BaseSearchForm.vb in the Solution Explorer to make the form active in the Design View (Visual Studio's large central window). Alternatively, click on the form in this central window, making it active. The properties window should now show the full compliment of available properties for the form.

5. Change the Text property from Form1 to Product / Supplier Search Utility, noting how the TitleBar of the form changes to reflect the property's new value.

6. Change the (Name) property of the form to BaseSearchForm, and finally enter 800, 600 for the Size property to enlarge the form to a size sufficient to hold all the controls we shall be adding. 800 X 600 is the typical screen size that most people have their monitor settings displaying as a minimum. Making the form size larger than 800 X 600 means that some portions of the screen will be cut off for many users.

7. Now, let's walk through the process of placing the controls on the form, starting with the Search Method. Open up the Toolbox normally tucked away on the left-hand side of the screen. Place one Label and one ComboBox on the form and set their properties as follows:

Control	(Name)	Text	Additional Remarks
`Label1`	`lblSearchMethod`	Please choose what you would like to search for:	Resize the label to display the entire contents. Move `ComboBox1` immediately after the label so they are aligned. Change the Modifiers property from Assembly to Family. This will allow the ComboBox and its properties to be modified in inherited child forms.
`ComboBox1`	`cboSearchMethod`	<blank>	Set the DropDownStyle property to DropDownList.

At this point, we should have something resembling the following:

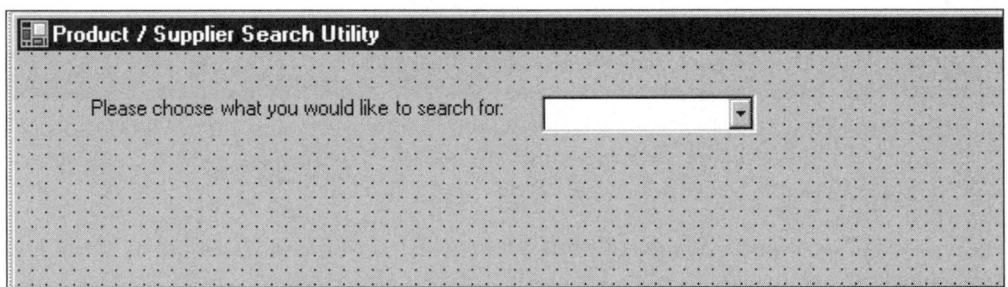

8. Add a GroupBox control to the form, to contain the controls for selecting the specific search criteria. Make sure the GroupBox is selected and place seven Labels, six ComboBoxes, and six TextBoxes on it, as shown in the screenshot opposite. You may find the quickest way to do this is to place the first of each control type on the form, select it, then copy, paste, and drag it to create the remaining controls:

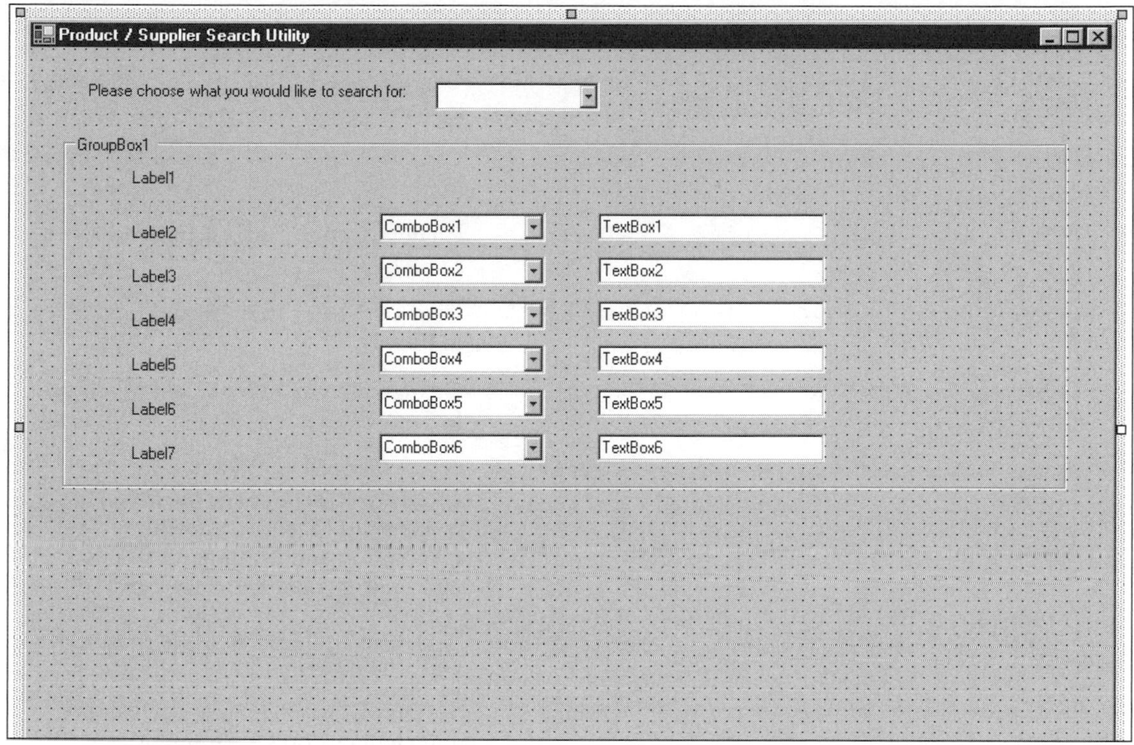

9. Name and label the controls in `GroupBox1`, according to the following table:

Control	(Name)	Text	Additional Remarks
`GroupBox1`	`grpSearchCriteria`	Search Criteria	Change the Modifiers property to Family. This will allow this `GroupBox` and its properties to be modified in inherited child forms.
`Label1`	`lblSearchCriteria`	Please specify one or more search criteria:	Change the Size property to 256, 23 so the complete text is shown.
`Label2`	`lblCriteria1`	<blank>	Change the Size property to 160, 16 so that it will be big enough to hold all the text. Also, change the Modifiers property to Family to allow the Label and its properties to be modified in inherited child forms.

Table continued on following page

Control	(Name)	Text	Additional Remarks
Label3	lblCriteria2	<blank>	Change Size to 160, 16, and Modifiers to Family.
Label4	lblCriteria3	<blank>	Change Size to 160, 16, and Modifiers to Family.
Label5	lblCriteria4	<blank>	Change Size to 160, 16, and Modifiers to Family.
Label6	lblCriteria5	<blank>	Change Size to 160, 16, and Modifiers to Family.
Label7	lblCriteria6	<blank>	Change Size to 160, 16, and Modifiers to Family.
ComboBox1	cboCriteria1	<blank>	Set the DropDownStyle property to DropDownList. Change the Modifiers property to Family to allow the ComboBox and its properties to be modified in inherited child forms.
ComboBox2	cboCriteria2	<blank>	Set DropDownStyle to DropDownList and change Modifiers to Family.
ComboBox3	cboCriteria3	<blank>	Set DropDownStyle to DropDownList and change Modifiers to Family.
ComboBox4	cboCriteria4	<blank>	Set DropDownStyle to DropDownList and change Modifiers to Family.
ComboBox5	cboCriteria5	<blank>	Set DropDownStyle to DropDownList and change Modifiers to Family.
ComboBox6	cboCriteria6	<blank>	Set DropDownStyle to DropDownList and change Modifiers to Family.
TextBox1	txtCriteria1	<blank>	Change the Size property to 168, 20 so that it will be large enough for the user's search criteria. Change the Modifiers property to Family to allow the TextBox and its properties to be modified in inherited child forms.
TextBox2	txtCriteria2	<blank>	Change Size to 168, 20 and Modifiers to Family.
TextBox3	txtCriteria3	<blank>	Change Size to 168, 20 and Modifiers to Family.
TextBox4	txtCriteria4	<blank>	Change Size to 168, 20 and Modifiers to Family.

Control	(Name)	Text	Additional Remarks
`TextBox5`	`txtCriteria5`	<blank>	Change Size to 168, 20 and Modifiers to Family.
`TextBox6`	`txtCriteria6`	<blank>	Change Size to 168, 20 and Modifiers to Family.

After making the above changes, our form should look like this:

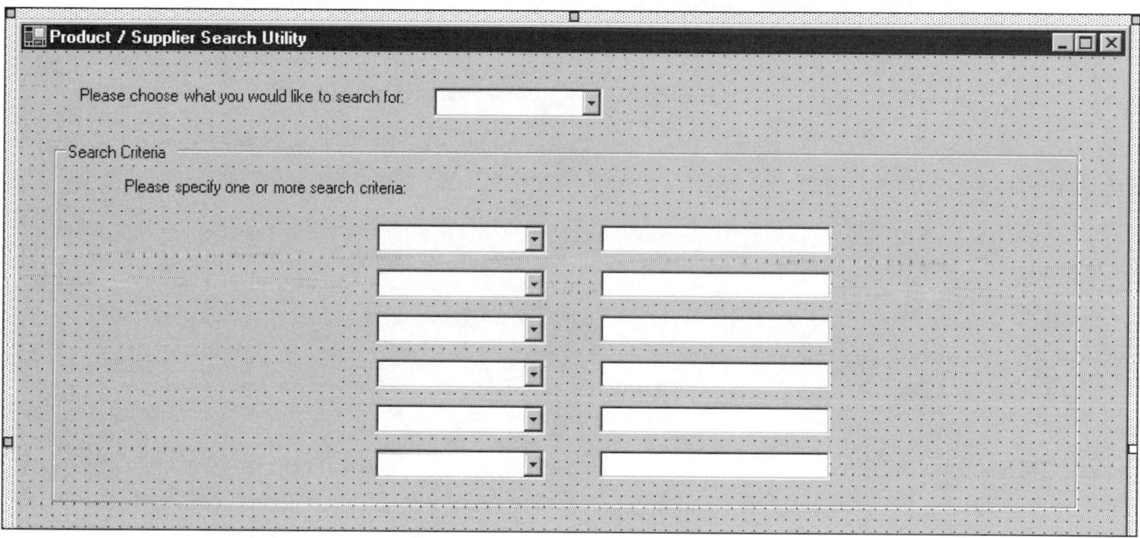

10. Place two Buttons and one DataGrid control on the form in the space beneath the Search Criteria GroupBox, and set the properties of the new controls as follows:

Control	Name	Text	Additional Changes
`Button1`	`btnSearch`	Search	Change the Modifiers property to Family to allow the Button and its properties to be modified in inherited child forms.
`Button2`	`btnClear`	Clear	Change Modifiers to Family.
`DataGrid1`	`dgdResults`	N/A	Change Modifiers to Family.

Note that DataGrid controls don't have a `Text` property. We should now have a form like this:

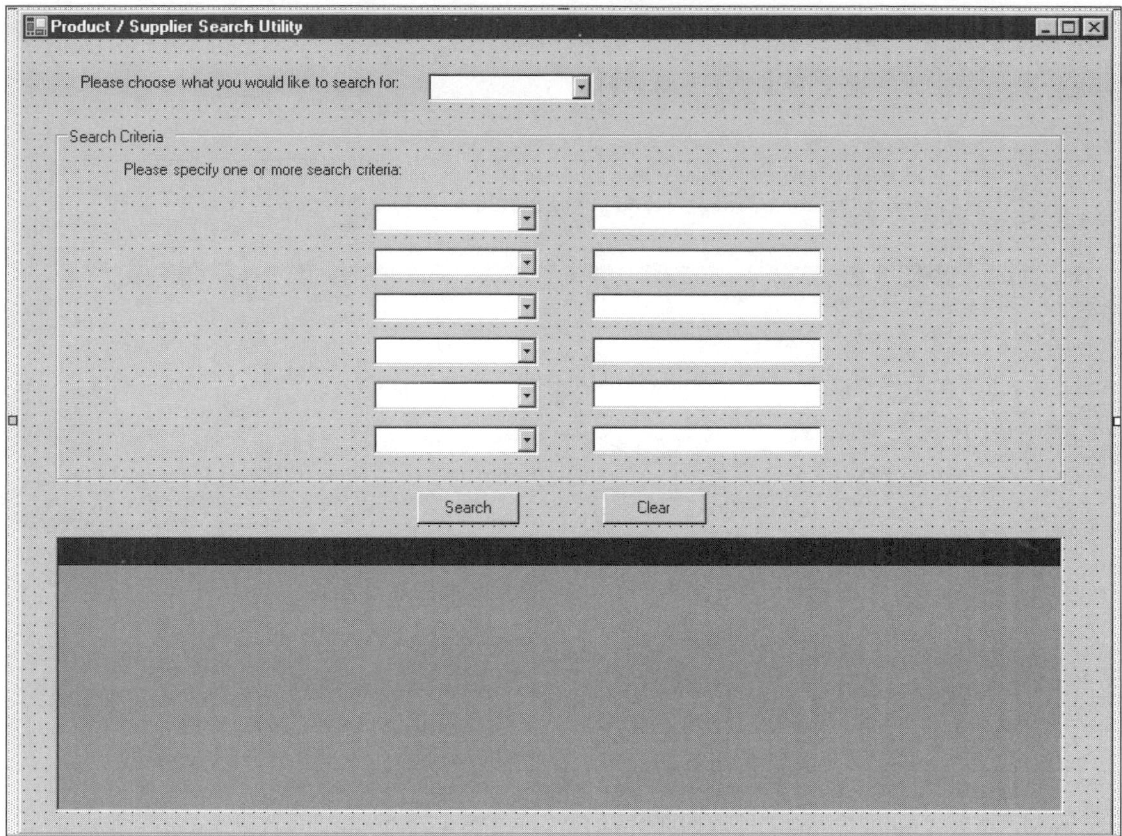

11. Next, set the tab stop properties so that when the user tabs from one field to the next, it happens in the proper sequence. From the View menu, select Tab Order. Click the number next to each of the controls in the search criteria group box in order, beginning with the "Please specify one or more search criteria" label and continuing from left to right so that the controls are numbered as shown below. When finished setting the tab order, from the View menu, select Tab Order to turn off the visual indicator showing where the tab stops are located.

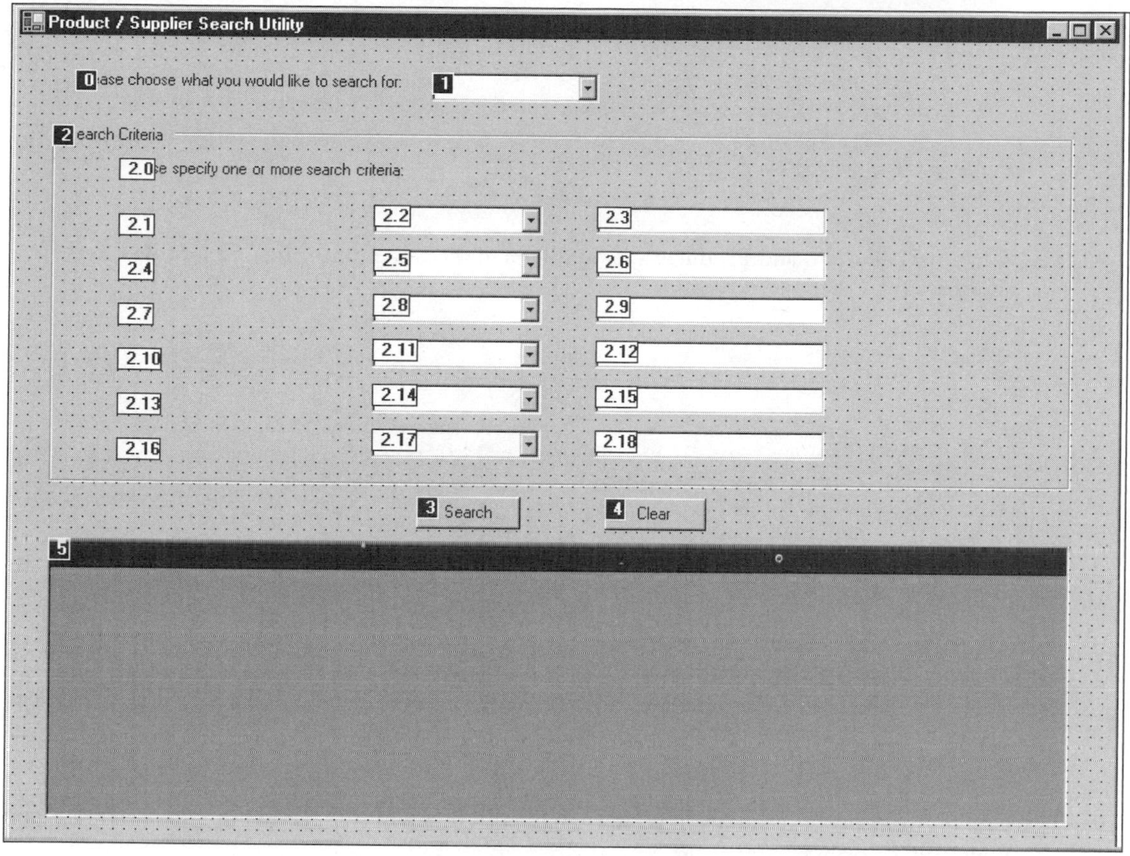

12. Always make sure to select **File | Save All** to save your changes at regular intervals.

13. Now that we have the user interface elements completed on the `BaseSearchForm`, let's put the code under the form that all search forms will have in common. To get to the code view, either double-click on the form or right-click on the form in Solution Explorer and choose **View Code**. Place these lines of code directly beneath the `Inherits System.Windows.Forms.Form` statement in the code:

```
Protected Const PROD = "Products"
Protected Const SUPP = "Suppliers"
Protected Const CONN = "user id=sa;password=xxxxx;initial " & _
              "catalog=NorthwindSQL;server=goz3"

Protected dsData As DataSet
Protected dsResults As DataSet
Protected adapterResults As New SqlClient.SqlDataAdapter()
```

14. Next, add a generic error handling procedure that will be used to display the error message to the user:

```
Sub UnhandledExceptionHandler()

    'Display an error to the user.
    MsgBox("An error occurred. Error Number: " & Err.Number & _
          " Description: " & Err.Description & " Source: " & Err.Source)

End Sub
```

15. Add a procedure to add Products and Suppliers to the `SearchMethod` ComboBox as choices.

```
Sub AddSearchMethod()

    Try
        'If the form has not been loaded before, then populate the
        'search choices in the drop-down list.
        If cboSearchMethod.Items.Count = 0 Then
            cboSearchMethod.Items.Add(PROD)
            cboSearchMethod.Items.Add(SUPP)
        End If

    Catch
        'error handling goes here
        UnhandledExceptionHandler()
    End Try

End Sub
```

16. Create two procedures that will populate a ComboBox with the search options. Place this code under the `BaseSearchForm`:

```
Sub AddCharDropDownCriteria(ByVal cboIn As ComboBox)

    Try
        'Add these values to the combo box passed in.
        'that is, to ComboBoxes searching against character fields
        cboIn.Items.Add("Equals")
        cboIn.Items.Add("Starts With")
        cboIn.Items.Add("Ends With")
        cboIn.Items.Add("Contains")

    Catch
        'Error handling goes here.
        UnhandledExceptionHandler()
    End Try

End Sub
```

```
Sub AddNumericDropDownCriteria(ByVal cboIn As ComboBox)

    Try
```

```
            'Add these values to the ComboBox passed in.
            'that is, to combo boxes searching against numeric fields

            cboIn.Items.Add("Equals")
            cboIn.Items.Add("Greater Than")
            cboIn.Items.Add("Less Than")

        Catch
            'Error handling goes here.
            UnhandledExceptionHandler()
        End Try

    End Sub
```

We will later call these procedures from the Search Products and Search Suppliers Forms to populate the ComboBoxes.

17. Finally, double-click the Clear button on your form and add the following code to the `Click` event:

```
    Private Sub btnClear_Click(ByVal sender As System.Object, ByVal e As _
                System.EventArgs) Handles btnClear.Click

        'Clear the search criteria.

        Try

            txtCriteria1.Text = ""
            txtCriteria2.Text = ""
            txtCriteria3.Text = ""
            txtCriteria4.Text = ""
            txtCriteria5.Text = ""
            txtCriteria6.Text = ""

            dgdResults.DataSource = Nothing
            dsResults = Nothing

        Catch
            'Error handling goes here.
            UnhandledExceptionHandler()
        End Try

    End Sub
```

18. This is a good point to save our work again using File | Save All. By regularly saving our project, we minimize the loss we would suffer in the event of a system crash.

19. Now that the code for our `BaseSearchForm` is complete, it is time to build (rebuild) the project. To do so, select Build | Rebuild All. This will compile the project and make sure no compiler errors exist and will also update the appropriate project files with newer build information.

How It Works

In this section, we created a project for the `BaseSearchForm`. The project was changed to a Class Library instead of a Windows Application to designate that it is to be used for inheritance purposes and not as a Windows Application on its own. We then created the user interface elements for the form that all search forms will have in common. Likewise, we also added the generic procedures for handling form errors, populating the search criteria and methods, etc. Since these features are the same regardless of whether you are searching for a product or a supplier, the base form is the appropriate place to include them.

First, we added the form constant and variable declarations.

```
Protected Const PROD = "Products"
Protected Const SUPP = "Suppliers"
Protected Const CONN = "user id=sa;password=xxxxx;initial " & _
                "catalog=NorthwindSQL;server=goz3"

Protected dsData As DataSet
Protected dsResults As DataSet
Protected adapterResults As New SqlClient.SqlDataAdapter()
```

The first three lines above declare constants for the Products, Suppliers, and the database connection string. The next three lines of code declare variables for two DataSets, which will hold the search results and code tables and a data adapter that will be used to work with the DataSets.

Note in the step above, we set up the connection string constant `CONN`, and you will need to replace the username and password with your own, and the server parameter (currently `goz3`) with the name of your SQL Server. To find out your Server's name, just open up the SQL Server Service Manager by clicking on its icon in the System Tray in the task bar, and read the name from the **Server** drop-down box.

We added a procedure to add Products and Suppliers to the Search Method ComboBoxes to allow the user to switch between the Products and Suppliers Search Screens. This will be called from each form to populate the Search Method ComboBox.

```
Sub AddSearchMethod()

    Try
        'If the form has not been loaded before, then populate the
        'search choices in the drop-down list.
        If cboSearchMethod.Items.Count = 0 Then
            cboSearchMethod.Items.Add(PROD)
            cboSearchMethod.Items.Add(SUPP)
        End If

    Catch
        'Error handling goes here.
        UnhandledExceptionHandler()
    End Try

End Sub
```

Try...Catch...Finally can be used in your Visual Basic .NET code to catch exceptions. You place the Try...Catch...Finally block of code around the code where an exception might occur. The Try statement comes before the block of code, the Catch statement is where you specify the type of errors to look for or just have a generic error handler for all errors. The above code shows an example of a generic handler that raises all errors. The optional Finally statement follows the Catch statement and contains cleanup code that should always execute. It is possible to use multiple Catch statements in our error handling code. For example, you might want to put a Catch statement for each error that you want to handle individually and then a generic Catch statement to handle all other errors. Suppose that you suspect that a "Divide by Zero" error might occur and you want to handle for it. You can use a Catch statement that reads something like this:

```
Catch excDivideByZero As System.OverFlowException
```

and then a generic Catch statement that contains what to do in all other situations. It is also important to mention that you can have multiple Try...Catch...Finally blocks in a procedure. You simply wrap the section of code where you want to trap errors with these statements.

Next, we created procedures to populate the Search Criteria ComboBoxes on the Search Screens. The ComboBoxes in the Product Search Criteria and Supplier Search Criteria GroupBoxes are to be populated with values such as "Starts With", "Ends With", "Equals", "Contains", "Greater Than", or "Less Than".

```
Sub AddCharDropDownCriteria(ByVal cboIn As ComboBox)

    Try
        'Add these values to the ComboBox passed in.
        'that is, to combo boxes searching against character fields.
        cboIn.Items.Add("Equals")
        cboIn.Items.Add("Starts With")
        cboIn.Items.Add("Ends With")
        cboIn.Items.Add("Contains")

    Catch
        'Error handling goes here.
        UnhandledExceptionHandler()
    End Try

End Sub
```

The AddCharDropDownCriteria procedure adds the following four items to the ComboBox passed in: Equals, Starts With, Ends With, and Contains. These options are relevant to ComboBoxes that will be used to search text fields, while the AddNumericDropDownCriteria method, below, is suitable for populating ComboBoxes associated with numeric fields. An example of a text field is the product name and an example of a numeric field is the product ID.

```
Sub AddNumericDropDownCriteria(ByVal cboIn As ComboBox)

    Try

        'Add these values to the ComboBox passed in.
        'that is, to ComboBoxes searching against numeric fields.
```

```
            cboIn.Items.Add("Equals")
            cboIn.Items.Add("Greater Than")
            cboIn.Items.Add("Less Than")

        Catch
            'Error handling goes here.
            UnhandledExceptionHandler()
        End Try

    End Sub
```

This will give users great flexibility in determining the precise records to retrieve from the database. For example, they could look up all products that contain the word "butter" anywhere in the product name by choosing Contains in the Product Name ComboBox and entering butter in the associated TextBox.

Lastly, we added the code for the `Click` event for the Clear button. When the user clicks the Clear button on the form, the criteria in each TextBox should be cleared as well as any records in the DataGrid.

```
        'Clear the search criteria.

        Try

            txtCriteria1.Text = ""
            txtCriteria2.Text = ""
            txtCriteria3.Text = ""
            txtCriteria4.Text = ""
            txtCriteria5.Text = ""
            txtCriteria6.Text = ""

            dgdResults.DataSource = Nothing
            dsResults = Nothing
```

With the base form created, we are now in a position to create the specific Products and Suppliers Search Screens that will inherit from this common set of functionality. We will then specify the few items that are different to customize the searches for either products or suppliers. You will soon see how visual inheritance saves extra coding effort because you do not repeat basically the same code or controls multiple times just to accomplish something nearly the same on a different form. Instead, you build from the core functionality and then make the few adjustments necessary for the particular search form. Let's now see how this works by creating a new project with two forms that inherit from the `BaseSearchForm`.

Inheriting from the Base Search Form

Now, we will create a new project for our main Product Management System. After creating the project, we will add two forms that inherit from the BaseSearchForm we created in the prior section and specify the Product Search Screen as the startup form. In the next section, we will move on to implementing the specific functionality that makes the Products Search Screen unique.

Try It Out – Creating a New Project and Inheriting from the Base Search Form

1. Select File | New | Project, and select Visual Basic Projects and then Windows Application. Browse to the same directory where you created the base forms project. Name this project MainApp and click OK.

2. Add the BaseForms project to the MainApp solution. Right-click the MainApp solution name in the Solution Explorer. From the pop-up menu, choose Add | Existing Project. On the dialog box that appears, select the Browse button and navigate to the BaseForms project directory. Select the BaseForms.vbproj project file and click OK. You should see that the BaseForms project has been added to the current solution.

3. In the Solution Explorer, right-click on the MainApp project name and select Add | Add Inherited Form. Alternatively, select Project | Add Inherited Form. Give the inherited form the name frmSearchProducts.vb as it will serve as the Products Search Screen.

4. The Inheritance Picker dialog box will appear, as shown below. Select the BaseSearchForm in the list and click OK. This adds the Products Search Screen to the project as a child inheriting from the BaseSearchForm.

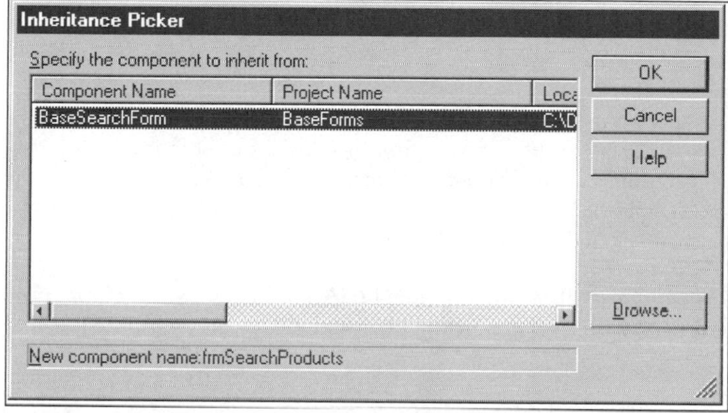

5. Next, add the Suppliers Search Form. In the Solution Explorer, right-click on the MainApp project name and select Add | Add Inherited Form. In the alternative, select Project | Add Inherited Form. Give the inherited form the name frmSearchSuppliers.vb.

6. On the Inheritance Picker dialog box, select the BaseSearchForm component and click OK. This designates that the new form will inherit functionality from the BaseSearchForm.

7. Delete Form1.vb from the MainApp project by right-clicking the file in Solution Explorer, and selecting Delete.

8. Change the Startup Form for the MainApp project to frmSearchProducts. Select the MainApp project in Solution Explorer, right-click, and choose Properties from the pop-up menu. On the dialog box that appears, change the Startup Object field from Form1 to frmSearchProducts and click OK to accept the change.

9. Save all changes to the solution by using File | Save All. The solution should look like the following at this point:

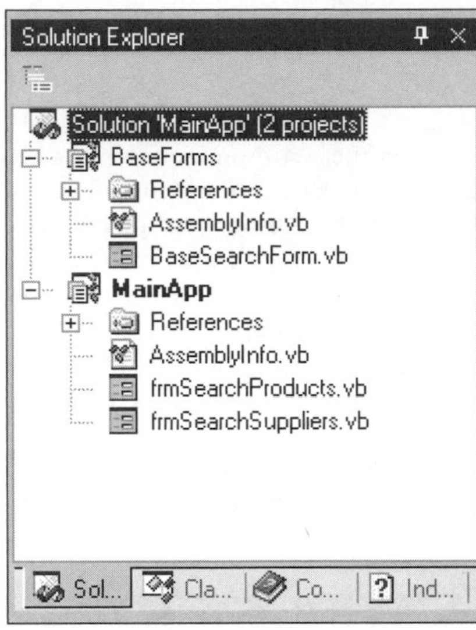

How It Works

We created a new project for the main application and then added the BaseForms project to the MainApp solution, so both the BaseForms and MainApp projects exist in one solution. Using the Inheritance Picker, we then added two forms to the MainApp project that inherit from the `BaseSearchForm`. After adding the two new forms, we deleted the Form1 default form that got added when the project was created. Next, we assigned the `frmSearchProducts` form to be the startup project.

These two child forms inherit all of the functionality from the `BaseSearchForm`. If you double-click on either of the forms, you will see something like the following:

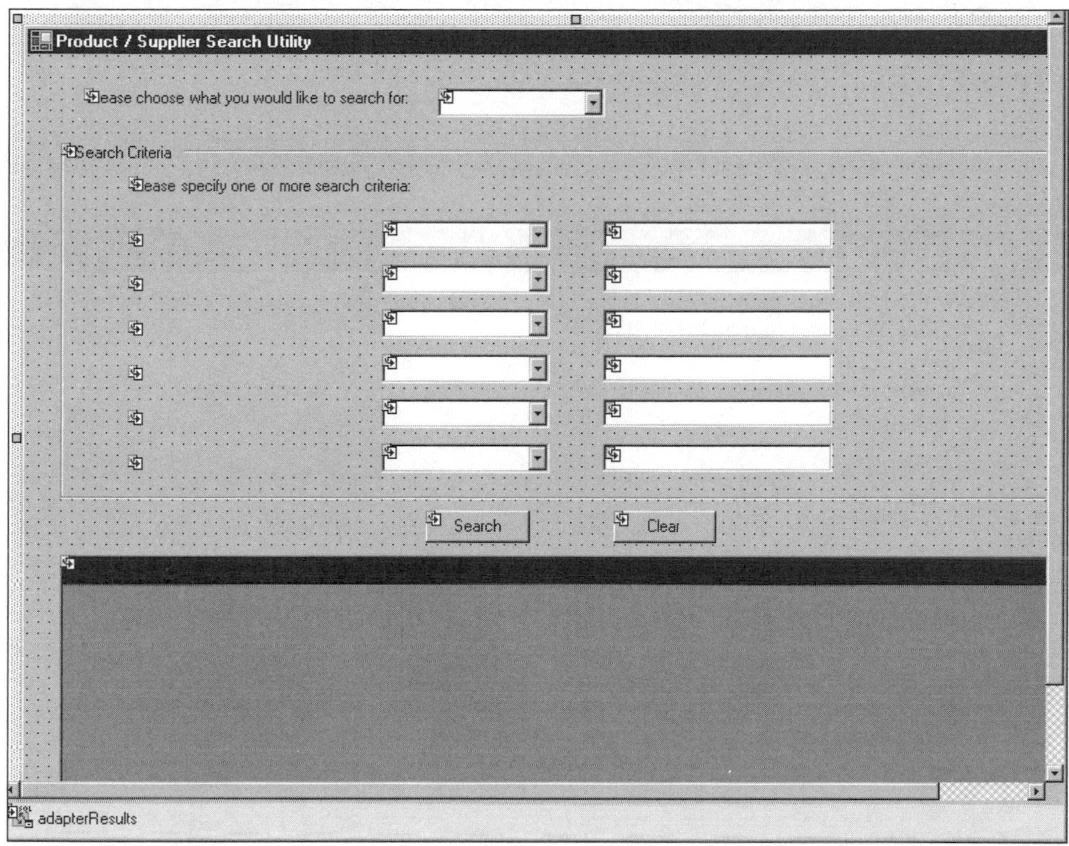

Notice how the `frmSearchProduct` form shown above looks exactly like the `BaseSearchForm` we created. The arrows on each control as shown above designate that the control is inherited from another form (versus being one added to this form specifically). If you view the code under this form, you will see these lines of code at the top of the code section:

```
Public Class frmSearchProducts
    Inherits BaseForms.BaseSearchForm
```

These lines specifically declare that the `frmSearchProducts` form is inheriting the functionality of the `BaseForms.BaseSearchForm`. This code was automatically created by Visual Basic .NET when the Inheritance Picker was used to specify which form to inherit from. Recall that we earlier discussed that such a line of code can be added to any class (form or otherwise) to inherit functionality from another class.

If you press F5 or select Debug | Start, then the Products Search Form will appear and will look just like the form above, only it will be in run mode (instead of design mode).

Now that we have the Product and Supplier Search screens inheriting their base functionality from the `BaseSearchForm`, we are ready to implement the customizations for each of them that make them unique.

Implementing the Unique Functionality of the Products Search Form

In this section, we will customize the Products Search Form by adding a small amount of code that will implement some of the additional functionality it requires. Other specific features will be added later in this chapter and in the next chapter.

Try It Out – Creating Specific Code for the Products Search Form

1. Add the following code to the `frmSearchProducts.vb` code section to allow selection of the Search Screen (either Products or Suppliers):

```
Private Sub cboSearchMethod_SelectedIndexChanged(ByVal sender As _
            System.Object, ByVal e As System.EventArgs) Handles _
            cboSearchMethod.SelectedIndexChanged

    Try

        'If the user wants to search by Suppliers, then open the
        'Suppliers form.
        'Otherwise, it will just remain on the Products search as it is
        'now.
        If cboSearchMethod.Text = SUPP Then
            Dim frmSuppliers As New frmSearchSuppliers()
            frmSuppliers.Show()
        End If

    Catch
        'Error handling goes here.
        UnhandledExceptionHandler()
    End Try

End Sub
```

2. Add the following code:

```
Private Sub frmSearchProducts_Load(ByVal sender As System.Object, _
        ByVal e As System.EventArgs) Handles MyBase.Load

    Try

        'Set the title of the form.
         Me.Text = "Product Search Utility"

        'Populate the search method drop-down list.
         AddSearchMethod()

        'Set products as the default selected (since this is the
        'Products search form).
        cboSearchMethod.Text = PROD
```

```
            'Populate the drop-down lists on the Products Group Box
            'with the proper values
            'Product Id
            AddNumericDropDownCriteria(cbocriteria1)
            'Product Name
            AddCharDropDownCriteria(cbocriteria2)
            'Supplier Company Name
            AddCharDropDownCriteria(cbocriteria3)
            'Category Name
            AddCharDropDownCriteria(cbocriteria4)
            'Unit Price
            AddNumericDropDownCriteria(cbocriteria5)
            'Units In Stock
            AddNumericDropDownCriteria(cbocriteria6)

            'Populate the corresponding labels with a
            'descriptive label.
            lblcriteria1.Text = "Product Id:"
            lblcriteria2.Text = "Product Name:"
            lblcriteria3.Text = "Supplier Company Name:"
            lblcriteria4.Text = "Category Name:"
            lblcriteria5.Text = "Unit Price:"
            lblcriteria6.Text = "Units In Stock:"

            'Assign the proper label to the GroupBox.
            grpsearchcriteria.Text = "Products Search Criteria"

        Catch
            'Error handling goes here.
            UnhandledExceptionHandler()
        End Try

    End Sub
```

How It Works

The first code section we added allows the user to switch to the Suppliers Search Screen to perform a search on Suppliers.

```
'If the user wants to search by Suppliers, then open the
'Suppliers form.
'Otherwise, it will just remain on the Products search as it is
'now.
If cboSearchMethod.Text = SUPP Then
    Dim frmSuppliers As New frmSearchSuppliers()
    frmSuppliers.Show()
End If
```

When the user changes the search method to Suppliers, that code will execute and will create and display a Suppliers form.

When the Products Search Screen loads, several customizations need to take place, such as displaying the proper labels for each search criteria, populating the search criteria ComboBoxes with the correct type of criteria options, etc. Next, we added the code to populate the search criteria ComboBoxes with the appropriate values, such as allowing `ProductId` (a numeric field) to be searched on `Equals`, `Greater Than`, or `Less Than` and for `ProductName` (a character field) to be searched on `Equals`, `Starts With`, `Ends With`, or `Contains`.

```
'Populate the drop-down lists on the Products Group Box
'with the proper values.
'Product Id
AddNumericDropDownCriteria(cbocriteria1)
'Product Name
AddCharDropDownCriteria(cbocriteria2)
'Supplier Company Name
AddCharDropDownCriteria(cbocriteria3)
'Category Name
AddCharDropDownCriteria(cbocriteria4)
'Unit Price
AddNumericDropDownCriteria(cbocriteria5)
'Units In Stock
AddNumericDropDownCriteria(cbocriteria6)
```

Recall that the `AddCharDropDownCriteria` and `AddNumericDropDownCriteria` procedures were created as part of the code for the base form and we are calling it from here. Can you see why we put the code for these two routines as part of the base form but we put the calls to it on the Product Search Screen? It is because the calls to the two procedures will be different for products and suppliers, as the fields those screens allow you to search for are not the same.

Then we customized the labels on the Products Search Screen as appropriate for products, such as to allow the user to search by `Product Id`, `Product Name`, etc.

```
'Populate the corresponding labels with a
'descriptive label.
lblcriteria1.Text = "Product Id:"
lblcriteria2.Text = "Product Name:"
lblcriteria3.Text = "Supplier Company Name:"
lblcriteria4.Text = "Category Name:"
lblcriteria5.Text = "Unit Price:"
lblcriteria6.Text = "Units In Stock:"
```

If you run the project at this point, you will see that the Products Search opens by default and contains the values in the drop-down lists that got populated above. An example of this is shown opposite:

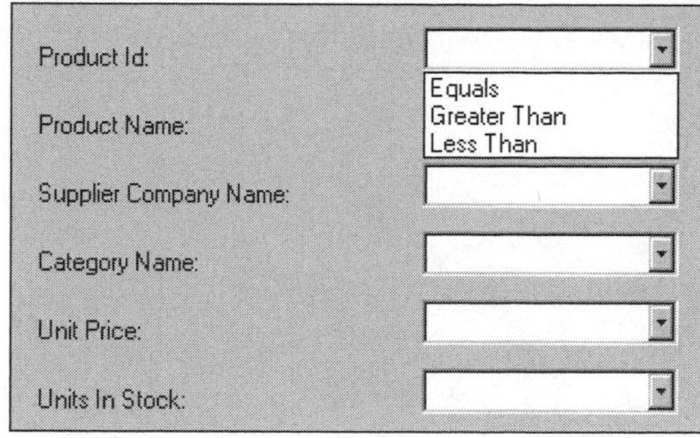

You will also be able to select Suppliers as a search method and a Suppliers Search Screen will appear. However, it does not yet have the values for the ComboBoxes as we haven't implemented them. Let's do that now, shall we?

Implementing the Unique Functionality of the Suppliers Search Form

In this section, we will customize the Suppliers Search Form by adding code that will implement some of the additional functionality that it requires. As with the Products Search Form, other specific features will be added later in this chapter and in the next chapter.

Try It Out – Creating Specific Code for the Suppliers Search Form

1. The following code should be placed on the `frmSearchSuppliers.vb` form:

```
    Private Sub cboSearchMethod_SelectedIndexChanged(ByVal sender As
            System.Object, ByVal e As System.EventArgs) Handles _
            cboSearchMethod.SelectedIndexChanged

        Try

            'If the user wants to search by Products, then open the Products
            'form. Otherwise, it will just remain on the Suppliers search as
            'it is now.
            If cboSearchMethod.Text = PROD Then
                Dim frmProducts As New frmSearchProducts()
                frmProducts.Show()
            End If

        Catch
            'Error handling goes here.
            UnhandledExceptionHandler()
        End Try

End Sub
```

2. Now, add this section of code so that the appropriate labels and search criteria choices are displayed for supplier searches:

```
    Private Sub frmSearchSuppliers_Load(ByVal sender As System.Object, _
            ByVal e As System.EventArgs) Handles MyBase.Load

        Try
            'Set the title of the form.
            Me.Text = "Supplier Search Utility"

            'Populate the search method drop-down list.
            AddSearchMethod()

            'Set suppliers as the default selected (since this is the
            'Suppliers search form).
            cboSearchMethod.Text = SUPP

            'Populate the drop-down lists on the Suppliers Group Box
            'with the proper values.
            'Supplier Id
            AddNumericDropDownCriteria(cbocriteria1)
            'Company Name
            AddCharDropDownCriteria(cbocriteria2)
            'Contact Name
            AddCharDropDownCriteria(cbocriteria3)
            'City
            AddCharDropDownCriteria(cbocriteria4)
            'Region (State)
            AddCharDropDownCriteria(cbocriteria5)
            'Postal Code
            AddCharDropDownCriteria(cbocriteria6)

            'Populate the corresponding labels with a
            'descriptive label.
            lblcriteria1.Text = "Supplier Id:"
            lblcriteria2.Text = "Company Name:"
            lblcriteria3.Text = "Contact Name:"
            lblcriteria4.Text = "City:"
            lblcriteria5.Text = "Region (State):"
            lblcriteria6.Text = "Postal Code:"

            'Assign the proper label to the GroupBox
            grpsearchcriteria.Text = "Suppliers Search Criteria"

        Catch
            'Error handling goes here.
            UnhandledExceptionHandler()
        End Try

    End Sub
```

How It Works

You can see that this code functions in the same manner as the code we placed under the Products Search Form, but that this one contains the specifics for the Suppliers Search Form. You are hopefully starting to see, at this point, how to make decisions about what to place under your base form and what is a customization that goes in the child forms.

If you want to run the project, go ahead and do so. The Product Search Utility still appears first but, now, when you open the Suppliers Search Utility form, you will see that the ComboBoxes are populated with values.

Click on the X in the top right corner to close the application and return to the Form Design view. Now that we have created the basic user interface for the Search Screens, we are ready to move on to learn about the `DataSet`. Once we understand how the `DataSet` works, we can create the code to retrieve the records from the database that match the criteria provided by the user.

Using the DataSet to Retrieve Data

In chapters 5 and 6, we introduced the `DataSet` and discussed how a `DataSet` object represents an in-memory store of data that retains no connection to the database from which it was populated. We also saw how to retrieve data into a `DataSet` by placing a `SqlDataAdapter` on the form and then using the Data Adapter Configuration Wizard to configure it. Now, we are going to look at the `DataSet` in more detail, including details of the object model as well as how to create a `DataSet` programmatically as opposed to with a Wizard.

The DataSet Object

As we saw in the last chapter, `DataSets` are designed to be disconnected from the data source that provides their contents, and that a `DataSet`, by virtue of its in-memory nature, allows rapid manipulation of data. The `DataSet` Object Model consists of the following objects:

- `DataSet` – an in-memory store of data
- `DataTable` – an in-memory store of a database table (which doesn't have to come directly from a single table in the database – it can be based on the results of a `SELECT` statement joining multiple tables)
- `DataRow` – allows for management of rows in a `DataTable`
- `DataColumn` – defines the columns of a `DataTable`
- `DataRelation` – allows two `DataTables` to be associated with each other
- `DataView` – creates a view on a subset of the data - covered in greater detail in Chapter 8

The best way to learn about these is to dive right in and see how they can be used in practice in our Products Management System!

Populating a DataSet from Multiple Tables and Relating Them to Each Other

In this section, we will write code to populate a `DataSet` that, in later chapters, will be used as a code table to display certain values in ListBoxes. But don't worry about that detail yet. Instead, concentrate on understanding how the `DataSet` works.

Try It Out – Populating a DataSet from Stored Procedures and Adding Relationships

1. Add a class module to the MainApp project. In the Solution Explorer, right-click on the MainApp project name and select Add | Add Class. Alternatively, select Project | Add Class. Give the class the name `clsDatabase.vb`.

2. Open the `clsDatabase` class in the project and add these two statements at the top of the class declaration (prior to the `Public Class clsDatabase` statement):

```
Imports System.Data
Imports System.Data.SqlClient
```

3. Next, we need a generic function that will populate a `DataSet` with the results of a stored procedure or SQL statement. Place the following `PopulateDataSetTable` function into the `clsDatabase` class:

```
    Function PopulateDataSetTable(ByVal strConnection As String, ByVal _
             strTableName As String, ByVal strSQLorStoredProc As String, _
             ByVal blnStoredProcedure As Boolean, _
             ByRef dsDataSet As DataSet) As DataSet

        '*************************************************************
        'Create a table in the DataSet and fill it with the specified
        'table in the database from calling a stored procedure or
        'executing a SQL statement (depending on whether
        'blnStoredProcedure is true or false; if true - run stored
        'procedure; if false, run SQL statement).
        '*************************************************************

        Try

            Dim sqlConn As New SqlClient.SqlConnection(strConnection)
            sqlConn.Open()

            Dim adapterProducts As New SqlClient.SqlDataAdapter()

            adapterProducts.TableMappings.Add("Table", strTableName)
            Dim cmdTable As SqlClient.SqlCommand = New _
                        SqlClient.SqlCommand(strSQLorStoredProc, _
                        sqlConn)

            'Run stored procedure or SQL statement accordingly.
            If blnStoredProcedure Then
                cmdTable.CommandType = CommandType.StoredProcedure
            Else
```

```
            cmdTable.CommandType = CommandType.Text
        End If

        adapterProducts.SelectCommand = cmdTable

        'Fill the DataSet with the table information as specified in
        'the stored procedure or from the results of the SQL statement.
        adapterProducts.Fill(dsDataSet)

        sqlConn.Close()

        Return dsDataSet

    Catch
        'Error handling goes here.
        UnhandledExceptionHandler()
    End Try

End Function
```

4. We are now going to create a generic function that creates a relationship between two tables in a `DataSet`. Place the following function, `PopulateDataSetRelationship`, into the `clsDatabase` class.

```
Function PopulateDataSetRelationship(ByVal strTable1 As String, ByVal _
         strTable2 As String, ByVal strColumnFromTable1 As String, _
         ByVal strColumnFromTable2 As String, ByVal _
         strRelationshipName As String, ByRef dsDataSet As DataSet) _
         As DataSet

    '*************************************************************
    'The purpose of this function is to create a relationship between
    'two tables in a DataSet.
    '*************************************************************

    Try

        Dim drRelation As DataRelation
        Dim dcCol1 As DataColumn
        Dim dcCol2 As DataColumn

        dcCol1 = _
              dsDataSet.Tables(strTable1).Columns(strColumnFromTable1)
        dcCol2 = _
              dsDataSet.Tables(strTable2).Columns(strColumnFromTable2)
        drRelation = New System.Data.DataRelation _
                   (strRelationshipName, dcCol1, dcCol2)
        dsDataSet.Relations.Add(drRelation)

        Return dsDataSet

    Catch
```

```
            'Error handling goes here.
            UnhandledExceptionHandler()
        End Try

    End Function
```

5. Place the following function `LoadCompleteDataSet` into the `clsDatabase` class.

```
Function LoadCompleteDataSet (ByVal strConnection As String) As DataSet

        '*****************************************************************
        'The purpose of this function is to populate a DataSet with
        'the local tables from the Products, Suppliers, and Categories
        'tables in the database.  This is an example of a DataSet that
        'uses relations among the tables.
        '*****************************************************************

        Try
            Dim dsData As New DataSet()

            Dim blnRunStoredProc As Boolean = True

            'Create a Products table in the DataSet.
            dsData = PopulateDataSetTable(strConnection, "Products", _
                     "spRetrieveProducts", blnRunStoredProc, dsData)

            'Create a Suppliers table in the DataSet.
            dsData = PopulateDataSetTable(strConnection, "Suppliers", _
                     "spRetrieveSuppliers", blnRunStoredProc, dsData)

            'Create a Categories table in the DataSet.
            dsData = PopulateDataSetTable(strConnection, "Categories", _
                     "spRetrieveCategories", blnRunStoredProc, dsData)

            'Create the relationship between Products and Suppliers tables.
            dsData = PopulateDataSetRelationship("Suppliers", "Products", _
                    "SupplierId", "SupplierId", "ProductsVsSuppliers", _
                     dsData)

            'Create the relationship between Products and Categories tables.
            dsData = PopulateDataSetRelationship("Categories", "Products", _
                    "CategoryId", "CategoryId", "ProductsVsCategories", _
                     dsData)

            WriteCompleteDataSetToOutputWindow(dsData)

            Return dsData

        Catch
            'Error handling goes here.
            UnhandledExceptionHandler()
        End Try

    End Function
```

6. Three stored procedures are used to retrieve the data from the `Products`, `Suppliers`, and `Categories` tables. Create the stored procedure `spRetrieveProducts` shown below using Server Explorer, as described in detail in Chapter 4. In short, navigate to the **SQL Servers** node in Server Explorer and expand the tree down until you can select the **NorthwindSQL** database. Under the NorthwindSQL database, right-click on the **Stored Procedures** node and select **New Stored Procedure**. Place the code below in the **NewStored Procedure** window that is opened:

```
CREATE PROCEDURE dbo.spRetrieveProducts
(
@ProductId int = NULL
)
/*
If the ProductId is not present, then return all products.  Otherwise, return only
that product.
*/
AS
IF @ProductId IS NULL
    BEGIN
       SELECT * FROM Products
   END
ELSE
    BEGIN
        SELECT * FROM Products WHERE ProductId = @ProductId
    END

RETURN
```

7. Next, create the stored procedure `spRetrieveSuppliers`, as shown below:

```
CREATE PROCEDURE dbo.spRetrieveSuppliers
(
@SupplierId int = NULL
)
/*
If the SupplierId is not present, then return all suppliers.  Otherwise, return
only that supplier.
*/
AS
IF @SupplierId IS NULL
    BEGIN
       SELECT * FROM Suppliers
   END
ELSE
    BEGIN
        SELECT * FROM Suppliers WHERE SupplierId = @SupplierId
    END

RETURN
```

8. Then add the stored procedure `spRetrieveCategories`, as shown overleaf:

```
CREATE PROCEDURE dbo.spRetrieveCategories
AS
   SELECT * FROM categories
   RETURN
```

9. Next, add this procedure to the `clsDatabase` class. This procedure gets called from the `LoadCompleteDataSet` function created previously and outputs the `DataSet` information to the Output window.

```
    Sub WriteCompleteDataSetToOutputWindow(ByVal dsData As DataSet)
        '*****************************************************************
        'Write data to the output window from the DataSet.
        '*****************************************************************

        Try

            Dim oRow As DataRow
            Dim strRecord As String

            'Write some data in the Products table to the Output window
            'to show that the data is there.
            For Each oRow In dsData.Tables("Products").Rows
                strRecord = "Product Id: " & oRow("ProductId").ToString()
                strRecord = strRecord & "  Product Name: "
                strRecord = strRecord & oRow("ProductName").ToString()
                strRecord = strRecord & "  Supplier Id: "
                strRecord = strRecord & oRow("SupplierId").ToString()
                Console.WriteLine(strRecord)

            Next

            'Write some data in the Suppliers table to the Output window
            'to show that the data is there.
            For Each oRow In dsData.Tables("Suppliers").Rows
                strRecord = "Supplier Id: " & oRow("SupplierId").ToString()
                strRecord = strRecord & "  Company Name: "
                strRecord = strRecord & oRow("CompanyName").ToString()
                strRecord = strRecord & "  Contact Name: "
                strRecord = strRecord & oRow("ContactName").ToString()
                Console.WriteLine(strRecord)
            Next

            'Write some data in the Categories table to the Output window
            'to show that the data is there.
            For Each oRow In dsData.Tables("Categories").Rows
                strRecord = "Category Id: " & oRow("CategoryId").ToString()
                strRecord = strRecord & "  Category Name: "
                strRecord = strRecord & oRow("CategoryName").ToString()
                strRecord = strRecord & "  Description: "
                strRecord = strRecord & oRow("Description").ToString()
                Console.WriteLine(strRecord)
            Next
```

```
        Catch
            'Error handling goes here.
            UnhandledExceptionHandler()
        End Try

    End Sub
```

10. Finally, add the `UnhandledExceptionHandler` to the `clsDatabase` class

```
    Sub UnhandledExceptionHandler()

        'Display an error to the user.
        MsgBox("An error occurred. Error Number: " & Err.Number & _
              " Description: " & Err.Description & " Source: " & Err.Source)

    End Sub
```

How It Works

In this section, first we created a new class, `clsDatabase.vb`, and added the following namespaces:

```
Imports System.Data
Imports System.Data.SqlClient
```

The `DataSet` features we will be using come from these two namespaces. If you do not have these references in your class module, then some of the code that follows will generate a compiler error when you try to build your project as they are required to locate certain classes and methods. The first namespace (`System.Data`) is for general data access, and the second namespace (`System.Data.SqlClient`) is SQL Server specific.

Next we added a generic routine that populates a `DataSet` with the results of a stored procedure or SQL statement.

```
Dim sqlConn As New SqlClient.SqlConnection(strConnection)
sqlConn.Open()

Dim adapterProducts As New SqlClient.SqlDataAdapter()

adapterProducts.TableMappings.Add("Table", strTableName)
Dim cmdTable As SqlClient.SqlCommand = New _
            SqlClient.SqlCommand(strSQLorStoredProc, _
            sqlConn)

'Run stored procedure or SQL statement accordingly.
If blnStoredProcedure Then
    cmdTable.CommandType = CommandType.StoredProcedure
Else
    cmdTable.CommandType = CommandType.Text
End If
```

```
adapterProducts.SelectCommand = cmdTable

'Fill the DataSet with the table information as specified in
'the stored procedure or from the results of the SQL statement.
adapterProducts.Fill(dsDataSet)
```

In the code snippet from the `PopulateDataSetTable` function above, notice how a `SqlConnection` is declared first, and then opened. Then, a new `SqlDataAdapter` is declared. `SqlDataAdapter` is the class used to fill and update `DataSets`. Note that `OleDbDataAdapter` can also be used, and it works with OLE DB data sources, including SQL Server. `SqlDataAdapter` on the other hand only works with SQL Server databases but, in such cases, it outperforms `OleDbDataAdapter`.

Next, table mappings are defined for the adapter. The primary purpose of a table mapping is to specify what the table in the `DataSet` should be called, regardless of the source it is coming from. The first parameter to the `Add` method is the source table and the second is the destination table. The source table is the table in the data source to retrieve information from while the destination table is the table in the `DataSet` that the data goes into. When populating the `DataSet` from a stored procedure or SQL statement, simply specifying the default value of `"Table"` for the source table is sufficient.

```
Dim adapterProducts As New SqlClient.SqlDataAdapter()

adapterProducts.TableMappings.Add("Table", strTableName)
Dim cmdTable As SqlClient.SqlCommand = New _
            SqlClient.SqlCommand(strSQLorStoredProc, _
            sqlConn)
```

A `Command` object is declared next to define the SQL statement or stored procedure to base the `DataSet` table on, as well as which database connection to use. The `Command` object is then associated with the adapter, which is how the adapter is made aware of from where to retrieve the results.

```
'Run stored procedure or SQL statement accordingly.
If blnStoredProcedure Then
    cmdTable.CommandType = CommandType.StoredProcedure
Else
    cmdTable.CommandType = CommandType.Text
End If

adapterProducts.SelectCommand = cmdTable
```

Finally, using the `DataAdapter`, the `DataSet` can be populated from the SQL statement or stored procedure.

```
'Fill the data set with the table information as specified in
'the stored procedure or from the results of the SQL statement.
adapterProducts.Fill(dsDataSet)

sqlConn.Close()
```

After creating the generic function to populate a DataSet, we then created a function called PopulateDataSetRelationship to relate two tables in a DataSet together. Recall that a DataSet is an in-memory copy of information. It can contain tables that are totally independent from the source, once placed in memory. Thus, even though relationships may exist in a database, when you populate such information into a DataSet, those relationships do not carry over between tables. You can create relationships between tables in your DataSet so that tables in the in-memory copy relate to each other.

This example makes use of the DataRelation and DataColumn objects. After the DataColumns to be related are specified (as columns already present in the DataSet), then the DataRelation object creates the relationship.

```
Dim drRelation As DataRelation
Dim dcCol1 As DataColumn
Dim dcCol2 As DataColumn

dcCol1 = _
       dsDataSet.Tables(strTable1).Columns(strColumnFromTable1)
dcCol2 = _
       dsDataSet.Tables(strTable2).Columns(strColumnFromTable2)
drRelation = New System.Data.DataRelation _
            (strRelationshipName, dcCol1, dcCol2)
dsDataSet.Relations.Add(drRelation)
```

In the above code, dcCol1 is the first table in the DataRelation method's parameters, and dcCol2 is the second. This means that dcCol1 is the **parent table**, and dcCol2 is the **child table**. A table is known as the parent table because it is the one that ensures the uniqueness of the key field on which this relationship hinges. If you were to reverse the order of these parameters, then you would likely get a run-time error about non-unique columns.

Now that we have our generic functions in place to populate a DataSet from a stored procedure or SQL statement, and one to create relationships in a DataSet, we're ready to populate a DataSet with information from the Products, Suppliers, and Categories tables. We created a LoadCompleteDataSet function to populate the DataSet that will be used in the application to store some values to populate the ComboBoxes. We sometimes refer to these as code tables.

Notice how we get to make use of the generic functions we created before to populate the DataSet. We populate the Products, Suppliers, and Categories tables in the DataSet by calling the PopulateDataSetTable function and passing the proper parameters, one of them being the stored procedure to run to retrieve the records.

```
'Create a Products table in the DataSet
dsData = PopulateDataSetTable(strConnection, "Products", _
         "spRetrieveProducts", blnRunStoredProc, dsData)

'Create a Suppliers table in the DataSet
dsData = PopulateDataSetTable(strConnection, "Suppliers", _
         "spRetrieveSuppliers", blnRunStoredProc, dsData)

'Create a Categories table in the DataSet
dsData = PopulateDataSetTable(strConnection, "Categories", _
         "spRetrieveCategories", blnRunStoredProc, dsData)

'Create the relationship between Products and Suppliers tables
```

```
dsData = PopulateDataSetRelationship("Suppliers", "Products", _
        "SupplierId", "SupplierId", "ProductsVsSuppliers", _
         dsData)

'Create the relationship between Products and Categories tables
dsData = PopulateDataSetRelationship("Categories", "Products", _
        "CategoryId", "CategoryId", "ProductsVsCategories", _
         dsData)

WriteCompleteDataSetToOutputWindow(dsData)
```

Stored procedures should be used to retrieve data whenever possible because they are precompiled on the database server and contain an execution plan which tells SQL Server how to execute them. This means that they execute faster than a SQL statement being passed on the fly to the database. Thus, retrieving values to populate our first `DataSet` was handled using stored procedures instead of a SQL statement in Visual Basic .NET code.

Later, we will look at an example of when you might need to use a SQL statement in the code instead of a stored procedure. Such cases occur typically when it would be extremely difficult, if not impossible, to determine the SQL statement up front such that it could be stored in a stored procedure. In instances like that, it makes sense to just create the SQL statement in the Visual Basic .NET code and pass the SQL statement to the database.

After populating the `DataSet`, we then created the relationships between the tables. Near the end of the `PopulateDataSetTable` function is a call to the `WriteCompleteDataSetToOutputWindow` procedure. We can comment the call to this out later but, in this chapter, we keep it in to verify that the `DataSet` is being correctly populated with the results of the query.

Let's have a quick look at what this procedure accomplishes:

```
Dim oRow As DataRow
Dim strRecord As String

'Write some data in the Products table to the Output window
'to show that the data is there.
For Each oRow In dsData.Tables("Products").Rows
    strRecord = "Product Id: " & oRow("ProductId").ToString()
    strRecord = strRecord & "  Product Name: "
    strRecord = strRecord & oRow("ProductName").ToString()
    strRecord = strRecord & "  Supplier Id: "
    strRecord = strRecord & oRow("SupplierId").ToString()
    Console.WriteLine(strRecord)

Next
```

In this case, we used the `DataRow` object to manipulate the `DataSet` and output all rows but only certain columns to the Output window.

Lastly, we added the `UnhandledExceptionHandler` to the `clsDatabase` class. This procedure will handle all unhandled exceptions that get raised in the `clsDatabase` class. This can be modified to handle errors in the `clsDatabase` class in whatever manner you desire.

It is very important that you understand what we just did in this section. We populated a DataSet with all of the records in the Products, Suppliers, and Categories tables and then related them together.

As you know, a DataSet is an in-memory copy of data. This means that it consumes memory based on the amount of records in your DataSet. The procedures we created in this section can be used in instances where your recordset is small, but you would never want to populate a DataSet with thousands of records. We just used this for illustration purposes to show you the concept of a DataSet and relationships between tables in the DataSet. In practice, you have to make good judgment calls based on the number of records being returned to determine whether this is really a good idea or not.

Now, let's move on to creating the code that will populate a DataSet from a SQL Statement and then on to writing the code to bring everything together so that it executes when the user specifies search criteria and clicks the Search button.

Populating a DataSet from a SQL Statement

Now we are ready to create a generic function that will populate a DataSet by executing a SQL statement that is passed in. We will then call this function later to have it execute the SQL statement that gets generated by the search criteria specified by the user.

Try It Out – Populating a DataSet from a Dynamic SQL Statement

1. This code below should be placed under the code for the clsDatabase.vb class:

```
Function LoadSearchDataSet(ByVal strConnection As String, ByVal strSQL _
      As String) As DataSet

     '*****************************************************************
     'The purpose of this function is to create and populate a DataSet
     'based on a SQL statement passed in to the function.
     '*****************************************************************
     Try

         Dim dsData As New DataSet()

         'Call the table in the local DataSet "results" since the values
         'may be coming from multiple tables.
         Dim strTableName As String = "Results"

         Dim blnRunStoredProc As Boolean = False

         dsData = PopulateDataSetTable(strConnection, strTableName, _
             strSQL, blnRunStoredProc, dsData)

         WriteSampleDataToOutputWindow(dsData)

         'Return the DataSet to the calling procedure.
         Return dsData

     Catch
         'Error handling goes here.
         UnhandledExceptionHandler()
```

```
        End Try

    End Function
```

2. This code should also be placed under the code for the `clsDatabase.vb` class:

```
    Sub WriteSampleDataToOutputWindow(ByVal dsdata As DataSet)

        '*****************************************************************
        'Write data to the output window from the DataSet
        '*****************************************************************

        Try

            Dim oRow As DataRow
            Dim oColumn As DataColumn

            Dim strRecord As String

            'Write some data in the Output window
            'to show that the data is there and that the SQL statement
            'worked.

            For Each oRow In dsdata.Tables("Results").Rows

                strRecord = oRow(0).ToString()
                strRecord = strRecord & "    " & oRow(1).ToString()
                strRecord = strRecord & "    " & oRow(2).ToString()
                strRecord = strRecord & "    " & oRow(3).ToString()
                strRecord = strRecord & "    " & oRow(4).ToString()
                Console.WriteLine(strRecord)
            Next

        Catch

            'Error handling goes here.
            UnhandledExceptionHandler()
        End Try

    End Sub
```

How It Works

The `LoadSearchDataSet` function calls the `PopulateDataSetTable` function with the parameter specifying that it is not a stored procedure but, rather, a SQL statement that the `DataSet` will be based upon.

```
            Dim dsData As New DataSet()

            'Call the table in the local DataSet "results" since the values
            'may be coming from multiple tables.
            Dim strTableName As String = "Results"
```

```
Dim blnRunStoredProc As Boolean = False

dsData = PopulateDataSetTable(strConnection, strTableName, _
    strSQL, blnRunStoredProc, dsData)
```

After creating the DataSet, a call is made to the WriteSampleDataToOutputWindow procedure.

```
WriteSampleDataToOutputWindow(dsData)
```

This procedure is called to write some sample data to the Output window to verify that the search results were populated correctly, based on the criteria specified by the user.

```
Dim oRow As DataRow
Dim oColumn As DataColumn

Dim strRecord As String

'Write some data in the Output window
'to show that the data is there and that the SQL statement
'worked.

For Each oRow In dsdata.Tables("Results").Rows

    strRecord = oRow(0).ToString()
    strRecord = strRecord & "    " & oRow(1).ToString()
    strRecord = strRecord & "    " & oRow(2).ToString()
    strRecord = strRecord & "    " & oRow(3).ToString()
    strRecord = strRecord & "    " & oRow(4).ToString()
    Console.WriteLine(strRecord)
Next
```

This procedure call can be commented out later but, for now, we want to see that our search results are coming back correctly.

We are now ready to write the code to generate the dynamic SQL statement based on the criteria specified by the user. In the process, we will modify the search forms so they call all of the code we created in the past two sections to populate the DataSets.

Building the SQL Statement Based on User Input

In this section, we will write the code to generate a SQL statement dynamically based on the criteria specified by the user on either of the search forms.

Try It Out – Creating a Dynamic SQL Statement Based on User Input

1. Add the following function to clsDatabase.vb:

```
    Function PadQuotes(ByVal strIn As String) As String
        '*********************************************************************
'The purpose of this (very short but important) function is to search for
'the occurrence of single quotes within a string and to replace any
```

```
'single quotes with two singles quotes in a row, so that, when executing
'the SQL statement, an error will not occur due to the database thinking
'it has reached the end of the field value. In SQL Server and some other
'databases, if you put such a delimiter twice in a row when passing a
'string SQL statement for it to execute (versus a stored procedure where
'this doesn't apply), it knows that you want to use it once - versus that
'it symbolizes the end of the value. Example: Grandma's Boysenberry then
'becomes Grandma''s Boysenberry as the database expects.
'**********************************************************************
        Try

            PadQuotes = strIn.Replace("'", "''")

        Catch
            'Error handling goes here.
            UnhandledExceptionHandler()
        End Try

    End Function
```

2. Next, add this code to the `clsDatabase.vb` class. This code will build the `WHERE` clause of the SQL statement for our search screens.

```
    Function BuildSQLWhereClause(ByVal strTableName As String, ByVal _
        strQueryOperator As String, ByVal strSearchValue As String, _
        ByVal blnPriorWhereClause As Boolean, ByVal strWhereClause As _
        String, ByVal blnNumberField As Boolean) As String

'**********************************************************************
'The purpose of this function is to add the parameters passed in to
'the WHERE clause of the SQL Statement.
'**********************************************************************

        Try

            Dim strWhere As String = strWhereClause
            Dim strDelimiter1 As String
            Dim strDelimiter2 As String

            If blnPriorWhereClause = False Then
                strWhere = " WHERE "
            Else
                strWhere = strWhere & " AND "
            End If

            Select Case strQueryOperator
                Case "Equals"
                    If blnNumberField Then
                        strDelimiter1 = " = "
                        strDelimiter2 = ""
                    Else
                        strDelimiter1 = " = '"
```

```
                strDelimiter2 = "' "
            End If

        Case "Starts With"
            strDelimiter1 = " LIKE '"
            strDelimiter2 = "%' "

        Case "Ends With"
            strDelimiter1 = " LIKE '%"
            strDelimiter2 = "' "

        Case "Contains"
            strDelimiter1 = " LIKE '%"
            strDelimiter2 = "%'"

        Case "Greater Than"
            strDelimiter1 = " > "
            strDelimiter2 = ""

        Case "Less Than"
            strDelimiter1 = " < "
            strDelimiter2 = ""

    End Select

    'Add the new criteria to the WHERE clause of the SQL Statement.
    'Note that the PadQuotes function is also being called to make
    'sure that if the user has a single quote in their search value,
    'it will put an additional quote so the database doesn't
    'generate an error.

    strWhere = strWhere & strTableName & strDelimiter1 & _
                PadQuotes(strSearchValue) & strDelimiter2

    Return strWhere

Catch
    'Error handling goes here.
    UnhandledExceptionHandler()
End Try

End Function
```

3. Next, add this function to `clsDatabase.vb` that will be used to build the `SELECT` and `FROM` clause of the dynamic SQL statement:

```
    Function BuildSQLSelectFromClause(ByVal strSearchMethod As String) _
        As String

'************************************************************************
'The purpose of this function is to create the SELECT FROM clause for
'the SQL statement depending on whether the search is for Products
```

```
'or Suppliers.
'*************************************************************************

        Try

            Dim strSelectFrom As String

            Select Case strSearchMethod

                Case "Products"
                    'Select the products information and the descriptions
                    '(Product Name and Category Name) from suppliers and
                    'categories table.
                    strSelectFrom = "SELECT p.ProductId as ProductId, " & _
                       "p.ProductName " & _
                       "as ProductName, p.SupplierId as SupplierId," & _
                       "s.CompanyName as CompanyName, p.CategoryId " & _
                       "as CategoryId, c.CategoryName as CategoryName, " & _
                       "p.QuantityPerUnit as QuantityPerUnit, " & _
                       "p.UnitPrice as UnitPrice, p.UnitsInStock " & _
                        "as UnitsInStock, p.UnitsOnOrder as " & _
                        "UnitsOnOrder, p.ReorderLevel as " & _
                        "ReorderLevel, p.Discontinued as " & _
                        "Discontinued " & _
                        "FROM Products p " & _
                        "INNER JOIN Suppliers s ON p.SupplierId = " & _
                        "s.SupplierId " & _
                        "INNER JOIN Categories c on p.CategoryId = " & _
                        "c.CategoryId"

                Case "Suppliers"
                    'Since we don't need to join to multiple tables, we can
                    'just select everything from the Suppliers table without
                    'listing the columns all out specifically.
                    strSelectFrom = "SELECT * FROM Suppliers"
            End Select

            Return strSelectFrom

        Catch
            'Error handling goes here.
            UnhandledExceptionHandler()
        End Try

    End Function
```

4. Save all of your changes to the MainApp solution and close the solution. Next, open the BaseForms solution. Add the following code to the `BaseSearchForm`. Don't worry, we'll explain it momentarily – it isn't as complicated as you might think. Go ahead and add it to the `BaseSearchForm` for now:

```
Delegate Function WhereClauseDelegate(ByVal strFieldName As String, _
              ByVal strMatchCriteria As String, _
              ByVal strFilterCriteria As String, _
              ByVal blnPriorWhere As Boolean, _
              ByVal strWhereCriteria As String, _
              ByVal blnNumberField As Boolean) As String

  Sub CheckSearchCriteria(ByVal strMatchCriteria As String, ByVal _
              strFilterCriteria As String, _
              ByVal strFieldName As String, ByRef strWhereCriteria _
              As String, ByRef blnPriorWhere As Boolean, ByVal _
              blnNumberField As Boolean, ByVal BuildWhere As _
              WhereClauseDelegate)

'**************************************************************************
'If the user filled out both a value for match criteria (Starts With, Ends
'With, etc.) and a criteria to search for in the corresponding textbox,
'then that criteria needs to be added to the WHERE clause of the SQL
'statement.
'
'Using an advanced feature called DELEGATION, this function receives a
'pointer to the clsDatabase.BuildSQLWhereClause method and invokes it with
'the Invoke statement below. Delegation really isn't hard to understand - in
'simplest terms, it allows you to pass a method as a parameter and then
'call that method.
'**************************************************************************

      If strMatchCriteria <> "" And strFilterCriteria <> "" Then
          strWhereCriteria = BuildWhere.Invoke _
              (strFieldName, strMatchCriteria, strFilterCriteria, _
               blnPriorWhere, strWhereCriteria, blnNumberField)
          blnPriorWhere = True
      End If

  End Sub
```

5. Select **Build | Rebuild All** and rebuild the BaseForms project. Then, save all of your changes and close the solution. You can next reopen the MainApp solution.

6. Now, you are ready to add some code to the Search Forms to have them read the criteria that the user typed in and build the SQL statement accordingly. On `frmSearchProducts.vb`, add the following function:

```
  Function BuildSQLStatement() As String

'*******************************************************************
'The purpose of this function is to build the SQL statement based
'on the criteria specified by the user on the Products form.
'*******************************************************************

      Try
```

```
            Dim strSQL As String = ""
            Dim strSelectFromCriteria As String = ""
            Dim strWhereCriteria As String = ""
            Dim blnPriorWhere As Boolean = False
            Dim blnNumericField As Boolean = False
            Dim clsDb As New clsDatabase()

           strSelectFromCriteria = _
                   clsDb.BuildSQLSelectFromClause("Products")
            'Check the search criteria and add to the WHERE clause if it was
            'specified. Do this for each set of criteria on the form.

            CheckSearchCriteria(cbocriteria1.Text, txtcriteria1.Text, _
                    "ProductId", strWhereCriteria, blnPriorWhere, "true", _
                    AddressOf clsDb.BuildSQLWhereClause)

            CheckSearchCriteria(cbocriteria2.Text, txtcriteria2.Text, _
                    "ProductName", strWhereCriteria, blnPriorWhere, _
                    "false", AddressOf clsDb.BuildSQLWhereClause)

            CheckSearchCriteria(cbocriteria3.Text, txtcriteria3.Text, _
                    "CompanyName", strWhereCriteria, blnPriorWhere, _
                    "false", AddressOf clsDb.BuildSQLWhereClause)

            CheckSearchCriteria(cbocriteria4.Text, txtcriteria4.Text, _
                    "CategoryName", strWhereCriteria, blnPriorWhere, _
                    "false", AddressOf clsDb.BuildSQLWhereClause)

            CheckSearchCriteria(cbocriteria5.Text, txtcriteria5.Text, _
                    "UnitPrice", strWhereCriteria, blnPriorWhere, _
                    "true", AddressOf clsDb.BuildSQLWhereClause)

            CheckSearchCriteria(cbocriteria6.Text, txtcriteria6.Text, _
                    "UnitsInStock", strWhereCriteria, blnPriorWhere, _
                    "true", AddressOf clsDb.BuildSQLWhereClause)

            'Put the SELECT, FROM, and WHERE clauses together into one
            'string.
            strSQL = strSelectFromCriteria & strWhereCriteria

            'Remove this message box after finished testing SQL syntax
            MsgBox("The SQL Statement is: " & strSQL)

            clsDb = Nothing

            Return strSQL

        Catch
            'Error handling goes here.
            UnhandledExceptionHandler()
        End Try

    End Function
```

7. Next, add a `BuildSQLStatement` function to the `frmSearchSuppliers.vb` form. This function contains the specific details for the Suppliers form and is different to that which was used for the Products form.

```
    Function BuildSQLStatement() As String

'*********************************************************************
'The purpose of this function is to build the SQL statement based
'on the criteria specified by the user on the Suppliers form.
'*********************************************************************

        Try

            Dim strSQL As String = ""
            Dim strSelectFromCriteria As String = ""
            Dim strWhereCriteria As String = ""
            Dim blnPriorWhere As Boolean = False
            Dim blnNumericField As Boolean = False
            Dim clsDb As New clsDatabase()

            strSelectFromCriteria = _
                  clsDb.BuildSQLSelectFromClause("Suppliers")

            'Check the search criteria and add to the WHERE clause if
            'it was specified. Do this for each set of criteria on the
            'form

            CheckSearchCriteria(cbocriteria1.Text, txtcriteria1.Text, _
                        "SupplierId", strWhereCriteria, blnPriorWhere, _
                    "true", AddressOf clsDb.BuildSQLWhereClause)

            CheckSearchCriteria(cbocriteria2.Text, txtcriteria2.Text, _
                    "CompanyName", strWhereCriteria, blnPriorWhere, _
                    "false", AddressOf clsDb.BuildSQLWhereClause)

            CheckSearchCriteria(cbocriteria3.Text, txtcriteria3.Text, _
                    "ContactName", strWhereCriteria, blnPriorWhere, _
                    "false", AddressOf clsDb.BuildSQLWhereClause)

            CheckSearchCriteria(cbocriteria4.Text, txtcriteria4.Text, _
                    "City", strWhereCriteria, blnPriorWhere, _
                    "false", AddressOf clsDb.BuildSQLWhereClause)

            CheckSearchCriteria(cbocriteria5.Text, txtcriteria5.Text, _
                    "Region", strWhereCriteria, blnPriorWhere, _
                    "false", AddressOf clsDb.BuildSQLWhereClause)

            CheckSearchCriteria(cbocriteria6.Text, txtcriteria6.Text, _
                    "PostalCode", strWhereCriteria, blnPriorWhere, _
                    "false", AddressOf clsDb.BuildSQLWhereClause)

            'Put the SELECT, FROM, and WHERE clauses together into one
            'string
```

```
            strSQL = strSelectFromCriteria & strWhereCriteria

            'Remove this message box after finished testing SQL syntax
            MsgBox("The SQL Statement is: " & strSQL)

            clsDb = Nothing

            Return strSQL

        Catch
            'Error handling goes here
            UnhandledExceptionHandler()
        End Try

    End Function
```

8. Last of all, add the following code to *both* the Products and Suppliers forms (`frmSearchProducts.vb` and `frmSearchSuppliers.vb`):

```
    Private Sub btnSearch_Click(ByVal sender As System.Object, ByVal e As _
                System.EventArgs) Handles btnSearch.Click

        Try

            Dim custCB As SqlClient.SqlCommandBuilder = New _
                         SqlClient.SqlCommandBuilder(adapterResults)
            Dim clsdatabase As New clsDatabase()
            Dim strSQL As String = ""

            'Load a DataSet with the complete Products, Suppliers, and
            'categories tables (to be used later as code tables to display
            'choices in a list, etc.).
            dsData = clsdatabase.LoadCompleteDataSet(CONN)

            'Load a DataSet with the search results based on the criteria
            'specified by the user on the form.
            strSQL = BuildSQLStatement()
            dsResults = clsdatabase.LoadSearchDataSet(CONN, strSQL)

        Catch
            'Error handling goes here.
            UnhandledExceptionHandler()
        End Try

    End Sub
```

How It Works

Before building the functions to dynamically generate the SQL statements, we first digressed momentarily to an important topic that can often be overlooked in database programming: the problem of the single quote character in strings. This character needs special treatment, and a poorly designed application will fail if the user attempts to use a string containing a single quote (apostrophe) for a database search query. This is because SQL uses single quotes to denote the beginning and end of a query string (that is, it's a string delimiter in SQL) and, if the user uses them within their own input, there is a real risk that the system will crash throwing an error. In order to use a single quote in a string as an apostrophe, SQL Server and many other database platforms require you to use two single quotes in a row instead of one. In this way, they are able to distinguish between a string delimiter and an apostrophe.

Of course, most users of databases are blissfully unaware of the double apostrophe requirement, and so they should be. However, it's not difficult for us, the application designers, to get around this potential hitch – by writing a function that you can call to transform any user search strings into this "two quotes in a row" format. Below is the single line of code that we used to create the `PadQuotes` function in `clsDatabase`:

```
PadQuotes = strIn.Replace("'", "''")
```

You only need to use the `PadQuotes` function when creating and executing SQL statements from Visual Basic .NET. If you are passing parameters to stored procedures, as we will see in Chapter 9, you do not need to pad the quotes, since SQL Server handles this for you automatically.

After creating the `PadQuotes` function, we then created the function to build the `WHERE` clause of our dynamic SQL statement. This is the most tricky part of this chapter (but, as you'll see, it's really not that complicated), where we dynamically built a `WHERE` clause based on the criteria specified by the user on the Search Screen.

Let's have a look at the `BuildSQLWhereClause` function in more detail to see how it works.

```
Dim strWhere As String = strWhereClause
Dim strDelimiter1 As String
Dim strDelimiter2 As String

If blnPriorWhereClause = False Then
    strWhere = " WHERE "
Else
    strWhere = strWhere & " AND "
End If
```

If a `WHERE` clause already exists, then the keyword `WHERE` does not need to be added again. After making the check for the prior `WHERE` clause, we add the following code:

```
Select Case strQueryOperator
    Case "Equals"
        If blnNumberField Then
            strDelimiter1 = " = "
            strDelimiter2 = ""
        Else
```

```
                strDelimiter1 = " = '"
                strDelimiter2 = "' "
            End If

        Case "Starts With"
            strDelimiter1 = " LIKE '"
            strDelimiter2 = "%' "
```

Notice how delimiters are assigned depending on the Search Operator being used (`Equals`, `Starts With`, `Ends With`, `Greater Than`, etc.). `Equals` is a special case that can apply to both strings and numbers, but the others apply to one or the other. Since `Equals` can apply to both data types but requires a different syntax for each, we wrap the `Equals` portion with an `If` statement that sets the delimiter accordingly (value wrapped in single quotes for strings and without the single quotes for numbers).

These delimiters will be incorporated into the SQL string at the end of the function to construct a fully functional SQL statement that meets the required syntax. Notice how the line at the end that assembles the complete `WHERE` clause also calls the `PadQuotes` function:

```
strWhere = strWhere & strTableName & strDelimiter1 & _
              PadQuotes(strSearchValue) & strDelimiter2
```

After creating the function to build the `WHERE` clause, we then created the function for building the `SELECT` and `FROM` clauses of the SQL statement.

```
Dim strSelectFrom As String

Select Case strSearchMethod

    Case "Products"
        'Select the products information and the descriptions
        '(Product Name and Category Name) from suppliers and
        'categories table.
        strSelectFrom = "SELECT p.ProductId as ProductId, " & _
            "p.ProductName " & _
            "as ProductName, p.SupplierId as SupplierId," & _
            "s.CompanyName as CompanyName, p.CategoryId " & _
            "as CategoryId, c.CategoryName as CategoryName, " & _
            "p.QuantityPerUnit as QuantityPerUnit, " & _
            "p.UnitPrice as UnitPrice, p.UnitsInStock " & _
             "as UnitsInStock, p.UnitsOnOrder as " & _
             "UnitsOnOrder, p.ReorderLevel as " & _
             "ReorderLevel, p.Discontinued as " & _
             "Discontinued " & _
             "FROM Products p " & _
             "INNER JOIN Suppliers s ON p.SupplierId = " & _
             "s.SupplierId " & _
             "INNER JOIN Categories c on p.CategoryId = " & _
             "c.CategoryId"

    Case "Suppliers"
        'Since we don't need to join to multiple tables, we can
        'just select everything from the Suppliers table without
```

```
                'listing the columns all out specifically.
                strSelectFrom = "SELECT * FROM Suppliers"
        End Select

        Return strSelectFrom
```

As you can see from above, the `BuildSQLSelectFromClause` function uses the Visual Basic `Select Case` construct to generate the SQL code that pulls data from either the `Products` or `Suppliers` tables depending on the user's request. If the user is searching for products, then the SQL `SELECT FROM` statement is generated that extracts data from three tables: `Products`, `Suppliers`, and `Categories`. The `Suppliers` and `Categories` tables are joined to get the required descriptions.

With the `Suppliers` table, we simply create a SQL statement that selects all rows and columns in the table, since we don't need to join to other tables like we did with Products. The SQL syntax we use here should be familiar from Chapter 3 – don't confuse the Visual Basic `Select` statement with SQL's `SELECT` clause however!

Our next step was to open the BaseForms solution and place a `Delegate Function` and a procedure on the `BaseSearchForm`. Let's look at this in greater detail to see exactly how it works. Don't be intimidated. In a moment you will learn an advanced technique (delegation) and it isn't as difficult to understand as it first appears.

In the `BaseSearchForm`, we first declared the `WhereClauseDelegate` function as a `Delegate Function`, as shown below:

```
Delegate Function WhereClauseDelegate(ByVal strFieldName As String, _
              ByVal strMatchCriteria As String, _
              ByVal strFilterCriteria As String, _
              ByVal blnPriorWhere As Boolean, _
              ByVal strWhereCriteria As String, _
              ByVal blnNumberField As Boolean) As String
```

A **delegate**, in simplest terms, allows you to pass a procedure or function as a parameter into another procedure or function, which then invokes it. There are times when you would rather pass a procedure as a parameter to a generic method and invoke it, versus writing the specific code in the method to invoke it directly. In order for delegation to work, the procedure or function that you are calling must have the exact same *type* of parameters in the exact same *order* (that is, it must have the same **signature**) as in the declaration of the delegate (as shown in the example above). Delegation is useful when you don't want to call the exact same procedure each time – a different action is required – but when those procedures have the same parameters.

So, in our case, we want to use delegation to invoke the `BuildSQLWhereClause` function in the `clsDatabase` class. The `BuildSQLWhereClause` function must match with the `WhereClauseDelegate` signature in order for this to work. The parameter names do not have to match exactly, but the order and data types must match. And, indeed, they do have matching signatures, as you can see below:

```
Function BuildSQLWhereClause(ByVal strTableName As String, ByVal _
    strQueryOperator As String, ByVal strSearchValue As String, _
```

```
ByVal blnPriorWhereClause As Boolean, ByVal strWhereClause As _
String, ByVal blnNumberField As Boolean) As String
```

As you already know, we could have invoked the `BuildSQLWhereClause` method directly, as in the line of code below:

```
strWhereCriteria = clsDatabase.BuildSQLWhereClause _
     (strFieldName, strMatchCriteria, strFilterCriteria, _
      blnPriorWhere, strWhereCriteria, blnNumberField)
```

Instead, we decided to use delegation so that the `clsDatabase.BuildSQLWhereClause` could be passed into the `CheckSearchCriteria` procedure as a parameter. This is useful in our scenario because we don't have a reference to the `clsDatabase` class in the BaseForms project. By just passing the procedure that we want to call as a parameter, we have enough information to invoke it. Notice that the `CheckSearchCriteria` procedure below has a parameter being passed in called `BuildWhere` of the type `WhereClauseDelegate`.

```
Sub CheckSearchCriteria(ByVal strMatchCriteria As String, ByVal _
           strFilterCriteria As String, _
           ByVal strFieldName As String, ByRef strWhereCriteria _
           As String, ByRef blnPriorWhere As Boolean, ByVal _
           blnNumberField As Boolean, ByVal BuildWhere As _
           WhereClauseDelegate)
```

`BuildWhere` must receive a pointer to the address of a procedure or function that matches the same signature as the delegate declaration. You don't have to know in great detail what we mean by a pointer, but just understand that it means it will contain a reference to an address in memory where that procedure or function can be found. We will see in a moment how to designate a pointer to the `BuildSQLWhereClause` method that must be passed as a parameter.

Next, the `CheckSearchCriteria` procedure checks to see if the user filled out both a match criteria (`Starts With`, `Equals`, etc.) and the criteria they want to search for. If they did, then the `Delegate` function gets invoked with the `Invoke` method, which, in our case, will be the `BuildSQLWhereClause` method.

```
    If strMatchCriteria <> "" And strFilterCriteria <> "" Then
        strWhereCriteria = BuildWhere.Invoke _
             (strFieldName, strMatchCriteria, strFilterCriteria, _
              blnPriorWhere, strWhereCriteria, blnNumberField)
        blnPriorWhere = True
    End If

End Sub
```

After saving these changes to the BaseForms solution, we then opened up the MainApp and placed code under the Products and Suppliers search forms to create the `BuildSQLStatement` functions. If we take just a snippet from the function used on the Products Search Screen, we can look at how it works and hence understand the remaining code sections which all follow a similar pattern. In the code opposite, the first line declares a new instance of the `clsDatabase` to allow us to invoke the methods used to build our SQL clauses. Then, the second line calls the `BuildSQLSelectFromClause` to build the `SelectFrom` part of the SQL statement.

```
Dim clsDb As New clsDatabase()

strSelectFromCriteria = _
        clsDb.BuildSQLSelectFromClause("Products")
```

Finally, here is where our delegation comes in. For each search criteria on the form, we call the `CheckSearchCriteria` procedure and pass it all of the parameters it expects, including a pointer to the `clsDb.BuildSQLWhereClause` method. Since we already have `clsDb` declared in this procedure as a new instance of `clsDatabase`, all we have to do – to pass a pointer to its `BuildSQLWhereClause` method as a parameter – is to place an `AddressOf` statement before `clsDb`. This tells Visual Basic .NET to pass a pointer to the location in memory where that method resides, so that the `Delegate` function can then know where to find it.

```
'Check the search criteria and add to the WHERE clause if it was
'specified. Do this for each set of criteria on the form

CheckSearchCriteria(cbocriteria1.Text, txtcriteria1.Text, _
       "ProductId", strWhereCriteria, blnPriorWhere, "true", _
       AddressOf clsDb.BuildSQLWhereClause)
```

That's the basic idea of how delegation works. It really isn't as complicated as it might seem on first glance, is it? Delegation is a powerful feature that can be used in many other ways not even covered here. The most important concept for you to take away about delegation is that it allows you to pass a procedure or function as a parameter to another procedure or method that then invokes it.

The last step we took was to add code to the `btnSearch Click` event that fires when the user clicks the **Search** button (on either search form) so that the search executes.

```
Dim custCB As SqlClient.SqlCommandBuilder = New _
           SqlClient.SqlCommandBuilder(adapterResults)
Dim clsdatabase As New clsDatabase()
Dim strSQL As String = ""

'Load a DataSet with the complete Products, Suppliers, and
'categories tables (to be used later as code tables to display
'choices in a list, etc.).
dsData = clsdatabase.LoadCompleteDataSet(CONN)

'Load a DataSet with the search results based on the criteria
'specified by the user on the form.
strSQL = BuildSQLStatement()
dsResults = clsdatabase.LoadSearchDataSet(CONN, strSQL)
```

Notice that, when the user clicks the **Search** button, the first `DataSet` is populated to hold the code tables, then the SQL statement is built dynamically and, lastly, the second `DataSet` is populated by the results of the search. This is where it brings together all of the functions and procedures we've been creating throughout this chapter.

Hopefully, you are wondering why you had to copy the same code twice and place it under both the Products and Suppliers search forms versus just putting it under the BaseForm (since the code was identical for both). The reason it was done this way is a result of a design choice that was made early on – to have the Base Forms in a different project. If we put this `Click` event code in the `BaseSearchForm`, then the `clsDatabase` class would have needed to be present in that project as well, since we are creating an instance of it in the code.

Or, alternatively, the `Click` event could have been added to the base and then the `clsDatabase` class referenced from another project in which it resides. Since the `clsDatabase` resides in the MainApp, it didn't make sense to put the reference back to the MainApp in the BaseForms project. You may think of other ways that this duplication could have been avoided. If so, great! This means that you are aware of the impact of certain design choices and how you should avoid code duplication whenever possible.

Wait a minute! Can you think of a third way that we could have done this? We could have used delegation in the same way that we did for `BuildSQLWhereClause`, to have the procedures passed in as a parameter. Throughout the process of building the Product Management System, you will learn many different ways to accomplish the same aim, which will provide you with good exposure to several of the object-oriented concepts new in Visual Basic .NET.

Let's take a quick look at an example so that you can see visually how this works. Suppose you have the Products Search Utility form open and you specify the following criteria - Product Name Contains the word berry:

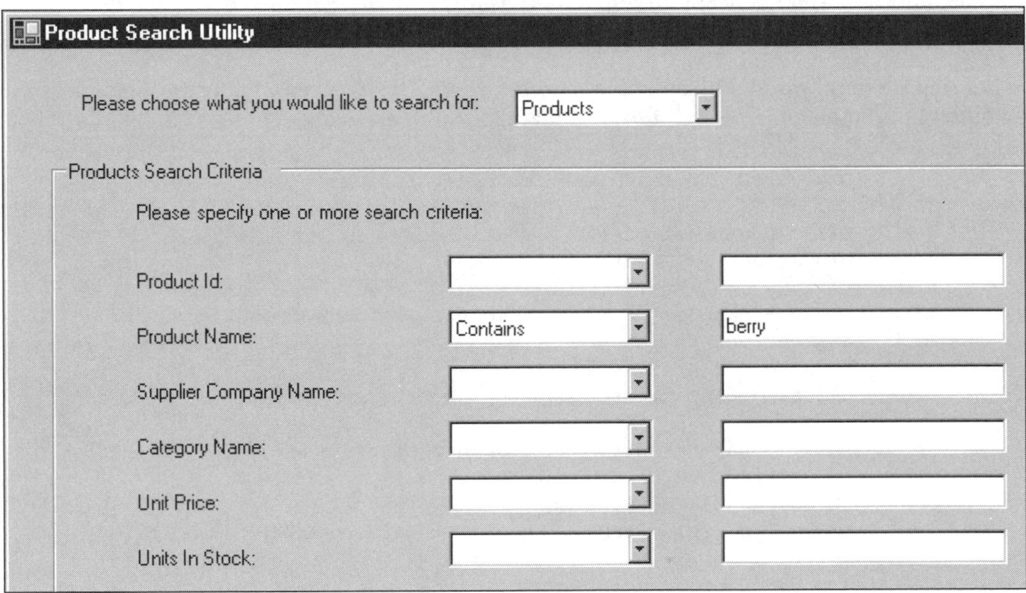

After clicking the Search button on the form, you should then see some results in the Output window similar to those shown opposite:

```
Output
Debug
Product Id: 1  Product Name: Chai  Supplier Id: 1
Product Id: 2  Product Name: Chang  Supplier Id: 2
Product Id: 3  Product Name: Aniseed Syrup  Supplier Id: 1
Product Id: 4  Product Name: Chef Anton's Cajun Seasoning  Supplier Id: 2
Product Id: 5  Product Name: Chef Anton's Gumbo Mix  Supplier Id: 2
Product Id: 6  Product Name: Grandma's Boysenberry Spread  Supplier Id: 3
Product Id: 7  Product Name: Uncle Bob's Organic Dried Pears  Supplier Id: 3
Product Id: 8  Product Name: Northwoods Cranberry Sauce  Supplier Id: 3
Product Id: 9  Product Name: Mishi Kobe Niku  Supplier Id: 4
Product Id: 10  Product Name: Ikura  Supplier Id: 4
Product Id: 11  Product Name: Queso Cabrales  Supplier Id: 5
Product Id: 12  Product Name: Queso Manchego La Pastora  Supplier Id: 5
Product Id: 13  Product Name: Konbu  Supplier Id: 6
Product Id: 14  Product Name: Tofu  Supplier Id: 6
Product Id: 15  Product Name: Genen Shouyu  Supplier Id: 6
Product Id: 16  Product Name: Pavlova  Supplier Id: 7
Product Id: 17  Product Name: Alice Mutton  Supplier Id: 7
```

By the way, if the Visual Studio Output window isn't visible, bring it up by selecting View | Other Windows | Output. If you're getting different behavior when you run a query, verify that your project contains all the code functions required and that they don't contain any errors, and try again.

Next, you should see a message box like the following appear to specify the dynamic SQL statement that was generated from your code:

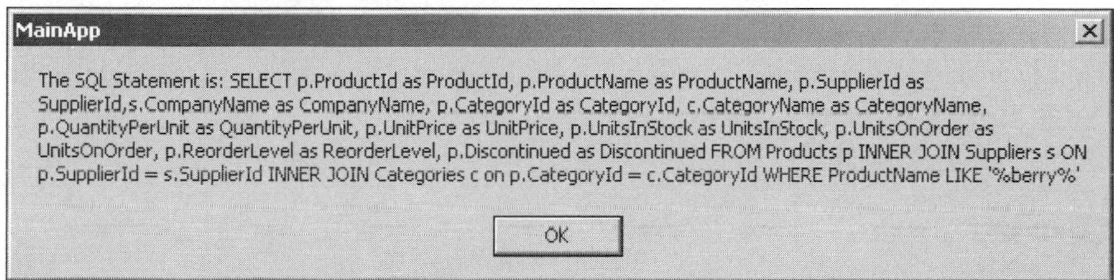
MainApp
The SQL Statement is: SELECT p.ProductId as ProductId, p.ProductName as ProductName, p.SupplierId as SupplierId,s.CompanyName as CompanyName, p.CategoryId as CategoryId, c.CategoryName as CategoryName, p.QuantityPerUnit as QuantityPerUnit, p.UnitPrice as UnitPrice, p.UnitsInStock as UnitsInStock, p.UnitsOnOrder as UnitsOnOrder, p.ReorderLevel as ReorderLevel, p.Discontinued as Discontinued FROM Products p INNER JOIN Suppliers s ON p.SupplierId = s.SupplierId INNER JOIN Categories c on p.CategoryId = c.CategoryId WHERE ProductName LIKE '%berry%'
OK

You can take this message box line of code out of the BuildSQLStatement functions when you are comfortable that it is working correctly. Lastly, you should see the results of the search in the Output window directly beneath that which was shown first:

```
Output
Debug
Category Id: 3  Category Name: Confections  Description: Desserts, candies, and sweet breads
Category Id: 4  Category Name: Dairy Products  Description: Cheeses
Category Id: 5  Category Name: Grains/Cereals  Description: Breads, crackers, pasta, and cereal
Category Id: 6  Category Name: Meat/Poultry  Description: Prepared meats
Category Id: 7  Category Name: Produce  Description: Dried fruit and bean curd
Category Id: 8  Category Name: Seafood  Description: Seaweed and fish
6   Grandma's Boysenberry Spread   3   Grandma Kelly's Homestead   2
8   Northwoods Cranberry Sauce   3   Grandma Kelly's Homestead   2
```

In other words, in the figure above, the last two records in the Output window are those returned by the search criteria (Product Names containing the word berry anywhere in them). The other results are from the prior function that wrote the results of the code tables to the window (as shown a moment ago).

Summary

In this chapter, we have covered a lot of ground and have made some great progress in building our Product Management System. We have also learned how to build a `DataSet` based on criteria specified by the user in the Search Screen. In particular, we covered the following:

- An introduction to the Product Management System
- A roadmap of the four Product Management System chapters
- Designing the Search Screen to allow for ad-hoc searching of Products and Suppliers
- How to populate a `DataSet` programmatically
- Using stored procedures to fill a `DataSet` with complete tables and then creating relationships between the tables
- Dynamically building a SQL statement based on user input
- Filling a `DataSet` with the results of the SQL statement
- Verifying the results in the Output window
- A quick look at using delegates

We put these new skills to work by creating a `DataSet` and building a Search Screen that generates the correct SQL statement according to the user's criteria. In the next chapter, we move on to discover how we can display data in a `DataSet` on screen using data binding, as we continue to build the Product Management System.

Exercises

1. What is a `DataSet`?
2. Name some `DataSet` objects and describe what they are used for.
3. Can a `DataSet` be based on a selection of information from multiple tables – or is it restricted to just a single table at a time?
4. When should we use stored procedures to retrieve data versus a SQL statement in the code itself?
5. What is the SQL statement that would be assembled when the user asks to see all seafood products under $10?
6. Why do we need to take special care when handling quotes within user input? Does this apply with stored procedures too?
7. What is the difference between `SqlDataAdapter` and `OleDbDataAdapter`?

Answers are available at http://p2p.wrox.com/exercises/.

Data Binding

In this chapter, we pick up where we left off in Chapter 7 to continue the development process of our Product Management System. During this chapter, we look in detail at how to bind the records in a `DataSet` to controls on a Form. We will implement the display of results in the `DataGrid` at the bottom of the Search Screen. We will also build the Add/View/Edit Products and Add/View/Edit Suppliers Screens and implement the logic to open those screens when a particular row in the search results is selected. The specific topics we will cover include:

- Simple and complex data binding
- Building the Add/View/Edit Products and Suppliers Screens
- Using the `ErrorProvider` control to validate user input
- Using `DataViews` to filter and sort data in the `DataSet`
- Using the `DataReader` to return a single record

After the summary of the above concepts, there are the usual questions to consolidate your grasp of these techniques.

Simple Versus Complex Data Binding

Data binding is the process of binding a control to a `DataSet` so that the control has ready access to the data in the `DataSet`. This technique is generally employed to display the data on screen using a particular control.

Simple data binding is when just a single value in a `DataSet` is bound to an item such as a property of a control or form. Any property of a component can be bound to any value in a `DataSet`. This type of simple data binding is also called **Property Binding**. An example of this would be binding the `Text` property of a TextBox to the `ProductName` column of the Products table in the `DataSet`.

Complex data binding allows you to bind more than one data element and typically more than one record in a `DataSet` to a control on the form. Some common examples of controls that support complex data binding include: `DataGrid`, `ComboBox`, `ListBox`, and `ErrorProvider` controls.

To further illustrate both simple and complex binding concepts, let's now modify our Product Management System to bind several different on-screen controls to our `DataSets`.

Binding the Results To the DataGrid

In Chapter 7, we created two `DataSets`: `dsData` to hold the `Products`, `Suppliers`, and `Categories` tables and `dsResults` to hold the results produced by the search requested by the user. You may recall that we displayed the data from the two `DataSets` in the Output window to demonstrate that they were indeed populated, but we did not display any data on the form itself.

The main objective of the Search Screen in the Product Management System is to display information that matches the user's search criteria. We shall use the form's `DataGrid` as the primary means to display these results, and we will implement that code in a moment. However, to fully demonstrate the hierarchical `DataGrid` control, I would like to digress momentarily and make it bind to `dsData` instead, which contains complete information from the three tables mentioned. After showing you how the hierarchical `DataGrid` works by populating it with data from `dsData`, we will then get back on track and make it display the search results data contained in `dsResults`.

Try It Out – Binding Data to a DataGrid

1. Open the MainApp solution for the Product Management System that you created in Chapter 7.

2. Double-click on the `frmSearchProducts.vb` file in the Solution Explorer to open in Design View.

3. Scroll to the end of the `btnSearch_Click` event and add the highlighted line of code as shown below:

```
        'Load a Dataset with the search results based on the criteria
        'specified by the user on the form.
        strSQL = BuildSQLStatement()
        dsResults = clsdatabase.LoadSearchDataSet(CONN, strSQL)

        dgdResults.DataSource = dsData

    Catch
        'Error handling goes here.
        UnhandledExceptionHandler()
    End Try
```

4. Run the program by selecting **Debug | Start** (or simply pressing the *F5* key). The Products Search Screen should then appear. Leave the search criteria fields blank. The search criteria values are not important at this point because, for now, we're not going to display any search results but rather the contents of the `dsData DataSet`. Go ahead and click the **Search** button.

5. When the Search button is clicked, we see almost the same thing as previously: a Message Box appears showing the SQL query that is to be performed, and some data comes up in the Output window. But, most importantly, we now have some data appearing in the `DataGrid` as a result of the line of code we just added. But – wait – there isn't any data there. All that we do see is a plus sign (+) in the left portion of the `DataGrid`.

6. Click the plus sign to expand the hierarchy of the `DataGrid`, and a screen like this will appear:

Product Search Utility
Please choose what you would like to search for: Products
Products Search Criteria
Please specify one or more search criteria:
Product Id:
Product Name:
Supplier Company Name:
Category Name:
Unit Price:
Units In Stock:
Search
Clear
Products
Suppliers
Categories

7. Click on one of the table names listed to view the data contained in within it. If you choose the Products link from the list, you would see something like this:

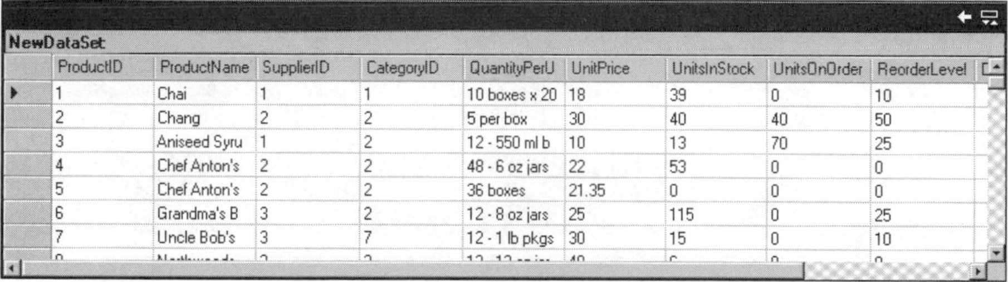

NewDataSet

ProductID	ProductName	SupplierID	CategoryID	QuantityPerU	UnitPrice	UnitsInStock	UnitsOnOrder	ReorderLevel
1	Chai	1	1	10 boxes x 20	18	39	0	10
2	Chang	2	2	5 per box	30	40	40	50
3	Aniseed Syru	1	2	12 - 550 ml b	10	13	70	25
4	Chef Anton's	2	2	48 - 6 oz jars	22	53	0	0
5	Chef Anton's	2	2	36 boxes	21.35	0	0	0
6	Grandma's B	3	2	12 - 8 oz jars	25	115	0	25
7	Uncle Bob's	3	7	12 - 1 lb pkgs	30	15	0	10

8. To navigate back to the table list, click the left (back) arrow button that you can see in the `DataGrid`'s top right corner. Play about with it for a few minutes to get a good feel of how it works.

How It Works

As this example should demonstrate, it is really quite easy to bind a `DataSet` to a `DataGrid` – all it requires is to set the `DataSource` property of the `DataGrid` to the name of the `DataSet` containing the information you wish to display:

```
dgdResults.DataSource = dsData
```

As `dgdResults` is the name of your `DataGrid`, this line binds the `DataGrid` to the `DataSet` called `dsData`.

As a hierarchical control, the `DataGrid` supports complex binding and can display data from multiple fields, records, and tables. A hierarchical `DataGrid` allows you to display results from multiple tables contained in the same `DataSet`. You can then navigate through the `DataSet` hierarchy graphically and view the records contained in each table in the `DataSet`. Furthermore, when table relationships exist in the `DataSet`, the hierarchical `DataGrid` allows you to expand a given record and then see the records that relate to it. Let's take a moment to see how this works.

For starters, navigate back to the top level where you see the list of the three tables: Products, Suppliers, and Categories. Then, select Suppliers from the list to see all of the records in the Suppliers table in the `DataSet`. Notice how there is a plus sign next to each record in the Suppliers list. This designates that there is a relationship to each of those records that exists with another table in the `DataSet`. Expand the first record by clicking on the plus sign. It should look like:

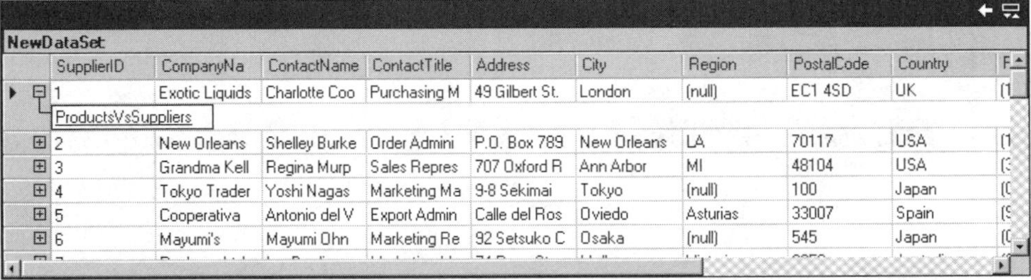

Next, click on the ProductsVsSuppliers link that was displayed upon expanding the record. You will then see a list of all products with the SupplierID of 1, as shown here:

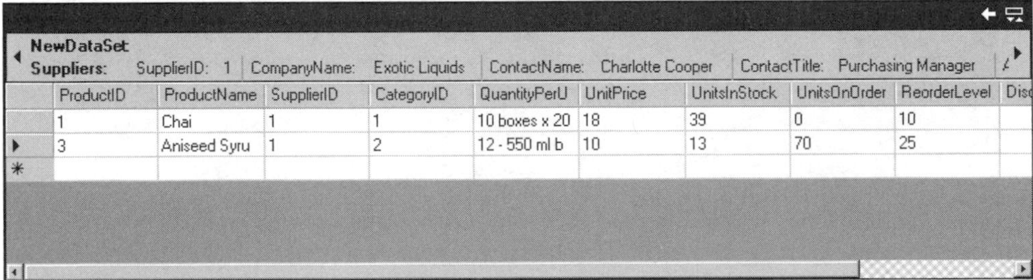

Did the name ProductsVsSuppliers sound familiar to you? Recall in Chapter 7 when we created the `dsData DataSet` and then created table relationships between the tables? That is where this table relationship is coming from. If we hadn't gone through the steps of relating the tables in the `DataSet`, then the relationship wouldn't appear under each Suppliers record.

I hope this little experiment has given you a pretty good feel for how a hierarchical DataGrid works and how powerful it can be.

Displaying the Search Results in the DataGrid

Now, we are going to get back on track and have the DataGrid display the results of the search itself. You will be amazed at how easy this task is.

At this point, you may wish to comment out the lines that display the Message Box if you don't want to see the SQL statements any more. These lines, you may remember, were inserted at the end of the BuildSQLStatement function in the frmSearchProducts.vb and frmSearchSuppliers.vb forms. Simply place a single quote (') at the front of this line to comment it out. You could, of course, delete it entirely, but there's no harm in leaving it there – it saves a little time if you should need it again, say when upgrading the system at a later date. If you wish, you can do the same for the statements in the LoadCompleteDataSet and LoadSearchDataSet functions that call the Output functions to write data to the Output window. These functions can be found in the clsDatabase.vb module. Feel free to leave any of these debug lines intact if you prefer, until you're happy with how the program works. Of course, you'd never leave such code in a production application!

Try It Out – Binding Search Results To a DataGrid

1. Return to the frmSearchProducts.vb [Design] view of the form and double-click on the form to open up the code window. Note, since we are using visual inheritance, if you double-click on the Search button, it will think you want to create another instance of the btnSearch_Click event, which is not what we want. Thus, just open the code window by double-clicking on the form itself or by selecting the file in Solution Explorer and choosing View Code. Modify the line added to the btnSearch_Click event in Step 3 of the Try It Out above to the following:

```
        dgdResults.DataSource = dsResults
```

2. Next, go to the frmSearchSuppliers.vb [Design] view of the form and double-click somewhere on the form to open up the code window for the suppliers search form. Add the line of code at the same spot in this btnSearch_Click event as you did on the Products search screen. Recall that we have two different click events – one for each search form.

3. Run the program with Debug | Start to see the effect of this change. The Product Search Utility opens by default. Provide some dummy search criteria, such as all products with a Unit Price of Less Than $50, and click that Search button!

   Again you will see the plus sign (+) indicating that the tree of data contained in the DataGrid can be expanded. Clicking on the plus sign expands it to reveal a link to the Results table in the DataSet. Click the Results link to see the data returned by your search, all nicely formatted inside the DataGrid, as shown here:

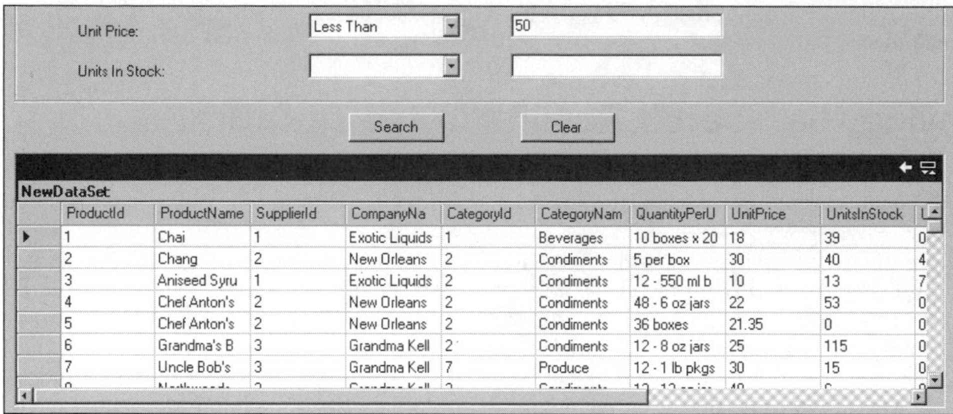

4. Stop the application and add the following two lines of code immediately beneath the line in the `btnSearch_Click` events for both the Products and Suppliers Search forms that we just modified above:

```
dgdResults.Expand(-1)
dgdResults.NavigateTo(0, "Results")
```

5. Run the application again to verify that the results should appear in the `DataGrid` pane immediately.

6. Try searching for some products and check that the records displayed match your criteria. As an example, suppose you want to buy something with berries in it. To do this, you can search for all products that contain the word "berry" and are less than $50 in price. Running such a search will return the following results:

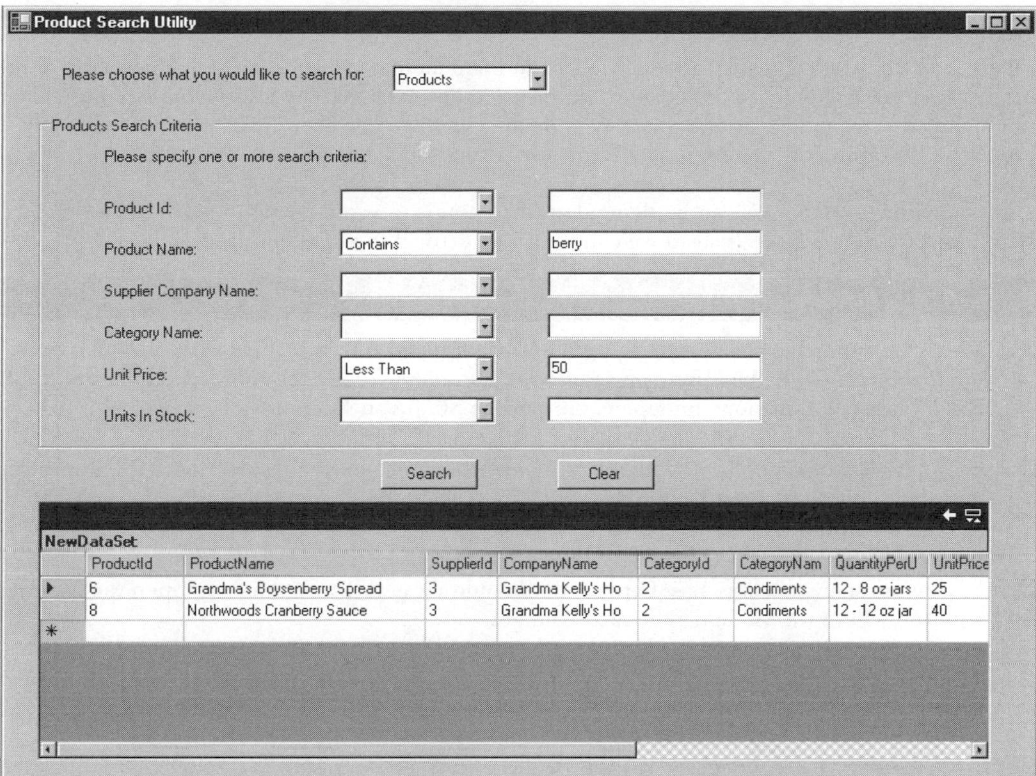

The two products that meet those criteria (containing the word berry and costing less than $50) are listed in the `DataGrid`: Grandma's Boysenberry Spread and Northwoods Cranberry Sauce. Run a couple of similar searches for suppliers too.

How It Works

All we've done here is to modify the `DataSource` property of the `DataGrid` so that it now binds to the `dsResults DataSet` rather than the `dsData` one.

```
dgdResults.DataSource = dsResults
```

We then modified the code so that the results would appear straight away, without the user having to use their mouse to navigate down through the hierarchy.

```
dgdResults.Expand(-1)
dgdResults.NavigateTo(0, "Results")
```

The `DataGrid`'s `Expand` method with an argument of -1 opens the `DataGrid` so that all table names in the `DataSet` are displayed, which in this case showed just the `Results` table. We then used the `NavigateTo` method to go to the first record of the `Results` table. When we now run a search, the results appeared in the `DataGrid` pane without having to click the mouse.

The Finishing Touches

By default, the `DataGrid` control allows you to edit the data that it displays by clicking on an item and entering a new value. Go ahead and try this out – notice however that the underlying database entries are not changed even though at first this may appear to be the case. Therefore, we want to disable this feature, as we are going to create separate forms for letting users edit data.

Also, another improvement we can implement at this point is to avoid trying to bind to the `DataSet` if the search returned no results. Instead we can return an error if this is attempted.

Try It Out – Form Enhancements

1. Close the Product Management System application and return to Visual Studio's design environment. Close the MainApp solution to completely close the solution. Open the BaseForms solution alone (independently of the MainApp solution).

2. From the BaseSearchForm.vb [Design] view, click once on the results `DataGrid` to select it, and then modify its ReadOnly property to True using the Properties window to the right of the main window.

3. Save your changes to the BaseForms solution and close it. You can now reopen the MainApp solution where we will make the next changes.

4. Modify your code from the last Try It Out on both the Product and Supplier Search forms to incorporate the `If...Else` statement as shown here:

```
If dsResults.Tables("Results").Rows.Count > 0 Then
        dgdResults.DataSource = dsResults
        dgdResults.Expand(-1)
        dgdResults.NavigateTo(0, "Results")
Else
        MsgBox("There were no records matching your search criteria.")
End If
```

5. Run a search that will not return any records and verify that this works for both the Products and Suppliers searches. For example, try searching for a Product with a `ProductId` that equals 5000. If your database doesn't have that `ProductId`, then you will get results like shown opposite:

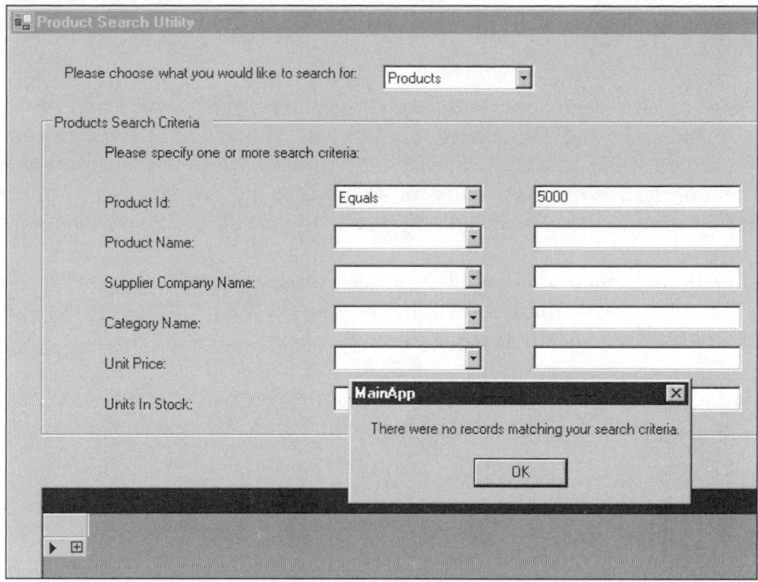

6. Next, run a search that returns results. You will again see that the results are displayed in the `DataGrid`, as in similar examples shown previously.

Congratulations! Your `DataGrid` displays the results matching the user's request neatly and accessibly, thanks to complex data binding.

How It Works

The first thing we did was to select the `DataGrid` in the BaseSearch Form and modify its ReadOnly property to True. We did this to prevent users from modifying any data that appears in the grid.

We made our first change on the BaseSearchForm so that all forms that inherit from it will have this property set already.

The reason for opening up the BaseForms solution alone is because, whenever making changes to base forms that are contained in another project, it is safest to perform the changes independently of the other project that uses those forms. With beta releases of Visual Studio .NET, changing the BaseSearchForm from within the MainApp resulted in Visual Studio locking up while it tried to follow all of the inheritance changes and resolve what had happened.

Then we wrapped the data-binding code we had just added a few moments ago inside an `If` statement, so that it only attempts to display data if there is indeed any data in the results `DataSet`.

```
If dsResults.Tables("Results").Rows.Count > 0 Then
        dgdResults.DataSource = dsResults
        dgdResults.Expand(-1)
        dgdResults.NavigateTo(0, "Results")
Else
        MsgBox("There were no records matching your search criteria.")
End If
```

If there was no data to be displayed, a Message Box containing an error message would appear to let the reader know.

Here are a couple of enhancements you should try to make on your own. First, you could implement the functionality to add an `Order By` clause to order by `ProductId` if it is a Product Search, or `SupplierId` if it is a Supplier Search. Currently, the records are being returned in whichever order the database gives them back in (which is usually in the order of the Primary Key, but not necessarily). It would be nice to be sure that the records will always be displayed in a particular sequence.

You might also like to implement the code that it takes to require at least one search criteria before the search will run. The way it works right now, if the user clicks the Search button without specifying any search criteria, it will return all of the records in the database (that is, there is no `WHERE` clause).

Now let's move on to the next stage and create the other screens required by the Product Management System. In doing so, we shall see simple data binding in action, and get further practice with complex data binding.

Creating the Base Add/View/Edit Form

We will again use visual inheritance and this time create a base Add/View/Edit form. In this section, we will create the form in our BaseForms solution. We will later inherit the common functionality from this base form and create a separate Add/View/Edit Products Screen and an Add/View/Edit Suppliers Screen that users must go to when they wish to change the data in the database tables in any way.

Try It Out – Creating the Base Add/View/Edit Form

1. Close the MainApp solution if it is presently open.

2. Open the BaseForms solution that contains just the BaseSearchForm at the present.

3. Add a new form to the project by selecting Project | Add Windows Form. Give the form a name of BaseDataForm.vb and click Open.

4. Double-click on BaseDataForm.vb in the Solution Explorer to make the form active in Design View. Alternatively, click on the form in this central window, making it active. The Properties window should now show the full compliment of available properties for the form.

5. Change the Text property from BaseDataForm to Product Management System, noting how the TitleBar of the form changes to reflect the property's new value.

6. Ensure that the (Name) property of the form is set to BaseDataForm and, finally, enter 800, 600 for the Size property. As we learned in Chapter 7, 800 X 600 is the typical screen size that most people have for their monitor settings as a minimum.

7. Now, let's walk through the process of placing the controls on the form, starting with the Labels and TextBoxes. Place twelve Labels and twelve TextBoxes on the form and set their properties as follows:

Control	(Name)	Text	Additional Remarks
Label1	lblField1		Change the Size property to 128, 23 so the complete text is shown. Change the Modifiers property from Assembly to Family to allow this Label and its properties to be modified in inherited child forms.
Label2	lblField2		Change Size to 128, 23 and Modifiers to Family.
Label3	lblField3		Change Size to 128, 23 and Modifiers to Family.
Label4	lblField4		Change Size to 128, 23 and Modifiers to Family.
Label5	lblField5		Change Size to 128, 23 and Modifiers to Family.
Label6	lblField6		Change Size to 128, 23 and Modifiers to Family.
Label7	lblField7		Change Size to 128, 23 and Modifiers to Family.
Label8	lblField8		Change Size to 128, 23 and Modifiers to Family.
Label9	lblField9		Change Size to 128, 23 and Modifiers to Family.
Label10	lblField10		Change Size to 128, 23 and Modifiers to Family.
Label11	lblField11		Change Size to 128, 23 and Modifiers to Family.
Label12	lblField12		Change Size to 128, 23 and Modifiers to Family.
TextBox1	txtField1	<blank>	Change the Size property to 136, 20 so that it will be large enough to display the data. Change the Modifiers property from Assembly to Family so this TextBox and its properties to be modified in inherited child forms.
TextBox2	txtField2	<blank>	Change the Size property to 216, 20. This field needs more room than the others as it will display either the `ProductName` or the `CompanyName` (depending on whether it is being used for Products or Suppliers). Change the Modifiers property from Assembly to Family.

Table continued on following page

Control	(Name)	Text	Additional Remarks
`TextBox3`	`txtField3`	<blank>	Change Size to 136, 20 and Modifiers to Family.
`TextBox4`	`txtField4`	<blank>	Change Size to 136, 20 and Modifiers to Family.
`TextBox5`	`txtField5`	<blank>	Change Size to 136, 20 and Modifiers to Family.
`TextBox6`	`txtField6`	<blank>	Change Size to 136, 20 and Modifiers to Family.
`TextBox7`	`txtField7`	<blank>	Change Size to 136, 20 and Modifiers to Family.
`TextBox8`	`txtField8`	<blank>	Change Size to 136, 20 and Modifiers to Family.
`TextBox9`	`txtField9`	<blank>	Change Size to 136, 20 and Modifiers to Family.
`TextBox10`	`txtField10`	<blank>	Change Size to 136, 20 and Modifiers to Family.
`TextBox11`	`txtField11`	<blank>	Change Size to 136, 20 and Modifiers to Family.
`TextBox12`	`txtField12`	<blank>	Change Size to 136, 20 and Modifiers to Family.

After making the above changes, our form should look like this:

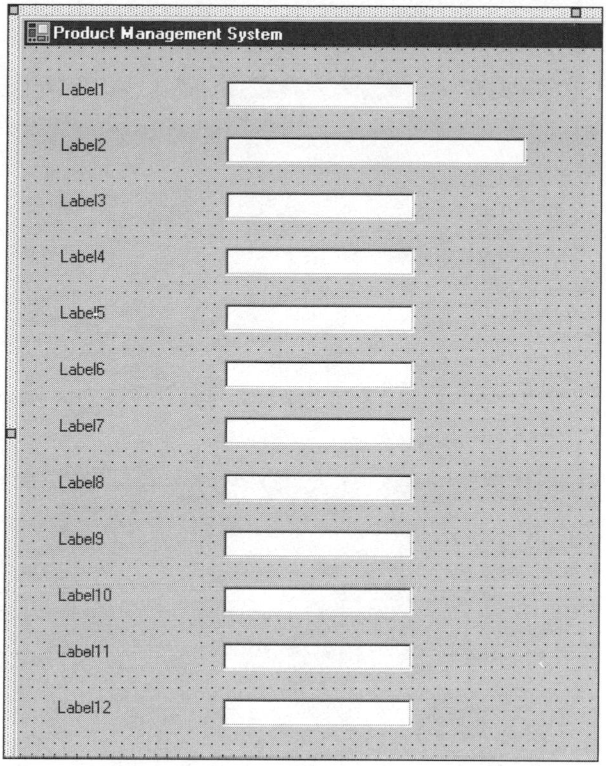

8. Now we need to add the Buttons for navigating through the records, adding records, saving changes, etc. Place five Buttons on the form and set their properties as follows:

Control	(Name)	Text	Additional Remarks
`Button1`	`btnPrevious`	Previous Record	Change the Size property to 144, 23 so the button text will be displayed without wrapping.
`Button2`	`btnNext`	Next Record	Change Size to 144, 23.
`Button3`	`btnAdd`	Add New Record	Change Size to 144, 23. Change the Modifiers property from Assembly to Family so this Button can be modified in the child forms that inherit from this base form.
`Button4`	`btnDelete`	Delete Current Record	Change Size to 144, 23.
`Button5`	`btnSave`	Save All Changes	Change Size to 144, 23. Change Modifiers to Family.

After adding the Buttons and setting the above properties, the form looks like the following:

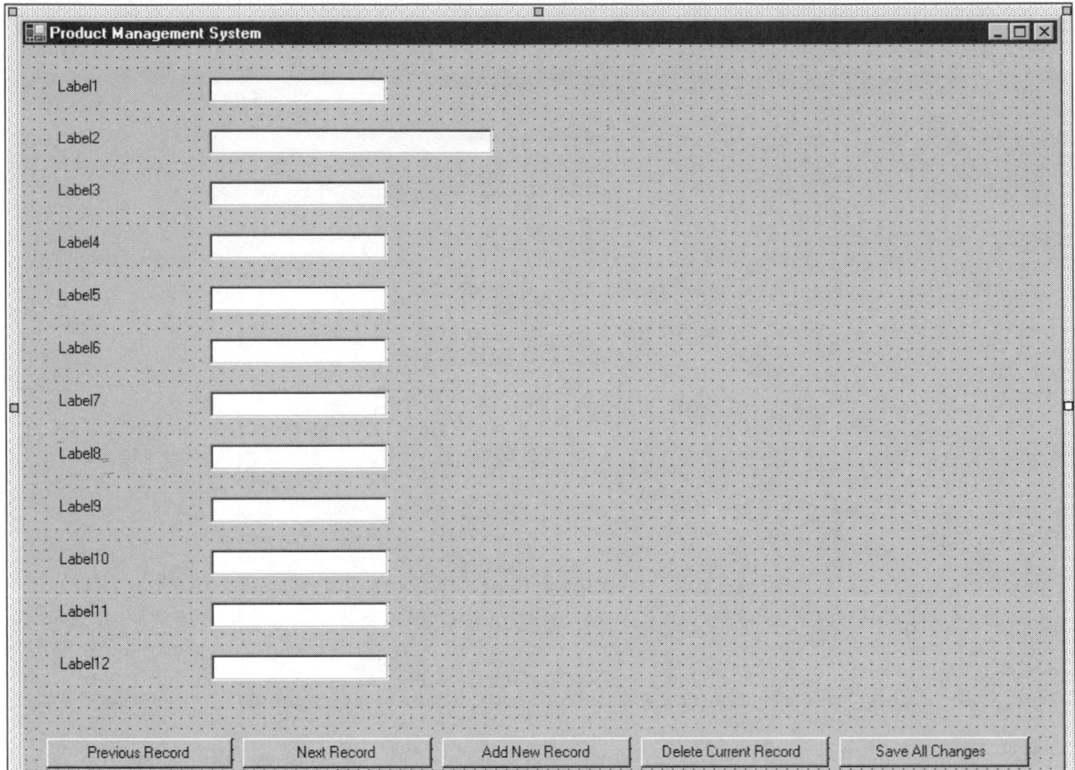

In this chapter we are only going to be looking at the Previous Record and Next Record Buttons. The others are going to be coded for in the next chapter.

9. Next, set the tab stop properties so that, when the user tabs from one field to the next, it happens in the proper sequence. See if you can remember how to do this from what you learned in Chapter 7. After you finish setting the tab stops, they should look like this:

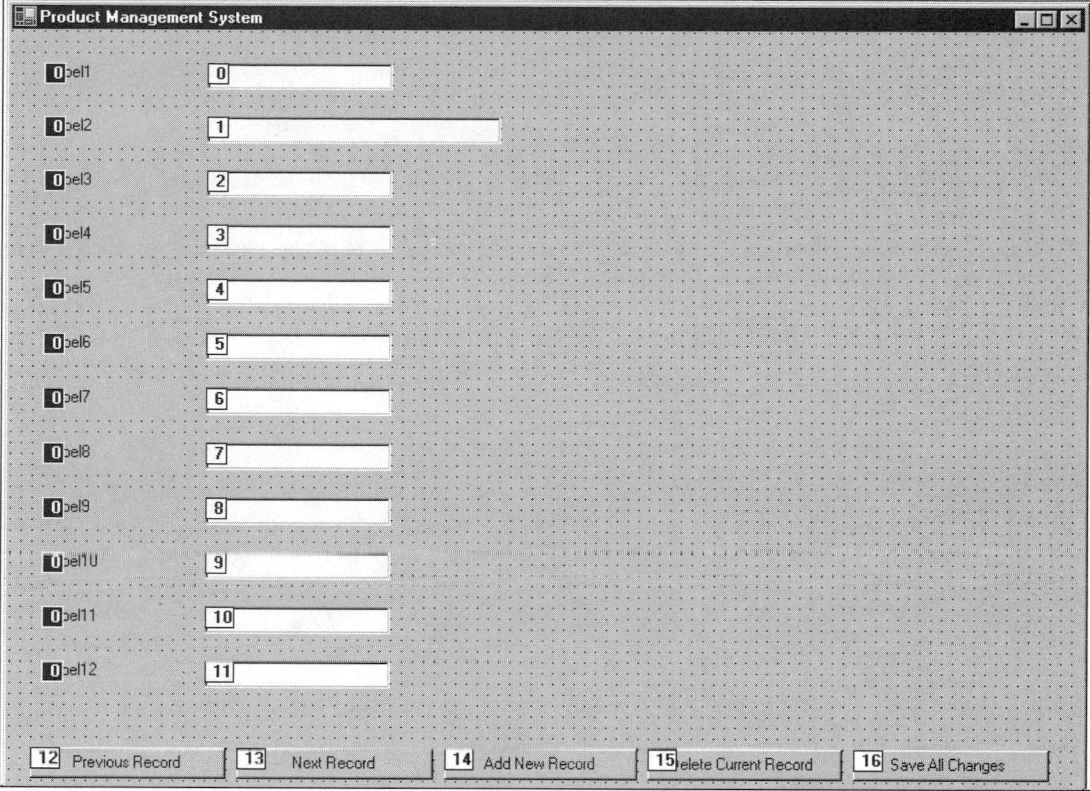

10. Select File | Save All to save all of your changes to the BaseForms solution thus far.

11. Now that we have the user interface elements completed on the base data form, let's put the code under the form that all data forms will have in common. To get to the code view, either double-click on the BaseDataForm or right-click on the form in Solution Explorer and choose View Code. Place these lines of code directly beneath the `Inherits System.Windows.Forms.Form` statement in the code:

```
Protected Const PROD = "Products"
Protected Const SUPP = "Suppliers"
Protected Const CONN = "user id=sa;password=xxxxx;initial " & _
                       "catalog=NorthwindSQL;server=goz3"

Protected dsSearchResults As DataSet
Protected dsCodeTables As DataSet
Protected intCurrentRec As Integer
Protected myBindingManagerBase As BindingManagerBase
```

12. Add the generic error handler to the form:

```
    Sub UnhandledExceptionHandler()

        'Display an error to the user.
        MsgBox("An error occurred. Error Number: " & Err.Number & _
            " Description: " & Err.Description & " Source: " & Err.Source)

    End Sub
```

13. Next, add a procedure that will be used to assign the values of the `DataSet` on the Search form to the local variables on the Data form:

```
   Sub AssignDataSet(ByVal dsResults As DataSet, ByVal dsData As DataSet, _
                     ByVal intCurrRow As Integer)
        Try

            'Assign the Datasets and current row values passed into the
            'local variables.
            dsSearchResults = dsResults
            dsCodeTables = dsData
            intCurrentRec = intCurrRow

        Catch
            'Handle errors.
            UnhandledExceptionHandler()
        End Try

    End Sub
```

14. Create the navigation procedures on the `BaseDataForm`:

```
    Sub MoveNext()
        Try
            'Increment the Position property value by one.
            myBindingManagerBase.Position += 1

        Catch
            'Handle errors.
            UnhandledExceptionHandler()
        End Try

    End Sub
```

```
    Sub MovePrevious()
        Try

            'Decrement the Position property value by one.
            myBindingManagerBase.Position -= 1

        Catch
            'Handle errors.
            UnhandledExceptionHandler()
```

```
        End Try

    End Sub
```

```
    Sub MoveFirst()
        Try

            'Go to the first item in the list.
            myBindingManagerBase.Position = 0

        Catch
            'Handle errors.
            UnhandledExceptionHandler()
        End Try

    End Sub
```

```
    Sub MoveLast()
        Try

            'Go to the last row in the list.
            myBindingManagerBase.Position = myBindingManagerBase.Count - 1

        Catch
            'Handle errors.
            UnhandledExceptionHandler()
        End Try

    End Sub
```

15. Create the events that will be fired when the user clicks the Next or Previous buttons on the form:

```
    Private Sub btnNext_Click(ByVal sender As System.Object, ByVal e As _
                              System.EventArgs) Handles btnNext.Click
        Try

            'Run the MoveNext procedure to move to the next record.
            MoveNext()

        Catch
            'Handle errors.
            UnhandledExceptionHandler()
        End Try

    End Sub
```

```
    Private Sub btnPrevious_Click(ByVal sender As System.Object, ByVal e _
                As System.EventArgs) Handles btnPrevious.Click
        Try
```

```
            'Run the MovePrevious procedure to move to the previous record.
            MovePrevious()

        Catch
            'Handle errors.
            UnhandledExceptionHandler()
        End Try

    End Sub
```

16. Add two generic procedures called `ReplaceControl` and `EnableDisable`:

```
    Sub ReplaceControl(ByVal ctlControl1 As Control, ByVal ctlControl2 As _
                       Control)

        'The purpose of this procedure is to replace one control at the
        'location of another control. Control 2 is the new control that you
        'want to replace Control 1. This is useful in instances such as
        'visual inheritance where you have a base form and need to slightly
        'customize it for only a few fields.

        Try

            Dim ptLocation As Point
            Dim szSize As Size

            'Place Control 2 in the exact location where Control 1 exists.
            ptLocation = ctlControl1.Location
            szSize = ctlControl1.Size
            ctlControl2.Location = ptLocation
            ctlControl2.Size = szSize
            ctlControl2.TabIndex = ctlControl1.TabIndex

            'Disable Control 1 since it is being replaced by Control 2.
            EnableDisable(ctlControl1, False)

        Catch
            'Handle errors.
            UnhandledExceptionHandler()
        End Try

    End Sub
```

```
    Sub EnableDisable(ByVal ctlControl As Control, ByVal blnEnable As _
                      Boolean)

        Try

            'Hide/disable fields or enable/make them visible based on
            'the parameters passed in.
            If blnEnable Then
```

```
                ctlControl.Visible = True
                ctlControl.Enabled = True
            Else
                ctlControl.Visible = False
                ctlControl.Enabled = False
            End If

        Catch
            'Handle errors.
            UnhandledExceptionHandler()
        End Try

    End Sub
```

17. This is a good point to save your work again using File | Save All.

18. Now that the code for our base data form is complete, it is time to rebuild the project. To do so, select Build | Rebuild All. This will compile the project and make sure no compiler errors exist, and will also update the appropriate project files with newer build information.

19. Close the BaseForms solution and open the MainApp solution, which we will be using momentarily.

How It Works

In this section, we created a Base Data Form. We created the user interface elements for the form that all Add/View/Edit forms will have in common.

Again, we started by placing the form constant and variable declarations:

```
    Protected Const PROD = "Products"
    Protected Const SUPP = "Suppliers"
    Protected Const CONN = "user id=sa;password=xxxxx;initial " & _
                           "catalog=NorthwindSQL;server=goz3"

    Protected dsSearchResults As DataSet
    Protected dsCodeTables As DataSet
    Protected intCurrentRec As Integer
    Protected myBindingManagerBase As BindingManagerBase
```

and then the generic error handler. Make sure to change the connection string constant so that it includes your username, password, and server.

Next, we added the class (form) variable declarations:

```
            dsSearchResults = dsResults
            dsCodeTables = dsData
            intCurrentRec = intCurrRow
```

- dsSearchResults holds a local copy of the Search Results DataSet
- dsCodeTables holds a local copy of the DataSet containing the complete three tables
- The intCurrentRec integer will store the position of the selected record on the Search Screen

Next, we added the procedures to move to the next position in the DataSet using the BindingManager, which associates a position with a DataSet. The myBindingManagerBase object will allow us to manipulate the local DataSets, such as moving to the next and previous records.

```
Sub MoveNext()
    Try
        'Increment the Position property value by one.
        myBindingManagerBase.Position += 1

    Catch
        'Handle errors.
        UnhandledExceptionHandler()
    End Try

End Sub
```

Similar code blocks were added to also allow us to move to the previous, first, and last records of the DataSet.

Then, we coded the Click events of the Next Record and Previous Record Buttons to allow us to move through the DataSet.

```
Private Sub btnNext_Click(ByVal sender As System.Object, ByVal e As _
                          System.EventArgs) Handles btnNext.Click
    Try

        'Run the MoveNext procedure to move to the next record.
        MoveNext()
```

In this case, the MoveNext procedure is called when the Next Record Button is clicked to enable us to move on by one record. In the case with the Previous Record Button, the MovePrevious procedure is called to move in the opposite direction.

Next, we added two procedures that are used to replace one control with another in the same location on the form. The ReplaceControl procedure is used to replace one control with another at the same place, which is useful when you need to customize a base form slightly for your new form:

```
        Dim ptLocation As Point
        Dim szSize As Size

        'Place Control 2 in the exact location where Control 1 exists.
        ptLocation = ctlControl1.Location
        szSize = ctlControl1.Size
        ctlControl2.Location = ptLocation
```

```
ctlControl2.Size = szSize
ctlControl2.TabIndex = ctlControl1.TabIndex

'Disable Control 1 since it is being replaced by Control 2.
EnableDisable(ctlControl1, False)
```

In order to disable the control being used, the `EnableDisable` procedure is called. This procedure hides or shows controls depending on which parameters are met in the current conditions:

```
'Hide/disable fields or enable/make them visible based on
'the parameters passed in.
If blnEnable Then
    ctlControl.Visible = True
    ctlControl.Enabled = True
Else
    ctlControl.Visible = False
    ctlControl.Enabled = False
End If
```

In this procedure, whether a control is enabled or not is linked to whether it is visible. In other words, if its `Visible` property is `True` then so is its `Enabled` property.

We will later use this to customize the form for Add/View/Edit Products so that two of the controls displayed will actually be ComboBoxes instead of the TextBoxes that are on the base data form. There will be more on this later; we just add these two procedures to the BaseDataForm for now. Since these features are the same regardless of whether you are managing Product or Supplier records, the base form is the appropriate place to include them.

With the base form created, we are now ready to create the specific Products and Suppliers Add/View/Edit screens that will inherit from this common set of functionality. We will then specify the few items that are different to customize each respective screen. This will build upon the visual inheritance principles that you learned in Chapter 7 and hopefully crystallize the concept in your mind.

Inheriting from the Base Data Form

We will add two forms to our MainApp project that inherit from the base data form we just created in the previous section. After adding the two new forms, we will move on to implementing the specific functionality that makes the Add/View/Edit Products screen unique.

Try It Out – Inheriting from the Base Data Form

1. In the Solution Explorer, right-click on the MainApp project name and select Add | Add Inherited Form. Alternatively, select Project | Add Inherited Form. Give the inherited form the name frmManageProducts.vb.

2. The Inheritance Picker dialog box will appear. Select the BaseDataForm in the list and click OK. This adds the Add/View/Edit Products Screen to the project as a child inheriting from the BaseDataForm.

3. Repeat these steps to add the Add/View/Edit Products Screen, giving it the name frmManageSuppliers.vb when prompted. This is a good chance to practice the step yourself to make sure you know how to do it. If necessary, refer back to steps 1 and 2 above.

4. Save all of your changes.

You may encounter an error message after selecting BaseDataForm *and clicking* OK. *This seems to be a bug which causes Visual Studio .NET to close. If you look in your MainApp folder, you should find that* `frmManageProducts.vb` */* `frmManageSuppliers.vb` *has actually been created. In this case, you need to open your MainApp project, right-click on the* MainApp *project name in Solution Explorer, and choose* Add Existing Item. *When you are given a list of items to choose from, click on the form you want to add (*`frmManageProducts.vb` */* `frmManageSuppliers.vb`*) and then* OK. *This should add the form to your project.*

How It Works

Like in Chapter 7, we used the Inheritance Picker to add two forms to the MainApp project that inherit from the BaseDataForm. The two child forms inherit all of the functionality from the BaseDataForm. If you double-click on either form to bring them up in Design View, you will see that they look identical to the BaseDataForm created in the prior section, only with the arrows indicating the controls that are inherited.

Now that we have the Add/View/Edit Products and Suppliers screens inheriting from the base functionality of the BaseDataForm, we are ready to implement the customizations for each of them that make them unique.

Implementing the Unique Functionality of the Add/View/Edit Products Form

In this section, we will customize the Add/View/Edit Products Form by adding a small amount of code that will implement some of the additional functionality that it requires. Other specific features will be added later.

Try It Out – Creating Specific Code for the Add/View/Edit Products Form

1. Open the code window for `frmManageProducts.vb` and place the following code at the top directly underneath the `Inherits BaseForms.BaseDataForm` statement.

```
Dim cboField3 As New ComboBox()
Dim cboField4 As New ComboBox()
Dim chkField10 As New CheckBox()
```

2. Next, add the `SetControls` procedure below:

```
Sub SetControls()

    Try
```

```
        'This procedure makes minor changes to customize the base
        'form to meet the specific needs of the Add/View/Update
        'Products form.

        'Assign the title to the form.
        Me.Text = "Add/View/Edit Products"

        'Assign the labels for the fields.
        lblField1.Text = "Product Id:"
        lblField2.Text = "Product Name:"
        lblField3.Text = "Supplier Id:"
        lblField4.Text = "Category Id:"
        lblField5.Text = "Quantity Per Unit:"
        lblField6.Text = "Unit Price:"
        lblField7.Text = "Units In Stock:"
        lblField8.Text = "Units On Order:"
        lblField9.Text = "Reorder Level:"
        lblField10.Text = "Discontinued:"

        'Hide/disable the labels and TextBoxes for fields 11 and 12
        'since we only need 10 fields on the Products Add/View/Update
        'form.
        EnableDisable(lblfield11, False)
        EnableDisable(txtfield11, False)
        EnableDisable(lblfield12, False)
        EnableDisable(txtfield12, False)

        'Field3 is the Supplier Id field and should be a ComboBox
        'instead of the default textbox. Put a ComboBox in the
        'exact location as the TextBox and disable the TextBox.
        ReplaceControl(txtField3, cboField3)

        'Field4 is the Category Id field and should be a ComboBox
        'instead of the default TextBox. Put a ComboBox in the
        'exact location as the TextBox and disable the TextBox.

        ReplaceControl(txtField4, cboField4)

        'Field10 is the Discontinued indicator and should be a CheckBox
        'instead of the default TextBox. Put a CheckBox in the exact
        'location as the TextBox and disable the TextBox.
        ReplaceControl(txtField10, chkField10)

        'Add the 3 new fields to the form controls so they will be
        'displayed.
        Me.Controls.Add(cboField3)
        Me.Controls.Add(cboField4)
        Me.Controls.Add(chkField10)

    Catch
        'Error handling goes here.
        UnhandledExceptionHandler()
```

```
        End Try

    End Sub
```

3. Now we are ready to put in the heart of the code that kicks everything off when the form loads. Note that this code still will not run after adding it because we have not specified when to open this form yet. That will be coming in the next section. For now, add this code to the `frmManageProducts.vb` form.

```
    Sub frmManageProducts_Load(ByVal sender As System.Object, ByVal e As _
                               System.EventArgs) Handles MyBase.Load

        Try

            'Customize the form to the specific needs of the Products
            'Add/View/Edit screen.
            SetControls()

            Dim oRow As DataRow

            'Loop through the CodeTables DataSet and populate the choices
            'in the SupplierId drop-down.
            For Each oRow In dsCodeTables.Tables("Suppliers").Rows
                cboField3.Items.Add(oRow("SupplierId").ToString())
            Next

            'Loop through the CodeTables DataSet and populate the choices
            'in the CategoryId drop-down.
            For Each oRow In dsCodeTables.Tables("Categories").Rows
                cboField4.Items.Add(oRow("CategoryId").ToString())
            Next

            'Bind each input field on the form to the corresponding item in
            'the search results DataSet.
            txtField1.DataBindings.Add(New Binding("Text", _
                          dsSearchResults, "results.ProductId"))
            txtField2.DataBindings.Add(New Binding("Text", _
                         dsSearchResults, "results.ProductName"))
            cboField3.DataBindings.Add(New Binding("Text", _
                         dsSearchResults, "results.SupplierId"))
            cboField4.DataBindings.Add(New Binding("Text", _
                            dsSearchResults, "results.CategoryId"))
            txtField5.DataBindings.Add(New Binding("Text", _
                            dsSearchResults, "results.QuantityPerUnit"))
            txtField6.DataBindings.Add(New Binding("Text", _
                            dsSearchResults, "results.UnitPrice"))
            txtField7.DataBindings.Add(New Binding("Text", _
                            dsSearchResults, "results.UnitsInStock"))
            txtField8.DataBindings.Add(New Binding("Text", _
                            dsSearchResults, "results.unitsonorder"))
            txtField9.DataBindings.Add(New Binding("Text", _
```

```
                    dsSearchResults, "results.ReorderLevel"))
        chkField10.DataBindings.Add(New Binding("Checked", _
                    dsSearchResults, "results.Discontinued"))

        'Set the ProductId to read-only since it is the key and should
        'not be changed.
        txtfield1.ReadOnly = True

        'Use the binding manager to manipulate the records in the
        'DataSet such as moving around the DataSet. In this case we're
        'setting the position to the selected record from the Search
        'Screen.
        myBindingManagerBase = BindingContext(dsSearchResults, _
                        "Results")
        myBindingManagerBase.Position = intCurrentRec

    Catch
        'Error handling goes here.
        UnhandledExceptionHandler()
    End Try

End Sub
```

How It Works

First, we added three control declarations (two `ComboBox`es and a `CheckBox`) that will be used on the form instead of three of the TextBoxes that the base form contains.

```
Dim cboField3 As New ComboBox()
Dim cboField4 As New ComboBox()
Dim chkField10 As New CheckBox()
```

We created a `SetControls` procedure that will customize the specific user interface elements for the Add/View/Edit Products form. For example, it will change the labels to indicate which `Products` fields are being displayed, as shown in the code snippet here:

```
        'Assign the labels for the fields.
        lblField1.Text = "Product Id:"
        lblField2.Text = "Product Name:"
        lblField3.Text = "Supplier Id:"
        lblField4.Text = "Category Id:"
```

`SetControls` will replace three TextBoxes that were on the base data form with ComboBoxes and a CheckBox instead. The base data form contains twelve TextBoxes and twelve Labels, but the Add/View/Edit Products screen only needs ten controls. Of the ten data input controls that it uses, only seven need to be TextBoxes. Two others need to be ComboBoxes to store the `SupplierId` and `CategoryId`, and the last one needs to be a CheckBox to display the `Discontinued` indicator.

```
        'Field3 is the Supplier Id field and should be a ComboBox
        'instead of the default TextBox. Put a ComboBox in the
```

```
'exact location as the TextBox and disable the TextBox.
ReplaceControl(txtfield3, cboField3)

'Field4 is the Category Id field and should be a ComboBox
'instead of the default TextBox. Put a ComboBox in the
'exact location as the TextBox and disable the TextBox.

ReplaceControl(txtfield4, cboField4)

'Field10 is the Discontinued indicator and should be a CheckBox
'instead of the default TextBox. Put a CheckBox in the exact
'location as the TextBox and disable the TextBox.
ReplaceControl(txtfield10, chkField10)

'Add the 3 new fields to the form controls so they will be
'displayed.
Me.Controls.Add(cboField3)
Me.Controls.Add(cboField4)
Me.Controls.Add(chkField10)
```

The reason why we created the base data form with twelve Labels and twelve TextBoxes is because that would require the least amount of code changes to customize the Products and Suppliers derivatives. The Add/View/Edit Suppliers form, as we will see momentarily, uses all twelve TextBoxes and thus requires fewer changes than the Products form.

Last of all, we added the `frmManageProducts_Load` event that gets called when the form loads to call the `SetControls` procedure. Also, it populates the ComboBoxes and binds the controls on the form to the appropriate fields in the `DataSet`. Let's look at how the ComboBoxes and data bindings work in more detail.

Using a `DataRow` variable, we loop through each record in the `Suppliers` table in the `dsData` code table `DataSet` and populate all `SupplierIds` that exist in the database in the `SupplierId` ComboBox:

```
Dim oRow As DataRow

'Loop through the CodeTables DataSet and populate the choices
'in the SupplierId drop-down.
For Each oRow In dsCodeTables.Tables("Suppliers").Rows
    cboField3.Items.Add(oRow("SupplierId").ToString())
Next
```

What this means is that when a user edits the `SupplierId` info for a given record, they will be able to assign it a value of any available `Supplier` in the database. Do not confuse this with the fact that, in a moment, we will bind the ComboBox to a field in the other `DataSet` so that the current value is displayed and it will be updated when it changes.

The same concept applies to the code for populating the `CategoryId` ComboBox. Each `CategoryId` in the `dsData` code table `DataSet` will be placed in the `CategoryId` ComboBox so the user will have the entire selection of `Categories` to choose from.

Next is a very important section to understand. This is where the data binding between some of the controls and the DataSet takes place. For each data entry field, we add a data binding that maps the property of the control on the form to a column in the dsSearchResults DataSet. For example, notice that we bind the ProductId in the dsSearchResults DataSet to the Text property of the txtfield1 control (which is used for the ProductId). Thus, any time the Text property of that control changes, it is updated in the DataSet automatically.

```
'Bind each input field on the form to the corresponding item in
'the search results DataSet.
txtField1.DataBindings.Add(New Binding("Text", _
                dsSearchResults, "results.ProductId"))
txtField2.DataBindings.Add(New Binding("Text", _
               dsSearchResults, "results.ProductName"))
cboField3.DataBindings.Add(New Binding("Text", _
               dsSearchResults, "results.SupplierId"))
cboField4.DataBindings.Add(New Binding("Text", _
                   dsSearchResults, "results.CategoryId"))
```

This is an example of simple binding – we are binding a control to just one element of a DataSet. The remaining code in this section follows a very similar pattern to bind each control on the form to the respective field in the DataSet. Notice that each field is bound to the Text property of each control with the exception of the final chkDiscontinued control. In that case, we bind to the Checked property, so that the CheckBox's ticked status will be set instead of its Text property:

```
chkField10.DataBindings.Add(New Binding("Checked", _
                   dsSearchResults, "results.Discontinued"))
```

Next, we assign the ProductId field to Read-Only so that it can't be changed:

```
'Set the ProductId to readonly since it is the key and should
'not be changed.
txtField1.ReadOnly = True
```

The last part of code to go in the Load event is to navigate to the selected record.

```
'Use the binding manager to manipulate the records in the
'DataSet such as moving around the DataSet. In this case we're
'setting the position to the selected record from the Search
'Screen.
myBindingManagerBase = BindingContext(dsSearchResults, _
                          "Results")
myBindingManagerBase.Position = intCurrentRec
```

What this does is to move to the record in the DataSet that was selected on the Search Screen. Since the controls are bound to the DataSet, the effect on the screen is that the selected record will become the current record when the form opens.

Now that we've completed some customizations for the Add/View/Edit Products Screen, let's make the appropriate adjustments to the Add/View/Edit Suppliers Screen.

Implementing the Unique Functionality of the Add/View/Edit Suppliers Form

Let's jump right in to assigning the specifics to the Add/View/Edit Suppliers Form.

Try It Out – Creating Specific Code for the Add/View/Edit Suppliers Form

1. Open the code window for `frmManageSuppliers.vb` and add the following procedure:

```
Sub SetControls()

    Try

        'This procedure makes minor changes to customize the base
        'form to meet the specific needs of the Add/View/Update
        'Suppliers form.

        'Assign the title to the form.
        Me.Text = "Add/View/Edit Suppliers"

        lblField1.Text = "Supplier Id:"
        lblField2.Text = "Company Name:"
        lblField3.Text = "Contact Name:"
        lblField4.Text = "Contact Title:"
        lblField5.Text = "Address:"
        lblField6.Text = "City:"
        lblField7.Text = "Region (State):"
        lblField8.Text = "Postal Code:"
        lblField9.Text = "Country:"
        lblField10.Text = "Phone:"
        lblField11.Text = "Fax:"
        lblField12.Text = "Home Page:"

    Catch
        'Error handling goes here.
        UnhandledExceptionHandler()
    End Try

End Sub
```

2. Next, add the code for the `frmManageSuppliers_Load` event:

```
Private Sub frmManageSuppliers_Load(ByVal sender As System.Object, _
        ByVal e As System.EventArgs) Handles MyBase.Load

    Try

        'Customize the form to the specific needs of the Suppliers
        'Add/View/Update screen.
        SetControls()
```

```
            'Bind each input field on the form to the corresponding item in
            'the search results DataSet.
            txtfield1.DataBindings.Add(New Binding("Text", _
                  dsSearchResults, "results.SupplierId"))
            txtField2.DataBindings.Add(New Binding("Text", _
                          dsSearchResults, "results.CompanyName"))
            txtfield3.DataBindings.Add(New Binding("Text", _
                          dsSearchResults, "results.ContactName"))
            txtfield4.DataBindings.Add(New Binding("Text", _
                          dsSearchResults, "results.ContactTitle"))
            txtfield5.DataBindings.Add(New Binding("Text", _
                     dsSearchResults, "results.Address"))
            txtfield6.DataBindings.Add(New Binding("Text", _
                     dsSearchResults, "results.City"))
            txtfield7.DataBindings.Add(New Binding("Text", _
                     dsSearchResults, "results.Region"))
            txtfield8.DataBindings.Add(New Binding("Text", _
                     dsSearchResults, "results.PostalCode"))
            txtfield9.DataBindings.Add(New Binding("Text", _
                     dsSearchResults, "results.Country"))
            txtfield10.DataBindings.Add(New Binding("Text", _
                     dsSearchResults, "results.Phone"))
            txtfield11.DataBindings.Add(New Binding("Text", _
                     dsSearchResults, "results.Fax"))
            txtfield12.DataBindings.Add(New Binding("Text", _
                     dsSearchResults, "results.HomePage"))

            'Set the Supplier ID to read-only so the user cannot edit it
            'since it is the key.
            txtfield1.ReadOnly = True

            'Use the binding manager to manipulate the records in the
            'DataSet such as moving around the DataSet. In this case we're
            'setting the position to the selected record from the Search
            'Screen.
            myBindingManagerBase = BindingContext(dsSearchResults, _
                                     "Results")
            myBindingManagerBase.Position = intCurrentRec

        Catch
            'Error handling goes here.
            UnhandledExceptionHandler()
        End Try

    End Sub
```

How It Works

As with the Products form, the `SetControls` procedure customizes the Add/View/Edit Suppliers form so that the appropriate labels are displayed, etc. The `frmManageSuppliers_Load` event then calls `SetControls` to customize the user interface accordingly, and then binds the `DataSet` columns to the appropriate TextBoxes on the form. The `SupplierId` field is set to `ReadOnly` and the `Binding Manager Base` is set to the current position. Since these concepts were explained in greater detail in the previous section, we do not need explain them again here.

Making the DataSets Accessible

Now we are ready to implement the code to open the forms with the selected record as the current record.

Next, we will add code to the `DoubleClick` event of the `DataGrid` for both Add/View/Edit Products and Suppliers forms so that, when the user double-clicks on a record in the grid, the Add/View/Edit Products or Add/View/Edit Suppliers screen appear as appropriate.

Try It Out – The Double-Click Event of the DataGrid

1. Let's start with making the appropriate changes to the `frmSearchProducts.vb` file. Insert the following code to accomplish this task:

```
Private Sub dgdResults_DoubleClick(ByVal sender As Object, ByVal e As _
    System.EventArgs) Handles dgdResults.DoubleClick

    Try

        'Use the BindingManagerBase to determine the current position of
        'the selected record.
        Dim bmGrid As BindingManagerBase
        bmGrid = BindingContext(dsResults, "Results")

        'Load Add/View/Update Suppliers screen.
        Dim frmProducts As New frmManageProducts()
        frmProducts.AssignDataSet(dsResults, dsData, _
                 bmGrid.Position)
        frmProducts.Show()

    Catch
        'Error handling goes here.
        UnhandledExceptionHandler()
    End Try

End Sub
```

2. Next, let's make the appropriate change to the `frmSearchSuppliers.vb` file so that it will open the Add/View/Edit Suppliers form when a result is double-clicked in the `DataGrid`. Insert the following code to accomplish this task:

```
Private Sub dgdResults_DoubleClick(ByVal sender As Object, ByVal e As _
        System.EventArgs) Handles dgdResults.DoubleClick

    Try

        'Use the BindingManagerBase to determine the current position of
        'the selected record.
        Dim bmGrid As BindingManagerBase
        bmGrid = BindingContext(dsResults, "Results")

        'Load Add/View/Update Suppliers screen.
```

```
            Dim frmSuppliers As New frmManageSuppliers()
            frmSuppliers.AssignDataSet(dsResults, dsData, _
                        bmGrid.Position)
            frmSuppliers.Show()

        Catch
            'Error handling goes here.
            UnhandledExceptionHandler()
        End Try

    End Sub
```

How It Works

First of all, notice that we declare a `BindingManagerBase` object to bind to the `dsResults` `DataSet`.

```
Dim bmGrid As BindingManagerBase
bmGrid = BindingContext(dsResults, "Results")
```

The `BindingManagerBase` class allows us to manage the synchronization of controls that are bound to the same data source. Imagine that we have a TextBox which is bound to the FirstName column in a Customers table, and a second TextBox which is bound to the LastName column. We need the two TextBoxes to be synchronized so that, when the user moves through customers' names, the LastName TextBox always shows the last name that corresponds with the first name displayed in the FirstName TextBox.

In our code here, we are using the `BindingManagerBase` object to determine the current position in a `DataSet`, by using its `Position` property:

```
Dim frmProducts As New frmManageProducts()
frmProducts.AssignDataSet(dsResults, dsData, _
        bmGrid.Position)
frmProducts.Show()
```

We can increment or decrement this property to move forwards or backwards through the `DataSet`. In this case, we use this property in the call to the `AssignDataSet` method of the product form, and will use a similar approach when we implement the code for the Suppliers Screen.

We then pass the position of the selected record to the Add/View/Edit Products form, which is then opened. Recall that the `AssignDataSet` method was created as part of the BaseDataForm.

Ready to Roll

Now that we have all the code to open the Add/View/Edit Products and Suppliers screens with the selected record, make sure you save your work and then we can test and see how well it works. Select Debug | Start to compile and run the program. Choose the Products option and specify a valid search criteria that will return some products – for example, Product Id Less Than 5. Then, in the results `DataGrid`, double-click on the left-hand column beside one of the product rows, as shown:

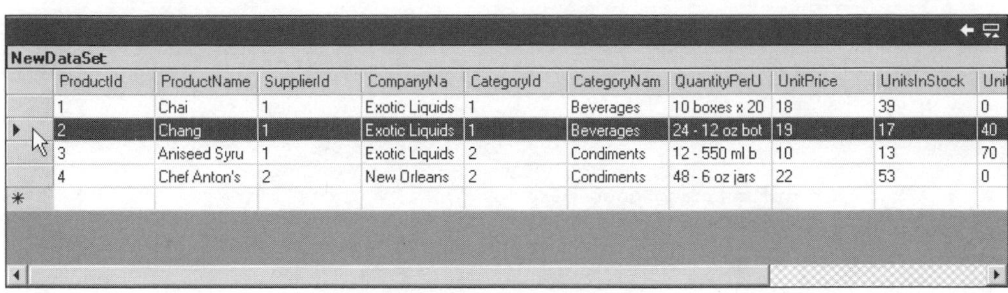

NewDataSet

	ProductId	ProductName	SupplierId	CompanyNa	CategoryId	CategoryNam	QuantityPerU	UnitPrice	UnitsInStock	Uni
	1	Chai	1	Exotic Liquids	1	Beverages	10 boxes x 20	18	39	0
▶	2	Chang	1	Exotic Liquids	1	Beverages	24 - 12 oz bot	19	17	40
	3	Aniseed Syru	1	Exotic Liquids	2	Condiments	12 - 550 ml b	10	13	70
	4	Chef Anton's	2	New Orleans	2	Condiments	48 - 6 oz jars	22	53	0
*										

The Add/View/Edit Products screen should appear with the selected record shown as the current record. Clicking on the Previous Record and Next Record buttons navigates forward and backward through the records returned by the search. An example of what the screen looks like is shown below:

Add/View/Edit Products

Product Id: 2

Product Name: Chang

Supplier Id: 2

Category Id: 2

Quantity Per Unit: 5 per box

Unit Price: 30

Units In Stock: 40

Units On Order: 40

Reorder Level: 50

Discontinued: ☑

Previous Record | Next Record | Add New Record | Delete Current Record | Save All Changes

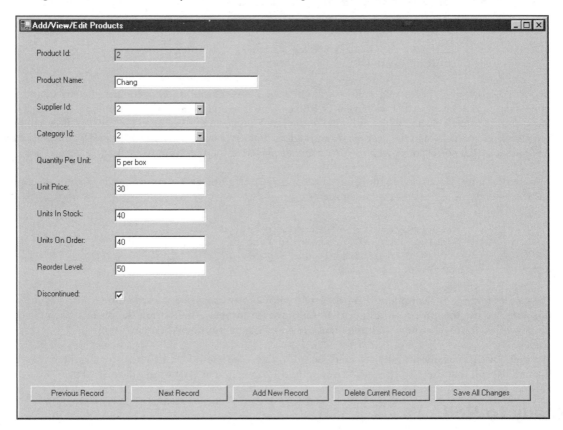

Next, let's repeat these steps to prove that the Suppliers form also works correctly. Close the Add/View/Edit Products form by clicking the X in the upper right-hand corner. From the Product Search Utility, select Suppliers as the Search Method from the ComboBox. The Supplier Search Utility should then appear. Again, specify some search criteria to return some records – for example, Supplier Id Less Than 5.

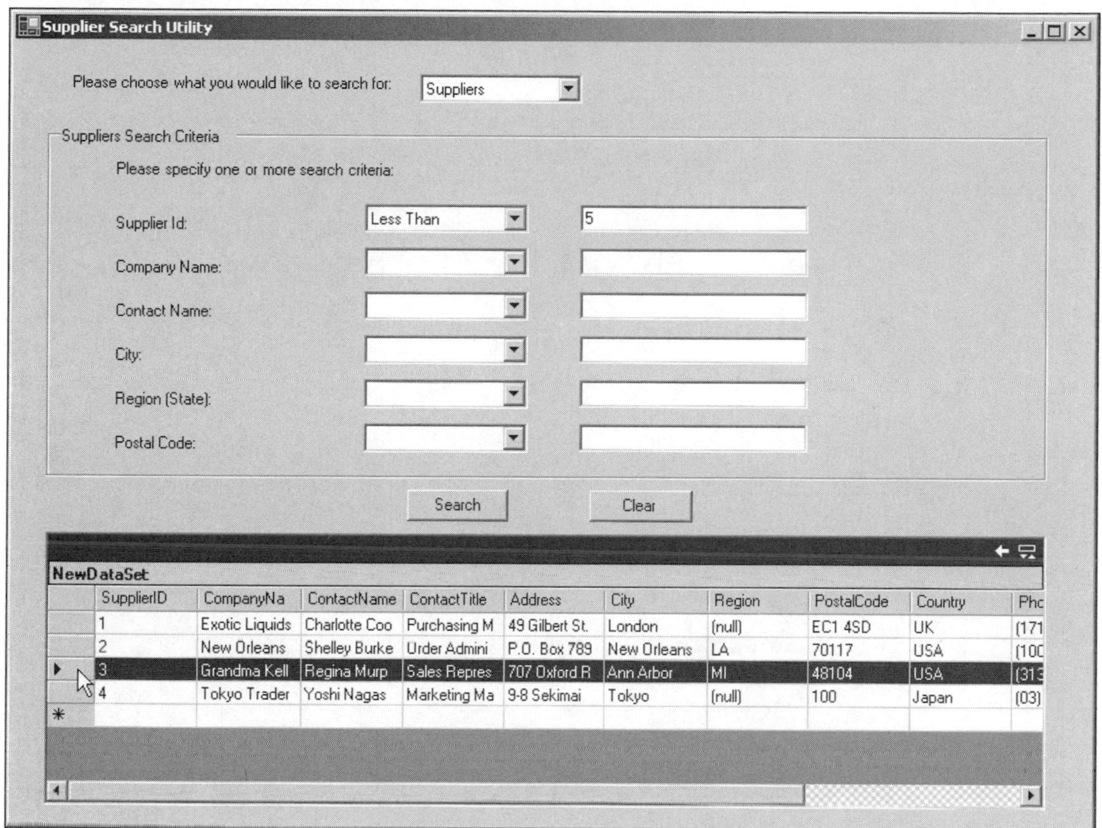

Then, double-click on the left-hand column beside one of the records and verify that the Add/View/Edit Suppliers form opens with that selected record. Also, use the Previous Record and Next Record Buttons to navigate through the results. An example of what this form might look like is shown overleaf.

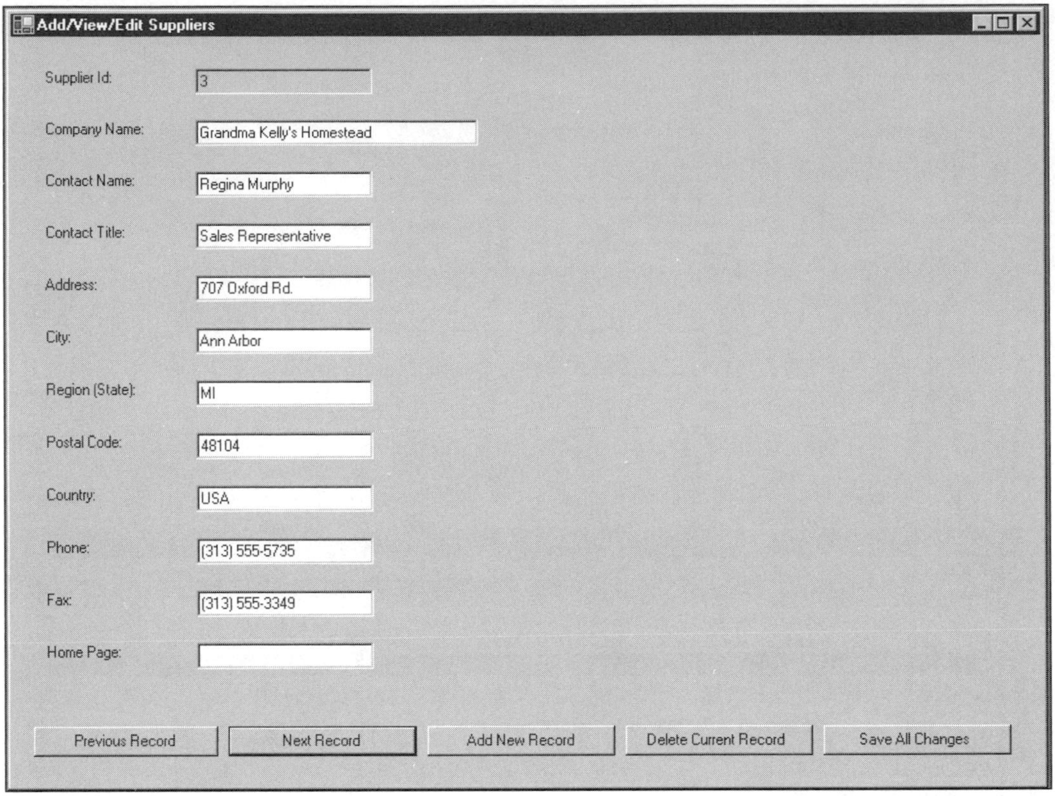

Add/View/Edit Suppliers
Supplier Id:
3
Company Name:
Grandma Kelly's Homestead
Contact Name:
Regina Murphy
Contact Title:
Sales Representative
Address:
707 Oxford Rd.
City:
Ann Arbor
Region (State):
MI
Postal Code:
48104
Country:
USA
Phone:
(313) 555-5735
Fax:
(313) 555-3349
Home Page:
Previous Record
Next Record
Add New Record
Delete Current Record
Save All Changes

Validating User Input

Now that we have our Add/View/Edit Products and Suppliers screens set up, let's investigate how we can validate user input using a complex binding technique. The `ErrorProvider` control can be bound to a `DataSet` to check for certain errors in the data entered by the user, and will give the user a suitable visual indicator in the event of a data entry error.

For instance, we may have some TextBoxes that are required fields, that is, the user cannot leave them blank. When such an error occurs, we can display a warning on screen – in the form of an **Alert Icon** – that informs the user of their mistake and allows them to address it. The final effect will look like this:

Product Name:
Please enter a value for this required field.
Supplier Id:
1

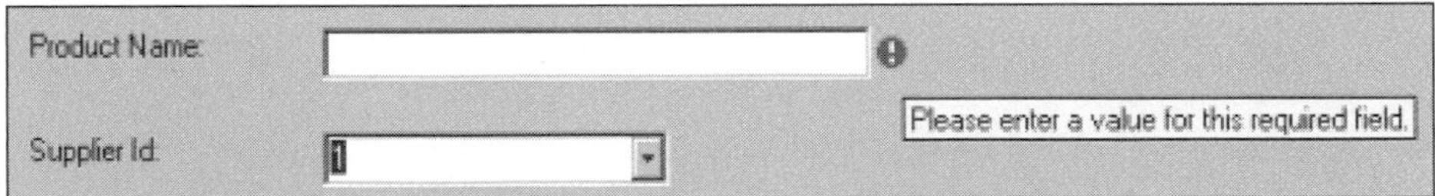

Validating a user's input like this is extremely useful because it makes using your application a lot less frustrating for the user. It can also help you to avoid writing a lot of code to deal with the many potential formats that users might input their data in.

In this section, we will see how the `ErrorProvider` control can validate user input and display alert icons when the user tries to enter faulty values into a control. We shall implement this capability for numeric fields and fields that must be entered for the `frmManageProducts` form and `frmManageSuppliers` forms to demonstrate how it works.

Try It Out – Incorporating the ErrorProvider Control in Our Application

1. Close the MainApp solution and open the BaseForms solution.

2. Drag and drop an `ErrorProvider` control from the Visual Studio Toolbox onto the `BaseDataForm` form. This should result in the `ErrorProvider1` control appearing in the Component Tray – the separate pane that appears at the bottom of the Designer, as shown below.

   Controls that do not appear on the form at runtime – like ErrorProvider controls (and Timer controls, for instance) – appear in this tray, rather than taking up space in the actual form Designer. The ErrorProvider control is invisible initially when the form appears in a running application, and only becomes visible if triggered by the user's input being incorrect.

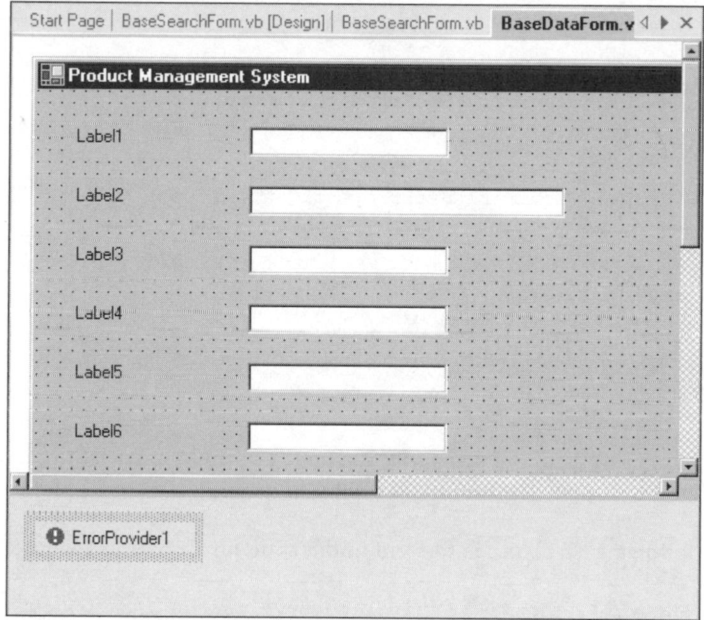

3. Change the **Modifiers** property of the `ErrorProvider1` control from **Assembly** to **Family**. This will allow us to change its properties in the child forms.

4. Add the following two procedures to the BaseDataForm:

```
Sub ValidateNumeric(ByVal ctlControl As Control)

    Try
```

```
        If Not IsNumeric(ctlControl.Text) Then
            'Set the error.
            ErrorProvider1.SetError(ctlControl, "Please enter a " & _
                                    "numeric value.")
        Else
            'Clear the error.
            ErrorProvider1.SetError(ctlControl, "")
        End If

    Catch
        'Handle errors.
        UnhandledExceptionHandler()
    End Try

End Sub
```

```
Sub ValidateNotBlank(ByVal ctlControl As Control)

    Try

        If ctlControl.Text = "" Then
            'Set the error.
            ErrorProvider1.SetError(ctlControl, _
                 "Please enter a value for this required field.")
        Else
            'Clear the error.
            ErrorProvider1.SetError(ctlControl, "")
        End If

    Catch
        'Handle errors.
        UnhandledExceptionHandler()
    End Try

End Sub
```

5. Save all changes to the BaseForms solution and recompile it. After it recompiles, then close the solution. Next, open the MainApp solution.

6. Place the following `Validating` event in the code for `frmManageProducts`:

```
Private Sub txtProductName_Validating(ByVal sender As Object, ByVal e _
            As System.ComponentModel.CancelEventArgs) Handles _
            txtField2.Validating

    Try
        ValidateNotBlank(txtField2)
    Catch
        'Error handling goes here.
        UnhandledExceptionHandler()
    End Try

End Sub
```

7. We can follow a similar procedure to add `Validating` events for the `txtUnitPrice`, `txtUnitsInStock`, `txtUnitsOnOrder`, and `txtReorderLevel` numeric fields, as below. This code should be placed in the code section of the `frmManageProducts` form.

```
Private Sub txtUnitPrice_Validating(ByVal sender As Object, ByVal e As _
               System.ComponentModel.CancelEventArgs) Handles _
               txtField6.Validating

    Try
        ValidateNumeric(txtField6)
    Catch
        'Error handling goes here.
        UnhandledExceptionHandler()
    End Try

End Sub
```

```
Private Sub txtUnitsInStock_Validating(ByVal sender As Object, ByVal e _
               As System.ComponentModel.CancelEventArgs) Handles _
               txtField7.Validating

    Try
        ValidateNumeric(txtField7)
    Catch
        'Error handling goes here.
        UnhandledExceptionHandler()
    End Try

End Sub
```

```
Private Sub txtUnitsOnOrder_Validating(ByVal sender As Object, ByVal _
                  e As System.ComponentModel.CancelEventArgs) Handles _
                  txtField8.Validating

    Try
        ValidateNumeric(txtField8)
    Catch
        'Error handling goes here.
        UnhandledExceptionHandler()
    End Try

End Sub
```

```
Private Sub txtReorderLevel_Validating(ByVal sender As Object, ByVal _
                   e As System.ComponentModel.CancelEventArgs) Handles _
                   txtField9.Validating

    Try
        ValidateNumeric(txtField9)
    Catch
```

```
            'Error handling goes here.
            UnhandledExceptionHandler()
        End Try

    End Sub
```

8. Next, add the following `Validating` event under the `frmManageSuppliers` form:

```
    Private Sub txtCompanyName_Validating(ByVal sender As Object, ByVal e _
                        As System.ComponentModel.CancelEventArgs) Handles _
                        txtField2.Validating

        Try
            ValidateNotBlank(txtField2)
        Catch
            'Error handling goes here.
            UnhandledExceptionHandler()
        End Try

    End Sub
```

9. Now we're ready to fire up our application and test out our new idiot-proofed fields. Run the project and do a Products search that will produce some results. Double-click on one of the results in the grid to bring up the Add/View/Edit Products screen. Then, tab to the Product Name field of the record that appears and delete the value that is there. When you now leave the Product Name field, say by tabbing to another field, an alert icon appears. If you move your mouse over the alert icon, a tooltip explaining the error appears as shown here:

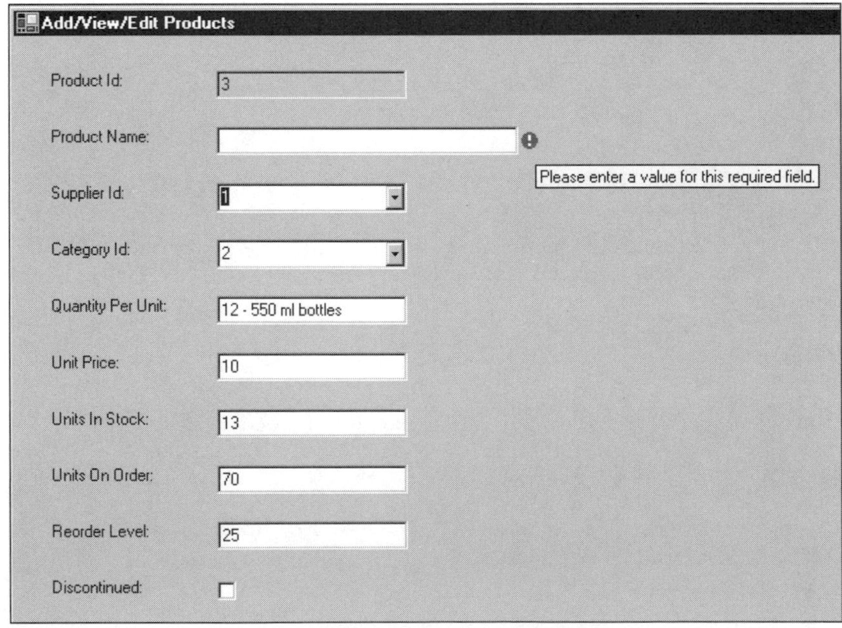

10. Try changing the numeric values to text values for the four numeric fields Unit Price, Units in Stock, Units on Order, and Reorder Level to verify that the expected alert icon appears corresponding to the `Validating` event we added for those controls.

How It Works

That's how easy it is to use the `ErrorProvider` control in conjunction with the `Validating` Event to check for invalid entries for a control.

To begin with we added an `ErrorProvider` to our BaseDataForm so its capabilities would be inherited by all child forms.

Next we created two generic validation controls that will be called from the inherited forms to conduct the validations. These procedures were added to ensure that only numeric values could be added and that the field wasn't left blank. `ValidateNumeric` and `ValidateNotBlank` are called by the `Validating` event of the Product and Suppliers Forms to test the values being inputted into the required fields.

We use the `Validating` event of a control to check for errors in the user input, and set an `ErrorProvider` error if we encounter something invalid. We started by creating code to validate the `ProductName` field. This is a required field and cannot be left blank. We then coded for the other required fields on the Products Form, and `CompanyName` on the Suppliers Form (the only required field there), with similar code blocks.

```
Private Sub txtProductName_Validating(ByVal sender As Object, ByVal e _
            As System.ComponentModel.CancelEventArgs) Handles _
            txtField2.Validating

    Try
        ValidateNotBlank(txtField2)
    Catch
        'Error handling goes here.
        UnhandledExceptionHandler()
    End Try

End Sub
```

The first line calls the `ValidateNotBlank` procedure to see if the `txtField2.Text` property is blank and, if so, that procedure calls the `ErrorProvider1 SetError` method with an appropriate error message for the alert icon to display. The parameters passed to the `SetError` method comprise this error message, preceded by the name of the control that the message applies to.

If, however, the user has entered correct data, then the error is cleared so that no alert icon will be displayed.

Notice how the event procedure is declared as `txtProductName_Validating` even though it handles the `txtField2.Validating` event. We can name the procedure for the event whatever we want, so as to make it more meaningful. In our case, it makes sense to give the event procedure a different name since `txtField2` doesn't tell us which field is being validated.

We could even have multiple event procedures that all fire when the same event (such as `txtField2.Validating`) occurs.

The `Validating` Event is fired when the focus moves away from a control (such as when you tab to another control). In previous versions of Visual Basic, it was hard to code a validating event that occurred before the control's `Click` event. Visual Basic .NET makes this easy.

Other Data Considerations

So far, we have looked at the basics of binding to `DataSets` using complex and simple binding methods. There are some other scenarios that are more involved than those we have looked at so far. For example, `DataViews` can be created on a `DataSet` to filter and sort data in meaningful ways. Secondly, the use of the `DataReader` class may often be preferable to `DataSets` due to the performance advantages that come from keeping just a single row in memory at a time. We will look at these more sophisticated techniques briefly in this section.

Using DataViews to Filter and Sort Data

`DataViews` provide a customized view of a `DataSet`. You can use `DataViews` to sort, search, and filter a `DataSet`. For example, suppose you want to show two different versions of the data in a `DataSet`, such as showing each employee only the suppliers they deal with. With a `DataView`, you can bind to an existing `DataSet` and then specify additional criteria to filter or sort on.

Let's look at a simple example of filtering our Search `DataSet` that is populated with the results of a search according to the user's criteria.

Try It Out – DataViews

1. Place a new Button on the `frmSearchProducts` form. Double-click on the Button and place the following code in its `Click` event.

```
Private Sub Button1_Click(ByVal sender As System.Object, ByVal e As _
        System.EventArgs) Handles Button1.Click

    'Create a new DataView and filter it based on the RowFilter
    'criteria.
    Dim dvView As New DataView()
    With dvView
        .Table = dsResults.Tables("results")
        .AllowDelete = True
        .AllowEdit = True
        .AllowNew = True
        .RowFilter = "SupplierId = '2'"
        .Sort = "ProductName ASC"
    End With

    'Display the results in the filtered view in the DataGrid.
    dgdResults.DataSource = dvView

End Sub
```

2. Let's see this in action. Run the project and perform a search on all products with a `ProductId` less than `5`:

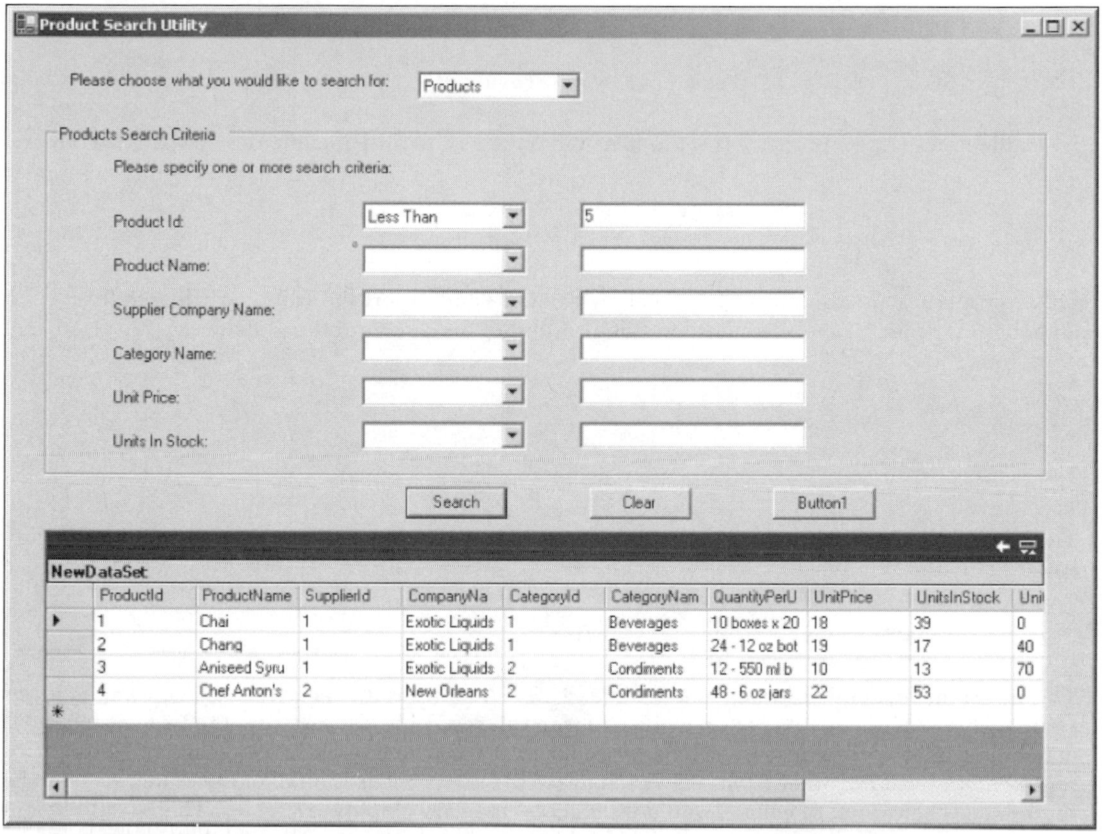

3. After the results are displayed in the grid, click on Button1 and run the filter. The data displayed in the `DataGrid` is then filtered according to the `DataView` such that only one record is displayed – the one where `SupplierId` is `2`.

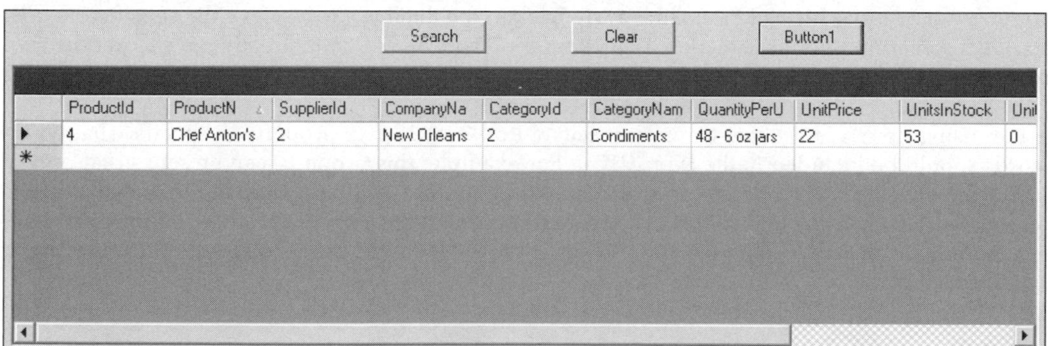

How It Works

Notice how a new DataView is declared and bound to the Results DataSet.

```
Dim dvView As New DataView()
With dvView
    .Table = dsResults.Tables("results")
```

Next, the RowFilter property is set to filter the DataSet to only include the SupplierId that equals 2.

```
    .RowFilter = "SupplierId = '2'"
```

Other properties are also set, such as to allow deletions and to sort the view according to the alphabetical order (or more accurately, ASCII order) of the ProductName field.

```
    .AllowDelete = True
    .AllowEdit = True
    .AllowNew = True
    .Sort = "ProductName ASC"
```

The last line in the event sets the DataGrid's DataSource property to make the grid display the data specified by the DataView.

```
dgdResults.DataSource = dvView
```

This is just one example of when to use DataViews. Another is for security reasons: when you want to restrict what records in a DataSet a given person can see. Take, for instance, the issue of salary. You may only want the employee to be able to see his salary and no one else's. The Human Resources representative, on the other hand, may need to see the salary records of all of the employees he/she represents. The owner, of course, would want access to every employee's salary. There could be one DataSet in an application that gets filtered in a number of different ways, like this, to display only certain records that the user has permission to view.

Another practical application of a DataView might be when you have one DataSet in memory that handles a larger set of information. You may need to filter the information for a quick analysis to meet a certain set of criteria. Instead of making a trip back to the database to retrieve the specific records you want, it is sometimes better to just do a quick filter on a DataSet you already have to get the records you need.

Besides using RowFilter, you can also specify a RowSetFilter property to specify what types of records should be included in the DataView. For example, this property can be set so that only added records appear in the DataView, or it can be set so that only original values are included in the DataView. This gives you an additional level of filtering of the DataSet, since not only can you apply the RowFilter property, but you can also apply the RowSetFilter property to further refine which rows are included.

Finally, while there are some controls that exist for data binding in web applications (that is, on web Forms), such web forms controls do not have the sophisticated features we have seen so far. For example, you can use a `DataGrid` in web forms to display data. The data must be based on a `DataView` created on an underlying `DataSet`. The reason it must be based on a `DataView` is because a `DataSet` can contain multiple tables and the web form can only display one table at a time. Thus, you create a `DataView` based on some information in the `DataSet` and bind the `DataGrid` control to the `DataSet`.

See how easy it is to create a `DataView` and filter and sort data in a variety of ways? You can be as creative as you like, and can devise `DataViews` for a number of helpful purposes, such as the ones suggested above. Now, though, let's move on to the last topic of the chapter.

Using the DataReader To Retrieve Single Rows

You can use the `DataReader` class to retrieve a read-only, forward-only set of data from a database. The `DataReader` can offer a significant increase in performance in an application because only a single record is ever in memory at a time. This might be a good option when you are returning very large amounts of data that may approach or even exceed available system resources. In general, you should always aim to use a `DataReader` when possible. It is faster than the `DataSet` because it is not retained in memory. Also, it is important to note that the `DataSet` actually goes through the `DataReader` to create its results. So you should be able to quickly see why the `DataSet` is slower and uses more resources. Not only does the `DataSet` have an extra layer to go through, but it stores all of the records locally in memory.

When performance is a big consideration, you should opt to use the `DataReader` if possible. You should always use the `DataReader` when you do not need an in-memory copy of the data. For example, if all you need to do is retrieve some records and take immediate action on them, use a `DataReader`. There is no reason to use the overhead of a `DataSet` to keep them in memory.

However, the `DataReader` has some limitations. It cannot bind to Windows Forms controls like we have been doing throughout this chapter. When using the `DataReader`, your code has to request, handle, and deal with each record individually (displaying it on screen, writing it to a file, and so on).

As we said earlier, the data in a `DataReader` is read-only and cannot be manipulated interactively, which is much more limited than the hierarchical `DataGrid` we have in our Product Management System.

Let's look at some sample code that does use a `DataReader`.

Try It Out – Using the DataReader

1. Place a new Button on the Search form, and add the following code to `frmSearchProducts.vb` for the Button's `Click` event:

```
Private Sub Button2_Click(ByVal sender As System.Object, ByVal e As _
            System.EventArgs) Handles Button2.Click

    Dim strConnection As String = "user id=sa;password=pwd;initial " & _
                                  "catalog=NorthwindSQL;server=goz3"

    Dim strSQL As String = "SELECT * FROM Products"
```

```
        Dim sqlConn As New SqlClient.SqlConnection(strConnection)
        sqlConn.Open()

        Dim myCommand As New SqlClient.SqlCommand(strSQL, sqlConn)
        myCommand.CommandType = CommandType.Text
        Dim myReader As SqlClient.SqlDataReader = myCommand.ExecuteReader()

        Do While myReader.Read
            Console.WriteLine("Product Id: " & myReader.GetInt32(0) & _
                    vbTab & "Product Name: " & myReader.GetString(1))
        Loop

        myReader.Close()
        sqlConn.Close()

    End Sub
```

2. Run the project and click on the Button to see all of the records from the Products table displayed in the Output window.

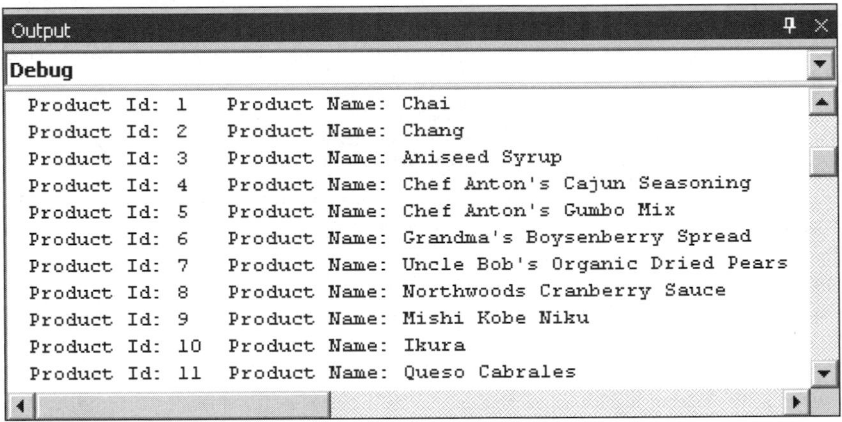

How It Works

The first part of the above code sets a connection string that includes all required information to connect to our SQL server database.

```
Dim strConnection As String = "user id=sa;password=pwd;initial " & _
                        "catalog=NorthwindSQL;server=goz3"
```

You will need to modify this line to work on your server.

The string defined in the next line specifies the SQL statement that we will use to choose records from our database that will populate our `DataReader`.

```
Dim strSQL As String = "SELECT * FROM Products"
```

Then, we open a new SQLConnection using the connection string.

```
Dim sqlConn As New SqlClient.SqlConnection(strConnection)
sqlConn.Open()
```

The myCommand data command is created by passing it the statement and connection strings. We can then use myCommand to cause the DataReader to execute the SQL statement that we want – in this case, to select all records from the Products table.

```
Dim myCommand As New SqlClient.SqlCommand(strSQL, sqlConn)
myCommand.CommandType = CommandType.Text
Dim myReader As SqlClient.SqlDataReader = myCommand.ExecuteReader()
```

However, as we learned previously, the DataReader retrieves the records one at a time in a forward-only and read-only format.

The last part of code retrieves each record in the DataReader one at a time and writes the Product ID and Product Name to the Output window using the Console.WriteLine method:

```
Do While myReader.Read
    Console.WriteLine("Product Id: " & myReader.GetInt32(0) & _
            vbTab & "Product Name: " & myReader.GetString(1))
Loop
```

Notice the use of the GetInt32 and GetString methods of the DataReader object. These methods can be used because we know the data types of the underlying data fields. By explicitly using the typed accessor methods in this way, we reduce the amount of type conversion that is required when retrieving the data.

Last of all, we have the line that closes the DataReader.

```
myReader.Close()
```

It is very important to note that a DataReader is open until you close the connection with such a line of code (or the object gets destroyed and thus the connection is closed at some point during garbage collection).

You can modify this simple example for your own purposes, but this should give you an idea of how a DataReader can be used to rapidly retrieve forward-only, read-only data. The most important idea to take away from this section is that you should use a DataReader whenever possible, and especially when an in-memory copy of data is not required.

Summary

In this chapter we've covered some crucial data-binding concepts as we further developed our Product Management System. We bound our search results to the `DataGrid` and added the functionality to allow the user to open a specific record in the results list on the Add/View/Edit Products or Suppliers screens. We specifically learned about:

- Complex data binding to bind controls to more than one element in a `DataSet`
- Simple data-binding to bind the property of a control to a single element in a `DataSet`
- Creating the Base Data Form for our Product Management System
- Creating the Add/View/Edit Products and Suppliers Screens that inherit functionality from the Base Data Form
- Customizing the Add/View/Edit Screens for their specific needs
- Validating user input using the `ErrorProvider` control
- Filtering and sorting data using `DataViews`
- Returning records using the `DataReader`

You should have a pretty good understanding of how to implement complex and simple data binding and should also have working Search Screens. In the next chapter, we will continue with the development of our application and begin implementing functionality to allow the user to update data from the Add/View/Edit Products and Suppliers screens.

Exercises

1. What is the difference between complex data binding and simple data binding? Where does property binding fit in?
2. Briefly describe the `ErrorProvider` control and what it can allow you to accomplish.
3. What is the purpose of a `DataView`?
4. Briefly describe the `DataReader` and when it can be used. Can you bind a `DataReader` to controls on a form such as a `DataGrid`? When should you use a `DataReader` versus a `DataSet`?

Answers are available at http://p2p.wrox.com/exercises/.

Updating the DataSet and Handling Errors

In this chapter, we continue developing our Product Management System where we left off in the previous chapter. We will focus on updating data in the DataSet and then on the underlying database based on changes made by the user. More specifically, we will learn about:

- Updating a DataSet based on user input
- Allowing the user to add, edit, and delete data in the DataSet on the Add/Edit/View Products and Suppliers screens
- Creating a second dataset that contains all changes made by invoking the GetChanges method
- Checking for errors in the changed dataset by checking the HasErrors property
- Saving the changes in the DataSet back to the database using Stored Procedures
- Accepting or rejecting the changes made based on whether the updates were successful
- Handling any errors that occur

Updating the Local Version of the DataSet

We now know that the DataSet is an in-memory copy of data that is not connected to the database from which its contents have come. Thus, if you modify the contents of a DataSet you are not actually updating the data in the underlying data store unless you take additional steps. We will start the latest round of changes to our Product Management System by adding code to enable changes to be made to the local DataSet. Then, we will implement the mechanism that saves all the changes back to the original data source when the user clicks the Save All button.

Modifying the Add/View/Edit Products and Suppliers Screens to Update the Local DataSet

In this section, we will modify `frmManageProducts.vb` and `frmManageSuppliers.vb` to enable the updating and deleting of data in the local `DataSet`.

Adding a New Record to the Local DataSet

Let's start with writing the code to add a new record to the local `DataSet` on both the Add/View/Edit Products and Add/View/Edit Suppliers forms.

Try It Out – Adding a New Record to the DataSet for the Products Screen

1. First, add this code to the `Click` event of the `btnAdd` Button on the `frmManageProducts` form:

```
Private Sub btnAdd_Click(ByVal sender As System.Object, ByVal e As _
        System.EventArgs) Handles btnAdd.Click

    Try

    'Use the NewRow to create a DataRow in the DataSet.
    Dim myRow As DataRow
    myRow = dsSearchResults.Tables("results").NewRow()
    myRow("ProductId") = "0"
    myRow("ProductName") = ""
    myRow("SupplierId") = "0"
    myRow("CategoryId") = "0"
    myRow("QuantityPerUnit") = ""
    myRow("UnitPrice") = "0"
    myRow("UnitsInStock") = "0"
    myRow("UnitsOnOrder") = "0"
    myRow("ReorderLevel") = "0"
    myRow("Discontinued") = "false"

    'Add the row with default values.
    dsSearchResults.Tables("results").Rows.Add(myRow)

    'Move to the newly added row so the user can fill in the new
    'information.
    MoveLast()

    'Make sure the frmManageProducts form stays on top.
    frmManageProducts.ActiveForm.TopMost = True

    'Set focus to the ProductName field on the form.
    txtField2.Focus()

    Catch
    'Error handling goes here.
    UnhandledExceptionHandler()
    End Try

End Sub
```

2. Next, we will add similar code to the `Click` event of the `btnAdd` Button on the `frmManageSuppliers` form:

```
Private Sub btnAdd_Click(ByVal sender As System.Object, ByVal e As _
            System.EventArgs) Handles btnAdd.Click

Try

    'Use the NewRow to create a DataRow in the DataSet.
    Dim myRow As DataRow
    myRow = dsSearchResults.Tables("results").NewRow()
    myRow("SupplierId") = 0
    myRow("CompanyName") = ""
    myRow("ContactName") = ""
    myRow("ContactTitle") = ""
    myRow("Address") = ""
    myRow("City") = ""
    myRow("Region") = ""
    myRow("PostalCode") = ""
    myRow("Country") = ""
    myRow("Phone") = ""
    myRow("Fax") = ""
    myRow("HomePage") = ""

    'Add the row with default values.
    dsSearchResults.Tables("results").Rows.Add(myRow)

    'Move to the newly added row so the user can fill in the new
    'information.
    MoveLast()

    'Make sure the frmManageSuppliers form stays on top.
    frmManageSuppliers.ActiveForm.TopMost = True

    'Set focus to the CompanyName field on the form.
    txtField2.Focus()

Catch
    'Error handling goes here.
    UnhandledExceptionHandler()
End Try
```

How It Works

The code segments first declare a new `DataRow`. The new `DataRow` is created using the `NewRow` method and then populated with default values (such as 0 for `ProductId`, `Null` for `ProductName`, etc.).

```
Dim myRow As DataRow
myRow = dsSearchResults.Tables("results").NewRow()
myRow("SupplierId") = 0
myRow("CompanyName") = ""
myRow("ContactName") = ""
myRow("ContactTitle") = ""
myRow("Address") = ""
myRow("City") = ""
myRow("Region") = ""
myRow("PostalCode") = ""
```

```
        myRow("Country") = ""
        myRow("Phone") = ""
        myRow("Fax") = ""
        myRow("HomePage") = ""
```

Next, the code adds that new row to the DataSet with default values by using the Add method:

```
dsSearchResults.Tables("results").Rows.Add(myRow)
```

It then moves to that newly added row by calling the MoveLast method:

```
MoveLast()
```

We finally set the focus to the ProductName or CustomerName field ready for the user to start filling in the details.

```
txtField2.Focus()
```

The main difference between the first set of code and the second is that the default values for the Products are different for Suppliers.

Deleting a Record in the Local DataSet

Next, let's move on to adding the code to delete the record in the local DataSet when the user clicks the Delete Button on either form.

Try It Out – Adding Code to Delete Records in the Local DataSet

1. Save all changes to the MainApp solution and then close it. Next, open the BaseForms solution. The Delete event is the same for both Products and Suppliers, so we are going to add it to the base form. Place the following code under the Click event for the Delete Button on the BaseDataForm.vb:

```
Private Sub btnDelete_Click(ByVal sender As System.Object, ByVal e As _
        System.EventArgs) Handles btnDelete.Click

Try

    'Delete the current row from the DataSet.
    Dim oRow As DataRow
    Dim oTable As DataTable
        Dim intResponse As Integer

        intResponse = MsgBox("Are you sure you want to delete the " & _
                "current record from the DataSet?", _
                MsgBoxStyle.YesNo, "Confirm Delete")

        'If they confirm they want to delete, then go ahead and remove
        'the record from the DataSet. Reminder that this still doesn't
        'delete it from the database. That occurs under the SaveAll
        'when all changes in the DataSet are updated in the database.
        If intResponse = vbYes Then
```

```
                oTable = dsSearchResults.Tables("results")
                oRow = oTable.Rows(myBindingManagerBase.Position)
                If Not oRow.RowState = DataRowState.Deleted Then _
                       oRow.Delete()

                'Make sure the frmManageXXX form stays on top.
                Me.ActiveForm.TopMost = True

                MovePrevious()
            End If

        Catch
            'Handle errors.
            UnhandledExceptionHandler()
        End Try

    End Sub
```

2. After you complete the changes above in the `BaseDataForm`, save the solution and rebuild the project by selecting Build | Rebuild All. Then you can close the BaseForms solution and return to the MainApp solution.

3. At this point, go ahead and run your project and conduct a search based on Products. Double-click on a record in the results grid to open the Add/View/Edit Products screen.

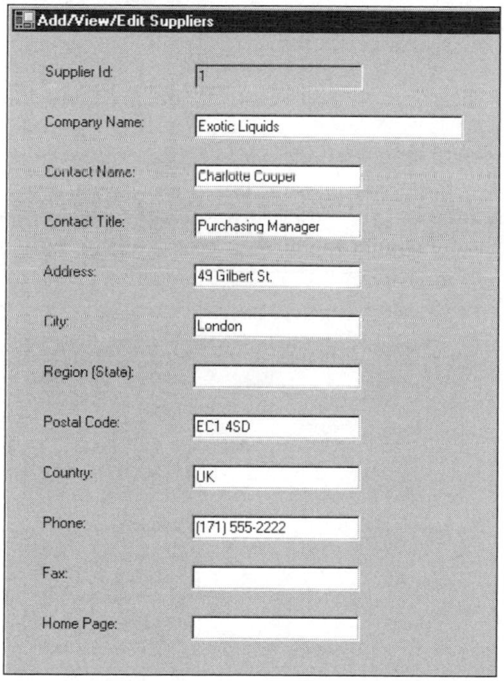

4. Make changes to the data and click the Next Record Button.

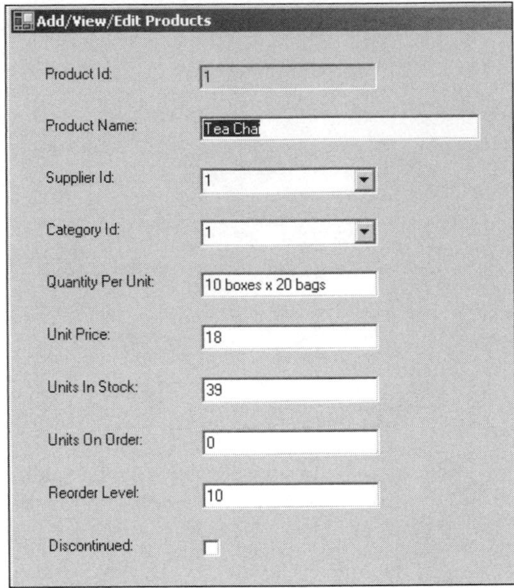

5. Move back and you will see that your changes are still in the local `DataSet`. Also, navigate to a record and click the Delete button.

Confirm Delete
Are you sure you want to delete the current record from the DataSet?
Yes No

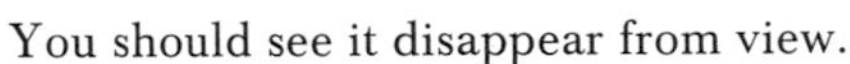
You should see it disappear from view.

6. Furthermore, when you click the Add New Record button, you should find that you are moved to a new record with blank values.

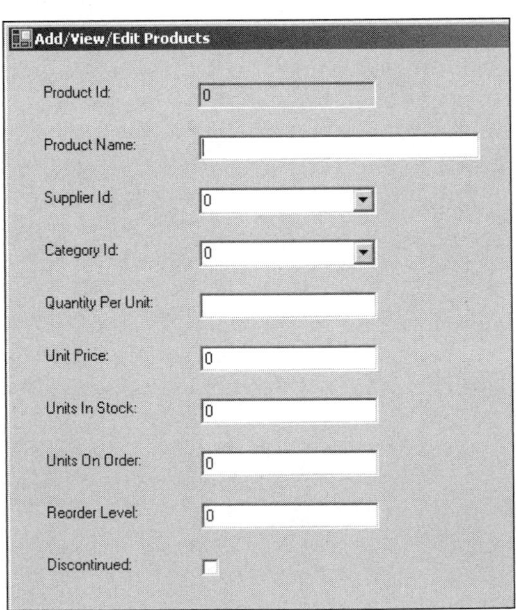

How It Works

The purpose of this code is to delete the current record from the local `DataSet` when the user clicks the Delete Button on either the Add/View/Edit Products or Suppliers forms. Before deleting the record, the user is prompted to confirm the deletion.

```
intResponse = MsgBox("Are you sure you want to delete the " & _
    "current record from the DataSet?", _
    MsgBoxStyle.YesNo, "Confirm Delete")
```

If they respond `Yes`, then the `Delete` method for the `DataRow` is called to delete the record from the `DataSet`.

```
If intResponse = vbYes Then
oTable = dsSearchResults.Tables("results")
oRow = oTable.Rows(myBindingManagerBase.Position)
If Not oRow.RowState = DataRowState.Deleted Then _
       oRow.Delete()
```

Recall that by deleting the record from the `DataSet`, the record still hasn't been deleted in the underlying database. Changes in the `DataSet` only get changed in the local in-memory copy of the data. We will later write the code to update the changes in the database itself.

Modifying an Existing Record in the Local DataSet

In order to modify an existing record in the local `DataSet`, there is no extra code that you have to implement. By having the simple binding to each control property (set up in Chapter 8), this happens automatically. In other words, if you navigate through the Add/View/Edit Products screen changing data, when you move back to the record, it will still have your changed value in that local copy. It has not been updated in the database, at that point, however.

Let's take a look at an example of this in action.

Try It Out – Modifying Records in the Local DataSet

1. Open the Suppliers Search Utility and run a search for all Suppliers with a Supplier ID less than 5. Double-click on one of the records in the list (Supplier ID 1 if you have it in your results) so that the Add/View/Edit Suppliers screen is shown with the selected record active, as shown overleaf:

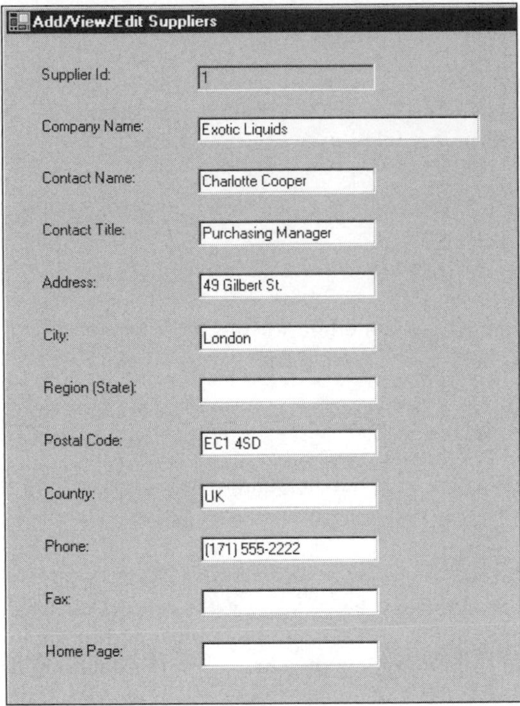

2. Take note of the current value for Company Name and Home Page. In the example above, the original value for the Company Name is Exotic Liquids and the Home Page is empty. Let's change the Company Name value to Exotic Liquids 2 and add a Home Page of www.somewhere.com. After making these changes, move to the next record by clicking the Next Record Button. Move to the previous record, and you should be back on the record you changed. Notice how the values contain the changes you just made:

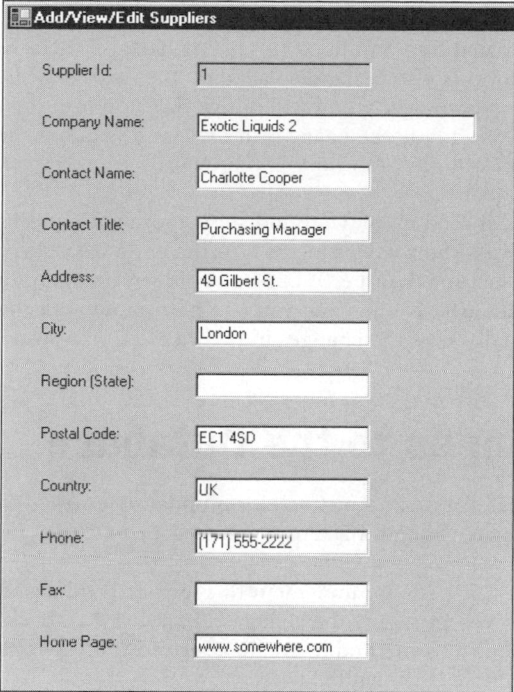

3. Close the Add/View/Edit Suppliers form and return to the Supplier Search Utility. You will even see that the record was updated in the `DataGrid`, as shown below:

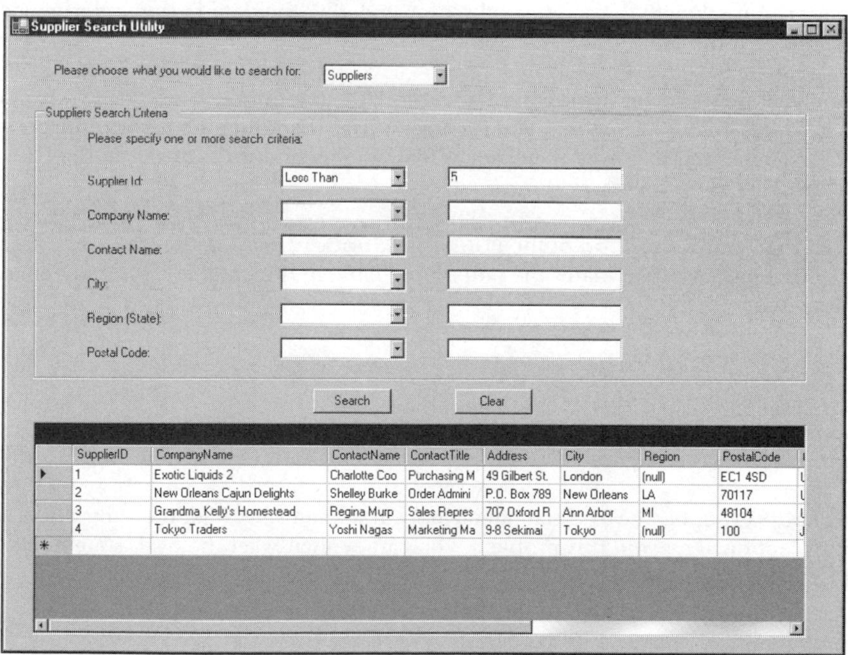

How It Works

The reason the value is updated here in the DataGrid is because the same DataGrid that you modified on the previous form is also being displayed on the Search Utility. However, if you click the Search Button to run your search again, you will notice that you lose the changes you made. Why is that the case? It is because you made the changes in the DataSet, but those changes were not saved to the database. When you click the Search Button, the records are retrieved from the database again.

Before moving on to the next section, play around some more with adding and deleting records in the DataSet as well as modifying their values to see how the code we've added to this point works. Try different variations so you can see that the DataSet is indeed being updated but, as soon as you refresh the DataSet, the values are lost. Then, when you're comfortable with the way it works, move on to the next section where we actually save the changes in the DataSet back to the database.

Saving the Changes to the Database

Now that you have the local DataSets on each form updating correctly, it's time to move on to the more complex part, saving the changes back to the database.

Before delving into the specific code to implement this for our Product Management System, let's first discuss the basic steps involved in saving the changes in a DataSet back to the database. First, you typically invoke the GetChanges method to create a second DataSet that contains only the records that have changed. An example is shown below:

```
dsChangedDataSet = dsdata.GetChanges()
```

It is much easier to work with the smaller subset for updating the data in the underlying database than it is when working with the full DataSet.

Second, you check for errors in the second DataSet by examining its HasErrors property, which indicates if anything in that DataSet contains errors. After handling the errors appropriately, you can invoke the Merge method to merge the changes from the second DataSet into the first, if your scenario dictates this to be necessary.

Then, you call the Update method of the SQLDataAdapter, passing the DataSet as an argument. The Update method actually updates the underlying table in the database with any changes (adds, inserts, or deletes).

```
myDataAdapter.Update(dsChangedDataSet,"Products")
```

When an application calls the Update method, the SQLDataAdapter examines the RowState property, and executes the required Insert, Update, or Delete statements against the database.

If the Insert, Update, or Delete statements have not been specified, then the Update method will generate an exception. To avoid this problem, you can explicitly set the SQL statements for the SQLDataAdapter, as shown opposite.

```
myDataAdapter.SelectCommand = "SELECT * FROM Products"
myDataAdapter.UpdateCommand = "UPDATE Products SET " & _
        "ProductName = 'Test' WHERE ProductId = 1"
myDataAdapter.InsertCommand = "INSERT INTO Products " & _
       "(ProductName,CategoryId) VALUES ('Test', 1) "
myDataAdapter.DeleteCommand = "DELETE FROM Products " & _
        " WHERE ProductId = 1"
```

The above lines of code would need to appear prior to the call to the `Update` method. Alternatively, you can create a `SqlCommandBuilder` object (which we looked at in Chapter 6) to have it automatically generate SQL statements for you. The `SqlCommandBuilder` object will only work with single-table updates (in other words, where Visual Basic .NET can determine the SQL statement for you). Here is an example:

```
Dim objCommandBuilder As New SQLCommandBuilder(myDataAdapter)
myDataAdapter.DeleteCommand = _
    objCommandBuilder.GetDeleteCommand()
myDataAdapter.UpdateCommand = _
    objCommandBuilder.GetUpdateCommand()
myDataAdapter.InsertCommand = _
    objCommandBuilder.GetInsertCommand()
```

If the updates were successful, you can invoke the `AcceptChanges` method on the `DataSet` and, alternatively, if they were not successful, you can invoke the `RejectChanges` method on the `DataSet`. These two methods only affect the local `DataSet` and not the data in the actual database.

Using the `Update` method, `AcceptChanges` and `RejectChanges` follow the principles of transactions. A transaction is a process that must either complete successfully or fail totally. We would not want the update process to finish halfway through, for instance. Transactions are covered in more detail in Chapter 10.

The above is the typical process flow for saving changes in a `DataSet` back to the database. However, there are some exceptions when all of these steps will not work. One example is when your `DataSet` was originally populated into a single table from the results of a `SELECT` statement joining multiple tables together. In such a case, you cannot invoke the `Update` method of the `SQLDataAdapter` object because it doesn't know which underlying table you want to update. Thus, you have to manually update the records in the database while looping through the changed `DataSet`.

If you recall, this is exactly the type of scenario we have with our Product Management System. The search results are based on a SQL statement that selects the records from multiple tables to make a single table in the `DataSet` called `Results`. Thus, instead of being able to easily update the database with changes in the `DataSet` just by invoking the `Update` method, we have to write our own looping code to perform the database changes. Let's get started and see exactly how that works.

Handling Changed Records

For starters, we need to handle existing records in the `DataSet` that have been modified.

Try It Out – Saving Changed Records in the DataSet to the Database

1. Place the following code under the `frmManageProducts.vb` form:

```
Private Sub btnSave_Click(ByVal sender As System.Object, ByVal e As _
          System.EventArgs) Handles btnSave.Click

    Try

        MoveFirst()

        Dim clsDb As New clsDatabase()

        clsDb.ProcessUpdates(CONN, PROD, dsSearchResults)

        clsDb = Nothing

        MsgBox("Save Completed.  If no other messages appeared " & _
            "indicating any errors, then all changes were successful.")

    Catch
        'Error handling goes here.
        UnhandledExceptionHandler()
    End Try
End Sub
```

2. Place this nearly identical code under the `frmManageSuppliers.vb` form:

```
Private Sub btnSave_Click(ByVal sender As System.Object, ByVal e As _
          System.EventArgs) Handles btnSave.Click

    Try

        MoveFirst()

        Dim clsDb As New clsDatabase()

        clsDb.ProcessUpdates(CONN, SUPP, dsSearchResults)
        clsDb = Nothing

        MsgBox("Save Completed.  If no other messages appeared " & _
            "indicating any errors, then all changes were successful.")

    Catch
        'Error handling goes here.
        UnhandledExceptionHandler()
    End Try
End Sub
```

3. Place the code for the `ProcessUpdates` method in `clsDatabase`:

```
Sub ProcessUpdates(ByVal strConnection As String, ByVal strUpdateTable _
              As String, ByRef dsdata As DataSet)
```

```
'*******************************************************************
'The purpose of this procedure is to call the database updates for
'Products or Suppliers based on the changes in the DataSet.
'The strUpdateTable variable passed in should be either "Products" or
'"Suppliers" for the value and depending on the value of it, the
'appropriate database updates will be called. This is a
'generic routine to keep code duplication to a minimum.
'*******************************************************************

    Try

        'Handle any changed records.
        If dsdata.HasChanges(DataRowState.Modified) Then
            Dim dsChangedDataSet As DataSet
            dsChangedDataSet = dsdata.GetChanges(DataRowState.Modified)

            If dsChangedDataSet.HasErrors Then
                HandleDataSetErrors(dsChangedDataSet)
            Else
                'Update the changes in the database.
                If strUpdateTable = "Products" Then
                    UpdateProductsInDb(strConnection, dsChangedDataSet)
                ElseIf strUpdateTable = "Suppliers" Then
                    UpdateSuppliersInDb(strConnection, dsChangedDataSet)
                End If

            End If

        End If
    Catch
        'Error handling goes here.
        UnhandledExceptionHandler()
    End Try
End Sub
```

4. Add the following procedure to the `clsDatabase`:

```
Sub HandleDataSetErrors(ByVal dsChanged As DataSet)

    Try

        'Invoke the GetAllErrors method to return an array of DataRow
        'objects with errors.

        Dim ErrorRows() As DataRow
        Dim oRow As DataRow

        ErrorRows = GetAllErrors(dsChanged)

        'On each DataRow, examine the RowError property.
        Dim i As Integer
        Dim strError As String

        strError = "The following errors occurred - "

        For i = 0 To ErrorRows.GetUpperBound(0)
            strError = strError & " Row Error: " & _
```

```
                    ErrorRows(i).RowError()
        Next
        Err.Raise(-5000, , strError)

    Catch
        'Error handling goes here.
        UnhandledExceptionHandler()
    End Try

End Sub
```

5. Then add the `GetAllErrors` function after the previous method:

```
Function GetAllErrors(ByVal rsChanges As DataSet) As DataRow()

    Try

        Dim rowsInError() As DataRow
        Dim myTable As DataTable
        Dim i As Integer
        Dim myCol As DataColumn

        For Each myTable In rsChanges.Tables
            ' See if the table has errors. If not, skip it.
            If myTable.HasErrors Then
                ' Get an array of all rows with errors.
                rowsInError = myTable.GetErrors()
            End If
        Next

        Return rowsInError

    Catch
        'Error handling goes here.
        UnhandledExceptionHandler()
    End Try

End Function
```

6. Create that `UpdateProductsInDb` procedure now, in `clsDatabase`:

```
Sub UpdateProductsInDb(ByVal strConnection As String, ByVal _
                       dsChangedDataSet As DataSet)

    '*****************************************************************
    'The purpose of this function is to update data in the Products
    'table based on information in a DataSet that changed.
    '*****************************************************************
    Try

        Dim oRow As DataRow
        Dim smallintDiscontinued As Int16
        Dim intRowsAffected As Integer

        For Each oRow In dsChangedDataSet.Tables("Results").Rows
```

```
            smallintDiscontinued = oRow("Discontinued")
            'Format to the format that SQL Server expects.
            'The equivalent to Boolean in SQL Server is BIT.
            'A Bit can have 1 for True or 0 for False.
            'A Boolean in VB can have -1 for True or 0 for False.
            If smallintDiscontinued = vbYes Then
                smallintDiscontinued = -1
            End If

            Dim cmdCommand As New SqlClient.SqlCommand()

            AddProductsInsertUpdateParameters(cmdCommand, oRow, _
                      smallintDiscontinued, True)
            intRowsAffected = ExecuteSPWithParameters(strConnection, _
                      "spUpdateProducts", cmdCommand)

        Next

    Catch
        'Error handling goes here.
        UnhandledExceptionHandler()
    End Try

End Sub
```

7. Add this procedure to `clsDatabase`.

```
Sub AddProductsInsertUpdateParameters(ByRef cmdCommand As _
        SqlClient.SqlCommand, ByVal oRow As DataRow, ByVal _
        smallintdiscontinued As Int16, ByVal blnAddProductId As _
        Boolean)

    'The purpose of this procedure is to add the parameters to the
    'command object that will be passed to the stored procedure for
    'Updating OR Inserting Products.

    Try

        Dim sqlparm As New SqlClient.SqlParameter()

        'If updating a record, then you will need to specify the ProductId.
        'If inserting, then one will not have been assigned yet (and
        'thus the insert stored procedure doesn't expect it as a '
        'parameter).
        If blnAddProductId Then
            sqlparm = cmdCommand.Parameters.Add("@ProductId", _
                      SqlDbType.Int)
            sqlparm.Value = oRow("ProductId")
        End If
        sqlparm = cmdCommand.Parameters.Add("@ProductName", _
                  SqlDbType.NVarChar, 40)
        sqlparm.Value = oRow("ProductName")
        sqlparm = cmdCommand.Parameters.Add("@SupplierId", _
                  SqlDbType.Int)
        sqlparm.Value = oRow("SupplierId")
        sqlparm = cmdCommand.Parameters.Add("@CategoryId", _
```

```
                SqlDbType.Int)
        sqlparm.Value = oRow("CategoryId")
        sqlparm = cmdCommand.Parameters.Add("@QuantityPerUnit", _
                SqlDbType.NVarChar, 20)
        sqlparm.Value = oRow("QuantityPerUnit")
        sqlparm = cmdCommand.Parameters.Add("@UnitPrice", _
                SqlDbType.Money)
        sqlparm.Value = oRow("UnitPrice")
        sqlparm = cmdCommand.Parameters.Add("@UnitsInStock", _
                SqlDbType.SmallInt)
        sqlparm.Value = oRow("UnitsInStock")
        sqlparm = cmdCommand.Parameters.Add("@UnitsOnOrder", _
                SqlDbType.SmallInt)
        sqlparm.Value = oRow("UnitsOnOrder")
        sqlparm = cmdCommand.Parameters.Add("@ReorderLevel", _
                SqlDbType.SmallInt)
        sqlparm.Value = oRow("ReorderLevel")
        sqlparm = cmdCommand.Parameters.Add("@Discontinued", _
                SqlDbType.Bit)
        sqlparm.Value = smallintdiscontinued

    Catch
        'Error handling goes here.
        UnhandledExceptionHandler()
    End Try

End Sub
```

8. Place the `ExecuteSPWithParameters` function in `clsDatabase` along with the others we've added so far:

```
Function ExecuteSPWithParameters(ByVal strConnection As String, ByVal _
         strSPName As String, ByVal cmdCommand As SqlCommand) As Integer

    'The purpose of this function is to execute a stored procedure with
    'parameters as passed in with the command object. The number of
    'rows affected is returned.

    Try

        Dim intRowsAffected As Integer
        Dim sqlConn As New SqlClient.SqlConnection(strConnection)
        sqlConn.Open()
        Dim cmdParms As SqlClient.SqlCommand = cmdCommand

        cmdParms.Connection = sqlConn
        cmdParms.CommandType = CommandType.StoredProcedure
        cmdParms.CommandText = strSPName

        'execute the stored procedure
        intRowsAffected = cmdParms.ExecuteNonQuery()
        sqlConn.Close()

        Return intRowsAffected

    Catch
        'Error handling goes here.
```

```
        UnhandledExceptionHandler()
    End Try

End Function
```

9. Next, create the `spUpdateProducts` stored procedure on the NorthwindSQL database, using Visual Studio .NET Server Explorer:

```
CREATE PROCEDURE dbo.spUpdateProducts
    (
  @ProductId int,
  @ProductName nvarchar(40),
  @SupplierId int,
  @CategoryId int,
  @QuantityPerUnit nvarchar(20),
  @UnitPrice money,
  @UnitsInStock smallint,
  @UnitsOnOrder smallint,
  @ReorderLevel smallint,
  @Discontinued bit
   )
AS
UPDATE Products set ProductName = @ProductName, SupplierId =
              @SupplierId, CategoryId  = @CategoryId, QuantityPerUnit =
              @QuantityPerUnit, UnitPrice = @UnitPrice, UnitsInStock =
              @UnitsInStock, UnitsOnOrder = @UnitsOnOrder,
              ReorderLevel = @ReorderLevel,
              Discontinued = @Discontinued
              WHERE ProductId = @ProductId
   RETURN
```

10. Now that we've completed the code for updating products in the database, let's move on to suppliers. Add the `UpdateSuppliersInDb` procedure to `clsDatabase`:

```
Sub UpdateSuppliersInDb(ByVal strConnection As String, ByVal _
                        dsChangedDataSet As DataSet)

    '*************************************************************
    'The purpose of this function is to update data in the Suppliers
    'table based on information in a DataSet that changed.
    '*************************************************************
    Try

        Dim oRow As DataRow
        Dim intRowsAffected As Integer

        For Each oRow In dsChangedDataSet.Tables("Results").Rows

            Dim cmdCommand As New SqlClient.SqlCommand()

            AddSuppliersInsertUpdateParameters(cmdCommand, oRow, _
                                  True)
            intRowsAffected = ExecuteSPWithParameters(strConnection, _
                                  "spUpdateSuppliers", cmdCommand)

        Next
```

```
    Catch
        'Error handling goes here.
        UnhandledExceptionHandler()
    End Try

End Sub
```

11. Add the `AddSuppliersInsertUpdateParameters` procedure to `clsDatabase`:

```
Sub AddSuppliersInsertUpdateParameters(ByRef cmdCommand As _
       SqlClient.SqlCommand, ByVal oRow As DataRow, ByVal _
       blnAddSupplierId As Boolean)

    'The purpose of this procedure is to add the parameters to the
    'command object that will be passed to the stored procedure for
    'updating or inserting Suppliers.

    Try

        Dim sqlparm As New SqlClient.SqlParameter()

        'If updating a record, then you will need to specify the SupplierId.
        'If inserting, then one will not have been assigned yet (and
        'thus the insert stored procedure doesn't expect it as a
        'parameter).
        If blnAddSupplierId Then
            sqlparm = cmdCommand.Parameters.Add("@SupplierId", _
                      SqlDbType.Int)
            sqlparm.Value = oRow("SupplierId")
        End If
        sqlparm = cmdCommand.Parameters.Add("@CompanyName", _
                  SqlDbType.NVarChar, 40)
        sqlparm.Value = oRow("CompanyName")
        sqlparm = cmdCommand.Parameters.Add("@ContactName", _
                  SqlDbType.NVarChar, 30)
        sqlparm.Value = oRow("ContactName")
        sqlparm = cmdCommand.Parameters.Add("@ContactTitle", _
                  SqlDbType.NVarChar, 30)
        sqlparm.Value = oRow("ContactTitle")
        sqlparm = cmdCommand.Parameters.Add("@Address", _
                  SqlDbType.NVarChar, 60)
        sqlparm.Value = oRow("Address")
        sqlparm = cmdCommand.Parameters.Add("@City", _
                  SqlDbType.NVarChar, 15)
        sqlparm.Value = oRow("City")
        sqlparm = cmdCommand.Parameters.Add("@Region", _
                  SqlDbType.NVarChar, 15)
        sqlparm.Value = oRow("Region")
        sqlparm = cmdCommand.Parameters.Add("@PostalCode", _
                  SqlDbType.NVarChar, 10)
        sqlparm.Value = oRow("PostalCode")
        sqlparm = cmdCommand.Parameters.Add("@Country", _
                  SqlDbType.NVarChar, 15)
        sqlparm.Value = oRow("Country")
        sqlparm = cmdCommand.Parameters.Add("@Phone", _
                  SqlDbType.NVarChar, 24)
```

```
            sqlparm.Value = oRow("Phone")
            sqlparm = cmdCommand.Parameters.Add("@Fax", _
                    SqlDbType.NVarChar, 24)
            sqlparm.Value = oRow("Fax")
            sqlparm = cmdCommand.Parameters.Add("@HomePage", _
                    SqlDbType.NText)
            sqlparm.Value = oRow("HomePage")

        Catch
            'Error handling goes here.
            UnhandledExceptionHandler()
        End Try

    End Sub
```

12. Next, create the `spUpdateSuppliers` stored procedure on the database:

```
CREATE PROCEDURE dbo.spUpdateSuppliers
    (
        @SupplierId int,
        @CompanyName nvarchar(40),
        @ContactName nvarchar(30),
        @ContactTitle nvarchar(30),
        @Address nvarchar(60),
        @City nvarchar(15),
        @Region nvarchar(15),
        @PostalCode nvarchar(10),
        @Country nvarchar(15),
        @Phone nvarchar(24),
        @Fax nvarchar(24),
        @HomePage ntext
    )
AS
    UPDATE Suppliers Set CompanyName = @CompanyName,
                    ContactName = @ContactName,
                      ContactTitle = @ContactTitle,
                    Address = @Address,
                    City = @City,
                    Region = @Region,
                    PostalCode = @PostalCode,
                    Country = @Country,
                    Phone = @Phone,
                    Fax = @Fax,
                    HomePage = @HomePage
WHERE SupplierId = @SupplierId
    RETURN
```

How It Works

We added a lot of code in this section. Don't get too overwhelmed – a lot of it is either repeated for the products and suppliers or is very similar. Recall that we first added the code to the `btnSave_Click` event to both the `frmManageProducts` and `frmManageSuppliers` forms. It creates an instance of the `clsDatabase` class and then calls the `ProcessUpdates` method to handle all of the changes in the `DataSet`.

```
Dim clsDb As New clsDatabase()
clsDb.ProcessUpdates(CONN, PROD, dsSearchResults)
clsDb = Nothing
MsgBox("Save Completed.  If no other messages appeared " & _
     "indicating any errors, then all changes were successful.")
```

The *only* difference in the two events is that the `SUPP` constant is passed as a parameter to `ProcessUpdates` instead of the `PROD` constant. This lets `ProcessUpdates` know whether the data to be updated applies to products or suppliers. This is another example of code that we could have made totally generic and placed on the base form since it is almost exactly the same for both child forms. However, since this references the `clsDatabase.vb` class module that isn't present in that base forms project, we duplicated it here rather than adding it to the base forms project or referencing it from that project. You may have other ideas on how we could have avoided this duplication; as there are multiple ways to do this.

Next, we added the `ProcessUpdates` method within which the `DataSet` is analyzed to see if it has any changes. `ProcessUpdates` method acts as the processor for calling the appropriate methods to update data in the database.

```
'Handle any changed records.
If dsdata.HasChanges(DataRowState.Modified) Then
    Dim dsChangedDataSet As DataSet
    dsChangedDataSet = dsdata.GetChanges(DataRowState.Modified)
```

The first line of code above checks the `HasChanges` property of the `DataSet` with the optional parameter `DataRowState.Modified` to determine if any changed records exist in the `DataSet`. If they do, then the `GetChanges` method is invoked to fill a new `DataSet` with only the records that changed.

```
    If dsChangedDataSet.HasErrors Then
        HandleDataSetErrors(dsChangedDataSet)
    Else
        'Update the changes in the database.
        If strUpdateTable = "Products" Then
            UpdateProductsInDb(strConnection, dsChangedDataSet)
        ElseIf strUpdateTable = "Suppliers" Then
            UpdateSuppliersInDb(strConnection, dsChangedDataSet)
        End If
```

The next section in the above code then checks to make sure that the `DataSet` doesn't contain any errors and proceeds with calling the `Update` procedures (depending on whether `Products` or `Suppliers` are being updated). For now, this method will only handle any changed records. We will modify it later in this chapter to handle deleted and inserted records too.

Next, we created a generic procedure in `clsDatabase`, called `HandleDataSetErrors`, which will loop through a `DataSet` and raise any errors that it encounters. The `GetAllErrors` method is invoked to return any `DataRow` objects with errors in an array.

```
Dim ErrorRows() As DataRow
Dim oRow As DataRow

ErrorRows = GetAllErrors(dsChanged)
```

```
'On each DataRow, examine the RowError property.
Dim i As Integer
Dim strError As String

strError = "The following errors occurred - "
```

Notice that an error number, `-5000`, is raised when the `DataSet` has errors. That number can be replaced with any appropriate error number and is just for demonstration purposes:

```
For i = 0 To ErrorRows.GetUpperBound(0)
    strError = strError & " Row Error: " & _
               ErrorRows(i).RowError()
Next
Err.Raise(-5000, , strError)
```

We then added the `GetAllErrors` function, which is called from `HandleDataSetErrors`, as shown above. This function checks each table in the `DataSet` to see if it has errors. If any errors are encountered, they are loaded into an array of `DataRows`.

```
For Each myTable In isChanges.Tables
    'See if the table has errors. If not, skip it.
    If myTable.HasErrors Then
        'Get an array of all rows with errors.
        rowsInError = myTable.GetErrors()
    End If
Next

Return rowsInError
```

The `ProcessUpdates` method created previously calls an `UpdateProductsInDb` procedure to take care of updating any changed product records. The `UpdateProductsInDb` and `UpdateSuppliersInDb` procedures both take care of calling the appropriate procedures to add the parameters that are to be passed to their respective stored procedures. Notice in the snippet below taken from `UpdateProductsInDb` that, for each row in the `DataSet`, the parameters are added to the `Command` object and then the stored procedure is executed:

```
For Each oRow In dsChangedDataSet.Tables("Results").Rows

    smallintDiscontinued = oRow("Discontinued")
    'Format to the format that SQL Server expects.
    'The equivalent to Boolean in SQL Server is BIT.
    'A Bit can have 1 for True or 0 for False.
    'A Boolean in VB can have -1 for True or 0 for False.
    If smallintDiscontinued = vbYes Then
        smallintDiscontinued = -1
    End If

    Dim cmdCommand As New SqlClient.SqlCommand()

    AddProductsInsertUpdateParameters(cmdCommand, oRow, _
              smallintDiscontinued, True)
    intRowsAffected = ExecuteSPWithParameters(strConnection, _
              "spUpdateProducts", cmdCommand)

Next
```

Further notice that we have to reformat the `Discontinued` value before passing it to the database. The value in Visual Basic .NET for a `Boolean` is different from that which SQL Server expects. A `True` in Visual Basic .NET is `-1` while, in SQL Server, a `bit` (which is the equivalent to `Boolean`) value of `True` is `+1`.

Before the stored procedure can be run to actually update the changes to the products/suppliers records in the database, we must first add the parameters to the `Command` object to pass to SQL Server to tell it which records to update. We will place the code to add these parameters in a procedure called `AddProductsInsertUpdateParameters` or `AddProductsInsertUpdateParameters`. The `Parameters.Add` method is being used to assign the parameters that the stored procedure expects to the corresponding values that came from the local `DataSet`. If we are adding a record, the record will not have a `ProductId` / `SupplierId` as one won't have been assigned yet. In this case, the stored procedure doesn't expect it for a parameter:

```
If blnAddProductId Then
    sqlparm = cmdCommand.Parameters.Add("@ProductId", _
              SqlDbType.Int)
    sqlparm.Value = oRow("ProductId")
End If
```

If a record is being inserted, then the `ProductId` / `SupplierId` needs to be specified with the rest of the parameters, as can be seen from the code snippet below:

```
sqlparm = cmdCommand.Parameters.Add("@ProductName", _
          SqlDbType.NVarChar, 40)
sqlparm.Value = oRow("ProductName")
sqlparm = cmdCommand.Parameters.Add("@SupplierId", _
          SqlDbType.Int)
sqlparm.Value = oRow("SupplierId")
```

Recall from earlier that we are handling the updates manually instead of just calling the `Update` method of the `DataSet`. That is because the `Results` table in our `DataSet` is based on more than one underlying table. It is for this reason that we loop through each record in the `DataSet` that contains the changes and execute the stored procedure to handle the update for that record.

Next, we added the `ExecuteSPWithParameters` function to `clsDatabase`. This is a generic function that will execute a stored procedure – with the parameters as passed with the `Command` object – and will return the number of rows affected. We will be able to call this function in multiple places:

```
Dim intRowsAffected As Integer
Dim sqlConn As New SqlClient.SqlConnection(strConnection)
sqlConn.Open()
Dim cmdParms As SqlClient.SqlCommand = cmdCommand

cmdParms.Connection = sqlConn
cmdParms.CommandType = CommandType.StoredProcedure
cmdParms.CommandText = strSPName

'Execute the stored procedure.
intRowsAffected = cmdParms.ExecuteNonQuery()
sqlConn.Close()

Return intRowsAffected
```

Finally, we added the `spUpdateProducts` and `spUpdateSuppliers` stored procedures to the NorthwindSQL database. These stored procedures accept all of the values in the products or suppliers table as parameters and then update the record for that `ProductId` or `SupplierId` with all of the values passed in:

```
CREATE PROCEDURE dbo.spUpdateProducts
    (
   @ProductId int,
   @ProductName nvarchar(40),
   @SupplierId int,
   @CategoryId int,
   @QuantityPerUnit nvarchar(20),
   @UnitPrice money,
   @UnitsInStock smallint,
   @UnitsOnOrder smallint,
   @ReorderLevel smallint,
   @Discontinued bit
    )
AS
UPDATE Products set ProductName = @ProductName, SupplierId =
              @SupplierId, CategoryId  = @CategoryId, QuantityPerUnit =
              @QuantityPerUnit, UnitPrice = @UnitPrice, UnitsInStock =
              @UnitsInStock, UnitsOnOrder = @UnitsOnOrder,
              ReorderLevel = @ReorderLevel,
              Discontinued = @Discontinued
              WHERE ProductId = @ProductId
   RETURN
```

That's it! We can now save changed records in the `DataSet` to the database. You may be asking, though, "What happens if two users try to update the same record at the same time?" In the next chapter we will cover how to handle concurrency conflicts that can occur when one user tries to change a record that another user has more recently changed.

Handling Deleted Records

Now that we have added the code to our in-progress application to handle records that have changed, let's move on to handling records that have been deleted from the local `DataSet`.

Try It Out – Removing Deleted Records in the DataSet from the Database

1. Add the following code in the `ProcessUpdates` procedure of `clsDatabase` immediately after the section for handling changed records and just above the `Catch` statement, as shown below:

```
End If

'Handle any deleted records.
If dsdata.HasChanges(DataRowState.Deleted) Then
    Dim dsDeletedDataSet As DataSet
    dsDeletedDataSet = dsdata.GetChanges(DataRowState.Deleted)

    If dsDeletedDataSet.HasErrors Then
        HandleDataSetErrors(dsDeletedDataSet)
    Else
```

```
                DeleteRecordsInDb(strConnection, dsDeletedDataSet, _
                                  strUpdateTable)
            End If
        End If

    Catch
        'Error handling goes here.
```

2. Next, add the `DeleteRecordsInDb` procedure to `clsDatabase`.

```
Sub DeleteRecordsInDb(ByVal strConnection As String, ByVal _
      dsDeletedDataSet As DataSet, ByVal strTableName As String)

    '*****************************************************************
    'The purpose of this function is to delete data in the Products
    'table based on information in a DataSet that was deleted.
    '*****************************************************************
    Try

        Dim oRow As DataRow
        Dim intRowsAffected As Integer

        For Each oRow In dsDeletedDataSet.Tables("Results").Rows

            Dim cmdCommand As New SqlClient.SqlCommand()

            'Reject changes so it will allow access to the ProductId.
            oRow.RejectChanges()

            If strTableName = "Products" Then
                AddDeleteParameters(cmdCommand, "@ProductId", _
                           oRow("ProductId"))
                intRowsAffected = _
                      ExecuteSPWithParameters(strConnection, _
                      "spDeleteProducts", cmdCommand)
            Else
                AddDeleteParameters(cmdCommand, "@SupplierId", _
                      oRow("SupplierId"))
                intRowsAffected = _
                      ExecuteSPWithParameters(strConnection, _
                      "spDeleteSuppliers", cmdCommand)
            End If

            'Turn around and delete it again.
            oRow.Delete()
        Next

    Catch
        'Error handling goes here.
        UnhandledExceptionHandler()
    End Try

End Sub
```

3. Place the `AddDeleteParameters` procedure in `clsDatabase` as well.

```
Sub AddDeleteParameters(ByRef cmdCommand As SqlClient.SqlCommand, _
        ByVal strVarName As String, ByVal intId As Integer)

    'The purpose of this procedure is to add the parameters to the
    'command object that will be passed to the stored procedure for
    'deleting Products or Suppliers. strVarname should be passed in as
    'the name of the parameter (e.g. @ProductId or @SupplierId) and
    'intId should be the unique ID to designate which record gets
    'deleted (e.g. ProductId or SupplierId).

    Try

        Dim sqlparm As New SqlClient.SqlParameter()

        sqlparm = cmdCommand.Parameters.Add(strVarName, SqlDbType.Int)
        sqlparm.Value = intId

    Catch
        'Error handling goes here.
        UnhandledExceptionHandler()
    End Try

End Sub
```

4. Create the `spDeleteProducts` stored procedure in the NorthwindSQL database to delete the specified product record.

```
CREATE PROCEDURE dbo.spDeleteProducts
   (
  @ProductId int
   )
AS
   DELETE FROM Products where ProductId = @ProductId
   RETURN
```

5. Create the `spDeleteSuppliers` stored procedure to delete the specified supplier record.

```
CREATE PROCEDURE dbo.spDeleteSuppliers
   (
  @SupplierId int
   )
AS
   DELETE FROM Suppliers where SupplierId = @SupplierId
   RETURN
```

How It Works

Recall that the user clicking the Save Button kicks off the `ProcessUpdates` method. We added code to the `ProcessUpdates` method to have it check for and handle any records that were deleted from the `DataSet`. If any deleted records exist, then a new `DataSet` containing only the deleted records is created.

```
If dsdata.HasChanges(DataRowState.Deleted) Then
Dim dsDeletedDataSet As DataSet
dsDeletedDataSet = dsdata.GetChanges(DataRowState.Deleted)
```

```
        If dsDeletedDataSet.HasErrors Then
            HandleDataSetErrors(dsDeletedDataSet)
        Else
```

The DeleteRecordsInDb procedure is then called to actually delete those records from the database, assuming no errors are contained in the DataSet.

```
            DeleteRecordsInDb(strConnection, dsDeletedDataSet, _
                                  strUpdateTable)
        End If
    End If
```

Then, we added the DeleteRecordsInDb procedure to clsDatabase. This procedure will call the appropriate procedures to add the parameters to the Command object and then execute the appropriate stored procedure depending on whether the delete is for products or suppliers. This function receives a DataSet as a parameter that contains records that should be deleted from the database.

```
    For Each oRow In dsDeletedDataSet.Tables("Results").Rows

        Dim cmdCommand As New SqlClient.SqlCommand()

        'Reject changes so it will allow access to the ProductId.
        oRow.RejectChanges()

        If strTableName = "Products" Then
            AddDeleteParameters(cmdCommand, "@ProductId", _
                        oRow("ProductId"))
            intRowsAffected = _
                  ExecuteSPWithParameters(strConnection, _
                  "spDeleteProducts", cmdCommand)
        Else
            AddDeleteParameters(cmdCommand, "@SupplierId", _
                  oRow("SupplierId"))
            intRowsAffected = _
                  ExecuteSPWithParameters(strConnection, _
                  "spDeleteSuppliers", cmdCommand)
        End If

        'Turn around and delete it again.
        oRow.Delete()
    Next
```

Notice in the code snippet above how it loops through each record and issues a delete statement against the database (by calling the delete stored procedure).

Further, note that a call to RejectChanges is made before the SQL statement and then the row is deleted again, two lines later. You are probably wondering – if it was deleted already, why we rejected the changes and then immediately deleted the record again. The reason is because, if you don't do it this way, you will receive an error when you try to create the strSQL statement saying that the item does not exist in the collection. So, by temporarily rejecting changes so the dynamic SQL statement can be built, and then immediately deleting it from the DataSet again, we overcome this issue.

We also added the AddDeleteParameters procedure to clsDatabase. It will add a single parameter to the Command object, which, in the case of both of our stored procedures, will be their respective IDs (ProductId or SupplierId). The name of the parameter is passed in using strVarname, and intId designates which record gets deleted using the unique ProductId or SupplierId.

```
Dim sqlparm As New SqlClient.SqlParameter()

sqlparm = cmdCommand.Parameters.Add(strVarName, SqlDbType.Int)
sqlparm.Value = intId
```

Finally, we created the stored procedures necessary to delete the specified record in either the Products or Suppliers table. The code below shows how the ProductId is used to specify which record is to be deleted from the Products table.

```
CREATE PROCEDURE dbo.spDeleteProducts
   (
  @ProductId int
   )
AS
   DELETE FROM Products where ProductId = @ProductId
   RETURN
```

The stored procedure for the Suppliers table works in exactly the same way as that given above for the Products table, with the obvious changes so that it refers to suppliers.

Handling Added Records

Now that we've handled updating existing records or deleting them, it's time to implement the code to add new records to the database.

Try It Out – Saving Added Records in the DataSet to the Database

1. Add the code below to the end of the ProcessUpdates procedure in clsDatabase above the Catch statement:

```
'Handle any new records.
If dsdata.HasChanges(DataRowState.Added) Then
    Dim dsAddedDataSet As DataSet
    dsAddedDataSet = dsdata.GetChanges(DataRowState.Added)

    If dsAddedDataSet.HasErrors Then
        HandleDataSetErrors(dsAddedDataSet)
    Else
        'Update the database with the new records.
        If strUpdateTable = "Products" Then
            InsertProductsInDb(strConnection, dsAddedDataSet)
        ElseIf strUpdateTable = "Suppliers" Then
            InsertSuppliersInDb(strConnection, dsAddedDataSet)
        End If

        'If the dsAddedDataSet was changed in the InsertXXXXInDb
        'method (because a new ProductId or SupplierId was
```

```
                'auto-generated by the database), then you will need to
                'update the Id for each record that was added.
                If dsAddedDataSet.HasChanges Then
                    Dim dsChangedAddedDataSet As DataSet
                    dsChangedAddedDataSet = _
                        dsAddedDataSet.GetChanges(DataRowState.Added)

                    'merge the dsChangedAddedDataSet with the
                    'dsSearchResults
                    dsdata.Merge(dsChangedAddedDataSet.GetChanges)
                    dsdata.AcceptChanges()

                    'Get rid of the duplicates that got created on merge
                    'because the primary key wasn't set yet (that is, delete
                    'the records that have a ProductId = 0 that are now
                    'in duplicate of the ones with the newly assigned
                    'ProductId.
                    Dim oRow As DataRow
                    For Each oRow In dsdata.Tables("results").Rows
                        If strUpdateTable = "Products" Then
                            If oRow("ProductId") = 0 Then
                                oRow.Delete()
                            End If
                        ElseIf strUpdateTable = "Suppliers" Then
                            If oRow("SupplierId") = 0 Then
                                oRow.Delete()
                            End If
                        End If

                    Next

                End If
            End If

        End If
```

2. Add the `InsertProductsInDb` procedure to `clsDatabase`:

```
Sub InsertProductsInDb(ByVal strConnection As String, ByVal _
                dsInsertedDataSet As DataSet)

    '****************************************************************
    'The purpose of this function is to insert data into the Products
    'table based on information in a DataSet that changed.
    '****************************************************************
    Try

        Dim oRow As DataRow
        Dim intRowsAffected As Integer
        Dim SmallIntDiscontinued As Int16

        For Each oRow In dsInsertedDataSet.Tables("Results").Rows

            Dim cmdCommand As New SqlClient.SqlCommand()

            SmallIntDiscontinued = oRow("Discontinued")
```

```
            'Format to the format that SQL Server expects.
            'The equivalent to Boolean in SQL Server is BIT.
            'A bit can have 1 for True or 0 for False.
            'A boolean in VB can have -1 for True or 0 for False.
            If SmallIntDiscontinued = vbYes Then
                SmallIntDiscontinued = -1
            End If

            AddProductsInsertUpdateParameters(cmdCommand, oRow, _
                        SmallIntDiscontinued, False)
            intRowsAffected = ExecuteSPWithParameters(strConnection, _
                        "spInsertProducts", cmdCommand)

            cmdCommand.Parameters.Clear()

            'Now we need to retrieve the ProductId that was auto-generated
            'by the database and include it in our DataSet.
            AddProductNameParameters(cmdCommand, oRow("ProductName"))
            intRowsAffected = ExecuteSPWithParameters(strConnection, _
                         "spGetProductIdByProductName", cmdCommand)

            'Retrieve the ProductId from the value returned by the
            'stored procedure and put it into our DataSet.
            oRow("ProductId") = _
                       cmdCommand.Parameters.Item("@ProductId").Value

        Next

    Catch
        'Error handling goes here.
        UnhandledExceptionHandler()
    End Try

End Sub
```

3. Add the `spInsertProducts` stored procedure to the database:

```
CREATE PROCEDURE dbo.spInsertProducts
      (
      @ProductName nvarchar(40),
      @SupplierId int,
      @CategoryId int,
      @QuantityPerUnit nvarchar(20),
      @UnitPrice money,
      @UnitsInStock smallint,
      @UnitsOnOrder smallint,
      @ReorderLevel smallint,
      @Discontinued bit
      )
AS
INSERT INTO Products (ProductName, SupplierId, CategoryId,
            QuantityPerUnit, UnitPrice, UnitsInStock, UnitsOnOrder,
            ReorderLevel, Discontinued)
VALUES (@ProductName, @SupplierId, @CategoryId,
            @QuantityPerUnit, @UnitPrice, @UnitsInStock, @UnitsOnOrder,
            @ReorderLevel, @Discontinued)
RETURN
```

4. Next, add the AddProductNameParameters procedure to clsDatabase:

```
Sub AddProductNameParameters(ByRef cmdCommand As sqlclient.SqlCommand, _
           ByVal strProductName As String)

    'The purpose of this procedure is to add the parameters to the
    'command object that will be passed to the stored procedure for
    'retrieving the ProductId that was just assigned.

    Try

        Dim sqlparm As New SqlClient.SqlParameter()

        sqlparm = cmdCommand.Parameters.Add("@ProductName", _
                  SqlDbType.NVarChar, 40)
        sqlparm.Value = strProductName

        sqlparm = cmdCommand.Parameters.Add("@ProductId", SqlDbType.Int)
        sqlparm.Direction = ParameterDirection.Output

    Catch
        'Error handling goes here.
        UnhandledExceptionHandler()
    End Try

End Sub
```

5. On the SQL Server database, add the spGetProductIdByProductName stored procedure:

```
CREATE PROCEDURE dbo.spGetProductIdByProductName
   (
  @ProductName nvarchar(40),
  @ProductId int OUTPUT
   )
AS
   SELECT    @ProductId = ProductId
   FROM      Products
   WHERE     ProductName = @ProductName
   RETURN
```

6. Next, add the procedure to handle Supplier updates, called InsertSuppliersInDb, to clsDatabase:

```
Sub InsertSuppliersInDb(ByVal strConnection As String, ByVal _
          dsInsertedDataSet As DataSet)

    '*****************************************************************
    'The purpose of this function is to insert data into the Suppliers
    'table based on information in a DataSet that changed.
    '*****************************************************************
    Try

        Dim oRow As DataRow
        Dim intRowsAffected As Integer
```

```
        For Each oRow In dsInsertedDataSet.Tables("Results").Rows

            Dim cmdCommand As New SqlClient.SqlCommand()

            AddSuppliersInsertUpdateParameters(cmdCommand, oRow, _
                     False)
            intRowsAffected = ExecuteSPWithParameters(strConnection, _
                    "spInsertSuppliers", cmdCommand)

            cmdCommand.Parameters.Clear()

            'Now we need to retrieve the SupplierId that was auto-generated
            'by the database and include it in our DataSet.
            AddSupplierCompanyNameParameters(cmdCommand, _
                      oRow("CompanyName"))
            intRowsAffected = ExecuteSPWithParameters(strConnection, _
                      "spGetSupplierIdByCompanyName", cmdCommand)

            'Retrieve the SupplierId from the value returned by the
            'stored procedure and put it into our DataSet.
            oRow("SupplierId") = _
                  cmdCommand.Parameters.Item("@SupplierId").Value

        Next

    Catch
        'Error handling goes here.
        UnhandledExceptionHandler()
    End Try

End Sub
```

7. Add the following stored procedure to the database - `spInsertSuppliers`:

```
CREATE PROCEDURE dbo.spInsertSuppliers
   (
  @CompanyName nvarchar(40),
  @ContactName nvarchar(30),
  @ContactTitle nvarchar(30),
  @Address nvarchar(60),
  @City nvarchar(15),
  @Region nvarchar(15),
  @PostalCode nvarchar(10),
  @Country nvarchar(15),
  @Phone nvarchar(24),
  @Fax nvarchar(24),
  @HomePage ntext
   )
AS
   INSERT INTO Suppliers (CompanyName, ContactName, ContactTitle,
            Address, City, Region, PostalCode, Country,
            Phone, Fax, HomePage)
VALUES (@CompanyName, @ContactName, @ContactTitle,
            @Address, @City, @Region, @PostalCode, @Country,
            @Phone, @Fax, @HomePage)
   RETURN
```

8. In the `clsDatabase` class, add a procedure, `AddSupplierCompanyNameParameters`, as shown below:

```
Sub AddSupplierCompanyNameParameters(ByRef cmdCommand As _
        sqlclient.SqlCommand, ByVal strCompanyName As String)

    'The purpose of this procedure is to add the parameters to the
    'command object that will be passed to the stored procedure for
    'retrieving the SupplierId that was just assigned.

    Try

        Dim sqlparm As New SqlClient.SqlParameter()

        sqlparm = cmdCommand.Parameters.Add("@CompanyName", _
                SqlDbType.NVarChar, 40)
        sqlparm.Value = strCompanyName

        sqlparm = cmdCommand.Parameters.Add("@SupplierId", _
                SqlDbType.Int)
        sqlparm.Direction = ParameterDirection.Output

    Catch
        'Error handling goes here.
        UnhandledExceptionHandler()
    End Try

End Sub
```

9. Next, add `spGetSupplierIdByCompanyName` as shown:

```
CREATE PROCEDURE dbo.spGetSupplierIdByCompanyName
   (
  @CompanyName nvarchar(40),
  @SupplierId int OUTPUT
   )
AS
   SELECT @SupplierId = SupplierId
 FROM Suppliers
 WHERE CompanyName = @CompanyName
RETURN
```

10. At the bottom of the `ProcessUpdates` procedure, add this code. It should immediately follow the code for adding new records in the step above and be immediately above the `Catch` statement:

```
            dsData.AcceptChanges()
```

11. Then, in the `Catch` statement, add this line of code underneath the line of code for the generic error handler:

```
            dsData.RejectChanges()
```

How It Works

We added code to the end of `ProcessUpdates` to create a new `DataSet` containing only the added records:

```
'Handle any new records.
If dsdata.HasChanges(DataRowState.Added) Then
    Dim dsAddedDataSet As DataSet
    dsAddedDataSet = dsdata.GetChanges(DataRowState.Added)

    If dsAddedDataSet.HasErrors Then
        HandleDataSetErrors(dsAddedDataSet)
    Else
        'Update the database with the new records.
        If strUpdateTable = "Products" Then
            InsertProductsInDb(strConnection, dsAddedDataSet)
        ElseIf strUpdateTable = "Suppliers" Then
            InsertSuppliersInDb(strConnection, dsAddedDataSet)
        End If

        'If the dsAddedDataSet was changed in the InsertXXXXInDb
        'method (because a new ProductId or SupplierId was
        'auto-generated by the database), then you will need to
        'update the Id for each record that was added.
        If dsAddedDataSet.HasChanges Then
            Dim dsChangedAddedDataSet As DataSet
            dsChangedAddedDataSet = _
                dsAddedDataSet.GetChanges(DataRowState.Added)
```

It then merges the changes made to populate the `ProductIds` (that got auto-assigned) back with the other local `DataSet`:

```
'Merge the dsChangedAddedDataSet with the
'dsSearchResults.
dsdata.Merge(dsChangedAddedDataSet.GetChanges)
dsdata.AcceptChanges()
```

Due to the fact that the original record that was added had a `ProductId` of 0 (since one had not yet been assigned), the merge created a duplicate of the same record. Thus, we need to manually loop through the `DataSet` and delete any rows that have a `ProductId` equal to zero:

```
'Get rid of the duplicates that got created on merge
'because the primary key wasn't set yet (that is, delete
'the records that have a ProductId = 0 that are now
'duplicates of the ones with the newly assigned
'ProductId.
Dim oRow As DataRow
For Each oRow In dsdata.Tables("results").Rows
    If strUpdateTable = "Products" Then
        If oRow("ProductId") = 0 Then
            oRow.Delete()
        End If
    ElseIf strUpdateTable = "Suppliers" Then
        If oRow("SupplierId") = 0 Then
            oRow.Delete()
        End If
    End If
```

We then call the `InsertProductsInDb` procedure to actually handle the inserts. It will loop through each added record, add the parameters, and execute the stored procedure to actually add the record to the database.

This function is a little more complicated than the two previous ones. It accepts a `DataSet` just like the other two containing records that are to be added to the database. However, it also contains code for retrieving the `ProductId` from the database that got auto-assigned. The `ProductId` field is the key in the Products table and is set to be auto-generated by SQL Server. Thus, when we issued the `Insert` statements, notice that the `ProductId` is blank. We therefore need to select the record that was just added to find out what `ProductId` was assigned. We can then update our local `DataSet` on the screen with the newly generated `ProductId`. An example of the code that does these tasks is shown below:

```
'Now we need to retrieve the ProductId that was auto-generated
'by the database and include it in our DataSet.
AddProductNameParameters(cmdCommand, oRow("ProductName"))
intRowsAffected = ExecuteSPWithParameters(strConnection, _
             "spGetProductIdByProductName", cmdCommand)

'Retrieve the ProductId from the value returned by the
'stored procedure and put it into our DataSet.
oRow("ProductId") = _
            cmdCommand.Parameters.Item("@ProductId").Value
```

Note that the `InsertSuppliersInDb` procedure follows a similar pattern in looking up the `SupplierId` after the new supplier record was added.

We created two stored procedures for the Products table and two for the Suppliers table. The `InsertProducts` stored procedure will add a new product record to the database:

```
INSERT INTO Products (ProductName, SupplierId, CategoryId,
            QuantityPerUnit, UnitPrice, UnitsInStock, UnitsOnOrder,
            ReorderLevel, Discontinued)
VALUES (@ProductName, @SupplierId, @CategoryId,
            @QuantityPerUnit, @UnitPrice, @UnitsInStock, @UnitsOnOrder,
            @ReorderLevel, @Discontinued)
```

The `GetProductIdByProductName` stored procedure will look up the `ProductId` based on a `ProductName`:

```
SELECT     @ProductId = ProductId
FROM       Products
WHERE      ProductName = @ProductName
```

The two stored procedures for the `Suppliers` table work in the same way but `GetSupplierIdByCompanyName` will actually look up the `SupplierId` based on a `CompanyName` passed in.

Next, we added the `AddProductNameParameters` procedure to `clsDatabase`. This procedure will add the appropriate parameters to the `Command` object that will later be used to retrieve the `ProductId` that was just assigned to the newly added record.

```
Dim sqlparm As New SqlClient.SqlParameter()

sqlparm = cmdCommand.Parameters.Add("@ProductName", _
          SqlDbType.NVarChar, 40)
sqlparm.Value = strProductName

sqlparm = cmdCommand.Parameters.Add("@ProductId", SqlDbType.Int)
sqlparm.Direction = ParameterDirection.Output
```

One parameter added is an input parameter (`ProductName`) and the other one is an output parameter (`ProductId`). Similarly, `AddSupplierCompanyNameParameters` handles adding parameters to the `Command` object for retrieving the `SupplierId` by `CompanyName`.

At the end of `ProcessUpdates` procedure, we added the line of code to call the `AcceptChanges` method of the `DataSet`.

```
dsData.AcceptChanges()
```

This line of code will accept changes in the `DataSet` so they will no longer keep being generated as changes. In other words, now that these changes have been saved to the database, the changes should be accepted in the `DataSet` so they will no longer be flagged as added, updated, or deleted. The `AcceptChanges` method resets all of the local trackers so that it is as though you are starting afresh without having made any changes. You can think of `AcceptChanges` as officially committing the changes to the `DataSet` (but not the underlying database).

Lastly, we added the `RejectChanges` method of the `DataSet` to the `Catch` statement.

```
dsData.RejectChanges()
```

This will reject all changes in the `DataSet` since an error occurred. This does not have any impact on the database, but simply puts the `DataSet` into a state where the added, inserted, and deleted records are still flagged as such.

Congratulations – you have now completed the code for saving your changes in the `DataSet` to the database. Let's test out the Add/View/Edit Products and Add/View/Edit Suppliers screens for adding, deleting, and updating items in the database.

Testing the New Capabilities of Our Forms

First, let's try running the same test we ran at the beginning of this chapter to see how the work we have done changes the result. Recall at the beginning how we ran a search, opened a record up on the Add/View/Edit Suppliers screen, edited some values, and then discovered that the changes were lost after rerunning the search. That was because we had only changed the local `DataSet` and had not saved the changes back to the database.

Try running that same test again. See if your changes are indeed saved to the database and if, when you rerun the search, the new values appear. As an example, open the supplier record and change the Company Name from Exotic Liquids to Exotic Liquids New. Also add a web site called www.somewhere.com. Click the Save All Changes Button and see what happens.

MainApp
Save Completed. If no other messages appeared indicating any errors, then all changes were successful.
OK

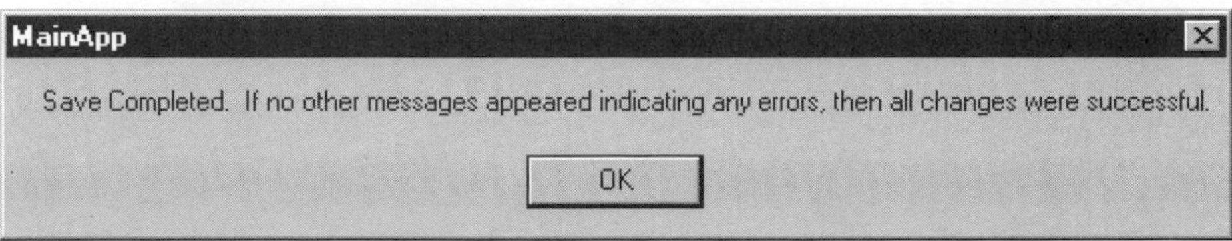

You should receive a message box like the one shown above indicating that your save completed successfully. Close this window and return to the search screen. Rerun your search again and see if, this time, your changes were saved to the database.

Next, let's try adding a new record. We want to see if the new record gets added to the database and if the new `SupplierId` is displayed on the form. Let's look at this in more detail so you can see what is going on. Run the search again with Supplier Id Less Than 5. You should get results similar to the following:

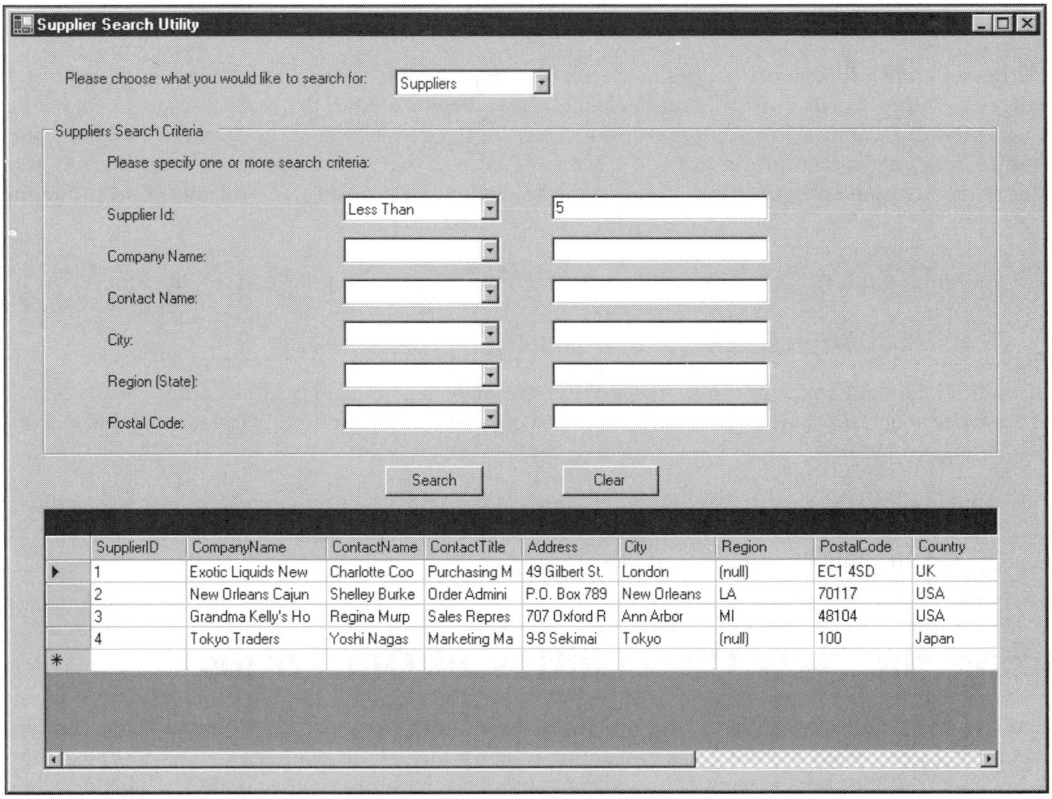

Supplier Search Utility
Please choose what you would like to search for:
Suppliers
Suppliers Search Criteria
Please specify one or more search criteria:
Supplier Id:
Less Than
5
Company Name:
Contact Name:
City:
Region (State):
Postal Code:
Search
Clear
SupplierID
CompanyName
ContactName
ContactTitle
Address
City
Region
PostalCode
Country
1 Exotic Liquids New Charlotte Coo Purchasing M 49 Gilbert St. London (null) EC1 4SD UK
2 New Orleans Cajun Shelley Burke Order Admini P.O. Box 789 New Orleans LA 70117 USA
3 Grandma Kelly's Ho Regina Murp Sales Repres 707 Oxford R Ann Arbor MI 48104 USA
4 Tokyo Traders Yoshi Nagas Marketing Ma 9-8 Sekimai Tokyo (null) 100 Japan

Double-click to open the first record so it will open in the Add/View/Edit Suppliers screen. Now, you are ready to click the Add New Record Button and add a new supplier to the `DataSet`. A blank record should appear with all fields blank except for the Supplier Id with a default value of 0. Fill in the information on the form such as in the example opposite:

It's time to actually commit these changes to the underlying database. Click the Save All Changes Button and see what happens. If all goes well, you should see the dialog box indicating that all changes were successful. You should also see that the record you added is now populated on the screen with a Supplier Id, as shown in the example overleaf:

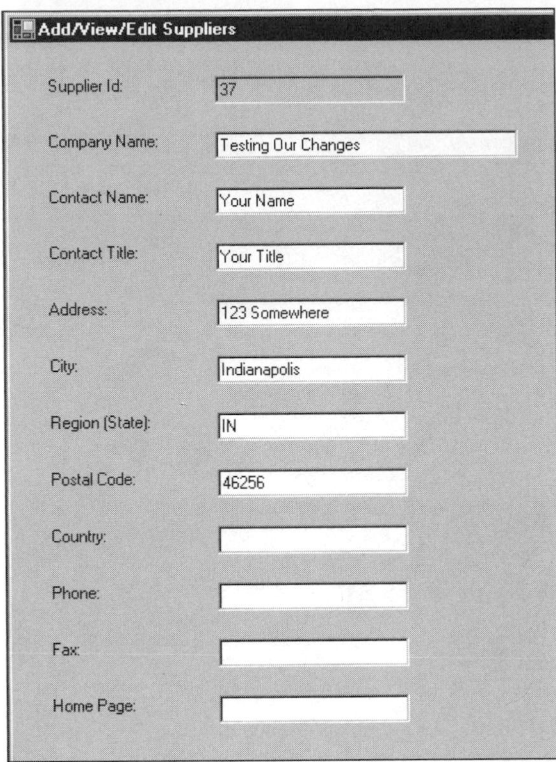

Next, click the Delete Button and confirm that you want to delete this record from the `DataSet`. Then, click the Save All Changes Button to save this change to the database. Run a search on the search screen including property criteria that would otherwise return that record to confirm that this record was indeed deleted from the database.

Play around with adding, updating, and deleting until you are comfortable with how it works. Try changing multiple records and then click Save All Changes and see if it updates all of them correctly. Congratulations! You just successfully updated the database based on changes made by the user on the screen!

Summary

In this chapter, we extended our Product Management System to include functionality to modify data on the Add/Edit/View Products and Suppliers screens. The user can work with the local copy, make changes to the `DataSet` and then, when completed, the changes are saved back to the database (upon clicking the Save All Changes Button). We specifically accomplished the following:

- Functionality on the Add/Edit/View Products and Suppliers screens to allow users to add, edit, and delete data in the `DataSet`
- Using the `GetChanges` method to create a second `DataSet` that contains all changes made

- Using the HasErrors property of the changed DataSet to check for errors
- Calling stored procedures to save the changed data in the DataSet back to the database
- Providing error handling to handle any errors that may occur
- Accepting or rejecting the changes made based on whether the updates were successful

In this chapter we covered some of the more complicated concepts of DataSets. Hopefully, you now have a good grasp on how to work with DataSets and to ultimately update the data back in the database. In the next chapter, we will handle conflict resolution, finish our Product Management System, and take a whirlwind tour of the completed application.

Exercises

1. What is the purpose of the GetChanges method of a DataSet?
2. Why could we not use the SQLDataAdapter to update the data in our Product Management System to make it easier?
3. What does the Merge method do?
4. What do the AcceptChanges and RejectChanges do?
5. What is the purpose of Try...Catch...End Try?

Answers are available at http://p2p.wrox.com/exercises/.

Conflict Resolution

In this chapter, we will finish up the Product Management System by implementing code to handle update conflicts that can occur when more than one person tries to update the same information at the same time. We will show when update conflicts can occur and how to handle them in your code. We will also look at other types of problems that can occur when updating data in a database, and how to use transactions to help resolve these problems. At the end of the chapter, we will then take a complete tour of the finished Product Management System that we've created. More specifically, we will cover:

- How update conflicts can occur
- What optimistic and pessimistic concurrency is
- Ways of implementing optimistic concurrency in general and with `DataSets` (the "Version Number" or "Timestamp" method and the "Saving All Values" method)
- What transactions are and how they work
- How a transaction's `Commit` and `Rollback` methods compare to the `AcceptChanges` and `RejectChanges` methods of the `DataSet`
- A complete tour of the Product Management System

As usual, we will end with a summary and some questions.

Handling Data Update Conflicts

Update conflicts can occur when one user attempts to update a record that another user has updated more recently. For example, in the disconnected world of data, suppose two different users have the same record in memory in their local `DataSet`. When one user changes the record, the other user still has the original (now outdated) copy in their local copy. When that second user then attempts to make an update, they could overwrite what the first user already changed.

Let's look at an example to demonstrate this concept. Suppose John Doe and Jane Smith are both using the Product Management System on two different computers. Further, suppose that John brings up the details for Boston Crab Meat on his **Products Add/View/Update** screen:

Product Name	Unit Price	Units in Stock	Units on Order	Reorder Level
Boston Crab Meat	18.40	123	0	30

When Jane opens her Products Add/View/Update screen, suppose she also sees the same information:

Product Name	Unit Price	Units in Stock	Units on Order	Reorder Level
Boston Crab Meat	18.40	123	0	30

John, who still has the Boston Crab Meat record on his screen, changes the Units in Stock to 120. He then saves this change to the database:

Product Name	Unit Price	Units in Stock	Units on Order	Reorder Level
Boston Crab Meat	18.40	**120**	0	30

Jane, still having the original record on her screen, changes the Units in Stock on her screen from the original 123 to 122, as shown below:

Product Name	Unit Price	Units in Stock	Units on Order	Reorder Level
Boston Crab Meat	18.40	**122**	0	30

When she presses the Save button, what will happen? Her value of 122 could overwrite John's recently updated value of 120. If our application doesn't handle update conflicts, you can have multiple users changing each other's data without realizing it. Ideally, the application needs some way of notifying Jane that the record has changed since she last opened it, so she can determine whether to continue with the save or not. In a more sophisticated application, she should also be provided with the values that have changed and how they compare to her values. She can then take action to update or cancel her changes based on this new information.

Note that it wouldn't matter which field for the Boston Crab Meat product Jane was trying to update (Units in Stock or some other field), she should still be made aware that a change to the record has occurred since she last opened the record. This is a good idea because the information another user changed could have an impact on whether she proceeds with her update. Even if the change was made to a different field, if Jane were to continue without realizing a change had been made, the field would be set back to the value Jane originally had for that field.

Handling update conflicts is a key consideration that should be part of your design decision from the beginning. In enterprise applications with hundreds or thousands of users simultaneously updating information, it would be extremely damaging to have users overwriting each other in a haphazard way. Work done could be lost and a lot of unnecessary confusion could be caused.

The simple examples in this section should convey the idea of update conflicts. Now that you understand what update conflicts actually are, let's look at some ways of dealing with them.

Handling Update Conflicts with Optimistic or Pessimistic Concurrency

In general, there are three ways to deal with updates in a database:

- With **last update wins**, no effort is made to compare updates made in the database with the original record. Under this scenario, both John Doe and Jane Smith's updates would succeed. John's update would be made and then Jane's update would be made, despite the fact that they overwrite each other. There may be certain situations when this method is appropriate; namely when, you want the last change to be the one that gets updated in the database. A specific example of this would be if you were storing stock ticker information in a database with multiple people updating the information constantly. In this situation, the last person to update the information is the one you want and you don't care about the fact that someone else may have just updated it a moment before.

- With **pessimistic concurrency**, a record is unavailable to other users while another user has it in edit mode. Until the user updates that record in the database, none of the other users can change it. It is locked while one user has it in edit mode. Using this method, the moment one user goes into edit mode, all other users are locked out of editing the record until the original user finishes.

- With **optimistic concurrency**, on the other hand, a record is unavailable to other users only for the short time that the data is actually being updated in the database. In other words, locks occur only in the moment during which the database is actually being accessed. The data is available any time between the start of the editing and when the attempt is made to update the database. The ideal case for the John Doe and Jane Smith example described earlier would be optimistic concurrency. John Doe updates the record but Jane Smith still has the old data on her screen. When she tries to save her changes to the database, she is notified that the record has changed since she started editing her copy of the data.

The ADO.NET data architecture, with the `DataSet` and `DataReader`, is based upon disconnected data and therefore employs either the last update wins or optimistic concurrency models. The pessimistic concurrency model is not applicable unless you write your own pessimistic locking logic. The `DataSet`, as you are aware, does not maintain a connection to the database but simply contains an in-memory copy of the data. Updates are made to the local in-memory copy and then those updates can be made in the database itself.

With the `DataReader`, you can retrieve a forward-only stream of data or can issue SQL statements or stored procedures to update data in the database. If the `DataReader` is used in an application to display data on the screen, then multiple users can have that information on their screens. If one of them then updates the record and saves the record back to the database, the other user will have an outdated record and not even be aware of it.

Due to the disconnected nature of both these update scenarios, it is possible that multiple users may overwrite each other's changes. Thus, you need to implement logic to handle the situations when the conflict arises. Alternatively (although usually not recommended), you could rely on the last update wins method and just let both changes be made to the database even though one person had just overwritten someone else's changes.

In the next section, we will look at the recommended approach: optimistic concurrency.

Implementing Optimistic Concurrency with DataSets

With optimistic concurrency, you have to write business logic to detect and handle situations when one user tries to save changes to a record that another user has already changed in the meantime. There are a couple of different ways to write business logic to determine when this happens.

Version Number or Timestamp Method

The first method for handling update conflicts is to use the **Version Number** or **Timestamp** method. For this approach to work, the table in the database you are updating must contain a version number or date/time field for when the record was last updated. The way that this approach works is as follows:

- The version or date/time value is saved on the client machine (either in a `DataSet` or a variable) when the record is initially retrieved.
- When the update is made, the record only gets updated in the database if the version or date/time values match identically.
- If they do not match, then you know that the record has changed in the meantime.

Under this approach, you must keep track of the original value for the version or last updated date/time value. When you are ready to update the database, you can compare against this original value to see if changes have been made more recently. If a conflict does occur, you should notify the user and ask how they want to proceed.

In enterprise applications, it is recommended that you implement a more sophisticated way of notifying users of the exact details of the conflict, such as a comparison of each field showing the value they entered versus the more current one in the database. They should be able to specify field by field which values to overwrite and which ones to preserve. The level of sophistication necessary just depends on the nature of the application. No matter how large or small the application, it is definitely a good idea to implement the basics of handling update conflicts, as we will be implementing for the Product Management System.

Without further hesitation, let's move on to seeing this method in action. The first thing we need to do is add the `LastUpdated` date/time field to be used later in our comparison methods.

Try It Out – Adding LastUpdated to NorthwindSQL

1. Navigate to the SQL Server NorthwindSQL database using Server Explorer. Expand the Tables node underneath the database and highlight the Products table. Right-click and select Design Table from the pop-up menu.

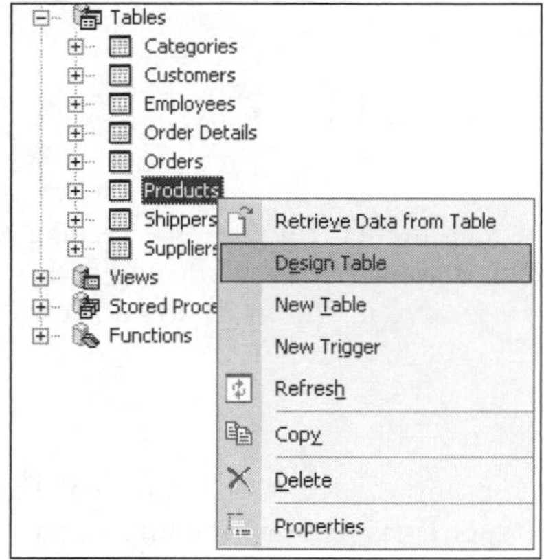

2. Scroll down to the end of the `Products` table in Design View and add a new column called `LastUpdated` with a data type of Date/Time.

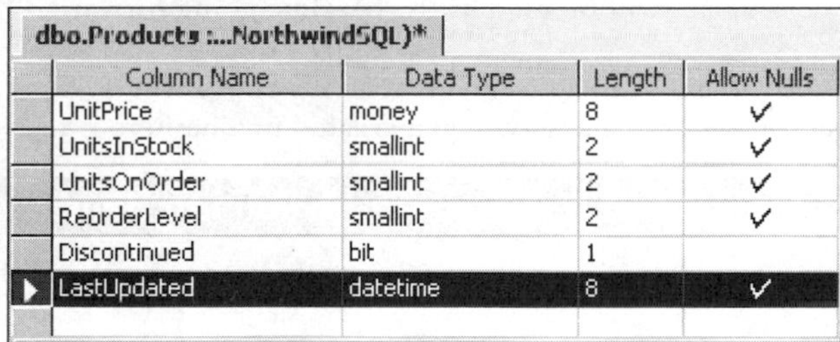

3. Close the Design View and save the changes to the `Products` table. Repeat these steps to add the `LastUpdated` column to the `Suppliers` table.

4. Right-click on the Views node and select New View. A window will open with a list of tables to add to your view. Just click on Close and you will be able to enter SQL statements into the view window.

5. Copy the following line of code over those already given in the view window:

```
UPDATE Products SET LastUpdated = GETDATE()
```

Right-click on the window and select Run.

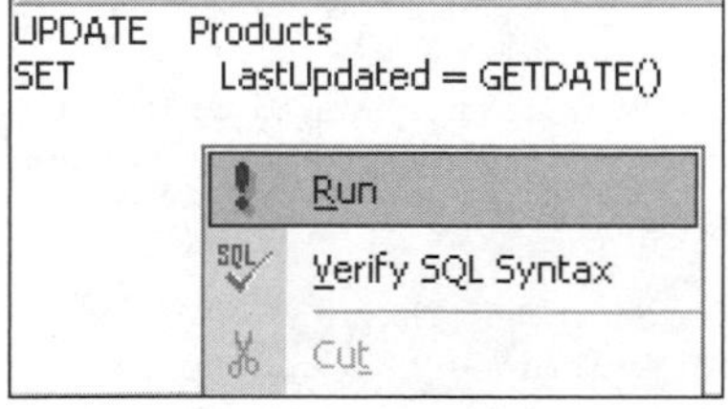

6. Now repeat with this line of code:

```
UPDATE Suppliers SET LastUpdated = GETDATE()
```

When you run these SQL statements, you will first receive a notice that they will not be able to be saved as views, which is fine. We are just using a view to run an interactive SQL statement and do not plan to save it. Click OK and a Message Box will appear telling you how many rows were affected.

How It Works

First, we modified the `Products` and `Suppliers` tables in the database to include a `LastUpdated` column that is a `Date/Time` data type. This is the column that stores the value of when the record was last updated. It will be used in our comparisons to see if another user has updated the record more recently.

After adding the new field to both tables, we then populated them with default values set to the current system date/time. We populated the `LastUpdated` fields in both tables to give a starting point for all future comparisons. These values will be used as the baseline going forward.

Next, we will add the code to the Product Management System to handle the update conflicts. Lastly, we will adjust the stored procedures that have been created in Chapters 7 and 9.

Try It Out – Modifying the Product Management System to Handle Update Conflicts

1. Add a `HandleUpdateConflicts` procedure to `clsDatabase`, as shown below:

```
Sub HandleUpdateConflicts(ByVal strconnection As String, _
                          ByVal strTableName As String, ByVal strName As _
                          String, ByVal orow As DataRow, optional ByVal _
                          smallintdiscontinued As Int16 = 0)

        'This procedure is used to handle update conflicts for Products
        'and Suppliers, based on whether "Products" or "Suppliers" is
        'passed in as the table name. The smallintdiscontinued field is
        'used with Products and is thus optional since Suppliers will not
        'make use of the field.

        Try

            Dim intResponse As Integer
            Dim intRowsAffected As Integer

            intResponse = MsgBox("Another user has changed this " & _
                    "record (" & strName & ") " & _
                    "since you last changed it.  Do you want to " & _
                    "overwrite their changes?", MsgBoxStyle.YesNo, _
                    "WARNING: Update Conflict")

            If intResponse = vbYes Then
                'Go ahead and issue the update statement without
```

```
                'requiring the exact match based on the original values.
                'Just update it based on the Id (Product Id or Supplier Id)
                'alone so their changes will overwrite the ones made by
                'someone else.
                Dim cmdCommand As New SqlClient.SqlCommand()
                If strTableName = "Products" Then
                  AddProductsInsertUpdateParameters(cmdCommand, orow, _
                             smallintdiscontinued, False, True)
                  intRowsAffected = ExecuteSPWithParameters(strconnection, _
                             "spUpdateProducts", cmdCommand)
                ElseIf strTableName = "Suppliers" Then
                  AddSuppliersInsertUpdateParameters(cmdCommand, orow, _
                             False, True)
                  intRowsAffected = ExecuteSPWithParameters(strconnection, _
                            "spUpdateSuppliers", cmdCommand)
                End If

                MsgBox(intRowsAffected & " record was updated " & _
                             "successfully to overwrite the other " & _
                             "record.", , "Update Conflict Handled")

            ElseIf intResponse = vbNo Then
                  'Let the user know their changes were not saved to the
                  'database since they clicked no. But go ahead and tell
                  'them how to see the current data.
                  MsgBox("Your changes were not saved to the database. " & _
                    "To see the " & _
                    "updated values as changed by another user, " & _
                    "please close the Add/View/Edit Products screen and " & _
                    "rerun your search again to see the new " & _
                    "values.", MsgBoxStyle.OKOnly, "Changes Not Made")
                End If

        Catch
            'Error handling goes here.
            UnhandledExceptionHandler()
        End Try

    End Sub
```

2. Modify the `AddProductsInsertUpdateParameters` procedure declaration line in `clsDatabase` and add the additional parameter at the end of the procedure above the `Catch` statement:

```
Sub AddProductsInsertUpdateParameters(ByRef cmdCommand As _
          SqlClient.SqlCommand, ByVal oRow As DataRow, ByVal _
          smallintdiscontinued As Int16, ByVal blnAddLastUpdated As _
          Boolean, ByVal blnAddProductId As Boolean)

...
```

```
'Only add the LastUpdated parameter if checking for conflicts
'(which applies when doing updates versus inserts). When
'specified, this parameter will insure that the record will be
'updated only if it hasn't changed.
'If unspecified, the record will be updated even if there was
'an update conflict (such as a user has chosen to overwrite the
'other changes).
'Note that this parameter isn't used for inserts, and in such
'cases we will not be checking for updates anyway (that is,.
'blnAddLastUpdated will be false) so this parameter will not be
'added.
If blnAddLastUpdated Then
    sqlparm = cmdCommand.Parameters.Add("@LastUpdated", _
              SqlDbType.DateTime)
    sqlparm.Value = oRow("LastUpdated")
End If
```

3. Modify the `AddSuppliersInsertUpdateParameters` procedure declaration in `clsDatabase` and add the additional parameter at the end of the procedure above the `Catch` statement:

```
Sub AddSuppliersInsertUpdateParameters(ByRef cmdCommand As _
          SqlClient.SqlCommand, ByVal oRow As DataRow, _
          ByVal blnAddLastUpdated As Boolean, ByVal _
          blnAddSupplierId As Boolean)
```

...

```
'Only add the LastUpdated parameter if checking for conflicts
'(which applies when doing updates versus inserts). When
'specified, this parameter will ensure that the record will be
'updated only if it hasn't changed.
'If unspecified, the record will be updated even if there was
'an update conflict (such as a user has chosen to overwrite the
'other changes).
'Note that this parameter isn't used for inserts, and in such
'cases we will not be checking for updates anyway (that is,
'blnAddLastUpdated will be false) so this parameter will not be
'added.
If blnAddLastUpdated Then
    sqlparm = cmdCommand.Parameters.Add("@LastUpdated", _
              SqlDbType.DateTime)
    sqlparm.Value = oRow("LastUpdated")
End If
```

4. Modify the call to `AddProductsInsertUpdateParameters` that is in the `UpdateProductsInDb` procedure in `clsDatabase` with the parameters shown below:

```
AddProductsInsertUpdateParameters(cmdCommand, oRow, _
        smallintDiscontinued, True, True)
```

5. Add the following lines of code to the end of the `UpdateProductsInDb` procedure in `clsDatabase` directly above the `Next` statement near the end of the procedure:

```
        'If the record was not updated, then there was most likely a
        'change made to that same record by another user
        'already...thus, handle the update conflict by letting the
        'user know that the record has changed.
        If intRowsAffected = 0 Then
            HandleUpdateConflicts(strConnection, _
                "Products", oRow("ProductName"), _
                oRow, smallintDiscontinued)
        End If
```

6. Modify the call to `AddProductsInsertUpdateParameters` that is in the `InsertProductsInDb` procedure in `clsDatabase` with the parameters shown below:

```
    AddProductsInsertUpdateParameters(cmdCommand, oRow, _
            SmallIntDiscontinued, False, False)
```

7. Modify the call to `AddSuppliersInsertUpdateParameters` that is in the `UpdateSuppliersInDb` procedure in `clsDatabase` with the parameters shown below:

```
    AddSuppliersInsertUpdateParameters(cmdCommand, oRow, True, True)
```

8. Add the following lines of code to the end of the `UpdateSuppliersInDb` procedure in `clsDatabase` directly above the `Next` statement near the end of the procedure:

```
        'If the record was not updated, then there was most likely a
        'change made to that same record by another user
        'already...thus, handle the update conflict by letting the
        'user know that the record has changed.
        If intRowsAffected = 0 Then
            HandleUpdateConflicts(strConnection, _
                    "Suppliers", oRow("CompanyName"), _
                    oRow)
        End If
```

9. Modify the call to `AddSuppliersInsertUpdateParameters` that is in the `InsertSuppliersInDb` procedure in `clsDatabase` with the parameters shown below:

```
    AddSuppliersInsertUpdateParameters(cmdCommand, oRow, False, False)
```

10. Modify the `BuildSQLSelectFromClause` procedure in `clsDatabase` to include the `LastUpdated` column as shown below:

```
        "as UnitsInStock, p.UnitsOnOrder as " & _
        "UnitsOnOrder, p.ReorderLevel as " & _
        "ReorderLevel, p.Discontinued as " & _
        "Discontinued, p.LastUpdated as LastUpdated " & _
        "FROM Products p " & _
```

How It Works

With the database tables modified and populated with the `LastUpdated` data, we then created the main procedure to handle the conflicts, called `HandleUpdateConflicts`. Let's look at this more carefully. First, notice that the `smallintdiscontinued` parameter passed to the procedure is set to `optional`.

```
Sub HandleUpdateConflicts(ByVal strconnection As String, _
                          ByVal strTableName As String, ByVal strName As _
                          String, ByVal orow As DataRow, optional ByVal _
                          smallintdiscontinued As Int16 = 0)
```

The reason it is `optional` is it only applies to handling update conflicts for products (not suppliers). When handling conflicts for suppliers, this value will not be passed in to the procedure. When specifying an `optional` parameter, you must also designate a default value for that parameter if it is not passed in to the procedure.

Next, we declare the procedure and some local variables that will be used to store the user's response and number of rows updated.

```
Dim intResponse As Integer
Dim intRowsAffected As Integer
```

The next line of code displays a Message Box to the user and prompts to see if they want to overwrite the changes the other user made. The user's response to this question is stored in the `intResponse` variable.

```
intResponse = MsgBox("Another user has changed this " & _
        "record (" & strName & ") " & _
        "since you last changed it.  Do you want to " & _
        "overwrite their changes?", MsgBoxStyle.YesNo, _
        "WARNING: Update Conflict")
```

If they answered `Yes` (they want to overwrite), the database will be updated. Different procedures are called depending on whether the update is for products or suppliers. The first procedure called is the one to add the parameters to the `Command` object that will be passed in to the stored procedure. Notice how, in this instance, the `LastUpdated Boolean` parameter is set to `False` in the call to `AddProductsInsertUpdateParameters`:

```
If strTableName = "Products" Then
  AddProductsInsertUpdateParameters(cmdCommand, orow, _
           smallintdiscontinued, False, True)
```

This indicates to that procedure to leave the last updated parameter off. This signals to the stored procedure that the database can be updated without worrying whether the record has been modified or not. The line that follows then executes the stored procedure to make the changes to the database:

```
intRowsAffected = ExecuteSPWithParameters(strconnection, _
          "spUpdateProducts", cmdCommand)
```

The same thing occurs for the Suppliers table if the update were to occur there instead of on the Products table, as can be seen here:

```
ElseIf strTableName = "Suppliers" Then
  AddSuppliersInsertUpdateParameters(cmdCommand, orow, _
             False, True)
  intRowsAffected = ExecuteSPWithParameters(strconnection, _
            "spUpdateSuppliers", cmdCommand)
End If
```

After the stored procedure runs, a message then gets displayed to the user indicating how many rows were successfully updated in the database in response to the update conflict:

```
MsgBox(intRowsAffected & " record was updated " & _
             "successfully to overwrite the other " & _
             "record.", , "Update Conflict Handled")
```

If the user responds No to the update conflict overwrite question, then they are simply notified that their change was not saved to the database:

```
MsgBox("Your changes were not saved to the database. " & _
 "To see the " & _
 "updated values as changed by another user, " & _
 "please close the Add/View/Edit Products screen and " & _
 "re-run your search again to see the new " & _
 "values.", MsgBoxStyle.OKOnly, "Changes Not Made")
```

After creating the HandleUpdateConflicts procedure, we make the changes in the clsDatabase class module to make use of this new procedure. First, the AddProductsInsertUpdateParameters procedure was modified. A new parameter was added to the procedure declaration to pass in the blnAddLastUpdated Boolean to the procedure:

```
smallintdiscontinued As Int16, ByVal blnAddLastUpdated As _
Boolean, ByVal blnAddProductId As Boolean)
```

Next, the procedure was modified to check the Boolean to see whether to add the LastUpdated parameter to the Command object.:

```
If blnAddLastUpdated Then
    sqlparm = cmdCommand.Parameters.Add("@LastUpdated", _
              SqlDbType.DateTime)
    sqlparm.Value = oRow("LastUpdated")
End If
```

Recall that the Command object gets passed to the stored procedure and includes the parameters that the stored procedure expects. If we are checking for update conflicts (that is, if blnAddLastUpdated is True), then this parameter needs to be added to the Command object. Similar modifications were made to the AddSuppliersInsertUpdateParameters to include this additional parameter.

Then, two changes were made to the UpdateProductsInDb procedure. The first change was to add the additional parameter to the call to AddProductsInsertUpdateParameters, as shown below:

```
AddProductsInsertUpdateParameters(cmdCommand, oRow, _
        smallintDiscontinued, True, True)
```

The parameter is set to True so that UpdateConflicts will be checked for when running the stored procedure against the database.

Then, we added the lines of code to actually call the new HandleUpdateConflicts procedure. If, as a result of the database update, zero records were updated, then we're assuming that another user has changed the record in the meantime.

```
If intRowsAffected = 0 Then
    HandleUpdateConflicts(strConnection, _
        "Products", oRow("ProductName"), _
        oRow, smallintDiscontinued)
End If
```

We also had to change the call to AddProductsInsertUpdateParameters in the InsertProductsInDb procedure, as shown below:

```
AddProductsInsertUpdateParameters(cmdCommand, oRow, _
        SmallIntDiscontinued, False, False)
```

In this instance, the blnLastUpdated value is set to False to indicate that we do not need to check for update conflicts. The reason we do not need to check for update conflicts on an insert is because the record has never been added before and thus no other user could have ever changed it. Similar changes to those above were then made to the appropriate suppliers procedures.

Finally, the BuildSQLSelectFromClause procedure was modified to select the LastUpdated parameter when retrieving values to populate the DataSet:

```
"Discontinued, p.LastUpdated as LastUpdated " & _
```

This value will be displayed in the DataGrid as well and will be used later to check the original value to see if any changes have indeed been made to the record.

Now that we have modified all of the procedures in clsDatabase, we need to do the same with the stored procedures.

Try It Out – Modifying the Stored Procedures

1. Modify the spUpdateProducts stored procedure in the SQL Server database as shown below. To modify the stored procedure, open the current spUpdateProducts stored procedure in Server Explorer and paste the statement shown opposite over the current code. When you save the changes to the stored procedure, it will be altered to include the new structure.

```
            @ReorderLevel smallint,
            @Discontinued bit,
            @LastUpdated datetime = NULL
        )
AS
/*
If LastUpdated is NULL then they want to update the record despite an update
conflict, etc. Otherwise, the record will be updated ONLY if the LastUpdated value
is the same in the database as it is in their local version (that is, that no one
updated it in the meantime).
*/
IF @LastUpdated IS NULL
    BEGIN
      UPDATE Products set ProductName = @ProductName, SupplierId =
                  @SupplierId, CategoryId  = @CategoryId, QuantityPerUnit =
                  @QuantityPerUnit, UnitPrice = @UnitPrice, UnitsInStock =
                  @UnitsInStock, UnitsOnOrder = @UnitsOnOrder, ReorderLevel
                  = @ReorderLevel, Discontinued = @Discontinued, LastUpdated
                  = GetDate()
     WHERE ProductId = @ProductId
   END
ELSE
   BEGIN
     UPDATE Products set ProductName = @ProductName, SupplierId =
                  @SupplierId, CategoryId  = @CategoryId, QuantityPerUnit =
                  @QuantityPerUnit, UnitPrice = @UnitPrice, UnitsInStock =
                  @UnitsInStock, UnitsOnOrder = @UnitsOnOrder, ReorderLevel
                  = @ReorderLevel, Discontinued = @Discontinued, LastUpdated
                  = GetDate()
    WHERE ProductId = @ProductId AND LastUpdated = @LastUpdated
   END
     RETURN
```

2. Modify the `spInsertProducts` stored procedure as shown below:

```
AS
     INSERT INTO Products (ProductName, SupplierId, CategoryId,
                QuantityPerUnit, UnitPrice, UnitsInStock, UnitsOnOrder,
                ReorderLevel, Discontinued, LastUpdated)
     VALUES (@ProductName, @SupplierId, @CategoryId,
                @QuantityPerUnit, @UnitPrice, @UnitsInStock, @UnitsOnOrder,
                @ReorderLevel, @Discontinued, GetDate())
     RETURN
```

3. Modify the `spUpdateSuppliers` stored procedure as shown below:

```
            @Fax nvarchar(24),
            @HomePage ntext,
            @LastUpdated datetime = NULL
        )
AS
```

```
/*
If LastUpdated is NULL then they want to update the record despite an update
conflict, etc. Otherwise, the record will be updated ONLY if the LastUpdated value
is the same in the database as it is in their local version (that is, that no one
updated it in the meantime).
*/
IF @LastUpdated IS NULL
    BEGIN
     UPDATE Suppliers Set CompanyName = @CompanyName, ContactName =
                    @ContactName, ContactTitle = @ContactTitle, Address =
                    @Address, City = @City, Region = @Region,
                    PostalCode = @PostalCode, Country = @Country, Phone =
                    @Phone, Fax = @Fax, HomePage = @HomePage, LastUpdated =
                    GetDate()
    WHERE SupplierId = @SupplierId
   END
ELSE
   BEGIN
     UPDATE Suppliers Set CompanyName = @CompanyName, ContactName =
                    @ContactName, ContactTitle = @ContactTitle, Address =
                    @Address, City = @City, Region = @Region,
                    PostalCode = @PostalCode, Country = @Country, Phone =
                    @Phone, Fax = @Fax, HomePage = @HomePage, LastUpdated =
                    GetDate()
    WHERE SupplierId = @SupplierId AND LastUpdated = @LastUpdated
   END
     RETURN
```

4. Modify the spInsertSuppliers stored procedure as shown below:

```
AS
     INSERT INTO Suppliers (CompanyName, ContactName, ContactTitle,
                Address, City, Region, PostalCode, Country,
                Phone, Fax, HomePage, LastUpdated)
      VALUES (@CompanyName, @ContactName, @ContactTitle,
                @Address, @City, @Region, @PostalCode, @Country,
                @Phone, @Fax, @HomePage, GetDate())
     RETURN
```

How It Works

After updating all of the appropriate procedures in the clsDatabase class, our last step was to update the four stored procedures: spUpdateProducts, spInsertProducts, spUpdateSuppliers, and spInsertSuppliers. The Update stored procedures are the most complicated, so let's look at them first.

The first change we made to the spUpdateProducts stored procedure was to add a parameter being passed in called @LastUpdated. This parameter then gets used in an IF...ELSE statement to determine which UPDATE statement to run against the database.

```
@LastUpdated datetime = NULL
```

If the `@LastUpdated` value is `NULL`, then the statement should simply update the record without regard to whether it has changed or not and re-assign the `LastUpdated` column to the current system date/time:

```
IF @LastUpdated IS NULL
    BEGIN
      UPDATE Products set ProductName = @ProductName, SupplierId =
                  @SupplierId, CategoryId  = @CategoryId, QuantityPerUnit =
                  @QuantityPerUnit, UnitPrice = @UnitPrice, UnitsInStock =
                  @UnitsInStock, UnitsOnOrder = @UnitsOnOrder, ReorderLevel
                  = @ReorderLevel, Discontinued = @Discontinued, LastUpdated
                  = GetDate()
     WHERE ProductId = @ProductId
   END
```

If, on the other hand, the `@LastUpdated` parameter is `NOT NULL`, then that means that the statement will check the `LastUpdated` column as part of the `WHERE` criteria. It will only update the record if the `LastUpdated` value matches with the original value (that is, that no other user has changed it since the record was originally retrieved for this user):

```
ELSE
   BEGIN
      UPDATE Products set ProductName = @ProductName, SupplierId =
                  @SupplierId, CategoryId  = @CategoryId, QuantityPerUnit =
                  @QuantityPerUnit, UnitPrice = @UnitPrice, UnitsInStock =
                  @UnitsInStock, UnitsOnOrder = @UnitsOnOrder, ReorderLevel
                  = @ReorderLevel, Discontinued = @Discontinued, LastUpdated
                  = GetDate()
   WHERE ProductId = @ProductId AND LastUpdated = @LastUpdated
  END
     RETURN
```

The changes to `spInsertProducts` stored procedure are much more simple than to the `spUpdateProducts` stored procedure. We just had to add the `LastUpdated` column to the insert statement so that, when new records are added to the database, the current system date/time is populated in the `LastUpdated` column:

```
ALTER PROCEDURE dbo.spInsertProducts
      INSERT INTO Products (ProductName, SupplierId, CategoryId,
                QuantityPerUnit, UnitPrice, UnitsInStock, UnitsOnOrder,
                ReorderLevel, Discontinued, LastUpdated)
     VALUES (@ProductName, @SupplierId, @CategoryId,
                @QuantityPerUnit, @UnitPrice, @UnitsInStock, @UnitsOnOrder,
                @ReorderLevel, @Discontinued, GetDate())
      RETURN
```

The same concepts as discussed above for the products stored procedures apply to the suppliers stored procedures so we will not discuss them here.

That's it. We've now added all of the necessary changes to the Product Management System to handle basic checking for update conflicts. As previously mentioned, the needs of your application may very well dictate more sophisticated handling of update conflicts. This is just the simplest example to get you started. The approach shown above does not do anything sophisticated in terms of showing you the exact values modified by the other user that are in conflict with the changes.

Furthermore, this approach makes an assumption, for the sake of demonstrating the concept in the simplest way possible, which may not always be true. It assumes that, if 0 records were updated, then there must have been an update conflict. Actually, there could have been 0 records updated for other reasons as well, such as a database error (for example, database no longer available, record that you're trying to update no longer exists, etc.). As a challenge, modify the program so that the only time the program thinks an update conflict occurred is in instances where one really did occur. Hint: you could add an extra call to the database to compare `LastUpdated` values. Now that you've gone through the whole process of creating the Product Management System, you should be able to figure out how to do this.

The example demonstrated here could have just as easily been modified to use a record Version Number field in the database instead of a `LastUpdated` date/time field. The exact same concept applies either way, but the `LastUpdated` field is actually more useful because it indicates the exact date/time that the record was most recently changed.

> *One thing that should definitely have been brought home to you by all this is the amount of effort required to change the application and database to deal with conflicts at this late stage. In a real-world project, as opposed to a tutorial like this, you would probably build in a* `LastUpdated` *column at the very beginning.*

Now that you have a good idea of how the Version or Timestamp method of handling update conflicts works, let's move on to learning about the Saving All Values approach.

The Saving All Values Method

In the previous section, we looked at the Version Number or Timestamp method of optimistic concurrency in great detail. We implemented the logic for the Product Management System to handle update conflicts using this method. Before moving on, let's briefly mention another possible way that you can handle update conflicts in your code, using the **Saving All Values** method to see if the record has changed. We will look at some code examples to demonstrate how this works, but will not implement this functionality in the Product Management System.

Under the **Saving All Values** method, you simply update the record only if all previous values still match. In other words, the `DataSet` keeps both versions of the record, the original value and the modified value. To save all values, you keep a copy of the original values before any edits are made to the data. You then use those original values as criteria in the `WHERE` clause of the `UPDATE` statement. If all of the original values in the `DataSet` match with what is currently in the database, then you know that no other user has modified it. You can then safely update the database with the new changes. If all of the values do not match, then you know that someone else has changed the information and that you need to notify the current user of the conflict.

There are two big changes in how this method differs from the first. The first major change is that you have to keep track of *all* of the original values instead of just the `LastUpdated` date/time field.

One way to do this is with the `DataRowVersion` attribute of the `DataSet`. The `DataRowVersion` attribute can be used to retrieve the original field values before any changes were made to the `DataSet`. These values will be stored in the local variables and then used later in the `UPDATE` statement to insure that we have an exact match before updating a record. The following example shows how you can use the `DataRowVersion` attribute:

```
'Retrieve all of the original values prior to the user changes.
'This will be used in the WHERE clause of the UPDATE statement
'to only update the record if no other user has updated the
'record in the meantime.

oColumn = dsChanges.Tables("Results").Columns("ProductName")
strProductName = padQuotes(oRow(oColumn, _
                 DataRowVersion.Original))
oColumn = dsChanges.Tables("Results").Columns("SupplierId")
intSupplierId = oRow(oColumn, DataRowVersion.Original)
oColumn = dsChanges.Tables("Results").Columns("CategoryId")
intCategoryId = oRow(oColumn, DataRowVersion.Original)
oColumn = dsChanges.Tables("Results").Columns("QuantityPerUnit")
strQuantityPerUnit = padQuotes(oRow(oColumn, _
                     DataRowVersion.Original))
oColumn = dsChanges.Tables("Results").Columns("UnitPrice")
decUnitPrice = oRow(oColumn, DataRowVersion.Original)
oColumn = dsChanges.Tables("Results").Columns("UnitsInStock")
intUnitsInStock = oRow(oColumn, DataRowVersion.Original)
oColumn = dsChanges.Tables("Results").Columns("UnitsOnOrder")
intUnitsOnOrder = oRow(oColumn, DataRowVersion.Original)
oColumn = dsChanges.Tables("Results").Columns("ReorderLevel")
intReorderLevel = oRow(oColumn, DataRowVersion.Original)
oColumn = dsChanges.Tables("Results").Columns("Discontinued")
intDiscontinued = oRow(oColumn, DataRowVersion.Original)
```

Notice how the values are retrieved from each column, one by one, using the `DataRowVersion.Original` property.

The next big change is to modify the stored procedure to accept the additional parameters and add those parameters to the `WHERE` clause to only update the record if all values are still the same. Before the stored procedure is called, you would have to modify the procedure that adds the parameters to the `Command` object to add parameters for all of the original values you have to pass in. You would then modify the stored procedure itself to accept these additional parameters and then make use of those parameters in the `WHERE` clause. We don't even have to look at the rest of these previously mentioned changes for you to see why this method takes more work than the Version Number or Timestamp method. You can see very quickly how much more coding effort is required to implement this approach.

This approach is very similar in concept to the Version Number or Timestamp approach, but in this scenario you must keep track of all of the original values and then check them against the database to determine whether a change has occurred. Recall with the Version Number or Timestamp method, you only have to store a single value: the Version Number or the Date/Time of when the record was last updated. For this reason, the Version Number or Timestamp method is more efficient and easier to implement than the Save All Values approach. Once a conflict is detected, you handle it in the same way regardless of which approach you are using. You will still have to implement the code to prompt the user as to how they want to proceed.

Transactions

In addition to update conflicts, updating the database can be problematic for other reasons. Problems arise if a user attempts to insert invalid data into a field, or into a database that is not presently online, etc. These issues are not update conflicts but are types of general errors.

Transactions can be used to handle many of these types of problems. A transaction is a sequence of tasks in which, if any one of the individual tasks fails, the whole sequence fails and the state of the system is returned to its state before the transaction began. The transaction can only succeed if every individual task succeeds, in which case the transaction is **committed**.

This concept is very important for database applications. Imagine the situation where a user changes 100 records in his/her local `DataSet` and then hits the Save button. Now imagine that the update process crashes halfway through, after saving only 50 records to the underlying database. The user might be aware of the error, but might not know exactly how many records were saved before the error occurred. This nasty situation can be avoided by making the update process into a transaction. If an error now occurs midway through updating the 100 records, then the whole process is classed as having failed and the 50 updates that have been saved are undone or **rolled back**, that is, the 50 updated records are returned to their original values before the transaction began. The user can be notified that the update failed, and can be safe in the knowledge that the database is exactly as it was before the transaction began, as if the transaction had never even been started.

Transactions in Database Applications

In this section, we will look at the steps involved with creating a database transaction and then some sample code to demonstrate the concept.

A summary of the steps to take advantage of transactions is:

- Create a local `Transaction` object and call the `BeginTransaction` method of the `Connection` object.
- Run the set of SQL statements.
- Call the `Commit` method of the `Transaction` object if everything succeeded, or call the `Rollback` method to cancel the transaction if errors occurred. You place the `Commit` at the end of the function and the `Rollback` in the error handler.

Let's take a look at a simple code example of how this works.

Try It Out – Transactions in Database Applications

1. Place a new Button on the Products Search screen with the following code in the Button's `Click` event:

```
Private Sub Button1_Click(ByVal sender As System.Object, & _
    ByVal e As System.EventArgs) Handles Button1.Click

    DemonstrateTransaction(CONN)

End Sub
```

2. Next, add the `DemonstrateTransaction` procedure to the form as well:

```
Sub DemonstrateTransaction(ByVal strConnection As String)
    '***************************************************************
    'The purpose of this function is to demonstrate how a transaction
    'works.
    '***************************************************************
    Dim strSQL As String
    Dim myConnection As New SqlClient.SqlConnection(strConnection)
    Dim myCommand As New SqlClient.SqlCommand(strSQL, myConnection)
    myCommand.Connection.Open()
    Dim myTrans As SqlClient.SqlTransaction = _
                myConnection.BeginTransaction()

    Try

        strSQL = "INSERT INTO Suppliers (ProductId, ProductName) " & _
                  "Values(10000, 'Test') "
        myCommand.CommandText = strSQL
        myCommand.ExecuteNonQuery()

        strSQL = "INSERT INTO Suppliers (ProductId, ProductName) " &
                  "Values(10000, 'Test Duplicate') "
        myCommand.CommandText = strSQL
        myCommand.ExecuteNonQuery()

        'If no errors have occurred, then commit all of the changes to
        'the database.
        myTrans.Commit()

    Catch

        'If any errors occur, then roll back the transaction.
        myTrans.Rollback()
        MsgBox("An error occurred with one of the database " & _
            "updates. None of the changes were saved to the " & _
            "database.")

    Finally
        'Close the database connection.
        myConnection.Close()

    End Try
End Sub
```

3. Run the Product Management System and click on the button just added to verify that you do indeed receive the error about the records not being updated. A Message Box like the following should appear:

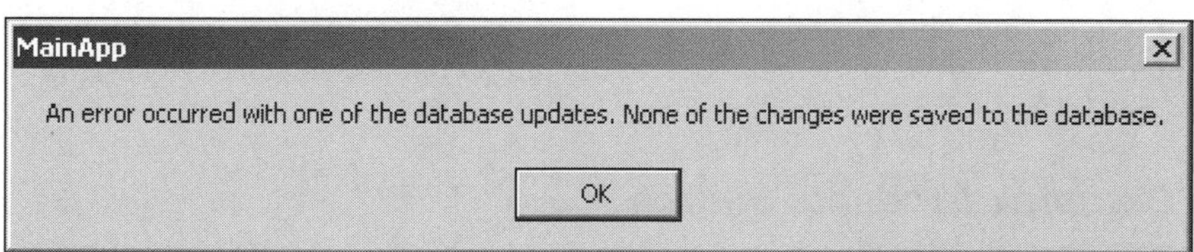

4. Also, run a search against the database to verify that neither record was added to the database.

How It Works

To begin with we added a new button to call our new procedure, `DemonstrateTransaction`, when it was clicked.

```
DemonstrateTransaction (CONN)
```

We then added the `DemonstrateTransaction` procedure. Notice how two `INSERT` statements are executed, with the second one trying to insert the same `ProductId` value into the database (which will generate a primary key violation because that primary key value already exists):

```
strSQL = "INSERT INTO Suppliers (ProductId, ProductName) " & _
         "Values(10000, 'Test') "
myCommand.CommandText = strSQL
myCommand.ExecuteNonQuery()

strSQL = "INSERT INTO Suppliers (ProductId, ProductName) " & _
         "Values(10000, 'Test Duplicate') "
myCommand.CommandText = strSQL
myCommand.ExecuteNonQuery()
```

Inline error handling is used to roll back the changes if an error occurs (`myTrans.Rollback()`). If an error does not occur, then the changes are committed to the database with the `Commit` method of the transaction object (`myTrans.Commit()`). Either way, the `Finally` statement will close the connection to the database.

> **The `DataSet` object's `AcceptChanges` and `RejectChanges` methods act like the `Transaction` object's `Commit` and `Rollback` methods. However, remember that with `DataSets` you are working with a local in-memory copy of the data. Any changes to the `DataSet` will not impact upon the data in the database until you issue separate commands to actually update the database.**

A detailed description of transactions is beyond the scope of this book. If you want more information on transactions, please look at Professional VB.NET (ISBN: 1861004974) by Wrox Press.

Product Management System Tour

It's now time to take that whirlwind tour of the Product Management System that you've been waiting for. In Chapters 7 to 10 we've implemented a lot of code to make our new system work. Let's give it a spin and see how it all looks together.

Running a Complex Products Search

Run the Product Management System and you will see the following screen:

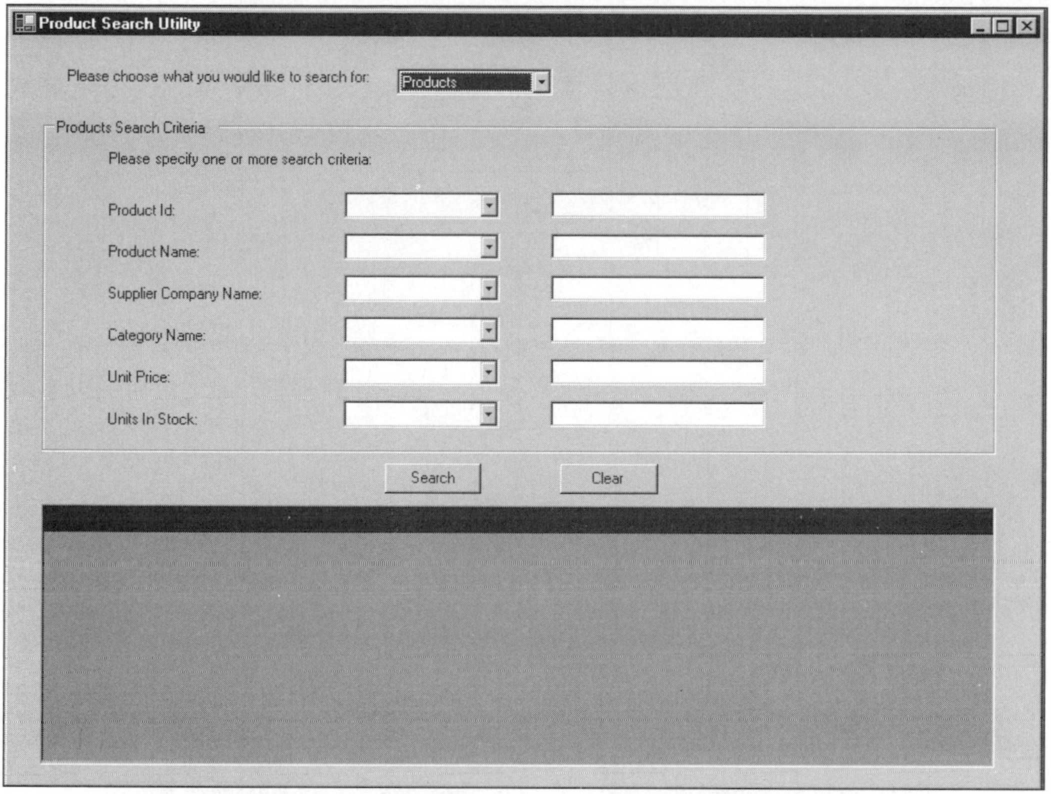

Fill in search criteria to search for all products that contain the word "berry" and which have a Unit Price of less than 50. Then click on the Search button:

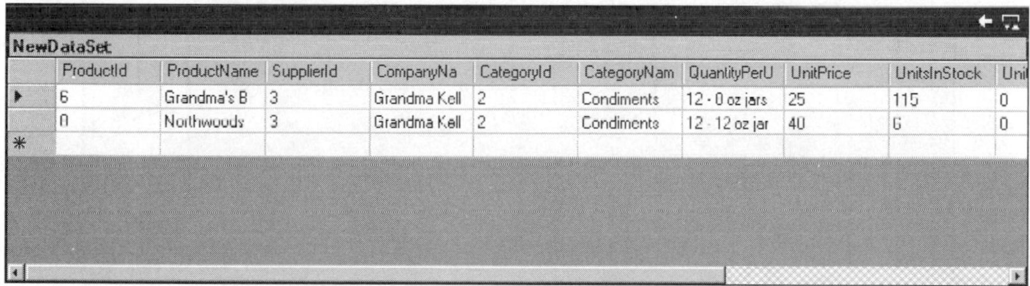

NewDataSet

	ProductId	ProductName	SupplierId	CompanyNa	CategoryId	CategoryNam	QuantityPerU	UnitPrice	UnitsInStock	Uni
▸	6	Grandma's B	3	Grandma Kell	2	Condiments	12 - 8 oz jars	25	115	0
	8	Northwoods	3	Grandma Kell	2	Condiments	12 - 12 oz jar	40	6	0
*										

Notice how the results are displayed in the `DataGrid` with two rows meeting the search criteria. Resize the data in the grid so you can see the `ProductName`. Double-click on the Grandma's Boysenberry Spread row.

Modifying Records Returned in the Search

The Add/View/Edit Products screen will appear, with Grandma's Boysenberry Spread as the current record as the one we selected:

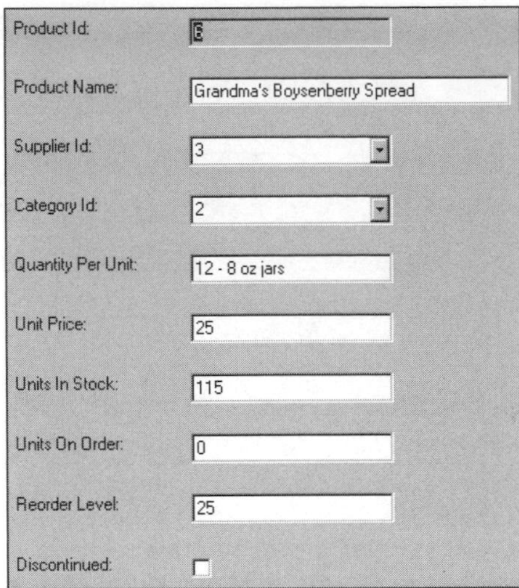

Change the Units In Stock value to 115 and click Save All Changes. Notice how the save succeeds. The `ProductName` (Grandma's Boysenberry Spread) contains an apostrophe and, if we had not implemented the `PadQuotes` function correctly, then the Save All Changes code would have failed.

Adding a New Record

After you've saved your changes to the Grandma's Boysenberry Spread entry, click the Add New Record button. The following screen will appear with empty or 0-valued fields:

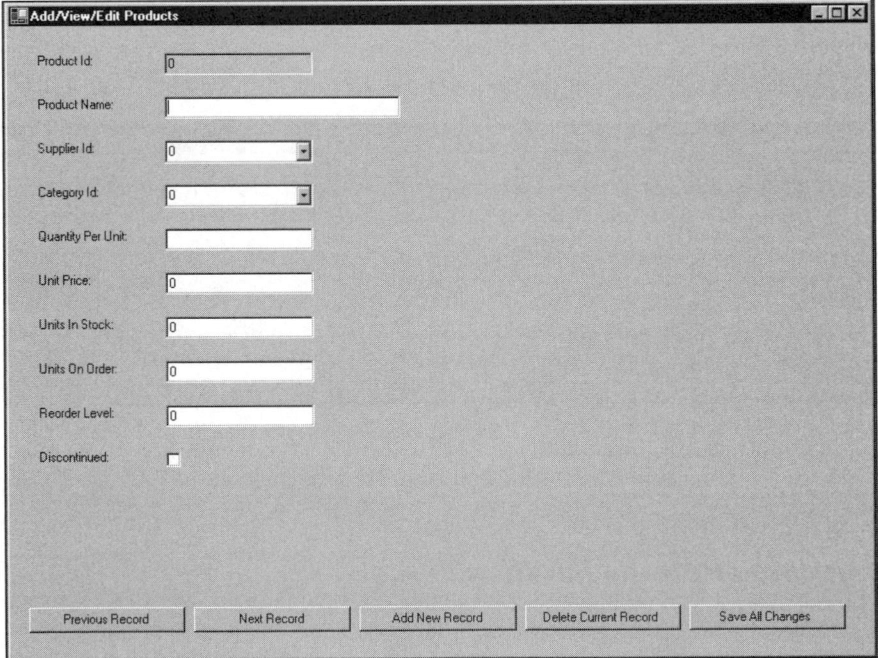

Fill in some information for your new product; such as in this example:

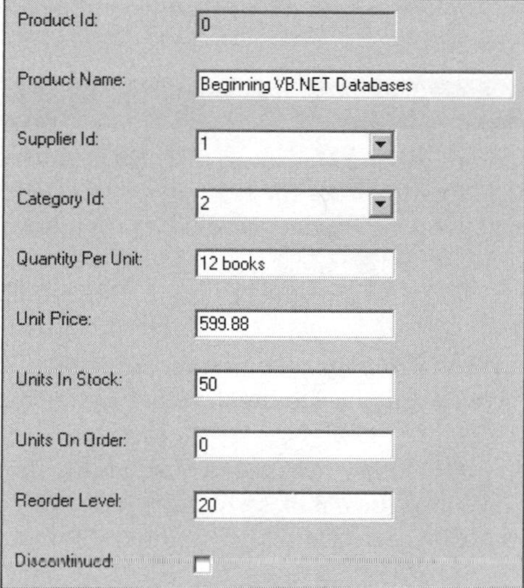

After filling in data for your new product, click the Save All Changes button. Navigate to the record you just added and you will notice that the Product Id for your new product now shows a number instead of the zero:

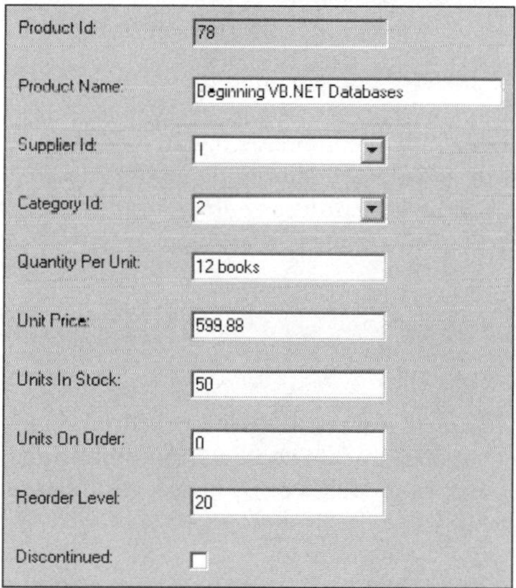

Recall that we implemented code to retrieve the system-assigned `ProductId` after the record is inserted into the database. We also added it to our local `DataSet`.

Generate an Update Conflict

Next, try running two different instances of the Product Management System side-by-side to generate an update conflict.

Try It Out – Generate an Update Conflict

1. Open the `bin` folder found in your `MainApp` folder. Double-click on the executable file (`MainApp` application file with a `.exe` file type) twice to open two instances of the program. This will allow you to generate an update conflict and see how it is handled.

2. Run the same search on both instances, for example Product Name Contains Tea.

3. Open up the Add/View/Edit screen for the first record, Chai Tea and change Units in Stock to 20 on one instance. Save the changes to the database by clicking Save All Changes.

4. Change the same field on the other instance (which, at this time, still has the original values) to 25 and attempt to save it to the database. What happens? You should receive a notification that an update conflict has occurred and a prompt to either cancel or overwrite:

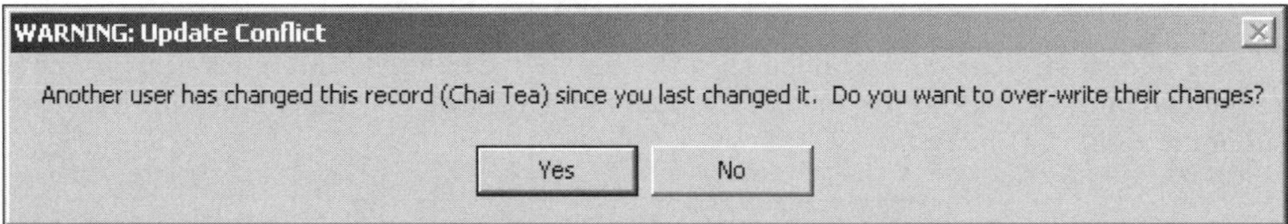

Congratulations! You have successfully implemented the Product Management System.

It'll be a useful learning experience for you to play around with the Product Management System. Run a variety of searches to see how the results are filtered depending on the criteria you specify. Open search windows and modify records, add new records, or delete records. Try typing invalid values in fields to see the alert icons powered by the `ErrorProvider` control.

Summary

In this chapter we have learned about how to deal with conflicts and errors that occur when you update data in the database. We have covered update conflicts and other database errors and how to handle them using optimistic concurrency approaches or by aggregating the data actions into transactions. We specifically covered these concepts:

- Update conflicts can occur when multiple persons try to update the same information at the same time
- How optimistic concurrency differs from pessimistic concurrency
- `DataSets` use the optimistic concurrency approach for handling update conflicts due to the disconnected nature of the data

- How to implement optimistic concurrency with the Saving All Values method
- What transactions are and how they can help deal with database errors that occur on inserts, updates, and deletes
- The `Transaction` object's `Commit` and `Rollback` affect the database but the `DataSet`'s `AcceptChanges` and `RejectChanges` only affect the local in-memory cache
- A whirlwind tour of the Product Management System

In this chapter, we have successfully completed the Product Management System that we started building in Chapter 7. We were able to apply database programming concepts to a realistic application that is typical of what you may be expected to create as a developer. In the next chapter, we will learn about web-based applications and ASP.NET.

Exercises

1. What is an update conflict?
2. What is the advantage of using optimistic concurrency to handle update conflicts versus the Last Update Wins method?
3. What is a transaction and when do you use one?
4. How do the `Transaction` object's `Commit` and `Rollback` methods differ from the `DataSet`'s `AcceptChanges` and `RejectChanges` methods?

Answers are available at http://p2p.wrox.com/exercises/.

ASP.NET

Way back in the mists of recent history, there was a time when Microsoft wasn't particularly interested in the Internet. In fact, for a while it looked like they were going to have nothing to do with the thing. But then certain strategists realized the importance that the Internet was likely to have, and managed to turn the company on a dime to start churning out web and Internet tools.

One technology that sprung out of this was Active Server Pages or ASP. This was, in this author's humble opinion, one of the best products ever to come out of Microsoft. Strangely, because Microsoft strategy was in a state of flux, it was released without much fanfare yet became as popular as it is today simply because developers loved it.

Essentially, ASP allows developers to write software that the user can access through a web browser rather than a separate program installed on their computer. Thanks to the nature of the Web, it allows developers to write server-specific, Microsoft platform code on the server, but as the application is "operated" through HTML, it's available to users on virtually any platform. Although this was, and is, possible without Microsoft technology, ASP supported the cut-down version of Visual Basic called VBScript. Coupled with very powerful and easy to use database access objects such as ADO, this made it possible for developers familiar with Visual Basic to build extremely powerful applications very quickly.

With the advent of .NET comes Active Server Pages .NET, or ASP.NET. This technology takes the best of ASP and enhances it to not only provide all of the power of .NET through the Framework classes, but also to incorporate the powerful control-centric paradigm for building applications that we've seen on the desktop. What this means is that if we want to put a button on a web page for the user to click, we can use the Toolbox to draw a button just as we would with a Windows Form. For this reason, the technology used to construct user interfaces in ASP.NET is known as "Web Forms".

In this chapter, we're going to take a look at ASP.NET and Web Forms. We'll show you how to build basic web pages as we create a small application that lets customers and salespeople check stock levels and prices over the Web. We then move on to take a look at how we can build a more complex application that lets us change data.

An Introduction

Visual Studio .NET has some great tools for developers of ASP.NET sites. However, to use these tools you'll need a web server either on your local computer or on your network so you can run the pages.

By default, the FrontPage Server Extensions 2000 are installed on your local machine along with the rest of the .NET Framework, providing that you have Internet Information Services installed before you install the Framework. This software allows a web site editing tool (like FrontPage or Visual Studio .NET) to connect to the server in order to upload pages or, alternatively, download existing pages for editing. In this chapter and the next, I'll assume that your computer does have the FrontPage Server Extensions 2000 correctly installed and enabled on your computer of choice.

In this chapter, we use the term `localhost` to refer to your own desktop computer. This is an Internet-specific term that means, basically, "the local computer". It is used to refer to the computer that is running the current application or web page itself.

Let's create an ASP.NET project now.

Try It Out – Creating the Project

1. Open Visual Studio .NET and create a new Visual Basic – ASP.NET Web Application project.

2. Set the name of the project to MyWebSite and make sure that the Location is set as http://localhost/

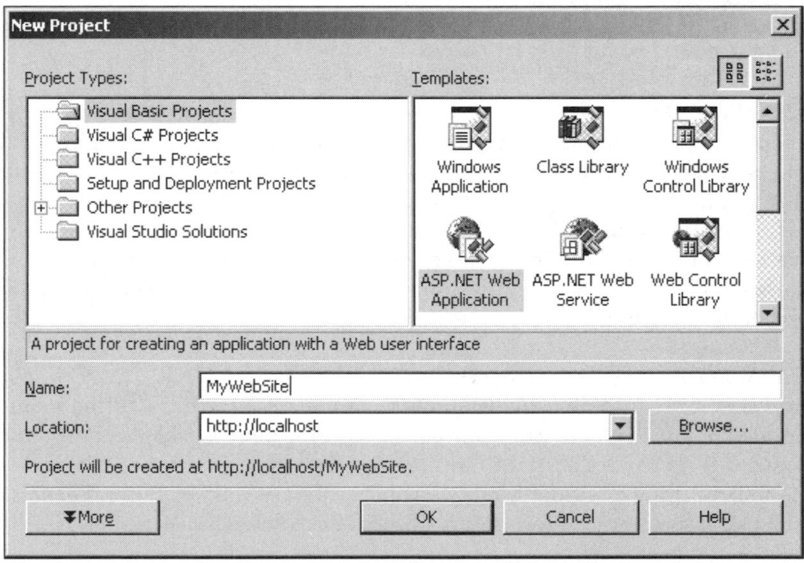

Notice the line under the Location box saying Project will be created at http://localhost/MyWebSite. This is important as we'll need to refer to this later, so keep it in mind.

3. Click the OK button to create your new project.

How It Works

At this point, Visual Studio .NET would have created your new project. The Solution Explorer, as with any other type of application, shows the files that make up the project.

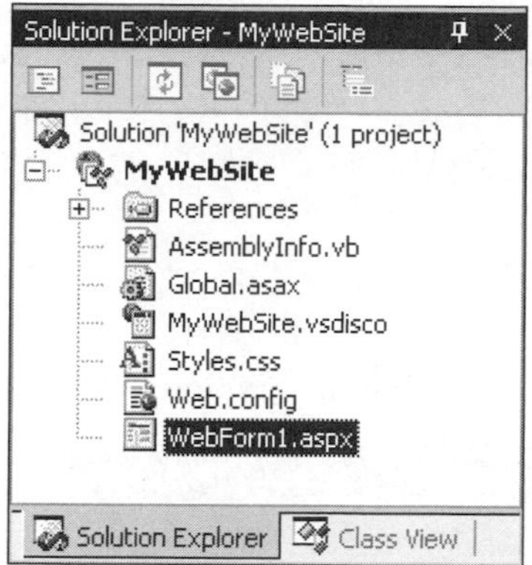

At this stage you can safely ignore most of these files. Right now, we're only concerned with the Web Form files, with an `.aspx` extension. These are the Web equivalent of Windows Forms.

Let's start off our first Web Form by adding a button that will do something when clicked.

Try It Out – Adding a Button to a Page

1. Right-click WebForm1 in the Solution Explorer and select View Designer to open it in Design view. Note the buttons at the bottom of the editor that tell us whether we are in Design or HTML view, and provide a quick way to switch from one mode to the other.

2. Using the Web Forms tab of the Toolbox, drag a Button control onto the page.

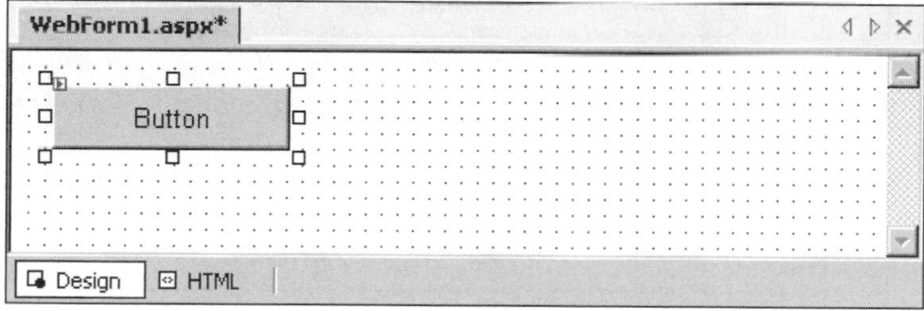

3. Open the Properties window as you would normally, and change the Button control's Text property to Press Me. Change the ID property to btnPressMe. Notice that Web Form controls do not have a Name property, but instead have an ID property. This is because Dynamic HTML (DHTML), a technology heavily used by ASP.NET, assumes that control names are referenced through a property called ID.

4. Double-click on the Button control. This will create a mouse click event handler, as you might expect, that we shall use to prove to the user that something has happened by changing the button text. Place the following code inside the `Click` handler:

```
Private Sub btnPressMe_Click(ByVal sender As System.Object, _
                             ByVal e As System.EventArgs)
                             Handles btnPressMe.Click

    ' Set the text...
    btnPressMe.Text = "Oh, that tickles!"

End Sub
```

5. Run the project. An instance of Internet Explorer will pop up and display our button.

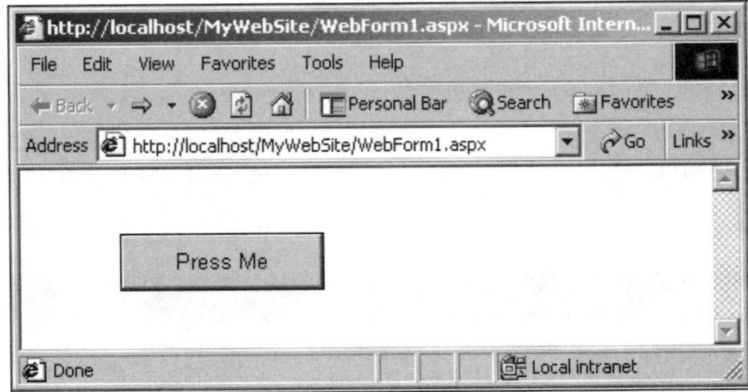

6. Now, press the button. You'll see this:

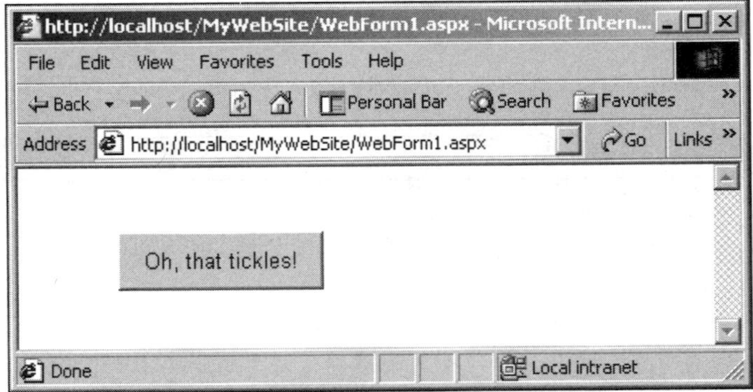

How It Works

You can see that the .NET approach to building forms for the Web is very similar to the approach when building forms for the desktop. We create a page, we add controls and we wire up events.

When the project is run, Internet Explorer is run, given the URL of the web application, namely http://localhost/MyWebSite/WebForm1.aspx.

You can see that this URL is built up from the details that we specified for our project earlier to create the full location of the project, including the server name (localhost), and of course the name of the form that we're using.

Suppliers and Products

As this book is all about working with databases, we'll delve into how we can present information taken from a database on an ASP.NET page. In this section, we'll produce a page that displays a list of suppliers. The user can select a supplier from the list to see all the products that that supplier deals with.

ASP.NET makes heavy use of data binding, but the way it works in ASP.NET can be a little tricky to understand. Take care to follow the instructions given carefully.

Try It Out – Showing a List of Suppliers

1. Using Solution Explorer, right-click on Global.asax and select View Code. At the top of the class definition, add the following:

```
Public Class Global
  Inherits System.Web.HttpApplication

  ' Constants
  Public Const DbString As String = _
    "integrated security=sspi;initial catalog=NorthwindSQL;data source=chimaera"
```

   Remember to change this database connection string to whatever works for your SQL setup.

2. Go back to the Solution Explorer, right-click on the MyWebSite project and select Add | Add Web Form. Call it Suppliers.

3. When the Designer appears, make sure you're in Design view, and add a new `DataList` control from the Toolbox to the form.

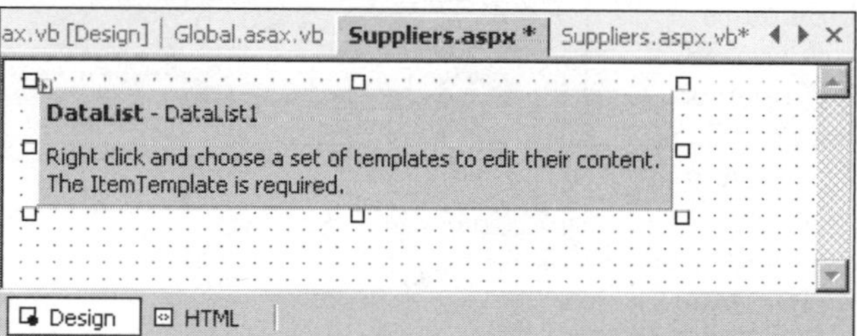

4. Change the ID property of the new control to lstSuppliers. As I mentioned before, data binding in Web Forms is a fairly odd process. The `DataList` control isn't capable of presenting the data by itself, so we need to place the control into a special mode that lets us add other controls to present the data.

   Right-click on the `DataList` control and select Edit Template | Item Templates. The control is now in a mode where we can add controls to present each item.

5. Drag a HyperLink control from the Toolbox onto the box in the `DataList` labelled ItemTemplate:

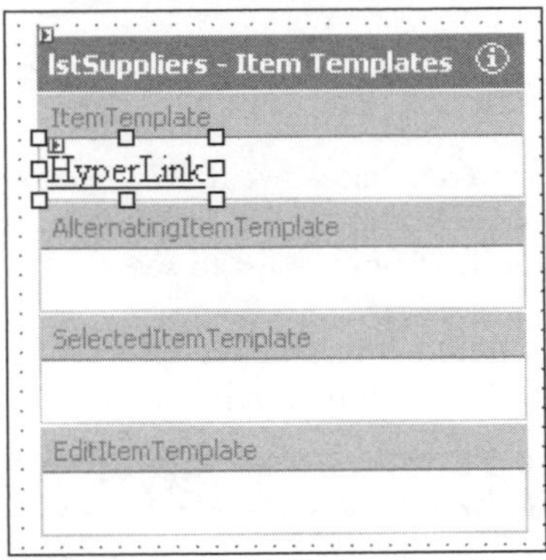

From this point on, to select the HyperLink *control, use the drop-down at the top of the* Properties *window rather than trying to click on the control in the Designer. This will make your life far less frustrating!*

Of the four areas in the editor, we're only interested in ItemTemplate. We can use AlternatingItemTemplate to display "every other item", which is useful on occasions where we want each line in the list to have an alternate background color. Although we're not going to use the selection or editing features here, SelectedItemTemplate is used when the item is selected and EditItemTemplate is used when the item is being edited.

6. Select the HyperLink control now. Change its ID property to lnkSupplier.

We now want to bind the row that we're working with to the Text property of the HyperLink control. Find the DataBindings property, which appears at the top of the Properties window in brackets. Click the ellipsis ("...") button to its right to make the window shown on the right appear. Select Text from the left-hand list, check Custom binding expression, and enter the code shown:

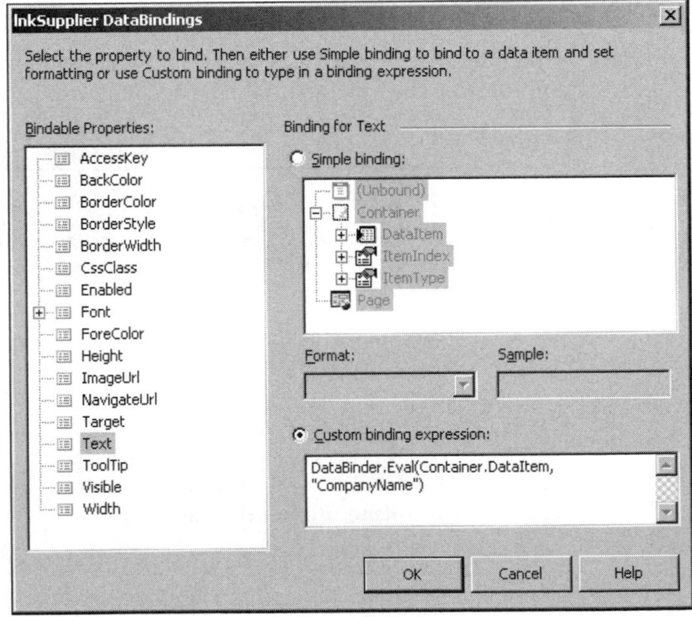

7. Click OK when you're happy you've entered the correct code. The displayed text of our HyperLinks is now bound to the CompanyName column of our data source. Later, we will be setting up URL links for these controls also, but for starters we'll just bind the Text property.

8. Next, we need to actually connect to the database and extract the list of suppliers. Double-click on the background of the form. This will open the `Load` event handler. Add this code:

```
Private Sub Page_Load(ByVal sender As System.Object, _
                      ByVal e As System.EventArgs) Handles MyBase.Load

    ' Connect to the database
    Dim connection As New SqlConnection(Global.DbString)
    connection.Open()

    ' Retrieve the suppliers
    Dim command As New SqlCommand("SELECT * FROM SUPPLIERS", connection)
    Dim reader As SqlDataReader = command.ExecuteReader()

    ' Bind the DataList to the SqlDataReader
    lstSuppliers.DataSource = reader
    lstSuppliers.DataBind()

    ' Close the SqlDataReader and release the SqlCommand object
    reader.Close()
    command.Dispose()

    ' Close the database connection
    connection.Close()

End Sub
```

9. Before we are ready to run the project, we need to add the following line to the beginning of `Suppliers.aspx.vb`, right at the top immediately preceding the `Page_Load` event:

```
Imports System.Data.SqlClient
```

10. Right-click on Suppliers.aspx in the Solution Explorer, and choose Set As Start Page. We're now ready to roll - choose Debug | Start, or press *F5*. You should see a list of suppliers displayed in your browser:

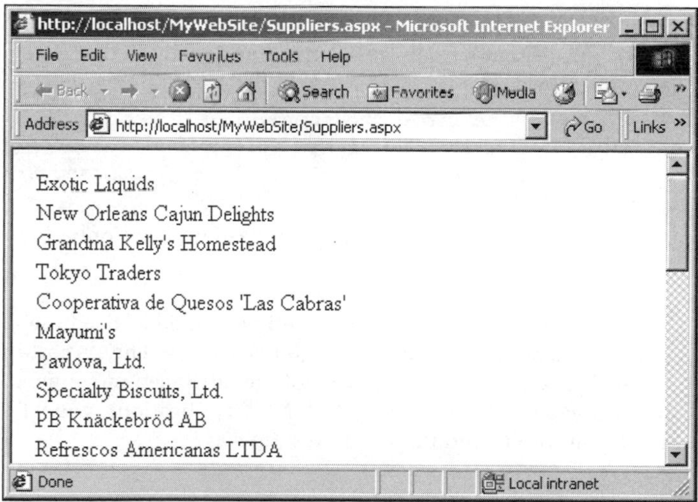

How It Works

First, we'll look at how we retrieved the supplier list. Then we'll take a look at how that list was displayed.

All ASP.NET projects can take advantage of `Global.asax`. This is a page that references a class called `Global` by default, and derives from `c`. This namespace defines events that we can catch and respond to, for example when the application is started (the first time that a page is requested after the server is rebooted) or whenever a user requests a page from the site. In our application, we've placed our connection string in the `Global.asax` page, and we can use that string constant from anywhere within our project to specify where our database can be found.

```
Public Class Global
  Inherits System.Web.HttpApplication

  ' Constants
  Public Const DbString As String = _
    "integrated security=sspi;initial catalog=NorthwindSQL;data source=chimaera"
```

When `Suppliers.aspx` is loaded, the `Page_Load` event is fired. `Suppliers.aspx.vb` defines a class called `Suppliers` that is associated with the `.aspx` page by the process known as "code behind". By default, Visual Studio creates all new Web Form pages in this way, deriving the associated classes from `System.Web.UI.Page`. Event-handling code that we write is placed in this class, and we can also add our own methods and properties. In our case, we use the code behind to extract data from a database. Notice how we're using the `DbString` constant defined in `Global.aspx`.

```
      ' Connect to the database
      Dim connection As New SqlConnection(Global.DbString)
      connection.Open()
```

Don't forget that almost everything happens on the server. When the page is requested, the `Suppliers.aspx` and `Suppliers.aspx.vb` files are both compiled and executed on the server with the ultimate goal of generating HTML that can be sent down to the client.

There are two important things to note here. Firstly, with ASP.NET, data binding is always read-only, which means that we can use a `DataReader` instead of a `DataSet`.

```
      ' Retrieve the suppliers
      Dim command As New SqlCommand("select * from suppliers", connection)
      Dim reader As SqlDataReader = command.ExecuteReader()
```

As described in Chapter 6, this provides fast, read-only, forward-only movement through the underlying data.

This type of database access is sometimes called a "fire hose" cursor, because you can quickly reel more out, but it's not really possible to go backwards. The `DataReader` consumes less memory and performs faster than a `DataSet` at the cost of the advanced movement and manipulation features supported by the `DataSet`. When creating ASP.NET applications, you will probably find that in the vast majority of cases you won't need these features anyway.

The other important thing to notice is that Web Form controls do not automatically data bind when the `DataSource` property is set, unlike Windows Forms. You must explicitly call the `DataBind` method when you want the control to bind.

```
' Bind the DataList to the SqlDataReader
lstSuppliers.DataSource = reader
lstSuppliers.DataBind()
```

Looking back at the `DataList` control, what happens is that for every data item in the source specified in the binding, new instances of any controls placed in the ItemTemplate area are created. In our case, these controls are `HyperLink` controls, the `DataBindings` property of which determines how data should be extracted from the current item to be bound and displayed on the control.

It's the `DataBinder.Eval` call that we set up in the lnkSupplier DataBindings dialog that performs the actual magic to associate the text of each `HyperLink` with the name of each supplier as it is pulled out of the database. The `Eval` method ("eval" being short for "evaluate") is a general purpose method used in data binding for extracting data from other objects. It's a shared method of the `System.Web.UI.DataBinder` object.

Let's have a closer look at that call now:

```
DataBinder.Eval (Container.DataItem, "CompanyName")
```

The first argument binds the `HyperLink`'s `Text` property to the `DataItem` property of the `HyperLink`'s container, which in this case is automatically set by ASP.NET to be our `DataList`. The second argument gives the name of a column, `CompanyName`, in the table that the control knows we're binding to.

Now we shall move on to enhance this code so that the user can click on a supplier to show the products they supply.

Try It Out – Binding URLs for the HyperLink Controls

1. Open `Suppliers.aspx` in Design view again. The `DataList` may be showing the text Databound several times, in which case you will need to right-click on it, and select Edit Template | Item Templates to make the `lnkSupplier` `HyperLink` control visible.

2. Select lnkSupplier from the drop-down list at the top of the Properties window. Open the lnkSupplier DataBindings dialog again by clicking on the ellipsis button of the DataBindings property. Click on NavigateUrl in the Bindable Properties pane, check Custom binding expression and add the expression shown:

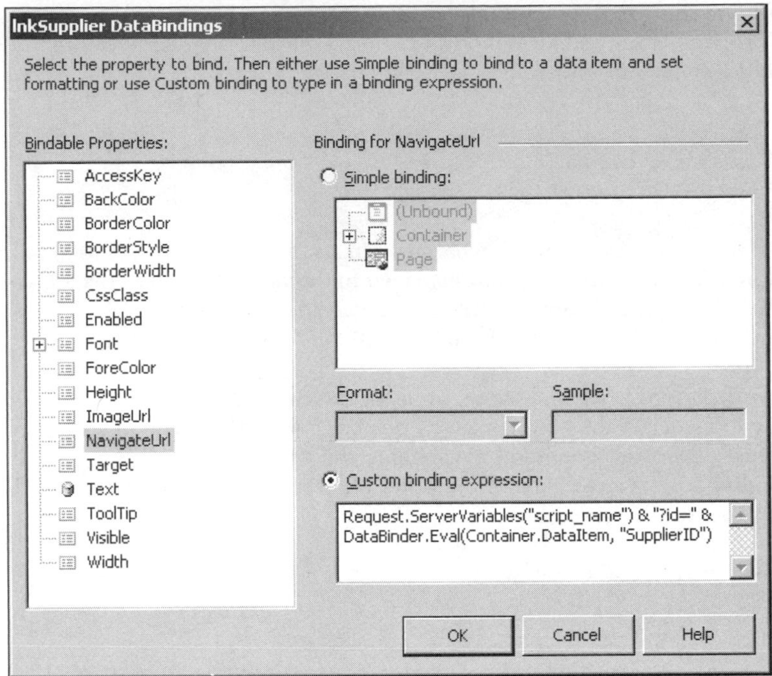

3. Click OK.

4. Now select DOCUMENT from the drop-down list at the top of the Properties window, and set the pageLayout property to FlowLayout. The DOCUMENT object refers to a DHTML object that's always present when we're working through the page. It provides access to the web page itself.

   Notice how the dots disappear from the form in Design view. Don't worry too much about what this means right now, as we will look at the differences between GridLayout and FlowLayout later in the chapter.

5. We shall display the product list for a supplier in a `DataGrid`. Make sure your cursor is to the right of the `DataList` and press *Return*. Drag a `DataGrid` from the Toolbox and place it underneath the `DataList`. Set its ID property to grdProducts.

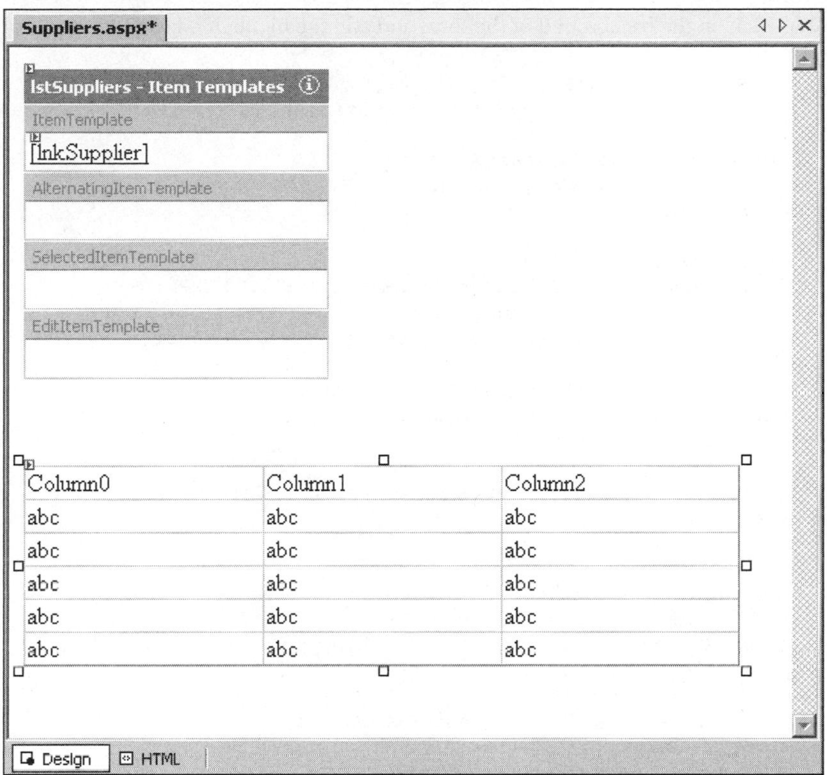

6. With the `DataGrid` selected, click on the Auto Format link in the Properties window.

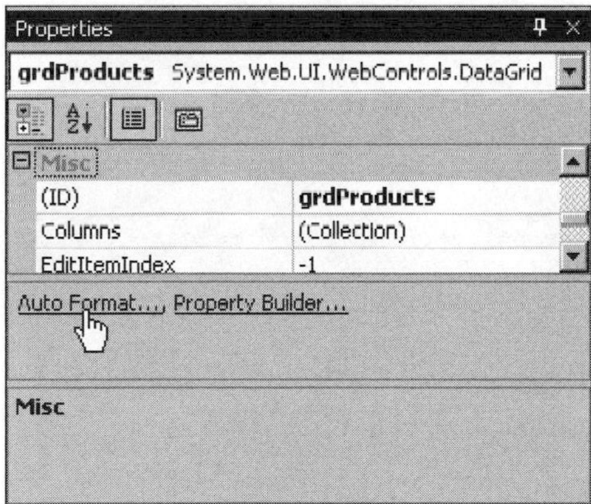

7. When you click Auto Format, a dialog should appear offering a selection of predefined formats that you can apply to the DataGrid. Choose a format that you like, I've gone for Professional 3.

8. Double-click on the background of the form and add the highlighted code to the `Page_Load` event:

```
Private Sub Page_Load(ByVal sender As System.Object, _
                         ByVal e As System.EventArgs) Handles MyBase.Load

    ' Connect to the database
    Dim connection As New SqlConnection(Global.DbString)
    connection.Open()

    ' Retrieve the suppliers
    Dim command As New SqlCommand("SELECT * FROM SUPPLIERS", _
                         connection)
    Dim reader As SqlDataReader = command.ExecuteReader()

    ' Bind the DataList to the SqlDataReader
    lstSuppliers.DataSource = reader
    lstSuppliers.DataBind()

    ' Close the SqlDataReader and release the SqlCommand object
    reader.Close()
    command.Dispose()

    Dim supplierId As Integer = 0
    ' If a supplier is selected...
    If Not Request.Params("id") Is Nothing Then

        ' ...Then get its ID
        supplierId = CInt(Request.Params("id"))

        ' Load their product details
        Dim productsCommand As New SqlCommand( _
                         "SELECT * FROM PRODUCTS WHERE SUPPLIERID=" & _
                         supplierId, connection)
        Dim productsReader As SqlDataReader = _
                         productsCommand.ExecuteReader()

        ' Bind the new SqlDataReader to the DataGrid
        grdProducts.DataSource = productsReader
        grdProducts.DataBind()

        ' Close the SqlDataReader and release the SqlCommand object
        productsReader.Close()
        productsCommand.Dispose()

    End If

    ' Close the database connection
    connection.Close()

End Sub
```

9. Now run the project. When you click on a supplier, the products that supplier deals with should show up in the `DataGrid`.

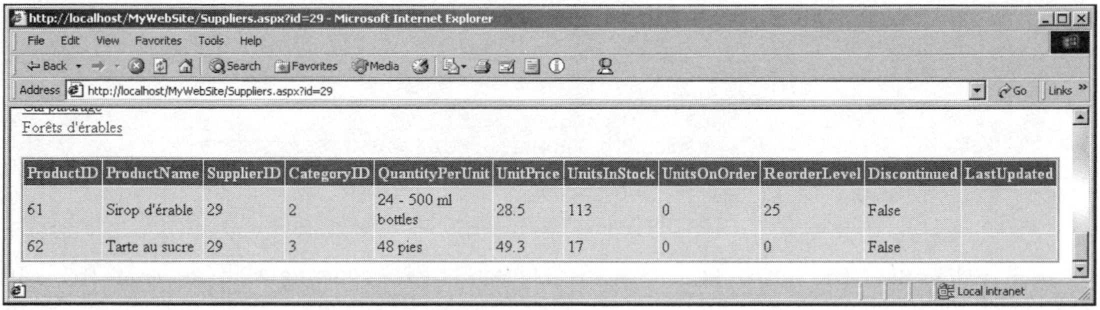
http://localhost/MyWebSite/Suppliers.aspx?id=29 - Microsoft Internet Explorer
File Edit View Favorites Tools Help
Address http://localhost/MyWebSite/Suppliers.aspx?id=29
Forêts d'érables
ProductID ProductName SupplierID CategoryID QuantityPerUnit UnitPrice UnitsInStock UnitsOnOrder ReorderLevel Discontinued LastUpdated
61 Sirop d'érable 29 2 24 - 500 ml bottles 28.5 113 0 25 False
62 Tarte au sucre 29 3 48 pies 49.3 17 0 0 False
Local intranet

How It Works

When the browser makes a request to the server, it must supply all necessary information for the server to accurately determine what the user wants. This information can be sent encoded in the URL for a requested page. For example, if we type the following URL into our browser:

http://localhost/MyWebSite/Suppliers.aspx

the server will return the list of suppliers. However, this URL:

http://localhost/MyWebSite/Suppliers.aspx?id=29

means the server should return the list of suppliers along with the products for the supplier with ID 29.

This process is called "passing parameters" to a page, and in this instance we've expressed the parameters as "query string variables". The query string is the term used to denote the portion of the URL following the question mark, which contains a list of name-value pairs. The name of every parameter is separated from its value by an equals sign. In this case, we have a variable called id and a value of 29. A query string can contain further parameters, each introduced by the ampersand character, as in this example:

http://www.wrox.com/Books/Books.asp?section=11_3&order=title

When we come to build the page we use the `Request` property of `System.Web.UI.Page` objects that serves the same purpose as the `Request` variable in old-style ASP. It returns an object of type `System.Web.HttpRequest` that is automatically populated with all the details supplied by the browser when the page request is made. In the code for the `Page_Load` event, we checked the `Params` property of `HttpRequest` to see if an `id` parameter had been supplied:

```
' If a supplier is selected...
If Not Request.Params("id") Is Nothing Then
```

If such a parameter is present, we extract it, not forgetting to convert it to an integer because all query string parameters are, as you may have guessed, passed in the form of a string. We can then use it in our SQL statement:

```
' ...Then get its ID
supplierId = CInt(Request.Params("id"))

' Load their product details
Dim productsCommand As New SqlCommand( _
                  "SELECT * FROM PRODUCTS WHERE SUPPLIERID=" & _
                   supplierId, connection)
Dim productsReader As SqlDataReader = _
                  productsCommand.ExecuteReader()
```

So where does the URL, such as http://localhost/MyWebSite/Suppliers.aspx?id=29, come from? It is produced by the binding we set for the `NavigateUrl` property of the `lnkSupplier HyperLink`, which specifies the destination URL to use when the `HyperLink` is clicked. Recall that we gave the following expression as the custom binding for that property:

```
Request.ServerVariables("script_name") & "?id=" & DataBinder.Eval(Container.DataItem, _
    "SupplierID")
```

This expression looks in the `Request` property of the page for a collection called `ServerVariables`, and extracts an item called `script_name`, that contains the name and path of the current `.aspx` file. We then just tack on the query string indicator followed by the variable name and an equals sign ("?id="). Lastly we have to append the ID of the supplier, which we do using `DataBinder.Eval` one more time.

Grid Layout vs. Flow Layout

Before we move on, now is a good time to look in some detail at what is meant by "grid layout" and "flow layout". The principle behind grid layout is to provide absolute control over where page elements are to be placed. In theory, this method gives you pixel perfect placement of where controls are to appear, and what the user sees in their browser will reflect exactly what you see in the Design view of your page.

In practice however, the Web does not lend itself to such precise specification of a page's layout. Imagine you have a list of ten items, and underneath it you want to show a grid of data. You can do this using grid layout, by providing precise coordinates for where you want the `DataGrid` to appear. That will work fine, but what if the list grows to twenty items? You would have to move the `DataGrid` accordingly otherwise it will overwrite the end of the list.

There's another crucial weakness with grid layout. Support for absolute positioning is very variable depending on the browser in use. In fact, you can only expect it to work 100% reliably when your users view your site using modern versions (version 5.0 and up) of Internet Explorer and Windows. Should they use a non-Microsoft browser or platform, or even some earlier IE version, you're risking your page being rendered at best haphazardly, and at worst completely illegibly.

The idea of flow layout is that controls are rendered on a page as and when they are defined. For example, in the above example, the browser would start by drawing the list at the top of the page, and when complete, would draw the grid underneath. Now, it no longer matters how many items that list contains, because the rendering will automatically cater for lists of any length. You lose precise control over the position of your controls, but your pages are more robust, and more compliant with older IE browsers and browsers from other vendors.

An Inventory Web Application

Now let's move on to create a practical ASP.NET business application that allows a salesperson, or customer, to search for products with a given name. We'll present a list of those products together with the current stock level and price.

Try It Out – Creating an Inventory Web Application

1. Create a new Web Form by right-clicking on MyWebSite in the Solution Explorer and selecting Add Web Form. Give it the name PriceCheck.

2. Make sure you're in Design view, and select DOCUMENT from the drop-down in the Properties window. Change the pageLayout property to FlowLayout. Again, you'll notice the dots disappear from the form.

3. From the Toolbox, drag and drop a Label control onto the middle of the Designer. You'll notice that it snaps to the top-left hand corner of the page. This is because flow layout starts in the top-left and works its way down the page to the bottom-right similarly to a word processing document.

4. Set the Text property of the Label to Enter a product name: including the final colon.

5. Now, click on the Designer and make sure the cursor appears to the right of the Label control. The cursor indicates where the next control will be placed, but we want to add the next control underneath the Label and not to its right. Hold down *Shift* and press *Return*. This will make the cursor drop to the line immediately below the Label. (What's actually happening here is that the editor is adding a <BR> tag at the end of the label control. BR is sort for "break" as in "line break" in HTML.)

6. Drag and drop a TextBox control from the Toolbox, noticing that it appears where the cursor was previously:

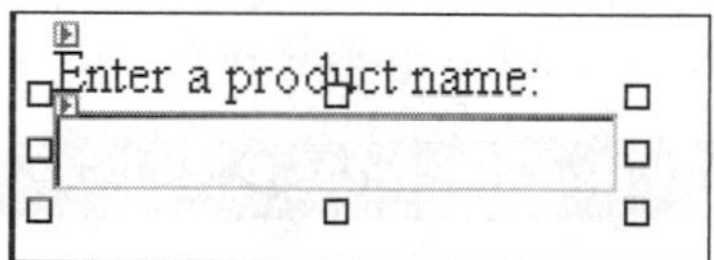

7. Change the ID property of the TextBox control to txtSearchFor, and set its Text property to Louisiana.

8. Click on the background of the form when done. The cursor should be flashing to the right of the TextBox. Press the space bar once, and drag a Button control onto the form:

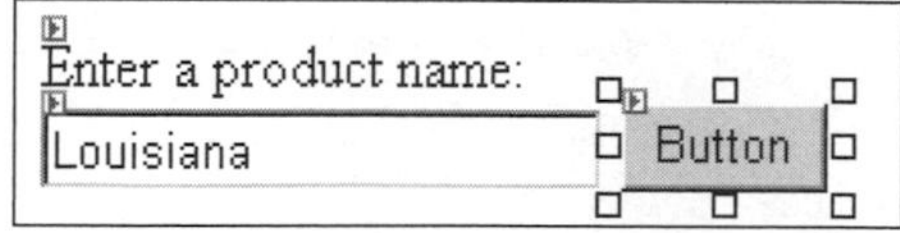

9. Set the Text property of the button to Go! and its ID property to btnSearch. Again, click on the background of the form.

10. Press *Return* but, this time, do not hold down *Shift*. Note how this has the effect of moving the cursor down two lines, rather than before when the cursor was positioned immediately below the Label control. This is known as a "paragraph" break and is achieved by Visual Studio adding a <P> tag to the page. Paragraph breaks always insert a blank line between itself and the line above.

11. Drag and drop a DataGrid control onto the form. Set its ID property to grdProducts, and again use the Auto Format link to choose an appearance to your taste.

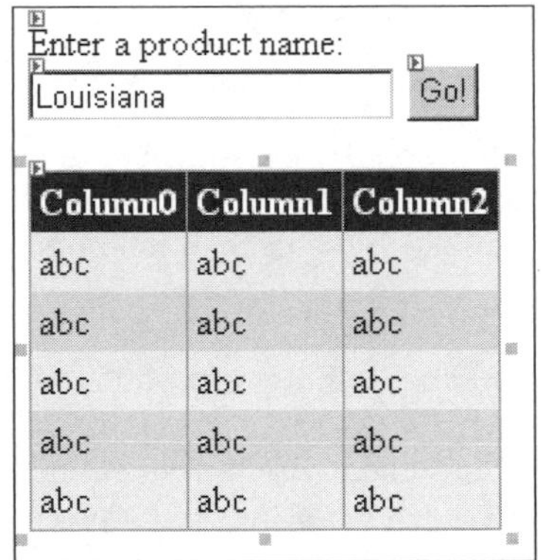

That's all we need to do as far as designing the page is concerned. The trick when you're working in "flow" mode is to get the cursor to the position where you want the next control. With experience, you will learn to master this technique, and you'll find that using the Designer becomes a lot easier.

Searching for Products

To perform the product search, all we need to do is wire up the Go! Button.

Try It Out – Adding a Click Event Handler in ASP.NET

1. Double-click on the Go! Button in the Designer, and add the code below for the Button's `Click` handler. Don't forget that we use the constant we defined on the `Global` class to get the database string for the connection.

```
Private Sub btnSearch_Click(ByVal sender As System.Object, _
                           ByVal e As System.EventArgs) Handles btnSearch.Click

    ' Connect to the database
    Dim connection As New SqlConnection(Global.DbString)
    connection.Open()

    ' Retrieve the items...
    Dim sql As String = _
```

```
            "SELECT productname, unitprice, unitsinstock FROM products " & _
            "WHERE productname LIKE '%" & Me.txtSearchFor.Text & "%'"
      Dim command As New SqlCommand(sql, connection)
      Dim reader As SqlDataReader = command.ExecuteReader()

      ' Bind the DataGrid to the SqlDataReader
      grdProducts.DataSource = reader
      grdProducts.DataBind()

      ' Close the SqlDataReader and release the SqlCommand object
      reader.Close()
      command.Dispose()

      ' Close the database connection
      connection.Close()

   End Sub
```

2. The page code has to import the `System.Data.SqlClient` namespace, so add the following to the top of the `PriceCheck.aspx.vb` file, as the very first line:

```
Imports System.Data.SqlClient
```

3. Right-click on PriceCheck.aspx in the Solution Explorer and select Set as Start Page. Now, run the project and click Go!. You should see this:

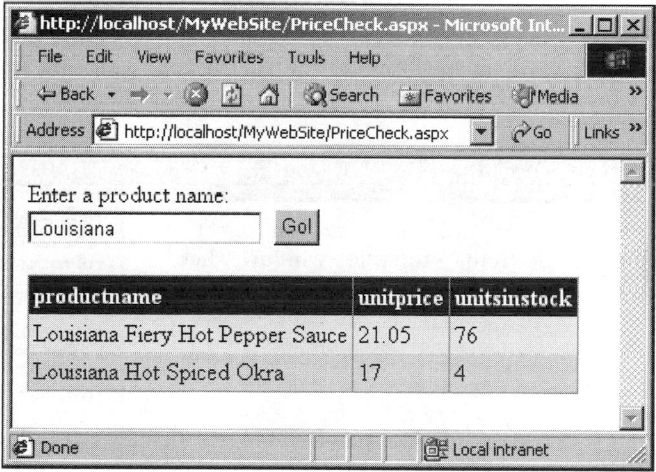

How It Works

What we're doing here is similar to the code we developed earlier in the chapter, retrieving data from a `SqlCommand` object by using a `SqlDataReader`:

```
Dim sql As String = _
      "SELECT productname, unitprice, unitsinstock FROM products " & _
      "WHERE productname LIKE '%" & Me.txtSearchFor.Text & "%'"
Dim command As New SqlCommand(sql, connection)
Dim reader As SqlDataReader = command.ExecuteReader()
```

and binding a display control (here we use the `DataGrid`) to that reader.

```
grdProducts.DataSource = reader
grdProducts.DataBind()
```

As can be seen, our SQL string contains a `LIKE` operator (this was explained in Chapter 3 if you need to refresh your memory).

However, although we do indeed see the results we want, they could be presented more attractively, and there are several ways for improving the presentation of data within a `DataGrid`. We look at these in the next section.

Improving Presentation of the DataGrid

By default, when given data to bind to, the `DataGrid` will give each of its columns the column name given by the data source for that column. This is why our columns are headed productname, unitprice and unitsinstock rather than having more descriptive and readable titles like Product Name, Unit Price and Units in Stock. We can provide such names quite easily.

> **As an alternative to the method you're about to see, you could add "aliases" to the columns in the SQL string itself. However, we are not going to go into this here as this section is designed to show you how you can control the appearance of the grid.**

Try It Out – Naming DataGrid Columns

1. Open `PriceCheck.aspx` in Design view, and select the `DataGrid` control. In the Properties window, click the link next to Auto Format entitled Property Builder.

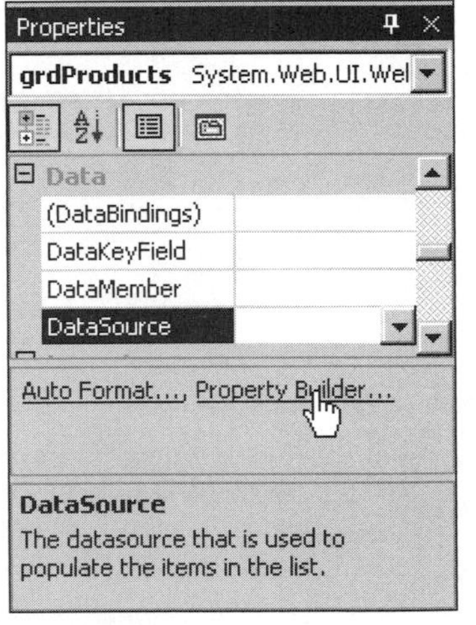

2. Select the Columns tab in the navigation bar running down the length of the left-hand side of the dialog. Uncheck the Create columns automatically at run time box. This tells the `DataGrid` control that we're going to tell it what columns should be on the grid, rather than expecting it to infer the results.

3. From the Available columns pane, select Bound Column and click the right-arrow button that appears next to that pane. This should enable the Header Text and Data Field boxes. Enter Product Name and productname respectively.

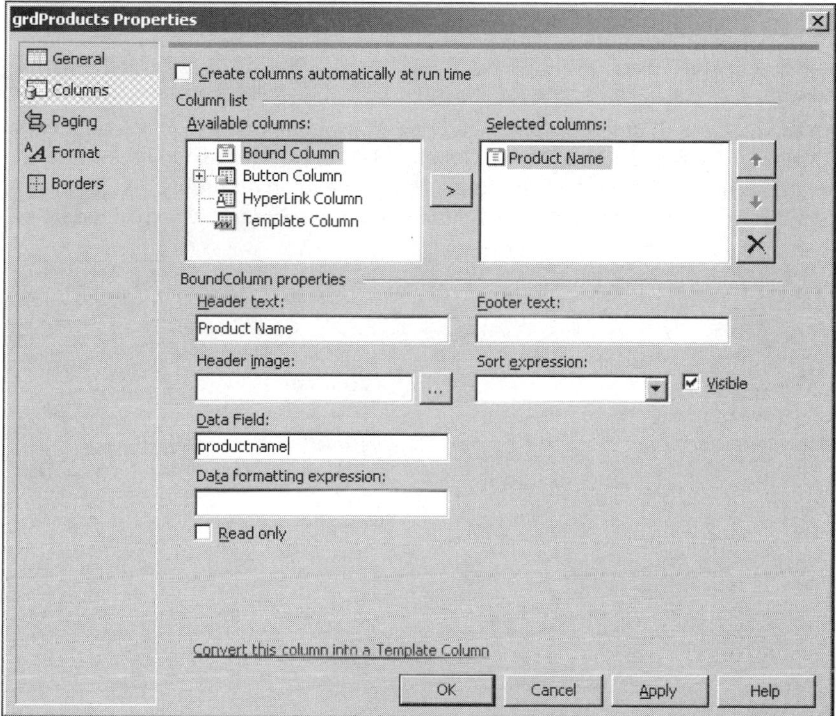

4. Click OK, and run the project. Now just the Product Name column appears in the DataGrid control:

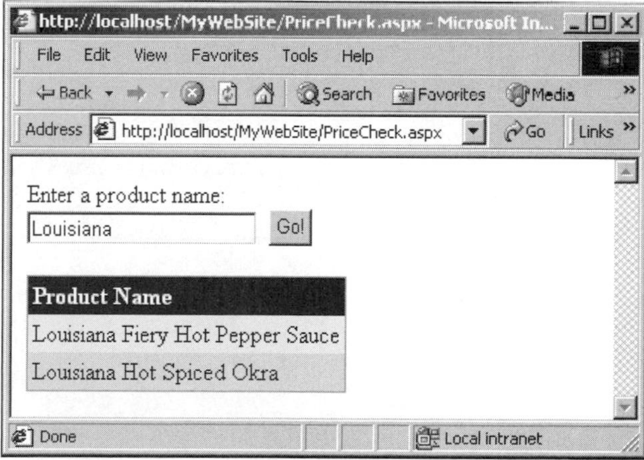

How It Works

Rather than telling the DataGrid to work out the columns for itself, thus displaying all available columns, we've specifically given it just a single column. We also specified a name for that column, Product Name, along with the name of the column in the data source that it should bind to, productname.

Adding a Unit Price Column

Let's look now at how to add a Unit Price column. Ideally, we would show the price as currency and we can do this by applying a format string to the column.

Try It Out – Adding a Currency Column

1. Open the Property Builder for the DataGrid control one more time. Change to the Columns view as before and add a new Bound Column. Set the Header text to Unit Price and the Data Field to unitprice. Insert {0:c} in the Data formatting expression box. This isn't just an extravagant two-way smiley: it also tells ASP.NET that this column is a currency, as explained later.

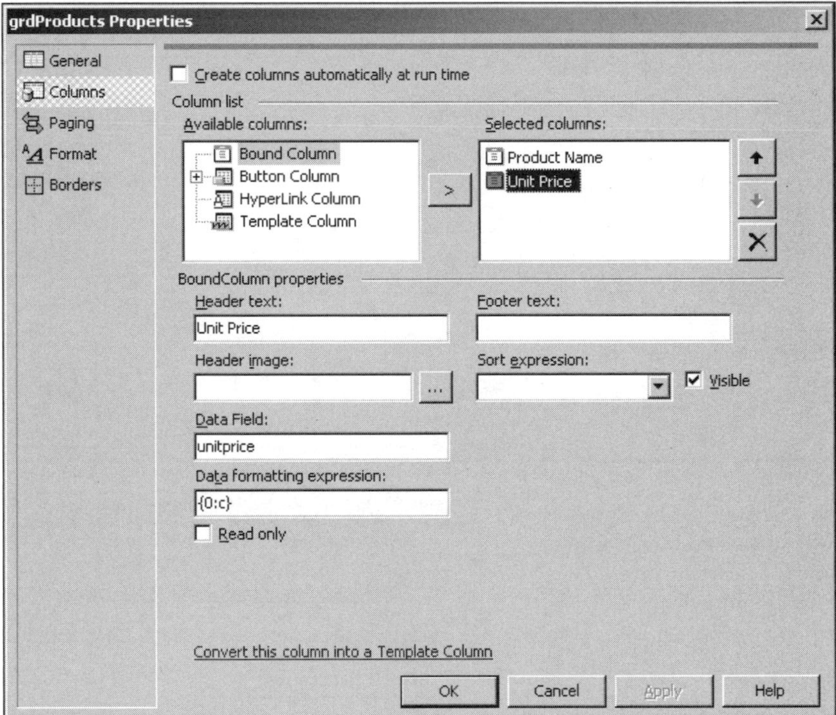

2. Click OK and run the project. You should see the following:

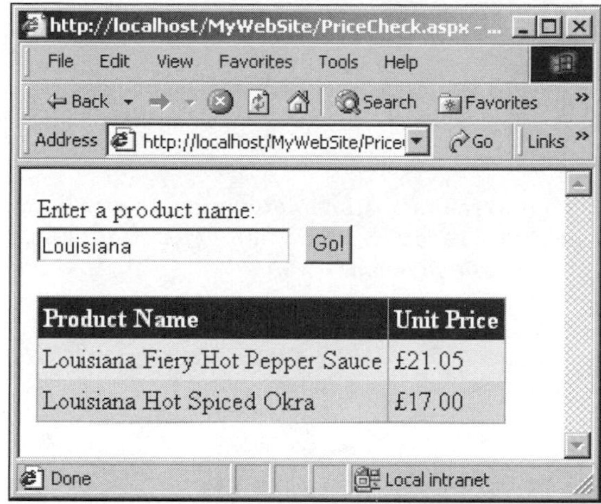

How It Works

The neat part here is the format string. The formatting codes it contains are universal throughout the Framework for converting values to strings. Here we used `{0:c}`, which means:

- Take the first (at index position 0) value that can be formatted from the corresponding data field, and render it as currency according to the current locale settings on the server. On this computer, the British Pound (£) is the local currency.

You can apply any valid formatting you want to a column. Follow the same formatting guidelines that apply to `String.Format`. String formatting is a relatively involved topic, so if you need more information, look up `System.String` in MSDN and find the `Format` method.

Adding an InStock Column

For our InStock column, rather than giving the actual number of items in stock, we want to say simply "Yes" or "No". There's no particular reason why our customers need to know exactly how many items are in stock, and in fact we could put ourselves at a competitive disadvantage if we advertised our current stock levels for all the world to see.

To create a column that displays "Yes" or "No" based on the value returned from the database requires us to create a method that will return "Yes" or "No" when given a quantity, and to then be able to call that method from a column.

Try It Out – Calling a Method from a Column

1. Open the code editor for `PriceCheck.aspx.vb` by right-clicking on `PriceCheck.aspx` in Solution Explorer and selecting View Code. Add the `IsInStock` method, which returns a Boolean indicating whether an item is in stock according to the stock level passed in as its argument.

```
' IsInStock - given a quantity, is the item in stock...
Public Function IsInStock(ByVal quantity As Integer) As Boolean
    If quantity > 0 Then
```

```
        Return True
    Else
        Return False
    End If
End Function
```

2. We also need functions to return a string representing the stock status of a product. Insert these two versions of `GetInStockString` into `PriceCheck.aspx.vb`, the first takes an integer, and the other takes a Boolean:

```
' GetInStockString - get a string indicating the status...
Public Function GetInStockString(ByVal quantity As Integer) As String
    Return GetInStockString(IsInStock(quantity))
End Function
```

```
Public Function GetInStockString(ByVal inStock As Boolean) As String
    If inStock = True Then
        Return "Yes"
    Else
        Return "No"
    End If
End Function
```

3. Open the Property Builder for the `DataGrid` control (go to the **Properties** window in the Design View), and select the **Columns** pane. From the **Available Columns** list, select **Template Column**, and click the right-arrow button to the right of the list. Set the **Header Text** for the column to **In Stock**:

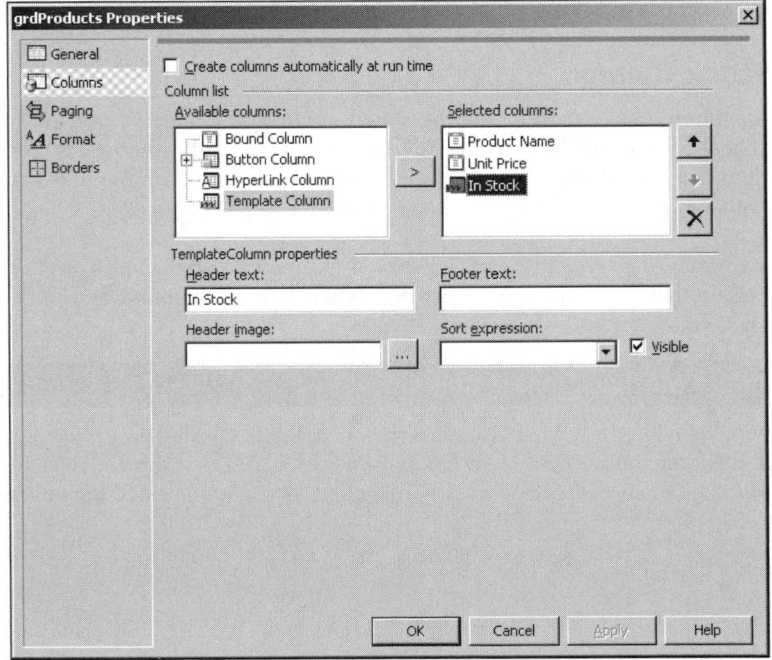

4. If you click OK, you'll see a new column in the `DataGrid`. You'll notice that the In Stock column doesn't say Databound. This is because we haven't defined what should appear in the column, only that something should appear. As we're about to see, we need to add new, data bound controls to this column.

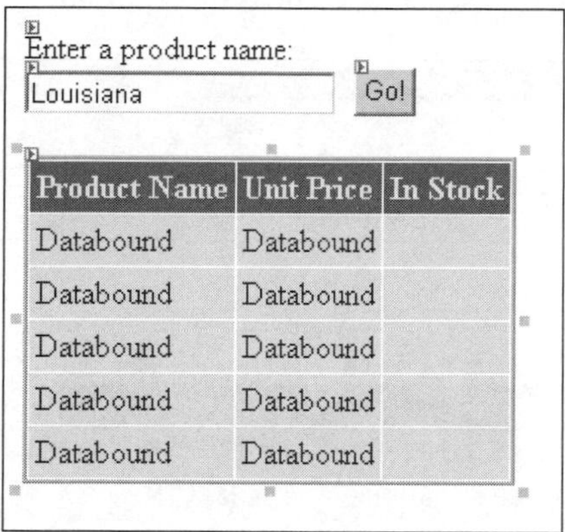

5. Right-click on the `DataGrid` and select Edit Template | Columns[2] In Stock. This will open a template editor very similar to the one we used back when we were displaying in a `DataList` control. Drag and drop a `Label` control from the Toolbox onto the ItemTemplate area as shown:

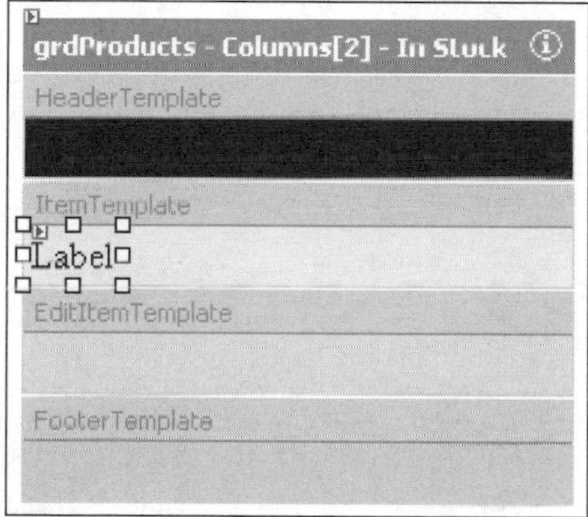

6. Change the ID property of the `Label` to lblInStock. Find the DataBindings property towards the top of the listed properties, and click the ellipsis button. Making sure that Text is selected in the left-hand list, check Custom binding expression, and enter the following expression in the box:

```
CType(Page, PriceCheck).GetInStockString(Container.DataItem("unitsinstock"))
```

Click the OK button to save the binding.

7. Now, set PriceCheck.aspx as the project's start page by right-clicking on `PriceCheck.aspx` in the Solution Explorer, and choosing Set As Start Page.

8. Run the project. Try different values in the product name field, and click on the Go! button. You should find that the stock status is correctly reported.

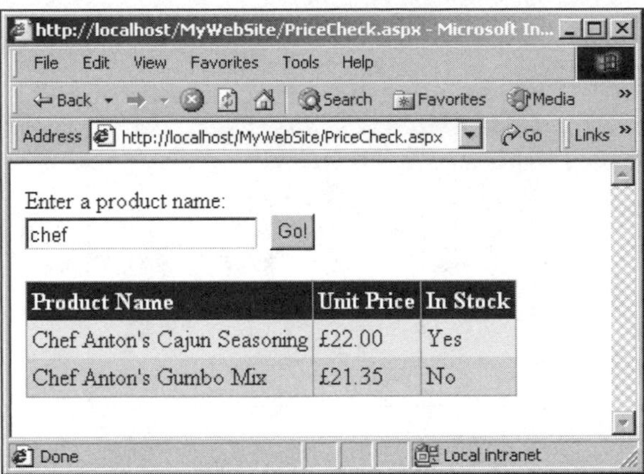

How It Works

Up to this point, we've exclusively dealt with default `DataGrid` behavior for the display of information from a database. Here we've added a couple of new methods to the class in the code behind `PriceCheck.aspx` to apply a little custom formatting to a field, converting it to either Yes or No.

The first method, `IsInStock`, returns a Boolean value when given a quantity:

```
If quantity > 0 Then
    Return True
Else
    Return False
End If
```

The second method, `GetInStockString`, takes that Boolean value and turns it into a string:

```
' GetInStockString - get a string indicating the status...
Public Function GetInStockString (ByVal quantity As Integer) As String
    Return GetInStockString(IsInStock (quantity))
End Function

Public Function GetInStockString(ByVal inStock As Boolean) As String
    If inStock = True Then
        Return "Yes"
    Else
        Return "No"
    End If
End Function
```

Template columns of DataGrids are a very powerful feature that lets us fully control the presentation of columns in a grid, and in this case we use such a column to call our GetInStockString method. Look again at that line we added as the custom binding expression for the DataGrid:

```
CType(Page, PriceCheck).GetInStockString(Container.DataItem("unitsinstock"))
```

We're using the Page property that returns a System.Web.UI.Page object. We cast that to a PriceCheck object using the CType function to access methods that we've placed in the inherited class, such as the GetInStockString method. We use Container.DataItem (remember that here the container is the DataGrid itself) to access the unitsinstock column, and send the value returned to GetInStockString to be converted to either Yes or No.

Paging

An age-old problem that faces web developers is that of presenting a single data source over multiple pages. Imagine you have 500 products that you need to display. Is it best to display a single page with all 500, or ten pages showing 50 products each? Usually, the latter is best as it makes the finished product more approachable to the user, and because a huge quantity of data isn't being sent all at once. It's much more suited to the low bandwidth world of the Internet.

Old style ASP lacked a simple way of presenting data in pages, which lead to a ridiculous position where virtually anyone representing tables of data using ASP had to roll their own code to allow the data to be presented in pages. However, ASP.NET has this functionality built-in, making the developer's life much easier. So, let's try adding paging capability to our DataGrid control.

Try It Out – Adding Paging

1. Make sure that PriceCheck.aspx is open in Design view, and go to the Property Builder for the DataGrid, but this time select Paging from the options down the right-hand side. Then check Allow Paging and set Page size to 10 rows.

2. Make sure the options in the lower page navigation section are set as in the following screenshot, in particular the Mode drop-down should be set to Page numbers:

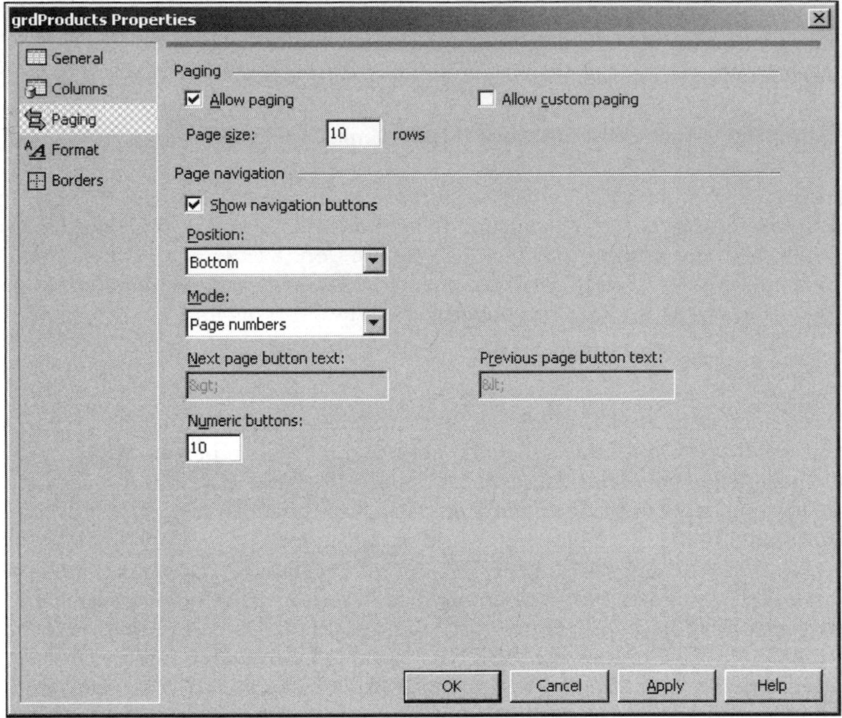

Click OK.

3. If you look at the `DataGrid` control on the designer, you'll notice that it now shows exactly ten rows and that a set of page navigation buttons has appeared at the bottom.

4. Make these changes to `btnSearch_Click` in `PriceCheck.aspx.vb`:

```
Private Sub btnSearch_Click(ByVal sender As System.Object, _
                    ByVal e As System.EventArgs) Handles btnSearch.Click
    BindData()
End Sub

Private Sub BindData()

    ' Connect to the database
    Dim connection As New SqlConnection(Global.DbString)
    connection.Open()

    ' Retrieve the items...
    Dim sql As String = _
          "SELECT productname, unitprice, unitsinstock FROM products " & _
          "WHERE productname LIKE '%" & Me.txtSearchFor.Text & "%'"
    Dim command As New SqlCommand(sql, connection)

    Dim dataset As New DataSet()
    Dim adapter As New SqlDataAdapter(command)
```

```
        adapter.Fill(dataset)
        adapter.Dispose()

        ' Bind the DataGrid to the SqlDataReader
        grdProducts.DataSource = dataset.Tables(0)
        grdProducts.DataBind()

        ' Release the SqlCommand object
        command.Dispose()

        ' Close the database connection
        connection.Close()

    End Sub
```

5. Using the drop-downs at the top of the central code pane, select **grdProducts** from the left-hand drop-down. From the right-hand drop-down, select **PageIndexChanged**, and add this code:

```
    Private Sub grdProducts_PageIndexChanged(ByVal source As Object, _
            ByVal e As System.Web.UI.WebControls.DataGridPageChangedEventArgs) _
            Handles grdProducts.PageIndexChanged

        ' Set the current page
        grdProducts.CurrentPageIndex = e.NewPageIndex

        ' Rebind to the grid
        BindData()

    End Sub
```

6. Run the project and enter a search term that will return a lot of products, for example just the letter **e**. You can now use the numbered links at the bottom of the DataGrid control to move through the data.

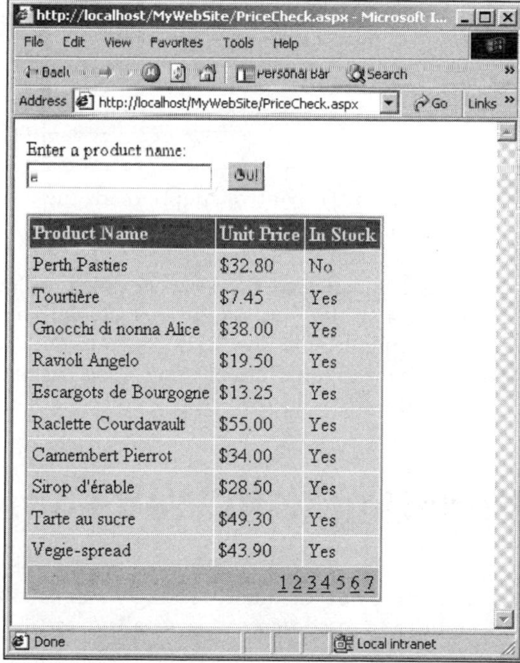

How It Works

Paging won't work with a DataReader object because it requires a control that allows both forward and backward movement through the data. We need to swap our DataReader for a DataAdapter.

```
Dim dataset As New DataSet()
Dim adapter As New SqlDataAdapter(command)
adapter.Fill(dataset)
adapter.Dispose()
```

However, there's another issue we must address. When the user navigates to another page of our data, we need to rebind the DataSet to its new contents. We can do this if we move the code from the btnSearch_Click event handler to a separate method called BindData. We can then call the BindData method from both the button's Click event, and the DataGrid's index changed event.

When a particular numbered link is clicked, the DataGrid doesn't display the new information automatically. Instead, it fires the PageIndexChanged event to let us handle the display ourselves. The code in that event updates the CurrentPageIndex property and reselects and rebinds the data.

```
' Set the current page
grdProducts.CurrentPageIndex = e.NewPageIndex

' Rebind to the grid
BindData()
```

What's important here is that the BindData method actually gets all of the data from the server on each call, which means that if you have 500 rows but only want to display ten, each time you make the call you're actually getting 490 more rows than you need to.

```
Dim sql As String = _
      "SELECT productname, unitprice, unitsinstock FROM products " & _
      "WHERE productname LIKE '%" & Me.txtSearchFor.Text & "%'"
```

(The DataGrid control simply reads the rows it needs from the Rows collection on the table that it's bound to.)

Using this paging method is very quick to develop, but not a great solution if you're really worried about scalability. (On an intranet site with a few dozen users, or on a small web site, it's fine providing that the underlying query isn't horrendously complex.) If you are worried about performance, you might want to look into caching – see *Beginning ASP.NET using VB.NET* by Wrox (ISBN 1861005040) – or developing your own paging code that gets just the data you need.

Updating with Web Forms

So far, we've used Web Forms to create a read-only view of a database. Web Forms are equally capable of creating new data and making changes to existing data. In this section, we'll put together an application to edit customer details over the Web.

Looking Up Customers

In the first part of this exercise, we'll build a basic page to edit the name of a company given a customer ID. We're not going to use data binding in this example for the sake of simplicity.

A crucial point in ASP.NET is that we're working in a disconnected environment unlike with Windows Forms where, if the user clicks a button, we can instantly respond and modify the UI (user interface) as appropriate. With Web Forms, the UI has to be constructed from scratch each time a change is made. We call this "stateless" because the application is unable to keep track of its own "state". For example, in a Windows Forms application if we click a button marked "Next" to view the "next" customer, we need to actually understand what the current customer is; this is stored in the application state. On the Web, because we have no state, we don't know what the "next" customer is because we have no state telling us what the "current" customer is. For this reason, every time we ask a web application to do something, we have to provide all the state it needs to make the request. If we want the "next" customer, we have to tell it what the "current" customer is when we make the request.

The issue is that as .NET developers we're used to storing state information in member variables. However, each time a request is made, a *new instance of the class is created.* So, if we store state in member variables, they're cleared every time the user makes a request for an updated copy of the page.

Fortunately, ASP.NET provides a way to store the values within controls from click to click: it's called **view state**, and controls automatically preserve it to an extent. Again, this isn't application state, only the state that applies to the page is stored. This means that if the user types "Hello" into a TextBox, .NET knows that when it updates the page it should add "Hello" to that TextBox again. That's how the `TextBox` for the customer ID managed to keep its `Text` property value intact even though we were clicking buttons on the form.

One way to solve this problem, and the method we're going use, is to create a control on the page expressly so we can use that control's "view state persistence" to retain values that we want to keep from page to page. We will keep this control visible so that we can see its value changing, but in real world applications you'd usually make it invisible to avoid cluttering the page.

> *Those of you who have put together HTML forms in the past will recognize this technique – it's conceptually similar to storing information in* `HIDDEN` *elements on a page.*

So let's create our basic form for changing the company name for a particular customer.

Try It Out – Editing a Database Field

1. Right-click on MyWebSite in Solution Explorer, and choose Add | Add Web Form. Call the new form EditCustomer, and add two `Buttons`, four `Labels` and two `TextBoxes` as shown:

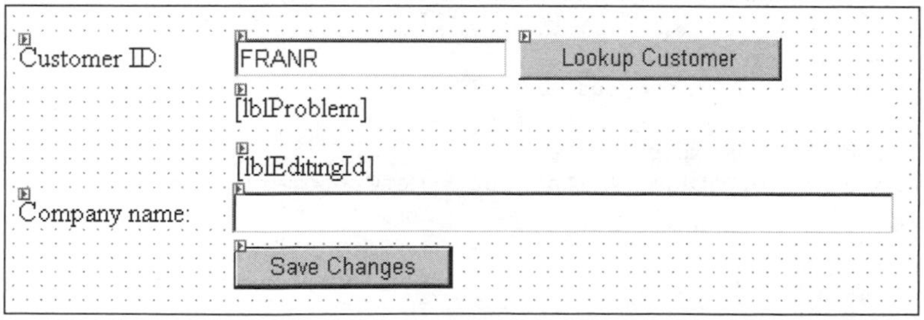

2. Two of the labels are used for describing each TextBox. Set properties for the controls as shown in the table below:

Control	Property	Value
First TextBox control	ID	txtCustomerId
	Text	FRANR
First Button control	ID	btnLookupCustomer
	Text	Lookup Customer
Label control marked [lblProblem]	ID	lblProblem
	Text	(Blank string)
	Width	379px
Label control marked [lblEditingId]	ID	lblEditingId
	Text	(Blank string)
Second TextBox control	ID	txtCompanyName
	Text	(Blank string)
Second Button control	ID	btnSaveChanges
	Text	Save Changes
	Visible	False

3. Double-click on the Look Up Customer button to create a new Click event handler, which will contain just one line of code:

```
Private Sub btnLookupCustomer_Click(ByVal sender As System.Object, _
              ByVal e As System.EventArgs) Handles btnLookupCustomer.Click
    BindData(txtCustomerId.Text)
End Sub
```

4. Add this method to the EditCustomer.aspx.vb file also:

```
' BindData - bind the data to the controls...
Public Sub BindData(ByVal customerId As String)

    ' Set Label Text
    lblEditingId.Text = customerId

    ' Get the customer
    Dim customerDataset As DataSet = GetCustomer(customerId)
```

```
        ' If the customer was found...
        If customerDataset.Tables(0).Rows.Count > 0 Then

            ' ...Reset the Label Text
            lblProblem.Text = ""
            btnSaveChanges.Visible = True

            ' Update the controls
            Dim customer As DataRow = customerDataset.Tables(0).Rows(0)
            txtCompanyName.Text = customer("companyname")

        Else

            ' ...Otherwise set an error message
            lblProblem.Text = "The customer ID '" & customerId & _
                              "' does not exist"
            btnSaveChanges.Visible = False

            ' Update the controls
            txtCompanyName.Text = ""

        End If

    End Sub
```

5. Follow it with two versions of the `GetCustomer` method. (The reason why we have two versions of this method will become apparent.)

```
    Public Function GetCustomer(ByVal customerId As String) As DataSet

        ' Call the other version of this method
        Dim adapter As SqlDataAdapter
        Dim customer As DataSet = GetCustomer(customerId, adapter)

        ' Dispose of the adapter
        adapter.Dispose()

        ' Return customer details
        Return customer

    End Function
```

```
    Public Function GetCustomer(ByVal customerId As String, _
                        ByRef adapter As SqlDataAdapter) As DataSet

        ' Connect to the database
        Dim connection As New SqlConnection(Global.DbString)
        connection.Open()

        ' Set up the SQL command object
```

```
        Dim command As New SqlCommand("SELECT customerid, companyname, " & _
                 "contactname, contacttitle, address, city, " & _
                 "region, postalcode, country, phone, fax " & _
                 "FROM customers WHERE customerid='" & customerId & "'", _
                  connection)

        ' Retrieve the data
        adapter = New SqlDataAdapter(command)

        ' Add a command builder
        Dim builder As New SqlCommandBuilder(adapter)

        ' Fill the DataSet
        Dim customer As New DataSet()
        adapter.Fill(customer)

        ' Disconnect
        connection.Close()

        ' Return customer details
        Return customer

    End Function
```

6. We must also import the `System.Data.SqlClient` namespace, so add the following line to the very top of `EditCustomer.aspx.vb`:

```
Imports System.Data.SqlClient
```

7. In Solution Explorer, right-click **EditCustomer.aspx** and select **Set As Start Page**, and run the project. Leaving the default of **FRANR** in the customer ID `TextBox`, click the **Look Up Customer** button. The customer ID isn't case-sensitive, but it must be an exact match.

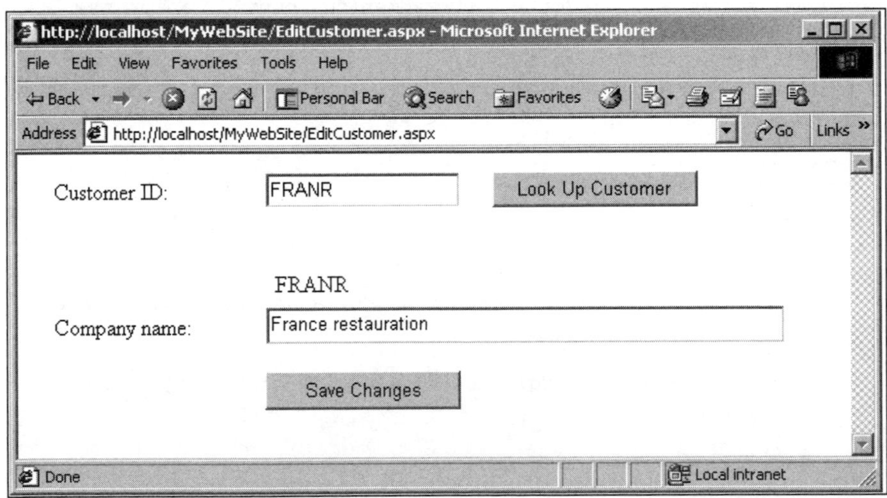

8. Change FRANR to SMURF, or some other customer ID that doesn't exist. Click the Look Up Customer button and you'll see a message saying that the customer ID does not exist:

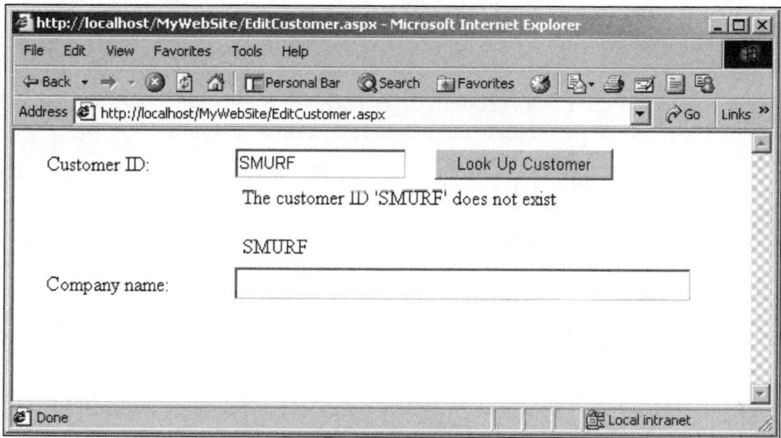

How It Works

When the Look Up Customer button is pressed, the `BindData` method is called to find the customer in the database and update the various form controls.

```
Private Sub btnLookupCustomer_Click(ByVal sender As System.Object, _
            ByVal e As System.EventArgs) Handles btnLookupCustomer.Click
    BindData(txtCustomerId.Text)
End Sub
```

The first thing the method does is set the `Text` property of `lblEditingId`, which keeps track of which customer is being edited for when Save Changes is clicked.

```
    lblEditingId.Text = customerId
```

When the Look Up Customer button is clicked, we go back to the server to tell it that the button has been clicked.

```
    Dim customerDataset As DataSet = GetCustomer(customerId)
```

We also pass the text in the TextBox back to the server. The event handling code on the server then stores the customer ID in the label control. All of this is crunched into a big block of HTML that's sent to the browser and displayed.

If you're wondering why we couldn't use the `Text` property of `txtCustomerId`, it's because if the user changed the value in this field and clicked Save Changes, we'd effectively end up saving the changes destined for the customer we originally specified over the top of the new customer that we've ended up specifying. These controls, that keep track of what we're doing and would normally be hidden in a production application, must be immutable by the user, that is, they may only be changed programmatically.

Once we've set the value, we call GetCustomer. We'll take a deeper look at this in a moment, but in essence, this method returns a DataSet containing the given customer.

After we've retrieved the DataSet, we look to see if it has any rows. If it does, we update the controls and show the Save Changes button:

```
' If the customer was found...
If customerDataset.Tables(0).Rows.Count > 0 Then

    ' ...Reset the Label Text
    lblProblem.Text = ""
    btnSaveChanges.Visible = True

    ' Update the controls
    Dim customer As DataRow = customerDataset.Tables(0).Rows(0)
    txtCompanyName.Text = customer("companyname")
```

If, on the other hand, it doesn't contain any rows, we display a message by setting the Text property of lblProblem, and hide the Save Changes button:

```
Else

    ' ...Otherwise set an error message
    lblProblem.Text = "The customer ID '" & customerId & _
                      "' does not exist"
    btnSaveChanges.Visible = False

    ' Update the controls
    txtCompanyName.Text = ""

End If
```

Ultimately, we want to update the data in the DataSet that was retrieved by the GetCustomer call. It's for this reason that we have a GetCustomer method that returns the SqlDataAdapter that retrieved the data. When Save Changes is clicked, we want to call the Update method of the adapter to commit the changes.

The first version of GetCustomer really just calls the other version of the method to retrieve the actual DataSet:

```
Dim adapter As SqlDataAdapter
Dim customer As DataSet = GetCustomer(customerId, adapter)
```

However, it does free up the adapter that is returned with a Dispose call:

```
adapter.Dispose()
```

The details of the customer in question are returned as a DataSet.

```
        Return customer
```

The second version is fairly conventional in the way it accesses the requested data. We create an adapter from a SQL command string:

```
        Dim connection As New SqlConnection(Global.DbString)
        connection.Open()

        ' Set up the SQL command object
        Dim command As New SqlCommand("SELECT customerid, companyname, " & _
                 "contactname, contacttitle, address, city, " & _
                 "region, postalcode, country, phone, fax " & _
                 "FROM customers WHERE customerid='" & customerId & "'", _
                  connection)

        ' Retrieve the data
        adapter = New SqlDataAdapter(command)

        ' Add a command builder
        Dim builder As New SqlCommandBuilder(adapter)
```

and use it to fill a DataSet.

```
        ' Fill the DataSet
        Dim customer As New DataSet()
        adapter.Fill(customer)
```

We need to have a SqlDataAdapter around to save the changes back to the database, which is what we're about to do now.

Saving Changes

Now that our application can display information that the user requests, we shall move on and add code to allow the user to make changes.

Try It Out – Saving Changes

1. Open EditCustomer.aspx in Design view, and double-click the Save Changes button. Add this code for the event handler:

```
    Private Sub btnSaveChanges_Click(ByVal sender As System.Object, _
                     ByVal e As System.EventArgs) Handles btnSaveChanges.Click

        ' Reload the customer
        Dim adapter As SqlDataAdapter
        Dim customerDataset As DataSet = GetCustomer(lblEditingId.Text, adapter)
        If customerDataset.Tables(0).Rows.Count = 0 Then
            adapter.Dispose()
            Return
        End If
```

```
        ' Update the DataGrid
        Dim customer As DataRow = customerDataset.Tables(0).Rows(0)
        customer("companyname") = txtCompanyName.Text

        ' Update the DataAdapter
        adapter.Update(customerDataset)

        ' Inform the user
        lblProblem.Text = "Your changes have been saved"
    End Sub
```

2. Run the project again. Click the **Look Up Customer** button, change the company name and click **Save Changes**. You'll notice that the value in the database has changed:

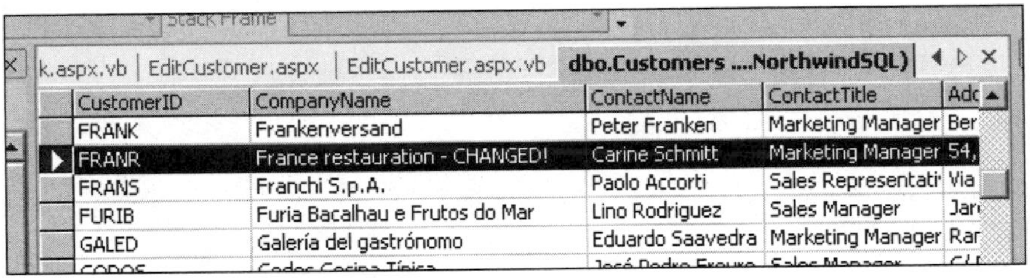

k.aspx.vb | EditCustomer.aspx | EditCustomer.aspx.vb | **dbo.Customers ....NorthwindSQL)**

CustomerID	CompanyName	ContactName	ContactTitle	Adc
FRANK	Frankenversand	Peter Franken	Marketing Manager	Ber
FRANR	France restauration - CHANGED!	Carine Schmitt	Marketing Manager	54,
FRANS	Franchi S.p.A.	Paolo Accorti	Sales Representati	Via
FURIB	Furia Bacalhau e Frutos do Mar	Lino Rodriguez	Sales Manager	Jar
GALED	Galería del gastrónomo	Eduardo Saavedra	Marketing Manager	Rar

How It Works

In this case, we've used the other version of `GetCustomer` to both retrieve the `DataSet` and retrieve the `SqlDataAdapter` that was used to populate the `DataSet` in the first place.

```
Dim adapter As SqlDataAdapter
Dim customerDataset As DataSet = GetCustomer(lblEditingId.Text, adapter)
```

Notice how we use the customer ID stored in the `Text` property of `lblEditingId`, which we know hasn't been changed since the **Lookup Customer** button was pressed.

The upshot? Whenever the **Save Changes** button is pressed, the value in the `Text` property of `txtCompanyName` is extracted and put into the `DataRow`. This marks the `DataRow` as needing to be updated.

```
' Update the DataGrid
Dim customer As DataRow = customerDataset.Tables(0).Rows(0)
customer("companyname") = txtCompanyName.Text
```

When `Update` is called, the changes are automatically saved.

```
' Update the DataAdapter
adapter.Update(customerDataset)
```

Finally, we informed the user that their changes were saved successfully:

```
lblProblem.Text = "Your changes have been saved"
```

Adding Other Fields

To consolidate what we've learnt up to now, in this section I shall quickly demonstrate how we could expand the application to show the other fields from the database. This was omitted earlier to keep the application simple, but I'd like to show how ASP.NET can let you rapidly add extra functionality to an existing web application.

Try It Out – Adding the Other Fields

1. Open `EditCustomer.aspx` in Design mode. Add two new Labels, and two new `TextBoxes` as below:

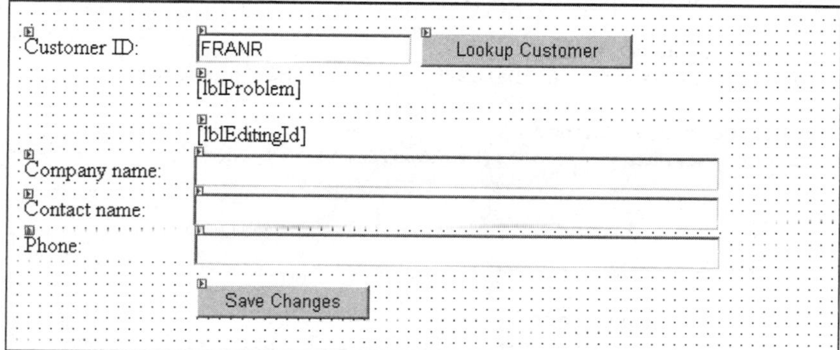

2. Change the properties of the new controls we have just added as listed in the following table:

Control	Property	Value
First `TextBox` control	ID	txtContactName
	Text	(blank)
	Width	379px
First `Label` control	ID	lblContactName
	Text	Lookup Customer
Second TextBox control	ID	txtPhone
	Text	(blank)
	Width	379px
Second Label control	ID	lblPhone
	Text	Phone:

3. There's quite a neat way to align multiple controls in Visual Studio .NET. First, click and drag a rubber band around all the text fields in question. You may need to right-click on the Toolbar and select Dialog Editor if it is not already visible. With all the TextBox controls selected, click the **Align Lefts** button, as highlighted here:

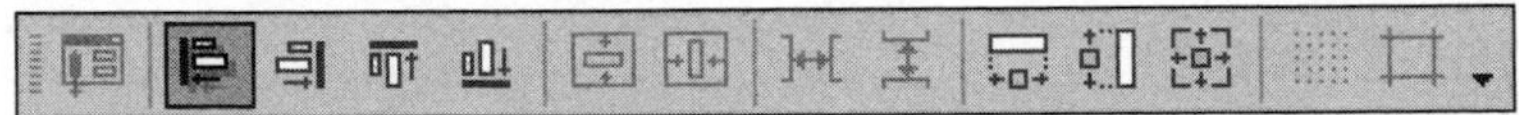

4. Repeat for the Label controls until they are all neatly arranged.

5. Open the `EditCustomer.aspx.vb` code page. Find the `BindData` method and add this code:

```
' BindData - bind the data to the controls...
Public Sub BindData(ByVal customerId As String)

    ' Set...
    lblEditingId.Text = customerId

    ' Get the customer...
    Dim customerDataset As DataSet = GetCustomer(customerId)

    ' Did we get anything?
    If customerDataset.Tables(0).Rows.Count > 0 Then

        ' Reset the text...
        lblProblem.Text = ""
        btnSaveChanges.Visible = True

        ' Update the controls...
        Dim customer As DataRow = customerDataset.Tables(0).Rows(0)
        txtCompanyName.Text = customer("companyname")
        txtContactName.Text = customer("contactname")
        txtPhone.Text = customer("phone")

    Else

        ' Set some problem text...
        lblProblem.Text = "The customer '" & customerId & "' does not exist"
        btnSaveChanges.Visible = False

        ' Update the controls...
        txtCompanyName.Text = ""
        txtContactName.Text = ""
        txtPhone.Text = ""

    End If

End Sub
```

6. Now, add this code to `btnSaveChanges_Click`:

```
Private Sub btnSaveChanges_Click(ByVal sender As System.Object, _
                ByVal e As System.EventArgs) Handles btnSaveChanges.Click

    ' Reload the customer...
    Dim adapter As SqlDataAdapter
```

```
        Dim customerDataset As DataSet = GetCustomer(lblEditingId.Text, adapter)
        If customerDataset.Tables(0).Rows.Count = 0 Then
            adapter.Dispose()
            Return
        End If

        ' Update...
        Dim customer As DataRow = customerDataset.Tables(0).Rows(0)
        customer("companyname") = txtCompanyName.Text
        customer("contactname") = txtContactName.Text
        customer("phone") = txtPhone.Text

        ' Update...
        adapter.Update(customerDataset)

        ' Tell the user...
        lblProblem.Text = "Your changes have been saved"

    End Sub
```

7. Run the project. You will now be able to make changes to any of the fields of a customer record:

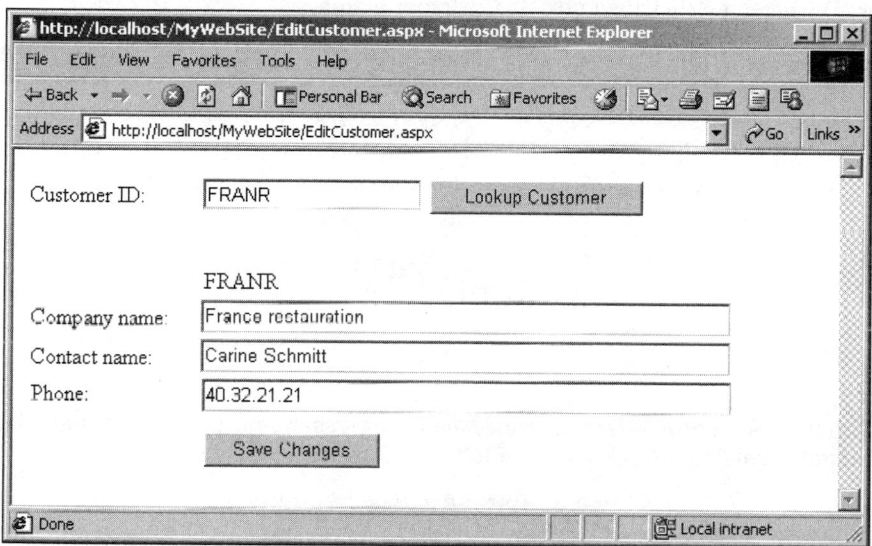

How It Works

All we have done here is add some further fields to our web page. Now when we look up the customer, we retrieve the contact name and telephone number of that company. This was done by adding the following lines to our `BindData` method:

```
txtContactName.Text = customer("contactname")
txtPhone.Text = customer("phone")
```

We are also able to make changes to these fields and save them as we added the following two lines to the `Click` event of our Save Changes button:

```
customer("contactname") = txtContactName.Text
customer("phone") = txtPhone.Text
```

Validating Data

The last thing we're going to look at in this chapter is data validation with ASP.NET. There are many situations in programming where validation is required, and web programming is no different. For example, you may have an application where the user must enter details for a customer record. You would want to ensure that a name is entered, and that the telephone number contains only digits for instance. If your applications don't provide some sort of built-in validation, if a user should enter incorrect details for some reason, they are liable to crash the application, or at best be presented with an unintelligible and ugly system error message.

In the next section, we shall add a validation control that checks to make sure that the user has entered a customer ID when they click the Look Up Customer button.

Try It Out – Checking a Field has been Supplied

1. Open `EditCustomer.aspx` in Design view. Drag a RequiredFieldValidator control from the Toolbox onto the form next to the Look Up Customer button:

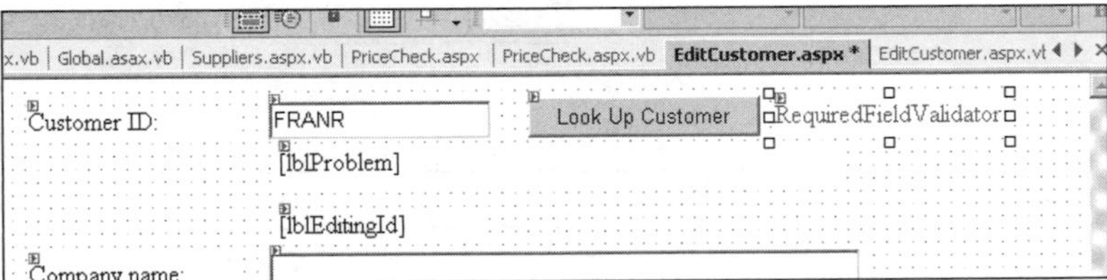

2. With the new control selected, change the ErrorMessage property to Required and set the ControlToValidate property in the Properties window to txtCustomerId.

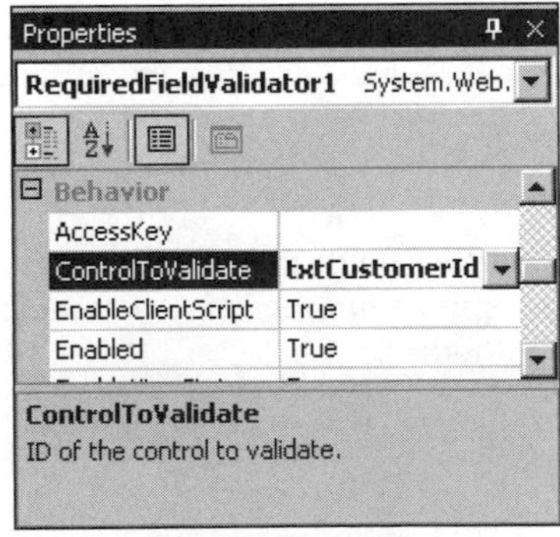

3. Run the project. Clear the `TextBox` and click the button. You should see an error message appear:

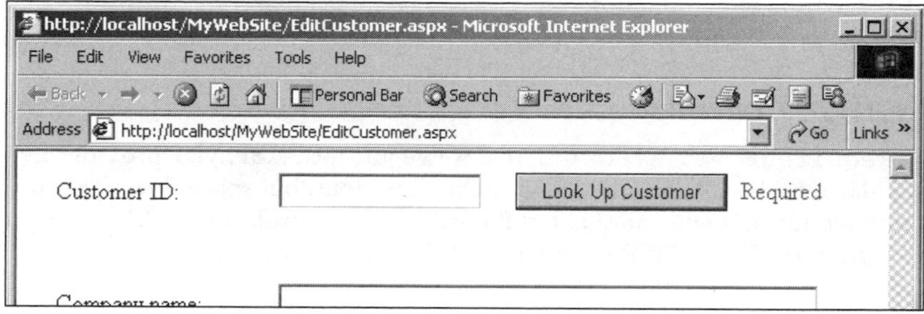

How It Works

When the server is required to do something with an ASP.NET page, it examines any validation controls on that page and checks that their validation rules have been satisfied. In our example, we added a `RequiredFieldValidator` to our web page. What this does is make the Customer ID TextBox a required field, or in other words, it cannot be left blank. If a Customer ID isn't entered into the TextBox, Required appears showing that there is an error with the data that has been entered.

Depending on the browser's capabilities, this doesn't necessarily involve a round-trip to the server. If you're using Internet Explorer 5 or above, you'll notice that the message appears the instant the button is pressed.

If you're building a web site, you want as many visitors as possible, but you want as little traffic as possible. What this means is if you have 1,000 visitors to your web site each day, you want those 1,000 visitors to make the *optimum* number of requests of the site. The word "optimum" is important here. Each web request, in effect, costs you money, not in terms of "usage fees", but in terms of infrastructure cost. Say you have a site that processes four million requests per day. It stands to reason that this server will need to be more powerful and probably require more labor to manage than a site that only gets fifty requests a day. In computing, "more powerful" typically leads to "more expensive", and that's where optimization fits in.

In the above example, when we first visit the page, we have one request. When we click "Lookup Customer", we have another request. When we click "Save Changes", we have yet one more. That's three in total. Now imagine that the user doesn't enter anything into the Customer ID field and clicks the button. Another request *could* (but actually isn't; more later) be made where the server sends back a message that says, "Customer ID required". At a worst case, this could lead to a 25% increase in the number of requests, and all for no advantage.

What JavaScript and Dynamic HTML (DHTML) do is allow us to do some of the processing on the client side. That's precisely what's happening here. The validation control is putting some JavaScript code in the page that says, "When the button is clicked, if the Customer ID field is empty, show the message." This happens without a round-trip to the server. In other words, we don't make this wasted request.

ASP.NET uses information passed in with the page request to determine whether or not the browser supports this kind of JavaScript code. If it does, the code is inserted and the page is optimized, all without you as the developer needing to understand what it does. If the browser does not (as is the case with "older" browsers; Microsoft refer to these as "down level" browsers), the old-school "re-request-the-page-and-insert-the-message" approach is used automatically.

The validation controls available in Windows Forms work in a different way, but follow a similar principle. By adding validation controls to Windows Forms, we're using the same technique of saying something like, "Make sure that TextBox has a value." Because we're guaranteed that code can always run on the desktop, there isn't this concept of choosing between using JavaScript or reprocessing the page.

Further Validation Controls

Including the `RequiredFieldValidator` that we've just met, ASP.NET provides five validation controls as standard. I'll briefly introduce you to the other four, but space doesn't permit showing how each works. If you'd like to know more about the validation controls, or ASP.NET in general, check out *Beginning ASP.NET using VB.NET* ISBN 1-861004-96-6 from Wrox Press.

RangeValidator

This control tests to see if a value is within a given numeric range. You provide upper and lower limits in the `MaximumValue` and `MinimumValue` properties.

CompareValidator

This control tests to see if a value fits a given expression. You provide the operator through the `Operator` property (`"equal"`, `"less than"`, and so on) and the type of value to compare is set by the `Type` property.

RegularExpressionValidator

This control tests to see if a value fits a given regular expression. For example, a telephone number field may need to only accept numbers in the form XXX-XXX-XXXX. You provide the regular expression that the value must match in the `ValidationExpression` property.

CustomValidator

We'll look in slightly more detail at the `CustomValidator` control, which uses a script function to test a given expression. It gives you maximum flexibility because you can customize the script function to do exactly what you want, but it always requires a round trip to the server. To use this type of control, you need to add a function to the `.aspx` page HTML code, which you can do by selecting HTML view in the Designer. The method has to be enclosed within `<SCRIPT>` tags, and must take the same parameters as the `MyServerValidation` function shown below. If the value tested meets the requirements of the script function then the `IsValid` member of the supplied `ServerValidateEventArgs` object is set to `True`.

```
<script runat=server language="vb">

   Sub MyServerValidation(ByVal source As Object, _
                          ByVal args As ServerValidateEventArgs)

      Try
         Dim i As Integer = Int32.Parse(args.Value);
         If i Mod 2 = 0 Then
            args.IsValid = True;
         Else
            args.IsValid = False;
         End If
```

```
        Catch
            args.IsValid = False;
        End Try

    End Sub

</script>
```

Summary

In this chapter, we took a look at how ASP.NET can be used to present data over the Web. Pretty quickly we were able to build powerful applications that extracted information from the NorthwindSQL database and presented it to the user.

Initially we looked at creating an ASP.NET project and building a basic Web Form. Then we went on to use the `DataList` control and saw how we could add controls (in particular, a `HyperLink` control) to the `ItemTemplate` area of that control. As the list was rendered, new link controls were automatically added for each value of the bound field.

We discussed the difference between grid layout and flow layout and learned that flow layout, although harder to use, usually gives the best results, especially when you need to support older or non-Microsoft browsers. We then wrote an application to perform a product search, presenting the results in a `DataGrid` control. We also covered ASP.NET's built-in `DataGrid` paging features and added a form to our project to allow us to edit the data and save the changes.

Finally, we went over how to validate any data that was entered in our form and the different validation methods available in Visual Basic .NET

Exercises

1. What is the `Global.asax` file used for and how do we make use of it?
2. Why doesn't the Web lend itself to control placement using Grid Layout?
3. Why doesn't the `DataReader` support paging?

Answers are available at http://p2p.wrox.com/exercises/.

ADO.NET and XML

In this chapter, we're going to be introducing the concept of Extensible Markup Language, or XML. For a while now, XML has been touted as an important technology for the storage and exchange of data and, with the advent of .NET, powerful XML functionality can be available to our application with minimal work.

In this chapter, we'll be looking at the essential nature of XML and see a few of the basic tools that are provided by .NET and ADO.NET for the creation and manipulation of XML data.

What is XML?

XML was invented as a technology for overcoming the problems involved in the relatively common activity of exchanging data between applications. However, XML is increasingly being used as a data storage and transport mechanism.

XML is one of those curious technologies that, while it seems scary to a newcomer, the principles are actually very easy to grasp. (Building an end-to-end solution using XML throughout can get a little tricky, however!) The classes available to us in the .NET Framework provide ways to read, write, and explore XML-formatted data very easily.

Despite its name, XML is probably best thought of not as a "language", but rather as a set of rules for defining markup languages. In order for applications to exchange data, the data has to be "marked up" in some way. This marking up allows an application receiving the data to make sense of it and use it in a useful manner. For example, if I give you a bit of data like this:

```
Disraeli
```

…how do we know what that data is? However, if I give you a little more information about the data, like this:

```
My Dog's Name: Disraeli
```

...then, using common sense, we can all understand what that bit of data represents. In the latter case, I've "marked up" the data. By using the English language, English-speaking readers at least can use the set of common sense rules that we all carry around in our heads to determine what I'm trying to say. XML is a "meta language" or, in other words, is self-describing – it gives the data *and* the rules to follow to determine what the data is.

As we said, XML is not a language but rather a set of standards and rules for creating your own markup languages. One of these rules is that XML documents must be **well-formed**. There are over a hundred rules for creating a well-formed XML document, but here are the three basic ones (luckily, the other ones are things you're unlikely to do anyway and so aren't of much importance):

- Every document must have exactly one top-level element.
- Elements must be closed in the reverse order that they were opened, that is, you can't do this:

  ```
  <ElementOne>Data<ElementTwo>MoreData</ElementOne></ElementTwo>
  ```

  ...because `ElementOne` is closed before `ElementTwo` is closed.
- Case sensitivity is important. `MyElement` is not the same as `mYeLEMENT`.

A Sample XML Document

XML is a fairly curious language because it seems a little "off planet" in concept until you actually start looking at some. Here is an XML document viewed in IE:

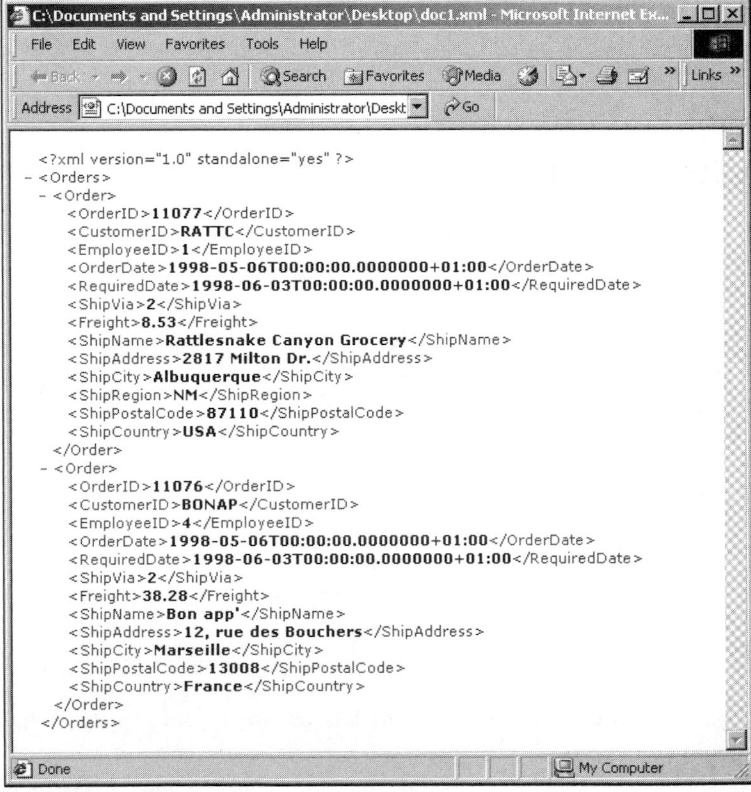

```
<?xml version="1.0" standalone="yes" ?>
- <Orders>
  - <Order>
      <OrderID>11077</OrderID>
      <CustomerID>RATTC</CustomerID>
      <EmployeeID>1</EmployeeID>
      <OrderDate>1998-05-06T00:00:00.0000000+01:00</OrderDate>
      <RequiredDate>1998-06-03T00:00:00.0000000+01:00</RequiredDate>
      <ShipVia>2</ShipVia>
      <Freight>8.53</Freight>
      <ShipName>Rattlesnake Canyon Grocery</ShipName>
      <ShipAddress>2817 Milton Dr.</ShipAddress>
      <ShipCity>Albuquerque</ShipCity>
      <ShipRegion>NM</ShipRegion>
      <ShipPostalCode>87110</ShipPostalCode>
      <ShipCountry>USA</ShipCountry>
    </Order>
  - <Order>
      <OrderID>11076</OrderID>
      <CustomerID>BONAP</CustomerID>
      <EmployeeID>4</EmployeeID>
      <OrderDate>1998-05-06T00:00:00.0000000+01:00</OrderDate>
      <RequiredDate>1998-06-03T00:00:00.0000000+01:00</RequiredDate>
      <ShipVia>2</ShipVia>
      <Freight>38.28</Freight>
      <ShipName>Bon app'</ShipName>
      <ShipAddress>12, rue des Bouchers</ShipAddress>
      <ShipCity>Marseille</ShipCity>
      <ShipPostalCode>13008</ShipPostalCode>
      <ShipCountry>France</ShipCountry>
    </Order>
  </Orders>
```

Those of you who have seen HTML code will notice that the XML files look very similar. That's because they both share a common ancestor. Standard Generalized Markup Language, or SGML, was the inspiration for both.

XML files work on the concept of tags and elements. A tag can either be a "start tag" or an "end tag" (or "both" – sometimes start and end tags are combined, but we'll see this later). Here's an example of a start tag:

```
<ShipCity>
```

...and here's an example of an end tag:

```
</ShipCity>
```

You can see that both kinds of tags start with a less-than sign and end with a greater-than sign. This is how tags are delimited. The name of the tag appears between these two signs, and, in this example, the name of the tag is `ShipCity`. The difference between a start tag and an end tag is that, on an end tag, the name is prefixed with a forward-slash character.

Together, a start tag and an end tag make an element. The text between the two tags is the data that belongs to the tag. For example:

```
<ShipCity>Albuquerque</ShipCity>
```

In this case, we have an **element** called `ShipCity`; the **value** of that element is `Albuquerque`.

Here are the elements that make up order 11077 as shown in our XML document:

- `<OrderID>11077</OrderID>`
- `<CustomerID>RATTC</CustomerID>`
- `<EmployeeID>1</EmployeeID>`
- `<OrderDate>1998-05-06T00:00:00.0000000+01:00</OrderDate>`
- `<RequiredDate>1998-06-03T00:00:00.0000000+01:00</RequiredDate>`
- `<ShipVia>2</ShipVia>`
- `<Freight>8.53</Freight>`
- `<ShipName>Rattlesnake Canyon Grocery</ShipName>`
- `<ShipAddress>2817 Milton Dr.</ShipAddress>`
- `<ShipCity>Albuquerque</ShipCity>`
- `<ShipRegion>NM</ShipRegion>`
- `<ShipPostalCode>87110</ShipPostalCode>`
- `<ShipCountry>USA</ShipCountry>`

Now life starts to get interesting. Elements can contain other elements. In this case, we have a start tag called `Order` and an end tag called `Order`.

```
<Order>
  <OrderID>11077</OrderID>
  <CustomerID>RATTC</CustomerID>
  <EmployeeID>1</EmployeeID>
  <OrderDate>1998-05-06T00:00:00.0000000+01:00</OrderDate>
  <RequiredDate>1998-06-03T00:00:00.0000000+01:00</RequiredDate>
  <ShipVia>2</ShipVia>
  <Freight>8.53</Freight>
  <ShipName>Rattlesnake Canyon Grocery</ShipName>
  <ShipAddress>2817 Milton Dr.</ShipAddress>
  <ShipCity>Albuquerque</ShipCity>
  <ShipRegion>NM</ShipRegion>
  <ShipPostalCode>87110</ShipPostalCode>
  <ShipCountry>USA</ShipCountry>
</Order>
```

Notice how the data that's contained within the `Order` element is a bunch of other elements. XML is hierarchical in nature, which means that the `Order` element contains a set of thirteen child elements, and each of those thirteen child elements represents one column from one particular row. The upshot of this is that if we have an `Order` element, we can drill down into its child elements to learn everything about the `Order` that we could possibly need to know.

If you look further into the document, you'll notice that each of the two `Order` elements is contained within a master `Orders` element. (I've omitted some elements here for clarity.)

```
<Orders>
  <Order>
   ...
  </Order>
  <Order>
   ...
  </Order>
</Orders>
```

Again, this means that, if we have an `Orders` element, we can assume that we have a list of orders contained within. We also know that each order is encapsulated in its own element called `Order`.

As we stated earlier, every XML document must have exactly one top-level element, called the **root** element. In this case, we do indeed have only one top-level element: `Orders`. If we omitted this element, the file would not be well-formed. For example, here's the same document again but without the single top-level element:

```
<Order>
 ...
</Order>
<Order>
 ...
</Order>
```

In this case, the document has two top-level elements. Under the rules of XML, this document is not well-formed – therefore it cannot be used.

Attributes

There is another way of introducing data into an XML file, although it's mainly used for "metadata", or data about the data. In this chapter, we're not going to concern ourselves with **attributes**, but here's a little information so you're aware of them. Take our `OrderID` element. If we wanted to indicate that this element was an ID column, we might add an `IsId` attribute that looks like this:

```
<OrderID IsId="True">11077</OrderID>
```

Attributes have the form of a `parameter="value"` pair, and sit within the opening tag of an element. We can have as many attributes as we like, and store any data that we like in them:

```
<OrderID IsId="True" AnotherAttribute="92384">11077</OrderID>
```

That's the basis behind XML. At this level, XML is mostly common sense and, I'm confident, pretty easy to understand. Because of this, what we'll do next is build the app that produces this output. This will bring the potentially fuzzy points of our discussion so far into sharp focus.

Creating an XML Document

In this chapter, we're going to be looking at an application that's capable of exporting the orders defined in the system to XML documents.

Try It Out – Creating the Project

1. Using Visual Studio .NET, create a new Visual Basic | Windows Application project and call it Order Export.

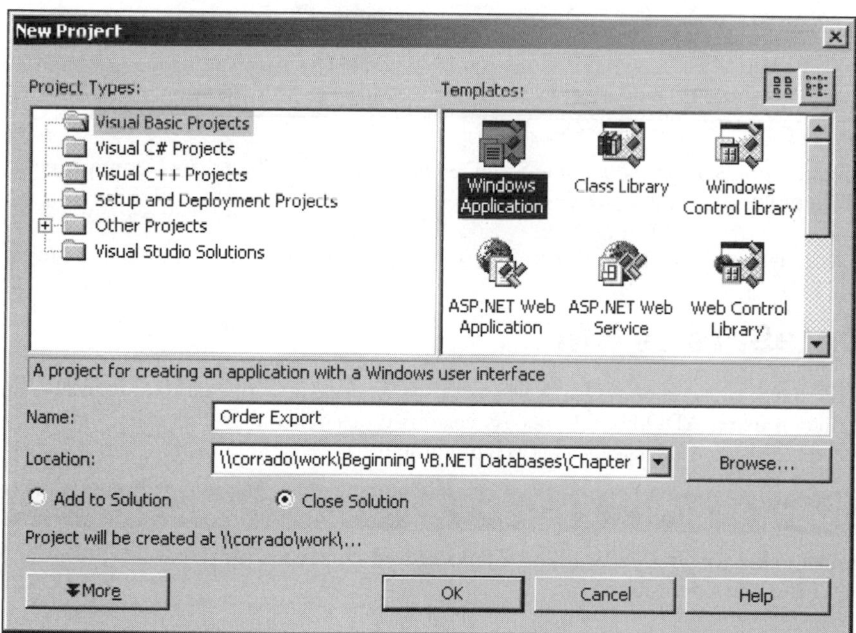

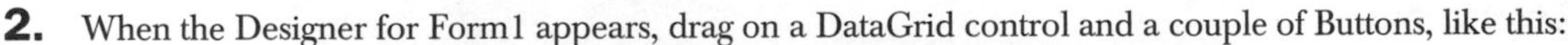

2. When the Designer for Form1 appears, drag on a DataGrid control and a couple of Buttons, like this:

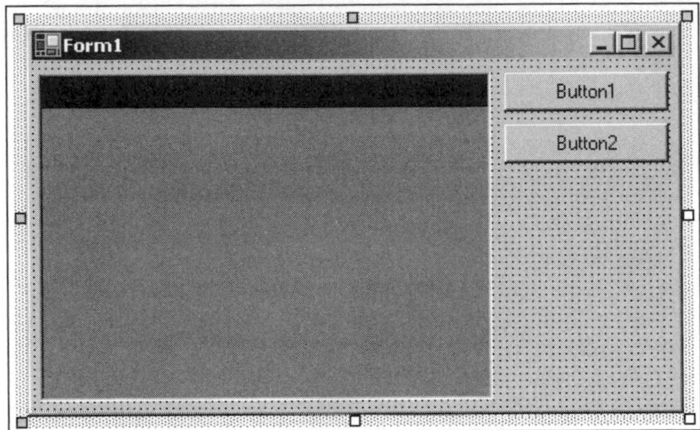

3. Change the properties for the controls in the Properties window, as shown below:

Control	Property	Value
Form1	Text	Northwind Order Export
	StartPosition	CenterScreen
DataGrid	Name	dgdOrders
	Anchor	Top, Bottom, Left, Right
Button1	Name	btnConnect
	Text	Connect
Button2	Name	btnSave
	Text	Save

4. Using the toolbox, drag on a new SaveFileDialog control. Change its Name property to dlgSaveFile.

That's the basic design of the form finished. Now we just need to add some business logic functionality.

Saving DataSets as XML

As ADO.NET has built-in support for XML – it uses XML as its internal data format – this gives us great flexibility in using ADO.NET to access various types of data. In this next section, we are going to look at how we can save `DataSets` as XML documents.

Try It Out – Saving an Order

1. Right-click on Form1 in Solution Explorer and click on View Code. Add this constant to the top of the class definition.

```
Public Class Form1
  Inherits System.Windows.Forms.Form

  ' Constants...
  Public Const DbString = _
   "integrated security=sspi;initial catalog=NorthwindSQL;data source=chimaera"
```

Remember, you *must* change the name of the server defined in `DbString` to whatever you actually use!

2. Again in the code editor, add this member:

```
Public Class Form1
  Inherits System.Windows.Forms.Form

  ' Members...
  Private _dataset As DataSet

  ' Constants...
  Public Const DbString = _
   "integrated security=sspi;initial catalog=NorthwindSQL;data source=chimaera"
```

3. Add these namespace import declarations:

```
Imports System.IO
Imports System.Xml
Imports System.Data.SqlClient

Public Class Form1
  Inherits System.Windows.Forms.Form
```

4. Flip back to the Designer and double-click on the **Connect** button. When the new `Click` event handler appears, add this code:

```
  Private Sub btnConnect_Click(ByVal sender As System.Object, _
            ByVal e As System.EventArgs) Handles btnConnect.Click

    ' Connect to the database...
    Dim connection As New sqlconnection(DbString)
    connection.Open()

    ' Create a new dataset
    Dim newDataset As New DataSet("Orders")

    ' Create a new table to hold the orders in...
    Dim ordersTable As New DataTable("Order")
    newDataset.Tables.Add(ordersTable)

    ' Load the last two orders from the database...
    Dim command As New SqlCommand("SELECT TOP 2 OrderID, CustomerID, " & _
            "EmployeeID, OrderDate, RequiredDate, ShippedDate, " & _
```

```
            "ShipVia, Freight, ShipName, ShipAddress, ShipCity, " & _
            "ShipRegion, ShipPostalCode, ShipCountry FROM Orders " & _
            "ORDER BY OrderID DESC", connection)

        ' Fill the DataSet...
        Dim adapter As New SqlDataAdapter(command)
        adapter.Fill(ordersTable)

        ' Set the DataSet property...
        Me.DataSet = newDataset

        ' Close the database...
        connection.Close()

    End Sub
```

5. Before you can run the project you'll need to add this property. This will provide a way for us to set up the data binding on the `DataGrid` when we need to display the data.

```
    ' DataSet property...
    Public Property DataSet() As DataSet
      Get
        Return _dataset
      End Get
      Set(ByVal Value As DataSet)

        ' Save it...
        _dataset = Value

        ' Bind...
        dgdOrders.DataSource = _dataset
        dgdOrders.DataMember = _dataset.Tables(0).TableName

      End Set
    End Property
```

6. Run the project and click the Connect button. You'll see something like this:

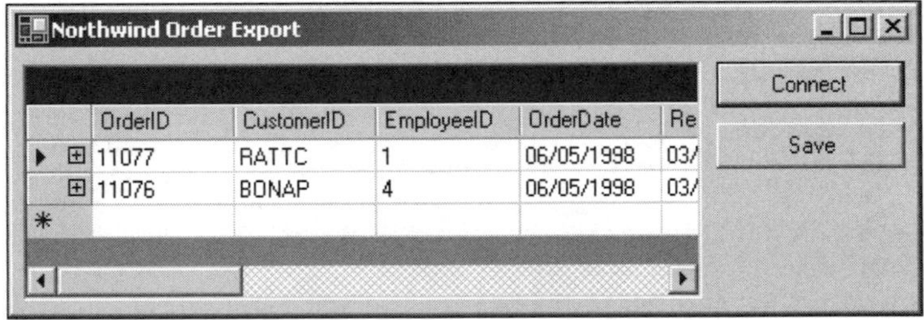

How It Works

Let's briefly walk through the code. Take your time – it's important that you get a good feel for what is going on.

When we come into the function, the first thing we do is open the database connection using the DbString constant that we previously defined.

```
    Private Sub btnConnect_Click(ByVal sender As System.Object, _
          ByVal e As System.EventArgs) Handles btnConnect.Click

      ' Connect to the database...
      Dim connection As New sqlconnection(DbString)
      connection.Open()
```

Once we have that, we create a new DataSet. We provide a name of Orders to this DataSet and the motivation for doing this will become apparent when we export the DataSet to an XML file.

```
      ' Create a new DataSet
      Dim newDataset As New DataSet("Orders")
```

Next, we create a new table within the DataSet called Order. Ultimately, in this example we want to create a set of linked tables within the DataSet and this is by far the easiest way of doing this. (For more information on this, see Chapter 7.)

```
      ' Create a new table to hold the orders in...
      Dim ordersTable As New DataTable("Order")
      newDataset.Tables.Add(ordersTable)
```

Next we create a command. We've embedded SQL code into this rather than using a stored procedure. This isn't *absolute* best practice, but I've done it here to expedite the creation of this sample. We've seen plenty of code that selects out from a stored procedure previously in the book, and we'll be seeing it again in the next two chapters.

```
      ' Load the last two orders from the database...
      Dim command As New SqlCommand("SELECT TOP 2 OrderID, CustomerID, " & _
              "EmployeeID, OrderDate, RequiredDate, ShippedDate, " & _
              "ShipVia, Freight, ShipName, ShipAddress, ShipCity, " & _
              "ShipRegion, ShipPostalCode, ShipCountry FROM Orders " & _
              "ORDER BY OrderID DESC", connection)
```

Once we've done that we create a new SqlDataAdapter object and get it to fill the new DataSet.

```
      ' Fill the DataSet...
      Dim adapter As New SqlDataAdapter(command)
      adapter.Fill(ordersTable)
```

As the last step, we set our own DataSet property to the value of the new DataSet. This has the effect of binding the new DataSet to the DataGrid control so that we can see the results.

```
      ' Set the DataSet property...
      Me.DataSet = newDataset

      ' Close the database...
      connection.Close()

    End Sub
```

Saving DataSets as XML

Our application can now get hold of orders from the database and display them on a form. What we have to do now is save them as XML.

Try It Out – Saving DataSets as XML

1. If the program is running, close it.

2. Open the Designer for Form1. Double-click on the Save button to create a new `Click` event handler. Add this code:

```
Private Sub btnSave_Click(ByVal sender As System.Object, _
            ByVal e As System.EventArgs) Handles btnSave.Click

   ' Do we have a DataSet?
   If Not DataSet Is Nothing Then

     ' Ask for a filename...
     dlgSaveFile.Filter = _
                "XML Files (*.xml)|*.xml|All Files (*.*)|*.*||"
     If dlgSaveFile.ShowDialog() = DialogResult.OK Then

       ' Save the DataSet...
       DataSet.WriteXml(dlgSaveFile.FileName)

     End If

   Else
     MsgBox ("You must connect to the database.")
   End If

End Sub
```

3. Run the project and click the Connect button. Then, click the Save button. You'll be prompted for a filename. Provide a filename somewhere on your local disk and click Save.

4. Next, using Windows Explorer, find the file and double-click it. It will open in Internet Explorer and you'll be able to see the contents.

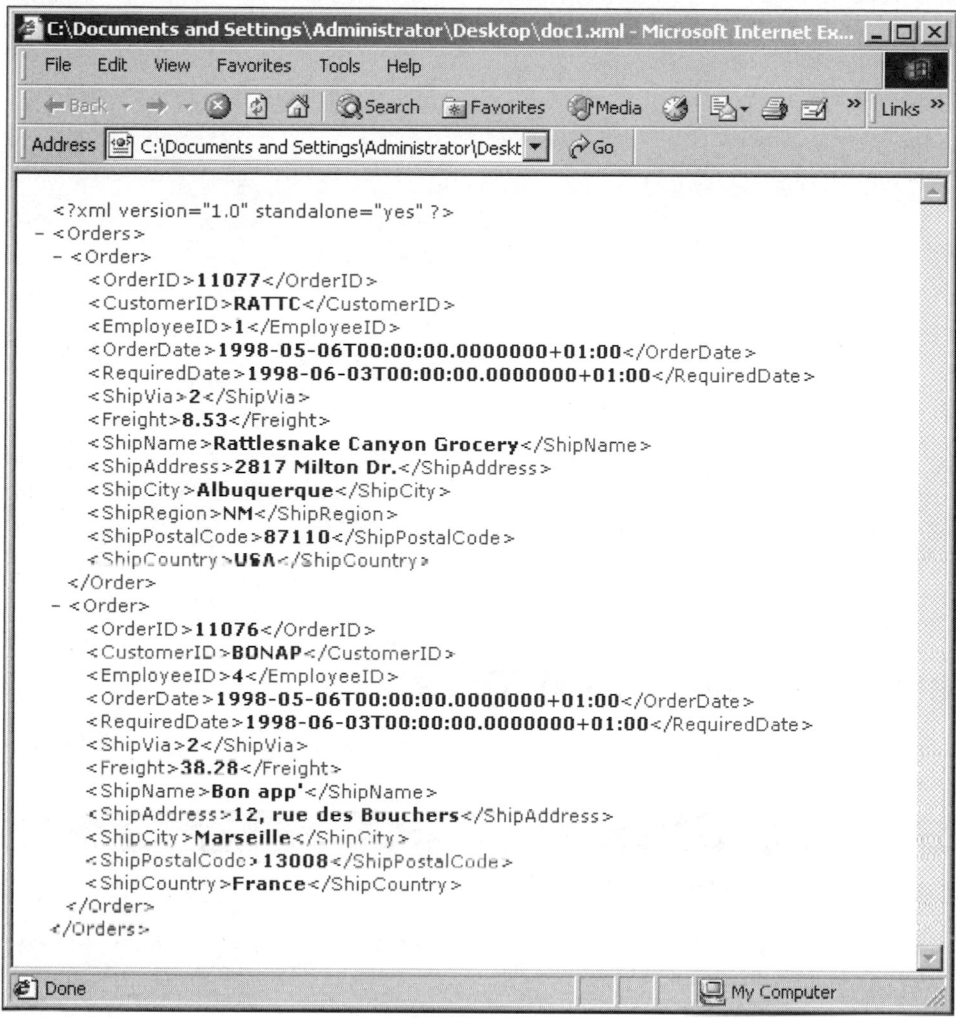

How It Works

What we have been given is a file containing an XML document that contains two orders. These two orders match, as you can see, the orders as they appear in the `DataGrid` control.

Producing an XML file from a `DataSet` is very easy. Once we know the name of the file that we want to save the `DataSet` to, we just call `WriteXml`.

```
Private Sub btnSave_Click(ByVal sender As System.Object, _
              ByVal e As System.EventArgs) Handles btnSave.Click

  ' Do we have a DataSet?
  If Not DataSet Is Nothing Then
```

```
    ' Ask for a filename...
    dlgSaveFile.Filter = _
                  "XML Files (*.xml)|*.xml|All Files (*.*)|*.*||"
    If dlgSaveFile.ShowDialog() = DialogResult.OK Then

      ' Save the DataSet...
      DataSet.WriteXml(dlgSaveFile.FileName)

    End If

  Else
    MsgBox ("You must connect to the database.")
  End If

End Sub
```

You can see that the names of each of the thirteen elements that make up the order match those defined in the database. You'll notice that `ShippedDate` is omitted from the list. That's because it has a `Null` value in the database and `Null` values are omitted from the XML.

Now let's look at why XML is such a useful tool for saving and transferring data.

Loading and Saving XML Data

Now that we know how to save a `DataSet` as XML, let's try and load the same XML file from disk and use it to populate the `DataGrid` control.

Try It Out – Loading XML Files

1. If the project is running, close it.

2. Using the Designer for Form1, draw on a new Button control. Set its Name property to btnLoad, Text property to Load and Anchor property to Top, Right.

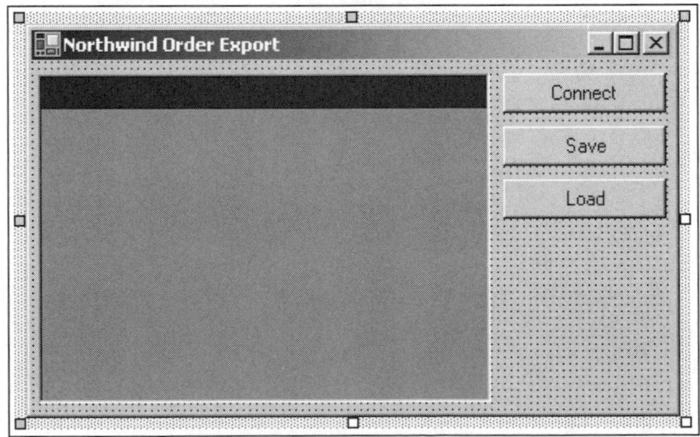

3. Again, using the Designer, draw on a new OpenFileDialog control. Change its Name property to dlgOpenFile.

4. Double-click on the Load button and add this code to the new `Click` event handler.

```
Private Sub btnLoad_Click(ByVal sender As System.Object, _
             ByVal e As System.EventArgs) Handles btnLoad.Click

  ' Display the dialog...
  dlgOpenFile.Filter = "XML Files (*.xml)|*.xml|All Files (*.*)|*.*||"
  If dlgOpenFile.ShowDialog() = DialogResult.OK Then

    ' Try and load...
    Try

      ' Create a new DataSet...
      Dim newDataset As New DataSet()

      ' Load...
      newDataset.ReadXml(dlgOpenFile.FileName)

      ' If we got here, we can load it...
      Me.DataSet = newDataset

    Catch ex As Exception
      MsgBox (ex.Message)
    End Try

  End If

End Sub
```

5. Run the project and click the Load button. (There's no need to click the Connect button.) Find the `.xml` file you saved before and click Open. The orders will be shown.

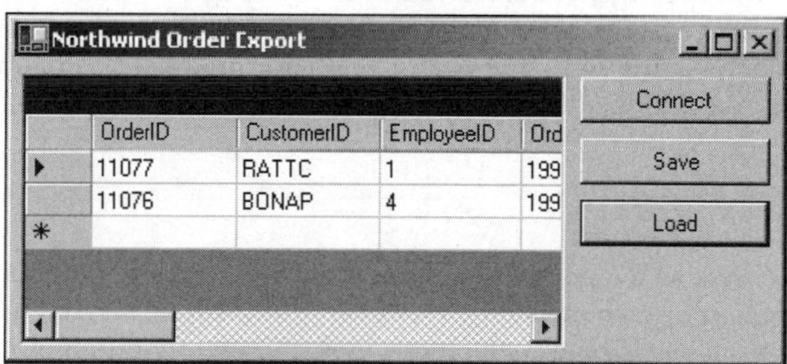

How It Works

With ADO.NET, Microsoft has tried to create a thick layer of abstraction between the database and the actual data.

Abstraction means "hiding the inner workings of" so, in this case, what ADO.NET is doing is managing all the hard work of saving a `DataSet` *to an XML file.*

Because of this abstraction, XML-formatted data stored in a file is treated in a similar way to the relational data stored in the database itself. So, we can load data from an XML file and it looks and "feels" the same as it does when we draw it from a database using the `System.Data.SqlClient` namespace.

Looking at the code, we can see that loading the data is no more complex than saving it:

```
Private Sub btnLoad_Click(ByVal sender As System.Object, _
              ByVal e As System.EventArgs) Handles btnLoad.Click

  ' Display the dialog...
  dlgOpenFile.Filter = "XML Files (*.xml)|*.xml|All Files (*.*)|*.*||"
  If dlgOpenFile.ShowDialog() = DialogResult.OK Then

    ' Try and load...
    Try

      ' Create a new DataSet...
      Dim newDataset As New DataSet()

      ' Load...
      newDataset.ReadXml(dlgOpenFile.FileName)

      ' If we got here, we can load it...
      Me.DataSet = newDataset

    Catch ex As Exception
      MsgBox(ex.Message)
    End Try

  End If

End Sub
```

What we have done is wrapped the `ReadXml` call in a `Try`...`Catch`. That's because we can't guarantee the user will select a valid XML file containing a `DataSet` that can be loaded. Apart from anything else, the user might select any file he or she chooses rather than a valid XML file that can be loaded into a `DataSet`. Now, let's take a look at how we can guarantee that the file we load always contains orders.

Schemas

One issue with XML is that, as we said before, it's a set of rules for defining markup languages. It is **extensible** – we can define our own elements. However, this also means that we need some way of understanding everyone else's elements, which can look completely different to our own. So we need to be able to define rules for XML documents that help them become as self-describing as possible. We need rules which let anyone reading the XML document understand that, for instance, "This XML file contains a list of orders as used by the NorthwindSQL database". Schemas provide a mechanism for defining rules that XML documents must adhere to, and which help everyone understand what the data held in an XML document actually is.

A schema defines how different elements can be put together to make a document of a certain type. This is done by using rules; in our XML document, we know the following rules apply:

- Our top-level element is called `Orders`.
- Our `Orders` element contains any number of `Order` elements, from zero to "infinity".
- Our `Order` element contains exactly thirteen elements, namely these and in the given order: `OrderID`, `CustomerID`, `EmployeeID`, `OrderDate`, `RequiredDate`, `ShippedDate` (if not `Null`), `ShipVia`, `Freight`, `ShipName`, `ShipAddress`, `ShipCity`, `ShipRegion`, `ShipPostalCode`, `ShipCountry`.

If we provide a schema that defines this structure along with our XML document, everyone will be able to understand the data contained within our document.

As we know, XML is a really useful technology for application integration and what a schema does is allow you to answer the question, "Does this XML file that a business partner gave me contain a list of orders specified in the manner that I am expecting?" If the answer is "Yes", the application can use the data and do something useful. If "No", the application can do something to tell the business partner that something is wrong with the file.

Schemas are a great way of making sure that, once you have a document, you can be confident that the document fits in with your business rules. Imagine you set up a piece of software that receives XML documents through e-mail or some other mechanism (we will look at a situation like this in the Case Study). Each of these documents contains an order from your customers, but you will need those documents to follow certain rules if your application is to be able to use them. For example, the document must contain a customer ID, a delivery address, and each line in the order must specify a product ID, a quantity, and a unit price.

Before you start processing an XML document, it's important to ask whether the document is **valid**, that is, whether it complies with the structure defined in your schema. We'll look at this concept in more detail later.

For now, the best way to understand schemas is to generate one, so let's do that now.

Try It Out – Generating a Schema

1. If the project is running, close it.

2. Open the code editor for Form1. Add this property:

```
' SchemaFilename - returns the file used to store a schema...
Public ReadOnly Property SchemaFilename() As String
  Get

    ' Get the app folder...
    Dim fileInfo As New FileInfo(Application.ExecutablePath)
    Dim folderName As String = fileInfo.DirectoryName

    ' Return the name...
    Return folderName & "\OrdersSchema.xml"

  End Get
End Property
```

3. Again using the code editor, find the definition for `btnConnect_Click`. Add this line just after you set the `DataSet` property:

```
...

    ' Set the DataSet property...
    Me.DataSet = newDataset

    ' Save the schema...
    newDataset.WriteXmlSchema(SchemaFilename)

    ' Close the database...
    connection.Close()

  End Sub
```

4. Run the project and click the Connect button. The two orders will be displayed as normal.

5. Find the folder where Visual Studio .NET creates the `Order_Export.exe` file. This will normally be in the `bin` folder directly beneath the folder in which you created the project.

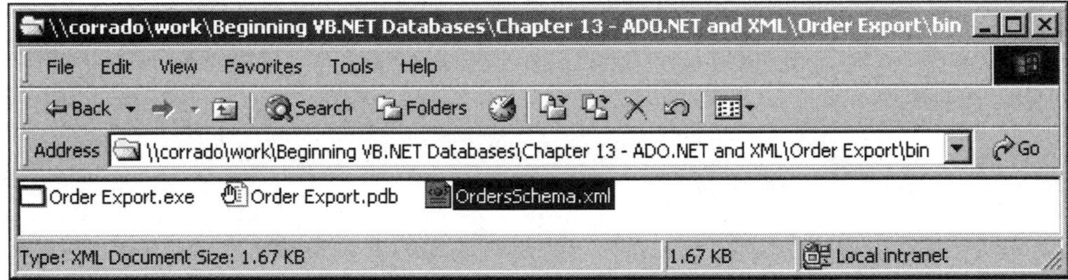

6. Double-click on the OrdersSchema.xml file. You'll see this:

Address C:\Documents and Settings\Administrator\Deskt Go

```
  <?xml version="1.0" standalone="yes" ?>
- <xsd:schema id="Orders" targetNamespace="" xmlns=""
    xmlns:xsd="http://www.w3.org/2001/XMLSchema"
    xmlns:msdata="urn:schemas-microsoft-com:xml-msdata">
  - <xsd:element name="Orders" msdata:IsDataSet="true"
      msdata:Locale="en-GB">
    - <xsd:complexType>
      - <xsd:choice maxOccurs="unbounded">
        - <xsd:element name="Order">
          - <xsd:complexType>
            - <xsd:sequence>
                <xsd:element name="OrderID"
                  type="xsd:int" minOccurs="0" />
                <xsd:element name="CustomerID"
                  type="xsd:string" minOccurs="0" />
                <xsd:element name="EmployeeID"
                  type="xsd:int" minOccurs="0" />
```

Done My Computer

How It Works

Creating the schema is no problem – the `DataSet` does it for us based on its understanding of the tables that it contains. We do this by calling `WriteXmlSchema`.

We're not going to learn about schemas in great detail as, by and large, it's easier to get .NET to generate them for us and use them. This, of course, doesn't apply if we've been given a schema to work to by a partner organization. We're only going to provide a brief overview of schemas here but XML is such an important language that you really will benefit from gaining a comprehensive understanding of it. A good place to start is by looking at *Beginning XML* (Wrox Press, ISBN 1861005598).

The first line of the file tells us that we're looking at an XML document, which also tells us that schemas are actually XML documents in their own right.

```
<?xml version="1.0" standalone="yes"?>
```

The next line defines the top-level element for an XML schema, `xsd:schema`. You'll notice that there are several attributes in this element:

```
<xsd:schema id="Orders" targetNamespace="" xmlns=""
xmlns:xsd="http://www.w3.org/2001/XMLSchema" xmlns:msdata="urn:schemas-microsoft-
com:xml-msdata">
```

The next element is the `xsd:element`. This is the first rule we define. In this case, we use the `name` attribute to define the rule, "The first element in the file will be called `Orders`." We can now see how the file is becoming self-describing:

```
<xsd:element name="Orders" msdata:IsDataSet="true" msdata:Locale="en-GB">
```

The next element is `xsd:complextype`. This tells us that the `Orders` element contains other elements:

```
<xsd:complexType>
```

This is followed by `xsd:choice`. These elements are used to add additional rules to the element that we're working with. In this case, we've said the `maxOccurs` is `unbounded`, meaning that there's no limit to the number of elements that `Orders` can contain:

```
<xsd:choice maxOccurs="unbounded">
```

Then we have an `xsd:element`. This creates the rule that "`Orders` contain `Order` elements."

```
<xsd:element name="Order">
```

Again, we can use `xsd:complexType` to beef this up to "`Orders` contain an unbounded number of `Order` elements."

```
<xsd:complexType>
```

xsd:sequence is then used to say that Order elements contain the following set of elements, in order.

```
<xsd:sequence>
```

Then we have the block of elements, each one representing a column in the Orders table. The attributes on each xsd:element tag tell us the name of the column, the type of the column, and the minimum times that each one will occur:

```
<xsd:element name="OrderID" type="xsd:int" minOccurs="0" />
<xsd:element name="CustomerID" type="xsd:string" minOccurs="0" />
<xsd:element name="EmployeeID" type="xsd:int" minOccurs="0" />
```

You'll notice that we appear to have omitted an end tag for each of the fourteen elements. That's because, if we end a start tag with a forward-slash, we're telling whoever is reading the XML not to expect an end tag as the element contains no data. This is a useful tool for saving space when writing XML files.

Finally, we close all of the elements that we have opened in reverse order:

```
      </xsd:sequence>
      </xsd:complexType>
    </xsd:element>
    </xsd:choice>
  </xsd:complexType>
  </xsd:element>
</xsd:schema>
```

Again, at this introductory level, the way an XML schema file is constructed is common sense and, like we said, it's usually easier to get .NET to create the schemas for us.

Let's look in more detail at why we need schemas.

Checking the Validity of a Document

Earlier in this chapter, we learned that an XML file must be well-formed. (We know that a document is well-formed because .NET will never load a document that isn't.) This is only half the battle because we need to know whether the data contained within fits the format that we require. If the data fits the format, we say that it is **valid**. Since we can use XML schemas to define rules, it follows that we are able to use XML schemas to determine the validity of an XML file.

Try It Out – Creating a DataSet from a Schema

1. If the project is running, close it.

2. Using the code editor for Form1, find the btnLoad_Click method. Add the highlighted line and comment out the ReadXml call, like this:

```
Private Sub btnLoad_Click(ByVal sender As System.Object, _
              ByVal e As System.EventArgs) Handles btnLoad.Click
```

```
    ' Display the dialog...
    dlgOpenFile.Filter = "XML Files (*.xml)|*.xml|All Files (*.*)|*.*||"
    If dlgOpenFile.ShowDialog() = DialogResult.OK Then

      ' Try and load...
      Try

        ' Create a new DataSet...
        Dim newDataset As New DataSet()

        ' Load the schema...
        newDataset.ReadXmlSchema(SchemaFilename)

        ' Load...
        ' newDataset.ReadXml(dlgOpenFile.FileName)

        ' If we got here, we can load it...
        Me.DataSet = newDataset

      Catch ex As Exception
        MsgBox(ex.Message)
      End Try

    End If

  End Sub
```

3. Run the project. Click the Load button and open the XML file you saved earlier. You should see this:

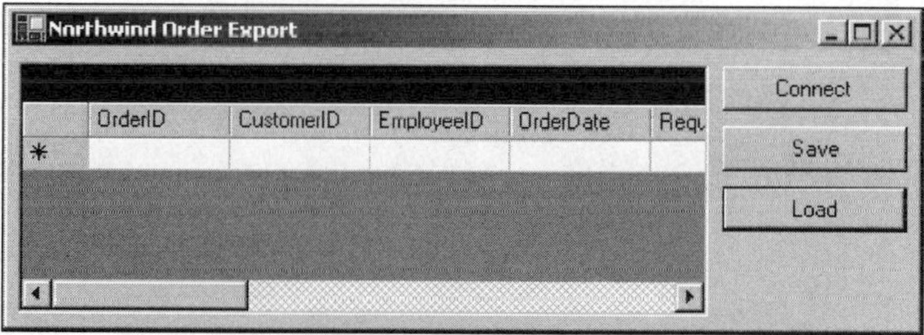

How It Works

What I'm trying to demonstrate here is that the schema file contains everything that the `DataSet` needs in order to generate the table and columns within that table, into which data can be loaded. Calling the `ReadXmlSchema` method to load the schema, but not calling `ReadXml` to read the actual data, creates a blank table with all the correct columns but no data.

The principle now is that, when we load the XML file using `ReadXml`, if the columns as they are defined in the XML file do not match the columns as defined in the schema, we can assume that the file is not valid and therefore we shouldn't try to process the data contained within it.

Checking Validity

Let's try that now.

Try It Out – Checking Validity

1. If the project is running, close it.

2. Using the code editor, find the `btnLoad_Click` method again. Take the comment out before `ReadXml`.

```
...

        ' Load the schema...
        newDataset.ReadXmlSchema(SchemaFilename)

        ' Load...
        newDataset.ReadXml(dlgOpenFile.FileName)

        ' If we got here, we can load it...
        Me.DataSet = newDataset

      Catch ex As Exception
        MsgBox(ex.Message)
      End Try

    End If

  End Sub
```

3. Run the project and click **Load**. You should see the data as normal.

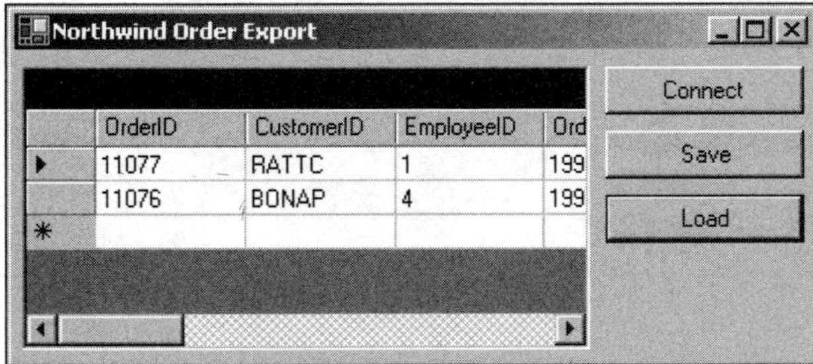

4. Find the XML file that we created previously and make a copy of it.

5. Now, open up a copy of Windows Notepad and open the *copy* of the XML file. Visual Studio .NET contains an XML editor if you'd prefer to use that. Change the name of the `Orders` start tag to `MyOrderList` and make the same change to the matching end tag. (I have shortened the file below for brevity.)

```
<?xml version="1.0" standalone="yes"?>
<MyOrdersList>
 <Order>
  <OrderID>11077</OrderID>
  <CustomerID>RATTC</CustomerID>

...

  <ShipCountry>France</ShipCountry>
 </Order>
</MyOrdersList>
```

6. To use the schema validation classes in Visual Basic .NET, we need to add a reference to the System.Xml.dll assembly as this contains the classes that we need for schema validation. To do this, stop the application from running and then, using Solution Explorer, right-click on the Order Export project and select Add Reference. This will open the Add Reference dialog box.

7. Using the list on the .NET tab. find the System.Xml.dll assembly. Select it, then click the Select button, and then OK.

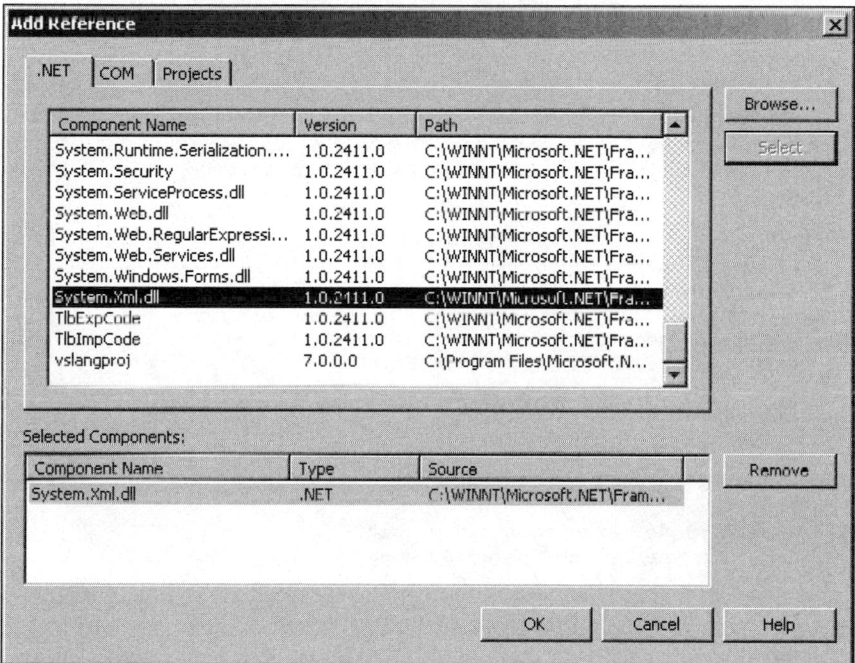

8. Next, open the code editor for `Form1`. Find the namespace import declarations at the top of the code listing and add this new one:

```
Imports System.IO
Imports System.Xml
Imports System.Xml.Schema
Imports System.Data.SqlClient
```

9. We need to make some changes to the `btnLoad_Click` implementation. Remove the `ReadXmlSchema` call and add this new code:

```
Private Sub btnLoad_Click(ByVal sender As System.Object, _
              ByVal e As System.EventArgs) Handles btnLoad.Click

  ' Display the dialog...
  dlgOpenFile.Filter = "XML Files (*.xml)|*.xml|All Files (*.*)|*.*||"
  If dlgOpenFile.ShowDialog() = DialogResult.OK Then

    ' Try and load...
    Try

      ' Create a new DataSet...
      Dim newDataset As New DataSet()

      ' Load the schema...
      newDataset.ReadXmlSchema(SchemaFilename)

      ' Create a validating reader...
      Dim reader As New XmlTextReader(dlgOpenFile.FileName)
      Dim validatingReader As New XmlValidatingReader(reader)

      ' Load our DataSet's schema into the reader...
      validatingReader.Schemas.Add(Nothing, SchemaFilename)

      ' Walk through the document element by element...
      Do While True
        If validatingReader.Read() = False Then Exit Do
      Loop

      ' Close...
      reader.Close()
      validatingReader.Close()

      ' Load the document...
      newDataset.ReadXml(dlgOpenFile.FileName)

      ' If we got here, we can load it...
      Me.DataSet = newDataset

    Catch ex As Exception

      ' What type of exception did we get?
      If ex.GetType Is GetType(XmlSchemaException) Then
        MsgBox ("The XML file is not valid: " & ex.Message)
      Else
        MsgBox("A general exception occured: " & ex.Message)
      End If

    End Try

  End If

End Sub
```

10. Now run the project. Click the Load button and open the *copy* of the XML file, the one that you changed. You should see a message similar to this:

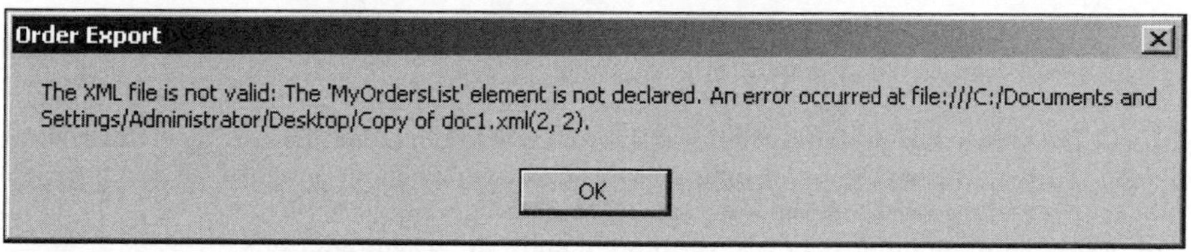

11. Click OK and press the **Load** button again. Open the original XML file and you should see the orders loaded as normal.

How It Works

By changing the copied file, we created a new XML document that didn't fit the rules as defined in the schema. The schema defined a rule that said, "The first element you come across will be called `Orders`" but, in the file, the first element is called `MyOrdersList`. The validation properly discovered the error and told us about it.

Because reading and validating an XML file takes longer and requires more resources than just reading it, by default the .NET classes that work with XML won't validate against a schema unless we specifically tell them to. To do this, we have to open the file manually using a `System.Xml.XmlTextReader` object. This class allows us to walk through the document piece-by-piece. We'll show exactly how this works in a little while.

```
Private Sub btnLoad_Click(ByVal sender As System.Object, _
              ByVal e As System.EventArgs) Handles btnLoad.Click

   ' Display the dialog...
   dlgOpenFile.Filter = "XML Files (*.xml)|*.xml|All Files (*.*)|*.*||"
   If dlgOpenFile.ShowDialog() = DialogResult.OK Then

     ' Try and load...
     Try

       ' Create a new DataSet...
       Dim newDataset As New DataSet()

       ' Load the schema...
       newDataset.ReadXmlSchema(SchemaFilename)

       ' Create a validating reader...
       Dim reader As New XmlTextReader(dialogOpenFile.FileName)
```

Once we have a reader, we create a `System.Xml.XmlValidatingReader` object. This type of object has the intelligence to determine if the XML file confirms to a schema that we give it.

```
       Dim validatingReader As New XmlValidatingReader(reader)
```

When the object is first created, it has no knowledge of any schemas, so we give it one:

```
' Load our DataSet's schema into the reader...
validatingReader.Schemas.Add(Nothing, SchemaFilename)
```

This is just half the battle though. We have to walk through the document element by element until something goes wrong. We use the `Read` method to walk through each node in the document and this method will return `False` when we reach the end. If something does go wrong, an exception will be thrown and, seeing as we're inside a `Try...Catch`, we'll know about this later on.

```
' Walk through the document element by element...
Do While True
  If validatingReader.Read() = False Then Exit Do
Loop
```

Once we've walked through the file we need to close both readers:

```
' Close...
reader.Close()
validatingReader.Close()
```

Once we get to this point, we're guaranteed that the document is valid so we can load it into the `DataSet` and set the `DataSet` property to display it on the `DataGrid`:

```
' Load the document...
newDataset.ReadXml(dlgOpenFile.FileName)

' If we got here, we can load it...
Me.DataSet = newDataset
```

So, what happens if an exception has been thrown? Well, we're going to get one of two possible types of exception: either a file can't be opened or something else goes wrong; or something specifically related to the validation happens. We can retrieve the `System.Type` object associated with the exception and choose what to do in each case.

```
      Catch ex As Exception
        ' What type of exception did we get?
        If ex.GetType Is GetType(XmlSchemaException) Then
          MsgBox("The XML file is not valid: " & ex.Message)
        Else
          MsgBox("A general exception occured: " & ex.Message)
        End If

      End Try

    End If

  End Sub
```

Relational Data

At this point we know how to load and save XML data directly using the `DataSet`. We also know how to generate schemas and how to use those schemas for validation. However, at this point, we've only seen what happens when we have a single table. As we've already seen in earlier chapters, the `DataGrid` control is capable of letting us navigate around different tables pretty easily.

In this section we'll extend what we have so that, when we have an order shown in the `DataGrid`, we can drill down to see the lines that make up that order.

Try It Out – Relating the "Order Details" Table

1. If the project is running, close it.

2. Using the code editor, find the code for `Form1`. Make these changes to `btnConnect_Click`.

```
Private Sub btnConnect_Click(ByVal sender As System.Object, _
                  ByVal e As System.EventArgs) Handles btnConnect.Click

  ' Connect to the database...
  Dim connection As New sqlconnection(DbString)
  connection.Open()

  ' Create a new dataset
  Dim newDataset As New DataSet("Orders")

  ' Create a new table to hold the orders in...
  Dim ordersTable As New DataTable("Order")
  newDataset.Tables.Add(ordersTable)

  ' Load the last two orders from the database...
  Dim command As New SqlCommand("SELECT TOP 2 OrderID, CustomerID, " & _
       "EmployeeID, OrderDate, RequiredDate, ShippedDate, " & _
       "ShipVia, Freight, ShipName, ShipAddress, ShipCity, " & _
       "ShipRegion, ShipPostalCode, ShipCountry FROM Orders " & _
       "ORDER BY OrderID DESC", connection)

  ' Fill the DataSet...
  Dim adapter As New SqlDataAdapter(command)
  adapter.Fill(ordersTable)

  ' Create a new table to hold the order details on...
  Dim detailsTable As New DataTable("Detail")
  newDataset.Tables.Add(detailsTable)

  ' Form a SQL string so that we only get the details that are
  ' included in the first table...
  Dim sql As String, row As DataRow
  For Each row In ordersTable.Rows

    ' Create a SQL snippet...
    If sql <> "" Then sql &= " or "
```

```
        sql &= "OrderID=" & row("orderid")

      Next

      ' Do we need to bother?
      If sql <> "" Then

        ' Create a new command...
        sql = "SELECT OrderID, ProductID, UnitPrice, Quantity, Discount " & _
                          "FROM [Order Details] WHERE " & sql
        Dim detailsCommand As New SqlCommand(sql, connection)

        ' Fill the new table...
        Dim detailsAdapter As New SqlDataAdapter(detailsCommand)
        detailsAdapter.Fill(detailsTable)

        ' Create the new relationship...
        newDataset.Relations.Add("Details", _
              ordersTable.Columns("OrderID"), detailsTable.Columns("OrderID"))

      End If

      ' Set the DataSet property...
      Me.DataSet = newDataset

      ' Save the schema...
      newDataset.WriteXmlSchema(SchemaFilename)

      ' Close the database...
      connection.Close()

    End Sub
```

3. Run the project and click **Connect**. You'll be able to use the "plus" buttons to show the **Details** link.

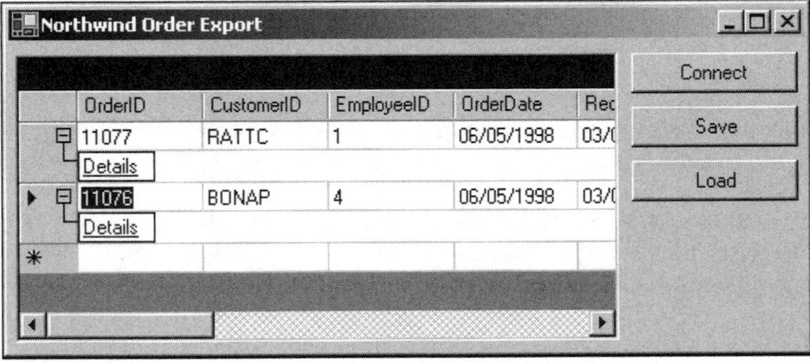

4. If you click on one of the **Details** links, you'll be able to see the related data.

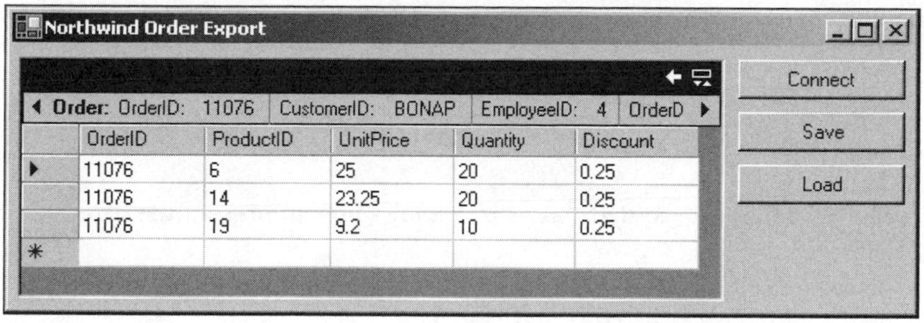

Northwind Order Export

Order: OrderID: 11076 | CustomerID: BONAP | EmployeeID: 4 | OrderD

OrderID	ProductID	UnitPrice	Quantity	Discount
11076	6	25	20	0.25
11076	14	23.25	20	0.25
11076	19	9.2	10	0.25

Connect

Save

Load

How It Works

None of that should be too new to you, as I'm sure you're comfortable with linking tables with `DataRelation` objects in this way. (See Chapter 7 for more details.)

It's worth taking a quick look at a portion of the code that we added. When we load a list of orders from the database into `ordersTable`, we need to load corresponding details in `detailsTable`. The way we do this is by looping through all the rows in `ordersTable` and creating a SQL snippet.

```
' Form a SQL string so that we only get the details that are
' included in the first table...
Dim sql As String, row As DataRow
For Each row In ordersTable.Rows

  ' Create a SQL snippet...
  If sql <> "" Then sql &= " or "
  sql &= "OrderID=" & row("orderid")

Next
```

Once we've been through that loop, our `sql` variable will be set to:

```
OrderID=11077 or OrderID=11076
```

We can combine this with the larger SQL statement to get this:

```
SELECT OrderID, ProductID, UnitPrice, Quantity, Discount FROM [Order Details]
   WHERE OrderID=11077 OR OrderID=11076
```

...and that's precisely what we do next.

```
' Do we need to bother?
If sql <> "" Then

  ' Create a new command...
  sql = "SELECT OrderID, ProductID, UnitPrice, Quantity, Discount " & _
              "FROM [Order Details] WHERE " & sql
  Dim detailsCommand As New SqlCommand(sql, connection)
```

Once we have the command, we can populate the detailsTable DataTable object as normal:

```
' Fill the new table...
Dim detailsAdapter As New SqlDataAdapter(detailsCommand)
detailsAdapter.Fill(detailsTable)
```

Finally, we create a relationship so that DataGrid knows how to present the data:

```
    ' Create the new relationship...
    newDataset.Relations.Add("Details", _
         ordersTable.Columns("OrderID"), detailsTable.Columns("OrderID"))

  End If
```

Now that we've proven we can load relational data, we need to look at what effect this has on our code to write the XML file.

Saving the DataSet

Saving the data isn't even worth a "Try It Out...How It Works"! Run the project, click **Connect**, and then click **Save**. Save the file with a different name to the one you used before.

Now find the file in Windows Explorer and open it. I've omitted quite a bit of XML here for brevity.

```
<Orders>
 <Order>
 <OrderID>11077</OrderID>
 <CustomerID>RATTC</CustomerID>
 <EmployeeID>1</EmployeeID>
 <OrderDate>1998-05-06T00:00:00.0000000+01:00</OrderDate>
 <RequiredDate>1998-06-03T00:00:00.0000000+01:00</RequiredDate>
 <ShipVia>2</ShipVia>
 <Freight>8.53</Freight>
 <ShipName>Rattlesnake Canyon Grocery</ShipName>
 <ShipAddress>2817 Milton Dr.</ShipAddress>
 <ShipCity>Albuquerque</ShipCity>
 <ShipRegion>NM</ShipRegion>
 <ShipPostalCode>87110</ShipPostalCode>
 <ShipCountry>USA</ShipCountry>
 </Order>
 <Order>
 ...
 </Order>
 <Detail>
 ...
 </Detail>
 <Detail>
 ...
 </Detail>
 <Detail>
```

```
  ...
  </Detail>
  <Detail>
  <OrderID>11077</OrderID>
  <ProductID>2</ProductID>
  <UnitPrice>19</UnitPrice>
  <Quantity>24</Quantity>
  <Discount>0.2</Discount>
  </Detail>
  ...
</Orders>
```

First of all, what's important here is noticing that we don't need to change the code that saves the `DataSet` as an XML file, even though we've changed the structure of the `DataSet`.

What's also important is that there's no physical link in the XML file between details and orders. It would make sense that the three `Detail` elements associated with order 11077 actually appeared *within* the `Order` element for 11077.

But, for now, just bear in mind that we've changed the structure of the `DataSet`, yet the data can still be written out as XML without any changes.

Loading the DataSet Again

OK, so when we clicked the Connect button, we made a call to `DataSet.WriteXmlSchema` and created a new schema. This schema contains the details for the `Detail` elements and also contains details of the relationship between `Order` and `Detail` elements.

If you open the `OrdersSchema.xml` file again, towards the bottom you'll find this:

```
<xsd:element name="Detail">
 <xsd:complexType>
 <xsd:sequence>
  <xsd:element name="OrderID" type="xsd:int" minOccurs="0" />
  <xsd:element name="ProductID" type="xsd:int" minOccurs="0" />
  <xsd:element name="UnitPrice" type="xsd:decimal" minOccurs="0" />
  <xsd:element name="Quantity" type="xsd:short" minOccurs="0" />
  <xsd:element name="Discount" type="xsd:float" minOccurs="0" />
 </xsd:sequence>
 </xsd:complexType>
</xsd:element>
```

Again, nothing complex there, we're just defining an element called `Detail` and specifying the five elements that it contains. Notice that `Detail` and `Order` appear as sibling elements in the document – they're at the same level. They'll appear as siblings to each other in the final XML document too.

Beneath, you'll see this:

```
<xsd:unique name="Constraint1">
 <xsd:selector xpath=".//Order" />
 <xsd:field xpath="OrderID" />
</xsd:unique>
```

This block is used to create a constraint, specifically one called `Constraint1` that's used to specify that the `OrderID` element contained within the `Order` element is unique.

Finally, you'll see this:

```
<xsd:keyref name="Details" refer="Constraint1">
 <xsd:selector xpath=".//Detail" />
 <xsd:field xpath="OrderID" />
</xsd:keyref>
```

What this tells us is that we have a relationship called `Details` that links `Constraint1` to the `OrderID` element within `Detail` elements. By definition, `Constraint1` refers to the `OrderID` element within `Order` elements and therefore we know that the `OrderID` in `Order` links to the `OrderID` in `Detail`.

Now, run the project and click **Connect** and then **Load**. You'll see this:

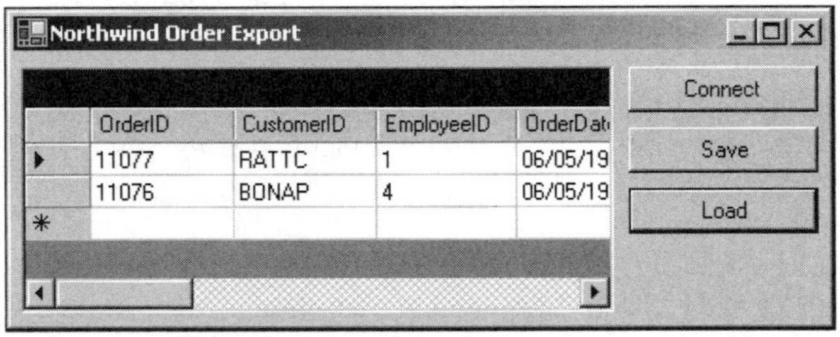

The trick here is that we've continued to use `ReadXmlSchema` as soon as the new `DataSet` is created. (I've omitted code here for brevity.)

```
Private Sub btnLoad_Click(ByVal sender As System.Object, _
            ByVal e As System.EventArgs) Handles btnLoad.Click

  ' Display the dialog...
  dlgOpenFile.Filter = "XML Files (*.xml)|*.xml|All Files (*.*)|*.*||"
  If dlgOpenFile.ShowDialog() = DialogResult.OK Then

    ' Try and load...
    Try

      ' Create a new DataSet...
      Dim newDataset As New DataSet()
```

```
        ' Load the schema...
        newDataset.ReadXmlSchema(SchemaFilename)

        ' Create a validating reader...
              ...

        ' If we got here, we can load it...
        Me.DataSet = newDataset

      Catch ex As Exception
            ...
      End Try

    End If

  End Sub
```

Because the schema contains details on the relationship between Orders and Order Details, when the data is loaded from XML, the relationship "sticks" and the `DataGrid` is able to present the information properly.

> **Remember, because we've created a new `OrdersSchema.xml` file, you won't be able to load the old XML files that don't contain `Detail` elements.**

XmlDataDocument

The last important class that we need to look at with respect to using XML with `DataSets` is `System.Xml.XmlDataDocument`.

`XmlDataDocument` "wraps" a `DataSet` but maintains a continuous connection between the document and the `Dataset`. This means that changes to the XML document are instantly reflected in the `DataSet` and changes to the `DataSet` are instantly reflected in the XML document.

In this section, we'll take a look at a couple of ways in which this object can be used.

Changing the XML Changes the DataSet

For this exercise, we'll imagine that we've been given an XML document that contains an order from a customer. However, we'll say that we've recently made some changes to our product portfolio and we're going to substitute some product IDs with other product IDs. What we'll do is go through the XML document element by element and do a search and replace.

In order to get this example working, you're going to have to look at the data stored in your copy of NorthwindSQL. We need to find a product ID.

Try It Out – Finding a Product ID

1. Run the project and click either the Connect or Load button to get some data.

2. Of the two orders you have, choose one. (I've chosen one with the least amount of detail rows associated with it.) Expand the details.

3. Look through the details and choose a product ID *that appears in the details list.* I've chosen 14 but, as I say, you'll need to choose one that appears in your list.

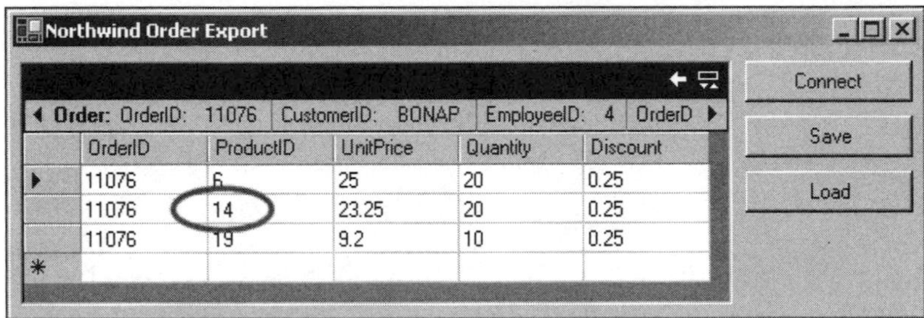

4. Note down the product ID. You'll need it in a moment.

Making Changes

Now that you have a product ID, you can start writing code!

Try It Out – Changing Data in an XmlDataDocument

1. If the project is running, close it.

2. Using Solution Explorer, right-click on the Order Export project and select Add | Add Class. Call the new class DataReplace.

3. When the code editor for `DataReplace` is opened, add this code:

```
Public Class DataReplace

   ' Members...
   Public ElementName As String
   Public LookFor As String
   Public ReplaceWith As String

End Class
```

4. Again, using Solution Explorer, create a new class called `DataReplaceCollection`. Add this code:

```
Public Class DataReplaceCollection
   Inherits CollectionBase
```

```
  ' Add - add an item...
  Public Sub Add(ByVal replace As DataReplace)
    list.Add(replace)
  End Sub

End Class
```

5. Next, open the code editor for `Form1`. Add this member:

```
Public Class Form1
  Inherits System.Windows.Forms.Form

  ' Members...
  Private _dataset As DataSet
  Private _document As XmlDataDocument
```

6. Find the `DataSet` property and add this code:

```
' DataSet property...
  Public Property DataSet() As DataSet
    Get
      Return _dataset
    End Get
    Set(ByVal Value As DataSet)

      ' Save it...
      _dataset = Value

      ' Bind...
      datagridOrders.DataSource = _dataset
      datagridOrders.DataMember = _dataset.Tables(0).TableName

      ' Create the document...
      _document = New XmlDataDocument(_dataset)

    End Set
  End Property
```

7. Next, add this property:

```
' Document property...
  Public ReadOnly Property Document() As XmlDataDocument
    Get
      Return _document
    End Get
  End Property
```

8. Now open the Designer for Form1. Draw on a new Button control. Change its Name property to btnReplace, Text property to Replace, and Anchor property to Top, Right.

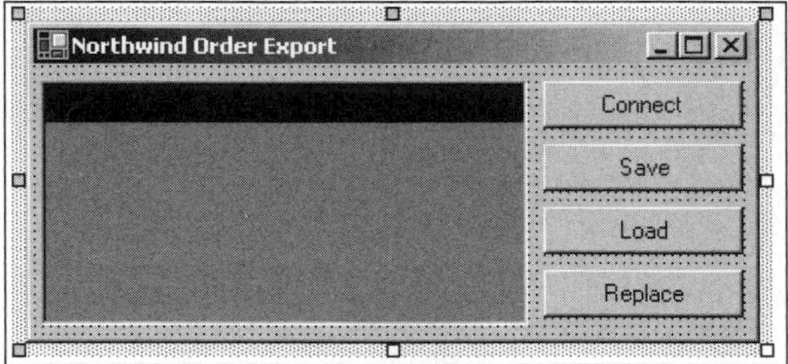

9. Double-click on the **Replace** button to create a new `Click` event handler. Add this code:

```
Private Sub btnReplace_Click(ByVal sender As System.Object, _
                ByVal e As System.EventArgs) Handles btnReplace.Click

    ' Create a collection...
    Dim replaceCollection As New DataReplaceCollection()

    ' What do we want to replace?
    Dim replace As New DataReplace()
    replace.ElementName = "ProductID"
    replace.LookFor = 14
    replace.ReplaceWith = 999
    replaceCollection.Add(replace)

    ' Do the replace...
    ReplaceData(replaceCollection)

  End Sub
```

10. In the above code sample, remember to replace this line:

```
replace.LookFor = 14
```

...with whatever product ID you noted down before.

11. Then, add this method:

```
Public Sub ReplaceData(ByVal replaceCollection As DataReplaceCollection)

    ' Turn off checking...
    Dim enforce As Boolean = DataSet.EnforceConstraints
    DataSet.EnforceConstraints = False

    ' Run the replace...
    DoReplace(replaceCollection, Document.FirstChild)

    ' Reset checking...
    DataSet.EnforceConstraints = enforce

  End Sub
```

12. Finally, add these two methods:

```
Protected Sub DoReplace(ByVal replaceCollection As DataReplaceCollection, _
                    ByVal node As XmlNode)
    DoReplace(replaceCollection, node, 0)
  End Sub
```

```
  Protected Sub DoReplace(ByVal replaceCollection As DataReplaceCollection, _
                    ByVal node As XmlNode)

    ' Go through the siblings...
    Do While Not node Is Nothing

      ' Do we have an element?
      If node.NodeType = XmlNodeType.Element Then

        ' Go through each one...
        Dim replace As DataReplace
        For Each replace In replaceCollection

          ' Does name match?
          If replace.ElementName = node.Name Then

            ' Compare node is the first child...
            Dim compareNode As XmlNode = node.FirstChild

            ' Compare the values...
            If compareNode.Value = replace.LookFor Then
              compareNode.Value = replace.ReplaceWith
            End If

            ' Quit...
            Exit For

          End If

        Next

        ' Walk down to the children...
        DoReplace(replaceCollection, node.FirstChild)

      End If

      ' Next...
      node = node.NextSibling()

    Loop

  End Sub
```

13. Run the project. Either click the Connect button to get data direct from the database or the Load button if you'd prefer to get the data from the file. (It doesn't matter which.)

14. Show the details for whichever order contains the product ID that you want to replace.

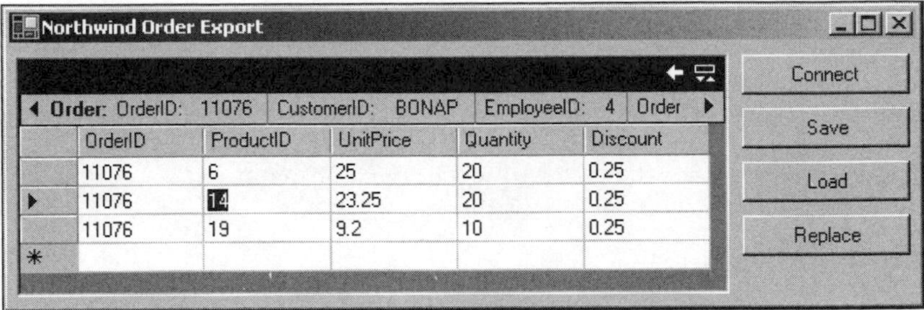

15. Click the Replace button. 14 will change to 999.

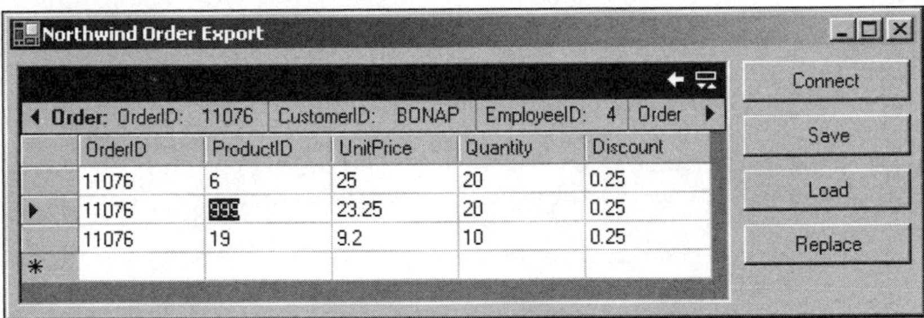

How It Works

`System.Data.DataSet` and `System.Xml.XmlDataDocument` work hand-in-hand. That's why we create a new `XmlDataDocument` whenever we set the `DataSet` property.

```
' DataSet property...
Public Property DataSet() As DataSet
  Get
    Return _dataset
  End Get
  Set(ByVal Value As DataSet)

    ' Save it...
    _dataset = Value

    ' Bind...
    datagridOrders.DataSource = _dataset
    datagridOrders.DataMember = _dataset.Tables(0).TableName

    ' Create the document...
    _document = New XmlDataDocument(_dataset)

  End Set
End Property
```

Basically, when we want to replace data, we can take one of two approaches. We could walk through each row of each table defined in the `DataSet` looking for columns with a particular name, comparing and changing values where necessary. I've used a similar approach but I'm walking through an XML document rather than a `DataSet`. Both techniques are equal, but what's important to see is that, as changes are made to the XML document, that change is *instantly* reflected in the `DataSet`. This is known as **synchronization**.

We've created a pretty flexible search and replace function here. We can provide a set of `DataReplace` objects to the `ReplaceData` method through a collection, so it can perform either a single search and replace in one call, or it can perform many. This would be useful if you maintained a list of substituted products. You can load the list, create `DataReplace` objects for each, and pass the collection to `ReplaceData`.

There are a number of ways that we can walk through an XML document, all of which work on a similar principle. Here we've gone with a fairly manual approach and built a pretty good recursive function that lets us go through the entire document with just one call made from within `ReplaceData`.

When `ReplaceData` is called, we can only make changes to the underlying `DataSet` if the `DataSet`'s `EnforceConstraints` property is set to `False`. When the function is called, we store the current value for this property and change it to `False`.

```
Public Sub ReplaceData(ByVal replaceCollection As DataReplaceCollection)

   ' Turn off checking...
   Dim enforce As Boolean = DataSet.EnforceConstraints
   DataSet.EnforceConstraints = False
```

Once we've done that, we call the protected `DoReplace` method, passing in the collection and the first "node" of the document. (More on nodes in a moment.)

```
   ' Run the replace...
   DoReplace(replaceCollection, Document.FirstChild)
```

Finally, we reset `EnforceConstraints` to whatever it was when we came in. This is good programming practice. If we need to change a property that some other part of the code or the caller him/herself might be dependent on, we should set it back to whatever it was when we're finished.

```
   ' Reset checking...
   DataSet.EnforceConstraints = enforce

End Sub
```

Nodes

XML documents work on the concept of nodes where each node is a "piece" of the document. A piece could be a start tag, an end tag, some data contained within two tags, or spaces and carriage returns that appear outside of the tags. (This latter part is known as **whitespace**.) What we want to do is start at the first node and walk through the entire document until we've seen all of them.

Walking through an XML document can be a little confusing, as you tend to end up jumping around all over the place. This diagram shows the jumps that happen between nodes.

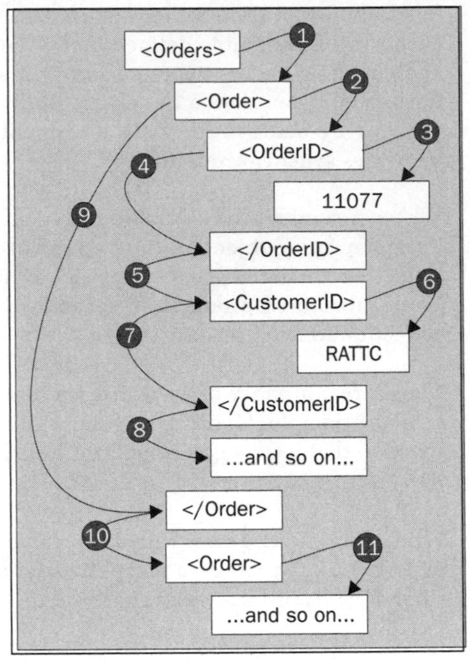

The first node we come to is the start tag for the top-level element: `<Orders>`. To walk through a document you have go through all of the child nodes of the node you're on, then, once you've exhausted the child nodes, you move to the next sibling along from you. Then the process repeats so you move to the sibling's first child, and so on and so forth. Eventually you will have traversed the entire document. To understand this, follow the jumps on the diagram in order.

That's what we're doing with our `DoReplace` method. We are given a `System.Xml.XmlNode` object that represents our current position. In the first instance, this will be the start tag of the top-level element. We'll see how this method is recursively called as we walk through the document.

```
Protected Sub DoReplace(ByVal replaceCollection As DataReplaceCollection, _
                        ByVal node As XmlNode )
```

What we do next is set up a loop that goes through the siblings. This has the effect of looking at the node that we were given through the `node` parameter first.

```
    ' Go through the siblings...
    Do While Not node Is Nothing
```

Straight away we look at the type of node that we have. If this is an `XmlNodeType.Element`, it's the start tag of an element. If we have an element, we go through each of the `DataReplace` objects comparing the values, looking for one whose `ElementName` property matches the `Name` property of the node. (And in our case we're looking for `ProductID`.)

```
        ' Do we have an element?
        If node.NodeType = XmlNodeType.Element Then

          ' Go through each one...
          Dim replace As DataReplace
          For Each replace In replaceCollection

            ' Does name match?
            If replace.ElementName = node.Name Then
```

Once we find that, we need to get hold of the first child of the node. In all cases, this will be a piece of text and we can compare the `Value` property of this child node to the `LookFor` property of the `DataReplace` object and, if need be, effect a change.

```
              ' Compare node is the first child...
              Dim compareNode As XmlNode = node.FirstChild

              ' Compare the values...
              If compareNode.Value = replace.LookFor Then
                compareNode.Value = replace.ReplaceWith
              End If

              ' Quit...
              Exit For

            End If

          Next
```

Once we've looked at the node, the rules about how we walk through a document dictate that we have to turn our attention to the child nodes. We call into the *same* function (recursion) but, this time, we pass the child node in as the node parameter. This has the slightly heady effect of running through the same function but this time we're looking at a different position on the tree. (This is one of the jumps that we saw in the diagram above.)

```
          ' Walk down to the children...
          DoReplace(replaceCollection, node.FirstChild)

        End If
```

Once we've gone through all of the children (and we would have effectively gone through all of the children's children and the children's children's children), we can move on to the sibling next to the one we've looked at.

```
      ' Next...
      node = node.NextSibling()

    Loop

  End Sub
```

Basically, the important part is the bit of code that sets the value in the node object. Here it is again:

```
' Go through each one...
Dim replace As DataReplace
For Each replace In replaceCollection

  ' Does name match?
  If replace.ElementName = node.Name Then

    ' Compare node is the first child...
    Dim compareNode As XmlNode = node.FirstChild

    ' Compare the values...
    If compareNode.Value = replace.LookFor Then
      compareNode.Value = replace.ReplaceWith
    End If

    ' Quit...
    Exit For

  End If

Next
```

Because the `DataSet` and `XmlDataDocument` are so closely tied, each `XmlNode` object that the `XmlDataDocument` object knows about is automatically linked to a particular column in a particular row in a particular table in the `DataSet`. Changing the `Value` property of the node automatically updates its counterpart in `DataSet`.

Changing the DataSet Changes the XML

So we've seen changes work one way. Let's see if we can make changes to the `DataSet` update the XML document.

To do this, we'll need to create a way of displaying the contents of the `XmlDataDocument` object from within our own code. We'll create a separate form containing a single ListBox control and add a method that will let us update the view whenever we suspect that the data in the `DataSet` has changed.

Try It Out – Changing DataSet Data

1. If the project is running, close it.

2. Using Solution Explorer, right-click on the Order Export project and select Add | Add Windows Form. Call the new form XmlDocumentView.

3. Paint on a new ListBox control. Set its Name property to lstNodes, IntegralHeight property to False and Anchor property to Top, Bottom, Left, Right.

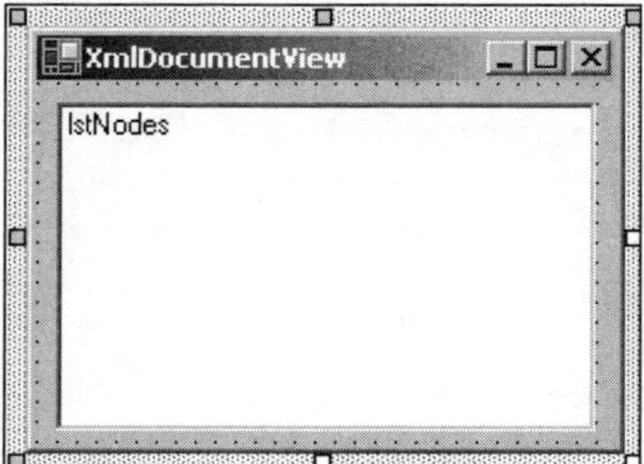

4. Open the code editor for the form. Add this namespace import declaration:

```
Imports System.Xml

Public Class XmlDocumentView
  Inherits System.Windows.Forms.Form
```

5. Next, add a new member to the class:

```
Public Class XmlDocumentView
  Inherits System.Windows.Forms.Form

  ' Members...
  Private _document As XmlDataDocument
```

6. Next, add this property:

```
' Document - document property...
  Public Property Document() As XmlDataDocument
    Get
      Return _document
    End Get
    Set(ByVal Value As XmlDataDocument)
      _document = Value
      UpdateView()
    End Set
  End Property
```

7. Finally, add these two methods:

```
' UpdateView - update the view...
  Public Sub UpdateView()

    ' Clear the list...
    lstNodes.Items.Clear()

    ' Do we have a document?
    If Not Document Is Nothing Then
```

```
      ' Start adding items...
      DoUpdateView(Document.FirstChild, 0)

    End If

  End Sub
```

```
  ' DoUpdateView - go through adding nodes...
  Protected Sub DoUpdateView(ByVal node As XmlNode, ByVal level As Integer)

    ' Go through the nodes...
    Do While Not node Is Nothing

      ' Create a new string...
      Dim nodeString As String = ""
      Dim n As Integer
      For n = 0 To level - 1
        nodeString &= "  "
      Next
      nodeString &= node.NodeType.ToString() & ":"
      If node.Value = "" Then
        nodeString &= node.Name
      Else
        nodeString &= node.Value
      End If

      ' Add it...
      lstNodes.Items.Add(nodeString)

      ' Do the children...
      DoUpdateView(node.FirstChild, level + 1)

      ' Next...
      node = node.NextSibling

    Loop

  End Sub
```

8. That's all we need to do in order to create a form that lets us view the current contents of an `XmlDataDocument` object.

9. Open the code editor for `Form1`. Add this member:

```
Public Class Form1
  Inherits System.Windows.Forms.Form

  ' Members...
  Private _dataset As DataSet
  Private _document As XmlDataDocument
  Private _documentView As XmlDocumentView
```

10. Flip over to the Designer for Form1 and double-click on the form background. This will create a new `Load` event handler. Add this code:

```
Private Sub Form1_Load(ByVal sender As System.Object, _
                ByVal e As System.EventArgs) Handles MyBase.Load

    ' Show the view...
    _documentView = New XmlDocumentView()
    _documentView.Show()

  End Sub
```

11. Find the `DataSet` property. Add this code:

```
...

        ' Create the document...
        _document = New XmlDataDocument(_dataset)

        ' Update the view...
        _documentView.Document = _document

      End Set
    End Property
```

12. Using the drop-down list in the top left-hand corner of the editor window, select dgdOrders. From the right-hand list select CurrentCellChanged.

13. When the new event handler has been created, add this code:

```
Private Sub dgdOrders_CurrentCellChanged(ByVal sender As Object, _
        ByVal e As System.EventArgs) Handles dgOrders.CurrentCellChanged
    _documentView.UpdateView()
  End Sub
```

14. Again, using the drop-down list, select (Overrides) from the left-hand list and select OnClosed from the right-hand list. Add this code:

```
Protected Overrides Sub OnClosed(ByVal e As System.EventArgs)
    _documentView.Close()
    _documentView = Nothing
  End Sub
```

15. Run the project. The new view window will appear. Click Load or Connect to load up the document and you'll notice that the list in the view window becomes populated with data.

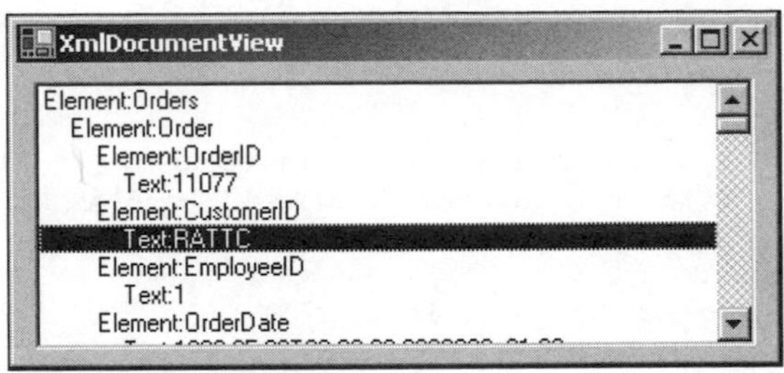

16. You can see here that I've selected the value contained within the `CustomerID` element for order 11077. Using the `DataGrid`, change this value to DIZZY.

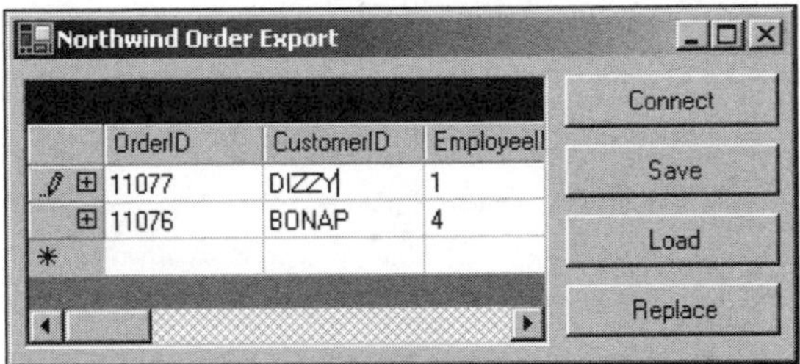

17. When you click outside of the cell or press *Return*, the changes will be made to the `DataSet` and the `CurrentCellChanged` event will be fired. You'll also notice that the XML document has also been updated.

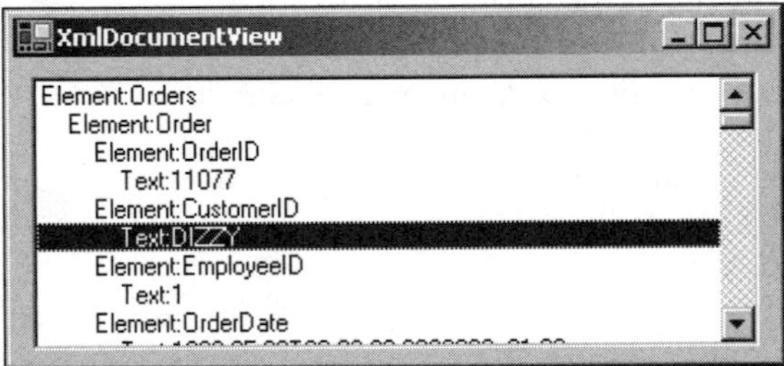

How It Works

So we've proved now that not only do changes to the `XmlDataDocument` object affect the `DataSet`, but also that the opposite is true.

It's worth looking at how we built up the view, as it's another example of how we can use recursion to walk through the nodes that make up the document. In fact, because we can see the results, it may make the process clearer if it's still a little foggy.

Again, when `DoUpdateView` is called, we pass in the node that represents the starting position. At first, this will be the start tag for the top-level element.

```
' DoUpdateView - go through adding nodes...
Protected Sub DoUpdateView(ByVal node As XmlNode, ByVal level As Integer)

  ' Go through the nodes...
  Do While Not node Is Nothing
```

For each one, we want to make up a string and add it to the ListBox. Depending on the level, we want to indent the string so on the first level there is no indentation, on the second level there's some indentation, on the third there's a little more, and so on. The level that we're working at will be passed in through the `level` parameter.

```
    ' Create a new string...
    Dim nodeString As String = ""
    Dim n As Integer
    For n = 0 To level - 1
      nodeString &= "   "
    Next
```

Once we've added an indent to a string, we can render the type that the node is. We then tack on either the name of the element or, if we have one, the current value.

```
    nodeString &= node.NodeType.ToString() & ":"
    If node.Value = "" Then
      nodeString &= node.Name
    Else
      nodeString &= node.Value
    End If
```

Then we can add the string to the ListBox:

```
    ' Add it...
    lstNodes.Items.Add(nodeString)
```

As before, as soon as we've done one element we need to call into the function again to do the children. We pass an incremented version of `level` into the function, and this lets us adjust the indentation.

```
    ' Do the children...
    DoUpdateView(node.FirstChild, level + 1)
```

After we've walked through the children, we can move onto the next sibling.

```
    ' Next...
    node = node.NextSibling

  Loop

End Sub
```

OK, so that's how the view is put together, and you can see that it follows the structure of the document as we see it displayed in Internet Explorer. (Using this method the end tags aren't displayed, but this is no big deal!) But, have we really proven that the objects are being synchronized, or are we showing that some funny business is going on?

If we look at the DataSet property, we can see that it's at that point that we set the Document property on our XmlDocumentView object.

```
' DataSet property...
Public Property DataSet() As DataSet
  Get
    Return _dataset
  End Get
  Set(ByVal Value As DataSet)

    ' Save it...
    _dataset = Value

    ' Bind...
    datagridOrders.DataSource = _dataset
    datagridOrders.DataMember = _dataset.Tables(0).TableName

    ' Create the document...
    _document = New XmlDataDocument(_dataset)

    ' Update the view...
    _documentView.Document = _document

  End Set
End Property
```

This is the only time this happens, and the only time that the DataSet property is set is after we've pressed the Connect or Load buttons.

When the current cell is changed on the DataGrid, we run this code:

```
Private Sub datagridOrders_CurrentCellChanged(ByVal sender As Object, _
      ByVal e As System.EventArgs) Handles datagridOrders.CurrentCellChanged
  _documentView.UpdateView()
End Sub
```

We know that this code just goes through the document that's stored in the DataSet public member on XmlDocumentView. As this isn't changing, the only reasonable conclusion that we can come to is that the DataSet is indeed updating the XmlDataDocument.

Simplifying Data Manipulation with Typed DataSets

Before we finish this chapter, we'll take a very quick look at how schemas let us define **typed** `DataSets`.

Typed `DataSets` can provide a more intuitive mechanism for the manipulation of data. A typed `DataSet` is bound to an XML Schema Definition (XSD) file. Schemas provide very rigorous definitions for the types of particular objects. In conjunction with the typed `DataSet`, they can allow access to the tables and columns of a `DataSet` using meaningful names. This not only improves the readability of your code, but also enables Visual Studio .NET's IntelliSense feature to make context-sensitive suggestions as you type in code.

You can think of this as a way to **early bind** to your `DataSet`, as opposed to the **late binding** that occurs with non-typed `DataSets`. Early binding is the ability to make Visual Basic .NET aware of the exact type of an object at design time, whereas late binding means the type of object will not be known until the code actually runs. With early binding, you have advantages such as IntelliSense and compilation checking that tell you whether certain features you are trying to use are actually supported.

Try It Out – Creating Typed DataSets from Existing Schemas

1. Generating a typed `DataSet` directly from an XSD schema is a very straightforward task. For example, save the following schema as `ProductsDataSet.xsd` somewhere on your computer:

```
<?xml version="1.0" encoding="utf-8" ?>
<xsd:schema id="ProductsDataSet"
targetNamespace="http://tempuri.org/ProductsDataSet.xsd"
elementFormDefault="qualified" xmlns="http://tempuri.org/ProductsDataSet.xsd"
xmlns:xsd="http://www.w3.org/2001/XMLSchema">
<xsd:element name="ProductsDataSet">
   <xsd:complexType>
     <xsd:sequence>
          <xsd:element name="ProductId" minOccurs="1" type="xsd:integer" />
       <xsd:element name="ProductName" minOccurs="1" type="xsd:string" />
       <xsd:element name="SupplierId" minOccurs="0" type="xsd:integer" />
       <xsd:element name="CategoryId" minOccurs="0" type="xsd:integer" />
      <xsd:element name="QuantityPerUnit" minOccurs="0" type="xsd:string" />
       <xsd:element name="UnitPrice" minOccurs="0" type="xsd:decimal" />
     <xsd:element name="UnitsInStock" minOccurs="0" type="xsd:integer" />
     <xsd:element name="UnitsOnOrder" minOccurs="0" type="xsd:integer" />
     <xsd:element name="ReorderLevel" minOccurs="0" type="xsd:integer" />
     <xsd:element name="Discontinued" minOccurs="0" type="xsd:byte" />
   </xsd:sequence>
   </xsd:complexType>
</xsd:element>
</xsd:schema>
```

2. In Visual Studio .NET, we can use this file to generate a typed `DataSet`, based on the type information it details. Start a completely new Windows Application project for this quick example. Then select Project | Add Existing Item.

3. In the Add Existing Item dialog box, browse to find the `ProductsDataSet.xsd` schema and open it.

4. In the Solution Explorer, double-click on the entry for the XML schema you just added. You will see a screen something like that shown below:

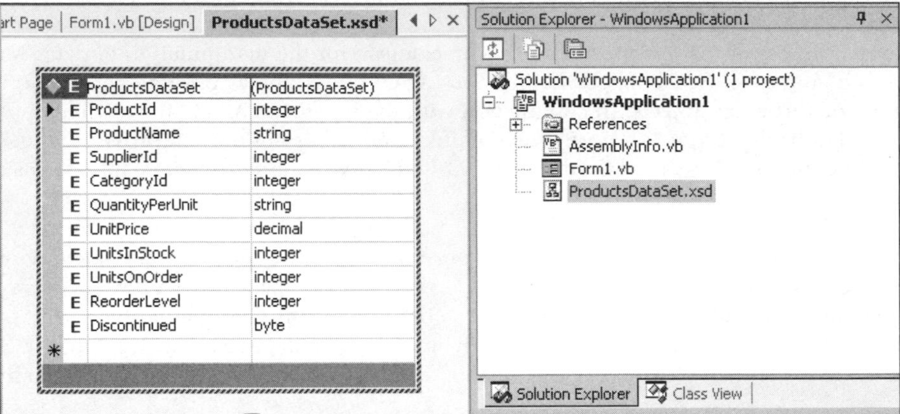

5. Notice how Visual Studio .NET takes the XSD schema and renders it visually on screen. If you want to see the file in its original XML format, just click on the XML tab at the bottom.

6. Select Schema from the menu and then choose Generate DataSet.

7. Click the Show All Files button in Solution Explorer to make all files visible.

8. If you expand the ProductsDataSet.xsd branch by clicking on the plus symbol to the left of the schema name, you will see a ProductsDataSet.vb and a ProductsDataSet.xsx file. If you open the code in ProductsDataSet.vb, you will see that it contains Visual Basic .NET code defining each element in the schema. ProductsDataSet.xsx is a file used by Visual Studio to determine information about how to display the schema in the designer.

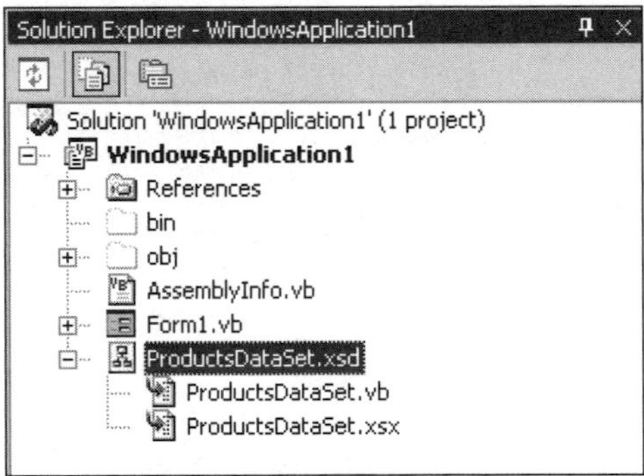

9. Let's now demonstrate that, by adding in this schema, we have enabled IntelliSense. Double-click on Form1 in the Designer and type the following lines into the `Form1_Load` event:

```
Dim dsTypedDataSet As New ProductsDataSet()
dsTypedDataSet.ProductsDataSet.ProductNameColumn
```

10. You should see that IntelliSense is now enabled and you can directly select the column names from the schema. You will find this much simpler and less error-prone to work with than having to remember column names unaided:

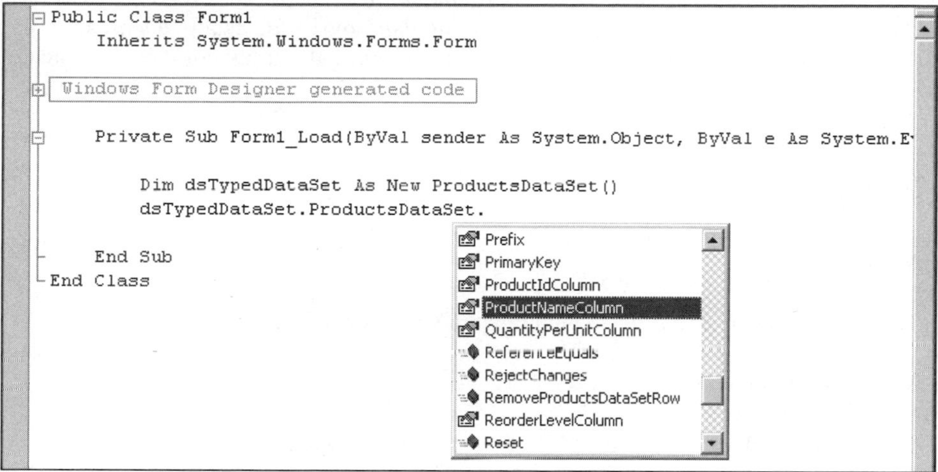

How It Works

By adding an existing XSD schema to our project, we can automatically generate a typed `DataSet` from the schema.

Using a typed `DataSet` provides a number of advantages. It provides you with a specification up front about how the `DataSet` should look. It also gives the advantage of IntelliSense, which suggests possible alternatives when typing a line of code. Your code also becomes more readable because you can use the column names in the `DataSet` inherently.

Summary

In this chapter, we initially saw a brief rundown of what XML is and learned that, at a basic level, it's based on common sense and is not particularly tricky to understand. We then took a look at how we can get the `System.Data.DataSet` class to generate an XML document with a single call to `WriteXml`. We dissected this document to learn more about how a document is made up of tags and elements. Next we saw how we could load that same file back into a `DataSet`.

Then we turned our attention to schemas, which are a way of defining the rules of a given document's construction – for example, "you'll see this element, followed by *n* occurrences of this element, etc.". We saw how we could create a schema using `WriteXmlSchema` and how we could validate a given XML document against a schema to determine its validity.

Next, we examined the `System.Xml.XmlDataDocument` class. This is a useful class that allows manipulation of the same basic data either through a `DataSet` object or through the `XmlDataDocument` itself.

Finally, we took a very quick look at typed `DataSets`.

That brings us to the end of our discussion on the basics of how ADO.NET can expose XML data to us and how we can manipulate that data. In the next chapter, we'll learn how Web Services work and, in Chapter 14, we'll see how XML can make an alternate data source for data in a similar way to the technique we've seen here. In the Case Study, we'll learn more about how different applications can share XML data.

Exercises

1. What is XML?
2. How can we get a `DataSet` to generate an XML document?
3. What's a schema?
4. How do we make sure that an XML file we receive is valid?
5. What's so useful about `XmlDataDocument`?

Answers are available at http://p2p.wrox.com/exercises/.

Web Services

Since .NET was first announced, Microsoft developers have been telling us all that the next big thing in Internet development will be the Web Service, especially since the release of .NET has made building Web Services a fairly trivial activity. In this chapter, we'll see how to build and use Web Services in our applications.

Traditionally, web sites are used by people. If I want to know the price of a book offered by a particular e-commerce site, I'll go to the site and find the book and see its price. If I want to compare their price with that of other vendors, I can visit a few other sites and do a manual comparison, or perhaps go to a site that compares values from a selection of sites for me.

A Web Service, on the other hand, is like a web site designed solely to be accessed by computers. To take the same example, our book vendor can enhance their web site to provide certain tools that computers can call over the Internet. Such a tool is known as a Web Service and, just like the objects you've already seen, Web Services expose "methods". In this case, we might have methods such as `GetPriceForBook` and `OrderBook`. Methods don't *have* to return a value, but all the ones we look at in this chapter do.

The main reason why Web Services are now a viable idea is the popularity of the Internet. Integrating computer systems is traditionally a complex and expensive affair. Without the Internet, if two companies want to link their computers, they would have to set up some kind of link just for the purpose. However, all the companies now have to do is connect to the Internet and use that for the exchange of data between their computers. Connectivity is much more straightforward, and integration of applications has been reduced to a software development issue.

However, it's still complex and expensive, and that's where Web Services come in. We all know how easy it is to build a web site. Thanks to the tools all platforms offer today, building complex web-based applications for everything from shopping to banking is now easy. The Web Service is the vehicle we can use to make integrating computer systems just as easy.

Imagine we want to provide a service that allows visitors to our site to tap in an ISBN and be presented with a list of the prices offered by a hundred different vendors. In an ideal world, each vendor would offer a Web Service exposing a method called `GetPriceForBook`, that takes an ISBN and returns a floating-point number representing the price. By the end of this chapter, you will be able to put together such a service in a single afternoon.

Now imagine we're trying to do that with conventional Internet tools. One way would be to perform "screen scrapes", where our application downloads each vendor's web page, and searches it to locate the price. The problem here is that not only will each vendor's page layout be quite different, and thus require custom code to extract the price, but the vendors may change the layout of the page we need at any time. This immediately breaks our screen scraping code, and we have to rewrite it to match the vendor's new site. Alternatively, we could negotiate with the vendor to obtain direct access to their computer system, but again we'd have to do custom integration work. Either way, you're looking at more than an afternoon's work!

In this chapter we'll see how to build a Web Service for our Northwind project to allow our customers to check the status of their orders over the Web. We'll also create a client application that uses this Web Service, and look at how to find other Web Services using UDDI (Universal Description, Discovery and Integration) and Web Service brokerages.

If you are interested in finding out more about the business benefits of Web Services, check out the Web Services Architect site at http://www.webservicesarchitect.com/.

Building a Web Service

As we're going to go to the trouble of building a Web Service, we might as well build one that satisfies a real-world business need. With the Northwind company, one thing that our customers may appreciate is to be able to check the status of their orders using the Web.

Providing this feature online brings major advantages for both parties. The company cuts down on the "Where is my order?" sort of enquiries as the customer can now find the information they need themselves. Customers, on the other hand, are reassured because they can check the status of the order 24 hours a day, seven days a week. Of course, this would be possible with traditional Web techniques – it's not the exclusive preserve of Web Services. However, a Web Service offers the advantage that we can easily access this remote functionality from as many of our own intranet, Internet, server, or desktop applications as we need.

Designing Our Web Service

To design our Web Service, we must first decide precisely what functionality to offer our customers. We want to provide a way for our customers to check the status of their orders, including what products the order contained, whether it has been shipped yet and, if so, when and how it was shipped.

One thing to note is that we can add more functionality to the Web Service later on – we're not fixed by the decisions we make today, although we want to insure any updates are 'backwards compatible' with the older version to avoid inconveniencing our existing users. This means we can roll out a fairly limited service today, and roll out improved or enhanced functionality at a later date based on feedback from the users.

A Web Service is in essence just a set of methods that can be called over the Internet. If we knew what our order number was and wanted the shipping date, we might create a method that looked like this:

```
Function GetShippingDateForOrder(ByVal orderId As Integer) As Date
```

If that method were to be implemented on an object installed on our local computer, we'd have no problem understanding what was going on. We pass in an order ID, the object looks up the shipping details, and returns the date to the caller. In principle, a Web Service works exactly the same, except that the code is now hosted on a web server that exposes it to requests originating over the Internet.

When a call is carried out on a local computer, both .NET and COM components use various proprietary tricks to make the call happen. Due to their cross-platform nature however, Web Service calls use a combination of open standards. As you probably know, web servers use HTTP, the Hypertext Transfer Protocol, to receive and respond to requests. This protocol can transfer either plain text or binary files. For example, the HTML that makes up web pages is transmitted as plain text, whereas images, executable files, and so on are transmitted as binary files.

Web Services are based on the exchange of SOAP (Simple Object Access Protocol) documents. SOAP documents follow XML formatting, meaning that they are plain text and can be readily exchanged over HTTP.

Whenever a call is made to a Web Service, the request is wrapped up as a SOAP message and sent over the Internet to the web server. The web server has a mechanism that takes the request and passes it to the software that powers the Web Service. The software then prepares the response, wraps it up as another SOAP message, and returns it to the client that made the call, again via the web server.

Web Services are not a proprietary Microsoft innovation. All the major platform vendors are releasing Web Service implementations based on a combination of HTTP and SOAP. Because the underlying standard followed on every platform is the same, a Web Service running on a UNIX computer can be accessed by a machine using Windows 2000, and vice versa. This is great for us because it means that, even though we're developing our system on the Windows platform, our customers will be able to access them regardless of which particular computer and operating system they may be using.

Try It Out – Building a Web Service

1. We can use a wizard to create a Web Service project for us. Open Visual Studio .NET and select New | Project from the menu.

2. From the Templates list on the right, select ASP.NET Web Service. Enter the name of the project as NorthwindWebService, and click OK:

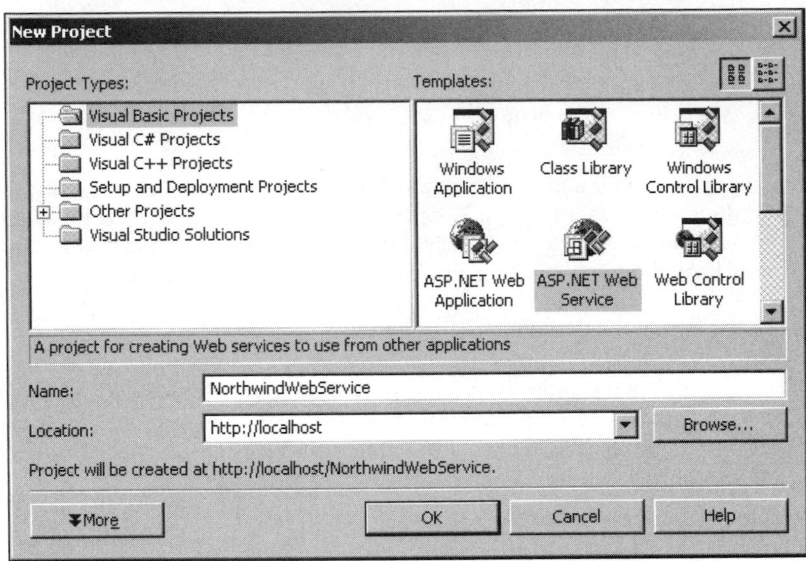

Try not to enter spaces or other odd characters into the project name because the name will form part of the URL that's used to access the Web Service. As URLs are restricted as to the characters that they may contain, Visual Studio .NET replaces any non-alphanumeric characters or spaces with underscores. This can make your Web Service URL appear quite different to what you intended.

If you can, use your local computer as the server required in the Location box. (Remember that localhost refers to the computer you're working on.) This will make following the exercises later a little easier.

A dialog will appear telling you that the new project is being created. It disappears as soon as the project has been successfully created.

3. If you look at Solution Explorer, you'll notice a number of new files that have been created. You may need to select View | Solution Explorer from the menu if it's not already visible:

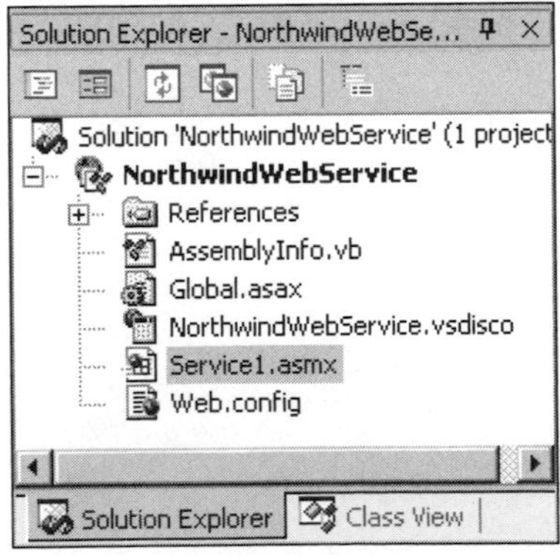

The file we're particularly interested in here is the `Service1.asmx` file. This is the default Web Services file that gets created for us, and that will contain our Web Service's main code.

4. Right-click Service1.asmx and select View Code, which opens the `Service1.asmx.vb` code file.

5. You'll notice three lines commented out. Remove the comments to produce:

```
' WEB SERVICE EXAMPLE
' The HelloWorld() example service returns the string Hello World.
' To build, uncomment the following lines then save and build the project.
' To test this web service, ensure that the .asmx file is the start page
' and press F5.
'
<WebMethod()> Public Function HelloWorld() As String
   HelloWorld = "Hello World"
End Function
```

6. Run the project by selecting Debug | Start from the menu, or hitting *F5*. Our `Service1.asmx` file should be set as the Start Page by default, so Internet Explorer should appear showing something like this:

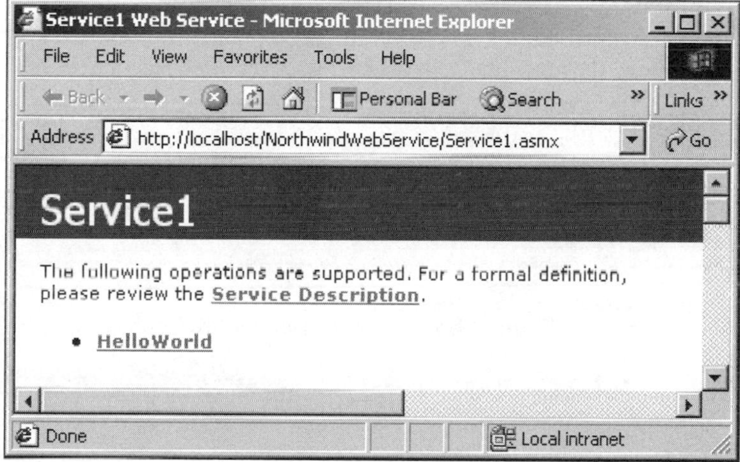

What we see here is a list of the methods that Service1.asmx exposes. At the moment, there is only one: HelloWorld, the method that we uncommented in step 5.

Below the method listing are messages about changing the default namespace. You can ignore this for now, as we revisit the "namespace" issue later in the chapter.

7. Now click on HelloWorld, taking us to a page for testing the method:

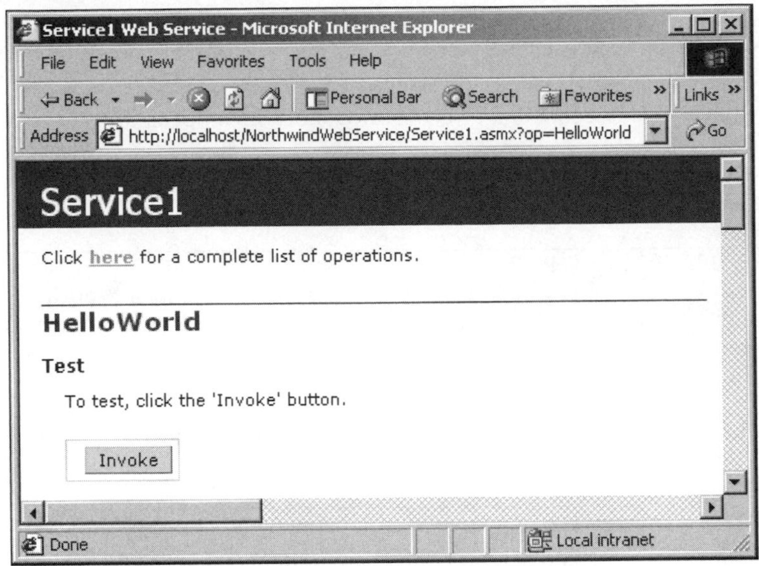

Beneath the Invoke button, you'll notice some notes about SOAP, HTTP GET, and HTTP POST. You can safely ignore these for the time being.

8. Now, click the Invoke button and a new Internet Explorer window will appear containing the XML document as shown:

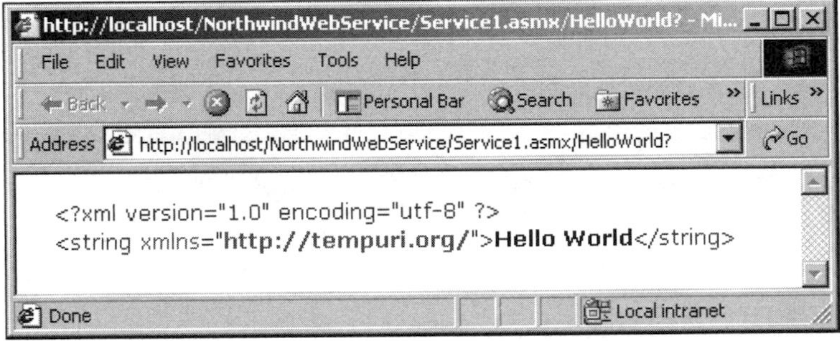

How It Works

Back in Chapter 11, when we looked at ASP.NET, one subject that came up was that of "code behind". When an application uses code behind, each page on the web server is associated with a code file containing the classes for building that page.

In normal ASP.NET projects, pages have the `.aspx` extension, but in an ASP.NET Web Service project, the extension is `.asmx`. ASMX comes from the term "Active Service Method", with the "X" a remnant from the days when ASP.NET was called "ASP+". The X in fact represents a plus-sign rotated through 45 degrees.

Like .aspx pages, .asmx pages actually comprise two files. One (Service1.asmx) is used for the pages that power the Web Service. The other (Service1.asmx.vb) is the code behind page specifying the actual methods for the Web Service. Unlike ASP.NET, you don't tend to do anything with the "in-front" page – everything is done in the code behind page.

The Service1.asmx.vb ASMX page contains this code:

```
Imports System.Web.Services


' Windows Form Designer-generated code region

Public Class Service1
  Inherits System.Web.Services.WebService

  ' WEB SERVICE EXAMPLE
  ' The HelloWorld() example service returns the string Hello World.
  ' To build, uncomment the following lines then save and build the project.
  ' To test this Web Service, ensure that the .asmx file is the start page
  ' and press F5.
  '
  <WebMethod()> Public Function HelloWorld() As String
    HelloWorld = "Hello World"
  End Function

End Class
```

You can see that the class is inherited from System.Web.Services.WebService. This is the class that automatically creates the user interface we saw in Internet Explorer that allowed us to invoke the HelloWorld method.

When we add methods to this class that we want to be made available over the Web, we have to add a WebMethod attribute, as shown below for our HelloWorld method:

```
<WebMethod()> Public Function HelloWorld() As String
```

When we first run the project, we navigate to this URL:

```
http://localhost/NorthwindWebService/Service1.asmx
```

When the page request is sent to IIS, the .asmx extension tells IIS to pass it on to ASP.NET for processing. ASP.NET looks at the page to determine the .vb file that contains the code that powers the Web Service. In our case, it is the file that contains the Service1 class we're currently working with.

At this point, Service1 must create a page to present details of the Web Service it represents. It knows that we haven't asked to actually run the Web Service at this point, so it looks through the class for all methods that have the WebMethod attribute set, and renders them on the page as the list of available methods:

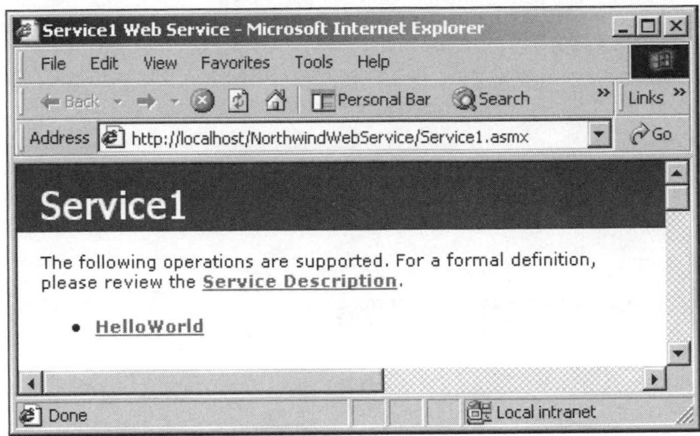

When we click HelloWorld, the `.asmx` page is again requested and IIS passes the request to ASP.NET for processing. This time, the URL used will be:

```
http://localhost/NorthwindWebService/Service1.asmx?op=HelloWorld
```

The `op` parameter at the end of the URL tells `Service1` to provide further details of the `HelloWorld` method. This it duly does, along with a button labeled Invoke. If our method had parameters, a form would also be produced for us to enter the values to use as parameters when we test the method.

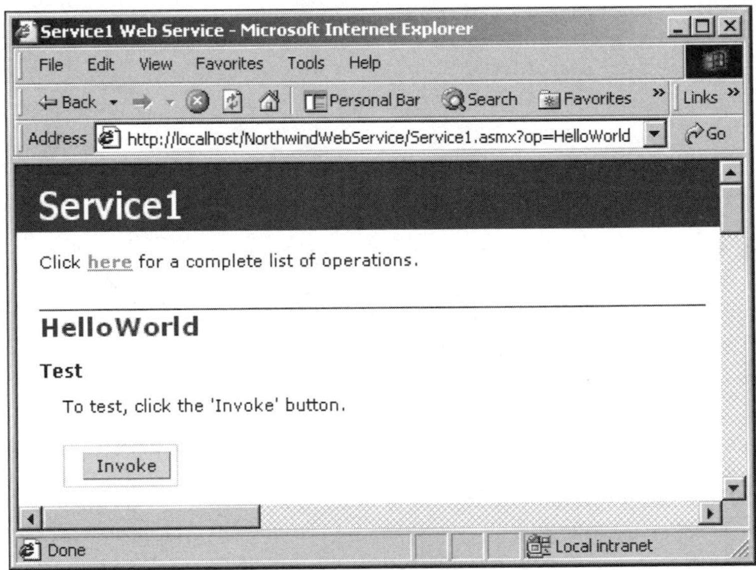

The Invoke button brings up a new browser window with this URL:

```
http://localhost/NorthwindWebService/Service1.asmx/HelloWorld?
```

This URL tells the Web Service to actually execute the `HelloWorld` method and package the return value as a SOAP document to be returned to the caller – in this case, us. The returned document contains only a single entry, which is the string that the `HelloWorld` implementation of `Service1` produced.

```
<?xml version="1.0" encoding="utf-8" ?>
<string xmlns="http://tempuri.org/">Hello World</string>
```

If we were using the Web Service in a real-world situation, we wouldn't really use the web interface we've seen in the last few screen shots. This interface is really only provided to test a Web Service. Later in the chapter, we look at how to use a Web Service from within our own applications.

Finding the Code

In Chapter 11, we mentioned how Visual Studio .NET will always create ASP.NET project files on the web server, rather than allowing us to nominate a folder on our local computer or file server. That's the case with Web Services too so, if we don't want to lose our work, we need to be able to find the files and copy them to a safer location, that is a location on our own network where we will be able to find them later.

In the vast majority of cases, your files will be contained in a subdirectory off the "IIS root" folder, typically `c:\inetpub\wwwroot`. So, as our project is called NorthwindWebService, our project files will be in a folder with a name similar to `c:\inetpub\wwwroot\NorthwindWebService`.

SOAP Namespaces

If you look at the first page that comes up when you run the project, you'll see a number of warnings about namespaces. These are there because we need to make sure that when our SOAP documents are passed around, the names and identifiers they use don't conflict with those in anyone else's documents. Namespaces provide a way for us to do this.

Using our own namespace makes the names used in our documents unique, and allows other people to use them and to uniquely identify responses from our Web Service with no danger of conflict with similar names used by their own systems. For example, we've already seen that our `HelloWorld` method returns a string back to the caller and that that string appears like this:

```
<string xmlns="http://tempuri.org/">Hello World</string>
```

The `xmlns` attribute tells the caller the namespace that that particular instance of `string` belongs to. In this case, the namespace is `http://tempuri.org/`, the default namespace Microsoft provide, and that we should replace with our own when we wish to deploy the service in a real-world environment.

Try It Out – Changing the Default Namespace

1. To change the default namespace, all we have to do is add an attribute to our class.

2. View the `Service1.asmx.vb` code. Add this `WebService` attribute to the class definition:

```
<WebService(Namespace:="http://wrox.com/1861005555/")> Public Class Service1
  Inherits System.Web.Services.WebService

  ' WEB SERVICE EXAMPLE
  ' The HelloWorld() example service returns the string Hello World.
  ' To build, uncomment the following lines, then save and build the project.
  ' To test this web service, ensure that the .asmx file is the start page
  ' and press F5.
  '
  <WebMethod()> Public Function HelloWorld() As String
    HelloWorld = "Hello World"
  End Function

End Class
```

3. Run the project. You'll notice that the warning message no longer appears on the first page.

4. If you click HelloWorld, and then the Invoke button when it appears, we'll get our new namespace given for the `string` element.

```
<?xml version="1.0" encoding="utf-8" ?>
<string xmlns="http://wrox.com/1861005555/">Hello World</string>
```

How It Works

We can use almost anything we like for the namespace. All we have to do is make sure it is unique so that everything that uses it will also be unique.

```
<WebService(Namespace:="http://wrox.com/1861005555/")> Public Class Service1
```

In this case, the wrox.com domain appended with the ISBN number of this book has been used because I can be fairly sure that it won't have been used by anyone else in this form.

Returning Shipping Details for an Order

Now let's have a go at building a Web Service with a practical use: to return an object that describes the status of an order, such as when it was placed, whether or not it's been shipped and, if so, what method it was shipped by. For this new service, we need a new `.asmx` file.

Try It Out – Creating a New ASMX File

1. In Solution Explorer, right-click the NorthwindWebService project and select Add | Add Web Service.

2. When the dialog appears, enter OrderQuery for the name, and click OK.

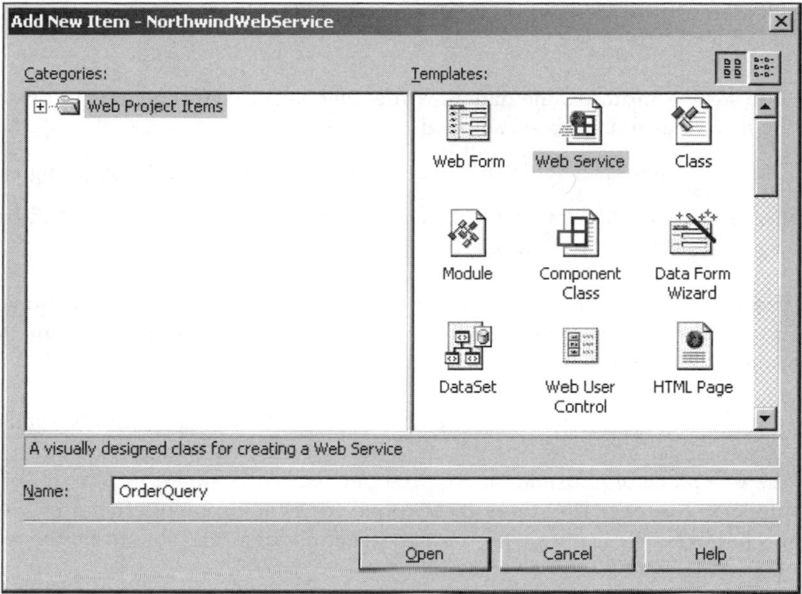

3. If we run the project, `Service1.asmx` will still be the page automatically loaded into Internet Explorer. We need to change the current start page, so right-click on OrderQuery.asmx in Solution Explorer, and select Set As Start Page.

4. Next let's change the default namespace. Right-click OrderQuery.asmx again, but this time select View Code. Add a `WebService` attribute to the class definition:

```
<WebService(Namespace:="http://wrox.com/1861005555")> Public Class OrderQuery
  Inherits System.Web.Services.WebService

End Class
```

That's all it takes: our new Web Service is set up and ready for us to add the code. We'll come back to this later, after addressing a couple of other important issues.

Returning Shipping Details

When our Web Service wants to return details to the caller, it's a good idea to pass back as much information as possible. Even though we can talk to a Web Service as if it were an object installed on the local machine, any calls we make are subject to the various problems that affect data moving over the Internet, so we want to get the job done with as few round trips as possible. Having one or two extra pieces of information on our client is not going to present any real problems, unlike the case where our client can't get the one or two pieces it does need due to network difficulties.

Luckily for us, we can return complex data structures from a Web Service method, so we're not limited to simple strings, numbers, and so on.

If we take a look at the Northwind `Orders` table, you'll notice there are quite a number of columns related to the shipping of the order, in particular:

- `ShippedDate` – indicates the date the order was shipped. If the value in this column is `Null`, then the order has not yet been shipped.
- `ShipVia` – references an ID in the `Shippers` table indicating the shipping company used.
- `ShipName` and various `Ship` address fields – indicates the company and address that the order was shipped to or will be shipped to.

If we want to find out if our order has been shipped, it's likely we'll want confirmation of the other details too. So instead of building a method that returns just the date, we'll build a method that returns all of that information in one hit.

The more object-oriented among you might be tempted to code several methods, such as `HasOrderShipped`, `GetOrderShippedDate`, and `GetOrderShipmentAddress`, each one returning just the one piece of information required in a particular situation. We're working with the less-than-reliable Web however, and those three round trips could potentially add a large impediment to our application's performance. That's why it would generally be preferable to do the whole job in one go.

Luckily for us, returning a set of information from a Web Service method is no more involved than returning just a single value. All we have to do is build a class with public properties for each value we want to return, so we could create a class called `ShippingDetailsResult` that exposes properties such as:

- `HasBeenShipped As Boolean`
- `ShippedDate As Date`
- `ShippingMethod As String`
- `ShippedToName As String`
- ...and so on.

Whatever we want our Web Service to return, there is the possibility that the request cannot be completed for some reason. Most often this will be because of a security problem – we'll discuss these in a moment. What we need is a common way to report problems. To follow good object-oriented design practices, we shall do this by building a separate class that our `ShippingDetailsResult` class can then inherit from. We'll call this class `WebServiceResult` and it will have two properties:

- `RequestOk As Boolean` – set `True` if the request was OK, `False` if not.
- `RequestProblem As String` – a string describing the problem if one occurred, for example, "Not allowed" or "Order not found".

Try It Out – Building the Result Class

1. To create the new class, right-click on the NorthwindWebService project in Solution Explorer and select Add | Add Class. Enter WebServiceResult as the class's name:

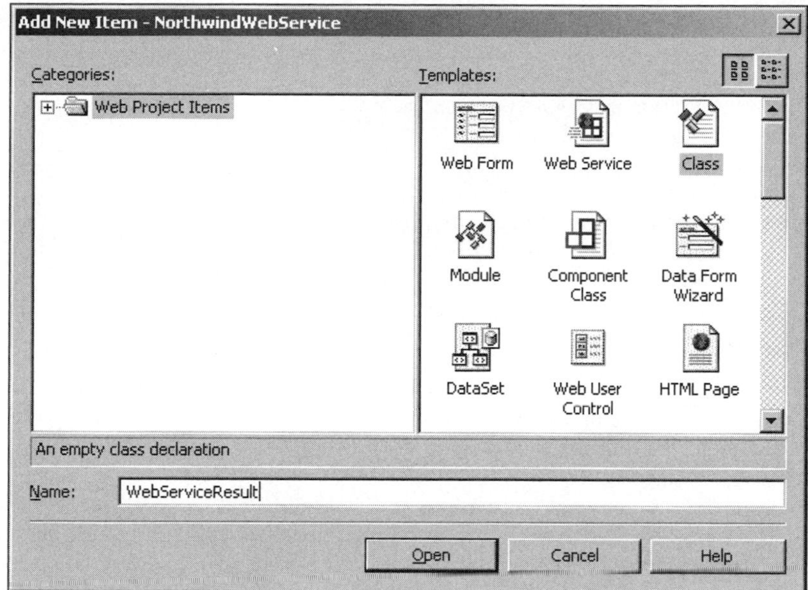

2. As we said, this class is going to have two properties. Add this code:

```
Public Class WebServiceResult

   ' members...
   Public RequestOk As Boolean
   Public RequestProblem As String

End Class
```

3. Now we can create the class that will actually be returned when we ask for the shipping details. In Solution Explorer, right-click the NorthwindWebService project again and select Add | Add Class. Give it the name ShippingDetailsResult.

4. This class needs to inherit from `WebServiceResult` and add various members to carry the order details over. Add this code to `ShippingDetailsResult`:

```
Public Class ShippingDetailsResult
   Inherits WebServiceResult

   ' members...
   Public HasBeenShipped As Boolean

   Public ShippedDate As Date
   Public ShippingMethod As String

   Public ShippedToName As String
   Public ShippedToAddress As String
```

```
    Public ShippedToCity As String
    Public ShippedToRegion As String
    Public ShippedToPostalCode As String
    Public ShippedToCountry As String

End Class
```

When we come to build our method to return the shipping details, it will be responsible for creating an instance of the `ShippingDetailsResult` object and populating its properties. After the object has been populated, ASP.NET sends it back to the caller to use as it wishes.

Security Considerations

There are important security considerations that Web Service developers must address to avoid headaches later on. The nature of the Web Services beast is that our methods are publicly available, so we have to take steps to prevent unauthorized people accessing sensitive information.

In our case, we especially don't want competitors to be able to steal our customer database by supplying random order IDs to our Web Service. There's nothing to stop a competitor building a little utility that continually calls GetShippingDetails with every order ID from 1 to 1,000,000. If the order ID is valid, the shipping address is returned, which is likely to be our customer's business address, thus giving our competitors a list of all our customers and their addresses.

A good technique for securing our service is to require a username and password pair to be supplied with the GetShippingDetails call. We can then check that the user making the request is indeed responsible for that order. However, building such a scheme is non-trivial and has several implications: for starters, we have to maintain a system that allows customers to register, issues them with forgotten passwords, and so on.

The GetShippingDetails Method

What we need to do now is build and test GetShippingDetails. This will involve a stored procedure that queries the database to find the shipping information and the code required to process the results.

Try It Out – Creating a Stored Procedure

1. We'll use Visual Studio .NET's built-in database administration features to add the stored procedure. Select View | Server Explorer from the menu and navigate down to the NorthwindSQL database under your database server. The screenshot shows my own server, called "chimaera":

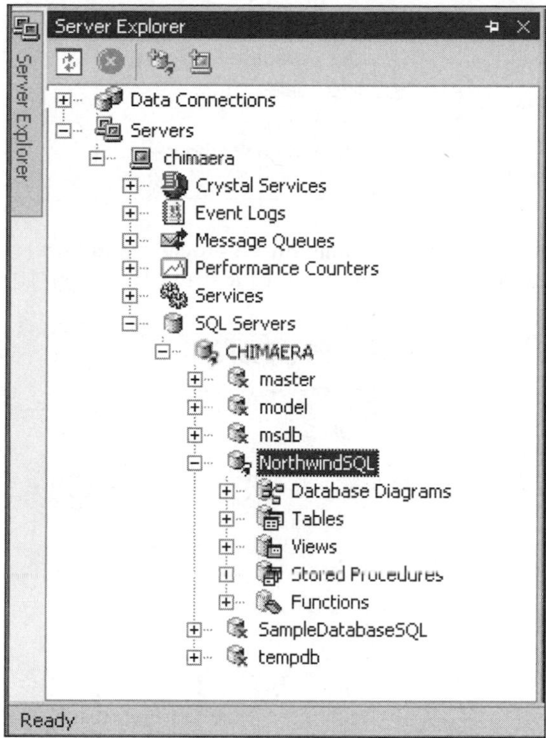

2. Right-click on the **Stored Procedures** object and select **New Stored Procedure**. A code window opens into which you should enter the SQL statement required.

3. Enter this code into the window, overwriting any text that Visual Studio .NET has added automatically:

```
Create Procedure GetShippingDetails
   (
      @orderId int
   )
As
   SELECT OrderID, PostalCode, ShippedDate, ShipVia, ShipName,
      ShipAddress, ShipCity, ShipRegion, ShipPostalCode, ShipCountry
      FROM Orders
         INNER JOIN Customers ON Orders.CustomerID = Customers.CustomerID
      WHERE OrderID=@orderId
   RETURN
```

4. Select **File | Save StoredProcedure1** from the menu. This will create the new stored procedure. If you expand the **Stored Procedures** node in Server Explorer, you should see the new **GetShippingDetails** stored procedure:

5. Right-click on the GetShippingDetails stored procedure in Server Explorer and select Run Stored Procedure. You'll be prompted for the order ID. Enter 10248 and click OK.

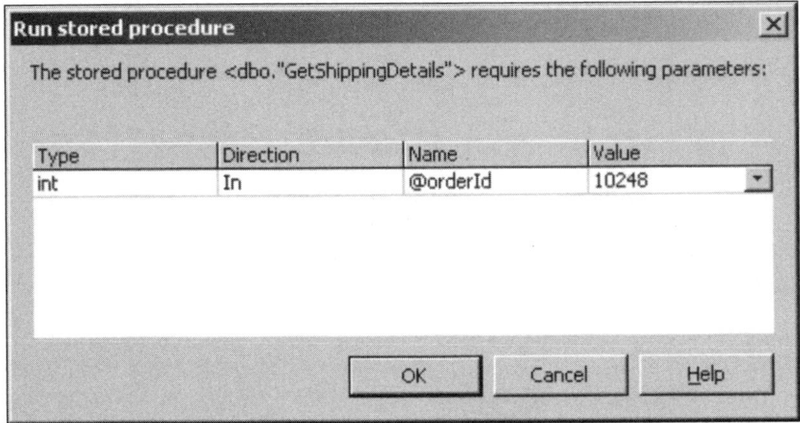

6. The Output window will appear containing the single row corresponding to the order ID supplied. If you can't see the Output window, select View | Other Windows | Output from the menu:

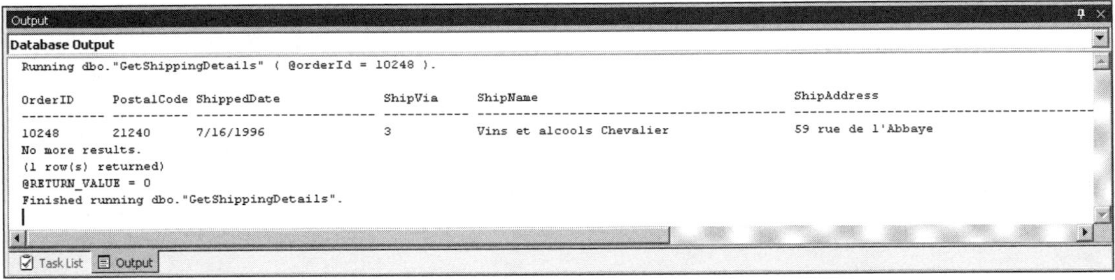

How It Works

You can see that the second column from the order ID returns the postal code of the customer. That's thanks to the `INNER JOIN` clause in the stored procedure. If PostalCode is the same as ShipPostalCode, that is because the customer's delivery address is the same as their business address.

For this customer to see the details of the order, they must provide the Web Service with both an order ID of 10248 and a postal code of 51100. With our somewhat rudimentary security scheme, if a postal code of 51100 is not entered, or if an order ID not linked to that address is provided, we return an error message, rather than the order details.

Building the GetShippingDetails Method

Now that we have the stored procedure, we can build the method.

Try It Out – Building a Web Method

1. Open Visual Studio .NET again, and locate the `OrderQuery` class in the code behind `OrderQuery.asmx`.

2. This method needs access to the various classes that provide SQL Server connectivity. At the top of `OrderQuery.asmx.vb`, add the line highlighted below:

```
Imports System.Data.SqlClient
Imports System.Web.Services
```

3. Next, add the `GetShippingDetails` method to `OrderQuery`:

```
  <WebMethod()> Public Function GetShippingDetails(ByVal orderId As Integer, _
                       ByVal customerZip As String) As ShippingDetailsResult

    ' Create a new object...
    Dim results As New ShippingDetailsResult()

    ' Be optimistic...
    results.RequestOk = True

    ' Establish a database connection...
    Dim connection As SqlConnection
    Dim reader As SqlDataReader
    Try
      connection = Connect()

      ' Create a command that will query the value we want...
      Dim command As New SqlCommand("GetShippingDetails", connection)
      command.CommandType = CommandType.StoredProcedure

      ' Add a parameter for the order ID...
      Dim param As SqlParameter = command.Parameters.Add("@orderId", _
                                       SqlDbType.Int)
      param.Direction = ParameterDirection.Input
      param.Value = orderId

      ' Execute it...
      reader = command.ExecuteReader()
      If reader.Read() = True Then

        ' Did the ZIP code match?
        If CStr(reader("ShipPostalCode")).ToLower = _
                                       customerZip.ToLower Then

          ' Did the order ship?
```

```
        If Not reader.IsDBNull(reader.GetOrdinal("ShippedDate")) Then

          ' It has been shipped...
          results.HasBeenShipped = True
          results.ShippedDate = reader("ShippedDate")

        Else

          ' The order has not shipped...
          results.HasBeenShipped = False

        End If

        ' We can populate the other data regardless...
        results.ShippedToName = reader("ShipName")
        results.ShippedToAddress = reader("ShipAddress")
        results.ShippedToCity = reader("ShipCity")
        If Not reader.IsDBNull(reader.GetOrdinal("ShipRegion")) _
                   Then results.ShippedToRegion = reader("ShipRegion")
        results.ShippedToPostalCode = reader("ShipPostalCode")
        results.ShippedToCountry = reader("ShipCountry")

      Else

        ' The ZIP code didn't match...
        results.RequestOk = False
        results.RequestProblem = _
                  "The ZIP code was invalid for this order."

      End If

    Else

      ' The order number was not found...
      results.RequestOk = False
      results.RequestProblem = "Order number '" & orderId & _
                                       "' was not found."

    End If

  Catch e As Exception

    ' Report that an exception occurred...
    ReportException(e, results)

  Finally
    If Not connection Is Nothing Then connection.Close()
    If Not reader Is Nothing Then reader.Close()

  End Try

  ' Return it...
  Return results

End Function
```

4. You may have spotted that call to the `Connect` method that opens the connection to our database. Placing it in a separate method like this makes it easier when we add new methods later. However, it needs a database connection string. We'll define this as a constant at the top of `OrderQuery`:

```
<WebService(Namespace:="http://wrox.com/1861005555")> Public Class OrderQuery
  Inherits System.Web.Services.WebService
```

```
  ' Constants...
  Protected Const DbString As String = "Integrated Security=SSPI;Data
Source=CHIMAERA;Initial Catalog=NorthwindSQL"
```

Notice that I've hard-coded in the database server name as `CHIMAERA` and the database name itself as `NorthwindSQL`. I've also used the SQL Server/MSDE integrated security provider. You'll need to change this string to suit your setup.

5. Now we can add the method to establish the database connection:

```
  ' Connect - connect to the database...
  Protected Function Connect() As SqlConnection

    ' create a new connection object...
    Dim connection As New SqlConnection(DbString)
    connection.Open()

    ' return the connection...
    Return connection

  End Function
```

6. You'll notice that towards the end of the method we call a function called `ReportException`. This method is quite simple, and tells the user about any errors that occur when the code runs. Add this code to `OrderQuery`:

```
  ' ReportException - report an exception when they occur...
  Protected Sub ReportException(ByVal e As Exception, _
                                ByRef result As ShippingDetailsResult)

    ' flag as failed and store the text...
    result.RequestOk = False
    result.RequestProblem = e.Message

  End Sub
```

We'll see later in the chapter how we can report exceptions to the system administrator. But for now, we'll just pass the exception back to the person using the Web Service.

How It Works

Let's run through the `GetShippingDetails` method. Firstly, we create a new `ShippingDetailsResult` object and we 'optimistically' set the `RequestOk` flag to `True`. If anything goes wrong, we change this to `False`.

```
<WebMethod()> Public Function GetShippingDetails(ByVal orderId As Integer, _
                  ByVal customerZip As String) As ShippingDetailsResult

  ' Create a new object
  Dim results As New ShippingDetailsResult()

  ' Be optimistic
  results.RequestOk = True
```

Once we have the object we can establish a database connection using our `Connect` method, placed inside a `Try...Catch` block. If anything goes wrong during our database interaction, an exception will be thrown that we can catch and act upon:

```
  ' Establish a database connection
  Dim connection As SqlConnection
  Dim reader As SqlDataReader
  Try
    connection = Connect()
```

To run the stored procedure, we need a `System.Data.SqlClient.SqlCommand` object. We pass this the name of the stored procedure, and the `SqlConnection` object:

```
    ' Create a command that will query the value we want...
    Dim command As New SqlCommand("GetShippingDetails", connection)
    command.CommandType = CommandType.StoredProcedure
```

To call the stored procedure, we need to create a parameter that references the `@orderId` parameter on the stored procedure. We give this the value passed into `GetShippingDetails` as the `orderId` parameter:

```
    ' add a parameter for the order ID...
    Dim param As SqlParameter = command.Parameters.Add("@orderId", _
                                     SqlDbType.Int)
    param.Direction = ParameterDirection.Input
    param.Value = orderId
```

Once we've configured the stored procedure, we execute it and move to the first row in the result set. If there is no row to read, the order ID supplied was invalid:

```
    ' execute it...
    reader = command.ExecuteReader()
    If reader.Read() = True Then
```

If there is a row to read, our first job is to look at the postal code we were passed. We use a case-insensitive comparison:

```
      ' did the ZIP code match?
      If CStr(reader("ShipPostalCode")).ToLower = _
                            customerZip.ToLower Then
```

If our `ShippedDate` column is `Null`, the order hasn't shipped yet. If not, then we can set the appropriate fields in our `ShippingDetailsResult` object.

```
' Did the order ship?
If Not reader.IsDBNull(reader.GetOrdinal("ShippedDate")) Then

  ' It has been shipped...
  results.HasBeenShipped = True
  results.ShippedDate = reader("ShippedDate")

Else

  ' The order has not shipped...
  results.HasBeenShipped = False

End If
```

Whether the order has been shipped or not, we populate the rest of the data. As `ShipRegion` can be `Null`, we test for this and don't add it to the results if it is:

```
' Populate the other data regardless...
results.ShippedToName = reader("ShipName")
results.ShippedToAddress = reader("ShipAddress")
results.ShippedToCity = reader("ShipCity")
If Not reader.IsDBNull(reader.GetOrdinal("ShipRegion")) _
               Then results.ShippedToRegion = reader("ShipRegion")
results.ShippedToPostalCode = reader("ShipPostalCode")
results.ShippedToCountry = reader("ShipCountry")
```

Now we look at the `Else` case when the postal code didn't match. If this is the case, we set the `ResultOk` property to `False` and tell the caller what happened:

```
Else

  ' The ZIP code didn't match...
  results.RequestOk = False
  results.RequestProblem = _
              "The ZIP code supplied does not match this order."

End If
```

Next comes the `Else` case to handle when a row could not be read, implying that order ID doesn't exist. We set `RequestOk` to `False`, and return a descriptive message:

```
Else

  ' the order number was not found...
  results.RequestOk = False
  results.RequestProblem = "Order number '" & orderId & _
                                                "' was not found."

End If
```

If an exception occurs, we need to pass it to our `ReportException` method. This method will automatically set `RequestOk` to `False` and pass the exception details back to the caller:

```
    Catch e As Exception

      ' report that an exception occurred...
      ReportException(e, results)
```

Irrespective of whether or not the method itself works, we need to make sure we close the `SqlConnection` and `SqlDataReader` object, if we managed to create them. By doing this in the `Finally` block of the `Try...Catch`, we guarantee that it will run:

```
    Finally
      If Not connection Is Nothing Then connection.Close()
      If Not reader Is Nothing Then reader.Close()

    End Try
```

Lastly, we return the `results` object:

```
    ' return it...
    Return results

  End Function
```

Our Web Service is now all built, and all that remains is to make sure it works.

Try It Out – Testing the Service

1. Run the project. You'll see a list of methods as before, but this time GetShippingDetails will be displayed:

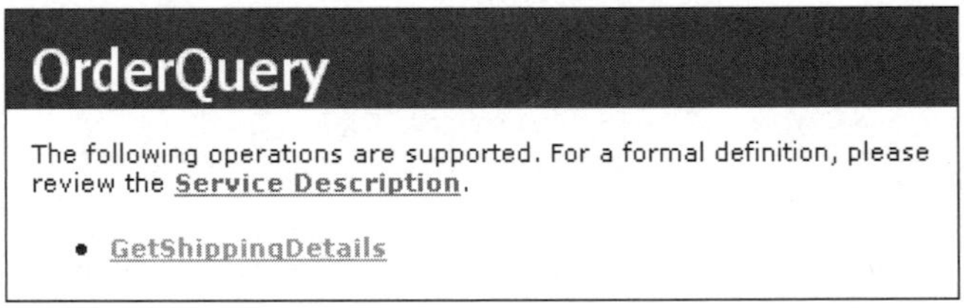

OrderQuery

The following operations are supported. For a formal definition, please review the **Service Description**.

- GetShippingDetails

2. Click GetShippingDetails. You'll be presented with a form that allows you to enter the parameters for the method call. Enter 10248 for the order ID and 51100 for the ZIP code and click the Invoke button:

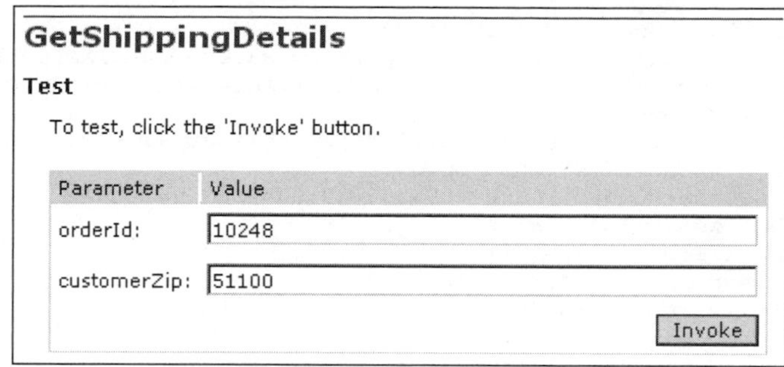

3. As normal, a new window will appear containing the results that the method would return to the client. Here's the XML that you should see:

```
 <?xml version="1.0" encoding="utf-8" ?>
- <ShippingDetailsResult xmlns:xsi="http://www.w3.org/2001/XMLSchema-instance"
xmlns:xsd="http://www.w3.org/2001/XMLSchema" xmlns="http://wrox.com/1861005555">
 <RequestOk>true</RequestOk>
 <RequestProblem xsi:nil="true" />
 <HasBeenShipped>true</HasBeenShipped>
 <ShippedDate>1996-07-16T00:00:00.0000000+01:00</ShippedDate>
 <ShippingMethod xsi:nil="true" />
 <ShippedToName>Vins et alcools Chevalier</ShippedToName>
 <ShippedToAddress>59 rue de l'Abbaye</ShippedToAddress>
 <ShippedToCity>Reims</ShippedToCity>
 <ShippedToRegion xsi:nil="true" />
 <ShippedToPostalCode>51100</ShippedToPostalCode>
 <ShippedToCountry>France</ShippedToCountry>
 </ShippingDetailsResult>
```

I've highlighted the RequestOk and HasBeenShipped entries that indicate that the request was processed without problem, and that the order has been shipped.

4. Now, close the results window and change the postal code to something invalid:

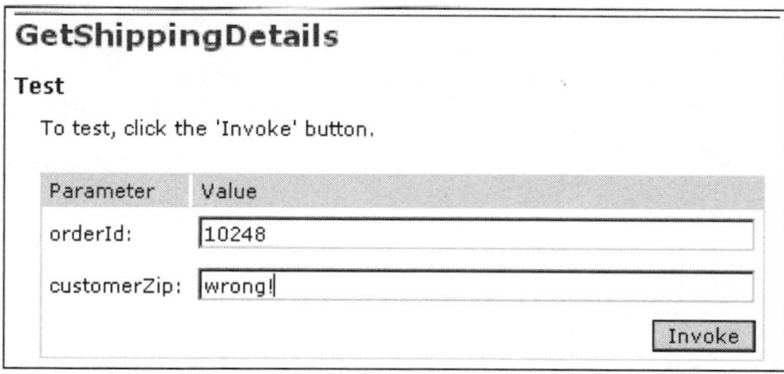

5. You'll now see that an error has been produced:

```
<?xml version="1.0" encoding="utf-8" ?>
- <ShippingDetailsResult xmlns:xsi="http://www.w3.org/2001/XMLSchema-instance"
xmlns:xsd="http://www.w3.org/2001/XMLSchema" xmlns="http://wrox.com/1861005555">
  <RequestOk>false</RequestOk>
  <RequestProblem>The ZIP code was invalid for this order.</RequestProblem>
  <HasBeenShipped>false</HasBeenShipped>
  <ShippedDate>0001-01-01T00:00:00.0000000-00:00</ShippedDate>
  <ShippingMethod xsi:nil="true" />
  <ShippedToName xsi:nil="true" />
  <ShippedToAddress xsi:nil="true" />
  <ShippedToCity xsi:nil="true" />
  <ShippedToRegion xsi:nil="true" />
  <ShippedToPostalCode xsi:nil="true" />
  <ShippedToCountry xsi:nil="true" />
  </ShippingDetailsResult>
```

This proves that our simple security scheme works. Unless the order ID and customer postal code match, the details are not returned. Note the `xsi:nil` attribute that indicates that a field doesn't have a value. Similar to SQL's `Null` value, it just means that there's no data for that entry. There's no such thing as a `Null` date, however. Hence, even though we provided no value, an arbitary date value still appears in the results.

6. Close the results window again, but this time enter an invalid order ID:

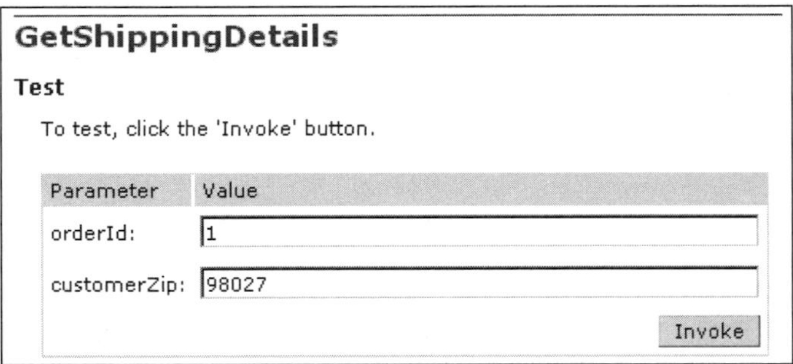

7. Again, an error will be returned:

```
<?xml version="1.0" encoding="utf-8" ?>
- <ShippingDetailsResult xmlns:xsi="http://www.w3.org/2001/XMLSchema-instance"
xmlns:xsd="http://www.w3.org/2001/XMLSchema" xmlns="http://wrox.com/1861005555">
  <RequestOk>false</RequestOk>
  <RequestProblem>Order number '1' was not found.</RequestProblem>
  <HasBeenShipped>false</HasBeenShipped>
  <ShippedDate>0001-01-01T00:00:00.0000000-00:00</ShippedDate>
  <ShippingMethod xsi:nil="true" />
  <ShippedToName xsi:nil="true" />
  <ShippedToAddress xsi:nil="true" />
  <ShippedToCity xsi:nil="true" />
  <ShippedToRegion xsi:nil="true" />
  <ShippedToPostalCode xsi:nil="true" />
  <ShippedToCountry xsi:nil="true" />
  </ShippingDetailsResult>
```

8. To test that the exception handling works, we'll need to create an exception. One way to do this is to alter the code so that it no longer works. Stop your Web Service, open `OrderQuery.asmx.vb`, and change the name of the stored procedure:

```
' create a command that will query the value we want...
  Dim command As New SqlCommand("DontGetShippingDetails", connection)
  command.CommandType = CommandType.StoredProcedure
```

9. Run the project again. Enter anything you like this time and an exception will be reported:

```
 <?xml version="1.0" encoding="utf-8" ?>
- <ShippingDetailsResult xmlns:xsi="http://www.w3.org/2001/XMLSchema-instance"
xmlns:xsd="http://www.w3.org/2001/XMLSchema" xmlns="http://wrox.com/1861005555">
 <RequestOk>false</RequestOk>
 <RequestProblem>Could not find stored procedure
'DontGetShippingDetails'.</RequestProblem>
 <HasBeenShipped>false</HasBeenShipped>
 <ShippedDate>0001-01-01T00:00:00.0000000-00:00</ShippedDate>
 <ShippingMethod xsi:nil="true" />
 <ShippedToName xsi:nil="true" />
 <ShippedToAddress xsi:nil="true" />
 <ShippedToCity xsi:nil="true" />
 <ShippedToRegion xsi:nil="true" />
 <ShippedToPostalCode xsi:nil="true" />
 <ShippedToCountry xsi:nil="true" />
 </ShippingDetailsResult>
```

At this point, we've fully tested the service and we can be fairly confident that it works as intended in all cases. All that remains now is to build a client application to use this Web Service.

Before you go on, remember to change the name of the stored procedure in `OrderQuery.GetShippingDetails` back to `GetShippingDetails` otherwise none of the remaining examples in this chapter will work.

Consuming a Web Service

Now that we've built our service and have managed to test it using the web interface in our browser, we can build a custom client to use or, more properly, **consume** it.

We could create a desktop application that lets our customers check the status of their orders. They simply enter an order number and their postal code, and the application displays the order details. Conceptually, there's no advantage to doing this over just having a form on our web site that customers can use to view their details, with no Web Service to be seen. So, in a way, if we were to offer our Web Service exclusively through a client application of our own, it would be a step backwards, as our customer now has to download that application, install it, and learn how to use it. Navigating to a traditional web page in their browser would be far easier.

The true power of Web Services, however, comes from the ease with which they can be integrated in an existing system. Say, for example, that our customer uses software they've written themselves for tracking stock. The application might show a list of all outstanding orders placed with their suppliers.

Our client could customize that software to automatically consume our Web Service and display live information about the status of outstanding orders. Once set up, there's no need to check our web site for that data – it is now seamlessly integrated into the existing package.

Unfortunately, it's not appropriate to show an example of how our Web Service could be integrated into an existing application, so in this exercise we'll build a dedicated client application to display the details of an order by using the Web Service. The principles behind the consuming process are the same irrespective of the final application. In a production situation, we would call this a "reference implementation", and it would be a good idea to make the source code available as a download too. It would help developers consume the Web Service from their own code with a minimum of hassle and, in this situation, hassle equates to phone calls and e-mails pestering you for help!

Try It Out – Building a Client Application

1. Open Visual Studio .NET and select File | New | Project from the menu. Select Windows Application from the Templates pane, and enter Northwind Order Status as the project title:

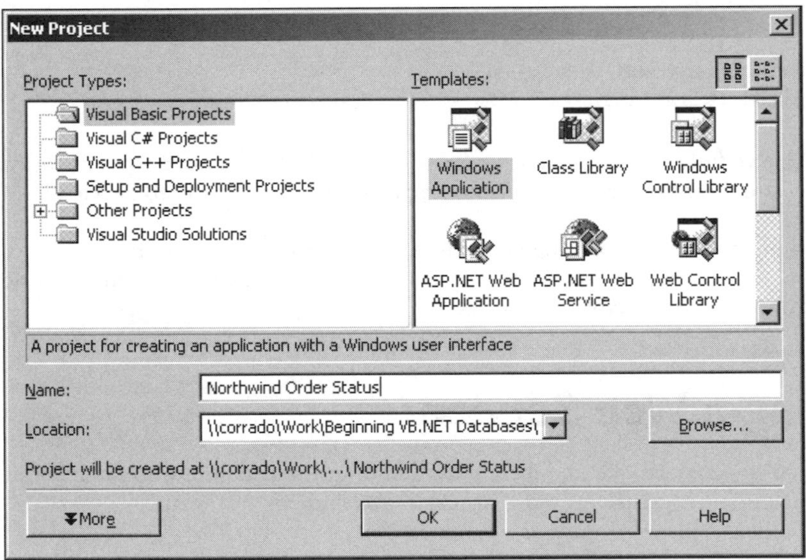

2. Once the project has been created, open the Form Designer and lay out some controls so that you have something that looks like this:

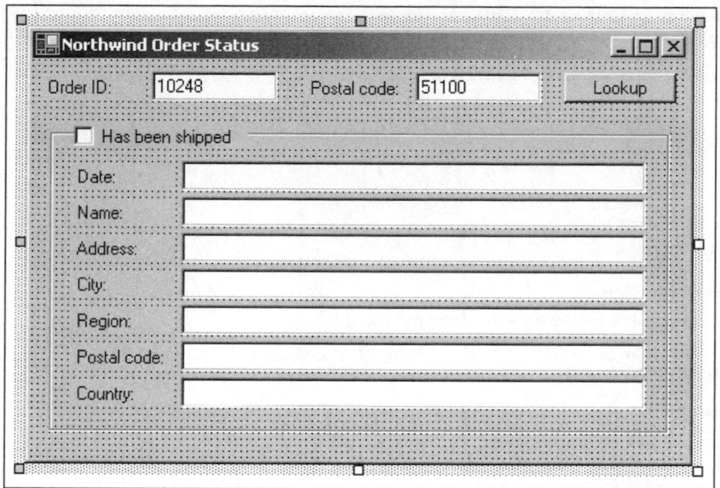

Working from left to right, and top to bottom, name your controls as follows:

- txtOrderId – also set the Text property to 10248
- txtZip – set the Text property to 51100
- btnLookup
- chkHasBeenShipped – set the Text property to Has been shipped
- txtShipDate
- txtName
- txtAddress
- txtCity
- txtRegion
- txtPostalCode
- txtCountry

I've used a group box to improve the aesthetics of the form, but you don't need to.

That's all there is to the form design. Before we wire up the code behind `btnLookup`, let's look at how to connect to our Web Service.

Try It Out – Adding a Web Reference

To use the Web Service, we need to add a "Web reference" to our project. This is simply a matter of pointing Visual Studio at the web server and selecting one of the Web Services hosted by the server.

1. Right-click on the Northwind Order Status project in Solution Explorer and click Add Web Reference. This will open the Add Web Reference dialog:

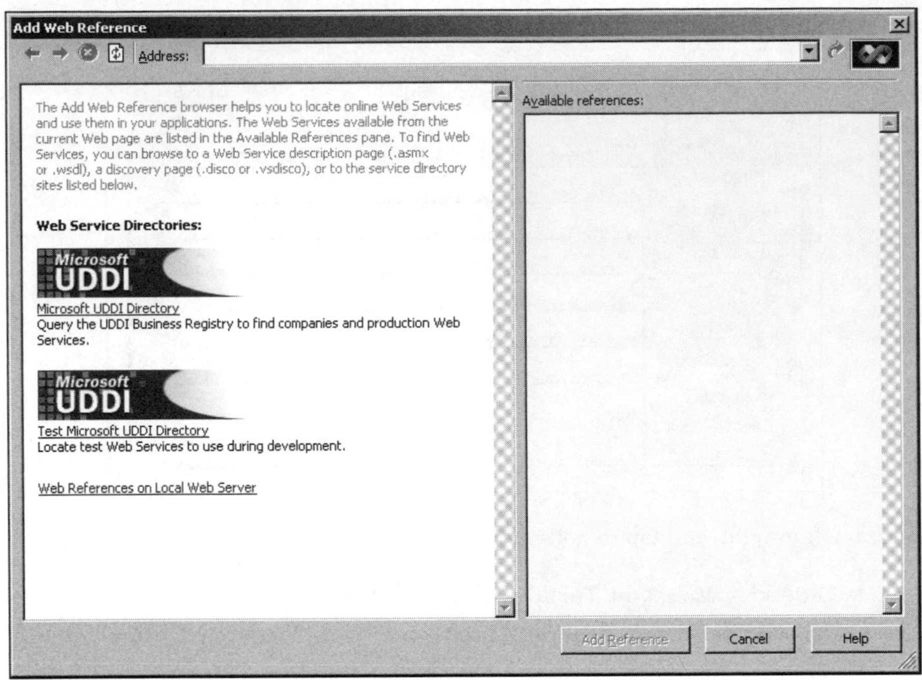

You can safely ignore the UDDI icons on the left-hand side. We'll be talking about UDDI a bit later, but for now it's not important.

2. Near the bottom of the left-hand pane is an entry marked Web References on Local Web Server. If you created your project on your local computer, click this.

   If you didn't, you're going to need to manually enter the URL. In the Address box at the top, enter the URL below, replacing machinename for your computer's name:

   http://machinename/default.vsdisco

   Click the little green arrow at the right of the Address box to load the references.

3. By default, the web server's root directory contains a file with a `.vsdisco` extension. "`disco`" is short for "discovery" and this file details the Web Services hosted on that computer. It should now appear in the left-hand pane as shown opposite:

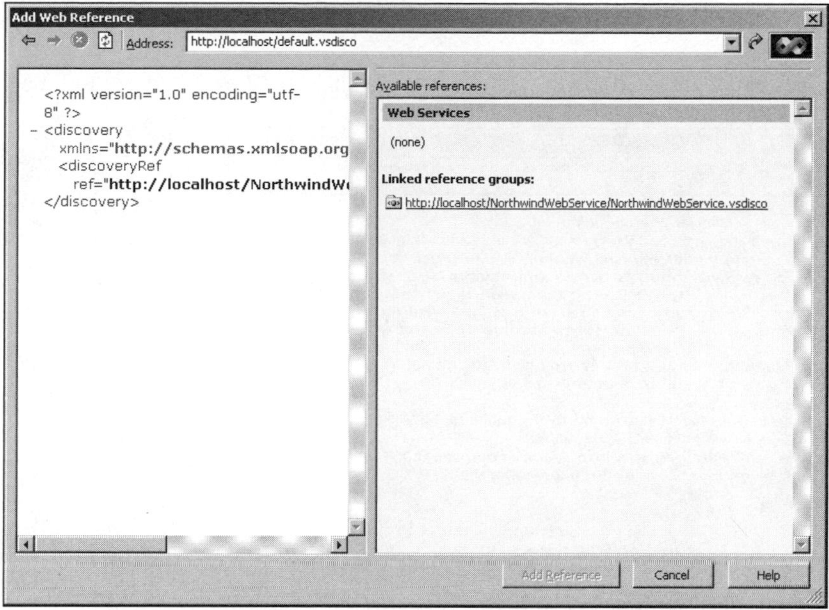

It is an XML file that lists the "reference groups", roughly analogous to our Visual Studio .NET projects. In the right-hand pane are listed the reference groups themselves. These groups contain the actual Web Services themselves.

4. Click the NorthwindWebService link in the right-hand pane to see the Web Services that the reference group contains:

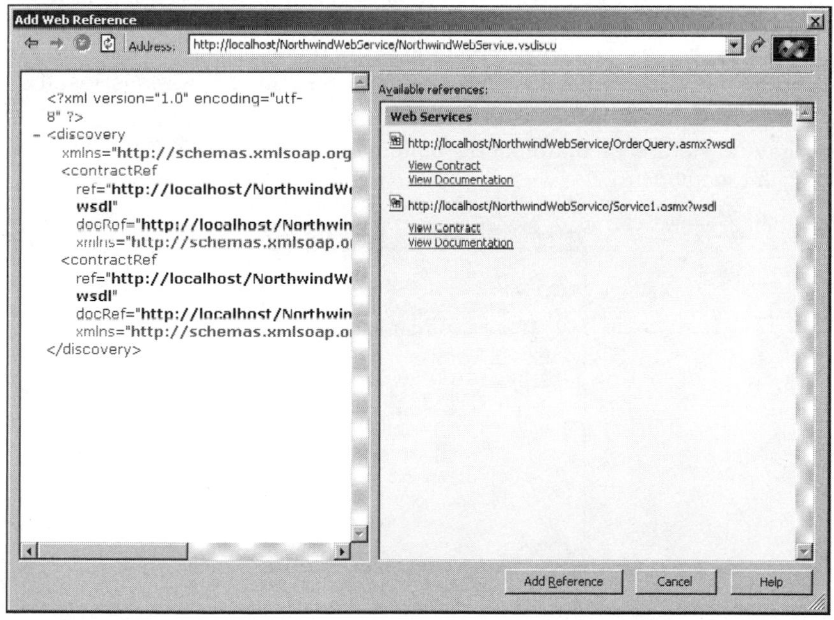

Note that our old "Hello, world!" service is still defined in `Service1.asmx`.

5. The one we're after is `OrderQuery.asmx`, so click the View Contract link below that entry:

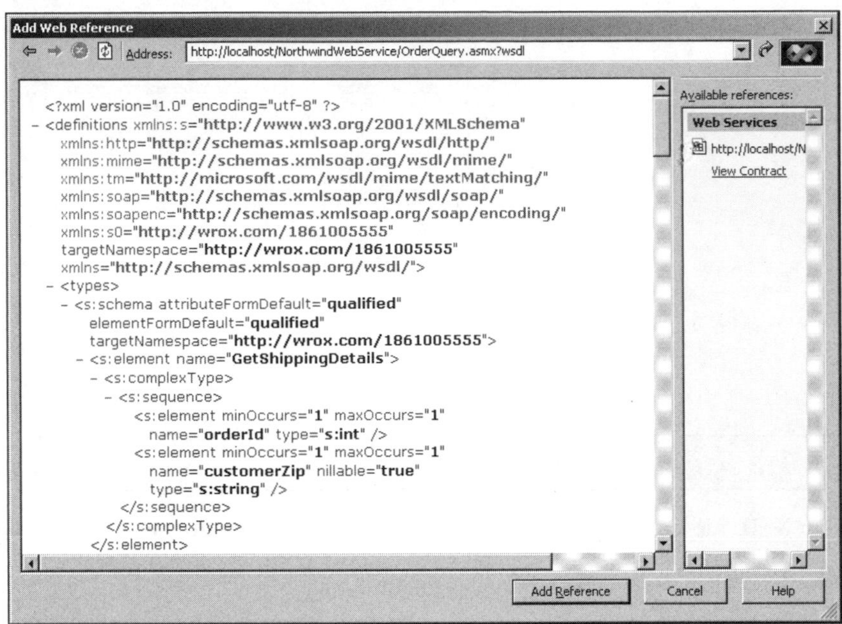

The XML that appears in the left-hand pane is the WSDL file that describes our Web Service. WSDL stands for "Web Services Description Language" and it is a standard way of describing how to talk to a Web Service. It details all the methods that the service supports, the parameters each takes, and what each returns. It also describes any complex types that are used, and in our case we have a single complex type: ShippingDetailsResult.

6. Click the Add Reference button at the bottom of the window. In Solution Explorer you'll see an entry for localhost:

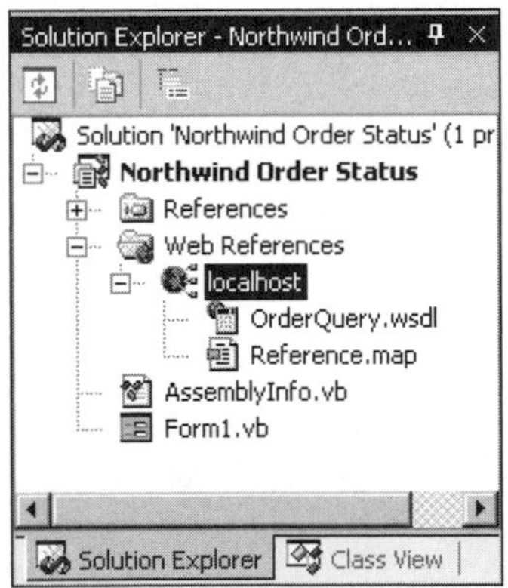

7. Before we finish, we can rename localhost to something more meaningful. Right-click on it within Solution Explorer, select Rename, and change the name to Northwind. Note that the name shown in Solution Explorer bears no relation to the URL used to access the Web Service. Although we've changed this to Northwind, internally it still points to localhost.

How It Works

Once we have the WSDL document corresponding to a Web Service, we can consume it. In this particular case, we used the point-and-click interface that forms part of the .NET discovery features to find the WSDL document for the particular Web Service we want.

The alternative is to be given a WSDL file direct. Usually, we'd expect someone to send us an e-mail containing a URL that points to their WSDL file but, as we'll see later in the chapter, we can use directories to find WSDL files that interest us.

Try It Out – Using the Web Reference

1. To use the web reference, we need to create a handler for the Click event of the Lookup button.

2. Double-click on the Lookup button on the Form Designer. This will bring up the code for the form, and automatically create a handler for the Click event.

3. Add this code:

```
Private Sub btnLookup_Click(ByVal sender As System.Object, _
            ByVal e As System.EventArgs) Handles btnLookup.Click

  ' clear the old details...
  chkHasBeenShipped.Checked = False
  txtShipDate.Text = ""
  txtName.Text = ""
  txtAddress.Text = ""
  txtCity.Text = ""
  txtRegion.Text = ""
  txtPostalCode.Text = ""
  txtCountry.Text = ""

  ' to connect to the Web Service, just create an instance of the
  ' object based on the reference that we added...
  Dim service As New Northwind.OrderQuery()

  ' now, we can just call methods on it...
  Dim result As Northwind.ShippingDetailsResult
  Try
    result = service.GetShippingDetails(txtOrderId.Text, txtZip.Text)
  Catch ex As Exception
    MsgBox("The Web service returned an error: " & ex.Message)
  End Try

  ' that's it! now we just use the object...
```

```
    If result.RequestOk = True Then

      ' set up the details...
      If result.HasBeenShipped = True Then
        chkHasBeenShipped.Checked = True
        txtShipDate.Text = result.ShippedDate.ToString
      End If

      ' set up the address details...
      txtName.Text = result.ShippedToName
      txtAddress.Text = result.ShippedToAddress
      txtCity.Text = result.ShippedToCity
      txtRegion.Text = result.ShippedToRegion
      txtPostalCode.Text = result.ShippedToPostalCode
      txtCountry.Text = result.ShippedToCountry

    Else

      ' report the problem...
      MsgBox("Order status could not be determined: " & _
                                                   result.RequestProblem)

    End If

  End Sub
```

4. Run the project. The form will appear and the Order ID and Postal code boxes will already be filled in. Click Lookup. You should see this:

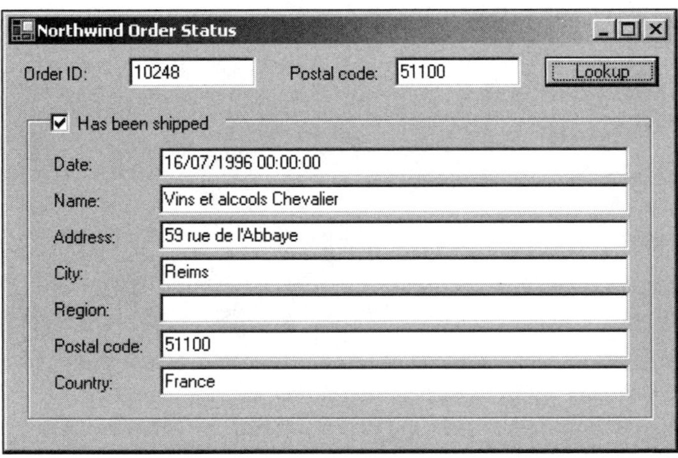

How It Works

Let's step through the code behind the Lookup button line by line.

The first thing we do is reset the details on the form. This means that if the order hasn't been shipped, or the Web Service cannot be found or returns an error, our form won't return invalid information:

```
Private Sub btnLookup_Click(ByVal sender As System.Object, _
                    ByVal e As System.EventArgs) Handles btnLookup.Click

  ' clear the old details...
  chkHasBeenShipped.Checked = False
  txtShipDate.Text = ""
  txtName.Text = ""
  txtAddress.Text = ""
  txtCity.Text = ""
  txtRegion.Text = ""
  txtPostalCode.Text = ""
  txtCountry.Text = ""
```

The next thing we do is to create an object that connects to the Web Service:

```
  ' to connect to the Web Service, just create an instance of the
  ' object based on the reference that we added...
  Dim service As New Northwind.OrderQuery()
```

Look back at the web references in Solution Explorer. Remember how we renamed localhost to Northwind? That allows us to create an instance of an object called `Northwind.OrderQuery`, rather than `localhost.OrderQuery`.

Visual Studio .NET is responsible for generating the code behind this object and there's no need to worry about what it's doing at this level. Suffice to say that we have a class that knows how to communicate with the Web Service.

Once we have a class that can connect to the service, we call the `GetShippingDetails` method. As you know, this returns a `ShippingDetailsResult` object:

```
  ' now, we can just call methods on it...
  Dim result As Northwind.ShippingDetailsResult
  Try
    result = service.GetShippingDetails(txtOrderId.Text, txtZip.Text)
  Catch ex As Exception
    MsgBox("The Web service returned an error: " & ex.Message)
  End Try
```

It's a good idea to wrap Web Service calls in a `Try...Catch` exception handler to trap the many things that can go wrong when calling a Web Service. If something does go wrong, `result` will be `Nothing`. Such events could include the Web Service itself not being available, problems with the local computer's Internet access, or unannounced changes to the parameters required by the Web Service. It won't catch internal errors to the Web Service, such as database errors, as these should be dealt with by the Web Service itself. Web Service owners should strive to insure that developers don't have to rework their own code if you add new methods or change its functionality. This can be quite a challenge, but it is very important to avoid putting off your customers.

So, if `result` isn't `Nothing`, we know that a valid set of results were returned from the server. If `RequestOk` is `True`, we know that some results were returned, rather than an error message, and thus we can update the details on the form:

```
        ' that's it! now we just use the object...
        If result.RequestOk = True Then

          ' set up the details...
          If result.HasBeenShipped = True Then
            chkHasBeenShipped.Checked = True
            txtShipDate.Text = result.ShippedDate.ToString
          End If

          ' set up the address details...
          txtName.Text = result.ShippedToName
          txtAddress.Text = result.ShippedToAddress
          txtCity.Text = result.ShippedToCity
          txtRegion.Text = result.ShippedToRegion
          txtPostalCode.Text = result.ShippedToPostalCode
          txtCountry.Text = result.ShippedToCountry
```

If ResultOk is False on the other hand, we need to report the error to the user:

```
        Else

          ' report the problem...
          MsgBox("Order status could not be determined: " & _
                                                  result.RequestProblem)

        End If

      End Sub
```

So what happens when the Click event actually fires? When we first create the Northwind.OrderQuery object, no information is actually sent over the Internet at all. Instead, preparations are performed for later calls to the method.

When the GetShippingResults method is called, the request is wrapped up as a SOAP message containing the name of the method and the parameters for the order ID and postal code. The Visual Studio .NET-generated OrderQuery object automatically does this for us. This same object then sends the message out over the Internet to the target Web Service.

IIS on the computer hosting the Web Service receives the request and, thanks to the .asmx extension within the URL, knows it has to pass it to ASP.NET. ASP.NET interprets the request, and fires up the OrderQuery object we built that powers the Web Service. The GetShippingResults method is called that creates a new ShippingDetailsResult object and populates it appropriately.

When we return from this method, it's down to ASP.NET to prepare a SOAP-formatted response describing the data contained within ShippingDetailsResult in XML form. The Visual Studio .NET-generated OrderQuery object on the client receives the message and recreates an actual instance of a ShippingDetailsResult object from the SOAP Response. One important thing to note is that the ShippingDetailsResult object is *not* the same as that on the server. Both are auto-generated by Visual Studio .NET; however, the client-side version simply makes the public properties and fields of the object available to the client. If the server ShippingDetailsResult object contains some clever functionality, we could not apply that functionality on the client.

If you require the rich functionality of your server objects to be made available to client applications, you need to use the technique of "remoting". See Professional VB.NET *(Wrox Press, ISBN 1861004974).*

So we end up, after the call, with a `ShippingDetailsResult` object on the client. We can then use its public properties just as we did on the server.

Testing More Eventualities

Let's take a look now at some more ways in which the service can be used. Start up the client again, keep the Order ID set to 10248, but change the Postal code to make it incorrect. Click Lookup, and you should be presented with a message like this:

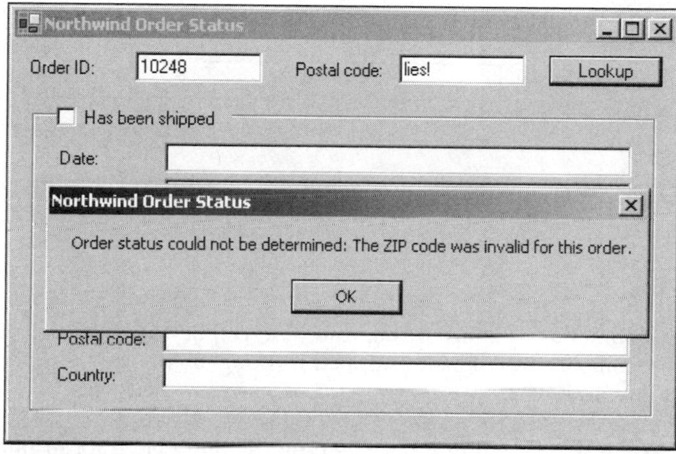

Now, try entering an Order ID that doesn't exist, like 1:

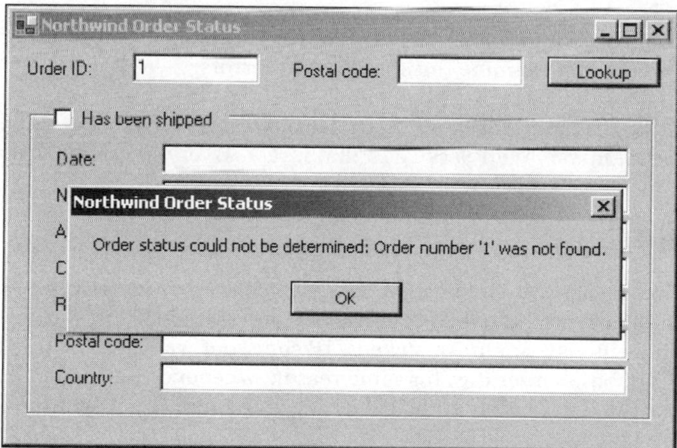

Finally, let's prove that we can look up other orders from the database, and check that if the order hasn't yet been shipped, Has been shipped remains unchecked. Enter an Order ID of 11019 and a Postal code of 1010:

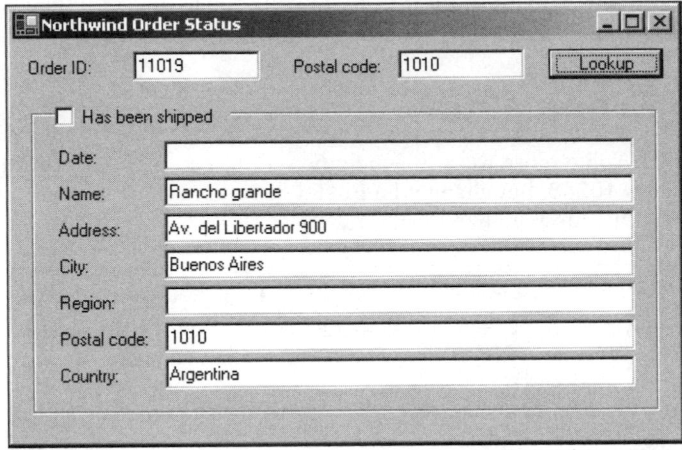

Error Logging

So how do we know if something's going wrong with our Web Service? We can either take the reactive approach and wait for someone to tell us it's stopped working, or we can be proactive and deliberately seek out and correct any problems.

Server applications like SQL Server and Exchange typically don't have a user interface – or, rather, their UI allows for administration tasks but is not one that sits on the desktop running continuously. Our Web Service may have a web interface for testing, but it doesn't run all the time.

When server applications want to report their status they traditionally do so using the "event log". A system administrator can then examine this event log for errors.

Writing to the Event Log is traditionally a non-trivial activity, but .NET has made it extremely easy. What we'll do now is set up our Web Service so that it reports any problems that occur in the event log.

Logging Problems

Our Web Service already has a method called `ReportException` that's called internally whenever an exception occurs. In the normal course of business, we don't need to report trivial problems, like an invalid order ID being entered, or a mismatched ZIP code, but we will need to watch for exceptions. For example, if our database server dies for some reason, whenever we try and connect we'll get an exception. If we report that exception in the event log, an administrator will see the problem and fix it.

Try It Out – Writing Exceptions To the Event Log

1. Open Visual Studio .NET and load the NorthwindWebService project from the web server. (Refer back to Chapter 11 for details on how to do this.)

2. We need to reference the `System.Diagnostics` and `System.Text` namespaces. Add the following directives to the top of the `OrderQuery.asmx.vb` code page:

```
Imports System.Data.SqlClient
Imports System.Web.Services
Imports System.Diagnostics
Imports System.Text
```

3. Add another constant to the `OrderQuery` class:

```
<WebService(Namespace:="http://wrox.com/1861005555")> Public Class OrderQuery
  Inherits System.Web.Services.WebService

  ' constants...
  Protected Const DbString As String = "Integrated Security=SSPI;" & _
                                       "Data Source=CHIMAERA,Initial Catalog=Northwind"
  Protected Const EventSourceName As String = "NorthwindWebService"
```

4. Now, locate the `ReportException` method. Add this code:

```
  ' ReportException - report an exception when they occur...
  Protected Sub ReportException(ByVal e As Exception, _
                                ByRef result As ShippingDetailsResult)

    ' flag as failed and store the text...
    result.RequestOk = False
    result.RequestProblem = e.Message

    ' before we can write to the log, we need to
    ' create an event source...
    Try
      EventLog.CreateEventSource(EventSourceName, "Application")
    Catch
    End Try

    ' create the message...
    Dim message As New StringBuilder("An exception has occured." & _
                                     ControlChars.CrLf)
    message.Append("Source: " & e.Source & ControlChars.CrLf)
    message.Append("Message: " & e.Message & ControlChars.CrLf)
    message.Append("Stack trace: " & e.StackTrace & ControlChars.CrLf)

    ' now, create a new event log object...
    Dim log As New EventLog()
    log.Source = EventSourceName
    log.WriteEntry(message.ToString, EventLogEntryType.Error, 1000)

  End Sub
```

5. To test the new functionality, we need to create an exception. An easy way to do this is to stop the database server. On the system tray next to the clock you should see the Desktop Engine Service Manager icon. Double-click on it, make sure the correct server name and the MSSQLServer service are selected, and click Stop:

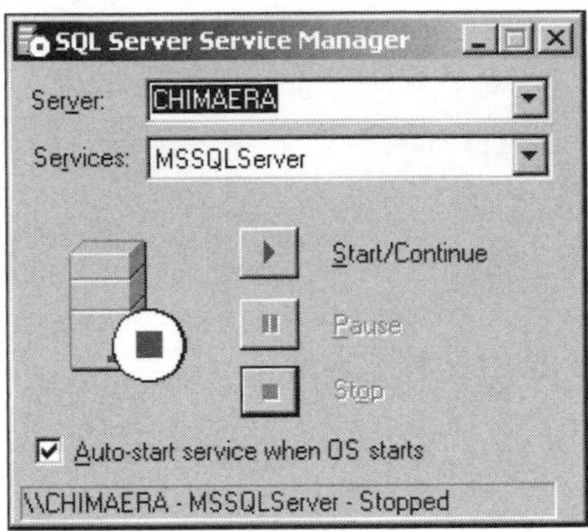

6. Now, run the project and run the `GetShippingDetails` method as normal. There will be a delay while the SQL connection times out but, eventually, you'll receive an error message:

```
<RequestOk>false</RequestOk>
<RequestProblem>SQL Server does not exist or access denied.</RequestProblem>
```

7. Let's now take a look at the event log. Click the Start button and select Settings | Control Panel | Administrative Tools | Computer Management. Expand the object tree until you see the Application event log:

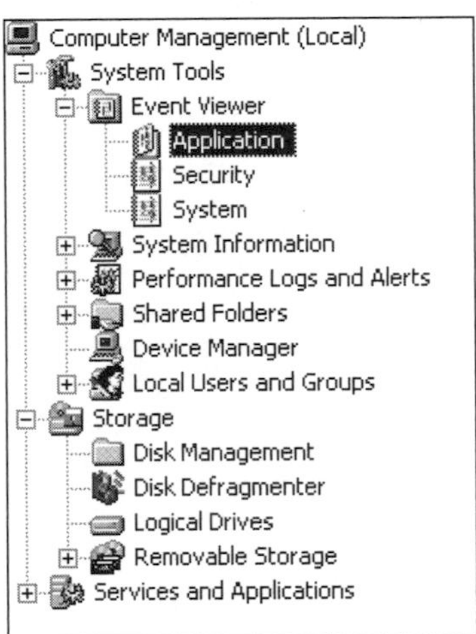

8. In the right-hand pane, you'll see a bunch of messages. You'll see one marked Error in the Type column, with NorthwindWebService specified in the Source column:

Type	Date	Time	Source
Error	25/06/2001	14:15:03	NorthwindWebService

9. Double-click the error and a window will appear with a Description box containing details of the exception. This should be enough for a system administrator or developer to rectify the problem:

```
An exception has occured.
Source: SQL Server Managed Provider
Message: SQL Server does not exist or access denied.
Stack trace:  at System.Data.SqlClient.SqlConnection.Open()
  at NorthwindWebService.OrderQuery.Connect() in
c:\inetpub\wwwroot\NorthwindWebService\OrderQuery.asmx.vb:line 131
  at NorthwindWebService.OrderQuery.GetShippingDetails(Int32 orderId, String customerZip)
in c:\inetpub\wwwroot\NorthwindWebService\OrderQuery.asmx.vb:line 54
```

How It Works

The event log implementation in .NET provides a really easy way for us to add messages to the event log. Before .NET, doing this in Visual Basic or C++ was a fairly painful process.

To write a message, we first set the event source that will appear in the Source column of the event viewer. The `System.Diagnostics.EventLog.CreateEventSource` method does this for us:

```
' ReportException - report an exception when it occurs...
Protected Sub ReportException(ByVal e As Exception, _
                              ByRef result As ShippingDetailsResult)

  ' flag as failed and store the text...
  result.RequestOk = False
  result.RequestProblem = e.Message

  ' before we can write to the log, we need to
  ' create an event source...
  Try
    EventLog.CreateEventSource(EventSourceName, "Application")
  Catch
  End Try
```

We wrap `CreateEventSource` up in a `Try...Catch` block to catch an exception if the source already exists.

> *The method called `Exists` can test if a source exists, but if the user clears the event log, it will incorrectly say that the source does not exist, resulting in an error.*

Once we have the source, we need to format the message. We use properties on the `System.Exception` object in conjunction with a `System.Text.StringBuilder`:

```
' create the message...
Dim message As New StringBuilder("An exception has occured." & _
                                  ControlChars.CrLf)
message.Append("Source: " & e.Source & ControlChars.CrLf)
message.Append("Message: " & e.Message & ControlChars.CrLf)
message.Append("Stack trace: " & e.StackTrace & ControlChars.CrLf)
```

Finally, we create a new `System.Diagnostics.EventLog` object and have it write our message to the event log:

```
    ' now, create a new event log object...
    Dim log As New EventLog()
    log.Source = EventSourceName
    log.WriteEntry(message.ToString, EventLogEntryType.Error, 1000)

  End Sub
```

With this functionality in place, if anything goes wrong with our Web Service after it's been made public, we will be alerted of any errors that occur so we may fix them.

Debugging SOAP

If you're doing a lot of work with Web Services, you'll eventually run into the situation where the service you're trying to use doesn't work exactly as intended. To find out more of what's going on, it can be useful to watch the SOAP envelopes as they pass between client and server.

There is a handy utility called "proxyTrace" that allows us to do this, and we shall have a look at this now. It's available as freeware from http://www.pocketsoap.com/, under the proxyTrace link. Download it now, and save it somewhere easy to find.

Try It Out – Watching SOAP Envelopes

1. Start proxyTrace. It will prompt you for a port. The default is 8080. If you've already got a proxy server installed on your computer, you'll have to choose another port. Most of you will have port 8080 available, so just click OK.

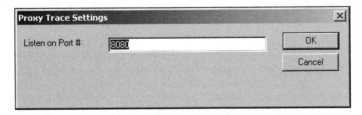

2. The proxyTrace application won't have much to say at the moment, but we'll need to set up our client to use the proxy server. Open the Northwind Order Status application, open Form1 in Design view, and double-click the Lookup button.

We need to set up the proxy server after we create the `Northwind.OrderQuery` object. Add this code to the `Click` event handler:

```
' to connect to the Web Service, just create an instance of the
' object based on the reference that we added...
Dim service As New Northwind.OrderQuery()

' create a connection to a proxy server...
service.Proxy = New System.Net.WebProxy("localhost", 8080)

' now, we can just call methods on it...
Dim result As Northwind.ShippingDetailsResult
Try
  result = service.GetShippingDetails(txtOrderId.Text, txtZip.Text)
Catch ex As Exception
  MsgBox("The Web service returned an error: " & ex.Message)
End Try
```

The last parameter to the WebProxy constructor is the port. If you weren't able to use port 8080, remember to change this to the port number you actually used.

3. Now, run the client. Click the Lookup button and the application should work as normal. However, the left-hand pane of proxyTrace should look like this:

Source IP	Destination	Time	Status	Bytes In	Bytes Out
127.0.0.1	localhost	12:13...	connected	3608	4114

If you click 127.0.0.1, the right-hand pane will display both the SOAP Request and the SOAP Response, the top entry being the Request and the bottom entry the Response.

You find a slew of data under VsDebuggingCausalityData. You can safely ignore this and, if you scroll down to the bottom of the top entry, you'll find the XML that constitutes the SOAP document sent to the server requesting the web method:

```
<?xml version="1.0" encoding="utf-8"?>
<soap:Envelope xmlns:soap="http://schemas.xmlsoap.org/soap/envelope/"
xmlns:xsi="http://www.w3.org/2001/XMLSchema-instance"
xmlns:xsd="http://www.w3.org/2001/XMLSchema">
 <soap:Body>
  <GetShippingDetails xmlns="http://wrox.com/1861005555">
   <orderId>10248</orderId>
   <customerZip>51100</customerZip>
  </GetShippingDetails>
 </soap:Body>
</soap:Envelope>
```

I've highlighted in gray the request to `GetShippingDetails`. You can see the parameters that we've passed through.

The response entry clearly shows us what was returned to the client:

```
<?xml version="1.0" encoding="utf-8"?>
<soap:Envelope xmlns:soap="http://schemas.xmlsoap.org/soap/envelope/"
xmlns:xsi="http://www.w3.org/2001/XMLSchema-instance"
xmlns:xsd="http://www.w3.org/2001/XMLSchema">
 <soap:Body>
  <GetShippingDetailsResponse xmlns="http://wrox.com/1861005555">
   <GetShippingDetailsResult>
    <RequestOk>true</RequestOk>
    <RequestProblem xsi:nil="true" />
    <HasBeenShipped>true</HasBeenShipped>
    <ShippedDate>1996-07-16T00:00:00.0000000+01:00</ShippedDate>
    <ShippingMethod xsi:nil="true" />
    <ShippedToName>Vins et alcools Chevalier</ShippedToName>
    <ShippedToAddress>59 rue de l'Abbaye</ShippedToAddress>
    <ShippedToCity>Reims</ShippedToCity>
    <ShippedToRegion xsi:nil="true" />
    <ShippedToPostalCode>51100</ShippedToPostalCode>
    <ShippedToCountry>France</ShippedToCountry>
   </GetShippingDetailsResult>
  </GetShippingDetailsResponse>
 </soap:Body>
</soap:Envelope>
```

Again, I've highlighted the important parts in gray. This XML will be used to populate our `ShippingDetailsResult` object on the client.

One thing to watch when using proxyTrace is that, if you send another request, another entry might not appear in the list on the left. Whenever a request is made, the connection remains open for a short time. (This makes communication more efficient.)

If you don't see the new request, but connected is shown in the Status column, you'll have to select another request in the list and then reselect the original one. Unfortunately, you can't just click on the blank area of the list to select nothing and then flip back again so, if you only have one request, close and restart proxyTrace.

How It Works

proxyTrace acts as a **proxy server**, intercepting and examining requests for web resources before forwarding them on to the server. Most proxy servers let you examine the data that they handle and that, of course, is the sole purpose of proxyTrace.

It is useful for situations when you're getting errors from a Web Service as you can determine whether or not the service is returning the expected response. If the Web Service does appear to be working properly, you know that the problem must lie in the client-side code.

In my experience, I've found the tool extremely useful for capturing errors returned from the Web Service. .NET doesn't properly trap SOAP Fault messages from some Web Service implementations, and comes up with some fairly cryptic messages, like this one:

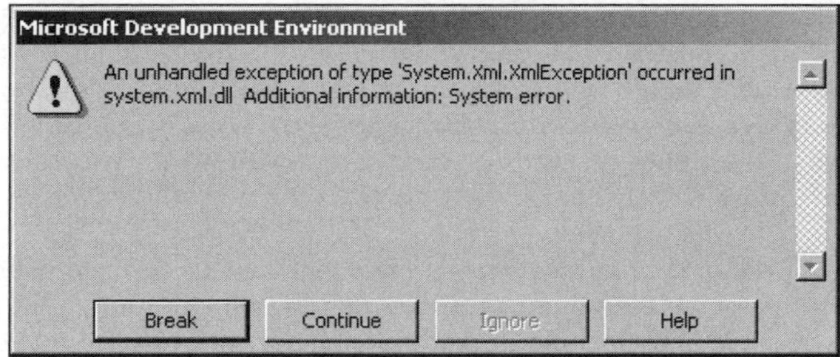

If you get an error similar to this when calling a web method, crack out proxyTrace and look at the response packet. You might find something like this:

```
<SOAP-ENV:Fault>
   <faultcode>SOAP-ENV:Client</faultcode>
   <faultstring>Client Error</faultstring>
   <faultactor>lcTk##SBA-CSOAPBusinessArea-SOAP</faultactor>
   <detail>
      <e:details xmlns:e="http://tempuri.org/">
         <message>ERR: Schema for that business area and process
         are missing</message>
         <errorcode>57126</errorcode>
      </e:details>
   </detail>
</SOAP-ENV:Fault>
```

If you get an error like this and can't figure out how to fix it, try contacting the Web Service owner for advice.

Directory Services

Although it's likely that, in time, you'll want to build your own Web Services, there are a growing selection of Web Services supplied by third-party sources for us to use.

The question remains, however, how to find these Web Services once companies have made them available.

In the next two sections, we'll take a look at how to use two kinds of directory services to find Web Services, namely UDDI and brokerages.

UDDI

UDDI, for Universal Description, Discovery, and Integration, is a type of directory geared towards business process integration. They are mainly used if you are looking for a business partner that provides some specific task, and who publishes a Web Service for that task.

The UDDI initiative was jointly launched by Microsoft, IBM, and Ariba in May 2001. Although all three organizations were to maintain sites that would allow searching and administration of a single directory, after a little over a month Ariba announced that Microsoft and IBM would be responsible for managing the directory. It's also expected that by the time this book is published, Hewlett-Packard will have another site. All of these sites synchronize their data so that it won't matter which of the two or more sites are used to query UDDI.

The ultimate goal of UDDI is to bring business partners together. Once they've done this, the companies can either interact in the usual way, that is through e-mails and phone calls, or they can use the directory to obtain the WSDL documents that describe the Web Service that each offers.

Let's take a look now at how a book distributor looking for potential new publishers might go about it. We'll also see how that publisher could find the Web Service that will allow orders to be placed automatically.

> **Although we're going to look at the case of a Web Service for distributors to place orders, the service doesn't really exist. This is a hypothetical scenario for demonstration purposes.**

Remember, the WSDL document is all you need to consume a Web Service, by following the same steps we took for the NorthwindWebService service.

Try It Out – Finding a Business Partner with UDDI

1. Microsoft and IBM each manage two directories. One is a live site that provides working business information and the other is a test site for testing how UDDI actually works. I've registered a sample set of services on the Microsoft UDDI test site. Open a web browser and go to http://test.uddi.microsoft.com/.

2. To find a business partner, you must either know their name, or know something about their business. In this hypothetical case, we're looking for book publishers. Standard Industry Classifications (SIC) codes can do this and, as long as you know the SIC code, tools on the site can find everyone in the specified category. Luckily, I happen to know that book publishing comes under Manufacturing | Printing and Publishing | Books and that the code we want is 2730.

   Click the Advanced Search link on the UDDI page, and enter the following:

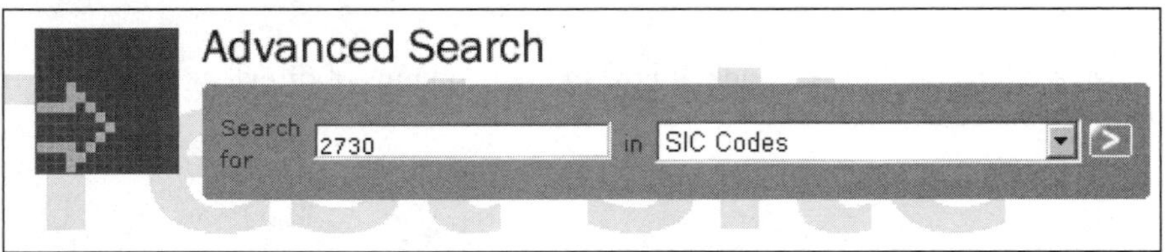

3. Click the arrow button next to the drop-down to bring up a list of businesses:

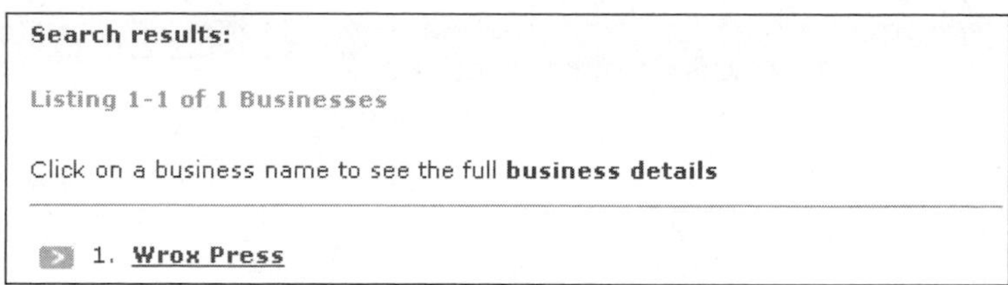
Search results:

Listing 1-1 of 1 Businesses

Click on a business name to see the full **business details**

1. Wrox Press

4. Click on Wrox Press. This will bring up the company listing. Half-way down the page you'll find an entry marked Services. This is a list of the services that the company offers. These aren't limited to Web Services, and can include traditional services offered by the company:

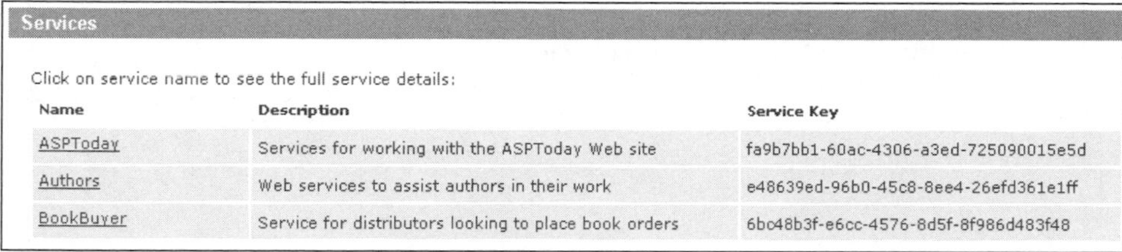
Services

Click on service name to see the full service details:

Name	Description	Service Key
ASPToday	Services for working with the ASPToday Web site	fa9b7bb1-60ac-4306-a3ed-725090015e5d
Authors	Web services to assist authors in their work	e48639ed-96b0-45c8-8ee4-26efd361e1ff
BookBuyer	Service for distributors looking to place book orders	6bc48b3f-e6cc-4576-8d5f-8f986d483f48

5. Click BookBuyer. This will bring up a list of bindings, which are particular to Web Services, and you'll find a single binding on this page that points to a WSDL file:

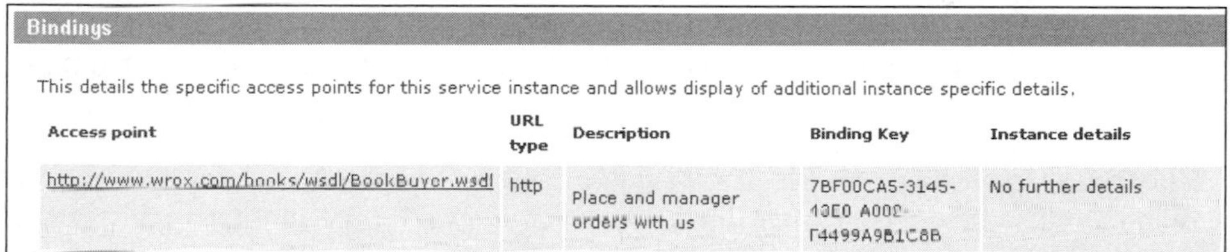
Bindings

This details the specific access points for this service instance and allows display of additional instance specific details.

Access point	URL type	Description	Binding Key	Instance details
http://www.wrox.com/books/wsdl/BookBuyer.wsdl	http	Place and manager orders with us	7BF00CA5-3145-43E0 A002-F4499A9B1C8B	No further details

6. Right-click on the URL of the WSDL file to bring up the context menu, and select Copy Shortcut.

7. Open Visual Studio .NET and select New Visual Basic project | Windows Application. Call it BookBuyer. The name doesn't matter too much because we'll throw it away after having used it to demonstrate the principles here.

8. Right-click on the BookBuyer project in Solution Explorer and select Add Web Reference.

9. Right-click the URL box at the top and select Paste. Click the green arrow. This will download the WSDL file from the Wrox site ready for use:

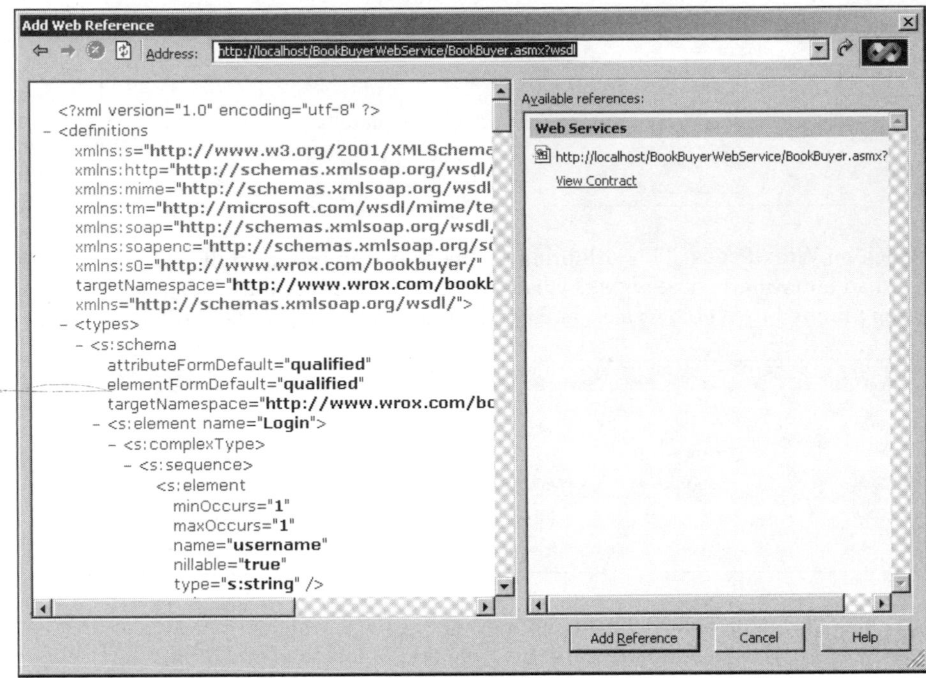

As the Web Service described by the WSDL file doesn't in reality exist, we'll stop our discussion here. Hopefully, though, you now understand how UDDI works. We use the tools supplied to find a business partner in the directory and, ultimately, a URL (a "binding") for their Web Service.

Had this been a real, existing Web Service, we'd just need to click the Add Reference button to get Visual Studio .NET to create the classes that consume the service. With those new classes in place, we could then start using the service straight away.

Web Service Brokerages

With UDDI, we saw an example of a Web Service directory that can help us find commercial business partners that expose Web Services as part of their line of business. This is just half the market. Over the coming months, we can expect to see companies deploy Web Services that add useful functionality to our applications. This is, after all, the central premise of Web Services – "software as services".

Microsoft's push into this area was initially dubbed Hailstorm, but is now known as ".NET My Services". This describes a set of common, fundamental services that web sites and desktop applications are likely to want to use. My Services will include the "Passport" concept and other central Internet-based services such as a diary, a file storage facility, and so on. At the time of writing, however, My Services is still very much hype, so we're not going to dwell on it here.

Another way to sift through the hundreds of Web Services coming on to the market is through a **Web Service brokerage**, such as Salcentral (http://www.salcentral.com/) or Grand Central (http://www.grandcentral.com/).

SMS Messaging

In this last section, we're going to use Salcentral to find a Web Service that we can call from our existing client application. Specifically, we're going to use their SMSMessaging Web Service. This Web Service can send a text message via SMS, the Short Message Service, to a handheld unit such as a compatible cell phone.

Without a suitable Web Service, this is a particularly tricky proposition that can entail physically connecting a cell phone to your computer and controlling it through the serial port, or integrating with a third-party SMS provider with none of the simplicity offered by a Web Service.

In many parts of the world, including Europe and Australia, SMS messaging is big business and a surprisingly popular way of communicating despite the cost – sending a message typically costs the sender between 10 and 20 cents per message. European phones support sending of SMS messages direct from the handset, whereas North American phones generally do not. Because of the inability of most North American phones to originate messages, SMS messaging is far less common here. However, it is a useful tool for communicating with your customers and employees when they're not physically in front of a connected computer.

Salcentral's SMS service is not a free service, but it has a free trial whereby you can send 20 messages for free while you're developing your application.

> *Wrox Press Ltd. in no way endorses Salcentral or its SMS Web Service and cannot accept any liability for loss or damage sustained as a result of using it.*

Registering for the Service

First of all, we have to register with Salcentral and sign up for their SMS Web Service, by following the instructions at http://www.salcentral.com/x/smsreg.asp. Make sure you note down the "Username" and "passkey" that you receive at the end of the process as they are needed when building your application.

Once we've registered for the service, we're ready to build our Windows application to access it.

Try It Out – Building the Project

1. Select New Visual Basic project | Windows Application. Call it SMS, and click OK.

2. When the Form Designer appears, change the Text property to SMS Messaging.

   Lay out controls on the form as shown here:

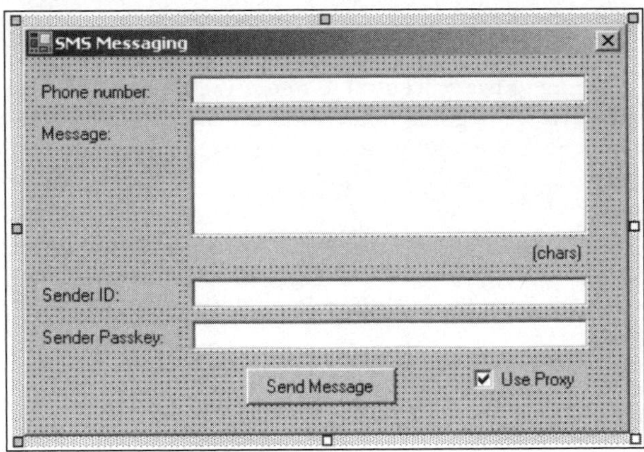

- The `TextBox` controls (from top to bottom) need to have their **Name** property set thus:
  - txtPhoneNumber
  - txtMessage – this control also needs its **Multiline** property set to **True**
  - txtSenderId
  - txtSendPasskey

  The `Label` control marked **(chars)** needs to have its **Name** property set to **lblChars**. Call the `CheckBox` **chkUseProxy** and set its **Checked** property to **True**. Also the button needs to be called **btnSendMessage**.

3. There is a limit to the number of characters that can be sent through to the service, so we want to keep the user informed of how much space is left for the message. The maximum length of the message is 120 characters and this includes the length of the sender ID, the word "from", and two spaces. Double-click on the `txtMessage` control and add the method call highlighted below to the event handler, followed by the `UpdateCharacterCount` method itself:

```
Private Sub txtMessage_TextChanged(ByVal sender As System.Object, _
           ByVal e As System.EventArgs) Handles txtMessage.TextChanged
  UpdateCharacterCount()
End Sub

Private Sub UpdateCharacterCount()

  ' add the number of chars...
  Dim numChars As Integer = " from ".Length
  numChars += txtMessage.Text.Length
  numChars += txtSenderId.Text.Length

  ' report the length...
  lblChars.Text = numChars & " characters"
  If numChars > 120 Then
```

```
    lblChars.ForeColor = Color.Red
  Else
    lblChars.ForeColor = SystemColors.ControlText
  End If

End Sub
```

4. Flip back to the Form Designer and double-click on the txtSenderId box. Add this code to the new event handler:

```
Private Sub txtSenderId_TextChanged(ByVal sender As System.Object, _
              ByVal e As System.EventArgs) Handles txtSenderId.TextChanged
  UpdateCharacterCount()
End Sub
```

Referencing the Web Service

Now that we've built the basic form, we are ready to add a reference to the SMS service on Salcentral's site.

Try It Out – Adding a Web Reference

1. Open your browser and go back to the http://www.salcentral.com/wrox/smsreg.asp page. On this page you'll find a link to the WSDL file describing the Web Service. It will look something like this:

   http://sal006.salnetwork.com:83/lucin/SMSMessaging/Process.xml

2. Select the entire URL with your mouse, and choose Edit | Copy from the menu.

3. Go back to Visual Studio . NET, right-click on the SMS project in Solution Explorer, and select Add Web Reference.

4. In the Address bar at the top, paste in the URL copied from Salcentral. Click the green arrow button. The WSDL file will be loaded and displayed in the left pane:

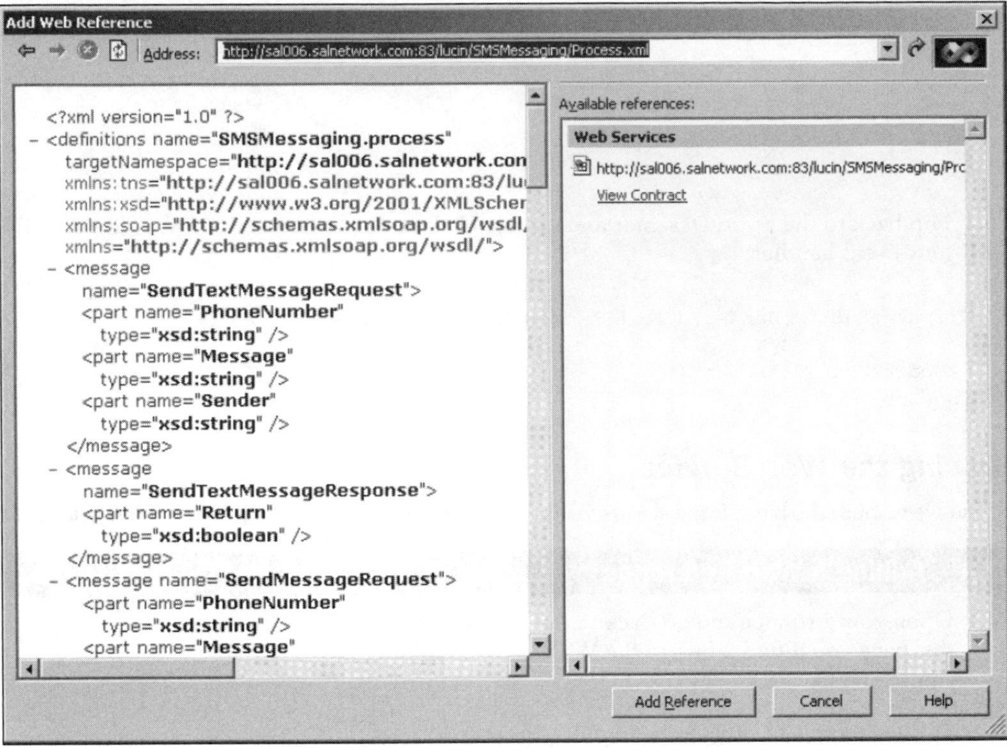

5. Click the Add Reference button to add a reference to the service to our project.

6. The new reference will appear as com.salnetwork.sal006 or something similar. Right-click on this and select Rename. Change the name to SMSService and press *Return*:

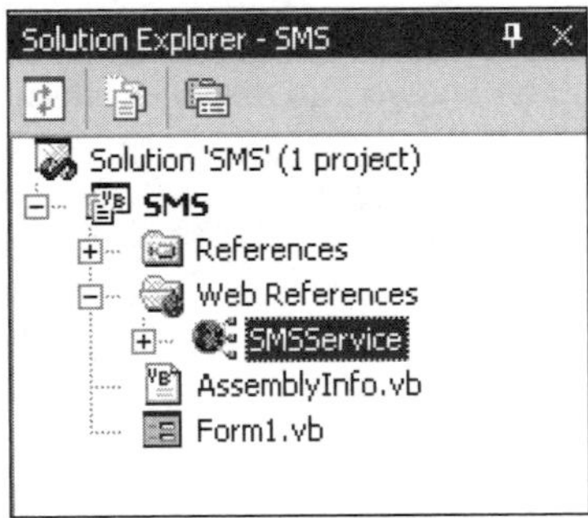

Sending Messages

With the reference added, Visual Studio .NET has automatically created a class to access the service, and all we have to do is create an instance of the class and call the `SendMessage` method.

Try It Out – Calling a Web Method

1. Open Form1 in Design view, and double-click on the Send Message button to create a new `Click` handler. Add this code:

```
Private Sub btnSendMessage_Click(ByVal sender As System.Object, _
            ByVal e As System.EventArgs) Handles btnSendMessage.Click

  ' create a new message box...
  Dim smsService As New SMSService.SMSMessagingprocessService()

  ' make sure the message goes through proxyTrace...
  If chkUseProxy.Checked = True Then
    smsService.Proxy = New System.Net.WebProxy("localhost", 8080)
  End If

  ' send the message...
  Try

    ' did we do it?
    Dim result As Boolean = smsService.SendMessage( _
                  txtPhoneNumber.Text, txtMessage.Text, _
                  txtSenderId.Text, txtSendPasskey.Text)
    If result = True Then
      MsgBox("The message was sent to " & txtPhoneNumber.Text & ".")
    Else
      MsgBox("The message could not be sent.")
    End If

  Catch ex As Exception

    ' we got an exception...
    MsgBox("An exception occured. " & ex.Message)

  End Try

End Sub
```

2. Open proxyTrace and tell it to connect to port 8080. (We covered proxyTrace earlier, so if you need a refresher go back a few pages.)

3. Run the project. Phone numbers have to be entered in international format. If necessary, this means you must drop the first zero of the number, and add a plus sign followed by the international dialing code for that country, for instance:

- For the US, numbers are prefixed with 1, so 06025551234 is +16025551234.
- For the UK, the dialing code is 44, so 07790123456 becomes +447790123456.

Enter any message you like, but remember to set the sender ID and passkey fields to whatever you were given at the end of the registration process:

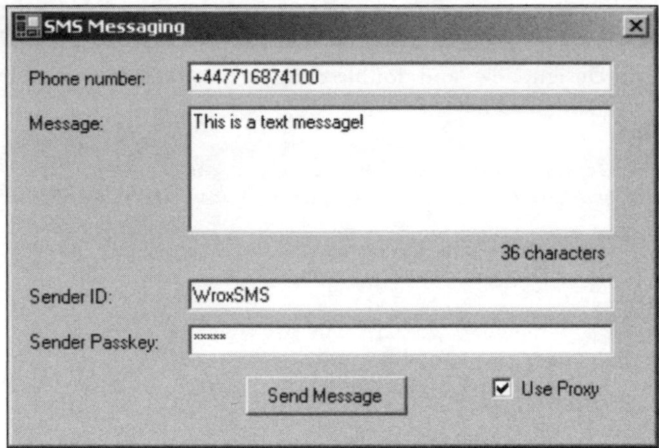

4. Click the Send Message button. If you see a message confirming that everything went OK, then great! If you didn't, you should get a message describing the problem.

How It Works

We've already seen how to create a connection to a Web Service just by creating a class, and here we use the same technique again:

```
Private Sub btnSendMessage_Click(ByVal sender As System.Object, _
              ByVal e As System.EventArgs) Handles btnSendMessage.Click

  ' Create a new message box
  Dim smsService As New SMSService.SMSMessagingprocessService()
```

This time, however, we've added a CheckBox to the form that allows us to control whether or not to use proxyTrace:

```
  ' Send the message via proxyTrace
  If chkUseProxy.Checked = True Then
    smsService.Proxy = New System.Net.WebProxy("localhost", 8080)
  End If
```

When we come to send the message, we simply extract the values from the four `TextBoxes` and pass them through to `SendMessage`:

```
  ' Send the message
  Try

    ' Did we do it?
    Dim result As Boolean = smsService.SendMessage( _
                            txtPhoneNumber.Text, txtMessage.Text, _
                            txtSenderId.Text, txtSendPasskey.Text)
    If result = True Then
```

```
      MsgBox("The message was sent to " & txtPhoneNumber.Text & ".")
    Else
      MsgBox("The message could not be sent.")
    End If
```

Everything is wrapped in a `Try...Catch` block, which helps us if something goes wrong. The "The message could not be sent" call is really redundant as, if the message could not be sent, an exception would be thrown, so this will never actually be called.

If an exception *is* thrown, we need to tinker with it a little to get the actual exception that was raised by the server. The layer of code between us and the Web Service will raise its own exception if something goes wrong, so we need to iterate through the `InnerException` property up to the last one. This will be the actual exception raised on the server. We didn't concern ourselves with this before as it was unlikely to happen, but here it's very real possibility and must be catered for:

```
  Catch ex As Exception

    ' We want the exception thrown by the service, not the .NET layer
    Do While Not ex.InnerException Is Nothing
      ex = ex.InnerException
    Loop
```

When we have the exception, we report it to the user.

```
    ' Report the exception
    MsgBox("An exception occured. " & ex.Message)

  End Try

End Sub
```

I hope that this section has shown you just how easy it is to find new Web Services and add some pretty cool functionality to your applications. All we had to do was use the Add Web Reference dialog, create an object, and call a method. Kid's stuff!

Summary

We started off this chapter by taking a look at what a Web Service is, and we likened a Web Service to a web site designed to be accessed by a computer rather than a person.

We then looked at how to build a Web Service, creating one as an example that would allow customers to view their own orders placed with the Northwind system. We devised and implemented a basic security system, and finally tested the service.

With our service created, we built a reference client implementation, using Visual Studio .NET's tools to automatically generate classes to consume the Web Service. After illustrating how simple this is, we looked at a debug tool to view the SOAP messages traveling between client and server and added extended error reporting to the service itself. To finish off, we looked at a number of ways of finding new Web Services.

Exercises

1. What does SOAP stand for?

2. How much harder is it to use complex types with a Web Service, as opposed to the simple types like Integer and String?

3. How can we find new Web Services that fulfill our business needs?

4. Why must we implement some form of security scheme on our services?

5. If you encounter unexpected problems when consuming a Web Service, what is a good first step to resolve the problem?

6. How do we consume a Web Service from a .NET project?

Answers are available at http://p2p.wrox.com/exercises/.

Disconnected Data

With .NET, Microsoft is trying to answer their critics and make deployment of Windows desktop applications far easier. Eventually, we'll get to a point where we can build an application for the local area network (LAN), deploy it "on demand" from a central web server, and let .NET worry about installation and security hassles. There is a natural extension to this paradigm – we can use .NET to build an application that works *identically* whether it's running on the LAN or running from an employee's DSL or cable modem connection.

This last line is specifically what we are going to look at in this chapter. Through this chapter, we are going to build an application that accesses a database either locally or by using a Web Service. Specifically, we are going to:

- Look at how and why we would want to use disconnected data
- Build a basic application to directly retrieve data
- Add functionality to our application to allow us to retrieve the data both directly and remotely
- Add the code to allow us to change any data and save the changes to the database

Disconnected Data Access

With the invention of the intranet, it finally became possible for an organization's computer systems to be made available without installing complex applications at many remote locations. As most modern organizations are powered by their applications, the intranet made it possible for employees to "unchain" themselves from their desk and start working from home, or access the same rich productivity tools from customer sites, hotel rooms, and Internet cafés.

However, there is a problem with intranet technologies – you're forced to use a web browser in order to use an intranet. Although web browser technology has come along in leaps and bounds in recent years, the user interface that you can build with a web browser is harder to develop and use than a traditional Visual Basic application.

Without using an intranet, the only way to make your organization's applications available outside of the LAN is to physically install it wherever you're working. This, in the world before .NET, was difficult, mainly because the choices Microsoft made with the architecture of their component solutions had the effect that installing applications was difficult. With DLL version conflicts and COM component problems, deploying applications in this way has always been complex. This explains part of the motivation for moving towards using intranet applications on the LAN rather than a standalone application. The deployment problems go away because all the user needs to do is point his or her browser at a URL to access the application.

Deploying applications with .NET is now so easy that, in theory, if you want to get your organization's desktop applications working on your home machine, all you have to do is follow a link on the web page and the application will be installed first time. Likewise, deployment and maintenance of applications within the organization becomes far easier too.

There is, however, one small caveat with this. Companies that care about security will separate their local network from the Internet by use of a firewall. This firewall lets employees send e-mail, browse the Web, and so on, but will not let intruders gain access to private company resources. Typically, your application's database will be "behind" the firewall, that is, accessible to employees but inaccessible to anyone outside of the LAN.

But, what happens when we put our application outside of the firewall? We won't be able to get at our data!

What we need to do is provide an alternative way for our application to get its data. In effect, we want to move away from the method of retrieving data whereby we are directly connected to the data. We want to start using a technique that allows the same application to get its data from a variety of different sources *without changing the client code.*

In this chapter, we'll build a client application that can automatically detect whether it has a direct connection to the database or not. If a direct connection cannot be made, it will get its data by connecting to a Web Service. If it can, it will connect directly and use the various classes in the `System.Data.SqlClient` namespace as we've already seen.

A Data Access Layer

In this application, we're going to build a data "provider". Rather than going directly through classes in the `System.Data.SqlClient` namespace, as we have been doing so far, we're going to access data through this provider. This provider will have the intelligence to know whether it should be drawing data directly from the database or through a Web Service.

We'll do this by inserting a layer between the application calls that require database access and the database itself. This layer will either connect directly to the database (through the `SqlClient` objects like we have been doing), or indirectly through a Web Service. This Web Service will then act as a proxy for the application's instructions, passing them on to the database in the usual way.

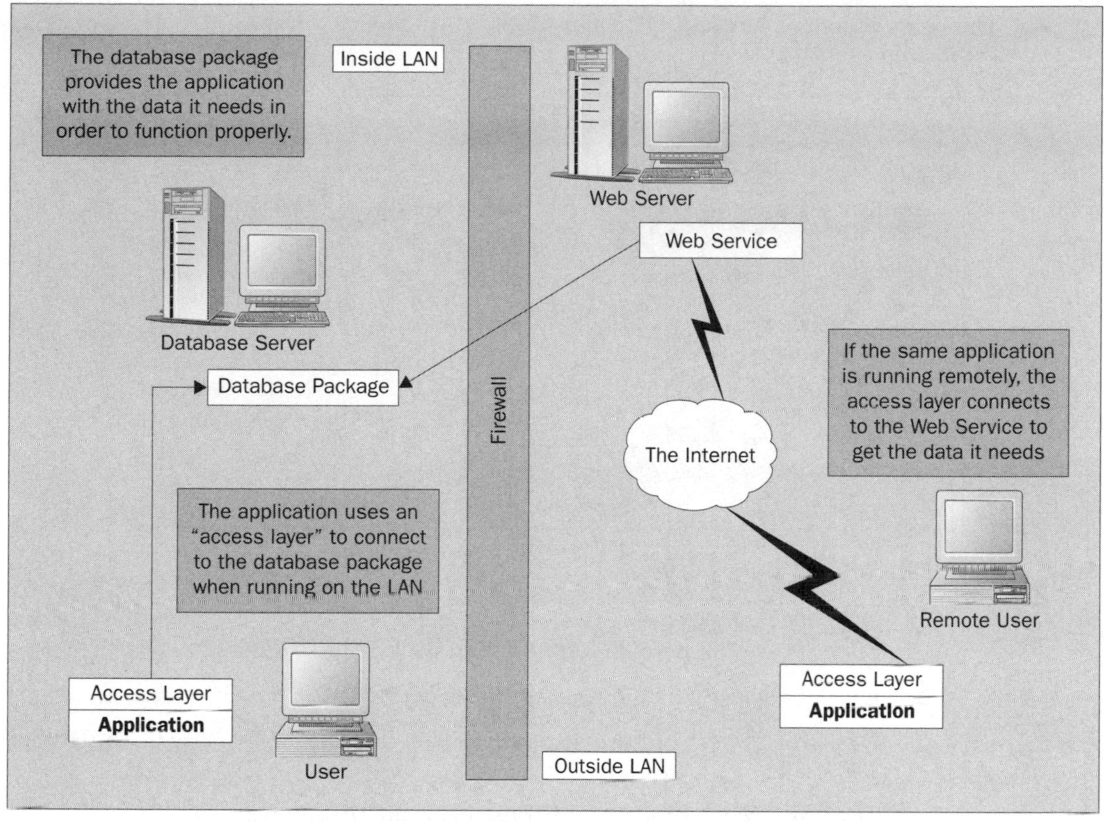

What this means is that we can build one application that works both inside and outside of the LAN. If the layer can make a direct connection to the database of choice, then it will work in "direct" mode. If the layer cannot connect directly, it will connect to a Web Service instead. We'll call this the "remote" mode.

Building the Application

In this chapter, we'll build a single desktop application for editing product information on the NorthwindSQL database. This application will use a data provider class to determine whether a direct or remote connection is required.

The first thing that we should do is to build the basic Product Editor application. This is a simple application to demonstrate the principle behind an application that can consume data from the provider that we'll build a little while later.

Try It Out – Building the Application

1. Open Visual Studio .NET and select File | New | Project from the menu. Create a new Visual Basic Windows Application project and call it Product Editor.

2. The Form designer for Form1 will automatically open. Layout a DataGrid, Label, TextBox, and Button control as shown here:

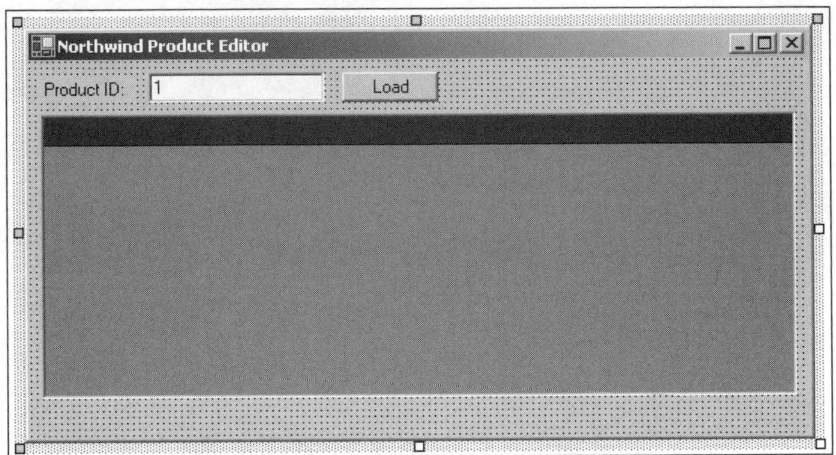

3. Change the properties of the controls like so:

    - Form1 – Text property to Northwind Product Editor
    - Label (Label1) – Text property to "Product ID:"
    - DataGrid – Name property to dgdProducts, and Anchor property to Top, Bottom, Left, Right
    - TextBox – Name property to txtProductId and Text property to "1"
    - Button – Name property to btnLoad, and Text property to "Load"

4. Using the Toolbox, paint on a StatusBar control. This kind of control automatically docks itself to the bottom of the form, so you might have to increase its height (with the Size property) to make it visible. Set its ShowPanels property to True.

5. Find the Panels property of the StatusBar control. Select it and an ellipsis ("...") button should appear. Click this to open the Collection Editor.

6. Press the Add button to add a new panel. Change these properties:

    - Name – change to pnlStatus
    - Text – change to Ready
    - AutoSize – change to Spring. This will cause the panel to adjust itself so that it is constantly just a little bigger than the size of the text contained within.

7. Press the Add button again to add another panel. Change these properties:

    - Name – change to pnlConnection

- Text – change this to Not connected
- AutoSize – change to Contents

8. After pressing OK, you should now see this:

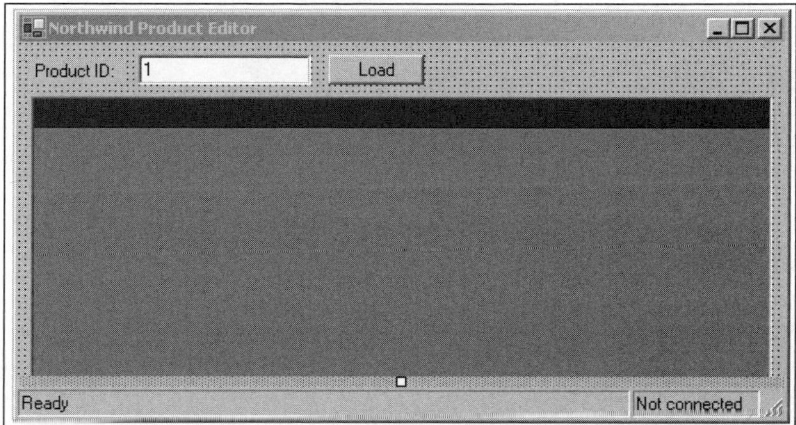

We're using the StatusBar control to indicate to the users of the application whether or not they are connected to the intranet and, if they are connected, whether they are connected directly or remotely.

9. Using Solution Explorer, open the code editor for Form1 by right-clicking on it and selecting View Code.

10. Add this property (we haven't shown the Windows Form Designer generated code here – don't delete it):

```
Public Class Form1
Inherits System.Windows.Forms.Form

    ' StatusText property...
Public Property StatusText() As String
    Get
        Return pnlStatus.Text
    End Get
    Set(ByVal Value As String)

        ' Put something default if we use blank...
        If Value = "" Then
            pnlStatus.Text = "Ready"
        Else
            pnlStatus.Text = Value
        End If

    End Set
End Property

End Class
```

11. Next, add these two methods:

```
    ' SetProcessText...
Public Sub SetProcessText(ByVal message As String)
    StatusText = message
    Me.Cursor = Cursors.WaitCursor
End Sub
```

```
    ' ResetProcessText...
Public Sub ResetProcessText()
    StatusText = ""
    Me.Cursor = Cursors.Default
End Sub
```

How It Works

In the last two steps, we've added code to control the way the StatusBar is updated. Firstly, we added a property, `StatusText`, that abstracts the `Text` property of `pnlStatus`.

```
    Get

        Return pnlStatus.Text

    End Get
```

If the `Status` property is set to a blank string, the text on the bar is set to `Ready`.

```
        If Value = "" Then
            pnlStatus.Text = "Ready"
        Else
            pnlStatus.Text = Value
        End If
```

Secondly, we added two methods to our form, `SetProcessText` and `ResetProcessText`. When the application is running, it periodically needs to "do something". If the task may take a while, the application will call these methods in order to set the text on the panel and also change the mouse cursor used by the form to an hourglass cursor and back to an arrow.

```
Public Sub SetProcessText(ByVal message As String)
    StatusText = message
    Me.Cursor = Cursors.WaitCursor
End Sub


Public Sub ResetProcessText()
    StatusText = ""
    Me.Cursor = Cursors.Default
End Sub
```

That will do for the basic form layout. Let's look now at how we can retrieve information from the database.

Retrieving Products

We're going to encapsulate all of the database functionality in a separate class library. The first step in achieving this goal is to put together a stored procedure that can return the product information to the caller.

Try It Out – Creating the Stored Procedure

1. To build the stored procedure, we'll use the Server Explorer in the usual way. If it is not already visible, open the Server Explorer by selecting View | Server Explorer from the menu.

2. We'll prefix the names of the stored procedures that we build as part of this exercise with the word "`Provider`". This will help us keep them separate from other stored procedures that may already be in the database.

3. Using the Server Explorer, drill down until you find the Stored Procedures node of the NorthwindSQL database. (In this screenshot, my server is called chimaera. Your machine will have a different name.)

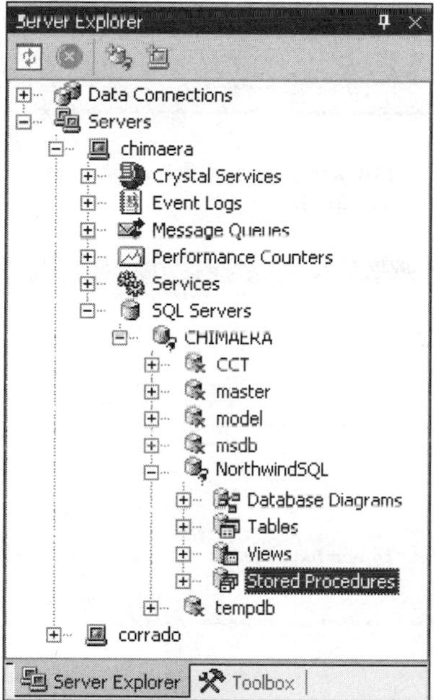

4. Right-click on the Stored Procedures node and select New Stored Procedure. Add this code in place of the existing code:

```
CREATE PROCEDURE dbo.ProviderGetProductDetails
(
  @productId INT
)
AS
```

```
SELECT ProductID, ProductName, SupplierID, CategoryID,
  QuantityPerUnit, UnitPrice, UnitsInStock,
  UnitsOnOrder, ReorderLevel, Discontinued
     FROM Products WHERE ProductID=@productId
```

5. Press Ctrl+S to commit the stored procedure to the database.

6. To test the stored procedure, right-click on the code editor and select Run Stored Procedure. When prompted, enter 1 for the product ID:

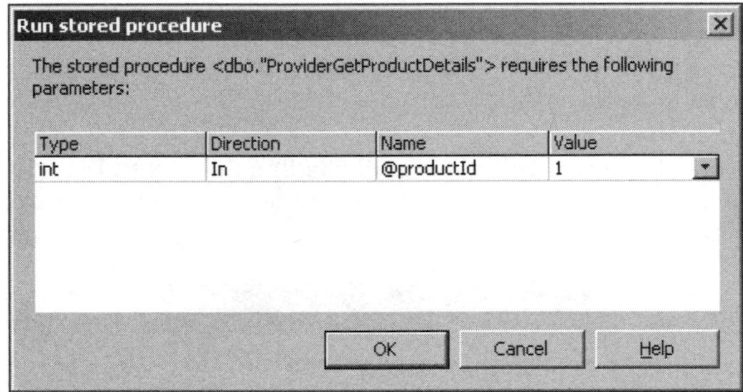

7. After pressing OK, the Output window should appear and the details of the product with a ProductID of 1 should be displayed:

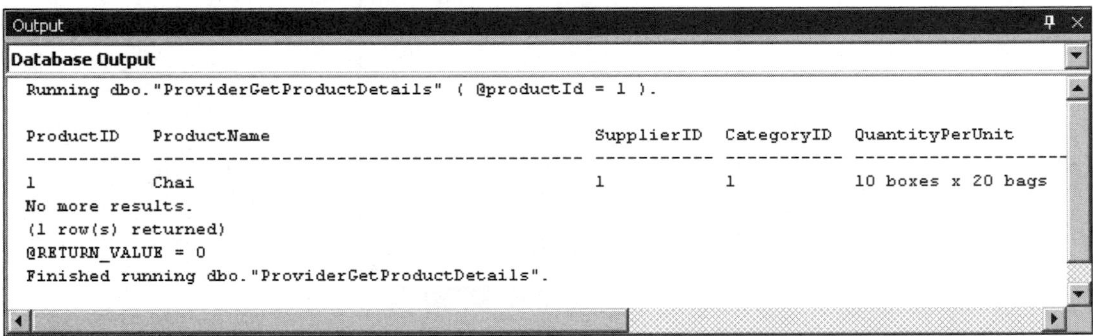

How It Works

What we've done here is put together a simple stored procedure that returns all rows from the `Products` table when given a particular `ProductID`.

```
SELECT ProductID, ProductName, SupplierID, CategoryID,
  QuantityPerUnit, UnitPrice, UnitsInStock,
  UnitsOnOrder, ReorderLevel, Discontinued
     FROM Products WHERE ProductID=@productId
```

In our application, the user will be expected to enter a Product ID and then click the Load button. We'll build this functionality in a moment but, when this happens, the `ProviderGetProductDetails` stored procedure that we've just built will be executed and the results returned.

The "Provider" Class

As we mentioned before, we're going to build a separate class library, called Northwind Provider, which our application will use to get data from the database. This library will be accessed through shared methods and properties in a class called `Provider`.

The `Provider` object will eventually have the intelligence to determine whether or not it needs to use a direct or remote connection. However, in the next few sections, we're going to manually tell it what it should be connecting to.

Architecturally speaking, we're going to build an **abstract** class that contains the various methods that the application will need: `GetProductDetails`, `GetAllSuppliers`, `SetProductDetails`, and so on. We'll then create two classes derived from this abstract class that actually know how to get the data that they've been asked for – one for direct connections and one for remote connections.

> *An **abstract** class is one that objects cannot be instantiated from directly. Instead, we have to create instances of a derived class, which inherits from the abstract class. Objects can then be instantiated from these derived classes.*

The first thing we need to do is create the new project that will contain the class library.

Try It Out – Creating the "Northwind Provider" Class Library

1. Using Solution Explorer, right-click on the Product Editor solution right at the top and select Add | New Project.

2. Make sure that a Visual Basic Class Library is selected as the project type and enter the name as Northwind Provider.

3. We want a better name for the class than Class1. Right-click on Class1 in the Solution Explorer, select Rename, and call it Provider. Then click on the View Code button and add this enumeration to Provider:

```
Public Class Provider

' Enumerations...
Public Enum ConnectionModes As Integer
    NotConnected = 0
    Direct = 1
    Remote = 2
End Enum

End Class
```

4. Now add these members:

```
Public Class Provider

' Enumerations...
Public Enum ConnectionModes As Integer
    NotConnected = 0
    Direct = 1
    Remote = 2
End Enum

    ' Members...
Private Shared _connectionMode As Provider.ConnectionModes = _
                        ConnectionModes.NotConnected

' Remember to change the data source to your server name!
Public Shared DbString As String = _
"Integrated Security=SSPI;Initial Catalog=NorthwindSQL;Data Source=CHIMAERA"

' Web Service...
Public Shared ServiceUrl As String = _
     "http://localhost/NorthwindProviderService/ProviderService.asmx"
Public Shared Proxy As System.NET.WebProxy

End Class
```

Remember! You'll need to change the `Data Source` member of the connection string from `CHIMAERA` (my computer) to whatever your computer is called.

5. Right-click on Northwind Provider and select Add | Add Class. Call the class ProviderConnection. Add this code, including the `MustInherit` keyword to the first line. This means that we cannot create instances of `ProviderConnection` classes directly. Instead, we have to derive from this class and create new instances of the derived classes.

```
Public MustInherit Class ProviderConnection

' Get the details for a product...
Public MustOverride Function GetProductDetails(ByVal _
                      productId As Long) As DataSet

End Class
```

6. Create another new class to Northwind Provider called DirectConnection. Add this code:

```
Imports System.Data.SqlClient

Public Class DirectConnection
    Inherits ProviderConnection

' Return the details for a product...
Public Overrides Function GetProductDetails(ByVal productId As Long) _
```

```
                    As System.Data.DataSet

End Function

End Class
```

How It Works

As you've probably guessed, GetProductDetails will run the stored procedure that we wrote a while ago and will return a DataSet, containing product information, back to the caller. How we get to that method illustrates most of the magic that we're discussing in this chapter!

The MustInherit keyword in the ProviderConnection class means that the ProviderConnection class can never be instantiated directly – it is an abstract class.

```
Public MustInherit Class ProviderConnection
```

In other words, it is impossible to create a ProviderConnection object based directly on that class. Instead, objects are instantiated through the DirectConnection subclass. This subclass will provide the functionality to call GetProductDetails when directly connected to the SQL Server Desktop Engine. Shortly, we will implement a second subclass of ProviderConnection called RemoteConnection. This subclass will handle the calling of GetProductDetails when using the Web Service to bypass the intranet's firewall.

Why do we have these two subclasses? Well, when other parts of the application want to call GetProductDetails, they need to get hold of a ProviderConnection object. By making ProviderConnection an abstract class, we can pass the caller either a DirectConnection object or a RemoteConnection object and the caller doesn't need to worry about which it is getting. Both types of object will behave in the same way, as far as the caller is concerned; their interfaces will be the same.

The MustOverride keyword in the GetProductDetails function means that the function must be overridden when used in derived classes.

```
Public MustOverride Function GetProductDetails(ByVal _
                    productId As Long) As DataSet
```

The GetProductsDetails function is going to be called by our derived classes, DirectConnection and RemoteConnection. As such, each of these classes must have a version of this function which overrides this one.

We'll stop the discussion of this step now and move on to implementing the ConnectionMode and Connection properties so that we can actually start getting some data back to prove the concept. We'll come back and explain what we've done here in more detail in a short while.

The ConnectionMode and Connection Properties

What we'll do next is build a shared Connection property on the Provider class that will return either DirectConnection or RemoteConnection. As this property is shared, it can be called from anywhere within the code (or its subsequent extensions or revisions).

Try It Out – Building the ConnectionMode and Connection Properties

1. The first thing we have to do is go back to the members of the `Provider` class and add this new member:

```
' Members...
Private Shared _connectionMode As Provider.ConnectionModes = _
                              ConnectionModes.NotConnected
Private Shared _connection As ProviderConnection
```

2. Next, add this shared property:

```
    ' ConnectionMode - what mode are we in?
Public Shared Property ConnectionMode() As Provider.ConnectionModes
    Get

        ' Return the connection mode that we've been given...
        Return _connectionMode

    End Get
    Set(ByVal Value As Provider.ConnectionModes)

        ' Set the connection mode...
        _connectionMode = Value

        ' Reset the connection...
        _connection = Nothing

    End Set
End Property
```

3. Then, add this shared property:

```
    ' Connection - do we have a connection object?
Public Shared Property Connection() As ProviderConnection
    Get

        ' Do we have a connection?
        If _connection Is Nothing Then

            ' Pick a mode...
            Select Case ConnectionMode

                Case ConnectionModes.Direct
                    _connection = New DirectConnection()

                Case Else
                    Throw New Exception("Connection mode not supported.")

            End Select
```

```
            End If

            ' Return what we have...
            Return _connection

        End Get
        Set(ByVal Value As ProviderConnection)
            _connection = Value
        End Set
    End Property
```

How It Works

The `Connection` property can be used whenever access to the database is required.

The first time this property is requested, `_connection` will be `Nothing`. When this happens, the `ConnectionMode` property is used to determine what kind of connection is being made.

```
    If _connection Is Nothing Then

                ' Pick a mode...
                Select Case ConnectionMode

                    Case ConnectionModes.Direct
                        _connection = New DirectConnection()
```

At this point, we only support `Direct`, so we create a new `DirectConnection` object and store that in `_connection`, whereupon it's returned to the caller.

This technique is called **Just In Time** (JIT) instantiation. It's a useful technique for keeping the resource footprint of your application small. The `Connection` object is only created the instant that it is needed and not before. Notice as well that, on subsequent calls, `_connection` will not be `Nothing` and therefore another object will not need to be created. This makes the call to the `Connection` property faster as it has less to do.

Returning Data

Implementing `GetProductDetails` is simply a matter of calling the stored procedure. However, to make life easier for us later on, we're going to build a number of protected methods that provide easy access to `DataSet` and `SqlDataAdapter` objects.

Try It Out – Returning Data

1. Add these two methods to `DirectConnection`:

```
    ' GetProductDetails - return the details for a product...
    Public Overrides Function GetProductDetails(ByVal productId As Long) _
                              As System.Data.DataSet
    End Function
```

```
    ' GetDataSet - run a stored procedure and get the results...
Protected Function GetDataSet(ByVal storedProcName As String, _
     ByVal dataSetName As String, ByVal paramName As String, _
     ByVal paramValue As Integer) As DataSet

    ' Create a connection to the database...
    Dim connection As New SqlConnection(Provider.DbString)
    connection.Open()

    ' Get the data adapter...
    Dim adapter As SqlDataAdapter
    adapter = GetDataAdapter(connection, storedProcName, paramName, paramValue)

    ' Create the dataset...
    Dim dataset As New DataSet(dataSetName)
    adapter.Fill(DataSet)

    ' Close...
    connection.Close()

    ' Return the dataset...
    Return DataSet

End Function
```

```
    ' GetDataAdapter - get the data adapter for the supplied stored proc...
Protected Function GetDataAdapter(ByVal connection As SqlConnection, _
  ByVal storedProcName As String, ByVal paramName As String, _
  ByVal paramValue As Integer) As SqlDataAdapter

    ' Create the command...
    Dim command As New SqlCommand(storedProcName, connection)
    command.CommandType = CommandType.StoredProcedure

    ' Add the parameter...
    Dim param As SqlParameter = _
           command.Parameters.Add(paramName, SqlDbType.Int)
    param.Direction = ParameterDirection.Input
    param.Value = paramValue

    ' Create an adapter from that...
    Return New SqlDataAdapter(command)

End Function
```

2. Next, add this code to `GetProductDetails` in the `DirectConnection` class:

```
    ' GetProductDetails - return the details for a product...
Public Overrides Function GetProductDetails(ByVal productId As Long) _
          As System.Data.DataSet
```

```
        ' Return the data...
    Return GetDataSet("ProviderGetProductDetails", _
                "Products", "@productId", productId)

End Function
```

Because we can't call `GetProductDetails` yet, we're going to hold off the explanation for a moment. We'll quickly go through the next stage and then go through all this in detail.

Try It Out – Calling GetProductDetails

1. In order to access the functionality of the objects in the class library, we have to add a reference to the Northwind Provider project. Using Solution Explorer, right-click on the Product Editor project and select Add Reference.

2. Select the Projects tab on the Add Reference dialog, click on the Northwind Provider project, and then on Select. Click OK when you've finished.

3. Open the code editor for Form1. At the very top of the class definition, add this namespace import directive.

```
Imports Northwind_Provider
```

4. From the Class Name drop-down list on the code editor window, select (Overrides). From the Method Name list, select OnLoad. Add this code to the event handler, and the associated property.

```
    Protected Overrides Sub OnLoad(ByVal e As System.EventArgs)
        ConnectionMode = Provider.ConnectionModes.Direct
    End Sub

    ' ConnectionMode property...
Public Property ConnectionMode() As Provider.ConnectionModes
    Get
        Return Provider.ConnectionMode
    End Get
    Set(ByVal Value As Provider.ConnectionModes)

        ' Set the mode...
        Provider.ConnectionMode = Value

        ' Update the display...
        pnlConnection.Text = Provider.Connection.ToString

    End Set
End Property
```

5. We need to add a member to `Form1` that can be used to hold the product `DataSet` that we get back from the provider and another member that can keep track of the `ProductID`. Add these members to the top of the class:

```
Public Class Form1
Inherits System.Windows.Forms.Form

    ' Members...
Public ProductDataSet As DataSet
Private _productId As Integer
```

6. Flip back to the Form Designer for Form1. Double-click on the Load button to create a new `Click` event handler. Add this code and associated `ProductId` property:

```
Private Sub btnLoad_Click(ByVal sender As System.Object, _
    ByVal e As System.EventArgs) Handles btnLoad.Click

    ' What productid do we want?
Dim newProductId As Integer
Try
    newProductId = CType(txtProductId.Text, Integer)
Catch
End Try

' Set it...
If newProductId <> 0 Then
    ProductId = newProductId
Else
    MsgBox("You must enter a valid product ID.")
End If

End Sub

Public Property ProductId() As Integer
Get
    Return _productId
End Get
Set(ByVal Value As Integer)

    ' Set the Id...
    _productId = Value

    ' Get the data...
    SetProcessText("Loading product information from " & _
    Provider.Connection.ToString & ".  Please wait...")
    ProductDataSet = Provider.Connection.GetProductDetails(_productId)
    ResetProcessText()

    ' Get the datagrid binding...
    dgdProducts.DataSource = ProductDataSet
    dgdProducts.DataMember = ProductDataSet.Tables(0).TableName

End Set
End Property
```

7. Run the project and click the Load button. You should see this:

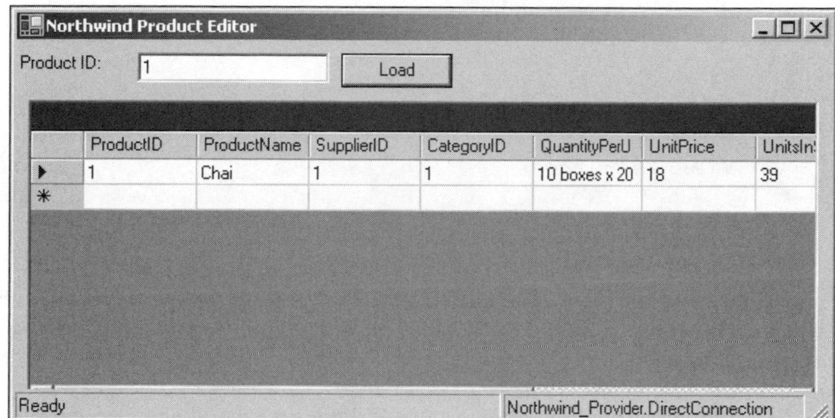

How It Works

The first thing that we do in the form is set its ConnectionMode property to Direct:

```
Protected Overrides Sub OnLoad(ByVal e As System.EventArgs)
    ConnectionMode = Provider.ConnectionModes.Direct
End Sub
```

This property in turn calls the shared ConnectionMode property of the Northwind_Provider.Provider class. After this call has been made, we then ask for the Connection property mainly because we want to get hold of its name to update the StatusBar:

```
    ' ConnectionMode property...
Public Property ConnectionMode() As Provider.ConnectionModes
    Get
        Return Provider.ConnectionMode
    End Get
    Set(ByVal Value As Provider.ConnectionModes)

        ' set the mode...
        Provider.ConnectionMode = Value

        ' update the display...
            pnlConnection.Text = Provider.Connection.ToString

    End Set
End Property
```

The first time Connection is requested from Northwind_Provider.Provider, a new DirectConnection object is created and passed back to the caller. The ToString method returns the name of the object, which we can see displayed on the status bar.

When the **Load** button is clicked, we go through a few hoops to make sure we've actually been given a valid integer value. If we have one, we pass it through to the `ProductId` property. The first thing this does is set the internal `_productId` member:

```
Public Property ProductId() As Integer
Get
    Return _productId
End Get
Set(ByVal Value As Integer)

    ' set the Id...
        _productId = Value
```

Once the member has been set, the `Provider.Connection` property is called again and the `DirectConnection` object is returned once more. Remember, we're actually getting a `ProviderConnection` object back that supports all of the methods we want but is nicely abstracted away from the implementation. Whether we have a `DirectConnection` or a `RemoteConnection` object, we don't need to know anything about the underlying process of actually getting the data. This is sometimes known by the term "polymorphism". Later, we'll actually be given a `RemoteConnection` object back and we won't have to change this code at all.

Once we have an object based on `ProviderConnection`, we call `GetProductDetails`. This returns a `DataSet` back to us, and we set up the binding on the `DataGrid` control so that the results are displayed:

```
            ' get the data...
        SetProcessText("Loading product information from " & _
           Provider.Connection.ToString & ".  Please wait...")
            ProductDataSet = Provider.Connection.GetProductDetails(_productId)
            ResetProcessText()

        ' set the datagrid binding...
            dgdProducts.DataSource = ProductDataSet
        dgdProducts.DataMember = ProductDataSet.Tables(0).TableName

    End Set
End Property
```

The text we display using the `SetProcessText` method appears on the status bar when data is loaded. However, the load process can be pretty fast, so you may not notice it appear.

The `GetProductDetails` method itself uses our `GetDataSet` helper method to quickly access and return a `DataSet` object.

```
    ' GetProductDetails - return the details for a product...
Public Overrides Function GetProductDetails(ByVal productId As Long) _
                      As System.Data.DataSet

        ' return the data...
    Return GetDataSet("ProviderGetProductDetails", "Products", _
                      "@productId", productId)

End Function
```

Calling `GetDataSet` is simply a matter of providing the name of the stored procedure, the name of the table that the stored procedure is based on (we'll use this later), and the parameter name and value, in this case `@productId` and whatever value was entered into the TextBox on the form. Our implementation of `GetDataSet` only supports a single stored procedure parameter; in order to call a stored procedure that has more than one parameter, you'll need to create an alternative version of the method with the additional parameters defined.

In turn, `GetDataSet` opens a connection to the database and calls the other internal helper function, `GetDataAdapter`.

```
    ' GetDataSet - run a stored procedure and get the results...
Protected Function GetDataSet(ByVal storedProcName As String, _
     ByVal dataSetName As String, ByVal paramName As String, _
     ByVal paramValue As Integer) As DataSet

        ' create a connection to the database...
    Dim connection As New SqlConnection(Provider.DbString)
    connection.Open()

    ' get the data adapter...
    Dim adapter As SqlDataAdaptor
    adapter = _
  GetDataAdapter(connection, storedProcName, paramName, paramValue)
```

Separating `GetDataSet` and `GetDataAdapter` out in this way will make updating the database much easier, as we'll see later.

Once we have the adapter, we fill and return the `DataSet` as usual:

```
        ' create the dataset...
    Dim dataset As New DataSet(dataSetName)
    adapter.Fill(DataSet)

    ' close...
    connection.Close()

    ' return the DataSet...
    Return dataset

End Function
```

To round off this discussion, we'll look at `GetDataAdapter`. All this method has to do is create a `SqlCommand`, add a parameter to it, and create a new `SqlDataAdapter`:

```
    ' GetDataAdapter - get the data adapter for the supplied stored proc...
Protected Function GetDataAdapter(ByVal connection As SqlConnection, _
  ByVal storedProcName As String, ByVal paramName As String, _
  ByVal paramValue As Integer) As SqlDataAdapter

    ' create the command...
```

```
        Dim command As New SqlCommand(storedProcName, connection)
        command.CommandType = CommandType.StoredProcedure

        ' add the parameter...
        Dim param As SqlParameter = _
               command.Parameters.Add(paramName, SqlDbType.Int)
        param.Direction = ParameterDirection.Input
        param.Value = paramValue

        ' create an adapter from that...
        Return New SqlDataAdapter(command)

    End Function
```

Now that we know how to get information back when we have a direct connection to the database, we'll take a look at how to get information back if we have a connection to the Web Service.

Overriding the ToString Method

Before we move on, let's clean up one tiny aspect of our application's look and feel.

At the moment, the status bar text doesn't say anything useful like "Direct" or "Remote". Instead, it says "Northwind_Provider.DirectConnection" which isn't very eloquent.

Try It Out – Overriding the ToString Method

1. Open the code editor for `DirectConnection`. Add this code to the class:

```
    ' ToString - provides better text...
Public Overrides Function ToString() As String
    Return "Direct"
End Function
```

2. Run the project. The status bar should now be a little more pleasing:

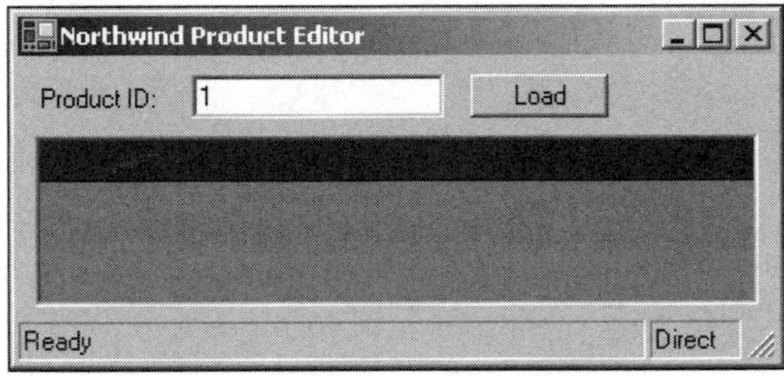

How It Works

All classes in .NET ultimately inherit from `System.Object`. This provides a few methods that all objects must support. In particular, this class defines a method called `ToString` that returns a string representation of the object.

By default, `ToString` returns the full name of the class, which is why before we saw Northwind_Provider.DirectConnection on the StatusBar. By overriding it as we've done in this way, we see Direct instead.

```
Public Overrides Function ToString() As String
    Return "Direct"
```

Remote Connections

Our motivation for building our database provider functionality in a separate class library should be becoming apparent now. We have created a set of classes that know how to get the information directly from a database connection. In theory, we should be able to create a Web Service and use the self-same `DirectConnection` object that we will have created to pass information back to the caller.

In a remote connection scenario, when our client application asks for the `Provider.Connection` property, it will get back a `RemoteConnection` object. As this object is based on the abstract `ProviderConnection` class, it will support all of the same methods that `DirectConnection` does. When a method on `RemoteConnection` is called, it will connect to the Web Service, whereupon the Web Service will ask for the `Provider.Connection` property from its local installation of the class library.

This local class library will be configured to always return a `DirectConnection` object. The Web Service will call the same method asked for on the `RemoteConnection` object and will return the data to the caller. All of this should happen without the user knowing what's happening, or the developer having to change any of the client code.

The first stage in this part of the process is to create the Web Service.

Try It Out – Creating the Web Service

1. Before we create the Web Service, we need to find out where the assembly containing the Northwind Provider project has been created. Using Solution Explorer, right-click on the Northwind Provider project and select Properties.

2. In the left hand list, select Configuration Properties and then select Build. The Output path entry will tell you where the `.dll` file containing the assembly has been created. Make a note of the path to this folder.

> **It might be the case that your output path simply reads bin\. In this case, to get the path to the solution, click the ellipsis button at the end of the Output path box. This will bring you into the bin folder and you should be able to work your way backwards through the folders in order to determine the path to this folder.**

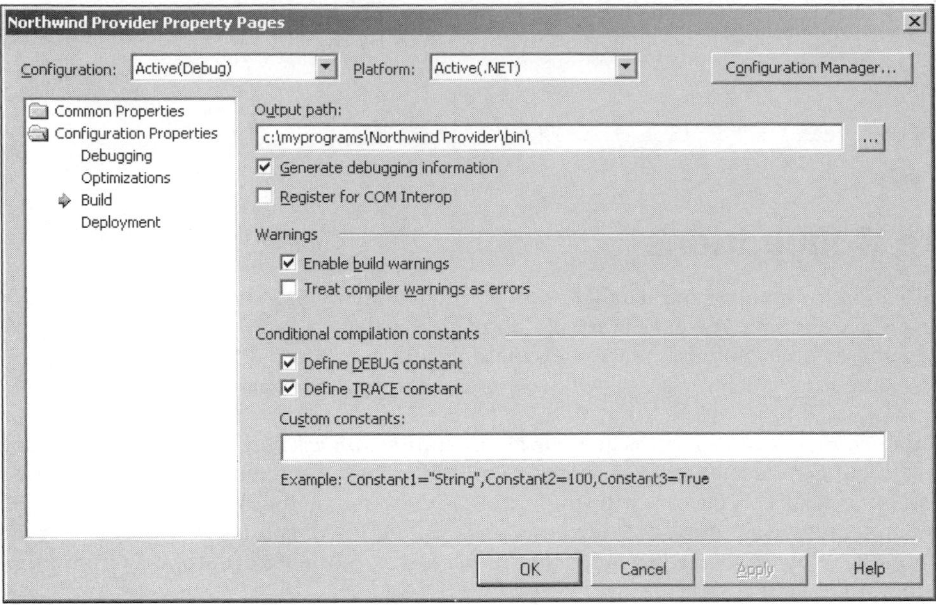

3. To create the Web Service, start another instance of Visual Studio. It will make life easier to have two copies of the environment side by side.

4. Select File | New | Project from the menu. Create a new Visual Basic ASP.NET Web Service application and call it NorthwindProviderService:

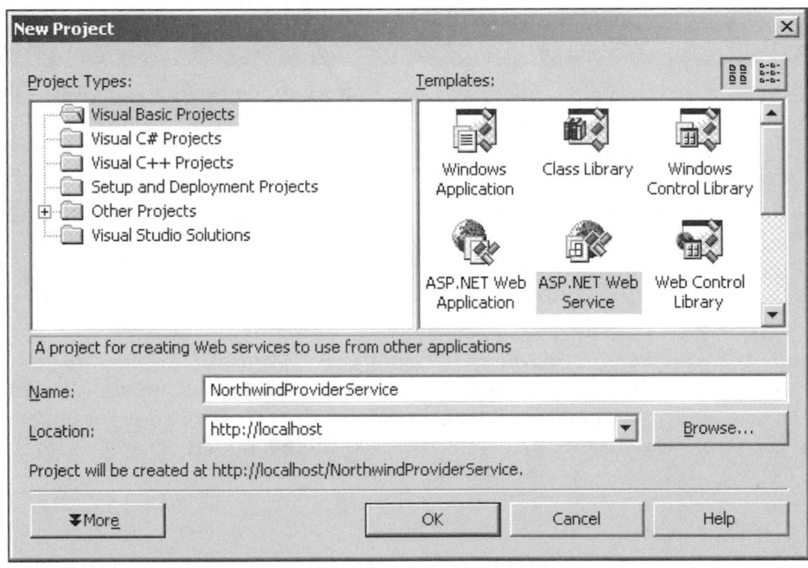

5. When the project has been created, right-click on Service1.asmx in Solution Explorer and choose Rename. Call the file ProviderService.asmx instead. Right-click on it once more and select Set As Start Page.

6. Right-click on the NorthwindProviderService project and select Add Reference.

7. When the Add Reference window appears, click the Browse button. Navigate to the folder containing the .dll file that the Northwind Provider assembly has been created in. You noted the path to this folder down earlier. Find the Northwind Provider.dll and add a reference to the project.

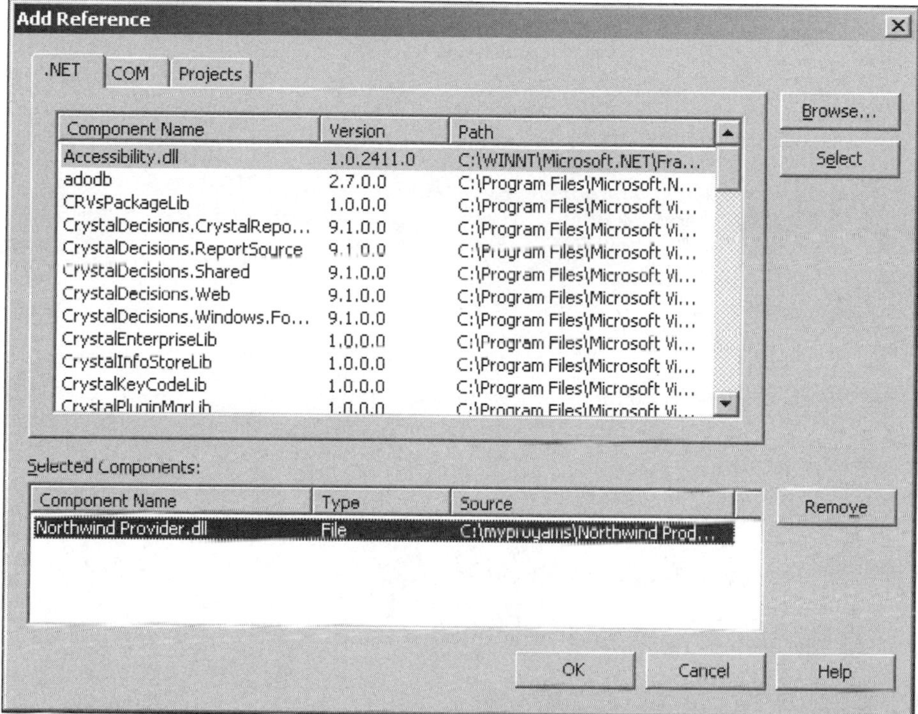

8. Open the code editor for ProviderService.asmx by right-clicking on it in Solution Explorer and selecting View Code.

9. Add this namespace import directive to the top of the code listing and rename the class to `ProviderService`:

```
Imports System.Web.Services
Imports Northwind_Provider

Public Class ProviderService
Inherits System.Web.Services.WebService
```

10. We need to add a namespace declaration to the service. If we don't do this, we can run into problems when and if we make the Web Service publicly available. Add this attribute to the ProviderService class definition:

```
<WebService(Namespace:="http://www.wrox.com/1861005555/")> _
Public Class ProviderService
Inherits System.Web.Services.WebService
```

11. Find the constructor for the ProviderService class. You might have to expand out the Windows Form Designer generated code region by clicking the little gray plus sign. Add this code:

```
    Public Sub New()
    MyBase.New()

    'This call is required by the Web Services Designer.
    InitializeComponent()

        ' check we have the correct connection type...
    If Provider.ConnectionMode <> Provider.ConnectionModes.Direct Then
        Provider.ConnectionMode = Provider.ConnectionModes.Direct
    End If

End Sub
```

12. Add this method after the block of Designer-generated code:

```
    ' GetProductDetails - make a call into the connection...
<WebMethod()> _
Public Function GetProductDetails(ByVal productId As Integer) As DataSet
    Return Provider.Connection.GetProductDetails(productId)
End Function
```

13. Run the project. As usual, you'll be given a list of the methods that the service supports:

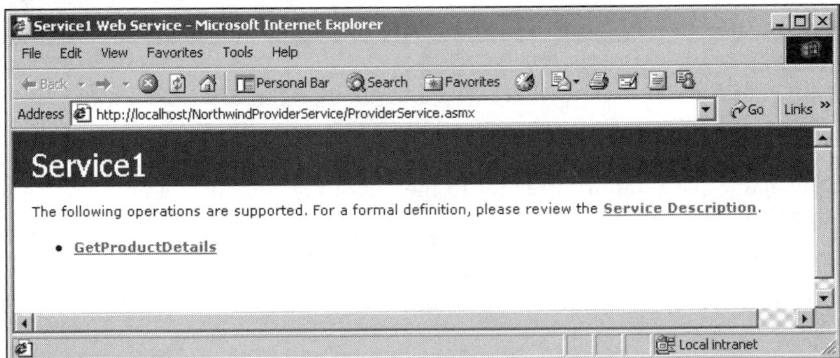

14. Click the GetProductDetails link to view the invocation form for the method. Enter the productId parameter as 1 and click Invoke.

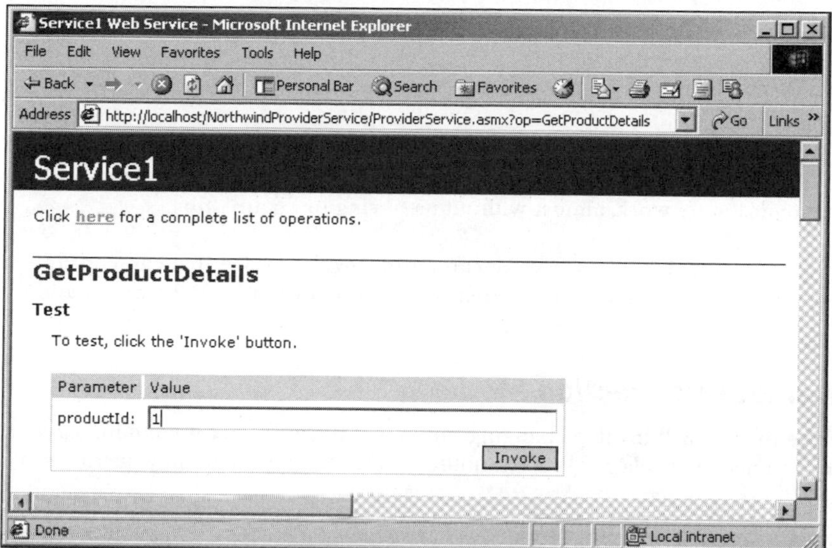

15. What you'll get back is a large lump of XML. This is the XML representation of the `DataSet` that we asked for, and it should look familiar to you after our work in the previous chapters.

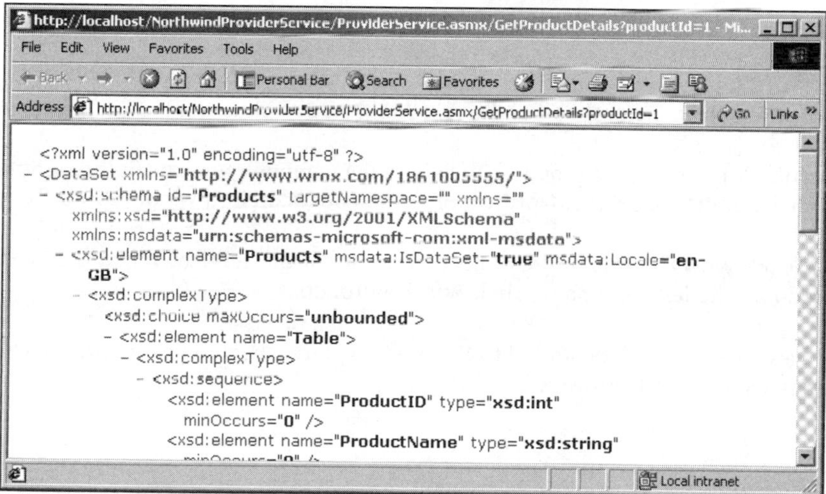

How It Works

What's important here is that the way we've called `GetProductDetails` in the Web Service method is virtually identical to the way that we've called it in the client application. Here's the way that it was called in the Web Service:

```
Return Provider.Connection.GetProductDetails(productId)
```

and here's the way it was called in the client application:

```
ProductDataSet = Provider.Connection.GetProductDetails(_productId)
```

The great news for us with all this is that we have to do literally nothing to get all of this working. .NET's Web Service implementation handles most of the stress involved in wrapping up a `DataSet` and passing it over the network, almost without us having to do anything.

Of course, all we've done is proven that we can build a Web Service that can consume the same objects that the client can. Now we have to prove that the client works in both the direct and remote connection modes.

Using the Remote Connection Mode

This part of the project will involve changing our class library so that it contains a reference to the Web Service and contains a new class called RemoteConnection. This will allow us to connect to the Web Service to get the remote data.

Try It Out – Updating the Class Library

1. We've finished with the Web Service for a while, so flip back to the Visual Studio .NET instance that contains the class library and client projects.

2. Firstly, we need to add a reference to the Web Service. Right-click on the Northwind Provider project in Solution Explorer and select Add Web Reference.

3. Click on the Web References on Local Web Server link in the bottom of the left-hand pane.

4. When the list of reference groups installed on the computer appears in the right-hand pane, find and click on http://localhost/NorthwindProviderService/NorthwindProviderService.disco.

5. Next, click View Contract to load the WDSL file for the service. When the WSDL file has loaded into the left-hand pane, click Add Reference.

6. The new reference will be added to Solution Explorer. Right-click it and select Rename. Change its name to NorthwindService.

7. Next, add a new class to the Northwind Provider project called `RemoteConnection`. Make the class derive from `ProviderConnection` like this:

```
Public Class RemoteConnection
    Inherits ProviderConnection

End Class
```

8. Ideally, we need to override `ToString` just like we did on `DirectConnection`. Add this method:

```
Public Overrides Function ToString() As String
    Return "Remote"
End Function
```

9. Add this method to `RemoteConnection`:

```
    ' GetService - return a service object...
Protected Function GetService() As NorthwindService.ProviderService

    ' Create an instance of the service...
    Dim service As New NorthwindService.ProviderService()

    ' Set the URL...
    service.Url = Provider.ServiceUrl

    ' Set the proxy...
    service.Proxy = Provider.Proxy

    ' Return the service...
    Return service

End Function
```

10. Finally, add this method:

```
    ' GetProductDetails - call the service's version of this...
Public Overrides Function GetProductDetails(ByVal productId As Long) _
                       As System.Data.DataSet

    ' Get the service...
    Dim service As NorthwindService.ProviderService = GetService()

    ' Call the remote method...
    Return service.GetProductDetails(productId)

End Function
```

How It Works

What we've done here is created a "sister" class to `DirectConnection` that also inherits from `ProviderConnection`. The ultimate goal is to be able to have an object in our application call the same `GetProductDetails` and not actually care whether `DirectConnection` is going directly to the database, or whether `RemoteConnection` is going through a Web Service.

The `GetService` method on `RemoteConnection` simply returns a new `NorthwindService.ProviderService` object that's configured to talk to the Web Service. This remote service also contains a `GetProductDetails` method, which ultimately talks to a `DirectConnection` object on the server to go and get the data. The data is returned from the service as a `DataSet` and we pass the data back to the caller. We will look at these methods in more detail at the end of the next section after we try running our application with a remote connection.

Creating RemoteConnection

At this point, we can create `DirectConnection` objects but not `RemoteConnection` objects.

Open the code editor for `Provider` and make this change to the `Connection` property:

```
            ' Pick a mode...
            Select Case ConnectionMode

                Case ConnectionModes.Direct
                    _connection = New DirectConnection()
                    Case ConnectionModes.Remote
                    _connection = New RemoteConnection()

                Case Else
                    Throw New Exception("Connection mode not supported.")
```

What this small change will do is make it possible for us to make `RemoteConnection` objects as well as `DirectConnection` objects, depending on the value stored in `ConnectionMode`. If we're "Direct", the property will return a `DirectConnection`. If we're "Remote", the property will return a `RemoteConnection`. Through `RemoteConnection`, we'll be able to gain access to the Web Service.

A Slight Change to the Client

Although I promised you that we wouldn't have to make changes to the client in order to get it working in remote mode, that was a white lie. We *do* have to change the `Load` event handler of `Form1` and tell it to change the `Provider.ConnectionMode` property.

Try It Out – Testing the Client

1. Open the code editor for `Form1` and find the `Load` event handler. Make this change:

```
Protected Overrides Sub OnLoad(ByVal e As System.EventArgs)
    ConnectionMode = Provider.ConnectionModes.Remote
End Sub
```

2. Run the project. If you click the **Load** button now, the Web Service will be used instead of the direct connection. (Notice that the connection type on the StatusBar is now shown as **Remote**.)

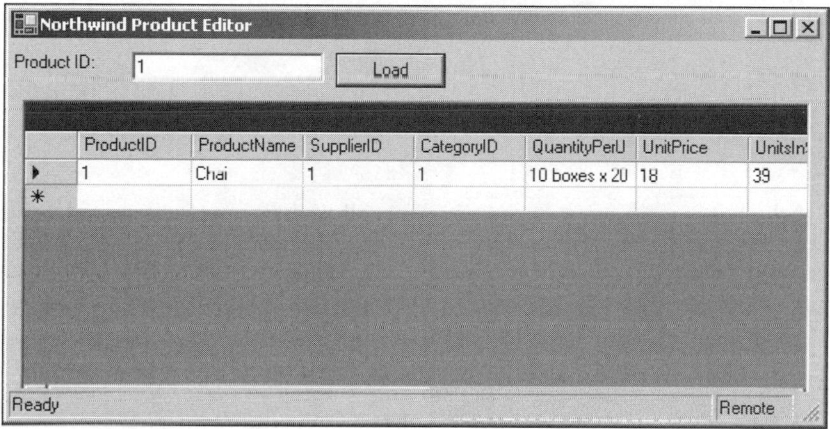

How It Works

With the `Provider.ConnectionMode` shared property set to `Remote`, any requests for the `Provider.Connection` shared property will return a `RemoteConnection` object, not a `DirectConnection` object.

When we call `GetProductDetails`, we'll be calling the method on the `RemoteConnection` object. The first thing this does is to call the `GetService` method to get hold of a `NorthwindService.ProviderService` object. (Visual Studio created this class automatically when we added the web reference to the project.)

```
    ' GetProductDetails - call the service's version of this...
Public Overrides Function GetProductDetails(ByVal productId As Long) _
                    As System.Data.DataSet

    ' Get the service...
    Dim service As NorthwindService.ProviderService = GetService()
```

Once it has the service, it calls the remote method, which, as we've seen, in turn causes the Web Service to call `GetProductDetails` on its installation of a `DirectConnection` object.

```
        ' Call the remote method...
        Return service.GetProductDetails(productId)

    End Function
```

Although we looked at Web Services in quite some detail in Chapter 13, we assumed that the proxy object would always contain the URL that we wanted to use for the service. In this instance, we're going to provide a mechanism that allows us to change the service URL. We don't *need* to do this for our application; it's just an illustration of a useful technique. For example, if we have an application that's used throughout the world, we might choose to geographically distribute our Web Service. Each client could be configured to connect to its "nearest", or "most accessible" one. By changing the value of one shared member in our application, we can redirect all traffic to a different Web Service.

The `Provider` class has shared members called `ServiceUrl` and `Proxy` that look like this:

```
        ' Web Service...
    Public Shared ServiceUrl As String = _
         "http://localhost/NorthwindProviderService/ProviderService.asmx"
    Public Shared Proxy As System.NET.WebProxy
```

By changing the value of `ServiceUrl`, we can direct all Web Service calls away from the URL that's hard-coded into the class library and to a different URL. (For this to work, the Web Service implementations at both URLs must be the same.) Our `GetService` method first creates an instance of a class that can talk to the Web Service, and then changes its URL property to whatever is specified in the shared `Provider.ServiceUrl` property:

```
        ' GetService - return a service object...
    Protected Function GetService() As NorthwindService.ProviderService

        ' Create an instance of the service...
        Dim service As New NorthwindService.ProviderService()

        ' Set the URL...
        service.Url = Provider.ServiceUrl
```

For good measure, we also configure `GetService` so that, if a `System.NET.WebProxy` object is stored in the shared `Provider.Proxy` property, the service will use that proxy. Remember that, in Chapter 13, we used "proxyTrace" to watch the SOAP messages passing between client and server.

```
            ' Set the proxy...
        service.Proxy = Provider.Proxy
```

Once that's done, we can return the object:

```
            ' Return the service...
        Return service
```

Switching Modes

Now that we can use both direct and remote connections, let's change our client application so that the user can choose which one he/she prefers to use.

In the real world, the user wouldn't typically be able to configure these settings. We're going to allow the user (us) to do it here so that we can test both of the modes easily. In the following section, we'll see how the application can determine for itself which is the best connection type to use.

Try It Out – Switching Modes

1. If the Product Editor program is running, close it.

2. Open the Form Designer for Form1. Add a CheckBox control to the top right-hand side of the form with its Text property set to "Use Service", Name to chkUseService, and Anchor to Top, Right.

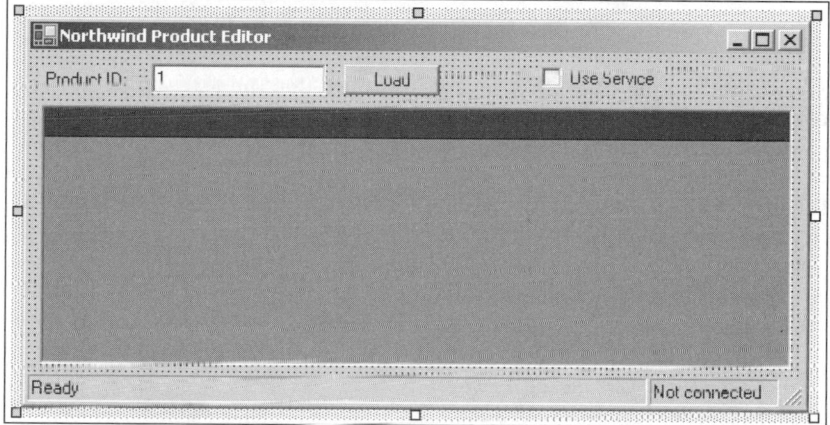

3. Open the code editor for Form1 and find the ConnectionMode property. Make these changes:

```
        ' Update the display...
        pnlConnection.Text = Provider.Connection.ToString

            ' Update the CheckBoxes...
        If Provider.ConnectionMode = Provider.ConnectionModes.Direct Then
            chkUseService.Checked = False
        Else
            chkUseService.Checked = True
        End If

    End Set
End Property
```

4. From the top-left drop-down list on the code editor, select chkUseService. From the right-hand list, select CheckedChanged. Add this code to the new event handler:

```
    Private Sub chkUseService_CheckedChanged(ByVal sender As Object, _
  ByVal e As System.EventArgs) Handles chkUseService.CheckedChanged

        ' Are we checked?
    If chkUseService.Checked = True Then
        ConnectionMode = Provider.ConnectionModes.Remote
    Else
        ConnectionMode = Provider.ConnectionModes.Direct
    End If

End Sub
```

5. Now run the application, you should find that you can use the Use Service CheckBox to flip between direct and remote connections.

How It Works

All we've done is wired up the CheckBox so that it will flip-flop the `Form1.ConnectionMode` mode property between Direct and Remote. This property also contains various calls to update the display, which is how we're updating the StatusBar.

We change the text on the status bar by watching for changes to the `ConnectionMode` property and setting the `Text` property of `pnlConnection`.

```
' Update the display...
pnlConnection.Text = Provider.Connection.ToString

    ' Update the check boxes...
If Provider.ConnectionMode = Provider.ConnectionModes.Direct Then
    chkUseService.Checked = False
Else
    chkUseService.Checked = True
End If
```

In the `CheckedChanged` event, the state of the CheckBox is evaluated and the `ConnectionMode` is determined. In this case, if the CheckBox is checked (`True`) then a Remote connection is used:

```
If chkUseService.Checked = True Then
    ConnectionMode = Provider.ConnectionModes.Remote
Else
    ConnectionMode = Provider.ConnectionModes.Direct
End If
```

Automatically Detecting the Connection Type

Detecting the connection type is simply a matter of going through the ProviderConnection objects in preferred order and asking if they can connect.

Try It Out – Automatically Detecting the Connection Type

1. Open the code editor for Provider. Add this enumeration and member to the top of the class definition:

```
' Enumerations...
Public Enum ConnectionModes As Integer
    NotConnected = 0
    Direct = 1
    Remote = 2
End Enum

Public Enum PreferredConnectionModes As Integer
    Unknown = 0
    Direct = 1
    Remote = 2
    NoneAvailable = -1
End Enum

'Members
Private Shared _connectionMode As Provider.ConnectionModes = _
                ConnectionModes.NotConnected
Private Shared _connection As ProviderConnection
Private Shared _preferredConnectionMode As Provider.PreferredConnectionModes
```

2. Open the code editor for ProviderConnection and add this code:

```
Public MustInherit Class ProviderConnection

' GetProductDetails - get the details for a product...
Public MustOverride Function GetProductDetails(ByVal productId As Long) _
                              As DataSet

    ' CanConnect - can we connect using these settings?
Public MustOverride Function CanConnect() As Boolean

End Class
```

3. Then, open the code editor for DirectConnection and add this code:

```
 ' CanConnect - try and make a connection...
Public Overrides Function CanConnect() As Boolean

    ' Try and connect to the database...
    Try

        ' Open a connection...
        Dim connection As New SqlConnection(Provider.DbString)
        connection.Open()
```

```
            ' We did it!
            connection.Close()
            Return True

        Catch
            Return False
        End Try

    End Function
```

Using an exception handler in this way is quite unusual – usually when we get an exception we do something with it. Instead, what we're doing here is saying, "If we can't connect to the database directly, return `False`." In our application, not being able to connect to a database isn't a critical issue because we can fail but still get our data from somewhere else. In most applications, it is critically important to be able to connect. So, here, we're not using the exception handler to "handle an exception" in a traditional sense, but rather we're using it to signal that a direct connection could not be made.

4. Open the code editor for RemoteConnection and add this code:

```
    Public Overrides Function CanConnect() As Boolean
        Return True
    End Function
```

5. Next, go back to the code editor for Provider and add this property:

```
    ' PreferredConnectionMode - try and make connections...
Public Shared Property PreferredConnectionMode() As PreferredConnectionModes
    Get

        ' Have we tried to look it up?
        If _preferredConnectionMode = PreferredConnectionModes.Unknown Then

            ' Try a database connection first...
            Dim testConnection As ProviderConnection = New DirectConnection()
            If testConnection.CanConnect = True Then

                ' We want direct!
                _preferredConnectionMode = PreferredConnectionModes.Direct

            Else

                ' Try the web connection...
                testConnection = New RemoteConnection()
                If testConnection.CanConnect = True Then

                    ' We want remote!
                    _preferredConnectionMode = _
                PreferredConnectionModes.Remote

                Else
```

```
                    ' There's nothing we can do...
                    _preferredConnectionMode = _
                  PreferredConnectionModes.NoneAvailable

                End If

            End If

        End If

        ' Return it...
        Return _PreferredConnectionMode

    End Get
    Set(ByVal Value As PreferredConnectionModes)
        _preferredConnectionMode = Value
    End Set
End Property
```

6. Also on Provider, add this method:

```
    ' CanConnect - can we connect to anything?
Public Shared Function CanConnect() As Boolean

    ' What's our PreferredConnectionMode?
    If PreferredConnectionMode <> PreferredConnectionModes.NoneAvailable Then
        Return True
    Else
        Return False
    End If

End Function
```

7. To round off the changes to the class library, find the `ConnectionMode` property and make these changes to the Get part. (I've omitted the Set part for clarity.)

```
    ' ConnectionMode - what mode are we in?
Public Shared Property ConnectionMode() As Provider.ConnectionModes
    Get

            ' Do we have a connection mode set?
        If _connectionMode = ConnectionModes.NotConnected Then

            ' Do we have a preferred connection mode?
            Select Case PreferredConnectionMode
                Case PreferredConnectionModes.Direct
                    _connectionMode = ConnectionModes.Direct
                Case PreferredConnectionModes.Remote
                    _connectionMode = ConnectionModes.Remote
```

```
            End Select

        End If

        ' Return the connection mode that we've been given...
        Return _connectionMode

    End Get
```

8. Now that we've changed everything we need to change about the class library, open the code editor for Form1 and find the OnLoad method. Make these changes:

```
    Protected Overrides Sub OnLoad(ByVal e As System.EventArgs)

        ' Can we connect?
    If Provider.CanConnect = False Then

        ' Tell the user and quit...
        MsgBox("A connection cannot be made to the database.")
        Application.Exit()

    Else

        ' Update the display...
        ConnectionMode = Provider.ConnectionMode

    End If

End Sub
```

9. Run the project and you should now see that the application defaults to a direct connection. That's because the database is running and we can make a direct connection to it.

10. Close the application.

11. However, if we stop the database service the application should default to a remote connection. Find the Service Manager. This will either be an icon like this in your task bar:

...or you'll have to run it by selecting **Start | Programs | SQL Server Desktop Engine | Service Manager**. Either way, open the Service Manager and click the "stop" button.

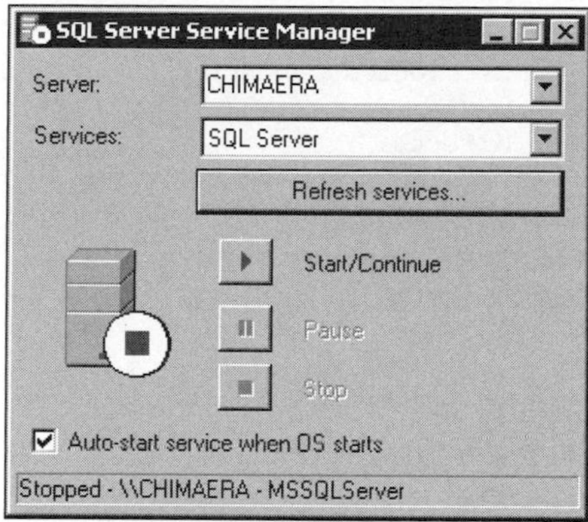

12. Run the project again and the application should fail to connect to the database server (it will take a moment for the connection to timeout, so the application won't appear immediately). It will fall-over and default to a remote connection.

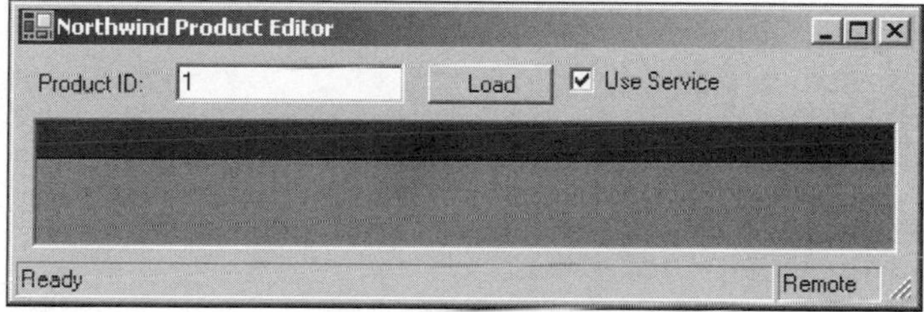

How It Works

The `PreferredConnectionMode` shared property on `Provider` has the intelligence to go through the available connection types in preferred order asking each one if it can connect. The first thing it does, though, is check to make sure that it hasn't been through this step before. As testing the different connections takes a while, we only ever want to do this once in the life of the application.

```
      Get

         ' Have we tried to look it up?
         If _preferredConnectionMode = PreferredConnectionModes.Unknown Then
```

If we've never tried to do this before (`_preferredConnectionMode` will be `Unknown`), we try and connect to the database, as this is the most preferred connection type.

```
               ' Try a database connection first...
           Dim testConnection As ProviderConnection = New DirectConnection()
```

The DirectConnection.CanConnect method itself will try and connect to the database specified using the shared Provider.DbString property, as we've already seen. If the connection can be made, we set the preferred mode to Direct.

```
                    If testConnection.CanConnect = True Then

                    ' We want direct!
                    _preferredConnectionMode = PreferredConnectionModes.Direct
```

If, however, CanConnect returns False we can assume that the connection is not available and so we try the same trick with RemoteConnection.

```
                    Else

                    ' Try the web connection...
                    testConnection = New RemoteConnection()
                    If testConnection.CanConnect = True Then

                        ' We want remote!
                        _preferredConnectionMode = _
                     PreferredConnectionModes.Remote
```

If this too fails, we indicate that we don't have any connections that we can use:

```
                    Else

                        ' There's nothing we can do...
                        _preferredConnectionMode = _
                     PreferredConnectionModes.NoneAvailable

                    End If

                End If

            End If
```

Finally, we return whatever value _preferredConnectionMode is set to.

```
                ' Return it...
            Return _preferredConnectionMode

        End Get
        Set(ByVal Value As PreferredConnectionModes)
            ...
        End Set
```

CanConnect examines the PreferredConnectionMode property and, seeing as this is the first method we call on Provider from within Form1, will trigger the above algorithm to try and find a connection type.

```
' What's our PreferredConnectionMode?
If PreferredConnectionMode <> PreferredConnectionModes.NoneAvailable Then
    Return True
Else
    Return False
End If
```

We can see here how `CanConnect` is called from within `Form1.OnLoad`. If the connection cannot be made, we display a message box and quit the application. Otherwise, we call the `Form1.ConnectionMode` property, which has the side-effect of updating the display.

```
' Can we connect?
If Provider.CanConnect = False Then

    ' Tell the user and quit...
    MsgBox("A connection cannot be made to the database.")
    Application.Exit()

Else

    ' Update the display...
    ConnectionMode = Provider.ConnectionMode

End If
```

The upshot of all of this is that `DirectConnection.CanConnect` is called first. If this succeeds, `PreferredConnectionMode` is set to `Direct`. If it fails, `RemoteConnection.CanConnect` is called. Right now, we have this configured to always succeed (that is, "`Return True`") so we'll always have a connection of some sort available.

Exception Handling

There's a chance that whenever we call a method on either of the `DirectConnection` or `RemoteConnection` objects that something could go wrong. We need to neatly handle any exceptions that may occur, so in this section we will be adding any exception handlers necessary.

Try It Out – Adding Exception Handling

1. Open the code editor for Form1. Add this method:

```
    ' HandleException...
Public Function HandleException(ByVal message As String, _
                    ByVal e As Exception)

    ' Drill down...
    Do While Not e.InnerException Is Nothing
        e = e.InnerException
    Loop

    ' Create a message...
```

```
    Dim builder As New System.Text.StringBuilder(message)
    builder.Append(ControlChars.CrLf)
    builder.Append(ControlChars.CrLf)
    builder.Append("An exception has occured:")
    builder.Append(ControlChars.CrLf)
    builder.Append(e.Message)
    builder.Append(ControlChars.CrLf)
    builder.Append(e.StackTrace)
    builder.Append(ControlChars.CrLf)
    builder.Append(ControlChars.CrLf)
    If Not Provider.Connection Is Nothing Then
        builder.Append("Connection in use: " & _
        Provider.Connection.ToString & " (" & _
        Provider.Connection.GetType.FullName & ")")
    Else
        builder.Append("A database connection cannot be established.")
    End If
    MsgBox(builder.ToString, MsgBoxStyle.Exclamation)

End Function
```

2. Next, find the `ProductId` property and add this `Try`...`Catch` block.

```
    Public Property ProductId() As Integer
    Get
        Return _productId
    End Get
    Set(ByVal Value As Integer)

        ' Set the Id...
        _productId = Value

        ' Get the data...
        SetProcessText("Loading product information from " & _
        Provider.Connection.ToString & ".  Please wait...")
            Try
                ProductDataSet = _
           Provider.Connection.GetProductDetails(_productId)
            Catch e As Exception
            HandleException( _
           "The product information could not be loaded.", e)
        End Try
            ResetProcessText()

   ' Set the datagrid binding...
        dgdProducts.DataSource = ProductDataSet
            If Not ProductDataSet Is Nothing Then
                dgdProducts.DataMember = ProductDataSet.Tables(0).TableName
            End If

    End Set
End Property
```

How It Works

Right now, nothing will throw an exception so you won't be able to see the message box. However, had something gone wrong, you would have seen something like this. (In this case, I've stopped the database server after the program has started and then clicked the Load button.)

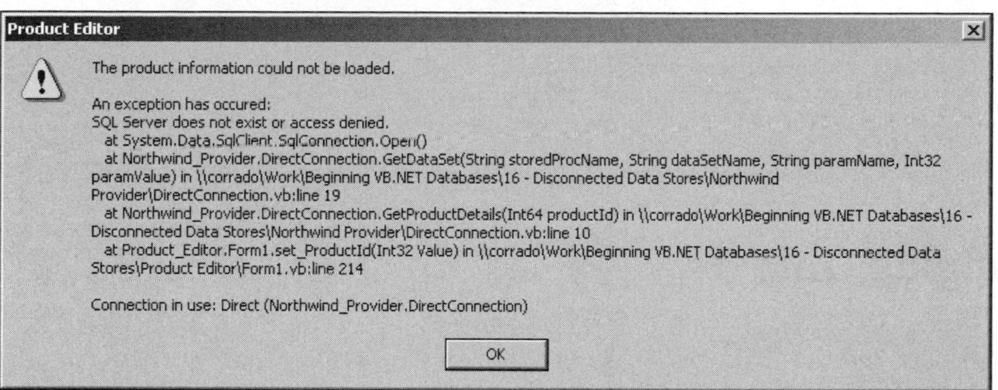

One thing to note, this kind of message is going to be of virtually no use in a real-world application. What you want to do is present some logical, helpful message to the user that will let them resolve the problem, or tell them that they can't. Our illustration here is just to show an example of exception handling without going too deeply into the problem.

When an exception is reported, it's often the case that the `Exception` object we get back actually contains another exception object, or they can be "nested". (This is particularly true when working with Web Services.) To find the original exception, the one where it all started to go wrong, we have to loop through the `InnerException` property on the `Exception` object itself. Each time we do this, we go further up the nested exceptions until eventually we find the "top-level" exception. This top-level exception is the one we want to tell the user about.

```
    ' Drill down...
Do While Not e.InnerException Is Nothing
    e = e.InnerException
Loop
```

The remainder of `HandleException` puts together a string to display a message box, as we've just seen.

So why did we have to change the `ProductId` property? Well, working with a Web Service is often a tricky thing to do. Firstly, they're often somewhere else on the Internet and may be inaccessible for any one of a thousand reasons. Secondly, they're owned by someone else, meaning that they can be changed without you knowing about it. If you imagine working with another team in your own organization, in a properly managed programming environment, one team shouldn't be able to break something you're using without you knowing about it. This doesn't necessarily hold for Web Services.

What we have to do is wrap the call to `GetProductDetails` in an exception handler. If, for some reason, we can't get the data back, we display a message to let the user know what's going on.

```
' Get the data...
SetProcessText("Loading product information from " & _
Provider.Connection.ToString & ".  Please wait...")

Try
    ProductDataSet = _
          Provider.Connection.GetProductDetails(_productId)
Catch e As Exception
    HandleException( _
          "The product information could not be loaded.", e)
End Try

ResetProcessText()
```

Changing Data

So far we've managed to prove that we can get information from both the direct and remote connections. We've yet to prove that we can make changes to the data in either mode.

The user can change any information he/she wants simply by making edits in the `DataGrid` control. As edits are made, the underlying `DataSet` object will be updated to reflect the new changes. All we have to do then is somehow pass the modified `DataSet` object back to the database, either directly or through the Web Service.

For simplicity's sake, any concurrency issues have been ignored in this chapter. For more information on concurrency, see Chapter 10.

One aspect of the UI for our application that's not very intuitive is the SupplierID column. At the moment, in order to change these values the user has to remember the entire list of suppliers and their associated IDs. A better way of doing this is to present a list of suppliers for the user to choose from.

In the first part of this next section, we'll look at presenting a list of suppliers to the user. The user will then be able to select a new supplier from the list. In the following section, we'll look at how to save changes to the database.

Before you go any further, remember to restart your SQL Server service otherwise you won't be able to get any data for your application.

Choosing Suppliers

In order to choose suppliers, we need to do three things: one, make a list of suppliers available to the client; two, present the list of suppliers; three, update the supplier when the user makes a change.

Building the "ProviderGetSuppliers" Stored Procedure

The first thing we'll do is to build a stored procedure that returns the entire list of suppliers.

Try It Out– Building "ProviderGetSuppliers"

1. Using the Server Explorer, create a new stored procedure with the following SQL code:

```
CREATE PROCEDURE dbo.ProviderGetSuppliers
AS
SELECT SupplierID, CompanyName, ContactName, ContactTitle,
  Address, City, Region, PostalCode, Country, Phone, Fax, HomePage
     FROM Suppliers ORDER BY CompanyName
```

2. Select File | Save Stored Procedure from the menu.

3. If you test the stored procedure, you should see a list of suppliers appear in the Output window.

Calling "ProviderGetSuppliers"

Both `DirectConnection` and `RemoteConnection` now need to be able to call this new stored procedure.

To let the user choose the supplier, we're going to pop up a separate form containing a list of suppliers. We're not specifically going to tie this form into suppliers; it will work with lists of anything that we choose.

Try It Out – Calling "ProviderGetSuppliers"

1. Open the code editor for `ProviderConnection`. Add this code:

```
Public MustInherit Class ProviderConnection

' GetProductDetails - get the details for a product...
Public MustOverride Function GetProductDetails(ByVal productId As Long) _
                              As DataSet

' CanConnect - can we connect using these settings?
Public MustOverride Function CanConnect() As Boolean

    ' GetSuppliers - get the entire supplier list...
Public MustOverride Function GetSuppliers() As DataSet

End Class
```

2. Next, open the code editor for `DirectConnection` and add this code:

```
    ' GetSuppliers - return a list of suppliers...
Public Overrides Function GetSuppliers() As System.Data.DataSet
    Return GetDataSet("ProviderGetSuppliers", "Suppliers")
End Function
```

3. At the moment, `GetDataSet` needs the name and value for a parameter to pass through to the stored procedure. There isn't one in this case, so we need to create an alternate, overloaded version of `GetDataSet`. Add this method to `DirectConnection`:

```
    ' GetDataSet - alternate version...
Protected Function GetDataSet(ByVal storedProcName, ByVal dataSetName) _
                                  As DataSet
    Return GetDataSet(storedProcName, dataSetName, "", 0)
End Function
```

4. When `GetDataSet` calls `GetDataAdapter`, `GetDataAdapter` will expect to receive a parameter, so what we need to do is change this method so that we don't *have* to supply a parameter, or rather if we don't, the method will gracefully handle the eventuality. Find the `GetDataAdapter` method and make this change:

```
' Create the command...
Dim command As New SqlCommand(storedProcName, connection)
command.CommandType = CommandType.StoredProcedure

    ' Do we have a parameter?
If paramName <> "" Then

    ' Add the parameter...
    Dim param As SqlParameter = _
       command.Parameters.Add(paramName, SqlDbType.Int)
    param.Direction = ParameterDirection.Input
    param.Value = paramValue

    End If

' Create an adapter from that...
Return New SqlDataAdapter(command)
```

5. Before we can run the project, we need to add a dummy implementation to `RemoteConnection`, otherwise we'll get a compilation error. We'll worry about implementing this properly in a moment, so for now open the code editor for `RemoteConnection` and add this code:

```
    Public Overrides Function GetSuppliers() As System.Data.DataSet

End Function
```

6. In the client, we'll need a form that we can display a list of suppliers in. Create a new form called Lookup. Set the SizeGripStyle property of the form to Hide.

7. Paint these controls onto the form and set their properties as follows:

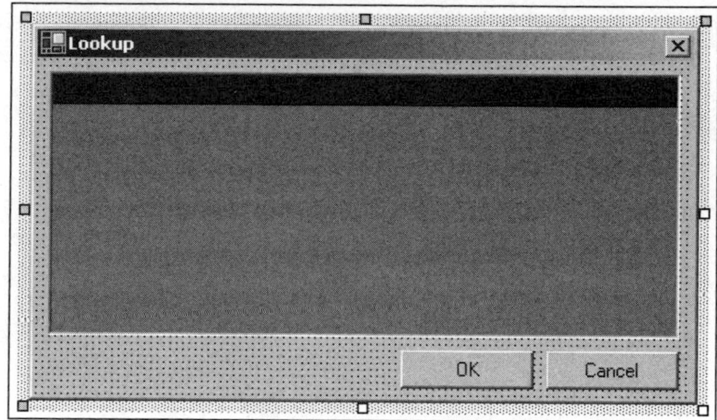

- Button1: Name to btnOk, DialogResult to OK, Anchor to Bottom, Right and Text to OK.
- Button2: Name to btnCancel, DialogResult to Cancel, Anchor to Bottom, Right and Text to Cancel.
- DataGrid: Name to dgdLookup, ReadOnly to True, Anchor to Top, Bottom, Left, Right.

8. Open the code editor for Lookup and add this private member and property:

```
Public Class Lookup
Inherits System.Windows.Forms.Form

    ' Members...
Private _dataSet As DataSet

' DataSet property...
Public Property DataSet() As DataSet
    Get
        Return _dataSet
    End Get
    Set(ByVal Value As DataSet)

        ' Store the DataSet...
        _dataSet = Value

        ' Update the data grid...
        dgdLookup.DataSource = _dataSet
        dgdLookup.DataMember = _dataSet.Tables(0).TableName

    End Set
End Property

End Class
```

9. Now we can turn our attention to displaying the Lookup form. Open the Form Designer for Form1 and add this button. Change the Name of the button to btnLookupSupplier and its Text to Lookup Supplier:

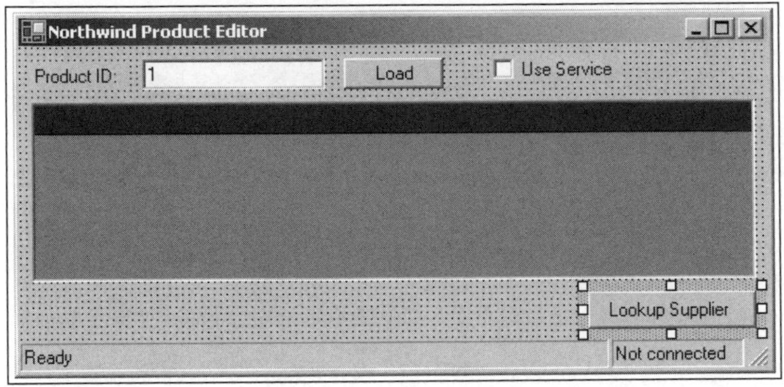

10. Double-click on the button to create a new `Click` handler. Add this code to the new event handler:

```
Private Sub btnLookupSupplier_Click(ByVal sender As System.Object, _
 ByVal e As System.EventArgs) Handles btnLookupSupplier.Click

    ' Get a list of suppliers back...
   Dim dataSetSuppliers As DataSet
   SetProcessText("Loading list of suppliers from " & _
    Provider.Connection.ToString & ".  Please wait...")
   Try
      dataSetSuppliers = Provider.Connection.GetSuppliers
   Catch ex As Exception
      HandleException("The supplier list could not be retrieved.", ex)
   End Try
   ResetProcessText()

   ' Did we get one?
   If Not dataSetSuppliers Is Nothing Then

      ' Create the form...
      Dim lookup As New Lookup()
      lookup.DataSet = dataSetSuppliers

      ' Show the dialog...
      If lookup.ShowDialog(Me) = DialogResult.OK Then

      End If

   End If

End Sub
```

11. Run the project and click the Lookup Supplier button. You should see this:

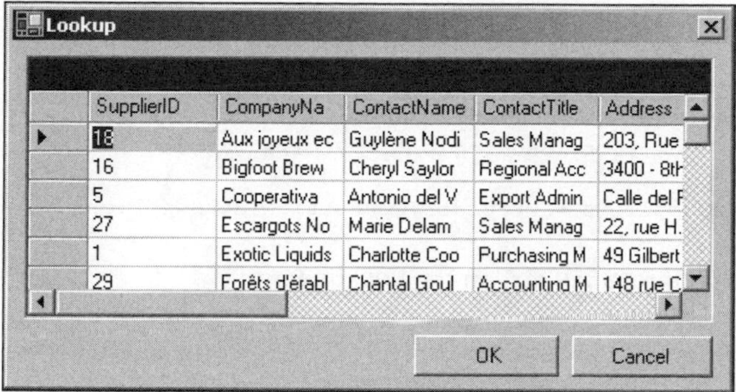

How It Works

The `GetSuppliers` method calls the `ProviderGetSuppliers` stored procedure in the database:

```
Return GetDataSet("ProviderGetSuppliers", "Suppliers")
```

That returns a list of suppliers in alphabetical order:

```
SELECT SupplierID, CompanyName, ContactName, ContactTitle,
  Address, City, Region, PostalCode, Country, Phone, Fax, HomePage
    FROM Suppliers ORDER BY CompanyName
```

We then pass this list over to the new Lookup form through the `DataSet` property where it updates the `DataGrid` control in the usual way. When we set the `DataSet` property of `Lookup`, what we do is bind the first table in the `DataSet` to the `DataGrid` control on the form.

```
' DataSet property...
Public Property DataSet() As DataSet
    Get
        Return _dataSet
    End Get
    Set(ByVal Value As DataSet)

        ' Store the DataSet...

        _dataSet = Value

        ' Update the data grid...
        dgdLookup.DataSource = _dataSet
        dgdLookup.DataMember = _dataSet.Tables(0).TableName

    End Set
End Property
```

Finally, we added a new button `Click` event to call the `GetSuppliers` method:

```
Dim dataSetSuppliers As DataSet
SetProcessText("Loading list of suppliers from " & _
 Provider.Connection.ToString & ".  Please wait...")
Try
    dataSetSuppliers = Provider.Connection.GetSuppliers
```

and list the suppliers on the `DataGrid` on the **Lookup** form:

```
Dim lookup As New Lookup()
lookup.DataSet = dataSetSuppliers
```

Changing the Selected Supplier

Although we've proven we can get a list of suppliers back, the **Lookup** form can show the suppliers, but doesn't let us select new suppliers. In addition, we need to highlight the currently selected supplier when the form first appears. Now, let's look at how we can resolve this.

Try It Out – Changing the Selected Supplier

1. If the program is running, close it.

2. Open the code editor for `Lookup`. Add this member that will hold the ID of the currently selected item. (Remember, the form is not specifically tied to displaying lists of suppliers, hence the name `_lookupId` rather than `_supplierId`.

```
    ' Members...
Private _dataSet As DataSet
    Private _lookupId As Integer
```

3. Next, add this property:

```
    Public Property LookupId() As Integer
    Get
        Return _lookupId
    End Get
    Set(ByVal Value As Integer)

        ' Store the Id...
        _lookupId = Value

        ' Find the selected item in the list...
        Dim row As DataRow, index As Integer = 0
        For Each row In _dataSet.Tables(0).Rows

            ' Does the Id match?
            If row.Item(0) = _lookupId Then
                dgdLookup.CurrentRowIndex = index
                Exit For
```

```
            End If

            ' Next...
            index += 1

        Next

    End Set
End Property
```

4. From the left-hand drop-down list, select dgdLookup. From the right-hand list, select CurrentCellChanged. Add this code to the new event handler:

```
    Private Sub datagridLookup_CurrentCellChanged(ByVal sender As Object, _
  ByVal e As System.EventArgs) Handles datagridLookup.CurrentCellChanged

        ' Get the current row...
    If dgdLookup.CurrentRowIndex >= 0 Then
        _lookupId = dgdLookup.Item(dgdLookup.CurrentRowIndex, 0)
    End If

End Sub
```

5. Open the code editor form Form1 and find the `btnLookupSupplier_Click` method. Make these changes:

```
    Private Sub btnLookupSupplier_Click(ByVal sender As System.Object, _
     ByVal e As System.EventArgs) Handles btnLookupSupplier.Click

        ' Firstly, we need the current supplierId...
    Dim supplierId As Integer, selectedRow As DataRow
    Try

        ' Get the product ID that's been selected...
        Dim selectedProductId As Integer
        selectedProductId = _
        dgdProducts.Item(dgdProducts.CurrentRowIndex, 0)

        ' Now, look through the DataSet for that item...
        Dim row As DataRow
        For Each row In ProductDataSet.Tables(0).Rows
            If row.Item(0) = selectedProductId Then
                selectedRow = row
                Exit For
            End If
        Next

        ' Did we get one?
        If Not selectedRow Is Nothing Then
            supplierId = selectedRow.Item("Supplierid")
```

```
            End If

        Catch
            MsgBox("You must select a product from the list.")
        End Try

        ' Did we get a supplier?
        If supplierId <> 0 Then

            ' Get a list of suppliers back...
            Dim dataSetSuppliers As DataSet
            SetProcessText("Loading list of suppliers from " & _
            Provider.Connection.ToString & ".  Please wait...")
            Try
                dataSetSuppliers = Provider.Connection.GetSuppliers
            Catch ex As Exception
                HandleException("The supplier list could not be retrieved.", ex)
            End Try
            ResetProcessText()

            ' Did we get one?
            If Not dataSetSuppliers Is Nothing Then

                ' Create the form...
                Dim lookup As New Lookup()
                lookup.DataSet = dataSetSuppliers
                    lookup.LookupId = supplierId

                ' Show the dialog...
                If lookup.ShowDialog(Me) = DialogResult.OK Then
                        selectedRow.Item("SupplierID") = lookup.LookupId
                    End If

            End If

        End If

    End Sub
```

6. Run the project. Click the Load button to load the product ID and click the Lookup Supplier button. You should notice that the currently chosen SupplierID in the `DataGrid` matches the newly selected supplier in the pop-up window.

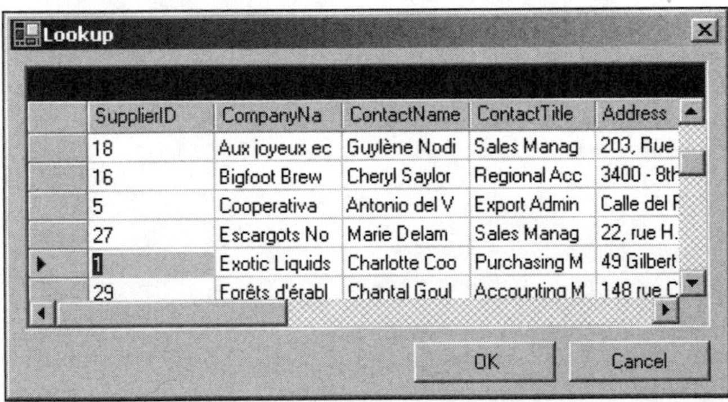

7. If you select another row and click OK, the SupplierID value on the original form will change to reflect the new selection.

How It Works

When the Lookup Supplier button on the original form is clicked, we use the `CurrentRowIndex` of the `DataGrid` to find out what product is selected. Although we've only seen one product in the `DataGrid` at a time, the client can handle multiple products.

The first thing we have to do is find the ID of the selected product. This will always be the first column of the currently selected row.

```
Dim supplierId As Integer, selectedRow As DataRow
Try

    ' Get the product ID that's been selected...
    Dim selectedProductId As Integer
    selectedProductId = _
    dgdProducts.Item(dgdProducts.CurrentRowIndex, 0)
```

Once we have the product ID, we need to find the relevant row in the `DataSet`. This, again, will be the item with the first column (actually, the "zeroth" column) that matches the product ID.

```
    ' Now, look through the DataSet for that Id...
    Dim row As DataRow
    For Each row In ProductDataSet.Tables(0).Rows
        If row.Item(0) = selectedProductId Then
            selectedRow = row
            Exit For
        End If
    Next
```

Once we have the row, we can use it to get the supplier ID.

```
    ' Did we get one?
    If Not selectedRow Is Nothing Then
        supplierId = selectedRow.Item("SupplierID")
    End If
```

If the user has selected a product, and the SupplierID column contains a valid, integer value, we can go ahead and display the Lookup form. After we give the Lookup form a list of suppliers, we also give it the chosen supplier ID by setting the `LookupId` property. (I've omitted some code here for brevity.)

```
            ' Create the form...
        Dim lookup As New Lookup()
        lookup.DataSet = dataSetSuppliers
            lookup.LookupId = supplierId

        ' Show the dialog...
```

```
            If lookup.ShowDialog(Me) = DialogResult.OK Then
                selectedRow.Item("SupplierID") = lookup.LookupId
            End If
```

In the Lookup form itself, setting the LookupId property will cause it to loop through the entire supplier list looking for the ID that we gave it. When it finds it, it changes the DataGrid's CurrentRowIndex property so that the relevant supplier is selected.

```
        Get
            Return _lookupId
        End Get
        Set(ByVal Value As Integer)

            ' Store the Id...
            _lookupId = Value

            ' Find the selected item in the list...
            Dim row As DataRow, index As Integer = 0
            For Each row In _dataSet.Tables(0).Rows

                ' Does the Id match?
                If row.Item(0) = _lookupId Then
                        datagridLookup.CurrentRowIndex = index
                        Exit For
                End If

                ' Next...
                index += 1

            Next

        End Set
```

As the user changes the selection, we update the _lookupId member so that it contains the ID of the currently selected row.

```
        Private Sub datagridLookup_CurrentCellChanged(ByVal sender As Object, _
      ByVal e As System.EventArgs) Handles datagridLookup.CurrentCellChanged

        ' Get the current row...
        If datagridLookup.CurrentRowIndex >= 0 Then
            _lookupId = datagridLookup.Item(datagridLookup.CurrentRowIndex, 0)
        End If

    End Sub
```

Looking back at the code in Form1 that displays the dialog, should the dialog return OK, we can use the LookupId property again to get the value of the _lookupId member and update the supplier ID.

```
                ' Create the form...
            Dim lookup As New Lookup()
            lookup.DataSet = dataSetSuppliers
            lookup.LookupId = supplierId
```

```
' Show the dialog...
If lookup.ShowDialog(Me) = DialogResult.OK Then
        selectedRow.Item("SupplierID") = lookup.LookupId
    End If
```

Calling "GetSuppliers" from the Web Service

If you check the Use Service checkbox and click Lookup Supplier, you'll notice that nothing happens. That's because we haven't updated the Web Service so that it is able to return a list of suppliers. We need to create a new method on the Web Service that `RemoteConnection` can use to get a list of suppliers.

Unlike the Product Editor project, the NorthwindProviderService project doesn't contain a reference to the Northwind Provider *project*. Instead, it contains a reference to the *assembly*. In Visual Studio .NET, changes made to a project are automatically reflected in any projects that have a reference to it. When we add new methods to `ProviderConnection`, the Product Editor code knows about the new methods instantly.

However, that doesn't hold true for referenced assemblies. At the moment, NorthwindProviderService knows nothing about the `GetSuppliers` method that we've added to `ProviderConnection`, therefore we cannot call `GetSuppliers`. To solve this problem, we have to remove the reference and add it again.

Try It Out – Updating the Web Service

1. If the program is running, close it and open the NorthwindProviderService project.

2. Using Solution Explorer, open up the References item beneath NorthwindProviderService.

3. Right-click Northwind Provider and select Remove.

4. Right-click References and select Add Reference. When the Add Reference dialog appears, select Browse.

5. Find and open the Northwind Provider.dll file. Click OK to add the assembly reference. At this point, Visual Studio will examine the assembly again and the `GetSupplier` method will be available.

6. View the code for ProviderService.asmx and add this method:

```
    ' GetSuppliers - return a list of suppliers...
<WebMethod()> Public Function GetSuppliers() As DataSet
    Return Provider.Connection.GetSuppliers()
End Function
```

7. Run the project and test that the new `GetSuppliers` method works.

8. Flip back to the Product Editor solution. Using Solution Explorer, find the NorthwindService Web Service reference under the Northwind Provider project.

9. Right-click NorthwindService and select Update Web Reference. Just as we needed to re-create the reference to Northwind Provider in the service project, we need to do a similar thing here so that the new `GetSuppliers` web method will be available to `RemoteConnection`.

10. Open the code editor for `RemoteConnection`. Find `GetSuppliers` and make this change:

```
    Public Overrides Function GetSuppliers() As System.Data.DataSet

         ' Get the service and call get suppliers...
    Dim service As NorthwindService.ProviderService = GetService()
    Return service.GetSuppliers()

End Function
```

11. Try running the project again and this time, change to Remote mode using the CheckBox and click Lookup Supplier. The list should come back exactly as it did over a direct connection.

How It Works

Previously, when we added the `GetSupplier` method to the abstract `ProviderConnection` class, to make the discussion easier to follow, we didn't bother adding an implementation to `RemoteConnection`, because this would have meant adding a new method to the NorthwindProviderService Web Service.

Since the start of the project, we've been trying to build the client in such a way that it doesn't care where its data is coming from. This is now paying dividends, because we had to make no changes to the client at all in order to convince it to get the data from the Web Service rather than directly from the database.

Saving Changes

The final part of this project involves saving the changes that the user makes to the product information back to the database. This not only includes saving the supplier ID using the Lookup form, but also dealing with changes to the other data that the `DataGrid` allows the user to edit.

Based on the work we've done in previous chapters, you may well be thinking that saving changes to a `DataSet` is easy. That's only half true. To transfer data between the database and the `DataSet` and back again, we need a `DataAdapter` object. However, we don't have one of these hanging around; whenever we use it, we get rid of it immediately after using it.

The reason why we get rid of it is because, although a `DataSet` can successfully pass through a Web Service, a `DataAdapter` cannot. As our architecture has to account for both direct and remote connections seamlessly, we cannot implement "special" features on each type of connection. Instead, we have to find a solution that works for both the direct and remote versions. In effect, we have to duplicate the functionality that the `DataAdapter` uses to update the database.

Imagine we have to update the `Products` table. (The actual algorithm we're going to put together will work on any `DataSet`, not just one drawn from the `Products` table.) Here's what we'll do:

- Create a new method called `SetProductDetails` on `ProviderConnection`. This method will accept a `DataSet` of rows drawn from the `Products` table. This will be known as the "Changed `DataSet`".
- We'll examine each row in the Changed `DataSet` in turn, looking for ones that have their `RowState` property set to `Modified`.
- When we find one, we'll get the same product back from the database. This time, however, we'll keep the `SqlDataAdapter` around and keep it bound to the `DataSet`. This new `DataSet` will be called the "Master `DataSet`".
- All of the columns in the applicable row in the Changed `DataSet` will be copied to the matching column in the Master `DataSet`.
- We'll use the `SqlDataAdapter` object's `Update` method to make the changes to the database itself.

This technique will work whether the Changed `DataSet` is passed directly to `DirectConnection` or through `RemoteConnection` and the Web Service. The only drawback is that we have to create two `SqlDataAdapter` objects whereas, if we only had to deal with a direct connection, we'd need just one.

Building "SetProductDetails"

The first thing we need to do is add `SetProductDetails` to the abstract `ProviderConnection` object.

Try It Out – Building "SetProductDetails"

1. Open the code editor for `ProviderConnection`. Add this method:

```
' GetSuppliers - get the entire supplier list...
Public MustOverride Function GetSuppliers() As DataSet

    ' SetProductDetails - set the details for products...
Public MustOverride Sub SetProductDetails(ByVal products As DataSet)

End Class
```

2. Open `RemoteConnection` and add "stub" method. As before, we'll come back and fill this in later.

```
    Public Overrides Sub SetProductDetails(ByVal products As System.Data.DataSet)

End Sub
```

3. Open `DirectConnection` and add this method:

```
    ' SetProductDetails - save changes to changed products...
Public Overrides Sub SetProductDetails(ByVal products As System.Data.DataSet)
    SaveChanges("ProviderGetProductDetails", "@productId", products)
End Sub
```

4. Then, add the `SaveChanges` method.

```
    ' SaveChanges - save changes to changed rows...
Protected Sub SaveChanges(ByVal selectStoredProc As String, _
                ByVal selectParamName As String, _
                ByVal changedDataSet As DataSet)

    ' Need to hold a database connection...
    Dim connection As New SqlConnection(Provider.DbString)
    connection.Open()

    ' Go through each row in the master DataSet...
    Dim changedRow As DataRow
    For Each changedRow In changedDataSet.Tables(0).Rows

        ' Has it changed?
        If changedRow.RowState = DataRowState.Modified Then

            ' Get the Id of the changes item...
            Dim changedId As Integer = changedRow.Item(0)

            ' Get the master row by using the adapter...
            Dim adapter As SqlDataAdapter = _
        GetDataAdapter(connection, selectStoredProc, _
        selectParamName, changedId)

            ' Create a command builder and bind it to the adapter...
            Dim builder As New SqlCommandBuilder(adapter)

            ' Fill a new dataset...
            Dim masterDataSet As New DataSet()
            adapter.Fill(masterDataSet)

            ' Get the row from this DataSet...
            Dim masterRow As DataRow = masterDataSet.Tables(0).Rows(0)

            ' Copy the changes from one to the other...
            Dim dataValue As Object, index As Integer
            index = 0
            For Each dataValue In changedRow.ItemArray
                masterRow.Item(index) = dataValue
                index += 1
            Next

            ' Tell the adapter to update...
            adapter.Update(masterDataSet)
```

```
        End If

    Next

    ' Close the connection...
    connection.Close()

End Sub
```

5. Open the Form Designer for Form1 and add a new button control next to the Load button. Change the Name property of the new button to btnSave.

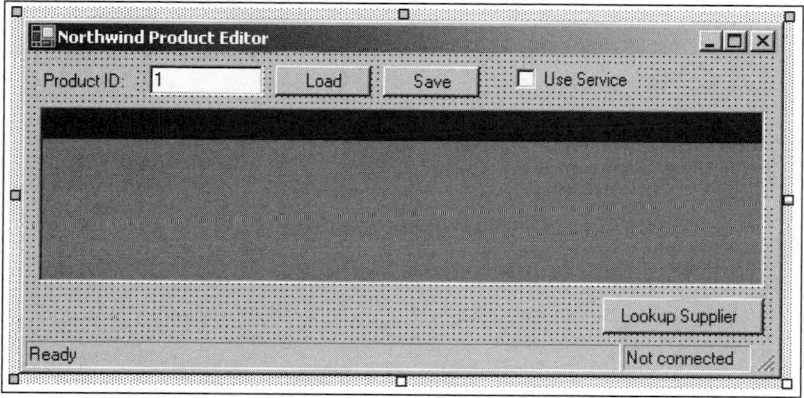

6. Double-click on the Save button to create a new `Click` event handler. Add this code:

```
Private Sub btnSave_Click(ByVal sender As System.Object, _
    ByVal e As System.EventArgs) Handles btnSave.Click

    ' Save changes...
    Provider.Connection.SetProductDetails(ProductDataSet)

    ' Report the save...
    MsgBox("The changes have been saved.")

End Sub
```

How It Works

We're going to hold off explaining how the code works until we can actually run `SetProductDetails`, which we'll do in a short while.

Testing the Changes

Before we run the project, we have to make sure that a primary key has been defined on the `Products` table. Without a primary key, `SqlCommandBuilder` will be unable to form the appropriate query to make the database changes. A primary key is necessary as the `SqlCommandBuilder` uses this information to generate the necessary SQL `WHERE` clause.

Try It Out – Checking the Primary Key and Testing the Code

1. Using the Server Explorer, find the Products table item within NorthwindSQL.

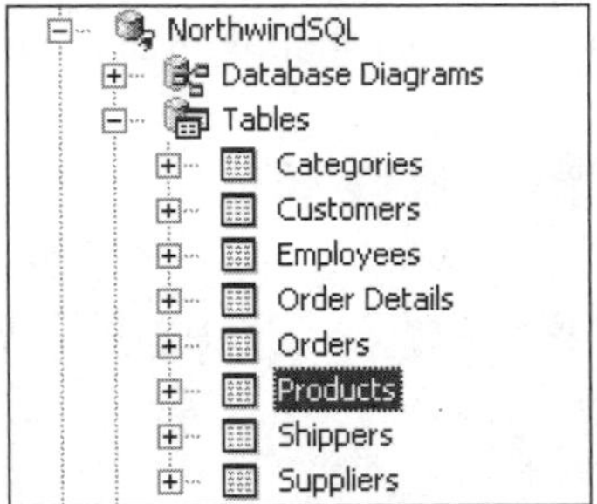

2. Right-click on Products and select Design Table.

3. If the ProductID column does not have a small key icon in the selection margin, right-click ProductID and select Set Primary Key. You should end up with something like this:

	Column Name	Data Type	Length	Allow Nulls
	ProductID	int	4	

4. Select File | Save Products from the menu to save the changes to the definition. Close down the definition window.

5. Click on the Products table in Server Explorer once more, and this time select Retrieve Data From Table. The first item should list a product with ID of 1 and a name of Chai.

	ProductID	ProductName	SupplierID
	1	Chai	1

6. Run the project. Click the Load button to load the product from the database and change the name to Chai Tea.

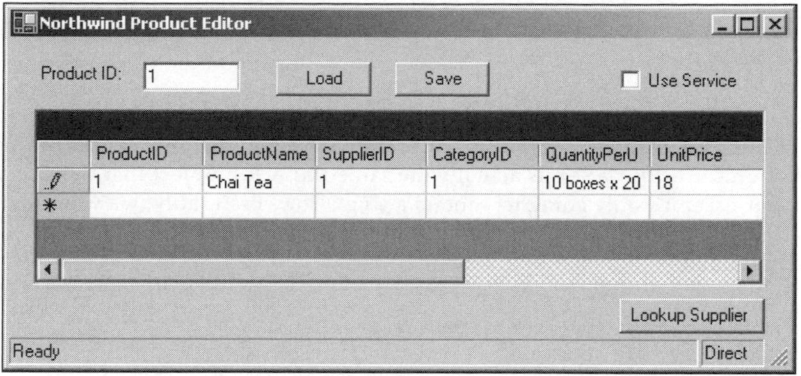

7. Click the Save button. You see a message box telling you that the changes have been saved.

8. Flip back to Visual Studio and find the listing of rows from the Products table again. Right-click on any column in any one of the rows and select Run. You should now see that the underlying database data is now the same as the values entered into the `DataGrid`.

	ProductID	ProductName	SupplierID
	1	Chai Tea	1

How It Works

Whenever changes are made to the edit control, the related `DataSet` is automatically updated. We hold the `DataSet` containing the products for editing in the `ProductDataSet` member.

When the Save button is clicked, we pass this `DataSet` over to the `SetProductDetails` member of the current `ProviderConnection` object, in this case `DirectConnection`.

```
    ' Save changes...
      Provider.Connection.SetProductDetails(ProductDataSet)

    ' Report the save...
    MsgBox("The changes have been saved.")
```

`SetProductDetails` defers processing of the changes to an internal helper method called `SaveChanges`. This method is a general-purpose function that isn't just tied to working with `DataSets` drawn from the `Products` table.

```
    ' SetProductDetails - save changes to changed products...
Public Overrides Sub SetProductDetails(_
                ByVal products As System.Data.DataSet)
        SaveChanges("ProviderGetProductDetails", "@productId", products)
    End Sub
```

Let's take a close look at `SaveChanges`. The first thing we need to do is establish a connection to the database.

```
Dim connection As New SqlConnection(Provider.DbString)
connection.Open()
```

Once we have the connection, we need to walk through each of the rows in the first table in the changedDataSet. We assume that the DataSet we've been given only supports a single table. Remember that changedDataSet is actually the same DataSet object that the DataGrid used for its binding so, in our case, it's only going to contain a single row. Preferably, we want the Product Editor application to handle multiple products. This method is prepared for the eventuality that we supply a list of multiple products.

```
' Go through each row in the master DataSet...
Dim changedRow As DataRow
For Each changedRow In changedDataSet.Tables(0).Rows
```

For each row, we check it to see if it has been modified. Notice we don't do anything if the row has been deleted or added (both of which we can check for using RowState).

```
    ' Has it changed?
    If changedRow.RowState = DataRowState.Modified Then
```

If the row has changed, we use the first column of the row to find the ID of the *item* that has been changed. In our case, this will be the ProductID.

```
        ' Get the Id of the changes item...
        Dim changedId As Integer = changedRow.Item(0)
```

When we called SaveChanges, we provided the name of the stored procedure used to get the row from the database in the first place ("ProviderGetProductDetails"), and also the name of the sole parameter on this stored procedure ("@productId"). GetDataAdapter will return a SqlDataAdapter object that is able to populate a DataSet with whatever is currently stored in the database for the provided ID.

```
        ' Get the master row by using the adapter...
        Dim adapter As SqlDataAdapter = _
       GetDataAdapter(connection, selectStoredProc, _
             selectParamName, changedId)
```

In order to update the database, we need a SqlCommandBuilder. This object is capable of automatically generating the SQL needed to update the database.

```
        ' We need to create a command builder and bind it...
        Dim builder As New SqlCommandBuilder(adapter)
```

The SqlDataAdapter can then be used to fill a new DataSet with whatever value is currently stored in the database. We also get the first row from the first table in this DataSet and this references the same product that the current value of changedRow references.

```
            ' Fill a new DataSet...
            Dim masterDataSet As New DataSet()
            adapter.Fill(masterDataSet)

            ' Get the row from this DataSet...
            Dim masterRow As DataRow = masterDataSet.Tables(0).Rows(0)
```

Once we have both rows, we copy the changed values into values stored against `masterRow`.

```
            ' Copy the changes from one to the other...
            Dim dataValue As Object, index As Integer
            index = 0
            For Each dataValue In changedRow.ItemArray
                masterRow.Item(index) = dataValue
                index += 1
            Next
```

At this point, what we effectively have is a copy of the new data that we were given but, this time, we have a `SqlDataAdapter` object that knows how to commit the changes to the database.

```
            ' Tell the adapter to update...
            adapter.Update(masterDataSet)

        End If
```

As the method can handle multiple rows, we keep looping and close the connection when we are finished.

```
        Next

        ' Close the connection...
        connection.Close()

    End Sub
```

Saving Changes Over the Web Service

To complete the functionality that we're going to explore with this application, we need to prove that we can save changes through the Web Service.

Try It Out – Saving Changes Over the Web Service

1. Open the Web Service project. Like we did before, delete the reference to Northwind Provider and add it again. Without this step, the service won't know anything about our new `SetProductDetails` method.

2. Open the code viewer for `ProviderService.asmx`. Add this new method:

```
    <WebMethod()> Public Sub SetProductDetails(ByVal products As DataSet)
    Provider.Connection.SetProductDetails(products)
End Sub
```

3. Build the project. Unless you do this, the new `SetProductDetails` method will not be available to the client application.

4. Flip back to the Northwind Provider project. Using Solution Explorer, find the NorthwindService Web Service reference group. Right-click on it and select Update Web Reference. Without this step, Northwind Provider wouldn't know about the `SetProductDetails` method that we just added to the service.

5. Next, open the code editor for `RemoteConnection`. Locate the dummy implementation for `SetProductDetails` and add this code:

```
    Public Overrides Sub SetProductDetails(_
            ByVal products As System.Data.DataSet)

        ' Get the service and call get suppliers...
    Dim service As NorthwindService.ProviderService = GetService()
    service.SetProductDetails(products)

End Sub
```

6. Run the project and check on the Use Service CheckBox. Database requests should now be routed through the Web Service. Make a change to the product that you load, click the Save button and use the Server Explorer to make sure that the changes have "stuck", like we did before.

How It Works

Again, adding functionality to the Web Service is simply an issue of forwarding requests of the web method to the existing method on `DirectConnection`.

```
    Dim service As NorthwindService.ProviderService = GetService()
    service.SetProductDetails(products)
```

.NET handles passing the `DataSet` over the Web Service and so, when we receive it at the other end, we can process it as normal.

Summary

In this chapter, we saw a technique for building a client application that is deployable both inside and outside of the company LAN. With .NET, a lot of the deployment hassles of traditional desktop applications go away, meaning that companies can return to building desktop applications with rich and powerful user interfaces, without having to decrease the functionality for use with Web browsers. web applications do not benefit from the same, rich user interface controls that desktop applications like those built with Windows Forms do.

We kicked off the application by introducing the concept of an access layer. Instead of connecting directly to the database, the application instead connects to this layer. The layer is able to "switch" between connecting directly to SQL Server Desktop Engine and connecting to a Web Service. This means that building the Web Service is simply a matter of creating a few methods that defer over to the existing access layer. Adding new methods to the layer is pretty trivial.

In building the application, we saw how to use the `DataGrid` control to display and edit product information. We also provided separate windows for looking up and changing supplier information. Finally, we solved the problem of saving changes back into the database even though we didn't have a `DataAdapter` object handy.

Exercises

1. What's the advantage of using the techniques that we've described in this chapter?
2. Why did we choose a Web Service as the alternative way of connecting to the database?
3. How did we detect if a database connection was available?
4. Why did we need to go through the complicated updating process that we saw in this chapter?

Answers are available at http://p2p.wrox.com/exercises/.

Case Study – B2B Application Integration Using XML

In this case study, we're going to build a Business-to-Business (B2B) application to process XML documents representing orders made by customers. The application will create the order on the Northwind system and return status information to the customer as XML.

This process was discussed back in the *Web Services* chapter (Chapter 13), and it is certainly possible to create a Web Service that customers can use to place orders with us. However, because Web Services are a relatively new technology, it's quite likely that we'd also need an "old school" method for automated order processing.

Today, this type of order processing often employs Electronic Data Interchange, or EDI. Like XML, this technology aims to facilitate business interactions that follow this pattern:

1. Organization "A" creates a document and passes it to Organization "B"
2. Organization "B" receives the document, processes it, and creates a response document
3. The response document is passed back to Organization "A"

However, EDI has a reputation for being woefully expensive and time-consuming to set up, so the automated order system we're going to concentrate on in this chapter will be XML-based. Here's what we're going to assume:

- Northwind (as the supplier) has defined an XML schema specifying how orders are to be organized. This schema describes elements for the customer's details and the shipping address, as well as the specific details of the order.
- The customer has a system that tracks stock levels in their warehouse. When stock levels for items supplied by Northwind fall below a certain point, those items are automatically ordered by constructing an order document based on Northwind's schema. The order document is then passed by some means to Northwind's computers to place the order.

- Once the document is received, it is processed and the order placed.
- Northwind also defines an XML schema for the response document. After the order has been placed, a response document is constructed and returned to the customer.

What's important here is how the documents are transferred. The Internet provides myriad techniques for communicating documents, including:

- Web Service interactions.
- FTP – Northwind could set up an FTP server that the customer connects to in order to upload orders. We can then scan for new orders and process them appropriately.
- Microsoft Message Queuing Service – this is a Windows feature that allows transfer of messages/documents between computers in a robust and reliable manner.
- E-mail – a variation on message queuing. We can use standard e-mail servers to transfer messages/documents.
- Web – we can use standard web servers for transferring messages over HTTP. (Note, this is a separate issue to Web Services.)
- Proprietary method – we can build our own method for the transfer of data.

We talk about some of these options in more detail later in this chapter. We're going to use the Web Services model at our end of the process, as we can assume that Northwind has .NET (although our customers may not), and this is perhaps the simplest method for our purposes. This isn't surprising really when you consider that Web Services were created to resolve these kinds of integration issues.

In this case study, we're going to look at building solutions to all four parts of this problem. We'll start off by looking at the schema.

Defining the Schema

In Chapter 13, we built a simple application that exported orders held in the `Orders` table from the database. You'll remember that the `DataSet` object exported the data in this format:

```
<?xml version="1.0">

<Orders>
 <Order>
 <OrderID>11077</OrderID>
 <CustomerID>RATTC</CustomerID>
 <EmployeeID>1</EmployeeID>
 <OrderDate>1998-05-06T00:00:00.0000000+01:00</OrderDate>
 <RequiredDate>1998-06-03T00:00:00.0000000+01:00</RequiredDate>
 <ShipVia>2</ShipVia>
 <Freight>8.53</Freight>
 <ShipName>Rattlesnake Canyon Grocery</ShipName>
 <ShipAddress>2817 Milton Dr.</ShipAddress>
```

```
    <ShipCity>Albuquerque</ShipCity>
    <ShipRegion>NM</ShipRegion>
    <ShipPostalCode>87110</ShipPostalCode>
    <ShipCountry>USA</ShipCountry>
    </Order>
    <Detail>
    <OrderID>11076</OrderID>
    <ProductID>6</ProductID>
    <UnitPrice>25</UnitPrice>
    <Quantity>20</Quantity>
    <Discount>0.25</Discount>
    </Detail>
    <Detail>
    <OrderID>11076</OrderID>
    <ProductID>14</ProductID>
    <UnitPrice>23.25</UnitPrice>
    <Quantity>20</Quantity>
    <Discount>0.25</Discount>
    </Detail>
   </Orders>
```

You may recall that I alluded to the fact that the format used in the `DataSet` doesn't really match the structure of the above XML document. To rectify this, it would be better to make the `<Detail>` elements "members" of the `<Order>` element, by placing them inside a `<Details>` node, like this:

```
<?xml version="1.0">

<Orders>
 <Order>
 <OrderID>11077</OrderID>
 <CustomerID>RATTC</CustomerID>
 <EmployeeID>1</EmployeeID>
 <OrderDate>1998-05-06T00:00:00.0000000+01:00</OrderDate>
 <RequiredDate>1998-06-03T00:00:00.0000000+01:00</RequiredDate>
 <ShipVia>2</ShipVia>
 <Freight>8.53</Freight>
 <ShipName>Rattlesnake Canyon Grocery</ShipName>
 <ShipAddress>2817 Milton Dr.</ShipAddress>
 <ShipCity>Albuquerque</ShipCity>
 <ShipRegion>NM</ShipRegion>
 <ShipPostalCode>87110</ShipPostalCode>
 <ShipCountry>USA</ShipCountry>
 <Details>
  <Detail>
  <OrderID>11076</OrderID>
  <ProductID>6</ProductID>
  <UnitPrice>25</UnitPrice>
  <Quantity>20</Quantity>
  <Discount>0.25</Discount>
  </Detail>
  <Detail>
```

```
      <OrderID>11076</OrderID>
      <ProductID>14</ProductID>
      <UnitPrice>23.25</UnitPrice>
      <Quantity>20</Quantity>
      <Discount>0.25</Discount>
      </Detail>
     </Details>
    </Order>
   </Orders>
```

The reason why the DataSet class doesn't do this kind of encapsulation, despite the fact that it could determine this structure based on the various DataRelation objects we could attach to it, is because the serialization code built into the DataSet class is optimized for data transfer, not representation. The code is used for passing the DataSet between server and client in Web Services and a very closely related technology called "Remoting". When we're sitting down to design an XML document, however, we want to design it so that its meaning is self-evident for anyone wishing to use it.

Here's a structure that better suits a B2B "customer talking to supplier" scenario:

```
<?xml version="1.0">

<Order>
 <CustomerID>RATTC</CustomerID>
 <PreferredShippingMethod>2</PreferredShippingMethod>
 <ResponseEmail>customer@pretendcompany.com</ResponseEmail>
 <ShippingAddress>
   <Name>Rattlesnake Canyon Grocery</Name>
   <Address>2817 Milton Dr.</Address>
   <City>Albuquerque</City>
   <Region>NM</Region>
   <PostalCode>87110</PostalCode>
   <Country>USA</Country>
 </ShippingAddress>
 <Details>
   <Detail>
     <ProductID>6</ProductID>
     <Quantity>20</Quantity>
   </Detail>
   <Detail>
     <ProductID>14</ProductID>
     <Quantity>20</Quantity>
   </Detail>
 </Details>
</Order>
```

Here's the rationale behind the design:

- We don't need an order ID or employee ID when placing orders. We generate the order IDs ourselves, and the employee ID we use depends on our policy. We can either give a customer the same employee ID, or we can pick one at random. In this example, we choose the latter option. We'll include those in the return document.

- To make our lives easier, we're not requiring a date to be provided either. This means that, when an order comes in, we can process it immediately rather than having to hold it for the given length of time before processing it. (This is a business decision – there's no technical reason why we can't do this.)
- When we've processed the order, we'll send the response back as an XML document contained within an e-mail message to the address given by the `<ResponseEmail>` element.
- We still ask for a preferred shipping method. We'll let the customer know what possible shipping methods are available and also inform them when the list changes.
- The shipping address has been encapsulated in a separate shipping address element. There isn't a strong reason for doing this – it just makes the document neater.
- The `<Detail>` elements are now contained within a `<Details>` element. Notice as well that we just want a product ID and a quantity. We'll determine the price at our end – we don't want the customer to specify any price that they fancy.

Now that we know what we want our XML document to look like, we can create an application that can produce an appropriate document containing an order.

Placing the Order

In this section we'll build a simple class library that allows us to create a dummy order that matches the XML document structure that we've already defined. This class library will contain two sets of classes: the first set describes the order request and the other describes the order response. Remember that there's no requirement that the names in the XML document need to match the names of the classes themselves. This is because we need to avoid naming conflicts. For example, both the request and response document will contain an `<Order>` element, but they both have very different meanings. The two key classes in our application that will mirror the XML documents are the `OrderRequest` and the `OrderResponse` classes:

- `OrderRequest` – describes the order being requested. Contains the customer's ID, the preferred shipping method, the shipping address, the response e-mail address, and a collection of `RequestDetail` objects.
    - `RequestDetail` – describes a line of the order and contains a product ID and quantity. Corresponds to the `<Detail>` element of the XML request document.
    - `RequestDetailCollection` – contains a collection of `RequestDetail` classes. These correspond to the `<Details>` element of the XML request document.

- `OrderResponse` – describes the response returned by the server. Contains the new order ID, the date the order was processed, an expected delivery date, the total charge for the order, and a collection of `ResponseDetail` objects.
    - `ResponseDetail` – describes an item included in the order, and matches the `<Detail>` element of the XML response document. Includes the product ID, the quantity, the price and any discount applied.

- ResponseDetailCollection – contains a collection of ResponseDetail classes. Corresponds to the <Details> element of the XML response document.

Let's begin building our project now. At this stage, we implement the RequestDetail object only and, when that's working as it should, we shall move on to the ResposeDetail object.

Try It Out – Building the Project

1. Open Visual Studio .NET and create a new Visual Basic | Class Library project. Call it NorthwindOrderGenerator.

2. Using Solution Explorer, delete the automatically created Class1.vb. Then right-click on NorthwindOrderGenerator, still using Solution Explorer, and select Add | Add Class, and call it OrderRequest.

3. Now, double-click on OrderRequest.vb and add these two namespace declarations to the top of the code listing:

```
Imports System.IO
Imports System.Xml

Public Class OrderRequest
```

4. Next, add this enumeration as a public property of the class:

```
Public Class OrderRequest

  ' ShippingMethod enum
  Public Enum ShippingMethod As Integer
    SpeedyExpress = 1
    UnitedPackage = 2
    FederalShipping = 3
  End Enum
```

5. Now, add these members:

```
Public Class OrderRequest

  ' ShippingMethod enum
  Public Enum ShippingMethod As Integer
    SpeedyExpress = 1
    UnitedPackage = 2
    FederalShipping = 3
  End Enum

  ' Members
```

```
  Public CustomerId As String
  Public PreferredShippingMethod As ShippingMethod
  Public ShippingAddress As New Address()
  Public Details As New RequestDetailCollection()
  Public ResponseEmail As String
```

6. Next, create a new class called **Address** using Solution Explorer. Add this code:

```
Imports System.Xml

Public Class Address

  ' Members
  Public Name As String
  Public Address As String
  Public City As String
  Public Region As String
  Public PostalCode As String
  Public Country As String

End Class
```

7. Create a third new class called **RequestDetail**, and add the following to its code file:

```
Imports System.Xml

Public Class RequestDetail

  ' Members
  Public ProductId As Integer
  Public Quantity As Integer

End Class
```

8. We'll create a strongly-typed collection to contain the `RequestDetail` objects. This way, we can inherit `System.Collections.CollectionBase`, and we then just need `Add` and `Remove` methods and an `Item` property. Create a new class called **RequestDetailCollection** and add this code:

```
Imports System.Xml

Public Class RequestDetailCollection
  Inherits CollectionBase

  ' Add - add detail
  Public Sub Add(ByVal detail As RequestDetail)
    list.Add(detail)
  End Sub
```

```
  Public Function Add(ByVal productId As Integer, _
                                 ByVal quantity As Integer) As RequestDetail

    ' Create a new detail
    Dim detail As New RequestDetail()
    detail.ProductId = productId
    detail.Quantity = quantity

    ' Add it
    Add(detail)

    ' Return it
    Return detail

  End Function

  Public Sub Remove(ByVal detail As RequestDetail)
    list.Remove(detail)
  End Sub

  Default Public Property Item(ByVal index As Integer) As RequestDetail
    Get
      Return list.Item(index)
    End Get
    Set(ByVal Value As RequestDetail)
      list.Item(index) = Value
    End Set
  End Property

End Class
```

9. These four classes can now be used to define an order. However, we need to get the objects to serialize themselves to XML, as this is far and away the easiest way of generating an XML document. Previously, the Framework objects we used could already perform their own serialization, so this is the first time we've done this.

   First of all, we need a method that can create a file. Open the code editor for OrderRequest and add this method:

```
  ' Save - save the order to a file
  Public Sub Save(ByVal filename As String)

    ' Do we need to delete the file?
    Dim info As New FileInfo(filename)
    If info.Exists Then info.Delete()

    ' Create the new file
    Dim stream As New FileStream(filename, FileMode.Create)

    ' Save it
    WriteXml(stream)
```

```
    ' Close the file
    stream.Close()

End Sub
```

10. Next, add these two methods:

```
' WriteXml - write XML to a stream
Public Sub WriteXml(ByVal stream As Stream)

    ' Create a writer
    Dim writer As New XmlTextWriter(stream, New System.Text.ASCIIEncoding())
    WriteXml(writer)
    writer.Close()

End Sub
```

```
Public Sub WriteXml(ByVal writer As XmlTextWriter)

    ' Start top-level tag
    writer.WriteStartElement("Order")

    ' Write the general details
    writer.WriteElementString("CustomerID", CustomerId)
    writer.WriteElementString("PreferredShippingMethod", _
                              PreferredShippingMethod)
    writer.WriteElementString("ResponseEmail", ResponseEmail)

    ' Write the address
    ShippingAddress.WriteXml("ShippingAddress", writer)

    ' Write the details
    Details.WriteXml(writer)

    ' Close top-level tag
    writer.WriteEndElement()

End Sub
```

11. Double-click on Address.vb in Solution Explorer to open it in the code editor. Add this method:

```
Public Sub WriteXml(ByVal elementName As String, _
                    ByVal writer As XmlTextWriter)

    ' Write the top-level tag
    writer.WriteStartElement(elementName)

    ' Write the details
    writer.WriteElementString("Name", Name)
```

```
    writer.WriteElementString("Address", Address)
    writer.WriteElementString("City", City)
    writer.WriteElementString("Region", Region)
    writer.WriteElementString("PostalCode", PostalCode)
    writer.WriteElementString("Country", Country)

    ' Close the top-level tag
    writer.WriteEndElement()

  End Sub
```

12. Open RequestDetailCollection.vb and add a `WriteXml` method there too:

```
  Public Sub WriteXml(ByVal writer As XmlTextWriter)

    ' Write the top-level tag
    writer.WriteStartElement("Details")

    ' Go through each detail
    Dim detail As RequestDetail
    For Each detail In InnerList
      detail.WriteXml(writer)
    Next

    ' Close the top-level tag
    writer.WriteEndElement()

  End Sub
```

13. We also need to implement a `WriteXml` method for the RequestDetail class:

```
  Public Sub WriteXml(ByVal writer As XmlTextWriter)

    ' Write the top-level tag
    writer.WriteStartElement("Detail")

    ' Write the details
    writer.WriteElementString("ProductID", ProductId)
    writer.WriteElementString("Quantity", Quantity)

    ' Close the top-level tag
    writer.WriteEndElement()

  End Sub
```

14. Now we have a set of objects that can be used to create an order and can also serialize themselves to XML. What we need now is a separate test application that can be used to create a dummy order document and save it to disk.

Using Solution Explorer, right-click on the NorthwindOrderGenerator solution object at the top of the tree and select Add | New Project.

15. Create a new Visual Basic | Windows Application project and call it Order Generator Test Client. We now need to add a reference to the NorthwindOrderGenerator project so right-click on the new project in Solution Explorer, and select Add Reference.

16. Change to the Projects tab. Ensure NorthwindOrderGenerator is highlighted in the top pane and click Select. It should now appear in the lower pane as shown. Click OK:

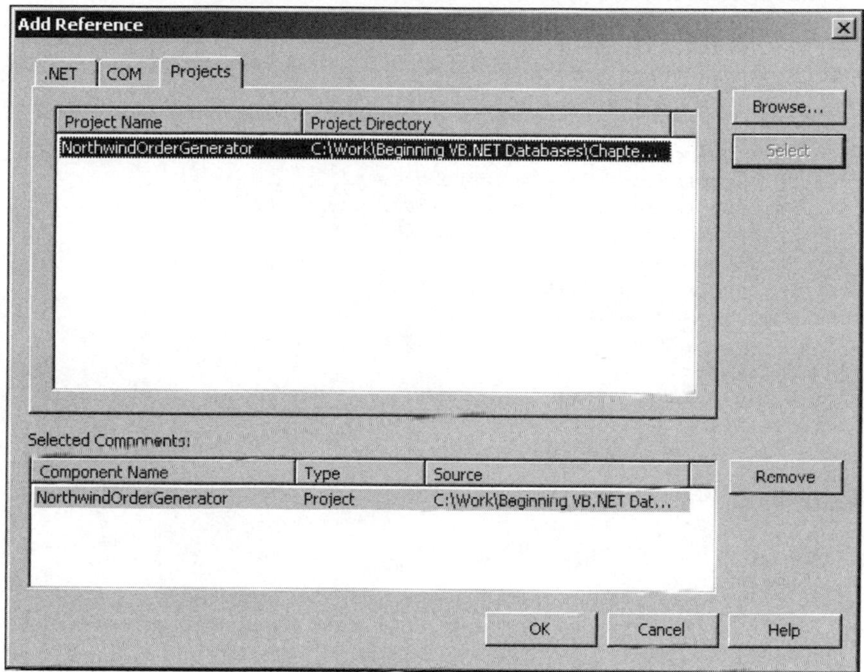

17. When Form1 appears in Design view, add a new `Button` control. Change its Name property to btnToFile and its Text property to Write Test Order to File:

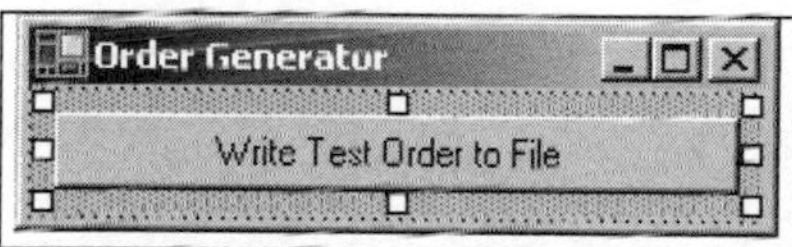

18. Using the Toolbox, add a new SaveFileDialog control to the form. Change its Name property to dlgSaveFile.

19. Double-click somewhere on Form1 to open the code editor. Right at the top, add this namespace reference:

```
Imports NorthwindOrderGenerator

Public Class Form1
  Inherits System.Windows.Forms.Form
```

20. Next, add this method to create a new `NorthwindOrderGenerator.OrderRequest` object populated with a dummy test order:

```
' CreateTestOrder - create a test order
Public Function CreateTestOrder() As OrderRequest

   ' Create a new order
   Dim order As New OrderRequest()
   order.CustomerId = "RATTC"
   order.PreferredShippingMethod = order.ShippingMethod.FederalShipping
   order.ResponseEmail = "wrox@matthewreynolds.com"

   ' Set up a shipping address
   order.ShippingAddress.Name = "Warehouse #2"
   order.ShippingAddress.Address = "1234 Nowhere Street"
   order.ShippingAddress.City = "Issaquah"
   order.ShippingAddress.Region = "WA"
   order.ShippingAddress.PostalCode = "98027"
   order.ShippingAddress.Country = "USA"

   ' Add details
   order.Details.Add(6, 10)
   order.Details.Add(14, 30)

   ' Return it
   Return order

End Function
```

21. Flip over to the Designer for Form1 and double-click on the `Button` control. Add this code to the new event handler:

```
Private Sub btnToFile_Click(ByVal sender As System.Object, _
                            ByVal e As System.EventArgs) Handles btnToFile.Click

   ' Show the dialog
   dlgSaveFile.Filter = "XML Files (*.xml)|*.xml|All Files (*.*)|*.*||"
   If dlgSaveFile.ShowDialog() = DialogResult.OK Then

      ' Create the order
      Dim testOrder As OrderRequest = CreateTestOrder()

      ' Save it
      testOrder.Save(dlgSaveFile.FileName)

      ' Inform the user
      MsgBox("The new order has been created at '" & _
              dlgSaveFile.FileName & "'.")

   End If

End Sub
```

22. Using Solution Explorer, right-click the Order Generator Test Client project and select Set as StartUp Project. Run the project.

23. When the form appears, click the button. A dialog prompts for a location to save the order document. I recommend creating a new folder called `C:\Automated Order Processor` on your local disk for this purpose.

Find the file using Windows Explorer and open it:

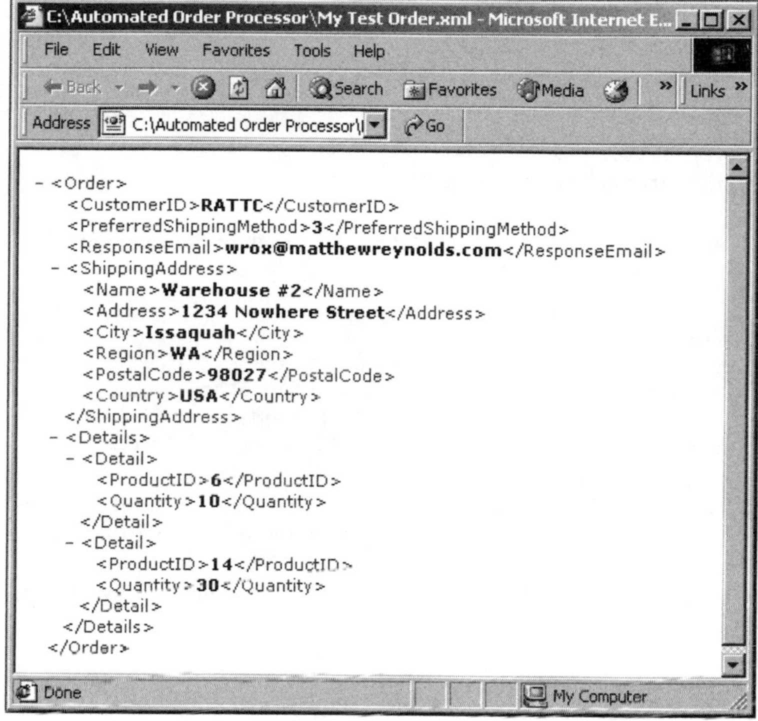

How It Works

You can see from the output in Internet Explorer that we've managed to create a file that matches the format defined earlier in the chapter.

The magic here is all due to the `XmlTextWriter` class, which lets us create our own XML very easily. Each of the classes that make up the order request can self-serialize to XML using their `WriteXml` method. The first one of these is the `OrderRequest` class, and its `WriteXml` method takes a `Stream` object. In our example, this `Stream` object is created by the `Save` method and is actually a `FileStream` object pointing to a file on disk.

Once we have a `Stream` object, we can use it to create an `XmlTextWriter` object, like this:

```
Public Sub WriteXml(ByVal stream As Stream)

  ' Create a writer
  Dim writer As New XmlTextWriter(stream, New System.Text.ASCIIEncoding())
  WriteXml(writer)
  writer.Close()

End Sub
```

Once we have the `XmlTextWriter`, we pass it to an overloaded version of `WriteXml`, which begins by writing the top-level `Order` start tag:

```
Public Sub WriteXml(ByVal writer As XmlTextWriter)

  ' Start top-level tag
  writer.WriteStartElement("Order")
```

We then use `WriteElementString` to add elements for each of the members that we want to include in the serialization:

```
  ' Write the general details
  writer.WriteElementString("CustomerID", CustomerId)
  writer.WriteElementString("PreferredShippingMethod", _
                            PreferredShippingMethod)
  writer.WriteElementString("ResponseEmail", ResponseEmail)
```

Although this method is called `WriteElementString`, there are no similar methods for other data types. As far as the `XmlTextWriter` is concerned, anything that gets written out is a string, because the underlying document is comprised of text. As Visual Basic .NET will implicitly convert data types by default, when we pass in an integer such as `CustomerId`, that value is converted to a string through an implicit call to `CustomerId.ToString`.

Once we've written the simple members, we call the `WriteXml` method on the `Address` and `RequestDetailCollection` classes:

```
  ' Write the address
  ShippingAddress.WriteXml("ShippingAddress", writer)

  ' Write the details
  Details.WriteXml(writer)
```

Finally, we close the top-level element. Notice that we don't have to specify the name of the element. The rules of well-formed XML dictate that tags must be closed in the reverse order to which they were opened (because elements may not overlap), so `XmlTextWriter` can deduce that the final call to `WriteEndElement` corresponds to the first call to `WriteStartElement`. Thus, if we had called `WriteStartElement` three times, we'd have to call `WriteEndElement` exactly three times also.

```
    ' Close top-level tag
    writer.WriteEndElement()

  End Sub
```

The WriteXml method of the Address object is similar, although you'll notice here that we pass in the name of the element that will contain the address data. That's because Address makes a good general-purpose object for requests and responses, to write both the shipping address and the invoice address, say:

```
  Public Sub WriteXml(ByVal elementName As String, _
                      ByVal writer As XmlTextWriter)

    ' Write the top-level tag
    writer.WriteStartElement(elementName)

    ' Write the details
    writer.WriteElementString("Name", Name)
    writer.WriteElementString("Address", Address)
    writer.WriteElementString("City", City)
    writer.WriteElementString("Region", Region)
    writer.WriteElementString("PostalCode", PostalCode)
    writer.WriteElementString("Country", Country)

    ' Close the top-level tag
    writer.WriteEndElement()

  End Sub
```

Again, similar code is used in RequestDetailCollection. For each RequestDetail object, note the call to the WriteXml method of RequestDetail. Also, note the use of InnerList, a protected property provided by CollectionBase to allow access to the underlying list. This property lets us iterate through all items in a collection from a method or property in a derived class.

```
  Public Sub WriteXml(ByVal writer As XmlTextWriter)

    ' Write the top-level tag
    writer.WriteStartElement("Details")

    ' Go through each detail
    Dim detail As RequestDetail
    For Each detail In InnerList
      detail.WriteXml(writer)
    Next

    ' Close the top-level tag
    writer.WriteEndElement()

  End Sub
```

Finally, the WriteXml method of the Detail class offers no surprises:

```
Public Sub WriteXml(ByVal writer As XmlTextWriter)

  ' Write the top-level tag
  writer.WriteStartElement("Detail")

  ' Write the details
  writer.WriteElementString("ProductID", ProductId)
  writer.WriteElementString("Quantity", Quantity)

  ' Close the top-level tag
  writer.WriteEndElement()

End Sub
```

In this section we've seen how to control serialization of objects and related objects to build an XML document that exactly suits our requirements. Later, we'll look at how to deserialize the objects from the XML document once it has been received.

Transferring the Document

So, once we've put together the XML document describing the order, how can we pass it to the supplier's (Northwind's) server for processing? There are many different techniques and we'll see some of them in this chapter.

Web Service

If we were asked to recommend a ".NET way" of transferring the document, we'd probably say a Web Service. We could configure an ASP.NET Web Service to run on a server and listen for incoming documents. Once a document was received, it could then be processed.

We demonstrate this technique fully in this chapter.

FTP

Of course, we can't guarantee that our customers will be using .NET, and we also can't guarantee that they're going to be able to use Web Services of any kind. One avenue open to us has been around almost as long as the Internet itself. File Transfer Protocol, or FTP, is a simple protocol that enables a two-way transfer of documents. (Generally, the Web is geared towards just downloading documents requested by a browser.)

.NET's support for FTP can, with a positive spin, be described as poor. Some even describe it as non-existent. Either way, it's hard to build .NET applications that use FTP, although in this chapter we'll have a go at receiving documents through FTP.

E-mail

Another message transfer mechanism with broad support is e-mail. On most platforms, it's very easy to send e-mail from an application once it's been composed. All we'd have to do is make our server monitor a mailbox for incoming messages and process them.

In this chapter's sample application, we're not going to listen for incoming mails but we are going to send a response out by e-mail once an order has been processed.

Message Queuing

Microsoft Message Queuing Service is designed for transferring messages between computers over potentially unreliable networks, such as the Internet. It's effectively a private e-mail server whereby a queue is set up on a destination computer and the source computer sends messages to that queue. The queue is monitored for incoming documents and each incoming document can then be processed.

We won't be looking at the Message Queuing Service here because it requires the server to run on a network with a Primary Domain Controller. If you're particularly interested in this facility, try Wrox's *Professional MTS & MSMQ Programming with VB and ASP* (ISBN 1861001460).

Proprietary

Another way of transferring documents would be to put together your own proprietary protocol and write your own server. With this technique you have ultimate control, but you're asking a lot of the people who want to use your service. Anyone wanting to transfer documents to you would need to either download a client you wrote to communicate with your service or write their own. It's likely that, when faced with such an option, your clients will harrumph loudly, "Can't I just use a Web Service or FTP or something!?"

Receiving and Processing the Order

Now that we can create an XML document containing the order (which will come from a Northwind customer), we need to turn our attention to the other end of the problem – how do we (at Northwind) receive the order, process it, and send a response.

What we want to do is offer a number of possibilities for how the file is transferred. Although a Web Service seems the obvious choice for transmitting the order details, as a relatively new technology, it's not smart to insist that our business partners and customers use it. They may be using a platform with relatively poor Web Service support, or simply do not have the resources to deploy a Web Service-based solution.

In the past, document transfers have commonly been done over FTP. A customer logs onto a special FTP site and uploads their file, which can be detected by a service at the supplier's end and added to the queue for processing. The beauty is that FTP is an old, established technology with native support in every computing platform. Well, every computing platform except .NET. For some reason, Microsoft has chosen not to include FTP support in the initial release of the Framework. This means that, in this case study, we cannot demonstrate how to transfer the file, but we can show what happens when it is received.

> **There are some FTP components available for old-school Windows DNA development. One free example is Server Object's ASPInet component available from http://www.serverobjects.com/.**

All FTP services work in the same way – you create a folder somewhere on your network and configure an FTP site that uses that folder as its "root". When the user connects to the FTP site, files are uploaded into that folder. So, if we create a folder called C:\Automated Order Processor\Inbound and configure an FTP site with this directory as its root, all uploaded files will then appear in C:\Automated Order Processor\Inbound.

In this section, we're going to create a service that monitors this folder for any new files – and remember that each new file contains exactly one order request document. We can simulate the action of the user uploading a file with an FTP client to copy files to the server, or simpler yet by manually copying the file with Windows Explorer. Unfortunately, we will not be able to get our test client that we've just built to automatically upload to FTP because of the lack of FTP support in .NET.

Creating the Service

Ideally, what we want to do is build a Windows Service on the computer that will monitor the `Inbound` directory. By creating a service we're actually creating a program that will run automatically whenever the computer is started, but more importantly will run when the user is not logged on.

For those of you unfamiliar with how a server works, most of the time they remain at the login screen. Nearly all of the tasks undertaken by the server – such as running a database, a web site, or making files accessible over the network – do not require user interaction and the safest way to leave a server is at the Windows login screen. In that way no one can change the server setup without a valid user name and password. Software that runs all the time, even while the login screen is displayed, is called a Windows Service.

Building a Windows Service in .NET is far easier than it was before. For ease of debugging and maintenance, however, we're going to build the project in three parts. We need:

- A class library that contains the code that powers the service. In our case, this will be code that monitors the `Inbound` folder, reads XML order request documents, updates the database, and prepares a response.
- A console application that can load the class library and display the results. We'll need this for debugging.
- A Windows Service that will load the class library but won't display the results. We would need this if we were to put the service into a production environment.

We'll use the console application to test and debug the service as we develop. As the "guts" of the service will be placed in the class library, when it's time to roll the system out in a production setting, we can get the Windows Service to load the same class library and everything should then work just as it did in the development lab.

First, we'll create the class library and the console application for debugging the project.

Try It Out – Building the "Automated Order Processor"

1. Open Visual Studio .NET. Create a new Windows Application | Class Library project, and call it Automated Order Processor.

2. Using Solution Explorer, delete Class1.vb, and create a new class called Processor.

   At the top of the Processor.vb code file, add these namespace declarations:

```
Imports System.IO
Imports System.Xml
Imports System.Xml.Schema
Imports System.Xml.Serialization

Public Class Processor
```

3. Add these members:

```
Public Class Processor

  ' Members
  Public Const InboundFolder As String = "C:\Automated Order Processor\Inbound"
  Public Shared DbString As String = "Initial Catalog=NorthwindSQL; _
                                      Data Source=NET-MONKEY\NetSDK;User ID=sa"
  Private _watcher As FileSystemWatcher
```

4. Add the start-up method:

```
  ' Start - start the watcher
  Public Sub Startup()

    ' Create a watcher
    _watcher = New FileSystemWatcher(InboundFolder)

    ' Create an event handler
    AddHandler _watcher.Created, AddressOf Me.ProcessOrder

    ' Start watching
    _watcher.Filter = "*.xml"
    _watcher.EnableRaisingEvents = True

    ' Tell the user
    Log("Monitoring '" & InboundFolder & "'")

  End Sub
```

5. Now, add the shut-down method:

```
' Stop - This method halts the watcher
Public Sub Shutdown()

  ' Stop the watcher
  If Not _watcher Is Nothing Then
    _watcher.EnableRaisingEvents = False
    _watcher = Nothing
    Log("Watcher closed")
  End If

End Sub
```

6. Then, add the method that writes information to the log file:

```
' Write log information
Public Sub Log(ByVal buf As String)
  Console.WriteLine(Date.Now.ToLongTimeString & ": " & buf)
End Sub
```

7. When we process the order, we have to prepare a response that can be sent back to the user. The easiest way is to create an OrderResponse class and associated classes just like we did for OrderRequest. It makes sense to add these classes to the existing NorthwindOrderGenerator library.

   Using Solution Explorer, right-click on the Automated Order Processor solution and select Add | Existing Project. Find and open `NorthwindOrderGenerator.vbproj`:

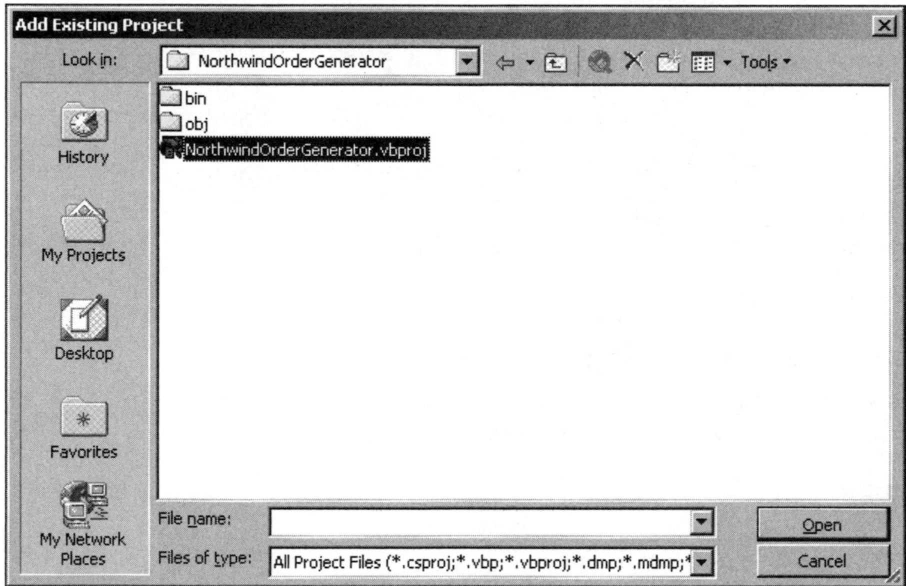

8. The Solution Explorer should now show the following:

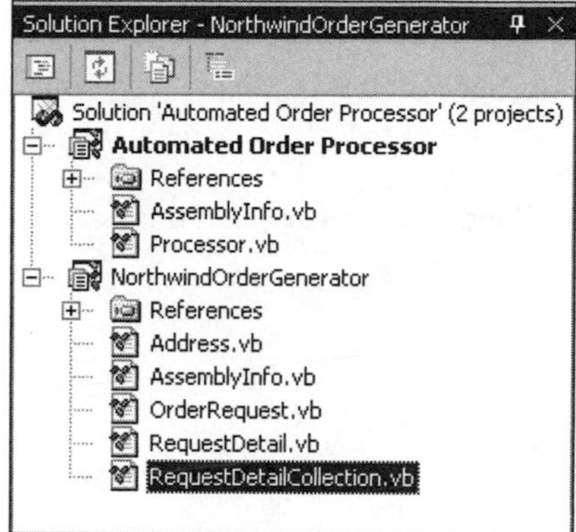

9. We must also tie the two projects together by adding a reference to NorthwindOrderGenerator from the Automated Order Processor object, otherwise the Automated Order Processor code will not be able to access the classes defined there. Right-click on the Automated Order Processor project and select Add Reference.

   Change to the Projects tab. Make sure NorthwindOrderGenerator is selected, click Select, and then OK.

10. Open Processor.vb in the code editor again. Add this namespace declaration:

```
Imports System.IO
Imports System.Xml
Imports System.Xml.Schema
Imports System.Xml.Serialization
Imports NorthwindOrderGenerator

Public Class Processor
```

11. Also add this method inside the `Processor` class:

```
  ' ProcessOrder - process an order
  Public Sub ProcessOrder(ByVal sender As Object, _
                          ByVal e As FileSystemEventArgs)

    ' Tell the user
    Log("Processing '" & e.FullPath & "'...")

    ' We'll do the processing here

    ' Tell the user
    Log("Finished '" & e.FullPath & "'...")

  End Sub
```

12. To run the solution, we need another project because class libraries cannot be started directly, and both projects in the solution are class libraries. Using Solution Explorer, right-click on the Automated Order Processor solution and select Add | Add New Project.

    Add a new Visual Basic | Console Application project. Call it Automated Order Processor Test Host.

13. When the code editor for Module1 appears, add this code:

```
Module Module1

  Sub Main()

    ' Start the processor
    Dim processor As New Automated_Order_Processor.Processor()
    processor.Startup()

    ' Wait
    Console.WriteLine()
    Console.WriteLine("Press Return to close the host")
    Console.ReadLine()

    ' Stop the processor
    processor.Shutdown()

  End Sub

End Module
```

14. One more thing before we can run the project – right-click on the new Automated Order Processor Test Host project in Solution Explorer and select Set as StartUp Project.

15. Now run the project. You should see this:

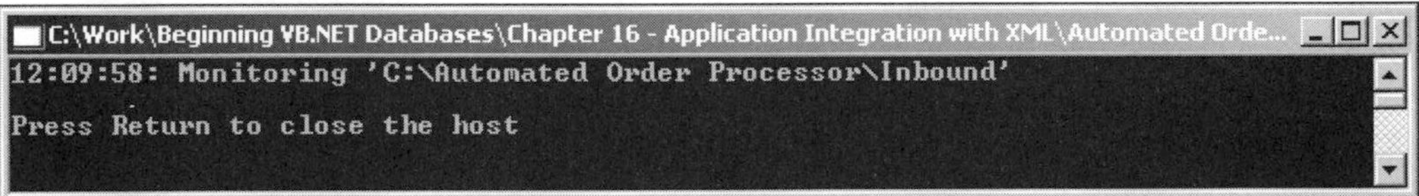

16. Now, using Windows Explorer, copy the XML file containing the test order that you saved previously in the `C:\Automated Order Processor\Inbound` folder. You should see this, indicating that the processor received an order:

```
C:\Work\Beginning VB.NET Databases\Chapter 16 - Application Integration with XML\Automated Orde...
12:09:58: Monitoring 'C:\Automated Order Processor\Inbound'

Press Return to close the host
12:11:54: Processing 'C:\Automated Order Processor\Inbound\my test order.xml'...

12:11:54: Finished 'C:\Automated Order Processor\Inbound\my test order.xml'...
```

How It Works

We've created a central library of functionality that will eventually contain everything related to the automatic processing of orders. For development purposes, we've created a console application project that creates an instance of the Processor class defined in this library, and told it to monitor the C:\Automated Order Processor\Inbound folder. Later in this chapter, we'll reuse this library in a Windows Service application.

For now, what's important here is the use of the System.IO.FileSystemWatcher class. This class can monitor a given folder for new files, changes to existing files, files being renamed, and files being deleted. In this case, it can notify us when a new order has been received.

The StartUp method is responsible for starting up the FileSystemWatcher. Here, we create a new instance of the class and provide the path to the Inbound folder, using the constant InboundFolder member defined at the beginning of the Processor class:

```
' Start - start the watcher
Public Sub Startup()

  ' Create a watcher
  _watcher = New FileSystemWatcher(InboundFolder)
```

We're only interested in listening for new files, so we add a handler to the object's Created event using the AddHandler keyword:

```
  ' Create an event handler
  AddHandler _watcher.Created, AddressOf Me.ProcessOrder
```

Also, as we're only interested in new XML files, we provide a filter for FileSystemWatcher so it only fires an event when the file has an extension of .xml:

```
  ' Start watching
  _watcher.Filter = "*.xml"
```

We then tell it to start raising events, and send a message to the log file:

```
  _watcher.EnableRaisingEvents = True

  ' Tell the user
  Log ("Monitoring '" & InboundFolder & "'")

End Sub
```

When using our Console Application, the Log method will direct its output to the console, giving us a way of seeing what's going on. We can leave these calls in when we eventually run this as a Windows Service, as the messages will not be shown as there will be no "console".

The FileSystemWatcher object stops listening when the EnabledRaisingEvents property is set to False:

```
' Stop - stop the watcher
Public Sub Shutdown()

  ' Stop the watcher
  If Not _watcher Is Nothing Then
    _watcher.EnableRaisingEvents = False
    _watcher = Nothing
    Log("Watcher closed")
  End If

End Sub
```

Whenever a new file is added (as was the case when we copied the file over), the `ProcessOrder` method will now be called as a result of the `Created` event being fired. The `FileSystemEventArgs` object passed through `e` contains the full path of the file that was added.

```
' ProcessOrder - process an order
Public Sub ProcessOrder(ByVal sender As Object, _
                        ByVal e As FileSystemEventArgs)

  ' Tell the user
  Log("Processing '" & e.FullPath & "'...")

  ' We'll do the processing here

  ' Tell the user
  Log("Finished '" & e.FullPath & "'...")

End Sub
```

One thing to note – if you try and copy the file into the `Inbound` directory again, you won't see the file get processed again. That's because we've configured `FileSystemWatcher` only to raise events when the file has been *created*, not changed. You'll need to delete the copy of the XML document and then copy the file if you want to repeat what we've just seen.

Responding To Order Requests

Now that we can detect when a new file has been received, we should look at processing the order and sending the response by e-mail. Unlike the Web Service model, e-mail gives us maximum flexibility – we don't have to process an order as soon as we receive it and if we want, we can collect all orders received in a day and process them as a single batch.

Imagine we receive an order for 100 widgets, but we only have 60. We ship 60, and create and e-mail an XML response document that informs the customer that 60 are on their way. We place the remaining 40 on back order and in a few days time when we receive stock, we create and e-mail another response document telling the customer that the remaining 40 are on the way.

This process is relatively complicated. We need to create another set of classes that describe an order response. As this response will contain information additional to the request document, we need another set of objects. To make our lives easier though, we'll use the `XmlSerializer` to turn these objects into an XML document, unlike for the request document where we did this "by hand".

The complicated part comes when we have to deserialize the request document and enter the information into the database. We'll come to this in the second part of this discussion.

Try It Out – Sending a Response

1. Using Solution Explorer, add a new class called OrderResponse to the NorthwindOrderGenerator project. Place this code inside it:

```
Imports System.Xml.Serialization

Public Class OrderResponse

  ' members
  Public Problem As ResponseProblem
  Public OrderId As Integer
  Public ProcessedDate As Date
  Public ExpectedDeliveryDate As Date
  Public Details As New ResponseDetailCollection()
  Public SubTotal As Single
  Public FreightCharge As Single
  Public Total As Single

End Class
```

2. When a problem occurs on the server (and in our case we're mainly talking about exceptions here), we'll need to encapsulate the problem in the response to the customer. Add a new class called ResponseProblem to the NorthwindOrderGenerator project containing the following code:

```
Public Class ResponseProblem

  ' Codes
  Public Enum ProblemCode As Integer
    Unknown = -1
    Exception = 0
  End Enum

  ' Members
  Public Code As ProblemCode = ProblemCode.Unknown
  Public Type As String
  Public Description As String

End Class
```

3. Next, add a new class called ResponseDetail to the NorthwindOrderGenerator project, and insert this code:

```
Public Class ResponseDetail

  ' Members
```

```
    Public ProductId As Integer
    Public Quantity As Integer
    Public UnitPrice As Single
    Public Discount As Single
    Public Total As Single

  End Class
```

4. To hold lists of ResponseDetail objects, we need our own collection. Add a new class called ResponseDetailCollection to the NorthwindOrderGenerator project with this code:

```
Public Class ResponseDetailCollection
  Inherits CollectionBase

  ' Add - add detail
  Public Sub Add(ByVal detail As ResponseDetail)
    list.Add(detail)
  End Sub

  ' Remove - remove detail
  Public Sub Remove(ByVal detail As ResponseDetail)
    list.Remove(detail)
  End Sub

  ' Item
  Default Public Property Item(ByVal index As Integer) As ResponseDetail
    Get
      Return list.Item(index)
    End Get
    Set(ByVal Value As ResponseDetail)
      list.Item(index) = Value
    End Set
  End Property

End Class
```

5. Open the code editor for Processor.vb. (Remember this is in the Automated Order Processor project.) Add these namespace declarations to the top of the code listing:

```
Imports System.IO
Imports System.Xml
Imports System.Xml.Schema
Imports System.Xml.Serialization
Imports System.Data.SqlClient
Imports System.Web
Imports System.Web.Mail
```

6. Add a new method:

```
Public Function ProcessOrder(ByVal filename As String) As OrderResponse

   ' Create an XML reader
   Dim reader As New XmlTextReader(filename)
   Dim response As OrderResponse = ProcessOrder(reader)
   reader.Close()

   ' Return
   Return response

End Function
```

7. Now add this method, but replace the e-mail address in the `SendResponse` method call with your own:

```
Public Function ProcessOrder(ByVal reader As XmlTextReader) As OrderResponse

   ' Create a new response
   Dim response As New OrderResponse()

   ' Add some dummy information for testing
   response.OrderId = 999
   response.ProcessedDate = Date.Now
   response.ExpectedDeliveryDate = Date.Now.AddDays(4)

   ' Add some dummy details
   Dim detail As New ResponseDetail()
   detail.ProductId = 4
   detail.Quantity = 1000
   detail.UnitPrice = 3.95
   detail.Total = detail.Quantity * detail.UnitPrice
   response.Details.Add(detail)

   ' Update the totals
   response.SubTotal = detail.Total
   response.FreightCharge = 10.5
   response.Total = response.SubTotal + response.FreightCharge

   ' Send e-mail
   SendResponse(response, "mytest@pretendcompany.com")

   ' Return the results
   Return response

End Function
```

8. Next, add this method:

```
' SendResponse - send the document by e-mail
Public Sub SendResponse(ByVal response As OrderResponse, _
```

```
                                ByVal emailAddress As String)

    ' Serialize the response object to a memory stream
    Dim stream As New MemoryStream()
    Dim serializer As New XmlSerializer(response.GetType)
    serializer.Serialize(stream, response)

    ' Convert the stream to a string
    stream.Seek(0, SeekOrigin.Begin)
    Dim reader As New StreamReader(stream)
    Dim responseXml As String = reader.ReadToEnd

    ' Close the stream and the reader
    reader.Close()
    stream.Close()

    ' Send the e-mail
    Try
      SmtpMail.Send("server@pretendcompany.com", emailAddress, _
                    "Status of Order #" & response.OrderId, responseXml)
      Log("Sent to '" & emailAddress & "'")
    Catch ex As Exception
      reportexception(ex)
    End Try

  End Sub
```

The `Send` method of `System.Web.Mail.SmtpMail` provides a quick way of sending e-mail. The parameters you need are the "from address", the "to address", the "subject", and the "message body" respectively.

9. Also, add this method:

```
  ' ReportException - log an exception
  Public Sub ReportException(ByVal ex As Exception)

    ' Get the innermost one
    Do While Not ex.InnerException Is Nothing
      ex = ex.InnerException
    Loop

    ' Report it
    Log("An exception occured: " & ex.Message)
    Console.WriteLine(ex.Source)
    Console.WriteLine(ex.StackTrace)

  End Sub
```

10. Go back to the original `ProcessOrder` method and add the highlighted code:

```
' ProcessOrder - process an order
Public Sub ProcessOrder(ByVal sender As Object, _
                        ByVal e As FileSystemEventArgs)

  ' tell the user
  Log("Processing '" & e.FullPath & "'...")

  ' we'll do the processing here
  Dim response As OrderResponse
  response = ProcessOrder(e.FullPath)

  ' tell the user
  Log("Finished '" & e.FullPath & "'...")

End Sub
```

11. Run the Automated Order Test Host project.

Using Windows Explorer, find the `Inbound` folder. Delete the copy of the XML document that you made previously, and copy the file again. You'll see this:

12. In a few minutes, you should receive the e-mail response. If not, there's probably something awry with your SMTP configuration. (This usually happens if your computer is behind a firewall, or you have incorrectly specified your SMTP server.)

13. If the e-mail does not appear, you can still see the message. Use Windows Explorer to open the c:\Inetpub\MailRoot\Queue folder, where unsent messages are kept:

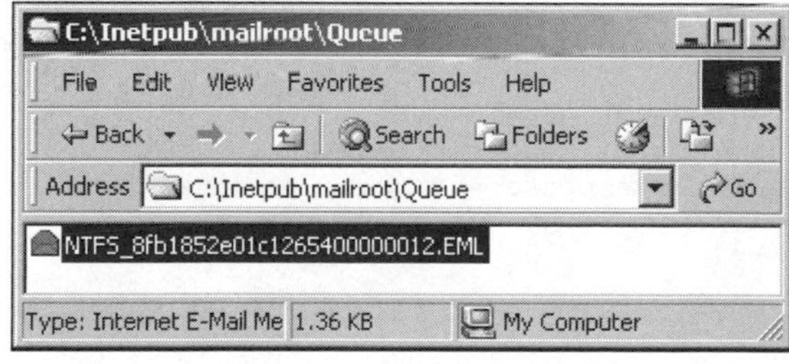

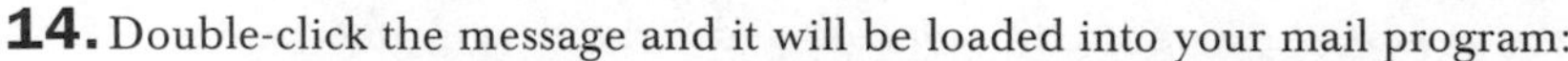

14. Double-click the message and it will be loaded into your mail program:

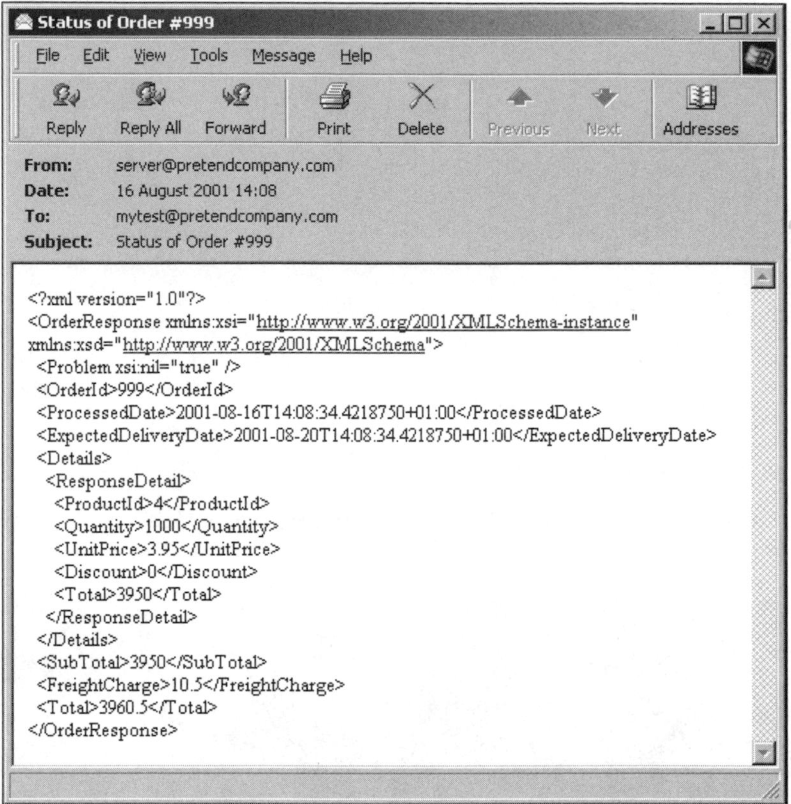

How It Works

In the first part of this exercise, we built a set of "response" objects similar to the ones that contain the order "requests".

When we detect that a new file has been added to the `Inbound` folder, our `ProcessOrder` method will be called by the `FileSystemWatcher` object's `Create` event. We create a new `XmlTextReader` object and pass that to another version of `ProcessOrder`:

```
Public Function ProcessOrder(ByVal filename As String) As OrderResponse

  ' Create an XML reader
  Dim reader As New XmlTextReader(filename)
  Dim response As OrderResponse = ProcessOrder(reader)
  reader.Close()

  ' Return
  Return response

End Function
```

This second version of `ProcessOrder` will eventually contain code to add the order to the database. For now, we create a dummy response with a fixed order ID and details:

```
Public Function ProcessOrder(ByVal reader As XmlTextReader) As OrderResponse

  ' Create a new response
  Dim response As New OrderResponse()

  ' Add some dummy information for testing
  response.OrderId = 999
  response.ProcessedDate = Date.Now
  response.ExpectedDeliveryDate = Date.Now.AddDays(4)

  ' Add some dummy details
  Dim detail As New ResponseDetail()
  detail.ProductId = 4
  detail.Quantity = 1000
  detail.UnitPrice = 3.95
  detail.Total = detail.Quantity * detail.UnitPrice
  response.Details.Add(detail)

  ' Update the totals
  response.SubTotal = detail.Total
  response.FreightCharge = 10.5
  response.Total = response.SubTotal + response.FreightCharge
```

After we've created the new `OrderResponse` object, we pass it over to the `SendResponse` method together with an e-mail address:

```
  ' Send e-mail
  SendResponse(response, "mytest@pretendcompany.com")

  ' Return the results
  Return response

End Function
```

We said before that we were going to use `System.Xml.Serialization.XmlSerializer` to turn the `OrderResponse` object into an XML document rather than doing the serialization ourselves. In most cases, `XmlSerializer` is used to save an object to a file but, in our case, we actually want to save it to a string. We have to create a `System.IO.MemoryStream` object to do this. This kind of stream works like standard `FileStream` objects, but rather than storing in a file on disk, `MemoryStream` uses an area of memory:

```
' SendResponse - send the document as e-mail
Public Sub SendResponse(ByVal response As OrderResponse, _
                        ByVal emailAddress As String)

  ' Serialize the response object to a memory stream
  Dim stream As New MemoryStream()
  Dim serializer As New XmlSerializer(response.GetType)
  serializer.Serialize(stream, response)
```

Once XmlSerializer has finished, we need to read the data back from the stream and into a string. We rewind the stream to the beginning, create a System.IO.StreamReader, and call ReadToEnd to extract the entire contents of the stream and return it as a string:

```
' Convert the stream to a string
stream.Seek(0, SeekOrigin.Begin)
Dim reader As New StreamReader(stream)
Dim responseXml As String = reader.ReadToEnd
```

Windows 2000 and .NET can send Internet e-mail through the SMTP Service using the System.Web.Mail.SmtpMail class. There isn't much to sending mail – we just need to specify a "from" address, a "to" address, a subject, and the message body through the shared Send method:

```
  ' Send the e-mail
  Try
    SmtpMail.Send("server@pretendcompany.com", emailAddress, _
                  "Status of Order #" & response.OrderId, responseXml)
    Log("Sent to '" & emailAddress & "'")
  Catch ex As Exception
    reportexception(ex)
  End Try

End Sub
```

Processing the Order

Now that we can create a response document and send it via e-mail, we can turn our attention to de-serializing the original request and saving the order in the database.

Try It Out – Processing the Order

1. If the project is still running, close it.

2. Open OrderRequest.vb, defined in the NorthwindOrderGenerator project, in the code editor and add the ReadXml method:

```
' ReadXml - load the order document
Public Sub ReadXml(ByVal reader As XmlTextReader)

  ' Read through the elements
  Do While True

    If reader.Read() = False Then
      Exit Do
    End If

    ' What node type do we have?
    Select Case reader.NodeType
```

```
        Case XmlNodeType.Element
          Select Case reader.Name

            Case "CustomerID"
              reader.Read()
              Me.CustomerId = reader.Value

            Case "PreferredShippingMethod"
              reader.Read()
              Me.PreferredShippingMethod = reader.Value

            Case "ResponseEmail"
              reader.Read()
              Me.ResponseEmail = reader.Value

            Case "ShippingAddress"
              Me.ShippingAddress.ReadXml(reader.Name, reader)

            Case "Details"
              Me.Details.ReadXml(reader)

          End Select

      End Select

    Loop

  End Sub
```

3. Now add a `ReadXml` method to the **Address.vb** code:

```
  ' ReadXml - read from an XML stream
  Public Sub ReadXml(ByVal elementName As String, _
                     ByVal reader As XmlTextReader)

    ' Loop
    Do While True

      ' Read
      If reader.Read() = False Then
        Exit Do
      End If

      ' What node type do we have?
      Select Case reader.NodeType

        Case XmlNodeType.Element

          ' What we do have?
          Select Case reader.Name
```

```
          Case "Name"
            reader.Read()
            Me.Name = reader.Value

          Case "Address"
            reader.Read()
            Me.Address = reader.Value

          Case "City"
            reader.Read()
            Me.City = reader.Value

          Case "Region"
            reader.Read()
            Me.Region = reader.Value

          Case "PostalCode"
            reader.Read()
            Me.PostalCode = reader.Value

          Case "Country"
            reader.Read()
            Me.Country = reader.Value

        End Select

      Case XmlNodeType.EndElement

        ' Have we reached the end of the element?
        If reader.Name = elementName Then
          Return
        End If

    End Select

  Loop

End Sub
```

4. Then add one to RequestDetailCollection.vb:

```
' ReadXml - read from an XML stream
Public Sub ReadXml(ByVal reader As XmlTextReader)

  ' Loop
  Do While True

    ' Read
    If reader.Read() = False Then
      Exit Do
```

```
      End If

      ' What node type do we have?
      Select Case reader.NodeType

        Case XmlNodeType.Element

          ' Do we have a detail element?
          If reader.Name = "Detail" Then

            ' Create one
            Dim detail As New RequestDetail()
            detail.ReadXml(reader)

            ' Add it
            Add(detail)

          End If

        Case XmlNodeType.EndElement

          ' Have we reached the end of the element?
          If reader.Name = "Details" Then
            Return
          End If

      End Select

    Loop

  End Sub
```

5. Finally, RequestDetail.vb needs a `ReadXml` method also:

```
  ' ReadXml - read from an XML stream
  Public Sub ReadXml(ByVal reader As XmlTextReader)

    ' Loop
    Do While True

      ' Read
      If reader.Read() = False Then
        Exit Do
      End If

      ' What node type do we have?
      Select Case reader.NodeType

        Case XmlNodeType.Element

          ' What do we have?
```

```
          Select Case reader.Name

            Case "ProductID"
              reader.Read()
              Me.ProductId = reader.Value

            Case "Quantity"
              reader.Read()
              Me.Quantity = reader.Value

          End Select

        Case XmlNodeType.EndElement

          ' Have we reached the end of the element?
          If reader.Name = "Detail" Then
            Return
          End If

      End Select

    Loop

  End Sub
```

6. Make these changes to the third overloaded `ProcessOrder` method in the Processor.vb file of the Automated Order Processor project. This code replaces the dummy code we used earlier:

```
  Public Function ProcessOrder(ByVal reader As XmlTextReader) As OrderResponse

    ' Create a new response
    Dim response As New OrderResponse()

    ' Load the order
    Try

      Dim request As New OrderRequest()
      request.ReadXml(reader)

      ' Connect to the database
      Dim connection As New SqlConnection(DbString)
      connection.Open()

      ' Set the date
      response.ProcessedDate = Date.Now
      response.ExpectedDeliveryDate = Date.Now.AddDays(3)

      ' Assume we have a fixed freight charge
      response.FreightCharge = 10.5

      ' Right, create a new order
```

```
        response.OrderId = CreateOrder(connection, request, _
                                       response.FreightCharge)

        ' Go through each detail
        Dim requestDetail As RequestDetail
        For Each requestDetail In request.Details

          ' Create a response detail
          Dim responseDetail As New ResponseDetail()
          response.Details.Add(responseDetail)

          ' Get the basic info
          responseDetail.ProductId = requestDetail.ProductId
          responseDetail.Quantity = requestDetail.Quantity

          ' Get the price
          Dim unitPrice As Single = _
                        GetProductPrice(connection, requestDetail.ProductId)
          responseDetail.Discount = 0.02
          responseDetail.UnitPrice = unitPrice * _
                                   (1 - responseDetail.Discount)
          responseDetail.Total = responseDetail.UnitPrice * _
                                 responseDetail.Quantity

          ' Add the detail
          AddOrderDetails(connection, response.OrderId, responseDetail)

          ' Adjust the charge of the order
          response.SubTotal += responseDetail.Total

        Next

        ' Update the total
        response.Total = response.SubTotal + response.FreightCharge

        ' Close the database connection
        connection.Close()

      Catch ex As Exception
        ReportException(ex)
      End Try

      ' Send e-mail
      SendResponse(response, "mytest@pretendcompany.com")

      ' Return the results
      Return response

    End Function
```

7. The next method we must add to Processor.vb is quite lengthy:

```
' CreateOrder - create a new order
Public Function CreateOrder(ByVal connection As SqlConnection, _
      ByVal order As OrderRequest, ByVal freightCharge As Single) As Integer

   ' Create a command
   Dim command As New SqlCommand("CreateOrder", connection)
   command.CommandType = CommandType.StoredProcedure

   ' Add parameters
   Dim customerIdParam As SqlParameter = _
      command.Parameters.Add("@CustomerId", SqlDbType.VarChar, 5)
   customerIdParam.Value = order.CustomerId
   Dim employeeIdParam As SqlParameter = _
      command.Parameters.Add("@employeeId", SqlDbType.Int)
   employeeIdParam.Value = GetRandomEmployeeId(connection)
   Dim shipViaParam As SqlParameter = _
      command.Parameters.Add("@shipVia", SqlDbType.Int)
   shipViaParam.Value = order.PreferredShippingMethod
   Dim emailParam As SqlParameter = _
      command.Parameters.Add("@email", SqlDbType.VarChar, 48)
   emailParam.Value = order.ResponseEmail
   Dim freightParam As SqlParameter = _
      command.Parameters.Add("@freight", SqlDbType.Float)
   freightParam.Value = freightCharge
   Dim shipNameParam As SqlParameter = _
      command.Parameters.Add("@shipName", SqlDbType.VarChar, 32)
   shipNameParam.Value = order.ShippingAddress.Name
   Dim shipAddressParam As SqlParameter = _
      command.Parameters.Add("@shipAddress", SqlDbType.VarChar, 32)
   shipAddressParam.Value = order.ShippingAddress.Address
   Dim shipCityParam As SqlParameter = _
      command.Parameters.Add("@shipCity", SqlDbType.VarChar, 32)
   shipCityParam.Value = order.ShippingAddress.City
   Dim shipRegionParam As SqlParameter = _
      command.Parameters.Add("@shipRegion", SqlDbType.VarChar, 32)
   shipRegionParam.Value = order.ShippingAddress.Region
   Dim shipPostalCodeParam As SqlParameter = _
      command.Parameters.Add("@shipPostalCode", SqlDbType.VarChar, 32)
   shipPostalCodeParam.Value = order.ShippingAddress.PostalCode
   Dim shipCountryParam As SqlParameter = _
      command.Parameters.Add("@shipCountry", SqlDbType.VarChar, 32)
   shipCountryParam.Value = order.ShippingAddress.Country

   ' Add a param for the return value
   Dim idParam As SqlParameter = _
            command.Parameters.Add("@id", SqlDbType.Int)
   idParam.Direction = ParameterDirection.ReturnValue

   ' Run it
   command.ExecuteNonQuery()

   ' Get the ID
   Dim orderId As Integer = idParam.Value
```

```
    ' Clean up
    command.Dispose()

    ' Return the ID
    Return orderId

  End Function
```

8. The `GetRandomEmployeeId` method assigns the order to an employee picked at random. In a real-world situation, particular employees would be designated to deal with certain accounts, but this will suffice for our example:

```
  ' GetRandomEmployeeId - pick an ID from those available
  Public Function GetRandomEmployeeId(ByVal connection As SqlConnection) _
                                      As Integer

    ' Fill a DataSet
    Dim adapter As New SqlDataAdapter("SELECT EmployeeID FROM Employees WHERE _
                                      ReportsTo IS NOT null", connection)
    Dim dataset As New DataSet()
    adapter.Fill(dataset)
    adapter.Dispose()

    ' Get the employee ID
    Dim index As Integer = _
                  New System.Random().Next(dataset.Tables(0).Rows.Count - 1)
    Dim employeeId As Integer = dataset.Tables(0).Rows(index).Item(0)

    ' Clean up
    dataset.Dispose()

    ' Return
    Return employeeId

  End Function
```

9. Add the `GetProductPrice` method:

```
  ' GetProductPrice - get the price of a product
  Public Function GetProductPrice(ByVal connection As SqlConnection, _
                                  ByVal productId As Integer) As Single

    ' Get an adapter and fill a DataSet
    Dim adapter As New SqlDataAdapter("SELECT unitprice FROM products WHERE _
                                      productid=" & productId, connection)
    Dim dataset As New DataSet()
    adapter.Fill(dataset)
    adapter.Dispose()
```

```
    ' Get the price
    Dim price As Single = dataset.Tables(0).Rows(0).Item(0)

    ' Clean up
    dataset.Dispose()

    ' Return it
    Return price

End Function
```

10. Next, the `AddOrderDetails` method:

```
' AddOrderDetails - add details to the order
Public Sub AddOrderDetails(ByVal connection As SqlConnection, _
                ByVal orderId As Integer, ByVal detail As ResponseDetail)

    ' Create a command
    Dim command As New SqlCommand("AddOrderDetails", connection)
    command.CommandType = CommandType.StoredProcedure

    ' Add parameters
    Dim orderIdParam As SqlParameter = _
                    command.Parameters.Add("@orderId", SqlDbType.Int)
    orderIdParam.Value = orderId
    Dim productIdParam As SqlParameter = _
                    command.Parameters.Add("@productId", SqlDbType.Int)
    productIdParam.Value = detail.ProductId
    Dim unitPriceParam As SqlParameter = _
                    command.Parameters.Add("@unitPrice", SqlDbType.Float)
    unitPriceParam.Value = detail.UnitPrice
    Dim quantityParam As SqlParameter = _
                    command.Parameters.Add("@quantity", SqlDbType.Int)
    quantityParam.Value = detail.Quantity
    Dim DiscountParam As SqlParameter = _
                    command.Parameters.Add("@discount", SqlDbType.Float)
    DiscountParam.Value = detail.Discount

    ' Run it
    command.ExecuteNonQuery()

    ' Close
    command.Dispose()

End Sub
```

11. You'll also need to create new stored procedures to commit the information to the database. Add the stored procedure opposite to the NorthwindSQL database using Server Explorer:

```
CREATE PROCEDURE CreateOrder
(
    @customerId varchar(5),
    @employeeId int,
    @shipVia int,
    @email varchar(48),
    @freight float,
    @shipName varchar(32),
    @shipAddress varchar(32),
    @shipCity varchar(32),
    @shipRegion varchar(32),
    @shipPostalCode varchar(32),
    @shipCountry varchar(32)
)
AS
    /* insert the order */
    INSERT INTO orders(customerid, employeeid, orderdate, requireddate, shipvia,
        freight, shipname, shipaddress, shipcity, shipregion, shippostalcode,
        shipcountry)
    VALUES (@customerid, @employeeid, getdate(), getdate(), @shipVia,
        @freight, @shipname, @shipaddress, @shipcity, @shipregion,
        @shippostalcode, @shipcountry)

    /* return the ID */
    return @@identity
```

12. Then, add this stored procedure:

```
CREATE PROCEDURE AddOrderDetails
(
    @orderId int,
    @productId int,
    @unitPrice float,
    @quantity int,
    @discount float
)
AS
    INSERT INTO [Order Details] (OrderID, ProductID, UnitPrice,
            Quantity, Discount)
        VALUES (@orderId, @productId, @unitPrice, @quantity, @discount)
```

13. Run the project and delete the XML file from the `Inbound` folder. Copy the original back there to trigger the order creation process.

You'll see this response document:

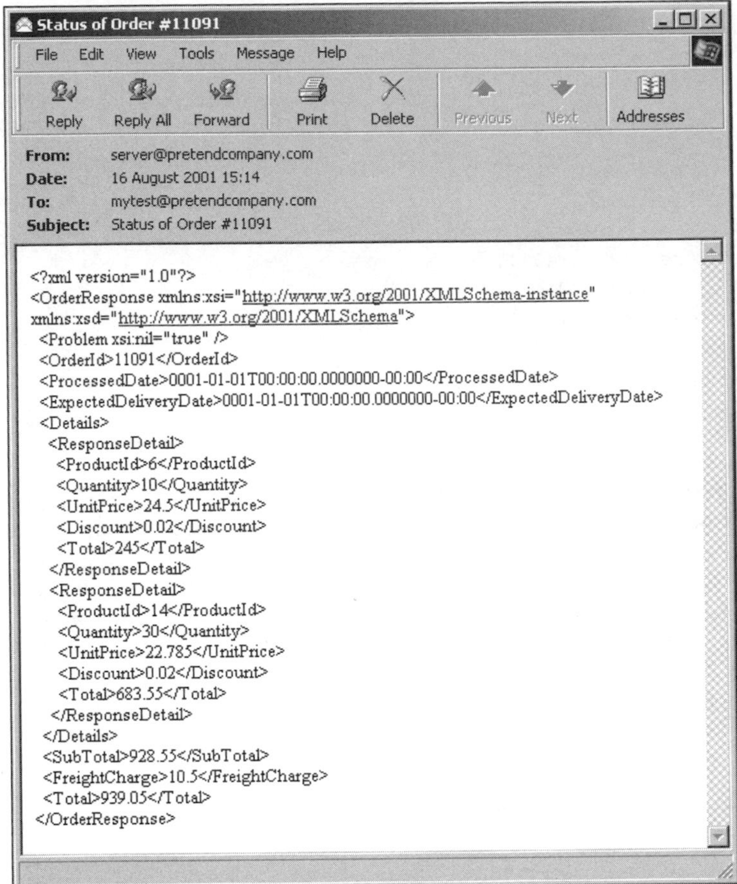

14. Now, when you examine the contents of the `Orders` table, you'll find the new order:

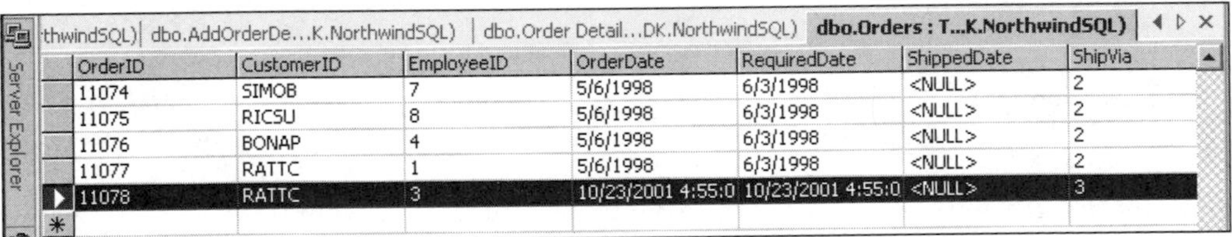

thwindSQL) | dbo.AddOrderDe...K.NorthwindSQL) | dbo.Order Detail...DK.NorthwindSQL) | **dbo.Orders : T...K.NorthwindSQL)**

OrderID	CustomerID	EmployeeID	OrderDate	RequiredDate	ShippedDate	ShipVia
11074	SIMOB	7	5/6/1998	6/3/1998	<NULL>	2
11075	RICSU	8	5/6/1998	6/3/1998	<NULL>	2
11076	BONAP	4	5/6/1998	6/3/1998	<NULL>	2
11077	RATTC	1	5/6/1998	6/3/1998	<NULL>	2
11078	RATTC	3	10/23/2001 4:55:0	10/23/2001 4:55:0	<NULL>	3

15. You'll also see the details in the Order Details table:

thwindSQL) | dbo.AddOrderDe...K.NorthwindSQL) | **dbo.Order Deta....NorthwindSQL)** | dbo.Orders : Ta...DK.NorthwindSQL)

OrderID	ProductID	UnitPrice	Quantity	Discount	upsize_ts
11077	66	17	1	0	<Binary>
11077	73	15	2	0.01	<Binary>
11077	75	7.75	4	0	<Binary>
11077	77	13	2	0	<Binary>
11078	6	24.5	10	0.02	<Binary>
11078	14	22.785	30	0.02	<Binary>

How It Works

The first problem to address is how to deserialize the order request from the XML document. We do this by building a `ReadXml` method to accompany the `WriteXml` method, using the `System.Xml.XmlTextReader` class as opposed to the `System.Xml.XmlTextWriter` class.

The `XmlTextReader` class works on the principle that XML files can be broken down into nodes. Each node defines a separate point in the document and can be roughly divided into four types. Note that here a node does not represent a single XML element and, in fact, an element such as `<dog>Rover</dog>` contains three nodes in total:

- Start tag
- End tag
- Value

Technically, there's also whitespace – the spaces, tabs, and new-line characters typically used between elements for readability – but we don't care too much about it here. We are only concerned with these three kinds of nodes. To take the first few lines of our order request document:

```
<Order>
 <CustomerID>RATTC</CustomerID>
 <PreferredShippingMethod>3</PreferredShippingMethod>
```

These elements are therefore broken down (or **parsed**) like so:

- Start tag: `Order`
- Whitespace
- Start tag: `CustomerID`
- Value: RATTC
- End tag: `CustomerID`
- Whitespace
- Start tag: `PreferredShippingMethod`
- Value: 3
- End tag: `PreferredShippingMethod`

`XmlTextReader` works by stepping between nodes and examining each one in turn. Each call to `Read` advances the pointer from one node to the next, and the `NodeType`, `Name`, and `Value` properties tell us what we're currently looking at. We need to determine when we start looking at an element, so we use `NodeType` to check for `XmlNodeType.Element`:

```
' ReadXml - load the order document
Public Sub ReadXml(ByVal reader As XmlTextReader)

   ' Read through the elements
```

```
    Do While True

      ' Read
      If reader.Read() = False Then
        Exit Do
      End If

      ' What node type do we have?
      Select Case reader.NodeType

        Case XmlNodeType.Element
```

Once we know we're looking at a start tag, we use a `Select Case` block to examine the name:

```
          Select Case reader.Name
```

If the element name is `CustomerID`, `PreferredShippingMethod`, or `ResponseEmail`, we have to advance the reader by one node to point at the value node following that XML tag, which contains the actual data for that element. We can then use `Value` to extract the data and store it in a variable:

```
            Case "CustomerID"
              reader.Read()
              Me.CustomerId = reader.Value

            Case "PreferredShippingMethod"
              reader.Read()
              Me.PreferredShippingMethod = reader.Value

            Case "ResponseEmail"
              reader.Read()
              Me.ResponseEmail = reader.Value
```

In the case of `ShippingAddress` and `Details`, we defer processing to the `ReadXml` method implemented on each of the classes. This is similar to how we dealt with serializing the other objects in `WriteXml`:

```
            Case "ShippingAddress"
              Me.ShippingAddress.ReadXml(reader.Name, reader)

            Case "Details"
              Me.Details.ReadXml(reader)

          End Select

      End Select

    Loop

  End Sub
```

By and large, deserializing an object in this way isn't difficult, but it is verbose. Look at the listing for ReadXml in Address and you'll see that it's a really long listing, although it's basically straightforward. This can be a nuisance for maintenance.

Processing the order by the ProcessOrder method is simply a matter of getting into a position where we can call methods that subsequently call stored procedures to add the rows to the database. First this method sets up a blank OrderResponse object, and then creates and loads an OrderRequest object from the XmlTextReader passed in:

```
Dim request As New OrderRequest()
request.ReadXml(reader)
```

We can then connect to the database. For simplicity, we apply a fixed shipping charge of $10.50 to each order:

```
' Assume we have a fixed freight charge
response.FreightCharge = 10.5
```

The CreateOrder method needs a database connection and an OrderRequest object. Most of the information that it needs to store in the database is contained within OrderRequest, with the notable exception of the freight charge, which we hard-coded above:

```
' Right, create a new order
response.OrderId = CreateOrder(connection, request, _
                               response.FreightCharge)
```

We can then look through each of the RequestDetail objects to find what has actually been ordered and add the details to the database:

```
' Go through each detail
Dim requestDetail As RequestDetail
For Each requestDetail In request.Details

  ' Create a response detail
  Dim responseDetail As New ResponseDetail()
  response.Details.Add(responseDetail)

  ' Get the basic info
  responseDetail.ProductId = requestDetail.ProductId
  responseDetail.Quantity = requestDetail.Quantity
```

We'll also apply a flat 2% discount for all orders placed through the online system. In a production situation, you'd probably use a scheme that required you to look up each customer and determine the discount that was appropriate for them:

```
  ' Get the price
  Dim unitPrice As Single = _
          GetProductPrice(connection, requestDetail.ProductId)
  responseDetail.Discount = 0.02
```

```
            responseDetail.UnitPrice = _
                    unitPrice * (1 - responseDetail.Discount)
            responseDetail.Total = _
                    responseDetail.UnitPrice * responseDetail.Quantity

            ' Add the detail
            AddOrderDetails(connection, response.OrderId, responseDetail)

            ' Adjust the charge of the order
            response.SubTotal += responseDetail.Total

          Next
```

After working through the detail, we can update the total:

```
          ' Update the total
          response.Total = response.SubTotal + response.FreightCharge
```

Finally, we close the database connection and send the response through e-mail as normal:

```
          ' Close the database connection
          connection.Close()

        Catch ex As Exception
          ReportException(ex)
        End Try

        ' Send e-mail
        SendResponse(response, "mytest@pretendcompany.com")

        ' Return the results
        Return response

      End Function
```

Building the Windows Service

At this point, we can accept orders through the online system. However, we're still using the test console application. What we'll do in this section is reuse the objects in the Automated Order Processor class library within a Windows Service.

Try It Out – Creating a Windows Service

1. If the project is running, close it.

2. Using Solution Explorer, add a new Visual Basic | Windows Service project. Call it Automated Order Processor Service:

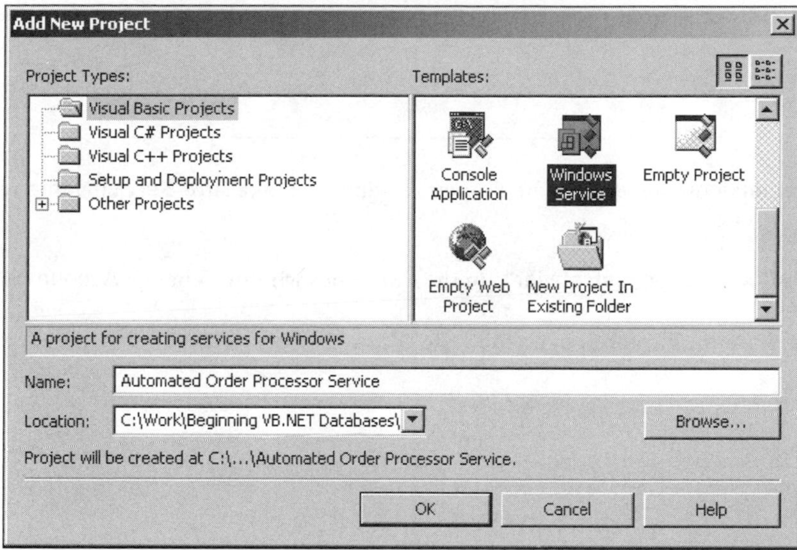

3. Right-click on the References object within the new project. Select Add Reference.

4. Change to the Projects tab. Select Automated Order Processor, click Select, and then click OK.

5. At this point, Visual Studio .NET should be showing the Designer for Service1.

   Display the Properties window for Service1 and change ServiceName to Automated Order Processor:

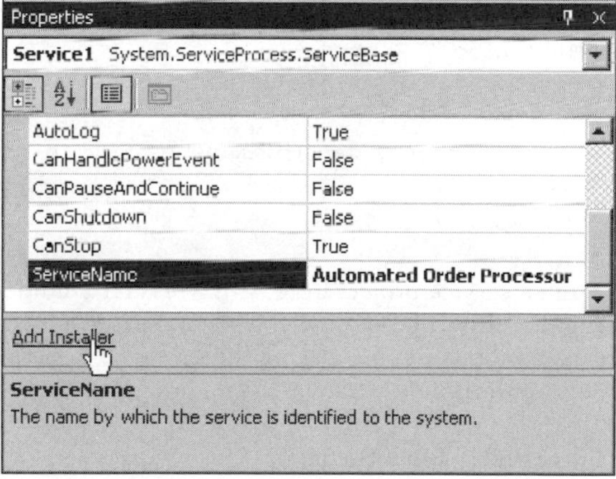

6. In the previous screenshot, the mouse cursor is over a link called Add Installer. Click this link.

   This will automatically create an installer for the service, a mechanism for installing the service on the computer, and it is essential for us to run it. This installer contains two objects: ServiceProcessInstaller1 and ServiceInstaller1:

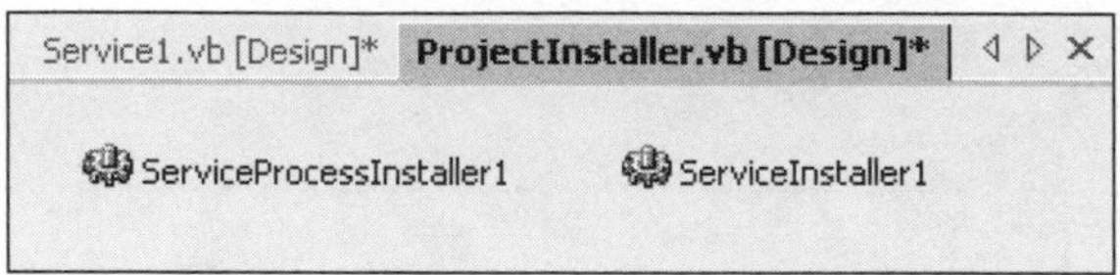

7. Select ServiceInstaller1. In the Properties window, make sure ServiceName reads Automated Order Processor.

8. Select ServiceProcessInstaller1. In the Properties window, change Account to LocalSystem.

9. Using Solution Explorer, open the code editor for Service1. Add this member:

```
Imports System.ServiceProcess

Public Class Service1
  Inherits System.ServiceProcess.ServiceBase

  ' Members
  Dim Processor As New Automated_Order_Processor.Processor()
```

10. Now, add this code to `OnStart`:

```
  Protected Overrides Sub OnStart(ByVal args() As String)
    ' Add code here to start your service. This method should set things
    ' in motion so your service can do its work.
    Processor.Startup()
  End Sub
```

11. Next, add this code to `OnStop`:

```
  Protected Overrides Sub OnStop()
    ' Add code here to perform any tear-down necessary to stop your service.
    Processor.Shutdown()
  End Sub
```

12. It's not possible to run a service project from within Visual Studio .NET. You have to build and install the service, and start it separately. This makes Windows Services awkward to debug, and is our main motivation for placing the guts of the service in a separate library so we can use a console application for testing.

13. From the menu, select Build | Build Solution.

14. Click the Windows Start button on the task bar. Select Programs | Microsoft Visual Studio .NET 7.0 | Visual Studio .NET Tools | Visual Studio .NET Command Prompt. This will open a new command prompt:

```
Visual Studio.NET Command Prompt
Setting environment for using Microsoft Visual C++.NET 7.0 tools.
(If you also have Visual C++ 6.0 installed and wish to use its tools
from the command line, run vcvars32.bat for Visual C++ 6.0.)

C:\Program Files\Common Files\System\MAPI\1033\nt>_
```

15. You can now run the `InstallUtil` utility for installing .NET services. Enter `InstallUtil` followed by the complete path to the service executable. Here's mine:

```
installutil "c:\Automated Order Processor\bin\Automated Order Processor
Service.exe"
```

16. Eventually, you'll see a message like this:

```
The Commit phase completed successfully.

The transacted install has completed.
```

17. Now, click the Windows Start button again. Select Settings | Control Panel. Open the Administrative Tools folder. Then, open the Services management console. You'll find the Automated Order Processor service listed there:

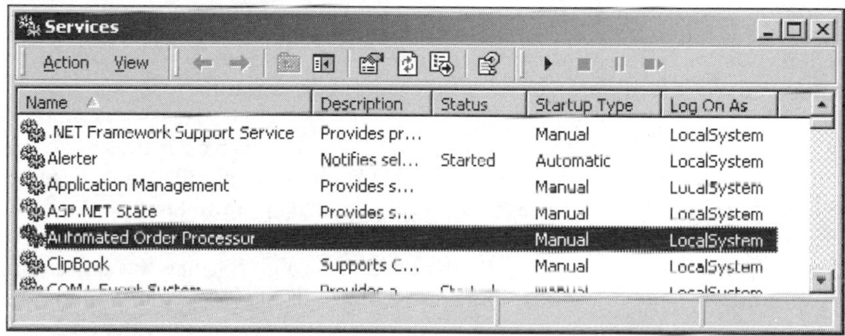

18. Right-click on the service and select Start. The service will start running.

19. Copy the XML request document into the `Inbound` folder. The service will process the order, but you won't see anything because service applications do not have a user interface. However, the e-mail confirming the order should soon arrive.

How It Works

As we mentioned before, a Windows Service is a special kind of Windows application that runs without presenting a user interface – it even runs when no user is logged in! We've created a separate project as a test console application for the same Automated Order Processor library.

Because Windows Service applications cannot be executed directly within Visual Studio, this separate test application is a good idea – we can develop and debug functionality using the console application to insure we're ready to deploy it as a Windows Service.

The rigmarole getting the Windows Service running stems from the fact that a service has to be installed before it can be started. The .NET Framework SDK provides the `InstallUtil` utility to install and uninstall .NET Windows Service applications. (To uninstall, run `InstallUtil` again but add the /u switch before the service executable's filename.)

Sending the Order via a Web Service

In this section we've concentrated on processing orders with legacy technology. At the start, we hinted that we could do the same thing with a Web Service. This is what we shall undertake in this section.

This means our complete application will support a full spread of technology:

- Customers using legacy systems unable to deploy Web Service solutions can generate an XML document according to our schema and send it over FTP.
- Customers using Windows DNA can generate the XML document and transmit it to the Web Service using the SOAP Toolkit available from MSDN.
- Customers using .NET can use the `NorthwindOrderGenerator` class library to generate new `OrderRequest` objects and use a method we'll add to this object called `Send` to transmit the order to our Web Service.
- Customers using a different platform can talk to the Web Service to send the request because Web Services are based on open standards with wide cross-platform support.

What we're going to do is tweak our `NorthwindOrderGenerator` class library so that it can communicate with a Web Service on the Internet. This Web Service will expose a single web method called `PlaceOrder` that takes an `OrderRequest` object as its parameter.

However, there are two ways we could handle the order our Web Service has gotten hold of it. One is to include the Automated Order Processor classes in the Web Service itself, and call `ProcessOrder` direct with the `OrderRequest` object supplied. Alternatively, we can take the `OrderRequest` object and serialize it to an XML file in the `Inbound` folder, whereupon the Windows Service will pick it up and process it as if it were received over FTP.

The only real consideration here is one of deployment. If we have only one part of the system responsible for processing the order, the system becomes simpler – everything enters through one point, is processed by the same code, and leaves by one point. If we make the Web Service capable of processing orders itself, everything is doubled, making the system more complex and hard to maintain. Therefore, we shall just have the Web Service drop the orders in XML format into the `Inbound` folder.

Try It Out – Building a Web Service

1. Using Solution Explorer, add a new Visual Basic | ASP.NET Web Service project to the solution. Call it NorthwindOrderWebService, and create it on the local machine if you can. (If you're lost, refer back to the discussion in Chapter 11 on how to set up Web Application projects.)

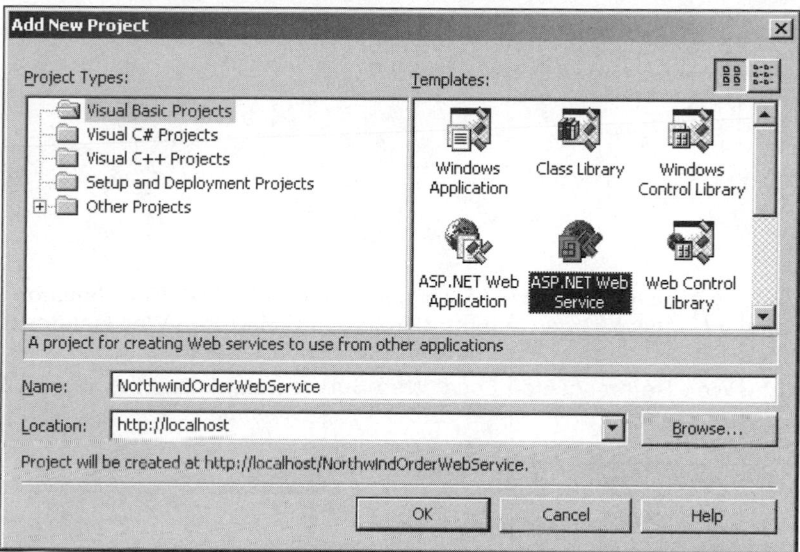

2. When the project has been created, right-click on the References object contained within the NorthwindOrderWebService project in Solution Explorer.

   Change to the Projects tab. Make sure NorthwindOrderGenerator is selected in the list, click Select, and then click OK.

3. Open Service1.asmx.vb in the code editor. Add these two namespace declarations to the top of the file:

```
Imports System.Web.Services
Imports System.IO
Imports NorthwindOrderGenerator

Public Class Service1
  Inherits System.Web.Services.WebService
```

4. Next, add this method:

```
  <WebMethod()> Public Sub PlaceOrder(ByVal orderXml As String)

    ' get a guaranteed unique ID string
    Dim guidString As String
```

```
    guidString = Guid.NewGuid.ToString()

    ' get a filename
    Dim filename As String
    filename = "c:\Automated Order Processor\Inbound\" & guidString & ".xml"

    ' save the file
    Dim stream As New FileStream(filename, FileMode.Create)
    Dim writer As New StreamWriter(stream)
    writer.Write(orderXml)
    writer.Flush()
    writer.Close()
    stream.Close()

  End Sub
```

5. That's all we have to do to get the Web Service running. Now, using Solution Explorer, right-click on the NorthwindOrderGenerator project and select Add Web Reference.

6. Click the Web References on Local Web Server link. A list of available Web Services will appear:

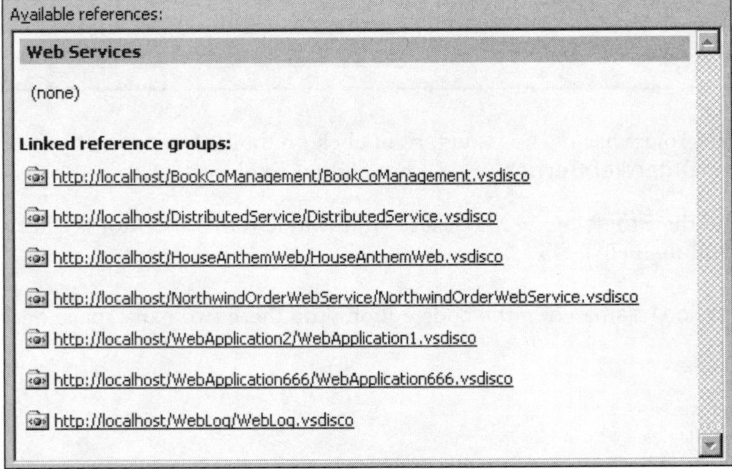

7. Click on the NorthwindOrderWebservice.vsdisco link, and click the Add Reference button that appears.

8. Rename the new localhost web reference OrderService:

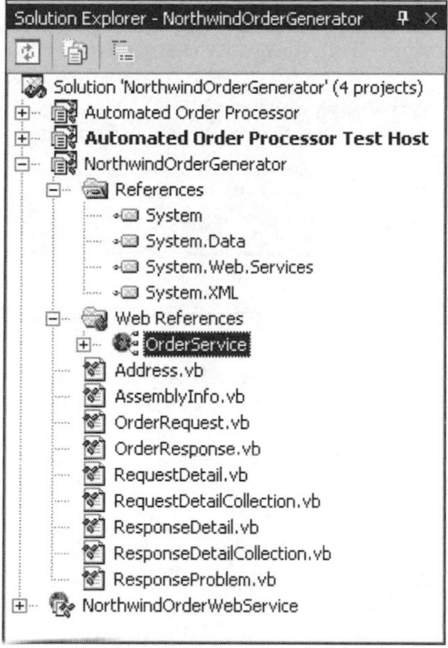

9. Now, add this method to the OrderRequest class:

```
' Send - send the order to the Web Service
Public Sub Send()

  ' Create a memory stream
  Dim memoryStream As New MemoryStream()

  ' Create an XML writer on the stream and write the document
  Dim writer As New XmlTextWriter(memoryStream, _
                                  New System.Text.ASCIIEncoding())
  WriteXml(writer)
  writer.Flush()

  ' Read the stream back
  memoryStream.Seek(0, SeekOrigin.Begin)
  Dim reader As New StreamReader(memoryStream)
  Dim orderXml As String = reader.ReadToEnd
  reader.Close()
  memoryStream.Close()

  ' Connect to the Web Service
  Dim service As New OrderService.Service1()
  service.PlaceOrder(orderXml)

End Sub
```

10. To test this next part out, you'll need to go all the way back to the Order Generator Test Client project that we built much earlier in the chapter. Add that project to the current solution. Right-click on it and select Set as StartUp Project.

11. Double-click Form1 to open the designer, and add a new button. Set its Text property to Send Test Order to Web Service, and change its Name property to btnToWeb.

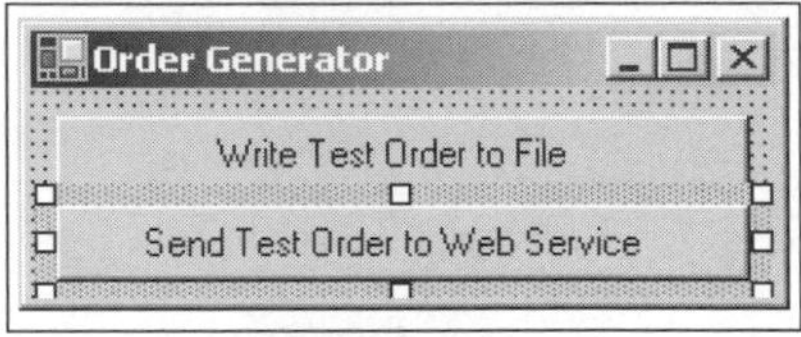

12. Double-click on the button. Add this code to the event handler:

```
Private Sub btnToWeb_Click(ByVal sender As System.Object, _
                           ByVal e As System.EventArgs) Handles btnToWeb.Click

  ' Create the test order
  Dim testOrder As OrderRequest = CreateTestOrder()

  ' Send it
  testOrder.Send()

  ' Tell the user
  MsgBox("The order was sent to the Web Service.")

End Sub
```

13. Make sure that the Automated Order Processor Service isn't running, and start up the project. Also, run the Test Host project so you can see what happens. Click the Send Test Order button and you'll see the Test Host report the fact that the order has been processed:

```
\\corrado\work\Beginning VB.NET Databases\Chapter 16 - Application Integration with XML\Automat...
11:56:40: Monitoring 'C:\Automated Order Processor\Inbound'

Press Return to close the host
11:57:35: Processing 'C:\Automated Order Processor\Inbound\a335c08f-1521-4ca2-bb
93-1f1b0de2e56b.xml'...
11:57:38: Sent to 'mytest@pretendcompany.com'
11:57:38: Finished 'C:\Automated Order Processor\Inbound\a335c08f-1521-4ca2-bb93
-1f1b0de2e56b.xml'...
_
```

How It Works

As mentioned before, we want to create a single route for orders however the XML describing the order was generated. In this exercise, we've added a method called `Send` to `OrderRequest`, which reuses our existing `WriteXml` method but captures the results in memory rather than writing them to disk. The `MemoryStream` object is conceptually similar to a `FileStream` but it outputs to a block of memory rather than to a disk file:

```
' Send - send the order to the Web Service
Public Sub Send()

  ' Create a memory stream
  Dim memoryStream As New MemoryStream()
```

```
        ' Create an XML writer on the stream and write the document
        Dim writer As New XmlTextWriter(memoryStream, _
                                        New System.Text.ASCIIEncoding())
        WriteXml(writer)
        writer.Flush()
```

Once `WriteXml` has written the XML, we then reset the stream to the beginning and use a `StreamReader` on it to read back everything that `WriteXml` had added. We store this in a string called `orderXml`:

```
        ' Read the stream back
        memoryStream.Seek(0, SeekOrigin.Begin)
        Dim reader As New StreamReader(memoryStream)
        Dim orderXml As String = reader.ReadToEnd
        reader.Close()
        memoryStream.Close()
```

With `orderXml` populated, we connect to the Web Service and pass it the XML string:

```
        ' Connect to the Web Service
        Dim service As New OrderService.Service1()
        service.PlaceOrder(orderXml)

    End Sub
```

At the other end, that is, inside the `PlaceOrder` method of the Web Service, we take the XML and write it out to a file. However, we need a unique filename, so we use `System.Guid` to create a guaranteed unique 128-bit number for the filename:

```
    <WebMethod()> Public Sub PlaceOrder(ByVal orderXml As String)

        ' Get a guaranteed unique ID string
        Dim guidString As String
        guidString = Guid.NewGuid.ToString()

        ' Get a filename
        Dim filename As String
        filename = "c:\Automated Order Processor\Inbound\" & guidString & ".xml"
```

Once we have the filename, we open the file and write out the XML passed in the `orderXml` parameter:

```
        ' Save the file
        Dim stream As New FileStream(filename, FileMode.Create)
        Dim writer As New StreamWriter(stream)
        writer.Write(orderXml)
        writer.Flush()
        writer.Close()
        stream.Close()

    End Sub
```

Once the file has been written to the `Inbound` folder, it's down to the service to pick it up. In this example, the Test Host picked up the order but, of course, this would work equally well with our Windows Service.

Summary

In this case study, we took a very detailed look at how we could build a system to receive and automatically process orders.

We started off by looking at the schema that we'd use to describe our orders. This was fairly straightforward, and comprised the shipping address, the customer ID, and order details. We built a new class library to generate and read an XML document that fitted the schema.

Once we had the document, we turned our attention to how to transfer it. There are a number of possibilities but, to maintain a single point of entry for documents coming into the system, a good idea is to create a folder on the server that we monitor for new files. This we did – we built a separate class library containing an order processor capable of monitoring a folder for incoming files. When a new file is detected, it is read and the order processed.

We then wrapped the order processor in a standalone Windows Service so that the order processing functionality would be available even if no-one is logged into the server. We finally built a Web Service that enables .NET-ready customers to transmit the order directly to us with a minimum of hassle.

Index

A Guide to the Index

The index is arranged hierarchically, in alphabetical order, with symbols preceding the letter A. Most second-level entries and many third-level entries also occur as first-level entries. This is to ensure that users will find the information they require however they choose to search for it.

Symbols

A

B

C

D

F

G

H

I

O

P

Q

R

T

U

V

W

X

Notes

Notes

Notes

Notes

Notes